Pillsbury's BEST 1000 Recipes

BEST of the BAKE-OFF® Collection

BEST of the BAKE-OFF

Edited and adapted by **Ann Pillsbury**
and the staff of Pillsbury's Home Service Kitchens

DRAWINGS BY SUZANNE SNIDER

Wiley Publishing, Inc

ISBN: 978-0470-39559-2

Manufactured in China

Facsimile Edition 2009

10 9 8 7 6 5 4 3 2 1

ACKNOWLEDGMENT

The "Best of the Bake-Off Collection" cook book has been made possible by the original recipe contributions of 1,000 of America's best home bakers, and the co-operation of Ann Pillsbury and her staff who have tested and adapted all recipes to assure you of their complete accuracy.

We're excited to bring you this treasured edition of *Pillsbury's Best of the Bake-Off® Collection*. All the recipes are exactly as they appeared in the original 1959 cookbook. Some ingredients have changed over the years so you will want to use today's ingredients and methods when making these recipes. Food safety concerns have also changed over the years, so please see below for Today's Food Safety information.

Today's Food Safety

Food safety concerns have changed over the years. We no longer can enjoy recipes using raw or under-cooked eggs. However, today we can substitute pasteurized eggs and safely enjoy these recipes. You can find cartons of pasteurized eggs in the refrigerator section of the grocery store. Or use a pasteurized fat-free cholesterol-free egg product. It is available in cartons in the refrigerator or freezer section of your grocery store.

Please use only pasteurized eggs in the recipes below that call for eggs. And remember, it will take up to twice as long to beat pasteurized egg whites to form stiff peaks.

WILEY

CONTENTS

Dear Friend:

This beautiful new cook book is our dream come true!

Between its covers are the 1,000 best baking recipes from the first ten Pillsbury Grand National BAKE-OFFS®.

Each recipe is a famous BAKE-OFF® prize winner. All are the personal creations of women just like you--women who love to bake. Pillsbury's BAKE-OFF® is actually a "back fence," and over it America's best recipes and ideas are exchanged and shared in true neighbor-to-neighbor fashion.

The preparation of this new cook book has been a joy and a delight for us. We hope its use will give you equal pleasure. Every recipe has been thoroughly tested, and bears the stamp of approval of the Pillsbury Home Service Kitchens. Each is written in a style you will find very easy to follow.

For your convenience and easy reference, all recipes have been arranged in sections. You'll find ideas and inspiration for every occasion, from every day family fare to the most elegant party dessert. In addition, we have included service ideas and baking hints to speed and simplify your work.

With this "Best of the Bake-Off® Collection," we hope you enjoy wonderful baking and eating . . . with the BEST recipes and Pillsbury's BEST flour.

Ann Pillsbury

Director
Pillsbury's Home Service Kitchens
Minneapolis 2, Minnesota

P.S. All the recipes in this book have been developed for use with Pillsbury's BEST Self-Rising Flour; a footnote after each recipe tells how the recipe may be adjusted when using Self-Rising Flour.

Pillsbury's BEST XXXX ALL PURPOSE FLOUR

BEST of the BAKE-OFF

PILLSBURY'S GRAND NATIONAL BAKE-OFF®

In 1949, homemakers across the nation paused in anticipation as 100 of America's best housewife-cooks walked excitedly into the Grand Ballroom of the Waldorf-Astoria hotel in New York. They were about to bake their best recipes for Pillsbury's first Grand National Recipe and Baking Contest.

The ladies were competing for $100,000 in prizes and the title "Cook of the Year". They were nervous. So were the sponsors. What, exactly, had been created? They all found out quickly enough. Next day the nation's press greeted the winning cook with a delighted front-page whoop and the BAKE-OFF® was established.

From then on a trip to the BAKE-OFF® has become the annual kitchen dream of millions of housewives. A thousand of them have made it so far, bringing their prize recipes; the carefully guarded family favorite, and the imaginative new creation. They brought them to share with the world.

Why do they come? Well, the money prizes *are* tempting. BAKE-OFF® prizes have bought new homes, financed college educations, and provided for many a "rainy day" project. But more than that, America's

outstanding cooks come for the fun and the drama—the once-in-lifetime chance to star in the show that's produced for them.

Pillsbury has a motive in all this baking madness. The company wants new recipes to help promote the use of its famous Pillsbury's Best Flour. What better place to find them than the recipe boxes of housewives who bake for the love of it?

So each spring for the past ten, Pillsbury has sent out the call for contestants. From the hundreds of thousands of hopefuls, the 100 best are selected for the finals. They earn their blue-ribbon pedigree the hard way. Preliminary judging is based on ease and speed of preparation, novelty or unusual characteristics, and general appeal. When the field is narrowed down to hundreds, professional home economists bake and rate them. The finalists are picked from the ratings by a professional judging firm.

Entering the BAKE-OFF® is simple. The cook has to be over 12 years old, and must use at least one-half cup of Pillsbury's Best Flour in her recipe. Anyone living in the United States (including the two newest states and Puerto Rico) is eligible. So are overseas members of America's Armed

Forces and their dependents. There have been some grandmothers and Girl Scouts, a Maryknoll sister and a lion hunter's wife. Some male cooks have entered—and won.

Nine of the ten Bake-Offs® have been held at the elegant Waldorf-Astoria hotel. In 1957 the contest moved west to the beautiful Beverly Hilton hotel in California. But wherever it is, it's still the BAKE-OFF®.

It's a wonderful trip, the contestants tell Pillsbury, even if they can't all win the big prize. The trip is as first class as Pillsbury can make it, right down to spending money.

The contestants arrive on Sunday and are greeted by members of the Pillsbury family and company officials. That evening they get acquainted at a dinner hosted by General Electric. It's an exciting beginning. Even those who have seen it before notice the first stirrings of adventure to come.

Next day there's no question about it. Adventure is here as the 100 finalists walk out onto the ballroom floor. Waiting are 100 new GE ranges, cooking utensils, and the most unusual ingredients ever gathered in one place (see photo inside front cover).

The cooks bake their recipes once and then once more. The sweet smell of successful baking is everywhere. Somebody is going to win—and in a closely guarded judging room off the ballroom floor a panel of professional home economists and prominent food editors makes the decisions. The competing entries are whisked to them as soon as the contestants complete their baking. They never know whose recipes they're evaluating. The room is off-limits to all but the judges. Pillsbury officials are notified only after judging is completed.

When it's over, tension slacks off. There's a supper party to attend and later a well-known television broadcast. The secret of the winners is locked up until next day.

Nobody yawns at the Awards Luncheon. It has stood the test of sophisticated New York and worldly-wise Hollywood. The genuine drama of announcing the winning BAKE-OFF® cooks has always produced gasps, tears and a near-swoon or two. There's glamour, too, in the sparkling ball-room setting (see photo inside back cover), television cameras, newspaper photographers, and the guest of honor—Mrs. Eleanor Roosevelt was the first, Miss Irene Dunne the latest—who awards the grand prize.

Everybody wins; the finalists all take home the GE range and mixer they use at the BAKE-OFF®. They all find they have won a place of honor among America's best cooks. The honor roll is here and so are the recipes—the 1,000 best.

PILLSBURY'S GRAND NATIONAL BAKE-OFF® JUDGES

Edith Barber—*New York Sun*
Anita Bennett—*Los Angeles Mirror-News*
Ruth Casa-Emellos—*New York Times*
Ruth Ellen Church—*Chicago Tribune*
Eleanor Crook—*The American Weekly, New York*
Iris Davenport—*Farm and Ranch Publishing Co.*
Pierre G. DeSautels—*Trans World Airlines*
Hazel Blair Dodd—*Los Angeles Herald & Express*
Virginia Dysard—*The Atlanta Constitution*
Violet Faulkner—*Washington Evening Star*
Esther Foley—*McFadden Publications, Inc.*
Dorothy Friedman—*Seventeen*
Mavis Gibbs—*Southern Planter*
Lila Gilliam—*The Progressive Farmer*
Cissy Gregg—*Louisville Courier-Journal*
Bertha Hahn—*Miami Daily News*
Eleanor Halderman—*Household, Capper's Farmer*
Florence LaGanke Harris—*The Cleveland Press*
Mary Hart—*Minneapolis Tribune*
Grace Hartley—*Atlanta Journal*
Sara L. Hervey—*Country Gentleman*
Kay Hillyard—*Sunset Magazine*

Marie Hulbert—*KOLN-TV, Lincoln, Nebraska*
Winnifred Jardine—*Salt Lake City Deseret News and Telegraph*
Myrna Johnston—*Better Homes & Gardens*
Marilyn Kaytor—*Look*
Helen Kelleher—*Capper's Farmer*
Maurine Kelley—*Seattle Post-Intelligencer*
Edna Kestal—*Forecast for Home Economists*
Dorothy Kirk—*Woman's Home Companion*
Ruth B. Lane—*Sunset Magazine*
Elinor Lee—*Washington Post and Times Herald*
Marian Manners—*Los Angeles Times*
Dorothy Marsh—*Good Housekeeping*
Catherine Nissly Maurer—*Farm Journal*
Jean McBride—*WWJ-TV, The Detroit News*
Josephine McCarthy—*WRCA-TV, New York*
Lois McCloskey—*Philadelphia Inquirer*
Jinx Falkenburg McCrary—*WNBC, New York*
Helen McCully—*McCall's*
Glenna McGinnis—*Woman's Day*
Marjorie Mills—*Boston Herald-Traveler*
Nell Nichols—*Farm Journal*

Clementine Paddleford—*New York Herald Tribune*
Alice Petersen—*New York Daily News*
Mary Presper—*Bride's Magazine*
Rosalie Riglin—*Farm Journal*
Helen M. Robertson—*Cleveland Plain Dealer*
Alice Sanderson—*Girl Scouts of the U.S.A.*
Wilma Sim—*KSD-TV, St. Louis Post Dispatch*
Dorothy Sinz—*Dallas Times-Herald*
Gloria Spitz—*Living for Young Homemakers*
Wilma Phillips Stewart—*Des Moines Register*
Vera Wilson Swope—*Co-Ed Magazine*
Demetria Taylor—*Parade*
Dorothy Thompson—*Chicago American*
June Towne—*The American Home*
Veronika Volpe—*Pittsburgh Post Gazette*
Beryl Walters—*Seventeen*
Gertrude Warren—*U.S. Dept. of Agriculture*
Adene Wilson—*Los Angeles Examiner*
Mary K. Wilson—*Brooklyn College*
Grace White—*Family Circle*
Norma Young—*KHJ, Hollywood*

HOW TO PERFECT THE ART OF BAKING

Baking is one of the most rewarding of all the arts! You can feel a glow of accomplishment when you put the finishing touches on a beautiful cake, take a shapely loaf of bread from the oven or treat your family to a batch of their favorite cookies.

The art of baking is not difficult to perfect! Recipes in this book have been tested and adapted by Ann Pillsbury and written in easy-to-follow Ann Pillsbury recipe style. Here and with each section you will find helpful baking tips.

KNOW YOUR INGREDIENTS

Choose good ingredients. You can't do a first-rate job with second-rate materials. All of the recipes in this book have been developed for use with Pillsbury's Best All Purpose Flour. When using Pillsbury's Best Self-Rising Flour (flour which has leavening ingredients and salt added), be sure to follow the directions given in the special footnote that has been included at the bottom of each recipe.

Be sure to use high-quality shortening. When using melted shortening allow it to cool before adding other ingredients.

For best results, eggs should be at room temperature; eggs beat much better if allowed to stand at room temperature no longer than 2 hours before they are used.

USE GOOD UTENSILS

Use standard measuring cups. The liquid measuring cup (a glass one is easiest to use) has a space above the 1-cup line so liquid will not spill. Nested metal measuring cups—¼, ⅓, ½ and 1 cup—are best for measuring dry ingredients or shortening. The measuring line is even with the top so measurements can be leveled off. *Use standard measuring spoons*—¼, ½ and 1 teaspoon and 1 tablespoon.

An electric mixer is a good right arm. Keep it on the counter where it is readily available. It can be used for combining ingredients, beating, creaming, blending, mixing and stirring (lowest speed). When using an electric mixer be sure to scrape the sides of the bowl occasionally for good blending.

An instance when a mixer should not be used is when cutting shortening into flour to form a crumb mixture; use a pastry blender or two knives. Also, a mixer is not recommended when you are making biscuits and muffins.

Other utensils: Use a flexible metal spatula for leveling off cup and spoon measurements, for frosting cakes and for loosening baked products from sides of pan.

Be sure that you use a mixing bowl that is large enough to allow dough or batter to be mixed with sweeping strokes.

A French knife or a sharp knife is a must to have on hand for chopping nuts and dicing fruit and vegetables. To use a French knife, keep tip of knife on board; raise and lower handle to chop or slice.

A kitchen scissors has a variety of uses—cutting dates, coconut, marshmallows, trimming pastry, etc.

MEASURING CORRECTLY IS IMPORTANT

All measurements in this book are level. Rounded or heaping measurements of ingredients change the "balance" of the recipe and may cause baking failures.

To measure flour: Sift once (onto a sheet of waxed paper), then gently spoon the sifted flour into the measuring cup and level off. Sift shortly before measuring as flour packs down when it stands.

To measure sugar: Fill the cup with *granulated sugar* and level it off. For *brown sugar*, if lumpy, roll between sheets of waxed paper since lumps will melt during baking and form holes. Pack brown sugar into the cup firmly so that it will keep the shape of the cup when it is turned out. Sift *confectioners' sugar* through a sieve or single-screen sifter to remove lumps; spoon lightly into measuring cup and level off.

When measuring butter, remember that one pound equals two cups. If you buy butter already divided into quarters, each quarter is exactly ½ cup. When packing butter firmly into measuring cup or spoon be sure it is soft and pliable so that air spaces do not develop; level with spatula.

To measure shortening: Firmly pack it into measuring cup or spoon and level off. Or measure it by the water displacement method; to measure ½ cup shortening, fill measuring cup to ½ cup level with water, add shortening, keeping it under water, until water reaches 1 cup mark, then pour off water.

Measure liquids in a glass measuring cup marked off in quarters and thirds. For accurate measurements pour liquid into cup on table and stoop to read at eye level. Greasing inside of measuring cup before measuring honey, syrup or molasses helps prevent it from sticking to the sides.

Measurement of eggs: If a recipe gives cup measurements when four or more eggs are called for, it is advisable to use the cup measurement since eggs vary in size.

PREPARE TO BAKE

Read the recipe carefully. Assemble the ingredients and utensils before you start. (Do not substitute ingredients.)

Preheat the oven. If your oven doesn't have a thermostat, or if you suspect it is not regulating accurately, use an oven thermometer to check on baking temperatures.

Measure correctly. Do not alter amounts of ingredients—when you make changes in amounts of ingredients you change the recipe!

Use the pan size specified in the recipe. Measure top inside length and width and inside depth. The recipes in this book specify whether pans should or should not be greased.

New metal baking pans should be scoured thoroughly with soap and a mild abrasive before using. To season, place in hot oven for a few minutes, then cool.

Mind your minutes—Check your recipe at the minimum baking time, then continue baking until desired brownness. Always bake near the center of the oven and use only one rack if possible. Pans should not touch each other or sides of oven. If it is necessary to use more than one rack, do not set pans on top rack directly above those on lower rack; stagger them to permit an even distribution of heat.

Oven temperatures—SLOW   250° to 325°

MODERATE	350° to 375°
MODERATELY HOT	400°
HOT	425° to 450°
VERY HOT	475° to 500°

Use Pillsbury's Best Flour Shaker to flour pastry cloth, bread board, meat and to make gravy and cream sauce.

PREPARATION OF INGREDIENTS

- To cut dates and marshmallows, dip scissors in hot water whenever there is any sticking.
- To chop candied fruit or raisins, coat with 1 tablespoon of the dry ingredients, or grease knife to prevent sticking.
- Drain maraschino cherries, crushed pineapple and other fruits thoroughly on absorbent paper such as paper toweling.
- To prepare orange sections, peel orange so that no white skin is left; loosen individual sections from membrane with sharp knife.
- To soften almonds and Brazil nuts for slicing, soak a few minutes in boiling water to cover.
- To blanch almonds, pour boiling water over them, simmer 2 to 3 minutes, then drain and slip skins off with fingers. Spread out on absorbent paper to dry.
- To toast coconut or nuts, bake at 375° for 5 to 7 minutes, stirring occasionally until golden brown.
- To tint coconut, combine 2 to 4 drops food coloring with a small amount of water. Toss with coconut until evenly colored.
- Melt chocolate over hot water. For small amounts, place chocolate in a small Pyrex dish that is sitting in a pan of boiling water. It is not necessary to cut chocolate into small pieces before melting.
- Crush peanut brittle and peppermint candy between sheets of waxed paper with a hammer.
- To make 1 cup strong coffee, dissolve 2 teaspoons instant coffee in 1 cup boiling water.
- To make 1 cup sour milk, combine 1½ to 2 tablespoons vinegar or lemon juice and milk to measure 1 cup. Let stand 5 minutes.
- To thicken cornstarch or flour mixtures, bring to boil over high heat, stirring constantly. Turn down to medium heat and continue cooking, stirring until mixture is thick.

BAKING TERMS

The following terms have definite meanings which you should know since they are used throughout this book.

Blend: To mix two or more ingredients together thoroughly.

Caramelize: To heat sugar slowly until it becomes brown in color. The darker the color, the stronger the flavor.

Combine: To mix ingredients together.

Cream: To work one or more ingredients until soft and creamy, using an electric mixer or a spoon or other implement. This generally applies to combination of shortening and sugar.

Cut: To incorporate shortening into dry ingredients with least amount of blending, using a pastry blender, pastry fork or two knives.

Dissolve: To make a solution from a dry and liquid ingredient.

Fold: To combine ingredients gently with wire whisk or slotted spoon using a down, across, up and over motion; this action is used when adding beaten egg whites or whipped cream to a mixture.

Knead: To fold dough over on itself and push with palms of hands; repeat rhythmically, turning dough one quarter way around each time.

Sauté: To brown or cook quickly in a small amount of fat until tender.

Scald: To heat a liquid to just below the boiling point.

Simmer: To cook slowly just at the boiling point.

Steam: To cook by contact with live steam in a closed container.

Stir in: To mix using a circular motion with a spoon or low speed of electric mixer.

HIGH ALTITUDE BAKING

If you live in an altitude of 3000 feet or over, you may have some baking problems and questions. Because each recipe is different in ingredient proportions, our hints must be general, but we hope you will find them helpful.

Cake recipes are often adjusted in altitudes above 3000 feet. Usually a decrease in leavening or sugar (or both) and an increase in liquid and flour are needed. The following table is merely a guide; it will be necessary for you to experiment in order to find the best adjustment for each recipe.

ADJUSTMENT	3000 FEET	5000 FEET	7000 FEET
Reduce **baking powder**			
For each teaspoon, decrease	⅛ teasp.	⅛ to ¼ teasp.	¼ to ½ teasp.
Reduce **sugar**			
for each cup, decrease	—	—	1 to 2 tablesp.
Increase **liquid**			
For each cup, add	1 to 2 tablesp.	2 to 3 tablesp.	3 to 4 tablesp.
Increase **flour**			
For each cup, add	—	—	1 to 2 tablesp.

A 10 to 15 degree increase in baking temperature may give better results with cupcakes and layer cakes.

When making rich cakes at high altitudes, it is sometimes necessary to reduce the shortening by 1 or 2 tablespoons.

Recipes using soda may require a very slight reduction of that leavening.

Foam-type cakes—sponge, angel food and chiffon—will require less beating of the eggs. In higher altitudes, the number of eggs may be increased. If eggs are overbeaten at high altitudes, the cake will be dry. Baking temperatures for foam cakes are increased slightly, 10 to 15 degrees for each 5000 foot altitude increase.

In altitudes over 3500 feet, self-rising flour is not recommended for use with cakes. However, it is still very satisfactory for biscuits and biscuit-type quick breads.

Yeast breads require little adjustment. At higher altitudes, the rising time may be reduced. Oven temperatures should be increased slightly, from 10 to 15 degrees. Loaves of bread are baked at 425°, higher than normal temperatures, for the first 10 to 15 minutes of baking time, then baked at normal temperature for the remainder of the baking period.

Cookies and pastry should require little or no change in high altitude areas.

MEASUREMENTS and EQUIVALENTS

3 teaspoons	1 tablespoon
2 tablespoons	⅛ cup
4 tablespoons	¼ cup
5⅓ tablespoons	⅓ cup
¾ cup plus 2 tablespoons	⅞ cup
16 tablespoons	1 cup
2 cups	1 pint
4 cups	1 quart
16 ounces	1 pound

1 pound sifted flour	about 4 cups
1 pound granulated sugar	2¼ cups
1 pound brown sugar	2 to 2¼ cups
1 pound sifted confectioners' sugar . . .	4 to 4¼ cups
1 pound butter or shortening	2 cups
1 square chocolate	1 ounce
¼ cup cocoa plus 2 teaspoons shortening . .	1 square chocolate
1 cup eggs	5 medium eggs
1 cup egg whites	8 medium eggs
1 cup egg yolks	12 to 14 medium eggs
1 pound cheese	4 cups shredded
8 ounces cream cheese, cottage cheese or sour cream	1 cup
1 medium lemon	3 tablespoons juice
1 medium orange	¼ to ½ cup juice
1 medium apple	1 cup slices
15 ounces raisins	3 cups
1 pound dates	2½ to 3 cups
1 pound pecans	4¼ cups
1 pound walnuts	4½ cups
½ pint whipping cream	2 cups whipped cream

1 No. 303 can (1 lb.)	2 cups
1 No. 2 can (1 lb. 4 oz.)	2½ cups
1 No. 2½ can (1 lb. 13 oz.)	3½ cups

FREEZING TIPS

Delicious baked food, ready for prompt serving to family and guests, is one of the delights of freezing. General hints which will help you to take advantage of your freezer are given here.

PACKAGING HINTS

Proper packaging is essential to maintain quality of the product to be stored. Freezing does not improve the product but simply maintains the original quality.

Wrapping materials should be: moisture-proof, strong and tough, odorless, tasteless, easy to handle, seal and label. Among the best are: polyethylene (plastic bags and plastic-coated freezer paper), heavy-duty aluminum foil and plastic film. Polyethylene melts at high temperatures, so use aluminum foil to wrap baked products which you plan to thaw in the oven.

A "druggist's wrap" is the method most often used for packaging. Place product in center of paper. Bring two longest sides together on top of product and fold these edges over about one inch. Fold as many times as necessary to bring paper tight and flat against top of product. Turn package over and fold corners toward each other, then fold ends over and stretch tight.

Freezer or masking tape is excellent for sealing and can be used to label and date packages. Aluminum foil is self-sealing; just use a strip of tape as a label. For polyethylene bags, tuck a label inside and seal by twisting tops and tying with rubber bands or "twist-ems."

Package foods in meal-size amounts for freezing.

BREADS

Yeast breads and quick breads can be frozen. Length of storage should not be more than three months. We recommend freezing the baked product. Unbaked dough may lose some of its rising capacity while in the frozen state; the bread when baked would be coarser in texture and smaller in volume.

To freeze: Remove baked product from pans to cool, then pack in meal-size amounts and freeze immediately. It should not stand out long between baking and freezing as this is the most rapid period of staling. However, never wrap breads while they are still warm.

To thaw: Leave breads in original wrappers. Unwrap just before serving. Thaw at room temperature on rack to allow good circulation of air. Thawing time will be 1 to 3 hours, depending on warmth of room and size of product. For warm rolls and coffee cakes, thaw in a 350° oven for 15 to 30 minutes.

CAKES

Cakes of any type, flavor or shape freeze well. Cakes may be frozen frosted or unfrosted, but unfrosted cakes keep longer, in better condition and are easier to wrap. Properly wrapped, unfrosted baked cakes remain in top condition for about 3 months. Frosted cakes may be stored 1 to 2 months. Fruitcakes may be stored considerably longer.

To freeze: Freeze a frosted cake before wrapping to set the frosting. It is well to store your cakes in cardboard boxes. Use crushed waxed paper to fill air spaces in the box. Then wrap, seal, label and date. Butter frostings (confectioners' sugar type) and fudge frostings are best for freezing. Boiled frostings freeze well, but are difficult to wrap. Place toothpicks in frosting to help prevent sticking.

To thaw: Unwrap frosted cakes, but leave unfrosted cakes wrapped. Thaw all cakes at room temperature on a rack to allow good circulation of air. Thawing time for cupcakes, 30 minutes; layers, 1 hour; and whole frosted cakes, 2 to 3 hours.

COOKIES

Bake cookies first, or freeze them unbaked, or just freeze the dough. When well packed, cookies and cookie dough may be stored in the freezer 6 to 12 months.

To freeze baked cookies: Bake cookies as usual, cool completely and wrap or place in freezer containers. (Pack very thin or fragile cookies in freezer containers to prevent breakage.) Fill empty spaces in containers with crumpled paper to protect cookies.

For freezer containers, use wide-mouthed screw-top glass jars, or canisters and coffee tins with tight covers sealed with masking tape. Or use commercial freezer containers—plastic with tight-fitting covers, heavy waxed cardboard or aluminum foil sealed with masking tape.

To wrap bar cookies for freezing, place on cardboard covered with waxed paper (or in a cardboard box); wrap securely with heavy-duty aluminum foil or self-sealing plastic film. Or place in plastic bags and seal with rubber bands.

Sturdy molded or drop cookies can be placed in plastic bags without cardboard and sealed.

To thaw baked cookies: Frozen baked cookies may be placed on serving plates immediately or thawed in container 15 minutes.

Large cookies or bars are better thawed in container 1 hour. (Thawing in the freezer container prevents moisture in the air from condensing on the cold cookies and making them soggy.)

To crisp pastry-type cookies, thaw in container for 15 minutes, then place on baking sheet and heat in oven 5 minutes.

To freeze unbaked cookies: Shape firm cookie dough according to recipe directions; arrange in a box in layers between aluminum foil or waxed paper. Wrap (or place in plastic bag), seal and freeze.

Shape soft cookie dough according to recipe directions, place on baking sheets and freeze. When hard, arrange in box, wrap, seal and store as for firm unbaked cookies.

No thawing period is necessary before baking frozen cookies.

To freeze cookie dough: Shape refrigerated cookie dough into rolls, wrap with heavy-duty aluminum foil, seal and freeze. On baking day slice immediately or thaw slightly in refrigerator until slicing is easy.

Wrap, seal and freeze bar cookie dough in the pan; bake without thawing. (This method cannot be used when two baking periods are required in the recipe.)

Pack other cookie doughs into freezer containers, seal and freeze. On baking day thaw to room temperature (or to temperature required for easiest handling); proceed according to recipe directions.

MAIN DISHES

Cooked foods should not be stored in the freezer longer than 2 to 3 months. If stored too long, some food flavors are lost, while others become too strong.

Preparation: When preparing a main dish especially for freezing, partially cook the vegetables; if completely cooked before freezing, they may become too soft and have a warmed-over flavor when reheated.

When making sauces and gravies for freezing, the fat and flour should be well blended and beaten until smooth to help avoid separation when thawed. If separation does occur, the ingredients recombine during heating.

Cool cooked foods promptly to prevent continued cooking and loss of flavor and to prevent growth of bacteria. To hasten cooling, partially submerge the pan of cooked food in a pan of ice water. Keep the saucepan covered to reduce loss of aroma and prevent contamination.

Packaging: Cooked foods may absorb off flavors in the freezer unless carefully wrapped and sealed. Many of these recipes may be frozen right in the baking dish, covered or wrapped well with aluminum foil or plastic film. In packaging meats in sauces, cover solid pieces well with the liquid to keep meat moist.

For fillings and sauces, choose from a variety of commercial freezer containers. Glass jars and metal shortening or coffee cans may be used. Be sure to cover and seal edges with tape.

To freeze leftover main dishes: Leave in serving dish or transfer to metal pan or freezer container. Cover well and freeze. To reheat, place frozen food in oven and heat at 400° for 45 to 60 minutes, depending upon the amount of food. If pastry topped, the dish may have to be partially covered after 30 minutes to prevent overbrowning.

Serving: Before serving, remove sauces or fillings from freezer containers and reheat in covered saucepan with a small amount of melted butter or in double boiler over boiling water. Thickened sauces and gravies have a tendency to become thicker when frozen, but may be thinned when reheated.

PIES

Chiffon, fruit, mince and unbaked pumpkin pies freeze well. Pie crust may be frozen baked or unbaked. Generally a storage period of 1 to 2 months is recommended. Custard and parfait pies are not suitable for freezing, and pie meringues shrink and become tough if frozen.

To freeze pie crust: Pastry may be frozen in bulk or rolled out to pastry circles. To freeze pastry circles, stack the circles between two sheets of waxed paper, wrap and seal as a group. When preparing more than one baked or unbaked pie shell for freezing, wrap individually, then stack with crumpled waxed paper between for protection.

To freeze pies: Pies may be frozen baked or unbaked. Prepare your crust and filling as directed in the recipes, using a regular pie pan or an aluminum foil pie pan. When preparing a fruit pie for freezing you may wish to use slightly more thickening than usual to prevent crust soakage. *Do not* slit the top crust of an unbaked pie before freezing. Allow chiffon and similar pies with uncooked fillings to set before freezing. Be sure baked pies are cool before wrapping.

Preparation: To wrap pies, baked or unbaked, cover them with paper plates to protect the tops. Wrap in moisture-vapor-proof material. Dispel as much air as possible and seal well. Label, date and place package level in the freezer. (If the pie seems too tender to handle, freeze before wrapping.)

Thawing: Chiffon and other refrigerator pies should be unwrapped and allowed to stand in the refrigerator 1 to 1½ hours.

Unwrap a frozen, baked pie and place in a 375° oven for 30 to 35 minutes until center is hot.

Unbaked pies should be unwrapped; slit top crust, then bake pie in a 425° oven for 40 to 50 minutes. Unwrap frozen unbaked pie shells and bake at 450° for 5 minutes. Then prick and bake 15 minutes longer.

Frozen baked pie shells need to be unwrapped and heated for 10 minutes at 375°, or they can thaw at room temperature.

Completely thaw bulk pastry and pastry circles; proceed according to recipe directions.

DESSERTS

Most desserts can be frozen following the directions for pies and cakes. Prepare extra shortcake or cream puffs to freeze. To thaw, heat in oven at 300° for about 10 to 15 minutes.

CREPES AND WAFFLES

Crepes should be frozen flat and unfilled. Crepes and waffles may be frozen in groups of 4 to 6. This way you may thaw as many or as few as you need. (If a large number are frozen together, thawing takes considerable time.) Fill and heat as directed in recipe.

To serve waffles: Pop them into your toaster, or heat in a 400° oven for 2 to 3 minutes until crisp.

YEAST BREADS

No menu is really complete without a serving of bread. What can be more satisfying than the sight of golden brown rolls or loaves and the fragrance of homemade bread? How proud you can be to say, "Yes, I made it myself. It was easy."

We have included general information with every step to help you make your breads perfect! However, this information should not be your only guide. Be sure to follow recipe directions carefully for each has been thoroughly tested to give the best results.

KNOW YOUR INGREDIENTS

The essential ingredients are few . . . flour, liquid, yeast, salt and sugar, and they combine to make breads that contain a valuable quantity of vitamins, minerals and useful proteins. (Average slice of bread = 63 calories.)

Flour is the chief ingredient. The inner portion of the wheat kernel, from which white flour is milled, makes the finest, lightest breads. Wheat is the only grain with proteins which produces gluten; this gives bread dough its elasticity and strength. Gluten stretches to form a meshlike framework that holds tiny gas bubbles formed by yeast.

Flours vary in the quantity and quality of their gluten. Good bread requires good flour. Pillsbury's Best Flour is milled to the same high quality standards at all times, so it can be depended upon to react in the same manner with each baking.

Liquid is essential for formation of gluten in the flour. Either water, fresh milk, dry or evaporated milk can be used. Water gives bread a hard crust, open texture and a wheaty flavor similar to the French breads. Milk produces bread that is more tender, nutritious and flavorful; it keeps better and toasts more quickly.

Yeast makes dough rise and gives bread its porous structure. It is a tiny living organism that utilizes sugar for its growth and produces tiny leavening gas bubbles.

There are two types of yeast on the market—dry and compressed. Both are easy to use and make good bread. Active dry yeast will stay fresh for several months stored on your shelf. Compressed yeast must be stored in the refrigerator not longer than a few weeks; it's good if it crumbles between the fingers when broken and has a fresh odor.

Check the expiration date of yeast, stamped on the back of dry yeast packets and the front of compressed yeast packages. Date may be number and day of month, such as 12/15 (December 15).

Salt gives flavor to bread and controls the action of the yeast. If salt is not added to the dough, rising takes place too rapidly and the bread will be coarse. If too much salt is added, the rising is too slow and the bread will be compact and fine.

Sugar provides food for the yeast. It also adds flavor and is partly responsible for a golden brown crust. Increasing the sugar hastens rising, but too much slows the action of the yeast.

Shortening is not necessary for bread. However, it improves the flavor, makes bread more tender, causes better browning and adds nutritional value.

Eggs give bread delicate texture and add flavor, color and richness.

STEPS IN BREADBAKING

Mixing is a must for well-shaped loaves of bread. Yeast cells must be distributed evenly throughout the dough; mixing accomplishes this.

Active dry yeast is softened in warm water, while lukewarm water is better for compressed yeast. To test, place a few drops of water on the inside of your wrist. Lukewarm water will feel neither warm nor cold; warm water will feel just slightly warm. Temperatures too hot kill yeast, and cold temperatures retard its growth.

Milk is scalded to destroy undesirable bacteria and enzymes that may interfere with the growth of the yeast. It must be cooled to lukewarm before being combined with softened yeast.

Kneading blends the ingredients and stretches the gluten into a fine elastic framework, which will hold the gas bubbles produced by the yeast when making bread by the straight dough or sponge dough methods.

To knead: Fold dough over on itself and push with palms of hands (photo A). Repeat process rhythmically, turning dough one quarter way around each time.

If the dough sticks, sprinkle kneading surface with additional flour. Do not knead in too much flour, as this makes a heavy dough that rises slowly and results in coarse-textured bread.

As kneading progresses, the dough loses its stickiness and rough appearance. It is sufficiently kneaded when smooth and satiny. To test, place dough in your hand for 15 seconds; it should not feel sticky. Pick up dough and examine closely; you'll see tiny bubbles under the tightly-stretched, satiny surface.

The dough is then rounded into a smooth ball and placed in a lightly-greased bowl. Turn dough over after placing it in bowl, so top surface of dough is lightly greased also. This will prevent crusting during rising.

Rising should not progress too rapidly or too slowly for good bread. Cold temperatures inhibit action of yeast; temperatures too warm speed yeast action, not allowing for other changes that make for good flavor and texture to take place in the dough.

The covered bowl of dough is placed in an 85° to 90° temperature away from drafts until dough has doubled in size. A steady warmth can be maintained in several ways:

- Place bowl of dough in pan of warm water; keep water warm throughout rising period.
- Place pan of hot water in bottom of unheated oven and bowl of dough on rack above it. Close oven door. (Dough does not have to be covered since steam from water keeps surface from drying.)
- Place dough in oven with pilot light; leave oven door open several inches.

To test amount of rising: Press two fingers deeply into dough (photo B). If impression remains and bubbles appear, the dough has risen sufficiently. No-knead and batter doughs are ready for shaping. If dough has been kneaded, punch it down by plunging your fist in center of dough, folding edges toward center. Turn dough upside down for second rising period (unless otherwise directed in recipe). When dough is light again, it is ready for shaping.

Shaping—(see Yeast Loaves, page 16, and Yeast Dinner Rolls, page 30, for shaping methods).

Baking—Gluten strands become more elastic and thin as dough rises. Bread must be baked before these strands become so thin that they break, allowing gas to escape. When this happens, the bread appears to have fallen and is coarse. On the other hand, bread that hasn't risen enough is small and heavy.

Baking sets the gluten and brings out the flavor. It also stops the rising; however, there is a 10 to 12 minute period just after the bread is placed in the oven when leavening gas in the dough expands. This quick rising is called "oven spring."

To test for doneness: Tap loaf with knuckles; if baked through, it sounds hollow. Baked breads are well browned and shrink slightly from sides of pan. When bread is baked, remove from pan immediately to prevent a soggy crust. Cool on wire rack.

Storage—Cool breads thoroughly before placing in bread box. Breads also store well in plastic bags or aluminum foil.

Bread should not be stored in the refrigerator unless you are having a problem with mold. Research recently has shown that refrigerator storage hastens staling.

Bread may be kept for several months in perfect condition in your freezer, wrapped in moisture-vapor proof material (plastic bags or aluminum foil).

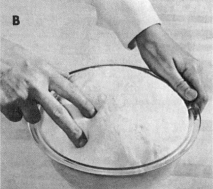

GENERAL HINTS

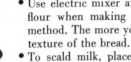

- Use electric mixer at low speed to blend in half of flour when making breads by no-knead or batter method. The more you beat the dough, the finer the texture of the bread.
- To scald milk, place in heavy saucepan or top of double boiler. Heat to a temperature just below boiling until small bubbles appear around edge and a "skin" forms over surface of milk.
- A cake of compressed yeast in these recipes refers to the ⅔ or the ⅗-ounce size, comparable to 1 packet of active dry yeast. Compressed yeast is also available in larger sizes.
- There are three most commonly used methods for making bread—

  Straight Dough Method is often used for homemade bread. All ingredients are combined at one time; the dough is kneaded and two rising periods are usually allowed.

  No-Knead Method is fairly new and saves time and labor. Only one mixing operation is involved and no kneading is necessary. Flour is blended with liquid ingredients, then the dough may be set aside to rise once before shaping. Total time to make and bake varies from 1 to 3 hours.

  Batter Dough Method is the quickest way to make homemade bread. Both kneading and shaping are eliminated; the soft dough is dropped or spread into baking pans. Usually one rising period is required.

- Use Pillsbury's Best Flour Shaker to flour kneading and rolling surface.
- When working with kneaded dough, mix in as much flour as you can, beating dough thoroughly. Adding flour in this method is hard work, especially when preparing a large recipe. It is possible to knead in the last portion of flour, using enough to obtain the proper handling consistency.

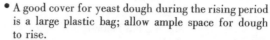

- A good cover for yeast dough during the rising period is a large plastic bag; allow ample space for dough to rise.

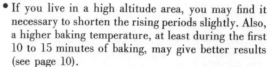

- If you live in a high altitude area, you may find it necessary to shorten the rising periods slightly. Also, a higher baking temperature, at least during the first 10 to 15 minutes of baking, may give better results (see page 10).

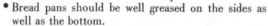

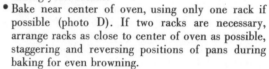

- Dull-finished pans should be used for breadbaking, as they absorb heat and give an even brown crust. Glass baking dishes may be used (photo C), as well as dull aluminum or dark metal pans.
- Bread pans should be well greased on the sides as well as the bottom.
- Preheat the oven to the specified temperature before baking yeast breads.
- Bake near center of oven, using only one rack if possible (photo D). If two racks are necessary, arrange racks as close to center of oven as possible, staggering and reversing positions of pans during baking for even browning.
- Some of these recipes specify that the dough may be refrigerated for several days and used as needed; be sure to cover dough well and place in coldest spot in your refrigerator.

C

D

YEAST LOAVES
—There are two basic methods for shaping yeast loaves.

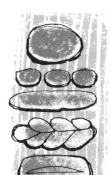

Rolling Pin Method
1. Roll dough for one loaf to 14x7-inch rectangle.
2. Roll tightly as for jelly roll, starting with 7-inch side.
3. Seal dough with heel of hand after each roll (photo A); seal edges and ends.
4. Place in pan, seam-side down.

Hand Method
1. Flatten dough for one loaf into 18x10-inch rectangle.
2. Fold one long side to center, pressing out air pockets (photo B); fold other side to overlap.
3. Fold both ends of dough (about ⅓ of length) and overlap in center; press out air each time.
4. Roll into loaf; seal edge well by pressing with heel of hand (photo C) and tucking edge under.
5. Place in pan, seam-side down.

Most of these recipes call for a 9x5x3-inch bread pan. However, the 8½x4½x2½-inch glass baking pans are very satisfactory for bread baking. Bread pans should be well greased on the sides as well as the bottoms.

For a crisp, glazed crust, brush before baking with mixture of slightly-beaten egg white and water.

To give softer crust and to help prevent crust from drying, brush tops of loaves lightly with butter or shortening after baking.

Use a good knife with a serrated edge to cut breads. Cut back and forth with a sawing motion.

County Fair Egg Bread
Senior Winner by Mrs. Philip Carlson, St. Helens, Oregon

Rich with eggs, this big bread recipe makes twenty-four moist, flavorful rolls—and a three-part loaf of bread, too!

BAKE at 375° for 15 to 20 minutes for rolls, 35 to 40 minutes for loaves   MAKES 2 dozen rolls and 1 loaf

Soften . . . . 2 packets active dry **yeast** (or 2 cakes compressed) in ½ cup warm **water**

Combine . . . . ⅓ cup **sugar**
    ½ cup **shortening**
    4 teaspoons **salt*** and
    2 cups hot scalded **milk** in large mixing bowl; stir to melt shortening. Add
    ½ cup cold **water.** Cool to lukewarm.

Stir in . . . . 4 beaten **eggs** and softened yeast.

Add . . . . 9 to 10 cups sifted **Pillsbury's Best All Purpose Flour*** gradually to form a stiff dough.

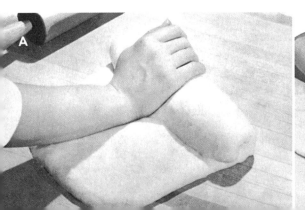

Knead . . . . on floured surface until smooth and satiny, 5 to 7 minutes. Place in greased bowl and cover.

Let rise . . . . in warm place (85°) until doubled, 1½ to 2 hours.

Punch down . . . . dough. Let rise 30 minutes.

Divide . . . . into three parts. Shape two parts into rolls 1½ to 2 inches in diameter. Place on greased baking sheets and let rise in warm place until light, about 45 minutes.

Shape . . . . remaining dough into 3 small loaves; place crosswise in one greased 9x5x3-inch pan. Let rise in warm place until light, about 1¼ hours.

Bake . . . . at 375°: 15 to 20 minutes for rolls; 35 to 40 minutes for loaf. While hot, brush with melted **butter**.

For use with Pillsbury's Best Self-Rising Flour, omit salt.

Egg Twist Loaves

Senior Winner by Fannie Thomas Greenberg, Chicago, Illinois

Nothing better than home-baked bread! Light in texture with attractive braid shaping, this recipe makes two golden loaves.

BAKE at 375° for 40 to 45 minutes   MAKES 2 loaves

Soften . . . . 2 packets active dry **yeast** (or 2 cakes compressed) in 2 cups warm **water** in large mixing bowl.

Combine . . . . ¼ cup **sugar**
4 teaspoons **salt*** and
¼ cup **salad oil** or melted shortening

Blend in . . . . . 3 slightly beaten **eggs** (reserve 1 tablespoon) and 3 cups sifted **Pillsbury's Best All Purpose Flour.*** Beat well.

Add . . . . 4½ to 5 cups sifted **Pillsbury's Best All Purpose Flour** gradually to form a stiff dough.

Knead . . . . on floured surface until smooth and satiny, 7 to 10 minutes. Place in greased bowl and cover.

Let rise . . . . in warm place (85°) until doubled, about 1½ hours.

Divide . . . . half of dough into three parts. Roll each part into a strip about 14 inches long. Braid the three strips together, sealing ends. Place braid in well-greased 9x5x3-inch pan. Repeat process with remaining dough. Cover.

Let rise . . . . in warm place until light, 45 to 60 minutes. Brush with reserved egg.

Bake . . . . at 375° for 40 to 45 minutes.

For use with Pillsbury's Best Self-Rising Flour, omit salt.

Golden-Crust Bread

Senior Winner

Sour cream adds tenderness to these loaves of white bread. You'll like the crisp, golden-brown crust edging the creamy-white slices.

BAKE at 375° for 40 to 45 minutes   MAKES 2 loaves

Soften . . . . 1 packet active dry **yeast** (or 1 cake compressed) in ¼ cup warm **water**

Combine . . . . . 1 cup **sour cream** (thick or commercial) and ¼ teaspoon **soda** in large mixing bowl.

Stir in . . . . . . 2 tablespoons **sugar**
1 tablespoon **salt***
2 tablespoons **butter** or margarine, melted
1 cup warm **water** and softened yeast.

Add . . . . . . 5½ to 6 cups sifted **Pillsbury's Best All Purpose Flour*** gradually to form a stiff dough.

Knead . . . . on floured surface until smooth and satiny, 5 to 7 minutes. Place in greased bowl and cover.

Let rise . . . . in warm place (85°) until doubled, 1½ to 2 hours.

Divide . . . . in half; form into balls. Cover; let stand 10 minutes.

Shape . . . . into loaves; place in greased 9x5x3-inch pans. Cover.

Let rise . . . . in warm place until light, about 1½ hours.

Bake . . . . at 375° for 40 to 45 minutes.

For use with Pillsbury's Best Self-Rising Flour, omit salt.

Crusty French Bread

Crusty French Bread

Senior Winner by Mrs. John Cabbell Roy, Birmingham, Alabama

This recipe came from a small cafe in Paris, France—a delicious, crispy, hard-crusted bread.

BAKE at 425° for 15 to 30 minutes, then at 350° for 30 minutes   MAKES 3 loaves

Combine . . . . . 1 tablespoon **shortening**
            1 tablespoon **salt**
            1 tablespoon **sugar** and
            1 cup **boiling water** in large mixing bowl.

Add . . . . 1 cup cold **water**. Cool to lukewarm.
Blend in . . . . . 1 packet active dry **yeast** (or 1 cake compressed). Let stand 5 minutes. Mix well.
Add . . . . 5 to 5½ cups sifted **Pillsbury's Best All Purpose Flour*** gradually to form a stiff dough, mixing well after each addition.
Knead . . . . on floured surface until smooth and satiny, about 5 minutes. Place in greased bowl and cover.
Let rise . . . . in warm place (85°) until doubled, about 1½ hours.
Shape . . . . into three oblong loaves about 10 inches long; place on greased baking sheet.
Let rise . . . . in warm place until light, about 1 hour.
Brush . . . . with slightly beaten **egg white**. With sharp knife, gently make three diagonal slashes across top.
Bake . . . . at 425° for 15 to 30 minutes, until golden brown, then at 350° for 30 minutes.

*Pillsbury's Best Self-Rising Flour is not recommended for use in this recipe.

French Onion Bread

Senior Third Prize Winner by Mrs. Thomas Maguire, Little Silver, New Jersey

Dry onion soup gives this bread an entirely new flavor . . . delicious fresh or toasted.

BAKE at 375° for 35 to 40 minutes   MAKES 2 loaves*

Soften . . . . 2 packets active dry **yeast** (or 2 cakes compressed) in ½ cup warm **water**
Combine . . . 1½ cups warm **water**
            3 tablespoons **sugar**
            2 tablespoons **shortening**, melted
            2 teaspoons **salt****
            1 package **dry onion soup** and softened yeast in large mixing bowl.
Add . . . . . . 5½ to 6 cups sifted **Pillsbury's Best All Purpose Flour**** gradually to form a stiff dough.

Knead	on floured surface until smooth and satiny, about 5 minutes. Place in greased bowl and cover.
Let rise	in warm place (85°) until doubled, about 1½ hours.
Punch down	dough. Let rise 30 minutes.
Divide	into two parts.* Shape into loaves and place in greased 9x5x3-inch pans. Cover.
Let rise	in warm place until light, about 1 hour.
Bake	at 375° for 35 to 40 minutes.*

*If desired, dough can be shaped into 18 hamburger buns. Let rise about 30 minutes; bake for 15 to 18 minutes.

**For use with Pillsbury's Best Self-Rising Flour, omit salt.

French Bread Braids

Senior Winner by Mrs. Lillie B. Eldredge, Glendale, Arizona

Typical French bread . . . crunchy-crusted, braided loaves (or dinner rolls, if you prefer) with a soft, downy texture.

BAKE at 425° for 15 minutes, then
    at 350° for 20 to 25 minutes

MAKES 3 loaves

Soften	1 packet active dry **yeast** (or 1 cake compressed) in ¼ cup warm **water**
Combine	2 cups warm **water**
	¼ cup **shortening**, melted
	1 tablespoon **salt**
	1 tablespoon **sugar** and softened yeast in large mixing bowl.
Add	7 to 7½ cups sifted **Pillsbury's Best All Purpose Flour*** gradually to form a stiff dough.
Knead	on floured surface until smooth and satiny, 5 to 8 minutes. Place in greased bowl and cover.
Let rise	in warm place (85°) until doubled, 1 to 1½ hours.
Punch down	dough. Let rise 30 minutes.
Divide	into three parts. Divide one part into three portions. Roll each portion into a strip about 14 inches long.

French Bread Braids

Braid the three strips together, sealing ends. Place braid on greased baking sheet. Repeat process with remaining parts. Cover.

Let rise	in warm place until light, 45 to 60 minutes.
Brush	tops of loaves with beaten **egg**. If desired, sprinkle with **poppy seeds** or sesame seeds.
Bake	at 425° for 15 minutes, then at 350° for 20 to 25 minutes.

*Pillsbury's Best Self-Rising Flour is not recommended for use in this recipe.

French Dinner Rolls: Divide dough into 24 equal parts and shape into rounds and ovals. Let rise and bake as directed above.

Herb and Butter Bread

Senior Winner by Mrs. Gust Johnson, Jamestown, New York

Handsome loaves of bread, fine textured with delicate brown interior and a just-right blend of herbs.

BAKE at 375° for 35 to 40 minutes   MAKES 2 loaves*

Brown . . . . . . ½ cup **butter** or margarine in saucepan.
Stir in . . . . . . ⅓ cup firmly packed **brown sugar**
          2 cups scalded **milk**
          1 tablespoon **salt****
          1 teaspoon **sweet basil**
          1 teaspoon **caraway seed** and
          ½ teaspoon **thyme.** Cool to lukewarm.
Soften . . . . 2 packets active dry **yeast** (or 2 cakes compressed) in
          ½ cup warm **water.** Add to lukewarm mixture.
Add . . . . 7½ to 8 cups sifted **Pillsbury's Best All Purpose Flour****
          gradually to form a stiff dough.

Herb and Butter Bread

Knead . . . . on floured surface until smooth and satiny, 5 to 8 minutes. Place in greased bowl and cover.
Let rise . . . . in warm place (85°) until doubled, about 1½ hours.
Punch down . . . . dough. Let rise 30 minutes.
Divide . . . . into two parts.* Shape into loaves. Place in greased 9x5x3-inch pans or 9-inch round layer pans. Cover.
Let rise . . . . in warm place until light, about 45 minutes.
Bake . . . . at 375° for 35 to 40 minutes.

   *Or divide into three parts; shape into loaves; place in greased 8x4x3-inch pans.
**For use with Pillsbury's Best Self-Rising Flour, omit salt.

Garlic Cheese Toast

Senior Winner by Lucy Collins, Long Beach, California

Toast this cheese loaf flavored with garlic; it's delicious with soups, vegetable salads or main dishes.

BAKE at 375° for 45 to 50 minutes   MAKES 1 loaf

Soften . . . . 1 packet active dry **yeast** (or 1 cake compressed) in
          ½ cup warm **water**
Combine . . . . ½ cup **milk**
          4 ounces (¾ cup) **Cheddar cheese,** cut in small pieces
          1 tablespoon **sugar** and
          1½ teaspoons **salt*** in saucepan. Heat until cheese melts. Pour into large mixing bowl. Cool to lukewarm.
Add . . . . 1 tablespoon finely chopped **garlic** and softened yeast.
Add . . . . 2½ cups sifted **Pillsbury's Best All Purpose Flour*** gradually; mix thoroughly.
Knead . . . . on lightly floured surface, about 5 minutes. Place in greased bowl and cover.
Let rise . . . . in warm place (85°) until doubled, about 1 hour.
Shape . . . . into loaf. Place in greased 9x5x3-inch pan.
Let rise . . . . in warm place until light, 30 to 60 minutes.
Bake . . . . at 375° for 45 to 50 minutes. Cool. Serve toasted.

*For use with Pillsbury's Best Self-Rising Flour, omit salt.

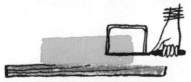

Chunk o' Cheese Bread

Second Grand Prize Winner by Mrs. Richard W. Ojakangas, Duluth, Minnesota

Two crusty round loaves with corn meal and molasses flavor . . . chunks of golden cheese are the added attraction in every slice.

BAKE at 350° for 45 to 55 minutes   MAKES 2 loaves

Combine . . . 1¾ cups **water**
½ cup **corn meal** and
2 teaspoons **salt*** in 2-quart saucepan. Bring to boil, stirring constantly; cook until slightly thickened. Remove from heat.

Add . . . . ½ cup **molasses** and
2 tablespoons **shortening.** Cool to lukewarm.

Soften . . . . 1 packet active dry **yeast** (or 1 cake compressed) in ½ cup warm **water** in large mixing bowl. Add corn meal mixture; blend thoroughly.

Add . . . . 4 to 5 cups sifted **Pillsbury's Best All Purpose Flour*** gradually to form a stiff dough.

Knead . . . . on well-floured surface until smooth and satiny, about 5 minutes. Place in greased bowl and cover.

Let rise . . . . in warm place (85°) until doubled, 1 to 1½ hours.

Cut . . . . 1 pound **American cheese** into ¼ to ½-inch cubes. Line two 8 or 9-inch round pans with 12-inch squares of aluminum foil, edges extending over pan; grease well.

Place . . . . dough on surface sprinkled with corn meal. Work cheese into dough, ¼ at a time, until cubes are evenly distributed. Divide into two parts.

Shape . . . . into round loaves, covering cheese cubes.

Let rise . . . . in warm place until light, about 1 hour.

Bake . . . . at 350° for 45 to 55 minutes.

*For use with Pillsbury's Best Self-Rising Flour, omit salt.

Chuck o' Cheese Bread

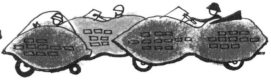

Peanut Butter Bread 'n' Rolls

Senior Winner by Mrs. Stanley B. Ashcroft, Assinippi, Massachusetts

Peanut butter is a surprise ingredient in this yeast dough. The recipe makes a dozen dinner rolls plus a loaf of bread.

BAKE at 350° for 40 to 45 minutes for bread,   MAKES 1 loaf
    at 375° for 20 to 25 minutes for rolls   and 1 dozen rolls

Soften........1 packet active dry **yeast** (or 1 cake compressed) in
     ¼ cup warm **water**
Combine.....½ cup firmly packed **brown sugar**
     ½ cup **peanut butter**
     2 teaspoons **salt*** and
     1½ cups scalded **milk** in large mixing bowl. Beat with
     rotary beater until smooth. Cool to lukewarm. Blend
     in softened yeast.
Add........4 to 4½ cups sifted **Pillsbury's Best All Purpose Flour***
     gradually to form a stiff dough.
Knead........on floured surface about 5 minutes. Place in greased
     bowl and cover.
Let rise........in warm place (85°) until doubled, about 2 hours.
Divide........in half. Shape one part into loaf and place in greased
     9x5x3-inch pan. Shape other part into 12 rolls. Place
     in greased muffin cups or on baking sheet. Cover.
Let rise........in warm place until light, about 1½ hours.
Bake.........bread at 350° for 40 to 45 minutes; rolls at 375°
     for 20 to 25 minutes.

For use with Pillsbury's Best Self-Rising Flour, omit salt; bake at 350°, decreasing baking time of bread to 35 to 40 minutes.

Caraway Bran Bread

Senior Winner by Mrs. Herbert Larson, Tamarack, Minnesota

Caraway seed and bran cereal are combined for a wonderful flavor.

BAKE at 375° for 40 to 45 minutes   MAKES 2 loaves

Soften.......1 packet active dry **yeast** (or 1 cake compressed) in
     ¼ cup warm **water**
Combine...1¼ cups **water**
     1 cup hot scalded **milk** and
     1 cup ready-to-eat **bran cereal** in large mixing bowl.
     Cool to lukewarm.
Blend in.....¼ cup dark **molasses**
     ¼ cup **shortening**, melted
     2 tablespoons **sugar**
     2 teaspoons **salt***
     1 teaspoon **caraway seed** and softened yeast.
Add.......5½ to 6 cups sifted **Pillsbury's Best All Purpose Flour***
     gradually to form a stiff dough.
Knead........on floured surface until smooth and satiny, 5 to 7
     minutes. Place in greased bowl and cover.
Let rise........in warm place (85°) until doubled, about 1½ hours.
Punch down....dough. Let rise 30 minutes.
Divide........in half; mold into two balls. Cover and let stand 15
     minutes. Shape into loaves; place in well-greased
     9x5x3-inch pans. Cover.
Let rise........in warm place until light, 45 to 60 minutes.
Bake.........at 375° for 40 to 45 minutes.

For use with Pillsbury's Best Self-Rising Flour, omit salt.

Sweet Nut Braid

Senior Winner by Mrs. E. Wingenbach, Carson, North Dakota

A delightful bread plain or toasted, with a nut filling for subtle flavor.

BAKE at 350° for 40 to 50 minutes   MAKES 2 loaves

Soften.......2 packets active dry **yeast** (or 2 cakes compressed) in
             ½ cup warm **water**
Combine....⅛ cup **butter** or margarine
           ⅛ cup **sugar**
           2½ teaspoons **salt*** and
           1 cup hot scalded **milk** in large mixing bowl. Cool to
           lukewarm.
Stir in.......2 unbeaten **eggs**
             1 tablespoon grated **lemon rind** and softened yeast.
Add.........5 to 5½ cups sifted **Pillsbury's Best All Purpose Flour***
            gradually to form a stiff dough.
Knead.......on floured surface until smooth and satiny, 5 to 8
            minutes. Place in greased bowl and cover.
Let rise........in warm place (85°) until doubled, about 1½ hours.
Cream......¼ cup **butter** or margarine. Gradually add
           1½ cups sifted **confectioners' sugar**
           1½ teaspoons **milk**
           1 teaspoon **vanilla** and
           ¼ teaspoon **nutmeg**, creaming well.
Roll out.......half of dough on floured surface to a 15x12-inch
              rectangle. Spread with half of creamed mixture.
              Sprinkle with
              ½ cup **nuts**, chopped. Cut into three 12x5-inch strips.
Roll.........each strip as for jelly roll, starting with 12-inch side;
            seal seam. Braid the three strips.
Place.........braid in well-greased 9x5x3-inch pan. Repeat with
             remaining dough.
Let rise........in warm place until light, about 1 hour.
Bake.........at 350° for 40 to 50 minutes.

*For use with Pillsbury's Best Self-Rising Flour, omit salt; decrease baking
time to 35 to 40 minutes.

Calico Carnival Bread

Junior Winner by Patricia Piper, Storden, Minnesota

*This rich, colorful loaf makes excellent open sandwiches when spread
with cream cheese.*

BAKE at 350° for 50 to 60 minutes   MAKES 1 loaf

Soften.......1 packet active dry **yeast** (or 1 cake compressed) in
             ¼ cup warm **water**
Combine....¼ cup **shortening**
           1 tablespoon **sugar**
           1½ teaspoons **salt*** and
           ¾ cup hot scalded **milk** in mixing bowl. Cool to
           lukewarm.
Add.........1 unbeaten **egg** and softened yeast.
Blend in....1¼ cups sifted **Pillsbury's Best All Purpose Flour;***
            mix well. Cover.
Let rise........in warm place (85°) until light, 45 to 60 minutes.
Stir in......½ to 1 cup **gumdrops**, cut (assorted fruit flavors)
            ¼ cup **raisins**
            ¼ cup **walnuts**, chopped, and
            2 cups sifted **Pillsbury's Best All Purpose Flour**; mix
            thoroughly.
Knead........on floured surface until smooth and satiny, 5 to 7
            minutes. Shape into loaf; place in greased 9x5x3-
            inch pan. Cover.
Let rise........in warm place until light, 1 to 1½ hours.
Bake.........at 350° for 50 to 60 minutes. Frost with **confection-
            ers' sugar icing**, if desired.

*For use with Pillsbury's Best Self-Rising Flour, omit salt.

Can-Pan Fruit Bread

Can-Pan Fruit Bread

Senior Winner by Mrs. Hildegard Chamberlain, Cambridge, Massachusetts

An Old World fruit bread with your choice of baking pans—perfect for Christmas gifts.

BAKE at 350°   MAKES 3 large or 6 small loaves

Soften . . . . 2 packets active dry **yeast** (or 2 cakes compressed) in
½ cup warm **water**
Combine . . . . ½ cup **sugar**
½ cup **shortening**
1 tablespoon **salt*** and
1½ cups hot scalded **milk** in large mixing bowl. Cool to lukewarm.

Add . . . . 2 beaten **eggs**
2 tablespoons **brandy flavoring** or **rum flavoring**
1 teaspoon **vanilla** and softened yeast.
Blend in . . . . . 4 cups sifted **Pillsbury's Best All Purpose Flour;***
mix well.
Let rise . . . . in warm place (85°) until doubled, about 1¼ hours.
Add . . . . 3 to 3½ cups sifted **Pillsbury's Best All Purpose Flour**
gradually to form a stiff dough.
Knead . . . . on floured surface until smooth and satiny, 5 to 8
minutes. Knead in
1½ cups chopped mixed **candied fruit**
½ cup chopped **candied cherries**
½ cup **raisins** and
½ cup blanched **almonds**, chopped
Let rise . . . . in warm place until doubled, about 1½ hours.
Shape . . . . dough as follows: (1) *Either* divide into three parts
and shape into round loaves. Place in three well-
greased 8 or 9-inch round layer pans or three
well-greased 3-pound shortening cans. (2) *Or* divide
into six parts, shape into round loaves and place in
six well-greased 1-pound coffee cans.
Let rise . . . . in warm place until dough fills pans and tops of
loaves are even with pan edges, about 1 hour.
Bake . . . . at 350°: large loaves for 50 to 60 minutes; small
loaves for 40 to 45 minutes. Remove from cans immediately and brush with beaten **egg**. If desired,
frost with **Vanilla Glaze,** page 326.
**For use with Pillsbury's Best Self-Rising Flour, omit salt.*

Scottish Currant Bread

Senior Winner by Mrs. Jessie A. Swan, Santa Barbara, California

Golden loaves of egg bread, generous with currants, so tasty with a refreshing orange flavor.

BAKE at 375° for 30 to 35 minutes, then **MAKES 2 loaves**
for 3 to 5 minutes

Soften . . . . 2 packets active dry **yeast** (or 2 cakes compressed) in
½ cup warm **water**

Combine . . . . ½ cup **butter** or margarine
⅓ cup **sugar**
1 tablespoon **salt*** and
½ cup hot scalded **milk** in large mixing bowl; stir to melt butter.

Stir in . . . . 2 unbeaten **eggs**
3 tablespoons grated **orange rind**
½ cup **orange juice** and softened yeast.

Add . . . . 6 to 6½ cups sifted **Pillsbury's Best All Purpose Flour*** gradually to form a stiff dough.

Knead . . . . on floured surface until smooth and satiny, 7 to 10 minutes. Place in greased bowl and cover.

Let rise . . . . in warm place (85°) until doubled, 1½ to 2 hours.

Divide . . . . dough into two parts. Roll out each part to an 18x7-inch rectangle. Sprinkle each with
½ cup dried **currants**. Roll tightly as for jelly roll, starting with 7-inch side. Seal edges and ends. Place in well-greased 9x5x3-inch pans, seam-side down.

Let rise . . . . in warm place until light, about 1½ hours.

Bake . . . . at 375° for 30 to 35 minutes. Combine
1 tablespoon **orange juice** and
1 tablespoon **sugar**. Brush tops of loaves; bake 3 to 5 minutes.

**For use with Pillsbury's Best Self-Rising Flour, omit salt.*

Up-to-Date Bread

Senior Winner by Mrs. Antoinette Jordan, Providence, Rhode Island

There's the rich flavor of dates and nuts in this dark yeast bread which is wonderful fresh or toasted. An orange glaze tops each loaf.

BAKE at 375° for 35 minutes, then **MAKES 3 loaves**
for 5 to 10 minutes

Heat . . . . 2 cups **milk** in top of double boiler over boiling water. Add 1½ cups **dates,** cut in pieces. Cook 10 minutes. Cool to lukewarm.

Soften . . . . 2 packets active dry **yeast** (or 2 cakes compressed) in
½ cup warm **water**

Combine . . . . . 2 tablespoons **sugar**
2 tablespoons **shortening**
1 tablespoon **salt*** and
1 cup hot scalded **milk** in large mixing bowl. Cool to lukewarm.

Add . . . . 1 cup **nuts**, ground or finely chopped, the date-milk mixture and softened yeast.

Blend in . . . . 8½ to 9 cups sifted **Pillsbury's Best All Purpose Flour*** to form a stiff dough.

Knead . . . . on floured surface until smooth and satiny, 8 to 10 minutes. Place in greased bowl and cover.

Let rise . . . . in warm place (85°) until doubled, about 2 hours.

Divide . . . . dough into 3 equal parts. Shape into loaves. Place in greased 9x5x3-inch pans. Cover.

Let rise . . . . in warm place until light, 45 to 60 minutes.

Bake . . . . at 375° for 35 minutes. Brush with Orange Glaze. Bake 5 to 10 minutes.

**For use with Pillsbury's Best Self-Rising Flour, omit salt.*

ORANGE GLAZE

Combine 2 tablespoons sugar and 2 tablespoons orange juice. Mix well.

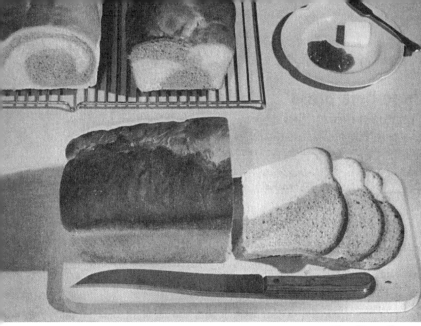

Two-Tone Loaves

Two-Tone Loaves

Senior Winner by Olive Foster Hoover, Takoma Park, Maryland

Whole wheat and white bread in the same loaf! You add whole wheat flour to half the dough, then shape the two together.

BAKE at 375° for 45 to 50 minutes   MAKES 3 loaves

Soften . . . . 2 packets active dry **yeast** (or 2 cakes compressed) in
         1 cup warm **water**
Combine . . . . ½ cup **sugar**
         ½ cup **shortening**
         2 tablespoons **salt*** and
         2 cups hot scalded **milk** in large mixing bowl. Stir to
         melt shortening. Cool to lukewarm by adding

         1 cup cold **water**; add softened yeast.
Add . . . . 4 cups sifted **Pillsbury's Best All Purpose Flour;***
         beat with mixer or rotary beater until smooth. Cover.
Let rise . . . . in warm place (85°) until doubled, about 1 hour.
Divide . . . . in half; place each half in large mixing bowl.
Blend . . . . . . 3½ to 4 cups sifted **Pillsbury's Best All Purpose Flour**
         into one part to form a stiff dough.
Stir . . . . ¼ cup dark **molasses** into second part. Then blend in
         2½ cups unsifted **Pillsbury's Whole Wheat (Graham)**
         Flour and
         1 to 1½ cups sifted **Pillsbury's Best All Purpose Flour**
         to form a stiff dough.
Knead . . . . on floured surface until smooth and satiny, 5 to 7
         minutes. Place each in greased bowl and cover.
Let rise . . . . in warm place until light, about 1½ hours.
Divide . . . . each dough into 3 equal parts. For each loaf, combine
         one light and one dark section, shaping into desired
         pattern. (See the suggestions below.) Press doughs
         firmly together to avoid air bubbles. Place each loaf
         in well-greased 9x5x3-inch pan. Cover.
Let rise . . . . in warm place until light, about 1 hour.
Bake . . . . at 375° for 45 to 50 minutes.
**For use with Pillsbury's Best Self-Rising Flour, omit salt.*

Pinwheel Loaf: Roll out or flatten one section of light dough and one section of dark dough to 12x8-inch rectangle; place one on top of the other. Roll up tightly, beginning with 8-inch edge.

Checkerboard Loaf: Shape 1½-inch balls from one section of each dough. Arrange in pan, alternating colors of dough. (Or alternate strips of dough the length of the pan.)

Half-and-Half Loaf: Shape one section of each dough into a strip about 8 inches long; press strips together, forming a loaf.

Patchwork Loaf: Combine small, irregularly shaped portions of one section of each dough, forming a loaf.

Party Rye Bread

Senior Winner by Mrs. George Grim, Olympia, Washington

Big, moist, sweet rye loaves, flavored with maple syrup, candied orange peel and anise seed.

BAKE at 350° for 15 minutes, then   MAKES 3 loaves
    at 300° for 30 to 40 minutes

Combine.....2 cups **milk**
       1¼ cups **maple syrup**
       ¼ cup **candied orange peel,** finely chopped
       ¼ cup **shortening** and
       4 teaspoons **anise seed** in double boiler. Heat over boiling water until milk is scalded. Cool to lukewarm.
Soften.......2 packets active dry **yeast** (or 2 cakes compressed) in
       1 cup warm **water** in large mixing bowl. Add lukewarm milk mixture.
Add........2 cups sifted **Pillsbury's Pure Medium Rye Flour** and
       1 tablespoon **salt;*** beat well. Let stand in warm place (85°) until covered with bubbles, 12 to 15 minutes.
Blend in.....3 cups sifted **Pillsbury's Pure Medium Rye Flour;** beat well.
Add........5 to 5½ cups sifted **Pillsbury's Best All Purpose Flour*** gradually to form a stiff dough.
Knead........on well-floured surface until smooth and satiny, 5 to 10 minutes. Place in greased bowl and cover.
Let rise........in warm place until doubled, 1½ to 2 hours.
Punch down....dough. Divide into 3 parts; mold into balls. Cover with bowl and let stand 30 minutes.
Shape........into 3 loaves; place each loaf in well-greased 9x5x3-inch pan. Let rise in warm place until light, 1 to 1½ hours. Using a very sharp knife, make diagonal slits ¼ inch deep and 3 inches apart across top of each loaf.
Bake.........at 350° for 15 minutes, then at 300° for 30 to 40 minutes.

*For use with Pillsbury's Best Self-Rising Flour, omit salt.

Dark Orange Raisin Bread

Senior Winner by Mrs. George Townsend, Spalding, Nebraska

A new, unusual flavor . . . caramelized sugar, raisins and orange rind in these dark loaves.

BAKE at 350° for 40 to 45 minutes   MAKES 3 loaves

Melt........¼ cup **sugar** in heavy skillet over low heat, stirring constantly, until sugar melts and turns dark golden brown. Add very slowly
       ⅓ cup hot **water,** a few drops at a time at first, stirring constantly until sugar is completely dissolved. Cool.
Soften.......2 packets active dry **yeast** (or 2 cakes compressed) in
       ½ cup warm **water** in large mixing bowl. Let stand 5 minutes.
Add........⅓ cup firmly packed **brown sugar**
       2 cups sifted **Pillsbury's Pure Medium Rye Flour**
       1 tablespoon **salt***
       1½ cups warm **water**
       ¼ cup **shortening,** melted
       1 cup **raisins**
       2 tablespoons grated **orange rind** and burnt sugar. Beat well.
Add........4 to 4½ cups sifted **Pillsbury's Best All Purpose Flour*** gradually to form a stiff dough.
Knead........on floured surface until smooth and satiny, 5 to 8 minutes. Place in a greased bowl and cover.
Let rise........in warm place (85°) until doubled, about 2 hours. Punch down and let rise 30 minutes.
Divide........dough into 3 parts. Shape into round or long loaves and place on greased baking sheets or in small loaf pans.
Let rise........in warm place until light, 30 to 60 minutes. Using a sharp knife, make three slits diagonally across the top of each loaf.
Bake.........at 350° for 40 to 45 minutes.

*For use with Pillsbury's Best Self-Rising Flour, omit salt.

No-Knead Golden Loaves

Junior Winner by Shirley Koller, Somerset, California

Bread-in-the-round . . . a moist loaf, easy to make.

BAKE at 400° for 40 to 45 minutes   MAKES 2 loaves

Combine . . . 1½ cups warm **water**
1 packet active dry **yeast** (or 1 cake compressed)
1 tablespoon **sugar**
1 tablespoon **shortening**, melted, and
2 teaspoons **salt*** in large mixing bowl. Let stand 5 minutes; mix well.

Add . . . . 4 to 4¼ cups sifted **Pillsbury's Best All Purpose Flour*** gradually to form a stiff dough, beating well after each addition. Cover.

Let rise . . . . in warm place (85°) until doubled, about 1½ hours.

Toss . . . . on well-floured surface to coat with flour. Divide in half; shape into 2 round loaves. Place in two 6-inch round casseroles, greased and sprinkled with **corn meal,** or place on greased baking sheet.

Let rise . . . . in warm place until light, 45 to 60 minutes. Brush with slightly beaten **egg white.**

Bake . . . . at 400° for 40 to 45 minutes.

For use with Pillsbury's Best Self-Rising Flour, omit salt.

No-Knead Holiday Bread

Junior Winner by Kathleen Boyd, Kenosha, Wisconsin

A No-Knead version of a traditional Danish Christmas bread, rich in raisins and candied fruit. It is simple to prepare—just one rising.

BAKE at 350° for 40 to 50 minutes   MAKES 1 loaf

Soften . . . . 1 packet active dry **yeast** (or 1 cake compressed) in ¼ cup warm **water**

Combine . . . . ¼ cup **sugar**

¼ cup **shortening**
1½ teaspoons **salt** and
½ cup hot scalded **milk** in large mixing bowl. Stir to melt shortening.

Add . . . . ¼ cup cold **water**
1 unbeaten **egg**
¾ cup **raisins**
1 cup (½ lb.) mixed **candied fruit** and softened yeast; mix well.

Add . . . . 3 to 3¼ cups sifted **Pillsbury's Best All Purpose Flour*** gradually; mix well. Cover; let stand 15 minutes.

Turn . . . . into well-greased 9x5x3-inch pan. Cover.

Let rise . . . . in warm place (85°) until light, about 1½ hours.

Bake . . . . at 350° for 40 to 50 minutes.

Pillsbury's Best Self-Rising Flour is not recommended for use in this recipe.

Old-Fashioned Nut Loaf

Senior Winner by Veronica Kmetz, Swoyerville, Pennsylvania

Slices of this festive, nut-sprinkled loaf reveal a spiral of coconut and chopped nuts.

BAKE at 350° for 40 to 45 minutes   MAKES 1 loaf

Soften . . . . 1 packet active dry **yeast** (or 1 cake compressed) in ¼ cup warm **water**

Heat . . . . ½ cup **milk** and

¼ cup **butter** or margarine until butter melts.

Combine.....2 unbeaten **egg yolks** (reserve whites for filling)
  ¼ cup **sugar** and
  1½ teaspoons **salt*** in large mixing bowl. Add milk mixture. Cool to lukewarm. Blend in softened yeast.

Add.......2¼ cups sifted **Pillsbury's Best All Purpose Flour***
  gradually, mixing well. Place in greased bowl and cover.

Let rise.......in warm place (85°) until doubled, about 2 hours. Prepare Nut Filling.

Roll out.......on floured surface to a 12x8-inch rectangle. Spread with Filling. Roll as for jelly roll, starting with 8-inch edge. Seal edge and ends. Place in greased 9x5x3-inch pan. Cover.

Let rise.......in warm place until light, about 1 hour. Brush with **milk**. Sprinkle with **sugar**.

Bake.........at 350° for 40 to 45 minutes.

For use with Pillsbury's Best Self-Rising Flour, omit salt.

NUT FILLING

Combine 2 slightly beaten egg whites, ¾ cup finely chopped pecans, filberts or other nuts, ¾ cup finely chopped coconut, 2 tablespoons sugar and ¼ teaspoon nutmeg. Mix well.

Golden Cake Bread

Second Grand Prize Winner by Mrs. L. M. Jehlik, Westchester, Illinois

Simple-to-make batter bread (no kneading or shaping), rich, with glossy crust and deliciously soft cake-like texture and flavor.

BAKE at 350° for 25 to 30 minutes   MAKES 2 loaves

Soften.......1 packet active dry **yeast** (or 1 cake compressed) in ¼ cup warm **water**

Combine....½ cup **butter** or margarine
  ½ cup **sugar** and

Golden Cake Bread

1 cup hot scalded **milk** in large mixing bowl. Cool to lukewarm.

Stir in.......2 slightly beaten **eggs** (reserving 1 tablespoon)
  2 teaspoons **vanilla**
  1 teaspoon **salt*** and softened yeast.

Add........4 to 4½ cups sifted **Pillsbury's Best All Purpose Flour***
  gradually to form a stiff batter, beating well after each addition. Cover.

Let rise.......in warm place (85°) until doubled, about 1 hour.

Beat down.....and let rise until doubled, about 45 minutes.

Turn..........into two well-greased 9x5x3 or 10x3½x2½-inch pans.

Let rise.......in warm place until light, about 45 minutes. Brush with reserved egg.

Bake.........at 350° for 25 to 30 minutes.

For use with Pillsbury's Best Self-Rising Flour, omit salt.

YEAST DINNER ROLLS

YEAST DINNER ROLLS may be made in many interesting shapings. If you like to experiment, try different shapings to vary your favorite roll recipes. Examples of some roll shapings to try may be found with these recipes:

Cloverleafs—Old Plantation Rolls, page 41
Crescents—Date-Bait Oatmeal Crescents, page 51
Pinwheels—Pinwheel Dinner Rolls, page 32
Curlicues—Mock Almond Danish Rolls, page 63
Fan Tans—Buttercrust Flake-Aparts, page 40
Parker House—Danish Ginger Rolls, page 44
Whirligigs—Honey Crust Whirligigs, page 35
Braids—Porch Supper Braids, page 36

Some other shapings you might like to try are:

Bow Knots—Roll small pieces of dough into 9-inch strips about ½ inch thick. Tie in loose knots. Place on greased baking sheets.

Finger Rolls—Shape medium-sized pieces of dough into rolls 4 inches long. Brush sides with melted butter. Place in two rows in greased 8x8x2 or 12x8x2-inch pans.

Speedy Cloverleafs—Shape dough into 2-inch balls. Place in greased muffin cups. With scissors, cut rolls in half, then in quarters, almost to the bottom.

Rolls may be brushed with a thin layer of melted butter or shortening; this helps retain the shape and lines of separation during rising and baking. To give dinner rolls a special touch, brush them with slightly-beaten egg white just before baking, and sprinkle generously with sesame, caraway, poppy or other seeds.

Rolls are usually removed from pans immediately and cooled on a wire rack. Most dinner rolls are best served warm.

Rolls may be reheated in several ways:
- Wrap in aluminum foil and heat in 350° oven.
- Place in brown paper bag sprinkled with water; heat in 350° oven.
- Place on small rack in large skillet; put 2 tablespoons water in bottom of pan. Cover and steam over low heat about 10 minutes.

Feather Light Dinner Buns

Senior Winner by Mrs. Robert E. Raymond, Cleveland, Ohio

Old-fashioned buns—tender and fluffy inside, brown and crusty outside.

BAKE at 400° for 12 to 15 minutes   MAKES 3 dozen

Combine....½ cup **sugar**
          ½ cup **shortening** and
          2 cups hot scalded **milk*** in large mixing bowl. Cool to lukewarm.

Add........1 cake compressed **yeast,** crumbled (or 1 packet active dry yeast dissolved in ¼ cup warm water).* Let stand 5 minutes.

Blend in.....2 cups sifted **Pillsbury's Best All Purpose Flour.*** Beat until smooth, about 1 minute. Cover.

Let rise........in warm place (85°) until doubled, about 2 hours.

Sift together 3¾ cups sifted **Pillsbury's Best All Purpose Flour**
          1 teaspoon **salt**
          ½ teaspoon double-acting **baking powder** and
          ½ teaspoon **soda.** Add gradually to the yeast mixture, beating well to form a stiff dough. (If necessary, blend in ¼ cup more flour.)

Knead........on floured surface until smooth and satiny, about 5 minutes.***

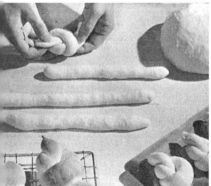

Bow Knots

Speedy Cloverleafs

Divide . . . . into 3 parts; cut each into 12 pieces. Shape each into a round roll and place on greased baking sheets about 3 inches apart. (Or form into Parker House, cloverleaf or other shape rolls.) Brush with melted **butter.** Cover.

Let rise . . . . in warm place until light, 1 to 1½ hours.

Bake . . . . at 400° for 12 to 15 minutes.

*Decrease milk to 1¾ cups if dry yeast is used.

**For use with Pillsbury's Best Self-Rising Flour, omit salt, baking powder, and soda.

***Dough may be stored in refrigerator up to 5 days and baked as needed.

Crusty Dinner Rolls

Best of Class Winner by Mrs. C. Arthur Reseland, Des Moines, Iowa

A crisp crust on the outside, but delicate and light inside.

BAKE at 400° for 20 to 25 minutes   MAKES 1½ to 2 dozen

Soften . . . . 1 packet active dry **yeast** (or 1 cake compressed) in ½ cup warm **water**

Combine . . . . . 1 tablespoon **sugar**
2 tablespoons **shortening**
1½ teaspoons **salt** and
½ cup **boiling water** in large mixing bowl. Cool to lukewarm. Add softened yeast.

Add . . . . 1 cup sifted **Pillsbury's Best All Purpose Flour*** and 2 stiffly beaten **egg whites**; mix thoroughly.

Add . . . . 2½ to 2¾ cups sifted **Pillsbury's Best All Purpose Flour** gradually to form a stiff dough.

Knead . . . . on floured surface until smooth and satiny, 3 to 5 minutes. Place in greased bowl and cover.

Let rise . . . . in warm place (85°) until doubled, 1 to 1½ hours.

Shape . . . . into round or oval-shaped rolls. Dip bottoms in **corn meal**; place on greased baking sheets.

Let rise . . . . in warm place until light, 1 to 1½ hours.

Combine . . . . . 1 **egg yolk** and
2 teaspoons **water**; brush carefully on rolls.

Bake . . . . at 400° for 20 to 25 minutes.

*Pillsbury's Best Self-Rising Flour is not recommended for use in this recipe.

Butter-Flake Rolls

Senior Winner by Mrs. A. R. Rodriguez, Franklinville, New York

These golden dinner rolls are so rich they literally flake apart.

BAKE at 375° for 12 to 15 minutes   MAKES 3 dozen

Soften . . . . 2 packets active dry **yeast** (or 2 cakes compressed) and 1 tablespoon **sugar** in ¾ cup warm **water**

Blend in . . . . . 1 cup sifted **Pillsbury's Best All Purpose Flour.*** Cover. Let rise in warm place (85°) until light and bubbly, 20 to 30 minutes.

Cream . . . . . . ½ cup **butter** or margarine in large mixing bowl. Add gradually ¼ cup **sugar**
1 teaspoon **salt** and
6 unbeaten **egg yolks,** creaming well. Add yeast mixture; mix well.

Add . . . . 3 cups sifted **Pillsbury's Best All Purpose Flour** gradually. Knead on floured surface about 30 strokes.

Place . . . . in greased bowl; cover and let rise until almost doubled, about 1½ hours.

Divide . . . . in half. Roll each half on floured surface to 18x6-inch rectangle. Spread center third with soft **butter.**

Fold . . . . one side of dough to overlap center. Spread with **butter.** Fold opposite side to overlap.

Roll out . . . . to 18x6-inch rectangle. Cut into 1-inch strips. Coil strips on well-greased baking sheet to form "snails."

Let rise . . . . in warm place until light, about 30 minutes.

Bake . . . . at 375° for 12 to 15 minutes.

*For use with Pillsbury's Best Self-Rising Flour, omit salt.

Pinwheel Dinner Rolls

Pinwheel Dinner Rolls

Senior Winner by Mrs. Frank A. Grenier, Dorchester, Massachusetts

You shape these dinner rolls simply by rolling the dough jelly-roll style, and slicing. No trick to it!

BAKE at 400° for 13 to 16 minutes   MAKES about 1½ dozen

Soften.......1 packet active dry **yeast** (or 1 cake compressed) in
            ½ cup warm **water**
Combine.....2 tablespoons **sugar**
            3 tablespoons **shortening**
            1½ teaspoons **salt*** and

½ cup hot scalded **milk** in large mixing bowl. Cool to
            lukewarm. Add softened yeast.
Add........3 to 3¼ cups sifted **Pillsbury's Best All Purpose Flour***
            gradually to form a stiff dough, beating well after
            each addition. Cover.
Let rise.......in warm place (85°) until doubled, 45 to 60 minutes.
Knead........on floured surface 20 strokes. Roll out to 18x9-inch
            rectangle. Brush with melted **butter.** Roll as for jelly
            roll, starting with 18-inch edge. Cut into 1-inch
            slices. Place on greased baking sheets 3 inches apart.
Let rise.......in warm place until light, 30 to 45 minutes.
Bake.........at 400° for 13 to 16 minutes.
For use with Pillsbury's Best Self-Rising Flour, omit salt.

Hot Butter-Flakes

Senior Winner by Mrs. Hazel Keeler, Chicago, Illinois

Buttery rolls that melt in your mouth! They're made by the Danish pastry method.

BAKE at 375° for 16 to 20 minutes   MAKES 32 rolls

Soften.......1 packet active dry **yeast** (or 1 cake compressed) in
            ¼ cup warm **water**
Sift together..2 cups sifted **Pillsbury's Best All Purpose Flour***
            1 tablespoon **sugar** and
            1 teaspoon **salt** into large mixing bowl.
Add........½ cup **milk** and softened yeast. Mix until all dry
            particles are moistened.
Knead........on floured surface until light and springy, 2 to 3
            minutes.
Roll out.......to a 14x8-inch rectangle.
Slice.......½ cup firm **butter** as thin as possible. Arrange one-
            fourth the sliced butter over half of dough. Refrigerate
            remaining butter.
Fold.........the unbuttered side over buttered side. Press down

firmly. Chill 10 minutes.

Repeat........rolling and folding process three more times, using remainder of butter. Wrap dough loosely in aluminum foil. Chill at least 3 hours.**

Divide........into 4 parts. Smooth edges of one part to make a circle.

Roll out......to a 10-inch circle. Cut into 8 wedges, using pastry wheel or knife. Roll wedge, starting with wide end and rolling to point. Place point-side down on ungreased baking sheet. Repeat process with remaining parts.

Bake.........at 375° for 16 to 20 minutes. Serve hot.

*For use with Pillsbury's Best Self-Rising Flour, omit salt.
**Dough may be stored in refrigerator up to 3 days and baked as needed.

Flaky Butter Brioche

Senior Winner by Sra. Amparo Feliciano, Ceiba, Puerto Rico

Light, delicate, flaky . . . these attractive, golden-yellow rolls look just like those from a French pastry shop.

BAKE at 350° for 20 to 25 minutes   MAKES 2 dozen

Soften.......1 packet active dry **yeast** (or 1 cake compressed) in ¼ cup warm **water**

Combine....½ cup **butter** or margarine, melted
⅓ cup **sugar**
1 teaspoon **salt**
2 well-beaten **eggs**
1 cup lukewarm scalded **milk** and softened yeast in large mixing bowl.

Blend in.....5 to 5½ cups sifted **Pillsbury's Best All Purpose Flour*** gradually; beat well after each addition.

Knead........on floured surface 2 minutes. Place in greased bowl and cover.

Let rise........in warm place (85°) until doubled, about 2 hours.

Flaky Butter Brioche

Shape........three-fourths of dough into two dozen 2-inch balls. Place in well-greased muffin cups or small tart shells. Shape remaining dough into two dozen ¾-inch balls, tapering one side to a point. Press deep indentation in large balls and insert pointed side of small rolls. Cover.

Let rise........in warm place until light, 45 to 60 minutes. If small balls roll to the side during rising, replace in center of large balls before baking.**

Bake.........at 350° for 20 to 25 minutes. Serve warm.

*For use with Pillsbury's Best Self-Rising Flour, omit salt.
**If desired, brush with mixture of 1 beaten egg yolk and 1 tablespoon cream.

Country Garden Pinwheels

Senior Winner by Mrs. Harvey Sparks, Kent, Washington

These dinner rolls have tangy chipped beef in the dough and chives rolled inside. So good with salads!

BAKE at 400° for 20 to 25 minutes   MAKES 1½ dozen

Soften . . . . 1 packet active dry **yeast** (or 1 cake compressed) in
                    ¼ cup warm **water**
Combine . . . . ¼ cup **shortening**
                    2 tablespoons **sugar**
                    1 teaspoon **salt*** and
                    1 cup hot scalded **milk** in large mixing bowl.
Add . . . . 3 ounces (1 cup) **dried beef,** cut fine, and
                    ½ cup **all bran cereal.** Cool to lukewarm.
Blend in . . . . . 1 unbeaten **egg** and softened yeast; mix well.
Add . . . . 3 to 3¾ cups sifted **Pillsbury's Best All Purpose Flour***

Country Garden Pinwheels

Knead . . . . on floured surface until smooth and satiny, 3 to 5
                     minutes. Place in greased bowl and cover.
Let rise . . . . in warm place (85°) until doubled, about 1½ hours.
Roll out . . . . on floured surface to 18x12-inch rectangle. Brush
                     with melted **butter;** sprinkle with
                     ¼ cup chopped **chives** or grated onion. Roll as for jelly
                     roll, starting with 18-inch edge.
Cut . . . . into 1-inch slices. Arrange cut-side down in greased
                     13x9x2-inch pan.
Let rise . . . . in warm place until light, about 1 hour.
Bake . . . . at 400° for 20 to 25 minutes.
*For use with Pillsbury's Best Self-Rising Flour, omit salt.

Hattie's Garden Crescents

Senior Winner by Mrs. Hattie Boutilier, Readfield, Maine

These tangy dinner rolls have a straight-from-the-garden appeal. Here's something different to perk up that luncheon or dinner.

BAKE at 400° for 15 to 20 minutes   MAKES 16 large rolls

Soften . . . . 1 packet active dry **yeast** (or 1 cake compressed) in
                    ¼ cup warm **water**
Combine . . . . ¼ cup **shortening**
                    1 tablespoon **sugar**
                    1½ teaspoons **salt*** and
                    ½ cup **boiling water.** Stir to melt shortening. Cool to
                    lukewarm by adding
                    ½ cup **tomato juice**
Stir in . . . . 1 tablespoon grated **onion**
                    1 tablespoon grated **celery**
                    1 tablespoon grated **carrot**
                    ½ teaspoon **garlic salt**
                    ½ teaspoon **sage** and softened yeast.
Add . . . . 3½ to 3¾ cups sifted **Pillsbury's Best All Purpose Flour***

gradually to form a dough. Mix thoroughly.

Knead . . . . on floured surface until smooth and satiny, 5 to 7 minutes. Place in greased bowl and cover.

Let rise . . . . in warm place (85°) until doubled, 45 to 60 minutes.

Divide . . . . dough into two parts. Roll each on floured surface to a 12-inch circle, about ¼ inch thick.

Sprinkle with . . . grated **Parmesan cheese.**

Cut . . . . each into 8 wedges. Roll wedge, starting with wide end and rolling to point. Place point-side down on greased baking sheet, curving to form crescent.

Let rise . . . . until light, 45 to 60 minutes.

Bake . . . . at 400° for 15 to 20 minutes.

For use with Pillsbury's Best Self-Rising Flour, omit salt and garlic salt.

Honey Crust Whirligigs

Senior Winner by Mrs. G. Warren Spaulding, Window Rock, Arizona

Fun to shape! Just wind a strip of dough around your finger and drop into a muffin cup.

BAKE at 400° for 12 to 15 minutes   MAKES 20 rolls

Cook . . . . 2 medium **potatoes,** diced, in 1 cup **water** until tender. Drain; reserve ¾ cup liquid. Mash potatoes and measure ¾ cup.*

Soften . . . . 1 packet active dry **yeast** (or 1 cake compressed) in ¼ cup warm **water**

Beat . . . . 2 **eggs** in large mixing bowl. Add ⅓ cup **shortening,** melted ¼ cup **sugar** 2½ teaspoons **salt,**** mashed potato, potato water and softened yeast. Mix well.

Blend in . . . . 4½ to 5 cups sifted **Pillsbury's Best All Purpose Flour**** to form a stiff dough.

Knead . . . . on floured surface until smooth and satiny, 5 to 7 minutes. Place in greased bowl and cover.

Honey Crust Whirligigs

Let rise . . . . in warm place (85°) until doubled, about 2 hours.

Divide . . . . dough in half. Roll out each on floured surface to a 15x10-inch rectangle. Cut into 10 strips, 10 inches long and 1½ inches wide. Wind each strip loosely around finger; drop into greased muffin cups on end or at angles. (Rolls take different shapes as they rise.) Cover.

Let rise . . . . in warm place until light, about 1 hour.

Blend . . . . ¼ cup soft **butter** or margarine with ¼ cup **honey.** Brush over rolls to be served the same day. (Omit on rolls to be stored.)

Bake . . . . at 400° for 12 to 15 minutes.

Three-fourths cup leftover mashed potato or prepared instant mashed potatoes and ¾ cup water (instead of "potato water") may be substituted.

**For use with Pillsbury's Best Self-Rising Flour, omit salt.*

Porch Supper Braids

Senior Winner by Mrs. John Lockley, Arlington, Virginia

These rich dinner rolls have a delicate anise flavor. Braid them and sprinkle with sesame seeds if you like—or shape your favorite way.

BAKE at 400° for 12 to 15 minutes   MAKES 2 dozen

Soften . . . . 1 packet active dry **yeast** (or 1 cake compressed) in
¼ cup warm **water**

Combine . . . . ¼ cup soft **butter** or margarine
3 tablespoons **sugar**
2 teaspoons **salt**
1 teaspoon **anise seed,** if desired, and
¾ cup hot scalded **milk** in large mixing bowl. Cool to lukewarm.

Add . . . . 1 well-beaten **egg** and softened yeast.

Blend in . . . . 3½ cups sifted **Pillsbury's Best All Purpose Flour***

Porch Supper Braids

Knead . . . . on floured surface until smooth and satiny, about 5 minutes. Place in greased bowl and cover.

Let rise . . . . in warm place (85°) until doubled, 1½ to 2 hours.

Roll out . . . . on lightly floured surface to ¼-inch thickness. Cut into 5x½-inch strips. Braid strips together in groups of 3, sealing ends. Place on greased baking sheets. Brush tops of rolls with beaten **egg;** sprinkle with **sesame seeds,** if desired.

Let rise . . . . in warm place until light, 30 to 45 minutes.

Bake . . . . at 400° for 12 to 15 minutes.

**For use with Pillsbury's Best Self-Rising Flour, omit salt.*

Corn Meal Fan-Tans

Junior Winner by Mrs. W. D. Davidson, Birmingham, Alabama

Light, tender and golden yeast rolls, in familiar fan-tan shape. Corn meal gives them an intriguing flavor, crunchy texture.

BAKE at 400° for 20 to 25 minutes   MAKES 2 dozen

Soften . . . . 1 packet active dry **yeast** (or 1 cake compressed) in
¼ cup warm **water**

Combine . . . 2½ cups **milk**
1 cup **yellow corn meal**
⅓ cup **shortening**
2 tablespoons **sugar** and
2 teaspoons **salt*** in top of double boiler. Cook over boiling water, stirring occasionally, until thick. Reduce heat; continue to cook 3 minutes. Turn into large mixing bowl. Cool to lukewarm.

Blend in . . . . . . 2 slightly beaten **eggs** and softened yeast.

Add . . . . 4 cups sifted **Pillsbury's Best All Purpose Flour*** gradually, mixing well.

Knead . . . . on floured surface until smooth, about 10 minutes. Place in greased bowl and cover.

Let rise . . . . in warm place (85°) until doubled, about 1 hour.

Roll out . . . . on floured surface to rectangle ¼ inch thick. Brush with melted **butter.**

Cut . . . . dough into strips 1 inch wide. Stack 5 or 6 strips together; cut into 2-inch pieces. Place each stack, cut-side down, in a greased muffin cup.

Let rise . . . . in warm place until light, 45 to 60 minutes.

Bake . . . . at 400° for 20 to 25 minutes.

For use with Pillsbury's Best Self-Rising Flour, decrease salt to 1 teaspoon.

Southern Corn Meal Rolls

Senior Winner by Mrs. H. H. Baird, Atlanta, Georgia

Crunchy, crusty corn meal rolls . . . simple to make. And they bake to a beautiful, deep golden brown.

BAKE at 400° for 15 to 20 minutes   MAKES about 2 dozen

Soften . . . . 1 packet active dry **yeast** (or 1 cake compressed) in ¼ cup warm **water**

Pour . . . . 1 cup **boiling water** over
1 cup **corn meal** in large mixing bowl. Cool to lukewarm.

Add . . . . ¾ cup lukewarm scalded **milk**
¼ cup **sugar**
2 teaspoons **salt***
½ cup **butter** or margarine, melted
1 unbeaten **egg** (or 2 egg yolks) and softened yeast; blend well.

Add . . . . 4 to 4½ cups sifted **Pillsbury's Best All Purpose Flour*** gradually to form a stiff dough.

Knead . . . . on floured surface until dough is smooth and springs back when pressed with fingers, 5 to 7 minutes. Place in greased bowl and cover.

Let rise . . . . in warm place (85°) until doubled, 1½ to 2 hours.

Divide . . . . into four parts. Cut one portion into six parts and each sixth into three. Shape each into a ball; place

in well-greased muffin cups, three to a cup. Repeat with remaining dough. Cover.

Let rise . . . . in warm place until light, about 1 hour.

Bake . . . . at 400° for 15 to 20 minutes.

For use with Pillsbury's Best Self-Rising Flour, omit salt.

Bit o' Rye Breadsticks

Senior Winner by Mrs. Charles E. Ham, Sidney, Nebraska

These rye breadsticks flavored with caraway seed, sage and celery seed would be wonderful with a buffet meal or spaghetti supper.

BAKE at 400° for 15 to 17 minutes   MAKES 3 dozen

Soften . . . . 1 packet active dry **yeast** (or 1 cake compressed) in 1 cup warm **water** in large mixing bowl.

Add . . . . 2 tablespoons **shortening,** melted and cooled
1 tablespoon **sugar**
2 teaspoons **salt***
2 teaspoons **caraway seed**
1 teaspoon **leaf sage** or ½ teaspoon ground sage and ½ teaspoon **celery seed**

Blend in . . . . . 1 unbeaten **egg**; beat well.

Add . . . . . . 2½ cups sifted **Pillsbury's Best All Purpose Flour*** and 1 cup sifted **Pillsbury's Pure Medium Rye Flour** gradually.

Knead . . . . on floured surface until smooth and elastic, about 5 minutes. Place in greased bowl and cover.

Let rise . . . . in warm place (85°) until doubled, about 1¼ hours.

Divide . . . . dough into three equal parts; cut each into 1 dozen pieces. Shape each into an 8-inch long "breadstick," about the thickness of a pencil. Place on greased baking sheets.

Let rise . . . . until light, about 1 hour. Brush with cold **water.**

Bake . . . . at 400° for 15 to 17 minutes.

For use with Pillsbury's Best Self-Rising Flour, omit salt.

Old-Fashioned Wheat Rolls

Senior Winner by Mrs. Wallace Baker, Great Falls, Montana

These light, fluffy wheat rolls really do have an old-fashioned flavor!

BAKE at 375° for 20 to 25 minutes   MAKES about 3 dozen

Soften . . . . 2 packets active dry **yeast** (or 2 cakes compressed) in
½ cup warm **water**
Combine . . . . ½ cup **sugar**
⅓ cup **shortening**
2 teaspoons **salt*** and
¾ cup **boiling water**** in large mixing bowl. Add
¾ cup **undiluted evaporated milk.** Cool to lukewarm.
Add . . . . 1 unbeaten **egg** and softened yeast.
Blend in . . . . 2½ cups sifted **Pillsbury's Best All Purpose Flour*** and
¾ cup unsifted **Pillsbury's Whole Wheat (Graham) Flour** or wheat germ. Mix until smooth.
Add . . . . 2½ to 3 cups sifted **Pillsbury's Best All Purpose Flour** gradually to form a stiff dough.

Old-Fashioned Wheat Rolls

Knead . . . . on floured surface until smooth and satiny, about 5 minutes. Place in greased bowl and cover.
Let rise . . . . in warm place (85°) until doubled, 1 to 1½ hours.
Shape . . . . into rolls as desired. Place in greased baking pans or muffin cups.
Let rise . . . . in warm place until light, 45 to 60 minutes.
Bake . . . . at 375° for 20 to 25 minutes for pan rolls, 15 to 20 minutes for rolls made in muffin cups.

**For use with Pillsbury's Best Self-Rising Flour, omit salt.*
***Or substitute 1½ cups hot scalded fresh milk for water and evaporated milk.*

Sophie's Flaky French Crescents

Senior Winner by Mrs. Robert O. Bache-Wiig, Waukesha, Wisconsin

You might find rolls like these in a French pastry shop.

BAKE at 400° for 10 to 14 minutes   MAKES 16 rolls

Soften . . . . 1 packet active dry **yeast** (or 1 cake compressed) in
¼ cup warm **water**
Combine . . . . . 2 tablespoons **sugar**
1 tablespoon **shortening**
1 teaspoon **salt*** and
¾ cup hot scalded **milk** in large mixing bowl. Cool to lukewarm.
Blend in . . . . . 1 well-beaten **egg** and softened yeast.
Add . . . . 2½ to 3 cups sifted **Pillsbury's Best All Purpose Flour*** gradually to form a stiff dough. Cover and chill at least 1½ hours.
Roll out . . . . on floured surface to a square, ¼ inch thick. Spread generously with soft **butter.**
Fold . . . . one end of dough over center. Fold opposite side over to make three layers. Then fold the ends over the center to make a small square. Chill ½ hour. Repeat rolling, folding and chilling process two more times, spreading with butter each time.

Divide . . . . .dough into two parts. Roll out each part on floured surface to a circle about ⅛ inch thick. Cut each into 8 wedges. Roll wedge, starting with wide end and rolling to point. Place point-side down on greased baking sheet, curving ends to form crescent.

Let rise . . . . . . .in warm place (85°) until light, 1 to 1½ hours.

Bake . . . . .at 400° for 10 to 14 minutes. While warm frost with Almond Icing, if desired.

For use with Pillsbury's Best Self-Rising Flour, omit salt.

ALMOND ICING

Combine 1 tablespoon milk, 1 tablespoon melted butter, 1 cup sifted confectioners' sugar, ½ teaspoon vanilla and ¼ cup finely chopped almonds or ¼ teaspoon almond extract. Mix thoroughly.

Country Company Rolls

Senior Winner

Save precious minutes in making the dough for these rich refrigerator rolls. Use an electric mixer, if you like; no kneading necessary.

BAKE at 400° for 12 to 15 minutes   MAKES 2 dozen

Soften . . . . . . .1 packet active dry **yeast** (or 1 cake compressed) in ½ cup warm **water**

Combine . . . . ½ cup **shortening** ⅓ cup **sugar** 2 teaspoons **salt*** and ¾ cup hot scalded **milk** in large mixing bowl. Cool to lukewarm.

Blend in . . . . . .1 unbeaten **egg** and softened yeast.

Add . . . . .4 cups sifted **Pillsbury's Best All Purpose Flour*** gradually; beat well after each addition. Cover.

Store . . . . .in refrigerator until ready to use (not over 2 days).**

Shape . . . . . . .into balls about 2 inches in diameter. Place in greased muffin cups. Brush with melted **butter.** Cover.

Let rise . . . . . . .in warm place (85°) until light, 2 to 2½ hours.

Bake . . . . .at 400° for 12 to 15 minutes.

For use with Pillsbury's Best Self-Rising Flour, omit salt.

**If desired, dough need not be refrigerated. Cover; let rise in warm place until doubled, about 1½ hours. Shape into rolls; let rise until light, 30 to 60 minutes. Bake as directed above.*

Table Talk Rolls

Senior Winner by Mrs. Dean Barney, Shoshone, Idaho

Tender, fluffy dinner buns with a light touch of lemon flavor.

BAKE at 375° for 15 to 20 minutes   MAKES about 2½ dozen

Soften . . . . . . .2 packets active dry **yeast** (or 2 cakes compressed) in ½ cup warm **water**

Combine . . . . ⅓ cup **sugar** 1 tablespoon **salt*** and ½ cup scalded **light cream** in large mixing bowl. Add ¼ cup cold **water.** Cool to lukewarm.

Blend in . . . . .2 unbeaten **eggs** 2 teaspoons grated **lemon rind** and softened yeast.

Add . . . . . . .4¼ to 4½ cups sifted **Pillsbury's Best All Purpose Flour*** gradually; beat well after each addition. Cover.

Let rise . . . . . . .in warm place (85°) until doubled, about 1½ hours.

Divide . . . . .dough into four parts. Pat each part on floured surface into a square ½ inch thick. Cut each into 6 or 8 rolls.

Coat . . . . .each with **flour.** Place on greased baking sheet.

Let rise . . . . . . .in warm place until light, 30 to 60 minutes.

Bake . . . . .at 375° for 15 to 20 minutes.

For use with Pillsbury's Best Self-Rising Flour, omit salt.

Buttercrust Flake-Aparts

Buttercrust Flake-Aparts

Senior Winner by Mrs. Paul W. Strebel, Hannibal, Missouri

These light, tender rolls separate easily into bite-size pieces.

BAKE at 400° for 15 to 20 minutes   MAKES about 20 rolls

Soften.......2 packets active dry **yeast** (or 2 cakes compressed) in
　　　　　　　¼ cup warm **water**
Combine....½ cup soft **butter** or margarine
　　　　　　　⅛ cup **sugar**
　　　　　　　2 teaspoons **salt*** and
　　　　　　　1¼ cups hot scalded **buttermilk** or sour milk in large
　　　　　　　mixing bowl. Cool to lukewarm.
Blend in.....½ teaspoon **soda** and softened yeast.
Add.......4½ to 5 cups sifted **Pillsbury's Best All Purpose Flour***

gradually; beat well after each addition. Cover.
Let rise........in warm place (85°) until doubled, about 1 hour.
Roll out.......on floured surface to a 15-inch square. Brush with
　　　　　　　melted **butter.** Cut into 1½-inch strips. Stack 5
　　　　　　　strips together and cut into 1½-inch pieces. Place
　　　　　　　each stack in greased muffin cup, cut-side down.
Let rise........in warm place until light, about 30 minutes.
Bake.........at 400° for 15 to 20 minutes. Serve warm.
**For use with Pillsbury's Best Self-Rising Flour, omit salt.*

Parmesan Honor Rolls

Junior Winner by Sally Sligar, Tucson, Arizona

Buttery cheese crescent rolls that melt in your mouth.

BAKE at 375° for 15 to 18 minutes   MAKES 40 rolls

Soften.......1 packet active dry **yeast** (or 1 cake compressed) in
　　　　　　　¼ cup warm **water**
Cut.........1 cup **butter** or margarine into
　　　　　　　3 cups sifted **Pillsbury's Best All Purpose Flour***
　　　　　　　until particles are the size of large peas.
Add........2 slightly beaten **eggs**
　　　　　　　1 cup lukewarm scalded **milk**
　　　　　　　¼ cup **sugar**
　　　　　　　1 teaspoon **salt** and softened yeast. Mix well.
Add.......1½ to 2 cups sifted **Pillsbury's Best All Purpose Flour**
　　　　　　　gradually to form a stiff dough. Mix well after each
　　　　　　　addition. Cover and chill 2 to 3 hours.**
Melt........⅓ cup **butter**
Divide........dough into 5 parts. Roll out one part on floured
　　　　　　　surface to a 9-inch circle.
Brush with....1 tablespoon of the melted butter; sprinkle with
　　　　　　　3 tablespoons grated **Parmesan cheese.** Cut into 8
　　　　　　　wedges. Roll wedge, starting with wide end and rolling
　　　　　　　to point. Place point-side down on greased baking

sheet. Repeat process with remaining parts (or make pinwheel rolls or fan tans).

Let rise . . . . in warm place (85°) until light, about 1 hour.

Bake . . . . at 375° for 15 to 18 minutes.

*For use with Pillsbury's Best Self-Rising Flour, increase the first addition of flour to 3½ cups and omit salt.

**Dough may be stored in refrigerator up to 4 days and baked as needed.

Old Plantation Rolls

Senior Winner by Mrs. William Edwin Baker, Colorado Springs, Colorado

You don't have to knead these rich, tender cloverleaf rolls . . . dough may be stored in your refrigerator and fresh rolls baked as needed.

BAKE at 400° for 15 to 20 minutes   **MAKES 2 dozen large rolls**

Soften . . . . 1 packet active dry **yeast** (or 1 cake compressed) in
¼ cup warm **water**

Combine . . . . ½ cup **shortening**
¼ cup **sugar** and
1 cup hot scalded **milk.** Stir to melt shortening. Add
¾ cup cold **water.** Cool to lukewarm.

Add . . . . 1 unbeaten **egg** and softened yeast.

Blend in . . . . . 3 cups sifted **Pillsbury's Best All Purpose Flour;*** let
stand 20 minutes.

Sift together 2½ cups sifted **Pillsbury's Best All Purpose Flour**
1½ teaspoons **salt**
1 teaspoon double-acting **baking powder** and
½ teaspoon **soda.** Blend into dough. Cover.

Let rise . . . . in warm place (85°) about 1 hour.

Toss . . . . dough on well-floured surface until coated with flour
and no longer sticky.

Shape . . . . into 24 cloverleaf rolls. Place in greased muffin cups.

Let rise . . . . in warm place until light, about 1 hour.

Bake . . . . at 400° for 15 to 20 minutes.

*For use with Pillsbury's Best Self-Rising Flour, omit salt, baking powder, soda.

Old Plantation Rolls

Gem Rolls

Gem Rolls

Senior Winner by Mrs. Victor W. Koepsell, Milwaukee, Wisconsin

Lucky cloverleafs sparkling with jelly are made from a No-Knead refrigerated yeast dough.

BAKE at 400° for 8 minutes, then   MAKES 2 dozen
for 4 to 7 minutes

Soften.......1 packet active dry **yeast** (or 1 cake compressed) in
⅓ cup warm **water**
Combine.....2 tablespoons **sugar**
2 tablespoons **shortening**
1½ teaspoons **salt*** and
¾ cup hot scalded **milk** in large mixing bowl. Cool to
lukewarm.

Stir in......½ cup riced or mashed **potatoes**
2 unbeaten **eggs** and softened yeast; mix well.
Add........4 to 4½ cups sifted **Pillsbury's Best All Purpose Flour***
gradually to form a stiff dough, mixing well after each
addition. Cover and chill 1 to 2 hours.
Roll out......chilled dough to a 12x8-inch rectangle. Brush with
1½ tablespoons melted **butter**. Mark dough into 2-inch
squares. Cut each square into four parts, shaping
each part into ball. Place in well-greased muffin cups,
four to a cup.
Let rise........in warm place (85°) until very light, about 1 hour.
Brush with melted **butter**.
Bake........at 400° for 8 minutes, until browning begins. Remove
from oven. Fill center of each roll with
1 teaspoon firm **jelly** or **jam**. Bake 4 to 7 minutes.

**For use with Pillsbury's Best Self-Rising Flour, omit salt.*

Caraway Rye Rolls

Senior Winner by Mrs. Marilyn Dunker, Redfield, South Dakota

No-Knead dinner rolls . . . just drop the soft dough into muffin cups, let rise, and bake.

BAKE at 400° for 15 to 20 minutes   MAKES 1½ to 2 dozen

Soften.......1 packet active dry **yeast** (or 1 cake compressed) in
⅓ cup warm **water**. Let stand 5 minutes.
Combine....⅓ cup **shortening**
1 cup hot scalded **buttermilk** or sour milk
⅓ cup **molasses**
1 teaspoon **salt*** and
2 teaspoons **caraway seed** in large mixing bowl. Mix

well. Cool to lukewarm.

Add . . . . 1 unbeaten **egg** and softened yeast.

Blend in . . . . . . 1 cup sifted **Pillsbury's Pure Medium Rye Flour**
1 teaspoon double-acting **baking powder** and
¼ teaspoon **soda.** Beat well.

Add . . . . 2½ to 3 cups sifted **Pillsbury's Best All Purpose Flour***
gradually to form a dough, mixing well after each
addition.

Fill . . . . well-greased muffin cups about one-half full.** Cover
and let rise in warm place (85°) until doubled, 1½
to 2 hours.

Bake . . . . at 400° for 15 to 20 minutes.

For use with Pillsbury's Best Self-Rising Flour, omit salt, baking powder, soda.

**If only one muffin pan is available, store remaining dough in refrigerator
while first rolls are baking.*

Three-Way Dinner Rolls

Senior Winner by Mrs. L. J. Wipperfurth, Madison, Wisconsin

*You get a section of plain roll, wheat roll and corn meal roll in every
one of these unusual cloverleafs.*

BAKE at 400° for 15 to 20 minutes   MAKES 2 dozen

Soften . . . . 1 packet active dry **yeast** (or 1 cake compressed) in
2 cups warm **water** in large mixing bowl.

Add . . . . ⅓ cup **sugar**
1 tablespoon **salt***
⅓ cup **shortening**, melted and cooled
2 beaten **eggs** and
3 cups sifted **Pillsbury's Best All Purpose Flour;***
beat until smooth.

Caraway Rye Rolls

Divide . . . . dough into 3 equal parts. To one part, add
½ cup **corn meal** and
½ to ⅔ cup sifted **Pillsbury's Best All Purpose Flour.**
To second part, add
1 cup unsifted **Pillsbury's Whole Wheat (Graham)
Flour.** To third part, add
1 to 1¼ cups sifted **Pillsbury's Best All Purpose Flour**

Let rise . . . . in warm place (85°) until doubled, about 1½ hours.

Toss . . . . each dough on well-floured surface until coated
with flour and no longer sticky.

Shape . . . . into cloverleaf rolls, placing one ball of each dough
in greased muffin cups.

Let rise . . . . in warm place until light, about 1 hour.

Bake . . . . at 400° for 15 to 20 minutes.

For use with Pillsbury's Best Self-Rising Flour, omit salt.

Herb Stickles

Bride First Prize Winner by Mrs. Marshall K. Ludwig, Forest Park, Illinois

Crisp bread sticks sprinkled with caraway seed and salt.

BAKE at 400° for 15 to 20 minutes   MAKES 16 sticks

Soften . . . . 1 packet active dry **yeast** (or 1 cake compressed) in 1 cup warm **water** in large mixing bowl.

Stir in . . . . 2 tablespoons **shortening,** melted
1 tablespoon **sugar**
1½ teaspoons **salt***
2 tablespoons chopped **chives**
1 tablespoon chopped **parsley** and
1 teaspoon **dill seed**

Add . . . . 2½ to 3 cups sifted **Pillsbury's Best All Purpose Flour*** gradually to form a stiff dough; beat well after each addition. Cover.

Let rise . . . . in warm place (85°) until doubled, about 1 hour.

Divide . . . . dough into four parts. Roll out one part on floured surface to an 8-inch square.

Cut . . . . into four 2-inch strips. Roll along 8-inch side to form sticks. Place on greased baking sheet. Brush with slightly beaten **egg.** Sprinkle with **salt** and **caraway seed.** Repeat process with remaining dough.

Let rise . . . . in warm place until light, 30 to 45 minutes.

Bake . . . . at 400° for 15 to 20 minutes. Serve warm.

For use with Pillsbury's Best Self-Rising Flour, omit salt in dough.

Danish Ginger Rolls

Senior Winner by Mrs. Edwin T. Tracy, Ogden, Utah

A family recipe brought from Denmark—rolls with subtle ginger flavor.

BAKE at 400° for 15 to 20 minutes   MAKES 1½ to 2 dozen

Soften . . . . 1 packet active dry **yeast** (or 1 cake compressed) in

Herb Stickles

Combine.....¼ cup warm **water**
3 tablespoons **sugar**
2 tablespoons **butter** or shortening
1½ teaspoons **salt***
1½ teaspoons **ginger** and
½ cup hot scalded **milk** in large mixing bowl. Cool to lukewarm.
Add.........2 well-beaten **eggs** and softened yeast.
Add.......3 to 3¼ cups sifted **Pillsbury's Best All Purpose Flour***
to form a stiff dough. Mix well. Cover.
Let rise.......in warm place (85°) until doubled, about 1 hour. Punch down. Let rise until light, about 30 minutes.
Roll out......on floured surface to about ¼-inch thickness. Cut into 3-inch rounds. Brush with melted **butter**. Mark a crease with dull edge of knife to one side of center of each round. Fold small part over large; press to seal. Place on greased baking sheet.
Let rise.......in warm place about 30 minutes.
Bake.........at 400° for 15 to 20 minutes.
For use with Pillsbury's Best Self-Rising Flour, omit salt.

Danish Ginger Rolls

English Oatwheels

Senior Winner by Mrs. F. Soroko, Minneapolis, Minnesota

English muffins to make ahead of time—and toast just before serving.

BAKE on moderately hot griddle   MAKES 1½ dozen
for 13 to 15 minutes

Soften.......1 packet active dry **yeast** (or 1 cake compressed) in ¼ cup warm **water**
Combine.....1 cup **boiling water** and
1 cup quick-cooking **rolled oats** in large mixing bowl. Stir until well blended. Cool to lukewarm.
Add........¼ cup **salad oil**
2 tablespoons **brown sugar**

2 tablespoons **molasses**
1 unbeaten **egg** and
1 teaspoon **salt;*** mix well. Stir in softened yeast.
Add........3 to 3¼ cups sifted **Pillsbury's Best All Purpose Flour***
gradually to form a stiff dough, beating well after each addition. Cover.
Let rest.......in warm place (85°) 30 minutes.
Roll out......on floured surface to ⅜-inch thickness. Cut into rounds with 3-inch cutter. Place on greased baking sheets sprinkled with **corn meal.**
Let rise.......in warm place until light, 30 to 45 minutes.
Bake.........slowly on moderately hot griddle (300°) until brown, about 7 minutes on each side. Split cooled muffins; toast cut sides and serve with **butter** and **jam** or jelly.
For use with Pillsbury's Best Self-Rising Flour, omit salt.

Parker House Wheat Rolls

Senior Winner by Mrs. A. L. Morrison, New Orleans, Louisiana

Whole wheat adds flavor, texture to these No-Knead "pocketbook" rolls.

BAKE at 400° for 12 to 15 minutes　　　　　MAKES 2½ dozen

Soften . . . . 1 packet active dry **yeast** (or 1 cake compressed) in
　　　　　　　½ cup warm **water**
Combine . . . . . 2 cups sifted **Pillsbury's Best All Purpose Flour*** and
　　　　　　　1 cup unsifted **Pillsbury's Whole Wheat (Graham)
　　　　　　　Flour.** Set aside.
Add . . . . ¼ cup **sugar** and
　　　　　　　1½ teaspoons **salt** gradually to
　　　　　　　½ cup **shortening,** creaming well.
Blend in . . . . . ½ cup **boiling water.** Cool to lukewarm.
Add . . . . 1 unbeaten **egg** and softened yeast; mix well.
Blend in . . . . the dry ingredients gradually; mix well. Cover.

Easy Cheesy Buns

Let rise . . . . in warm place (85°) until doubled, 1 to 1½ hours.
Roll out . . . . on floured surface to ¼-inch thickness. Cut with
　　　　　　　3-inch round cutter; brush with melted **butter.** Mark
　　　　　　　a crease with dull edge of knife to one side of center
　　　　　　　of each round. Fold small part over large; press to
　　　　　　　seal. Place on greased baking sheets.
Let rise . . . . in warm place until light, 45 to 60 minutes.
Bake . . . . at 400° for 12 to 15 minutes. Brush with melted **butter.**
*For use with Pillsbury's Best Self-Rising Flour, decrease salt to ½ teaspoon.

Easy Cheesy Buns

Bride First Prize Winner by Mrs. Raymond E. Myers, Milan, Illinois

*Make these silky-textured rolls on your busy day! Don't knead or shape
the rich yeast dough—just drop in muffin cups, let rise, and bake.*

BAKE at 375° for 12 to 15 minutes　　　　　MAKES 1 dozen

Soften . . . . 1 packet active dry **yeast** (or 1 cake compressed) in
　　　　　　　½ cup warm **water** in large mixing bowl. Let stand 5
　　　　　　　minutes.
Add . . . . ⅔ cup shredded soft **yellow cheese** or a cheese spread
　　　　　　　2 tablespoons **sugar**
　　　　　　　1 teaspoon **salt***
　　　　　　　1 unbeaten **egg**
　　　　　　　2 tablespoons **butter** or margarine, melted, and
　　　　　　　1 cup sifted **Pillsbury's Best All Purpose Flour.*** Beat
　　　　　　　2 minutes until cheese is well blended. (With mixer
　　　　　　　use a low speed.)
Add . . . . 1¼ to 1½ cups sifted **Pillsbury's Best All Purpose Flour**
　　　　　　　gradually to form a dough, mixing well after each
　　　　　　　addition.
Fill . . . . well-greased muffin cups one-half full. Cover and let
　　　　　　　rise in warm place (85°) until light, 1 to 1½ hours.
Bake . . . . at 375° for 12 to 15 minutes. Serve hot.
*For use with Pillsbury's Best Self-Rising Flour, omit salt.

Half-Time Spoon Rolls

Senior Third Prize Winner by Mrs. Robert G. Walker, Kenosha, Wisconsin

No kneading, no rolling, no shaping necessary for these moist, light dinner rolls—and so quick to make!

BAKE at 400° for 15 to 20 minutes   MAKES 1½ dozen

Soften.......1 packet active dry **yeast** (or 1 cake compressed) in ¼ cup warm **water**

Combine....⅛ cup **shortening**
         ¼ cup **sugar**
         1 teaspoon **salt*** and
         ¾ cup hot scalded **milk** in large mixing bowl. Cool to lukewarm by adding
         ½ cup cold **water**

Blend in.....1 unbeaten **egg** (or 2 egg whites) and softened yeast.

Add.......3½ cups sifted **Pillsbury's Best All Purpose Flour*** gradually, beating well after each addition. Cover.

Let rise........in warm place (85°) until doubled, 45 to 60 minutes.

Stir..........dough. Spoon into well-greased muffin cups, filling one-half full.

Let rise........in warm place until light, about 45 minutes.

Bake.........at 400° for 15 to 20 minutes.

*For use with Pillsbury's Best Self-Rising Flour, omit salt.

Honey Twin Rolls

Senior Winner by Mrs. Romer Bullington, Tyler, Texas

Here are honey-flavored rolls that you don't have to shape or knead. All you do is stir them up, let them rise, then spoon them into muffin cups.

BAKE at 400° for 12 to 15 minutes   MAKES 3 dozen

Soften.......2 packets active dry **yeast** (or 2 cakes compressed) in 1¾ cups warm **water** in large mixing bowl.

Add.......½ cup **honey**

Honey Twin Rolls

         ¼ cup **shortening,** melted
         1 well-beaten **egg** and
         2 teaspoons **salt***

Blend in.....4 cups sifted **Pillsbury's Best All Purpose Flour;*** beat 1 minute.

Add.........2 to 2¼ cups sifted **Pillsbury's Best All Purpose Flour** to form a stiff batter; beat well.**

Let rise........in warm place (85°) until doubled, 1 to 1½ hours.

Stir...........batter 1 minute. Drop into greased muffin cups, 2 spoonfuls per cup, forming twin rolls.

Let rise........in warm place until light, about 1 hour.

Bake.........at 400° for 12 to 15 minutes. Serve with **butter** and **honey,** if desired.

*For use with Pillsbury's Best Self-Rising Flour, omit salt.
**If desired, dough may be refrigerated up to two days.

YEAST SWEET ROLLS

YEAST SWEET ROLLS—To cut dough that has been rolled jelly-roll fashion, use sharp knife or heavy sewing thread. Place thread under dough; bring ends of thread up and around sides of dough; cross as if to tie, cutting dough into slices.

When baking "sticky" rolls on baking sheets, line sheets with aluminum foil (shiny-side down) to make cleaning easier.

When removing rolls with topping from baking pan, invert pan onto serving plate or wire rack with waxed paper underneath. Leave pan in place several minutes to allow syrup to drip over rolls.

Coffee-Time Cinnamon Rolls

Senior Winner by Mrs. Birdie M. LaHue, Kansas City, Kansas

It's no trick to shape these sweet rolls—cut them with a cookie cutter, dip them in sugar and cinnamon, and arrange in the pan.

BAKE at 375° for 25 to 30 minutes   MAKES two 8-inch round coffee cakes

Soften . . . . 1 packet active dry **yeast** (or 1 cake compressed) in
    2 tablespoons warm **water**
Combine . . . . . 2 tablespoons **sugar**
    2 tablespoons **shortening**
    1 teaspoon **salt*** and
    ½ cup hot scalded **milk** in large mixing bowl. Add ½ cup cold **water**. Cool to lukewarm.
Stir in . . . . softened yeast.
Blend in . . . . . 3 to 3¼ cups sifted **Pillsbury's Best All Purpose Flour*** to form a stiff dough.
Knead . . . . on floured surface until smooth and satiny, 3 to 4 minutes. Place in greased bowl and cover.
Let rise . . . . in warm place (85°) until doubled, 1 to 1½ hours.
Roll out . . . . to ¼-inch thickness on floured surface. Cut with floured 2-inch round cutter. Dip each roll in

⅓ cup **butter** or margarine, melted, then in mixture of
    ⅔ cup **sugar** and
    1½ teaspoons **cinnamon**
Arrange . . . . rolls around edges of greased 8-inch round pans, overlapping slightly. Place 5 rolls in center of each.
Let rise . . . . in warm place until light, about 45 minutes.
Bake . . . . at 375° for 25 to 30 minutes. Frost with **Vanilla Glaze**, page 326, if desired.

**For use with Pillsbury's Best Self-Rising Flour, omit salt.*

Pineapple Supreme Rolls

Bride Winner by Mrs. Harry R. McGahan, Tacoma, Washington

Cinnamon rolls baked upside down over a pineapple "topping."

BAKE at 375° for 20 to 25 minutes   MAKES about 15 rolls

Soften . . . . 1 packet active dry **yeast** (or 1 cake compressed) in
    ¼ cup warm **water**
Combine . . . . ¼ cup **sugar**
    2 tablespoons **shortening**
    2 teaspoons **salt*** and
    1 cup hot scalded **milk** in large mixing bowl. Cool to lukewarm.
Stir in . . . . 1 unbeaten **egg** and softened yeast.
Add . . . . 4 to 4½ cups sifted **Pillsbury's Best All Purpose Flour*** gradually to form a stiff dough.
Knead . . . . on floured surface until smooth and satiny, 3 to 5 minutes. Place in greased bowl and cover.
Let rise . . . . in warm place (85°) until doubled, 1½ to 2 hours. Punch down; let rise 30 minutes. Prepare Pineapple Topping.
Roll out . . . . on floured surface to a 16x12-inch rectangle. Brush with melted **butter**; sprinkle with mixture of
    ⅓ cup **sugar** and
    2 to 3 teaspoons **cinnamon**

Roll . . . . as for jelly roll, starting with 16-inch side. Cut into fifteen 1-inch slices. Place slices cut-side down over Topping. Cover.

Let rise . . . . in warm place until light, 45 to 60 minutes.

Bake . . . . at 375° for 20 to 25 minutes.

For use with Pillsbury's Best Self-Rising Flour, omit salt.

PINEAPPLE TOPPING

Melt ¼ cup butter in a 13x9x2-inch pan. Add ⅔ cup firmly packed brown sugar and 1 cup (No. 1 can, undrained) crushed pineapple.

Black Bottom Pecan Rolls

Senior Winner by Mrs. Peter Martenson, Richfield, Minnesota

Chocolate lovers will delight in these chocolate-caramel pecan rolls!

BAKE at 350° for 15 to 18 minutes   MAKES 2 dozen

Soften . . . . 1 packet active dry **yeast** (or 1 cake compressed) in ¼ cup warm **water**

Combine . . . . ½ cup **sugar**
1½ teaspoons **salt***
¾ cup lukewarm scalded **milk**
½ cup **salad oil**
1 unbeaten **egg** and
1 teaspoon **rum flavoring** or vanilla and softened yeast in large mixing bowl.

Add . . . . 4 to 4½ cups sifted **Pillsbury's Best All Purpose Flour*** gradually to form a stiff dough.

Knead . . . . on floured surface until smooth and satiny, 5 to 7 minutes. Place in greased bowl and cover.

Let rise . . . . in warm place (85°) until doubled, 2 to 2½ hours.

Combine . . . . ½ cup firmly packed **brown sugar**
2 to 3 tablespoons **cocoa**
3 tablespoons **light corn syrup**
2 tablespoons **butter,** melted

1 tablespoon **water** and
1 teaspoon **rum flavoring** or vanilla; blend well. Place 2 teaspoons mixture in 24 well-greased muffin cups.** Place 3 **pecan halves** in each cup.

Roll out . . . . on floured surface to a 24x9-inch rectangle. Brush with
2 tablespoons **butter** or margarine, melted

Combine . . . . ¼ cup firmly packed **brown sugar**
¼ cup **pecans,** chopped, and
1 tablespoon **cocoa**. Sprinkle over dough.

Roll . . . . as for jelly roll, starting with 24-inch side. Cut into 1-inch slices. Place in prepared muffin cups.

Let rise . . . . in warm place until light, about 1 hour.

Bake . . . . at 350° for 15 to 18 minutes. Cool 2 minutes, then invert on plate or rack.

For use with Pillsbury's Best Self-Rising Flour, omit salt.
**Or bake in two 9-inch round pans or 8-inch square pans 20 to 25 minutes.*

Black Bottom Pecan Rolls

Cinnamon Nut Crisps

Senior Second Prize Winner by Mrs. Joseph Terrill, Burlingame, Kansas

Brown sugar, raisins and nuts are rolled up inside rich yeast dough. They'll remind you of Danish crisps.

BAKE at 375° for 15 to 18 minutes   MAKES about 2 dozen

Soften.......1 packet active dry **yeast** (or 1 cake compressed) in
       ½ cup warm **water**
Combine.....2 well-beaten **eggs**
       1 cup lukewarm **cream**
       3 tablespoons **sugar**
       1½ teaspoons **salt***
       1 teaspoon **vanilla** and softened yeast in large mixing bowl.
Add.......4½ to 5 cups sifted **Pillsbury's Best All Purpose Flour***
       gradually to form a stiff dough.
Knead........on floured surface until smooth, 2 to 3 minutes. Place in greased bowl and cover.
Let rise........in warm place (85°) until doubled, about 1½ hours.
Roll out.......on floured surface to a 26x20-inch rectangle. Brush with
       2 tablespoons **butter,** melted
Combine.....1 cup firmly packed **brown sugar** and
       1 teaspoon **cinnamon**. Sprinkle half of mixture over dough.
Fold..........long sides to center; press down firmly. Fold in half lengthwise, making 4 layers. Seal edges.
Roll out.......to 26x12-inch rectangle. Brush with
       2 tablespoons **butter,** melted
Combine.....¾ cup blanched **almonds** or other nuts, finely chopped
       ⅓ cup **raisins**, chopped, and remaining brown sugar-cinnamon mixture. Sprinkle over dough.
Roll..........as for jelly roll, starting with 26-inch edge. Cut into 1-inch slices. Dip one cut side of each roll in flour and place floured-side up on surface sprinkled with **sugar**. Roll to ¼-inch thickness. Place on well-greased baking sheets, sugared-side up.**
Let rise........in warm place 15 minutes.
Bake..........at 375° for 15 to 18 minutes.

*For use with Pillsbury's Best Self-Rising Flour, omit salt.

**While first pans of rolls are baking, place extra rolls on waxed paper, sugared-side up, to rise. Transfer to baking sheet to bake. If necessary, rolls may rise longer than 15 minutes.*

Mocha Sundae Rolls

Senior Winner by Mrs. Stella M. Kvetcovsky, Newport, New Hampshire

Thin, crisp candy-like rolls with a coffee-nut flavor baked right in, and a cream cheese-marshmallow creme-chocolate topping.

BAKE at 350° for 15 minutes, then   MAKES about 1½ dozen
       for 5 to 6 minutes

Soften.......1 packet active dry **yeast** (or 1 cake compressed) in
       ¼ cup warm **water**
Cream......¼ cup **butter** or margarine. Add
       ½ cup **sugar**; mix well.
Blend in......1 unbeaten **egg**, mixing thoroughly.
Add.........4 teaspoons **instant coffee**
       ½ teaspoon **salt***
       ½ cup lukewarm scalded **milk** and softened yeast; mix well.
Add.........3 to 3½ cups sifted **Pillsbury's Best All Purpose Flour***
       gradually to form a dough.
Knead........on floured surface until smooth and satiny, 3 to 5 minutes. Place in greased bowl and cover.
Let rise........in warm place (85°) until light, about 2 hours.
Roll out......on floured surface to a 16x10-inch rectangle.
Brush with....2 tablespoons **butter,** melted. Combine
       ¾ cup firmly packed **brown sugar** and
       ¾ cup **pecans**, chopped; sprinkle over dough.
Roll..........as for jelly roll, starting with 10-inch side. Cut into

½-inch slices. Dip one cut side in **brown sugar**; place sugar-side down on greased baking sheet. Flatten to about ¼-inch thickness.

Let rise........in warm place 30 minutes.

Bake.........at 350° for 15 minutes. Remove from oven.

Spoon........about 1 teaspoonful of Cheese-Sundae Fluff in center of each. Sprinkle with
1 ounce shredded **German's sweet chocolate**. Bake 5 to 6 minutes.

For use with Pillsbury's Best Self-Rising Flour, omit salt.

CHEESE-SUNDAE FLUFF

Soften 3 tablespoons cream cheese. Blend in ¾ cup marshmallow creme.

Date-Bait Oatmeal Crescents

Senior Winner by Mrs. Marjorie M. Callison, Janesville, Wisconsin

Sweet rolls . . . unique in texture, with rolled oats in the dough. Inside, an easy-to-mix, uncooked filling of dates, nuts and lemon rind.

BAKE at 400° for 15 to 18 minutes*   MAKES 2 dozen

Soften........1 packet active dry **yeast** (or 1 cake compressed) in ¼ cup warm **water**

Combine.....1 cup quick-cooking **rolled oats**
1 cup **boiling water**
½ cup **shortening**
⅓ cup **sugar** and
1½ teaspoons **salt*** in large mixing bowl. Mix well. Cool to lukewarm.

Add.........1 unbeaten **egg** and softened yeast.

Add.......2½ to 3 cups sifted **Pillsbury's Best All Purpose Flour*** gradually to form a stiff dough.

Knead.......on floured surface until smooth and satiny, 3 to 5 minutes. Place in greased bowl and cover.

Let rise........in warm place (85°) until light, 1½ to 2 hours.

Date-Bait Oatmeal Crescents

Combine.....1 cup **dates,** cut fine
1 teaspoon grated **lemon rind** and
¾ cup **nuts,** finely chopped

Divide........dough into three parts. Roll out one part on floured surface to a 12-inch circle. Cut into 8 wedges.

Spread........a rounded teaspoonful of date mixture along wide end of each wedge. Roll to point, starting with wide end. Place point-side down on greased baking sheet, curving ends to form crescent. Repeat with remaining dough.

Let rise........until light, about 45 minutes.

Bake........at 400° for 15 to 18 minutes.* While warm, frost with **Vanilla Glaze**, page 326.

For use with Pillsbury's Best Self-Rising Flour, omit salt; decrease baking time to 12 to 15 minutes.

Almond Petals

Senior Winner by Mrs. Pauline Silver, New York, New York

Dainty, rose-shaped sweet rolls with almond filling inside each petal! Surprisingly simple to shape.

BAKE at 400° for 12 to 15 minutes   MAKES 3 dozen

Soften . . . . . . .1 packet active dry **yeast** (or 1 cake compressed) in
¼ cup warm **water**

Sift together . .3 cups sifted **Pillsbury's Best All Purpose Flour***
¼ cup **sugar** and
1¼ teaspoons **salt** into large mixing bowl.

Cut in . . . . . .⅓ cup **butter** or margarine until particles are fine.
Make a well in the center.

Add . . . . .1 beaten **egg**
½ cup **sour cream** (thick or commercial) and softened
yeast. Stir until well combined.

Almond Petals

Knead . . . . .on floured surface until smooth and satiny, 8 to 10
minutes. Place in greased bowl and cover.

Let rise . . . . .in warm place (85°) until doubled, about 2 hours.
Prepare Almond Filling.

Divide . . . . .dough into four parts. Cut each into nine pieces;
shape into flat rounds. Place about 1 teaspoon
Filling in center of each. Bring up edges of dough;
pinch together to enclose filling.

Roll . . . . .each ball on floured surface to an 8-inch long
"pencil;" flatten into a strip ¾ inch wide. Cut slits
at ½-inch intervals along one side, making slits
three-fourths through to opposite side. Begin at one
end and roll strip. Place on greased baking sheet with
cut ends up; turn ends down slightly.

Combine . . . . .2 tablespoons **sugar** and
¼ teaspoon **cinnamon**. Sprinkle over rolls.

Let rise . . . . .in warm place 15 minutes.

Bake . . . . .at 400° for 12 to 15 minutes.

*For use with Pillsbury's Best Self-Rising Flour, omit salt; decrease baking time to 10 to 12 minutes.

ALMOND FILLING

Cream 2 tablespoons butter with ½ cup sifted confectioners' sugar. Thin with 1 to 2 teaspoons water to form stiff paste. Blend in ½ cup almonds, ground, and 1 teaspoon almond extract. Refrigerate.

Whole Wheat Caramel Rolls

Senior Winner by Mrs. Norman L. Edie, Hamburg, New York

Caramel topping and nuts make whole wheat rolls a breakfast sensation.

BAKE at 350° for 25 to 30 minutes   MAKES 16 rolls

Soften . . . . . . .1 packet active dry **yeast** (or 1 cake compressed) in
¼ cup warm **water**

Combine . . . . .3 tablespoons **sugar**

2 tablespoons **shortening**
1 teaspoon **salt*** and
¾ cup hot scalded **milk** in large mixing bowl. Cool to lukewarm.

Stir in . . . . softened yeast.

Add . . . . 1⅛ cups unsifted **Pillsbury's Whole Wheat (Graham) Flour** and
1 to 1¼ cups sifted **Pillsbury's Best All Purpose Flour*** gradually to form a stiff dough.

Knead . . . . on floured surface until smooth and satiny, 3 to 5 minutes. Place in greased bowl and cover.

Let rise . . . . in warm place (85°) until doubled, 1 to 1½ hours.

Roll . . . . on floured surface to 16x12-inch rectangle.

Combine . . . . ⅓ cup **butter**, melted, and
1 cup firmly packed **brown sugar**. Spread over dough. Sprinkle with
½ cup **nuts**, chopped

Roll . . . . as for jelly roll, starting with 16-inch side. Cut into 1-inch slices. Place cut-side down in well-greased 9-inch square pan or muffin cups.

Let rise . . . . in warm place until light, about 1 hour.

Bake . . . . at 350° for 25 to 30 minutes. Cool 2 minutes, then invert on plate or rack.

*For use with Pillsbury's Best Self-Rising Flour, omit salt.

Ye Olde Saffron Braids

Senior Winner by Mrs. John Vuolle, Calumet, Michigan

Saffron lovers will find these fruited golden rolls very appetizing; omit the saffron if you prefer. A coffee-sugar glaze tops them.

BAKE at 350° for 12 to 15 minutes, then   MAKES 3 dozen
for 5 minutes

Combine . . . . ¼ teaspoon **saffron** and
¼ cup **boiling water.** Cool to lukewarm. Do not strain.

Combine . . . . ¾ cup lukewarm scalded **milk***
½ cup **sugar**
1 teaspoon **salt****
½ teaspoon ground **cardamom** and saffron in large mixing bowl.

Add . . . . 1 cake compressed **yeast**, crumbled (or 1 packet active dry yeast softened in ¼ cup warm water).* Let stand 5 minutes. Mix well.

Stir in . . . . . ⅓ cup **shortening**, melted and cooled
2 unbeaten **eggs**
½ cup **raisins** and
¼ cup **citron**, chopped fine. Mix well.

Add . . . . 3½ to 4 cups sifted **Pillsbury's Best All Purpose Flour**** gradually to form a stiff dough.

Knead . . . . on floured surface until smooth and satiny, about 5 minutes. Place in greased bowl and cover.

Let rise . . . . in warm place (85°) until doubled, about 2 hours.

Shape . . . . dough into ½-inch strips, 4 inches long. Seal top ends of three strips; braid and fasten ends. Place on greased baking sheets. Cover.

Let rise . . . . in warm place until light, 1 to 1½ hours.

Bake . . . . at 350° for 12 to 15 minutes. Remove from oven; brush with a mixture of
⅓ cup **sugar** and
2 tablespoons strong **coffee.** Bake 5 minutes.

*If dry yeast is used, decrease milk to ½ cup.

**For use with Pillsbury's Best Self-Rising Flour, omit salt.

Cinna-Rye Cloverleafs

Junior Winner by Ruth Massey, Cataula, Georgia

Hearty rolls with a hint of rye and a surprise filling in each section.

BAKE at 350° for 15 to 20 minutes   MAKES 16 rolls

Soften.......1 packet active dry **yeast** (or 1 cake compressed) in
        ¼ cup warm **water**

Combine....½ cup **bran flakes**
        ½ cup **sugar**
        ½ cup **shortening**
        1 teaspoon **salt*** and
        ¾ cup **boiling water** in large mixing bowl. Stir to melt
        shortening. Cool to lukewarm.

Blend in.....1 unbeaten **egg** and softened yeast.

Add........1 cup sifted **Pillsbury's Pure Medium Rye Flour** and
        3 to 3¼ cups sifted **Pillsbury's Best All Purpose Flour***
        gradually to form a stiff dough.

Knead........on floured surface until smooth and satiny, about
        5 minutes. Place in greased bowl and cover.

Let rise.......in warm place (85°) until doubled, 2 to 2½ hours.
        Prepare Cinnamon Filling.

Roll out......half of dough to 12x8-inch rectangle. Cut into 24
        two-inch squares. Place ½ teaspoon Filling in center
        of each square. Wrap dough around Filling and place
        balls in well-greased muffin cups, three to a cup.
        Repeat process with remaining dough.

Let rise........in warm place until light, about 1 hour.

Bake.........at 350° for 15 to 20 minutes.

*For use with Pillsbury's Best Self-Rising Flour, omit salt.

CINNAMON FILLING

Combine ⅓ cup firmly packed brown sugar, ⅓ cup raisins, ⅓ cup chopped nuts, ⅓ cup butter or margarine and 1½ teaspoons cinnamon.

Cinnamince Cider Buns

Senior Winner by Mrs. Kermit L. Sandefur, Overland Park, Kansas

Savory mincemeat, sweet apple cider and cinnamon combine for the festive filling of these No-Knead yeast rolls. Top with cider glaze.

BAKE at 350° for 30 to 35 minutes   MAKES 16 rolls

Soften.......1 packet active dry **yeast** (or 1 cake compressed) and
        3 tablespoons **sugar** in
        1 cup warm **water** in large mixing bowl.

Stir in.......1 cup sifted **Pillsbury's Best All Purpose Flour*** and
        1½ teaspoons **salt**. Beat until smooth.

Add........1 unbeaten **egg** and
        ¼ cup **shortening**, melted. Beat well.

Blend in.....3 cups sifted **Pillsbury's Best All Purpose Flour** to
        form a soft dough. Cover.

Let rise.......in warm place (85°) until doubled, 1½ to 2 hours.
        Prepare Mincemeat Filling. Knead dough 4 to 5
        strokes on floured surface. Roll out to 26x9-inch
        rectangle. Spread with Filling.

Combine....¼ cup firmly packed **brown sugar** and
        1½ teaspoons **cinnamon**; sprinkle over Filling. Dot with
        2 tablespoons **butter**.

Roll..........as for jelly roll, starting with 26-inch edge. Cut into
        1½-inch slices. Place cut-side down in two greased
        8-inch round layer pans. Cover.

Let rise........in warm place until light, 45 to 60 minutes.

Bake.........at 350° for 30 to 35 minutes. While warm, drizzle
        with Cider Glaze and garnish with chopped **mara-
        schino cherries**.

*For use with Pillsbury's Best Self-Rising Flour, omit salt.

MINCEMEAT FILLING

Place ½ package (½ cup) dry mincemeat in saucepan; break up slightly with spoon. Add ½ cup sweet apple cider; bring to boil. Boil vigorously 1 minute, stirring constantly. Cool, stirring occasionally.

CIDER GLAZE

Blend together ¾ cup sifted confectioners' sugar, ¾ teaspoon cinnamon and 1 tablespoon sweet apple cider. Gradually add 2 to 3 teaspoons apple cider to form a thin glaze.

Almond Rolls

Senior Winner by Mrs. Ralph Taylor, Greencastle, Indiana

Tender, almond-flavored sweet rolls are excellent with salad or make a favorite breakfast treat. Butter, eggs and sour cream make them extra rich.

BAKE at 350° for 15 to 20 minutes   MAKES 3 dozen

Soften.......1 packet active dry **yeast** (or 1 cake compressed) in
¼ cup warm **water**

Sift together 3¼ cups sifted **Pillsbury's Best All Purpose Flour*** and
1 teaspoon **salt** into large mixing bowl.

Cut in......½ cup **butter** or margarine and
¼ cup **shortening** until the size of small peas.

Beat........1 **egg** and
2 **egg yolks** in large mixing bowl.

Blend in.....⅔ cup **sour cream** (thick or commercial)
1 tablespoon **sugar**
1 teaspoon **almond extract** and softened yeast.

Add..........the dry ingredients; mix well. Cover; chill 2 hours.

Sprinkle.....⅔ cup firmly packed **brown sugar** on floured surface. Roll dough in sugar with rolling pin, folding over and rerolling until all sugar is used and dough is about ¼ inch thick.

Sprinkle.....½ cup **almonds,** chopped, over dough, pressing in with rolling pin.

Cut..........into 6x1-inch strips. Twist strips and form into circles. Place on greased baking sheets.

Let rise........in warm place (85°) until light, about 30 minutes.

Bake.........at 350° for 15 to 20 minutes.

*For use with Pillsbury's Best Self-Rising Flour, omit salt.

Sugar Swirls

Senior Winner by Mrs. George Uhal, Sr., Lakewood, Ohio

Golden pinwheels of buttery goodness—made rich with confectioners' sugar and nuts!

BAKE at 350° for 15 to 20 minutes   MAKES about 4½ dozen small rolls

Soften.......1 packet active dry **yeast** (or 1 cake compressed) in
¼ cup warm **water**

Cut..........1 cup **butter** or margarine into
4 cups sifted **Pillsbury's Best All Purpose Flour*** until particles are the size of small peas.

Combine.....5 unbeaten **egg yolks**
¾ cup **milk**
2 tablespoons **sugar**
1½ teaspoons **salt** and softened yeast. Add to flour mixture; mix well. Cover; chill at least 4 hours.

Combine...1½ cups sifted **confectioners' sugar** and
1 cup **nuts,** finely chopped

Divide........dough into three parts. On surface sprinkled with one-third the sugar-nut mixture, roll out one part to a 15-inch square.

Roll..........as for jelly roll; cut into ¾-inch pieces. Place cut-side down on greased baking sheets. Repeat with remaining dough.**

Let rise........in warm place (85°) until light, 30 to 45 minutes.

Bake.........at 350° for 15 to 20 minutes.

*For use with Pillsbury's Best Self-Rising Flour, omit salt.

**Dough may be stored in refrigerator up to 4 days and baked as needed.

BEST of the BAKE-OFF

No-Knead
Water-Rising
Twists
**Grand Prize Winner
of the First
Grand National
Bake-Off®**

No-Knead Water-Rising Twists

Grand Prize Winner by Mrs. Ralph E. Smafield, Detroit, Michigan

These sweet, tender nut rolls have a marvelous richness and delicacy. The ease and speed of making them will delight you.

BAKE at 375° for 12 to 15 minutes   MAKES 2 dozen

Combine . . . . ½ cup **shortening**
           3 tablespoons **sugar**
           1½ teaspoons **salt***
           1 teaspoon **vanilla** and
           ½ cup hot scalded **milk** in large mixing bowl. Cool to lukewarm.

Add . . . . 2 cakes compressed **yeast**, crumbled (or 2 packets active dry yeast softened in ¼ cup warm water; decrease milk to ¼ cup). Let stand 5 minutes.

Blend in . . . . 1½ cups sifted **Pillsbury's Best All Purpose Flour;*** beat until smooth. Cover. Let stand 15 minutes.

Add . . . . 3 unbeaten **eggs,** beating well after each.

Add . . . . 1½ cups sifted **Pillsbury's Best All Purpose Flour** gradually to form a soft dough.

Let rise . . . . in one of two ways: (1) *Either* tie dough in a tea towel, allowing ample space for dough to rise. Then place in large mixing bowl and fill with water (75° to 80°). Let stand until dough rises to top of water, 30 to 45 minutes. Remove from water. Dough will be soft and moist. (2) *Or* set covered dough in warm place (85°) about 30 minutes.

Combine . . . . ¾ cup **nuts,** chopped
           ½ cup **sugar** and
           1 teaspoon **cinnamon**

Divide . . . . dough into small pieces with a tablespoon. Roll each piece in sugar-nut mixture; stretch to about 8-inch length. Twist into desired shape. Place on greased baking sheet. Let stand 5 minutes.

Bake . . . . at 375° for 12 to 15 minutes.

For use with Pillsbury's Best Self-Rising Flour, omit salt.

Lucky Apple Coffee Cake

Senior Winner by Mrs. Jean L. Davis, Vienna, West Virginia

Diced apples are rolled up inside yeast dough. An orange juice, honey and spice mixture lines the pan, making a delicious glaze.

BAKE at 375° for 25 to 30 minutes   MAKES 1 dozen rolls

Soften . . . . 1 packet active dry **yeast** (or 1 cake compressed) in ¼ cup warm **water**

Combine . . . . ¼ cup **sugar**
           ¼ cup **shortening**
           2 teaspoons **salt*** and
           ½ cup hot scalded **milk** in large mixing bowl; stir to melt shortening.

Add . . . . ¼ cup cold **water**. Blend in 1 unbeaten **egg** and softened yeast.

Add . . . . 3 cups sifted **Pillsbury's Best All Purpose Flour*** gradually, beating well after each addition. Knead on floured surface a few strokes until smooth.

Roll out . . . . to a 12x8-inch rectangle.

Combine . . . . ½ cup **honey**
           2 tablespoons **sugar**
           1 tablespoon **flour**
           ½ teaspoon **cinnamon** and
           2 tablespoons **orange juice**. Spread 2 tablespoons mixture over dough. Spread remainder in well-greased 13x9x2-inch pan.

Sprinkle . . . . 1½ cups pared, finely diced **apples** over dough.

Combine . . . . . 2 tablespoons **sugar** and
           ½ teaspoon **cinnamon**. Sprinkle over apples. Dot with 1 tablespoon **butter**

Roll . . . . as for jelly roll, starting with 12-inch edge. Cut into 1-inch slices. Place cut-side down in pan.

Let rise . . . . in warm place (85°) until light, about 1½ hours.

Bake . . . . at 375° for 25 to 30 minutes. Invert on wire rack; cool 5 minutes before removing pan.

For use with Pillsbury's Best Self-Rising Flour, omit salt.

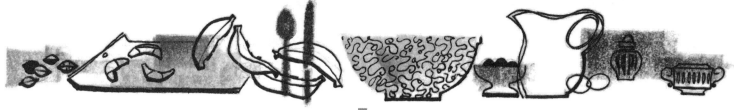

No-Knead Mocha Rolls

Senior Winner by Mrs. Garth Thornburg, Paonia, Colorado

Bohemian kolacky was the inspiration for these unusual rolls. They're flavored with coffee, and have an apricot filling.

BAKE at 375° for 12 to 15 minutes   MAKES 3 dozen

Soften.......1 packet active dry **yeast** (or 1 cake compressed) in
               ¼ cup warm **water**
Combine....⅛ cup **sugar**
               ¼ cup **shortening**
               1½ teaspoons **salt*** and
               ½ cup hot scalded **milk** in large mixing bowl. Stir to
               melt shortening.
Add........¼ cup cold strong **coffee**
               1 unbeaten **egg** and softened yeast.
Add.......3¼ cups sifted **Pillsbury's Best All Purpose Flour***
               gradually; mix well. Cover; let stand 15 minutes.
Roll out.......on floured surface to ¼-inch thickness. Cut with
               2-inch round cutter. Place on greased baking sheets.
Let rise........in warm place (85°) until light, about 1 hour.
               Prepare Apricot Filling.
Press.........fingers in center of each round to form a hollow.
               Fill each with a teaspoonful of Filling.
Bake.........at 375° for 12 to 15 minutes.
*For use with Pillsbury's Best Self-Rising Flour, omit salt.

APRICOT FILLING

Combine 3 tablespoons sugar and 2 teaspoons cornstarch in saucepan. Blend in 1 cup cooked apricots. Cook, stirring constantly, until thickened and clear. Stir in 1 teaspoon butter. Cool.

Golden Bananzas

Senior Winner by Mrs. Pazzino de'Pazzi, Hampton Bays, Long Island, N.Y.

Mashed bananas and buttermilk give these sweet rolls special flavor. They're topped with a simple glaze and a dusting of nutmeg.

BAKE at 375° for 15 to 18 minutes   MAKES 2 dozen

Soften.......1 packet active dry **yeast** (or 1 cake compressed) in
               ¼ cup warm **water**
Combine....⅛ cup **sugar**
               1½ teaspoons **salt***
               3 tablespoons **shortening** or salad oil and
               1 cup hot scalded **buttermilk** or sour milk in large
               mixing bowl. Cool to lukewarm.
Stir in.......½ teaspoon **soda***
               ¾ cup mashed ripe **banana** (1 large)
               1 unbeaten **egg** and softened yeast. Add
               2 to 4 drops **yellow food coloring**, if desired.
Add.......4¼ to 4¾ cups sifted **Pillsbury's Best All Purpose Flour***
               gradually to form a dough. Cover; let stand 5 minutes.
Roll out.......half of dough on floured surface to a 12x6-inch
               rectangle. Brush with melted **butter**. Fold lengthwise
               to form a 12x3-inch strip. Cut into 3x1-inch pieces;
               twist each 2 or 3 times. Place on greased baking
               sheets; curve to crescent shape. Repeat with remain-
               ing dough.
Let rise........in warm place (85°) until doubled, about 1 hour.
Bake.........at 375° for 15 to 18 minutes. While warm, spread
               with **Vanilla Glaze**, page 326; sprinkle lightly with
               nutmeg.
*For use with Pillsbury's Best Self-Rising Flour, omit salt and soda.

Prune Brunch Rolls

Senior Winner by Mrs. Joseph Rutkowski, Milwaukee, Wisconsin

These prune-and-nut-filled rolls are derived from kolacky, a traditional Bohemian sweet roll. But the method is modern—no kneading.

BAKE at 375° for 15 to 20 minutes   **MAKES about 3 dozen small rolls**

Soften . . . . 1 packet active dry **yeast** (or 1 cake compressed) in
⅓ cup warm **water**

Combine . . . . ⅓ cup **sugar**
¼ cup **shortening**
1½ teaspoons **salt*** and
¾ cup hot scalded **milk** in large mixing bowl. Cool to
lukewarm.

Blend in . . . . . 1 unbeaten **egg** and softened yeast.

Add . . . . 3 to 3¼ cups sifted **Pillsbury's Best All Purpose Flour***
gradually; beat well after each addition. Cover.

Let rise . . . . in warm place (85°) until doubled, about 1 hour.

Roll out . . . . . . on floured surface to ¼-inch thickness; cut into
rounds with 2½-inch cutter. Place on greased baking
sheets.

Let rise . . . . in warm place until light, about 1 hour.

Press . . . . fingers in center of each round to form a hollow.
Place a teaspoonful of Prune Filling and a teaspoonful of Cheese Filling in each hollow. Sprinkle with
chopped **nuts.**

Bake . . . . at 375° for 15 to 20 minutes.

*For use with Pillsbury's Best Self-Rising Flour, omit salt.

PRUNE FILLING

Combine 1 cup cut, cooked prunes (about ½ pound uncooked), 2
teaspoons grated orange rind, 3 tablespoons sugar and ¼ teaspoon
cinnamon.

CHEESE FILLING

Combine 1 cup creamed cottage cheese, ¼ cup sugar and ½ teaspoon
salt. Mix well.

Fruit-Filled Horns

Junior Winner by Dolores Thee, Savannah, Georgia

*These small, tender horns have an old-fashioned apricot filling.
Rich enough for dessert—ideal for between-meal snacks.*

BAKE at 400° for 10 to 12 minutes   **MAKES 2½ dozen**

Soften . . . . 1 packet active dry **yeast** (or 1 cake compressed) in
¼ cup warm **water**

Sift together . . 3 cups sifted **Pillsbury's Best All Purpose Flour***
1 cup sifted **confectioners' sugar** and
1½ teaspoons **salt** into large mixing bowl.

Cut in . . . . . . ¾ cup **shortening** until particles are fine.

Combine . . . . . 1 beaten **egg**
¼ cup undiluted **evaporated milk** and softened yeast.
Sprinkle over flour mixture, stirring with fork until
thoroughly combined. Cover.**

Let rise . . . . in warm place (85°) until doubled, about 1 hour.
Prepare Apricot-Nutmeg Filling.

Divide . . . . dough in half. Roll out each half on floured surface
to a 15x9-inch rectangle. Cut into 3-inch squares.
Place a teaspoon of Filling in center of each. Fold
two opposite corners to center to form a horn shape;
seal. Place on greased baking sheet.

Bake . . . . at 400° for 10 to 12 minutes.

*For use with Pillsbury's Best Self-Rising Flour, omit salt.
**If desired, dough may be refrigerated up to two days.

APRICOT-NUTMEG FILLING

Combine in saucepan 1½ cups dried apricots, cut into small pieces,
and ¾ cup water. Cook until tender. Add ¾ cup sugar, ¼ teaspoon
salt and ¼ teaspoon nutmeg. Cook until thickened; cool.

Starlight Sugar Crisps

Senior First Prize Winner by Mrs. Leland E. Ross, Roscommon, Michigan

Flaky, tender, sugared twists that you can serve as either a sweet roll or a cookie . . . these easily-made pastries are wonderful at a tea, or with afternoon coffee.

BAKE at 375° for 15 to 20 minutes   MAKES about 5 dozen

Soften . . . . 1 packet active dry **yeast** (or 1 cake compressed) in ¼ cup warm **water**

Sift together 3½ cups sifted **Pillsbury's Best All Purpose Flour*** and 1½ teaspoons **salt** into large mixing bowl.

Cut in . . . . . . ½ cup **butter** or margarine and ½ cup **shortening** until particles are fine.

Blend in . . . . . 2 beaten **eggs**
½ cup **sour cream** (thick or commercial)
1 teaspoon **vanilla** and softened yeast. Mix thoroughly. Cover; chill at least 2 hours.**

Combine . . . 1½ cups **sugar** and
2 teaspoons **vanilla**

Roll out . . . . half of chilled dough on surface sprinkled with about ½ cup of the vanilla sugar. Roll out to a 16x8-inch rectangle. Sprinkle with about 1 tablespoon of the vanilla sugar.

Fold . . . . one end of dough over center. Fold other end over to make three layers. Turn one-quarter of the way around and repeat rolling and folding twice, sprinkling surface with additional vanilla sugar each time as needed.

Roll out . . . . to a 16x8-inch rectangle about ¼ inch thick.

Cut . . . . into 4x1-inch strips. Twist each strip 2 or 3 times. Place on ungreased baking sheets. Repeat entire process with remaining dough.

Bake . . . . at 375° for 15 to 20 minutes.

*For use with Pillsbury's Best Self-Rising Flour, omit salt.

**If desired, dough may be stored in refrigerator up to four days and baked as needed.

Starlight Sugar Crisps

Apple Roll-Ups

Senior Winner by Lillian B. Ellis, La Grange, Illinois

Tempting cinnamon pinwheel rolls with apple slices rolled up inside.

BAKE at 400° for 25 to 30 minutes*   MAKES 2½ dozen

Soften.......1 packet active dry **yeast** (or 1 cake compressed) in
¼ cup warm **water**

Heat.......¼ cup **water** and
2 tablespoons **shortening** in saucepan until shortening melts.

Combine.....1 slightly beaten **egg**
½ cup undiluted **evaporated milk** or fresh milk
¼ cup **sugar**
2 teaspoons **salt**,* the shortening and softened yeast in large mixing bowl. Mix well.

Add.......3¼ cups sifted **Pillsbury's Best All Purpose Flour***
gradually, beating well after each addition. Cover.

Let rise........in warm place (85°) until doubled, about 1½ hours.

Roll out.......on floured surface to 15-inch square. Brush with
2 tablespoons **butter,** melted

Combine....⅓ cup **sugar** and
2 teaspoons **cinnamon**. Sprinkle over dough. Cut into 1-inch strips. Cut strips in half crosswise.

Drain.......1 No. 2 can **apple slices**. Place a slice on one end of strip; roll up half way. Add another slice on strip and continue rolling to end. Place rolls on greased baking sheets seam-side down. Repeat process with remaining strips.

Let rise........in warm place until light, about 1 hour.

Bake.........at 400° for 25 to 30 minutes. Serve warm.

For use with Pillsbury's Best Self-Rising Flour, omit salt; decrease baking time to 15 to 20 minutes.

Apricot Coconut Twists

Senior Winner by Mrs. Peggy Anne Laut, Jamaica, Long Island, New York

Easy-to-shape sweet rolls filled with a refreshing combination . . . tangy dried apricots, coconut and brown sugar. Chewy and full of flavor.

BAKE at 400° for 12 to 15 minutes   MAKES 1½ to 2 dozen

Soften.......1 packet active dry **yeast** (or 1 cake compressed) in
¼ cup warm **water**

Combine.....3 cups sifted **Pillsbury's Best All Purpose Flour***
¼ cup firmly packed **brown sugar** and
1 teaspoon **salt** in large mixing bowl.

Cut in......½ cup **butter** or margarine and
¾ cup creamed small-curd **cottage cheese** until particles are fine.

Add.........2 beaten **eggs** (reserve 1 tablespoon to brush tops)
1 teaspoon **vanilla** and softened yeast; blend well.

Roll out.......on floured surface to a 16x10-inch rectangle.

Brush with....2 tablespoons **butter,** melted. Spread Apri-coconut Filling over half of dough along 16-inch side. Fold uncovered dough over Filling.

Cut..........crosswise into strips ¾ inch wide. Twist each strip twice; place on greased baking sheet. Brush with reserved egg.

Let rise........in warm place (85°) until doubled, 45 to 60 minutes.

Bake.........at 400° for 12 to 15 minutes. Frost while warm with
Vanilla Glaze, page 326, if desired.

Pillsbury's Best Self-Rising Flour is not recommended for use in this recipe.

APRI-COCONUT FILLING

Cover ½ cup finely cut dried apricots with boiling water. Let stand 5 minutes; drain. Add ½ cup coconut, ⅓ cup firmly packed brown sugar, 2 tablespoons melted butter and ½ teaspoon vanilla. Mix well.

Beauty Bow Rolls

Best of Class Winner by Mrs. Donald J. Gillian, Tonawanda, New York

Rich, tender yeast rolls with a butter and almond filling. The "knots" are almonds. Crisp, yet tender, their flavor is truly delicious.

BAKE at 400° for 12 to 15 minutes   MAKES 2 dozen

Soften. . . . . . .1 packet active dry **yeast** (or 1 cake compressed) in
⅟₄ cup warm **water**
Combine. . . .¼ cup **sugar**
1 teaspoon **salt***
1 tablespoon grated **lemon rind**
¼ cup **shortening** and
½ cup hot scalded **milk** in large mixing bowl. Add
½ cup cold **water**. Cool to lukewarm.
Blend in. . . . .1 slightly beaten **egg** and softened yeast.
Add. . . . . . . .4 to 4½ cups sifted **Pillsbury's Best All Purpose Flour***

Beauty Bow Rolls

gradually; beat well after each addition. Cover.
Let rise. . . . . . .in warm place (85°) until almost doubled, 45 to 60 minutes.
Combine. . . . .¾ cup firmly packed **brown sugar**
⅓ cup **butter** or margarine, melted
2 tablespoons **flour** and
1 to 2 teaspoons **almond extract**; mix well.
Divide. . . . . . . .dough in half. Roll out each half on floured surface to 12x10-inch rectangle.
Spread. . . . . . .almond-butter mixture over dough. Roll as for jelly roll, starting with 12-inch edge. Cut into ½-inch slices. Arrange slices in pairs on greased baking sheet. Flatten to ¼-inch thickness and pinch each pair together to form a "bow."
Let rise. . . . . . .in warm place until light, 30 to 45 minutes. Pinch rounds together again.
Place. . . . .**blanched almond** in center of each "bow" for "knot." Brush tops of rolls lightly with **cream**.
Bake. . . . . . . .at 400° for 12 to 15 minutes.
*For use with Pillsbury's Best Self-Rising Flour, omit salt.

Sunday Best Sweet Rolls

Senior Winner by Rena Giblin, Buffalo, New York

These are much like Danish pastry. Cottage cheese gives them flavor.

BAKE at 400° for 12 to 15 minutes   MAKES about 1½ dozen

Soften. . . . . . .1 packet active dry **yeast** (or 1 cake compressed) in
¼ cup warm **water**
Sift together 2½ cups sifted **Pillsbury's Best All Purpose Flour***
¼ cup **sugar** and
1 teaspoon **salt** into large mixing bowl.
Cut in. . . . . .½ cup **butter** or margarine and
1 cup creamed small-curd **cottage cheese** until the particles are very fine.

Add . . . . 1 slightly beaten **egg** and softened yeast; mix well.
Roll out . . . . on well-floured surface to 14-inch square.
Combine . . . . ¾ cup firmly packed **brown sugar**
 3 tablespoons **butter** or margarine, melted
 ¼ teaspoon **salt**
 ½ teaspoon **almond extract**
 ½ teaspoon **vanilla** and
 ⅔ cup **nuts**, chopped. Sprinkle over dough.
Roll . . . . as for jelly roll. Cut into ¾-inch slices. Place cut-side down on greased baking sheet.
Let rise . . . . in warm place (85°) until light, about 1½ hours.
Bake . . . . at 400° for 12 to 15 minutes.
For use with Pillsbury's Best Self-Rising Flour, omit salt in dough.

Mock Almond Danish Rolls

Senior Winner by Mrs. Russell Johnson, Rockford, Illinois

Dainty hi-light rolls with a marzipan-like filling.

BAKE at 425° for 10 to 12 minutes   MAKES 2½ dozen

Cut . . . . ¼ cup **Pillsbury's Best All Purpose Flour** into ¾ cup **butter** or margarine. Form into ball. Chill 1 hour.
Crumble . . . . . 1 cake compressed **yeast**;* add ¼ cup **sugar**. Let stand 5 minutes.
Combine . . . . . 1 beaten **egg**
 ¾ cup **milk**
 1 teaspoon **salt**** and softened yeast.
Add . . . . 2½ to 3 cups sifted **Pillsbury's Best All Purpose Flour**** gradually to form a stiff dough. Beat well after each addition.
Roll out . . . . on well-floured surface to 12-inch square.
Roll . . . . flour-butter mixture on well-floured surface to a 10x5-inch rectangle; place in center of dough. Fold sides of dough to overlap over butter mixture. Cover. Let rest 30 minutes. Prepare Almond Crumb Filling.

Mock Almond Danish Rolls

Roll out . . . . . . to 12x10-inch rectangle. Spread with Filling.
Cut . . . . into 4x1-inch strips. Roll each strip to form a pinwheel.
Place . . . . in small muffin cups, lined with paper baking cups (tea-size cups).*** Cover.
Let rise . . . . in warm place (85°) until light, about 1½ hours.
Bake . . . . at 425° for 10 to 12 minutes.
 Or substitute 1 packet active dry yeast softened in ¼ cup warm water; decrease milk to ½ cup and add the ¼ cup sugar with milk.
 **For use with Pillsbury's Best Self-Rising Flour, omit salt.*
 ****Or place paper baking cups on ungreased baking sheet.*

ALMOND CRUMB FILLING

Combine 1 well-beaten egg, ½ cup sugar, ⅔ cup bread crumbs and 2 teaspoons almond extract. Blend thoroughly.

BEST of the BAKE-OFF

Ring-a-Lings
**Grand Prize Winner
of the Seventh
Grand National
Bake-Off®**

Ring-a-Lings

Grand Prize Winner by Mrs. Bertha E. Jorgensen, Portland, Oregon

Rolls rich and tender with filberts in the filling and a fresh orange glaze on top—full flavor in every bite. There's no kneading and they are surprisingly easy to shape.

BAKE at 375° for 15 minutes, then   MAKES 1½ to 2 dozen
for 5 minutes

Soften.......2 packets active dry **yeast** (or 2 cakes compressed) in
¼ cup warm **water**

Combine....⅓ cup **butter** or margarine and
¾ cup hot scalded **milk** in large mixing bowl. Cool to lukewarm.

Add........⅓ cup **sugar**
2 teaspoons **salt***
2 teaspoons grated **orange rind**
2 unbeaten **eggs** and softened yeast.

Add........4 to 4½ cups sifted **Pillsbury's Best All Purpose Flour***
gradually to form a stiff dough, beating well after each addition. Cover and let stand 30 minutes. Prepare Nut Filling.

Roll out.......on floured surface to a 22x12-inch rectangle. Spread half of dough along 22-inch side with Filling. Fold uncovered dough over Filling.

Cut..........into 1-inch strips (crosswise). Twist each strip 4 or 5 times. Then hold one end down on greased baking sheet for center of roll. Curl remaining strip around center on baking sheet as for a pinwheel, tucking other end under. Cover.

Let rise........in warm place (85°) until light and doubled, 45 to 60 minutes.

Bake.........at 375° for 15 minutes. Prepare glaze of
¼ cup **orange juice** and
3 tablespoons **sugar**. Brush tops of rolls. Bake 5 minutes.

*For use with Pillsbury's Best Self-Rising Flour, omit salt.

NUT FILLING

Cream ⅓ cup butter or margarine. Blend in 1 cup sifted confectioners' sugar. Add 1 cup filberts or hazelnuts, ground or chopped very fine. (Other nuts may be substituted.)

Cookie Buns

Senior Winner by Mrs. Rex H. Berry, Tipton, Iowa

Only one rising is necessary for these rich egg and sour cream yeast "cookies." And there's no shaping . . . just drop dough on baking sheet.

BAKE at 350° for 15 to 20 minutes   MAKES 5 dozen

Sift together..3 cups sifted **Pillsbury's Best All Purpose Flour*** and
1 teaspoon **salt**

Soften.......1 packet active dry **yeast** (or 1 cake compressed) in
¼ cup warm **water**

Blend.......½ cup **shortening**
¼ cup **sugar**
1 tablespoon grated **lemon rind** and
1 tablespoon **lemon juice**, creaming well.

Add........5 unbeaten **egg yolks** (or 2 whole eggs and 1 yolk)
¾ cup **sour cream** or sweet cream and softened yeast. Beat well.

Blend in.......the dry ingredients gradually; beat well after each addition.**

Drop.........by teaspoonfuls onto greased baking sheets. Cover.

Let rise........in warm place (85°) until doubled, 30 to 60 minutes. Brush with slightly beaten **egg white**; sprinkle generously with **sugar**.

Bake.........at 350° for 15 to 20 minutes. Serve warm.

*For use with Pillsbury's Best Self-Rising Flour, omit salt.
**Dough may be stored in refrigerator up to 5 days and baked as needed.

Yam-Yam Honey Buns

Best of Class Winner by Helen V. Zymalski, Miami, Florida

Light, airy nut-filled rolls with a delicate new sweet potato flavor and a honey-brown sugar-pecan topping.

BAKE at 375° for 25 to 30 minutes   MAKES 1 dozen large rolls

Soften . . . . 2 packets active dry **yeast** (or 2 cakes compressed) in ½ cup warm **sweet potato liquid** or water

Combine . . . . ½ cup mashed **sweet potatoes** or yams (canned or cooked)
  ¼ cup **sugar**
  3 tablespoons **butter** or shortening, melted
  2 teaspoons **salt***
  1 teaspoon **vanilla** and
  2 unbeaten **eggs** in large mixing bowl. Add softened yeast.

Yam-Yam Honey Buns

Add . . . . 3¼ to 3½ cups sifted **Pillsbury's Best All Purpose Flour*** gradually to form a stiff dough, beating well after each addition. Cover.

Let rise . . . . in warm place (85°) until doubled, about 1½ hours. Prepare Honey Nut Topping. Pour into greased 13x9x2-inch pan.** Sprinkle with
  ½ cup **pecans** or walnuts, chopped

Toss . . . . dough on well-floured surface until coated with flour and no longer sticky. Roll out to 24x8-inch rectangle.

Brush with . . . . 2 tablespoons **butter,** melted. Sprinkle with
  ¼ cup firmly packed **brown sugar** and
  ¼ cup **pecans** or walnuts, chopped

Roll . . . . as for jelly roll, starting with 24-inch side. Cut into twelve 2-inch slices. Place cut-side down over Topping. Cover.

Let rise . . . . in warm place until light, 30 to 45 minutes.

Bake . . . . at 375° for 25 to 30 minutes. Cool 2 minutes, then invert. Let stand 30 seconds.

*For use with Pillsbury's Best Self-Rising Flour, omit salt.

**Rolls may be baked in two 8 or 9-inch round layer pans for 20 to 25 minutes.

HONEY NUT TOPPING

Combine in saucepan ⅓ cup honey, ½ cup firmly packed brown sugar, ¼ cup butter or margarine and ¼ teaspoon salt. Bring to boil and cook, stirring constantly, to soft-ball stage (236°), about 1½ minutes.

Lemon Nut Rolls

Bride First Prize Winner by Mrs. Thomas May, Sykesville, Maryland

No-Knead potato rolls, featuring lemon in the bread, filling and glaze.

BAKE at 375° for 20 to 25 minutes   MAKES 16 rolls

Soften . . . . 1 packet active dry **yeast** (or 1 cake compressed) in ¼ cup warm **water**

Combine.... ⅛ cup **sugar**
⅛ cup **shortening**
½ cup **mashed potatoes***
1 teaspoon **salt**** and
½ cup hot scalded **milk** in large mixing bowl; stir until
well blended. Cool to lukewarm.

Stir in....... 1 unbeaten **egg**
1 teaspoon grated **lemon rind**
1 tablespoon **lemon juice** and softened yeast.

Add....... 3½ to 4 cups sifted **Pillsbury's Best All Purpose Flour****
gradually to form a stiff dough, beating well after
each addition. Cover.

Let rise....... in warm place (85°) until doubled, about 1 hour.

Roll out....... on well-floured surface to 16x12-inch rectangle.
Brush with
2 tablespoons **butter**, melted

Combine.... ¾ cup **sugar**
½ cup **pecans**, chopped, and
2 teaspoons grated **lemon rind**. Sprinkle over dough.

Roll.......... as for jelly roll, starting with 16-inch side. Cut into
sixteen 1-inch slices. Place cut-side down in two
well-greased 8 or 9-inch round layer pans. Cover.

Let rise....... in warm place until light, 30 to 45 minutes.

Bake......... at 375° for 20 to 25 minutes. While warm, drizzle
with Lemon Glaze.

*Use reconstituted instant mashed potatoes or leftover mashed potatoes.
**For use with Pillsbury's Best Self-Rising Flour, omit salt.

LEMON GLAZE

Blend together ½ cup sifted confectioners' sugar, 1 teaspoon grated
lemon rind, ½ teaspoon lemon juice and 1 tablespoon cream. Beat
until smooth.

Orange Glory Rolls

Junior Third Prize Winner by Mrs. Patrick Sullivan, Lawrence, Kansas

*Light, tender sweet rolls—with fresh-flavored orange filling! And the
dough can be refrigerated for later baking.*

BAKE at 375° for 15 to 20 minutes   MAKES 3 dozen

Combine.... ½ cup **butter** or margarine
2 cups **sugar**
1 cup **orange juice** and **pulp** and
¼ cup grated **orange rind** in saucepan. Boil 6 minutes,
stirring constantly. (If desired, 2½ cups orange
marmalade, heated with ½ cup butter, may be
substituted.)* Place 1 tablespoon mixture into each
well-greased muffin cup.**

Soften....... 2 packets active dry **yeast** (or 2 cakes compressed) in
½ cup warm **water**

Combine.... ½ cup **sugar**
¼ cup **shortening**
2 teaspoons **salt***** and
1 cup **boiling water** in large mixing bowl. Add
¾ cup cold **water**. Cool to lukewarm.

Blend in..... 2 unbeaten **eggs** and softened yeast.

Add....... 7½ to 8 cups sifted **Pillsbury's Best All Purpose Flour*****
gradually to form stiff dough; beat well.* Toss on
well-floured surface until no longer sticky.

Roll out....... one-third at a time on floured surface to a 12x10-
inch rectangle. Brush with melted **butter**. Roll as
for jelly roll, starting with 12-inch edge. Cut into
1-inch slices. Place in muffin cups, cut-side down.

Let rise....... in warm place (85°) until light, 45 to 60 minutes.

Bake......... at 375° for 15 to 20 minutes. Cool 30 seconds,
then invert, allowing sauce to drain onto rolls.

*Dough and sauce may be refrigerated up to three days. Reheat sauce.
**Rolls may be baked in greased 9-inch round or 8-inch square pans. Place
1 cup orange mixture and 12 rolls in a pan. Bake 20 to 25 minutes.
***For use with Pillsbury's Best Self-Rising Flour, omit salt.

Fan-Tasties

Senior Winner by Gladys D. Ellis, Jacksonville, Florida

Sweet raisin fan tan rolls with a delicate orange-raisin flavor . . . extra rich and good eating.

BAKE at 375° for 15 to 18 minutes   MAKES 1½ dozen

Soften . . . . 1 packet active dry **yeast** (or 1 cake compressed) in
     ¼ cup warm **water**
Sift together . . 4 cups sifted **Pillsbury's Best All Purpose Flour*** and
     2 teaspoons **salt** into large mixing bowl.
Cut in . . . . . . ½ cup **butter** or margarine and
     ½ cup **shortening** until particles are fine.
Combine . . . . . 2 well-beaten **eggs**
     1 cup **raisins**
     ⅔ cup **sour cream** (thick or commercial)

Fan-Tasties

     ¼ cup **sugar**
     1 tablespoon grated **orange rind**
     2 tablespoons **orange juice** and softened yeast.
Add . . . . to flour mixture; mix thoroughly. Cover; chill at
     least 2 hours.**
Combine . . . . . 1 tablespoon **orange juice** and
     2 tablespoons **butter,** melted
Roll out . . . . . . half of dough on floured surface to 14x10-inch
     rectangle. Brush with half of butter mixture, then
     sprinkle with half of Sugar Nut Filling.
Cut . . . . into five 14x2-inch strips. Stack the strips; cut into
     1½-inch pieces. Place each stack, cut-side down, in
     well-greased muffin cup. Repeat process with re-
     maining dough. Cover.
Let rise . . . . in warm place (85°) until light, 1½ to 2 hours.
Bake . . . . at 375° for 15 to 18 minutes.
  *For use with Pillsbury's Best Self-Rising Flour, omit salt.
  **Dough may be stored in refrigerator up to 4 days and baked as needed.*

SUGAR NUT FILLING

Combine ⅓ cup firmly packed brown sugar, ⅓ cup sifted confectioners' sugar, ⅔ cup chopped nuts and 1 teaspoon grated orange rind.

Blind Date Surprise Rolls

Junior Winner by Virginia McCammon, Rankin, Texas

There's a moist date-nut filling inside each of these extra-tender sweet rolls. Just one rising.

BAKE at 375° for 15 to 20 minutes   MAKES 1½ to 2 dozen

Soften . . . . 2 packets active dry **yeast** (or 2 cakes compressed) in
     ¼ cup warm **water** in large mixing bowl. Let stand 5
     minutes.
Add . . . . 1 cup lukewarm **sour cream** (thick or commercial)
     3 tablespoons **butter** or shortening, melted

¼ cup **sugar**
1½ teaspoons **salt*** and
1 unbeaten **egg.** Mix well.

Stir in . . . . .3½ cups sifted **Pillsbury's Best All Purpose Flour*** to form a stiff dough. Cover. Prepare Date Filling.

Roll out . . . . . . .on floured surface to a large rectangle ⅛ inch thick.

Cut . . . . .into 5x3-inch rectangles. Spread rounded teaspoonful warm Filling down center of each rectangle, leaving 1 inch at each end. Fold 5-inch sides to meet; seal edges. Place on greased baking sheet. Curl ends in to form "C." Cover.

Let rise . . . . . . .in warm place (85°) until light, about 45 minutes.

Bake . . . . .at 375° for 15 to 20 minutes. Cool 5 minutes. Spread with **Vanilla Glaze,** page 326.

For use with Pillsbury's Best Self-Rising Flour, omit salt.

DATE FILLING

Melt ¼ cup butter or margarine. Add ⅓ cup firmly packed brown sugar, ¾ cup finely cut dates, ¼ cup finely chopped nuts, ½ teaspoon cinnamon and ⅛ teaspoon nutmeg. Simmer over medium heat, stirring until thick (1 to 2 minutes). Cool slightly.

Sweet and Simple Buns

Senior Winner by Mrs. Ethel Johnson, Chico, California

Honey and cream in these No-Knead buns and a sugar-nut coating.

BAKE at 375° for 15 to 20 minutes   MAKES 2½ to 3 dozen

Soften . . . . . . .2 packets active dry **yeast** (or 2 cakes compressed) in ½ cup warm **water**

Combine . . . .¾ cup lukewarm scalded **whipping cream**
⅓ cup **honey**
2 tablespoons **butter,** melted
1 tablespoon **sugar**
2 teaspoons **salt***

2 **egg yolks** and softened yeast in large mixing bowl.

Add . . . . .4 to 4¼ cups sifted **Pillsbury's Best All Purpose Flour*** gradually to form stiff dough. Cover.

Let rise . . . . . . .in warm place (85°) until doubled, about 1½ hours.

Combine . . . . .1 cup **nuts,** finely chopped
¾ cup **sugar** and
1 teaspoon **cinnamon.** Set aside.

Drop . . . . .dough by tablespoonfuls into
2 slightly beaten **egg whites** and then into the nut mixture. Place 3 inches apart on greased baking sheets.** Cover.

Let rise . . . . . . .in warm place until light, about 45 minutes.

Bake . . . . .at 375° for 15 to 20 minutes. (While first rolls bake, refrigerate remaining dough.)

For use with Pillsbury's Best Self-Rising Flour, omit salt.
**Or stretch into 6 to 8-inch strips; twist into desired shapes.*

Sweet and Simple Buns

YEAST COFFEE CAKES

Rich Danish Coffee Cake

Senior Winner by Mrs. Elisabeth Peterson, Great Falls, Montana

Tender dough rich in butter, a filling of cookie or cake crumbs, fruits and nuts all add up to wonderful "Danish pastry."

BAKE at 375° for 25 to 30 minutes   MAKES 2 coffee cakes

Soften . . . . 1 cake compressed **yeast** in
                 ¾ cup lukewarm **milk.*** Set aside.

Measure . . . . . 2 cups sifted **Pillsbury's Best All Purpose Flour****
                 into large mixing bowl. Cut in
                 ¾ cup **butter** or margarine until particles are fine.

Add . . . . 3 tablespoons **sugar**
                 ½ teaspoon **salt**
                 1 beaten **egg** (reserve 1 tablespoon for topping) and
                 softened yeast. Mix thoroughly.

Blend in . . . . . ½ to 1 cup sifted **Pillsbury's Best All Purpose Flour**
                 to form a stiff dough.

Knead . . . . on floured surface until smooth and satiny, about 3
                 minutes. Cover.

Let rise . . . . in warm place (85°) 1 hour. Prepare Crumb Filling.

Divide . . . . dough in half. Roll one half into a strip 24 inches
                 long. Flatten until 5 inches wide. Spread half of
                 Filling down center of strip; fold both sides to center;
                 seal with fingers. Shape into a coil or pretzel on
                 lightly-greased baking sheet. Flatten slightly. Repeat
                 with remaining dough and filling. Cover.

Let stand . . . . . . at room temperature for 20 to 30 minutes.

Blend . . . . 1 tablespoon **water** with reserved egg. Brush coffee
                 cakes generously. Sprinkle with a mixture of

                 ¼ cup **sugar** and
                 ¼ cup blanched **almonds,** finely chopped

Bake . . . . at 375° for 25 to 30 minutes.

   **Or substitute 1 packet active dry yeast softened in ¼ cup warm water.
   Decrease milk to ½ cup and add with softened yeast.*
   ***For use with Pillsbury's Best Self-Rising Flour, omit salt.*

CRUMB FILLING

Prepare 1¼ cups sweet crumbs by crushing 6 coconut macaroons or other crisp cookies, graham crackers or dry cake. Add ¼ cup melted butter or margarine and ¼ cup sugar. Add 1 cup whole raisins, dates, coconut, finely cut, or chopped nuts. Mix thoroughly.

Raisin Apple Pair

Senior Winner by Mrs. Helen K. Perkins, Salt Lake City, Utah

Two coffee cakes shaped from refrigerated dough—with a tasty filling.

BAKE at 375° for 15 to 20 minutes   MAKES 2 coffee cakes

Soften . . . . 1 packet active dry **yeast** (or 1 cake compressed) in
                 ¼ cup warm **water**

Combine . . . . ⅓ cup **butter** or margarine
                 ¼ cup **sugar**
                 1 teaspoon **salt*** and
                 ¾ cup hot scalded **milk** in large mixing bowl; stir to
                 melt butter. Cool to lukewarm.

Stir in . . . . 1 beaten **egg** and softened yeast.

Add . . . . . . 3½ to 4 cups sifted **Pillsbury's Best All Purpose Flour***
                 gradually to form a stiff dough.

Knead . . . . on floured surface until smooth and satiny, 3 to 5
                 minutes. Place in greased bowl and cover. Chill at
                 least 2 hours.**

Roll out . . . . half of dough on floured surface to 12-inch square.
                 Place on greased baking sheet. Spread half of Raisin-
                 Apple Filling down center third of dough.

Cut . . . . dough diagonally at 1-inch intervals on both sides, herringbone fashion. Make cuts 3 inches long.

Fold . . . . opposite strips of dough over Filling, crossing in center. Seal ends of coffee cake. Repeat process with remaining dough.

Let rise . . . . in warm place (85°) until light, about 1 hour.*

Bake . . . . at 375° for 15 to 20 minutes. While warm, spread with **Vanilla Glaze,** page 326.

*Pillsbury's Best Self-Rising Flour is not recommended for use in this recipe.
**Dough may be stored in refrigerator up to 4 days and baked as needed.*

RAISIN-APPLE FILLING

Combine in saucepan 2½ cups pared, finely chopped apples, 1 cup raisins, ground, 1 cup firmly packed brown sugar, ½ teaspoon salt, and ½ teaspoon cinnamon. Boil 4 minutes, stirring constantly. Cool.

Sweet Petals

Senior Winner by Mrs. Grace Autrey, Denver, Colorado

A coffee cake for nibblers . . . break off a petal, and come back for more.

BAKE at 350° for 25 to 30 minutes   MAKES 1 coffee cake

Soften . . . . 1 packet active dry **yeast** (or 1 cake compressed) in ¼ cup warm **water**

Combine . . . . ¾ cup hot scalded **milk**
2 tablespoons **sugar**
3 tablespoons **shortening** and
1½ teaspoons **salt** in large mixing bowl. Cool to lukewarm.

Stir in . . . . the softened yeast.

Add . . . . 2½ to 3 cups sifted **Pillsbury's Best All Purpose Flour***
gradually to form a stiff dough.

Knead . . . . on floured surface until smooth and satiny, 3 to 5 minutes. Place in greased bowl and cover.

Let rise . . . . in warm place (85°) until doubled, about 1 hour.

Place . . . . a 15-inch sheet of aluminum foil, dull-side up, on baking sheet. Grease; turn up edges to form a 12-inch round pan.

Pinch off . . . . . small piece of dough, enough to roll into 6-inch strip, ½ inch thick. Dip in melted **butter** (½ cup in all), then in Cinnamon-Sugar Topping.

Wind . . . . into a flat coil in center of pan. Continue making strips, placing them close together to make a round, flat coffee cake. Cover.

Let rise . . . . in warm place until light, 45 to 60 minutes.

Bake . . . . at 350° for 25 to 30 minutes. Cool slightly. Combine ½ cup sifted **confectioners' sugar** with 1 to 2 teaspoons **milk** to make glaze. Drizzle over top.

For use with Pillsbury's Best Self Rising Flour, omit salt.

CINNAMON-SUGAR TOPPING

Combine ¾ cup sugar, ¼ cup firmly packed brown sugar, 2 teaspoons cinnamon and ¾ cup chopped nuts.

Sweet Petals

Honey-Kist Twist

Honey-Kist Twist

Senior Winner by Mrs. Maryellen Adgate, Washington, D. C.

From one rich yeast dough come three novel-shaped coffee cake swirls.

BAKE at 350° for 35 to 45 minutes*　　　　MAKES 3 coffee cakes

Soften . . . . 2 packets active dry **yeast** (or 2 cakes compressed) in
　　　　　　　½ cup warm **water**
Combine . . . . ½ cup **sugar**
　　　　　　　½ cup **butter** or margarine
　　　　　　　2 teaspoons **salt*** and
　　　　　　　1 cup hot scalded **milk** in large mixing bowl. Cool to
　　　　　　　lukewarm.
Stir in . . . . 1 unbeaten **egg**
　　　　　　　1 unbeaten **egg yolk** and softened yeast.
Add . . . . 6½ to 7 cups sifted **Pillsbury's Best All Purpose Flour***

gradually to form a stiff dough.
Knead . . . . on floured surface until smooth and satiny, about
　　　　　　　5 minutes. Place in greased bowl and cover.
Let rise . . . . in warm place (85°) until doubled, about 1 hour.
　　　　　　　Prepare Honey Topping.
Divide . . . . dough in three parts. Cut one part in half; roll each
　　　　　　　half into a 24-inch strip. Twist one strip; wind into
　　　　　　　a coil in center of 8 or 9-inch greased round layer
　　　　　　　pan. Twist second strip and coil around first strip to
　　　　　　　make a coffee cake. Repeat with remaining parts.
Spread . . . . each with one-third Topping; sprinkle each with
　　　　　　　¼ cup **pecans,** chopped
Let rise . . . . in warm place until light, 30 to 45 minutes.
Bake . . . . at 350° for 35 to 45 minutes.*

*For use with Pillsbury's Best Self-Rising Flour, omit salt; decrease baking
time to 25 to 30 minutes.*

HONEY TOPPING

Cream ¼ cup butter or margarine and 1 cup sifted confectioners' sugar.
Blend in 1 unbeaten egg white, ¼ cup honey and ½ teaspoon cardamom.

Vienna Coffee Bread

Junior Winner by Mrs. Irma Rosenzweig, Upton, Long Island, New York

Slice this loaf, and see the swirls of cinnamon-cocoa filling.

BAKE at 375° for 15 to 20 minutes　　　　MAKES 1 coffee cake

Combine . . . . ¼ cup **sugar**
　　　　　　　¼ cup **shortening**
　　　　　　　2 teaspoons **salt*** and
　　　　　　　½ cup hot scalded **milk**** in large mixing bowl. Cool to
　　　　　　　lukewarm.
Add . . . . 1 cake compressed **yeast,** crumbled (or 1 packet active
　　　　　　　dry yeast dissolved in ¼ cup warm water).** Let
　　　　　　　stand 5 minutes.

Blend in . . . . . 1 slightly beaten **egg**

Add . . . . 2¼ to 2½ cups sifted **Pillsbury's Best All Purpose Flour*** gradually to form a stiff dough.

Knead . . . . on floured surface until smooth and satiny, 3 to 4 minutes. Place in greased bowl and cover.

Let rise . . . . in warm place (85°) until doubled, 1½ to 2 hours.

Roll out . . . . on floured surface to a 12-inch square; combine
2 tablespoons **cocoa**
¼ cup **sugar** and
½ teaspoon **cinnamon.** Sprinkle over dough.

Roll . . . . as for jelly roll; place on greased baking sheet.

Let rise . . . . in warm place until light, about 1½ hours.

Bake . . . . at 375° for 15 to 20 minutes. While warm, sprinkle with **confectioners' sugar.**

*For use with Pillsbury's Best Self-Rising Flour, omit salt.

**If dry yeast is used, decrease milk to ¼ cup.

Merry-Go-Round Coffee Cake

Senior Winner by Mrs. Howard Graham, Charlotte, North Carolina

This festive coffee cake is just the thing for special holidays.

BAKE at 350° for 25 to 30 minutes   MAKES 1 coffee cake

Soften . . . . 1 packet active dry **yeast** (or 1 cake compressed) in 2 tablespoons warm **water**

Combine . . . . ¼ cup **sugar**
2 tablespoons **shortening**
1 teaspoon **salt** and
½ cup hot scalded **milk** in large mixing bowl. Cool to lukewarm.

Add . . . . 1 unbeaten **egg** and softened yeast.

Add . . . . 2½ to 3 cups sifted **Pillsbury's Best All Purpose Flour*** gradually to form a stiff dough.

Knead . . . . on floured surface until smooth and satiny, about 3 minutes. Place in greased bowl and cover.

Let rise . . . . in warm place (85°) until doubled, about 1 to 1½ hours. Roll out to 20x9-inch rectangle.

Combine . . . . ½ cup **jelly**
¼ cup chopped mixed **candied fruit**
¼ cup chopped **candied cherries**
¼ cup **raisins** and
¼ cup **nuts,** chopped. Spread over dough.

Roll . . . . as for jelly roll, starting with 20-inch edge. Seal edges well. Flatten roll slightly; cut lengthwise through center, dividing roll into two 20-inch strips. Turn cut sides up.

Place . . . . one strip on greased baking sheet. Loosely coil the strip pinwheel fashion, keeping cut edge up. Join second strip to end of first strip and continue winding the dough to make a 9-inch round coffee cake.

Let rise . . . . in warm place until light, 30 to 45 minutes.

Bake . . . . at 350° for 25 to 30 minutes.

*Pillsbury's Best Self-Rising Flour is not recommended for use in this recipe.

Merry-Go-Round Coffee Cake

Pineapple Raisin Tea Ring

Pineapple Raisin Tea Ring

Junior Winner by Carolyn Miller, Hickman Mills, Missouri

A simple-to-shape coffee cake with filling of pineapple, raisins, cinnamon and brown sugar.

BAKE at 375° for 20 to 25 minutes   MAKES 2 tea rings

Soften . . . . 2 packets active dry **yeast** (or 2 cakes compressed) in ¼ cup warm **water**

Combine . . . . ½ cup **sugar**
¼ cup **shortening**
1 teaspoon **salt*** and
1 cup hot scalded **milk** in large mixing bowl. Cool to lukewarm.

Stir in . . . . 2 unbeaten **eggs** and softened yeast.

Add . . . . 5 to 5½ cups sifted **Pillsbury's Best All Purpose Flour*** gradually to form a stiff dough.

Knead . . . . on floured surface until smooth and satiny, 5 to 8 minutes. Place in greased bowl and cover.

Let rise . . . . in warm place (85°) until doubled, 1 to 1½ hours. Prepare Pineapple Raisin Filling.

Divide . . . . dough in half. Roll out one portion on floured surface to 20x12-inch rectangle. Brush with melted **butter.** Spread with half the Filling to within 1 inch of one long side and to edge of other sides.

Combine . . . . ⅓ cup firmly packed **brown sugar** and 2 teaspoons **cinnamon;** sprinkle half over Filling on dough. Roll as for jelly roll, starting with covered 20-inch edge.

Shape . . . . into a ring on greased baking sheet. With scissors, make cuts 1 inch apart through top of ring to 1 inch from bottom. Alternate cut slices, bringing one to the center and the next to the outside of the ring. Cover. Repeat entire process with remaining dough.

Let rise . . . . in warm place until light, 45 to 60 minutes.

Bake . . . . at 375° for 20 to 25 minutes. While warm, frost with **Vanilla Glaze,** page 326. Garnish with chopped **nuts** and **maraschino cherry halves.**

*For use with Pillsbury's Best Self-Rising Flour, omit salt.

PINEAPPLE RAISIN FILLING

Combine in saucepan 1 No. 2 can crushed pineapple (1½ cups), well drained, ¾ cup sugar and 1 tablespoon cornstarch. Cook over medium heat until thick. Add ½ cup raisins; cool.

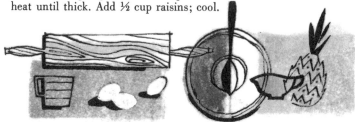

Easy Prune Braid

Bride Winner by Mrs. Herbert Sosedow, Delhi, New York

A prune-nut-lemon blend fills these two braided coffee cakes!

BAKE at 350° for 25 to 30 minutes   MAKES 2 coffee cakes

Soften . . . . . . .1 packet active dry **yeast** (or 1 cake compressed) in ¼ cup warm **water**

Combine . . . .¼ cup **sugar**
2 teaspoons **salt*** and
¾ cup scalded **milk** in large mixing bowl; stir to dissolve.

Stir in . . . . . . .1 tablespoon grated **lemon rind**
1 unbeaten **egg**
½ cup sifted **Pillsbury's Best All Purpose Flour*** and softened yeast.

Add . . . . .¼ cup **shortening,** melted; mix well.

Add . . . . .3 to 3¼ cups sifted **Pillsbury's Best All Purpose Flour** gradually to form a stiff dough.

Knead . . . . .on floured surface until smooth and satiny, 3 to 5 minutes. Place in greased bowl and cover.

Let rise . . . . .in warm place (85°) until doubled, 1½ to 2 hours. Meanwhile prepare Prune Filling.

Divide . . . . .in half. Divide first half into three portions; shape into balls.

Roll out . . . . . . .a portion of dough on floured surface to a 14x5-inch strip. Spread with ⅓ cup Filling to within ½ inch of edges. Moisten both ends and one side. Roll as for jelly roll, sealing ends and moistened side. Repeat with two more portions. Braid the three strips

Easy Prune Braid

together, sealing ends. Shape braid into a crescent on greased baking sheet.

Repeat . . . . .with remaining dough, making a second braided crescent.

Brush . . . . .braids with melted **butter** or cream. Sprinkle with mixture of
¼ cup **sugar** and
1 teaspoon **cinnamon**

Let rise . . . . .in warm place until light, about 45 minutes.

Bake . . . . .at 350° for 25 to 30 minutes.

**For use with Pillsbury's Best Self-Rising Flour, omit salt.*

PRUNE FILLING

Combine 2 cups cut, cooked prunes (about 1 pound uncooked), ¼ cup sugar, 2 tablespoons lemon juice and ½ cup nuts, finely chopped.

Sweetheart Coffee Cake

Junior Second Prize Winner by Marianne Louise Hirt, Lucas, Kansas

Shaping novelty with no special pans! Twin, heart-shaped coffee cakes . . . with cinnamon-sugar filling . . . or two other unique coffee breads.

BAKE at 350°   MAKES 2 coffee cakes

Soften . . . . 2 packets active dry **yeast** (or 2 cakes compressed) in ½ cup warm **water**

Combine . . . . ⅓ cup **sugar**
⅓ cup **butter** or shortening
2 teaspoons **salt*** and
⅔ cup hot scalded **milk** in large mixing bowl. Cool to lukewarm.

Stir in . . . . 2 unbeaten **eggs** and softened yeast.

Add . . . . 4¼ to 5 cups sifted **Pillsbury's Best All Purpose Flour*** gradually to form a stiff dough.

Knead . . . . on floured surface until smooth and satiny, about 5 minutes. Place in greased bowl and cover.

Let rise . . . . in warm place (85°) until doubled, about 1½ hours.

Combine . . . . . 1 cup **nuts,** chopped
1 cup **sugar** and
2 teaspoons **cinnamon**

Divide . . . . dough in half. Roll out one portion to a 15x10-inch rectangle. Brush with melted **butter.** Sprinkle with half of cinnamon-sugar mixture. Roll as for jelly roll, starting with 15-inch side.

Place . . . . on greased baking sheet. Fold half the roll on top of other half, sealing ends together. Starting at folded end, cut with scissors down center of roll to within 1 inch of other end. Turn cut halves flat on side, cut-side up, to form a heart. Repeat with remaining dough. (See following suggestions for other shaping variations.)

Let rise . . . . in warm place until light, about 45 minutes.

Bake . . . . at 350° for 25 to 30 minutes.

For use with Pillsbury's Best Self-Rising Flour, omit salt.

Sweetheart Coffee Cake

Fruit Braid: Combine ½ cup sugar and 1 teaspoon cinnamon. Coat ½ cup finely chopped candied fruit with 2 tablespoons cinnamon-sugar. Divide one portion of dough into three equal parts. Roll each part to a 12-inch strip. Sprinkle strips with half the candied fruit mixture. Braid the three strips together, seal ends and place in a 9x5x3-inch pan, well greased and coated with 1 tablespoon cinnamon-sugar. Brush with melted butter and sprinkle with 2 tablespoons cinnamon-sugar. Repeat with remaining dough. Let rise in warm place until light, about 1¼ hours. Bake 25 to 30 minutes.

Cherry Ring: Combine ⅔ cup sugar and 1 teaspoon cinnamon. Drain No. 303 can sour pie cherries. Roll out one portion of dough to a 15x10-inch rectangle. Brush with melted butter; sprinkle with half the cinnamon-sugar. Place half the well-drained cherries on dough. Roll as for jelly roll, starting with 15-inch side. Shape into ring in well-greased 9-inch round layer pan. Cut deep gashes 1 inch apart with scissors; turn each piece on side. Repeat with remaining dough. Let rise in warm place until light, about 1¼ hours. Bake 30 to 35 minutes. If desired, frost with **Vanilla Glaze,** page 326.

Sunflower Coffee Cake

Senior Winner by Mrs. Carl Lehnkering, Shullsburg, Wisconsin

Sunny and cheerful, this coffee cake is fun to make and easy to shape.

BAKE at 375° for 15 to 20 minutes   MAKES 2 coffee cakes

Soften . . . . 2 packets active dry **yeast** (or 2 cakes compressed) in
             ¼ cup warm **water**
Combine . . . . ½ cup lukewarm scalded **milk**
             ½ cup **water**
             ⅓ cup **shortening,** melted
             ½ cup **sugar**
             2 unbeaten **eggs**
             2 teaspoons **salt***
             ½ teaspoon **lemon extract** and softened yeast.

Add . . . . 5 to 5½ cups sifted **Pillsbury's Best All Purpose Flour***
             gradually to form a stiff dough.
Knead . . . . on floured surface until smooth and satiny, 3 to 5
             minutes. Place in greased bowl and cover.
Let rise . . . . in warm place (85°) until doubled, 1 to 1½ hours.
Roll out . . . . . . half of dough to about ½-inch thickness. Cut out 16
             "doughnuts."
Arrange . . . . . . doughnut "holes" in center of ungreased baking
             sheet; stretch "doughnuts" slightly; place around
             "holes," petal fashion. Make second coffee cake.
Let rise . . . . until light, about 1 hour. In center of each petal place
             ½ to 1 teaspoon **jam, jelly** or prepared **mincemeat.**
Bake . . . . at 375° for 15 to 20 minutes. Cool. Outline petals
             and frost centers of coffee cakes with **Vanilla Glaze,**
             page 326. Sprinkle each center with
             1 tablespoon finely chopped **nuts** and
             1 tablespoon **chocolate cake decorations,** if desired.

*Pillsbury's Best Self-Rising Flour is not recommended for use in this recipe.

Sunflower Coffee Cake

Almond Halo Coffee Cake

Senior Winner by Mrs. Sylvia Kosmatka, Milwaukee, Wisconsin

Makes 3 small, delicious, butter-rich golden-brown coffee cake rings. They're filled with a scrumptious almond-meringue mixture.

BAKE at 350° for 25 to 30 minutes   MAKES 3 coffee cakes

Soften.......1 packet active dry **yeast** (or 1 cake compressed) in
¼ cup warm **water**

Blend.......¾ cup soft **butter** or margarine with
¼ cup **sugar**
1 teaspoon **salt*** and
1 teaspoon **vanilla** in large mixing bowl.

Add........2 unbeaten **egg yolks** (reserve whites for Filling)
½ cup undiluted **evaporated milk** and softened yeast. Mix thoroughly.

Add........3 to 3¼ cups sifted **Pillsbury's Best All Purpose Flour***
gradually to form a stiff dough. Cover.

Let rise........in warm place (85°) 1 hour.

Chill..........about 1 hour. Prepare Almond Meringue Filling.

Divide........in 3 parts. Roll out one part on floured surface to 15x7-inch strip. Spread with one-third Filling, leaving ½ inch uncovered along one long edge; moisten edge.

Roll..........as for jelly roll; seal. Form into a circle on greased baking sheet; pinch ends together. Repeat with remaining dough and Filling.

Bake.........at 350° for 25 to 30 minutes.

Brush.........hot coffee cake with soft **butter** and sprinkle with **confectioners' sugar.**

For use with Pillsbury's Best Self-Rising Flour, omit salt.

ALMOND MERINGUE FILLING

Beat 2 egg whites with ⅛ teaspoon salt until soft mounds form. Gradually add ¾ cup sugar, beating until meringue stands in stiff, glossy peaks. Fold in ½ teaspoon almond extract and 1 cup unblanched almonds, ground or finely chopped.

Snow Ring

Senior Winner by Mrs. Harold W. Bockstahler, East Lansing, Michigan

Almonds, citron and currants are between the braids of this coffee cake.

BAKE at 350° for 25 to 30 minutes   MAKES 1 coffee cake

Soften.......1 packet active dry **yeast** (or 1 cake compressed) in
2 tablespoons warm **water**

Add........1 cup lukewarm scalded **milk**
2 teaspoons **sugar** and
1½ cups sifted **Pillsbury's Best All Purpose Flour.***
Beat until smooth.

Let rise........in warm place (85°) until light and bubbly, about 30 minutes.

Cream......½ cup **butter** or margarine with
1 cup sifted **confectioners' sugar.** Beat in
1 unbeaten **egg**
1 unbeaten **egg yolk** (reserve white) and
1½ teaspoons **salt.** Add to yeast-flour mixture.

Blend in....2½ cups sifted **Pillsbury's Best All Purpose Flour.** Beat 2 minutes.

Let rise........in warm place until doubled, about 1 hour. Punch down; let rise 30 minutes.

Divide........dough into 3 parts. Shape each into an 18-inch strip. Lay strips on floured surface; flatten slightly.

Place.......¼ cup blanched **almonds** down center of one strip.
¼ cup diced **citron** down center of next strip and
¼ cup **currants** down center of last strip. Seal edges.

Braid.........the three strips of dough; shape into ring on greased baking sheet. Insert
¼ cup **almonds** in dough between strips.

Let rise........in warm place until light, about 30 minutes.

Combine.....1 **egg white** and
1 tablespoon **water;** brush over dough.

Bake.........at 350° for 25 to 30 minutes. While warm, sprinkle with **confectioners' sugar.**

Pillsbury's Best Self-Rising Flour is not recommended for use in this recipe.

Blueberry Coffee Cake

Senior Winner by Mrs. Ruth E. Krick, Blue Island, Illinois

Blueberries in a coffee cake! One recipe makes two coffee cake rings.

BAKE at 375° for 25 to 30 minutes   MAKES 2 coffee cakes

Soften.......2 packets active dry **yeast** (or 2 cakes compressed) in ½ cup warm **water**

Combine....¼ cup **butter** or margarine
¼ cup **sugar**
1½ teaspoons **salt*** and
⅔ cup hot scalded **milk** in large mixing bowl. Cool to lukewarm.

Stir in.......1 unbeaten **egg** and softened yeast.

Add........4 to 4½ cups sifted **Pillsbury's Best All Purpose Flour*** gradually to form a stiff dough. Cover.

Let rise........in warm place (85°) until doubled, 1 to 1¼ hours. Prepare Blueberry Filling.

Divide........dough in half. Roll out one portion on floured surface to 18x9-inch rectangle. Brush with melted **butter.** Spread half of Filling over dough, spreading to edge of one long side, to within 2 inches of other long side and to within 1 inch of ends.

Roll..........as for jelly roll, starting with covered 18-inch edge. Seal ends. Form into circle (ends not joined) on greased baking sheet with edge of dough up; pinch to seal. Cut slits in top. Cover. Repeat with remaining dough and Filling.

Let rise........in warm place until light, about 45 minutes.

Brush........with **milk**; sprinkle with mixture of ¼ cup **sugar** and
1 tablespoon grated **lemon rind**

Bake........at 375° for 25 to 30 minutes.

*For use with Pillsbury's Best Self-Rising Flour, omit salt.

BLUEBERRY FILLING

Combine ½ cup sugar and 3 tablespoons cornstarch in saucepan.
Add 1 pint fresh blueberries or 1 package (10 to 12 oz.) frozen blueberries. (One 15-oz. can blueberries may be substituted; drain off ¼ cup liquid.) Add 2 tablespoons lemon juice; cook and stir until very thick. Stir in 1 tablespoon butter. Cool.

Topsy-Turvy Coffee Ring

Senior Winner by Mrs. Ray Arthur, Oak Ridge, Tennessee

Cinnamon rolls are arranged in a tube pan to make one big coffee cake.

BAKE at 350° for 35 to 45 minutes   MAKES 9-inch coffee ring

Soften.......1 packet active dry **yeast** (or 1 cake compressed) in ¼ cup warm **water**

Combine.....3 tablespoons **shortening,** melted
½ cup warm **buttermilk** or sour milk
⅛ cup **sugar** and
1½ teaspoons **salt*** in large mixing bowl. Cool to lukewarm.

Blend in.....2 well-beaten **eggs** and softened yeast.

Add........3 to 3¼ cups sifted **Pillsbury's Best All Purpose Flour*** gradually, beating well after each addition. Cover.

Let rise........in warm place (85°) until doubled, 1½ to 2 hours.

Roll out.......on floured surface to 20x12-inch rectangle. Spread with
¼ cup soft **butter** or margarine

Combine....⅓ cup firmly packed **brown sugar**
1 teaspoon **cinnamon**
¾ cup **raisins** and
⅛ cup **nuts,** chopped; sprinkle over dough.

Roll..........as for jelly roll. Cut into 2-inch slices. Arrange slices, cut-side down, in well-greased 9-inch tube pan.

Let rise........in warm place until light, 30 to 45 minutes.

Bake........at 350° for 35 to 45 minutes. While warm, frost with **Vanilla Glaze,** page 326.

*For use with Pillsbury's Best Self-Rising Flour, omit salt.

Two-Way Coffee Bread

Senior Winner by Mrs. Henry Roeschlein, Chicago, Illinois

One batch of dough makes both caramel-pecan coffee cake and rolls.

BAKE at 375° for 18 to 23 minutes   MAKES 9-inch coffee ring
and 1 dozen rolls

Soften . . . . 2 packets active dry **yeast** (or 2 cakes compressed) in
            1 cup warm **water**
Cream . . . . . . ½ cup **butter** or margarine
Stir in . . . . 2 unbeaten **eggs**
            ¼ cup **sugar**
            1½ teaspoons **salt***
            ½ cup **raisins**
            1 tablespoon grated **lemon rind** and softened yeast.
Add . . . . 3¾ cups sifted **Pillsbury's Best All Purpose Flour***
            gradually; beat well after each addition. Cover.
Let rise . . . . in warm place (85°) until doubled, about 1 hour.
Combine . . . . ¼ cup **butter** or margarine, melted
            ¾ cup firmly packed **brown sugar**
            ¼ cup **sugar**
            ½ cup **pecan halves** or pecans, coarsely chopped
            ¼ cup **light corn syrup**
            1 teaspoon **cinnamon** and
            2 tablespoons **water**. Place half of sugar-nut mixture
            in well-greased 9-inch ring mold. Place remaining
            sugar-nut mixture in 12 well-greased muffin cups.
Spread . . . . half of dough in ring mold. Divide remaining dough
            into 12 muffin cups.
Let rise . . . . in warm place until light, about 45 minutes.
Bake . . . . at 375° for 18 to 23 minutes. Turn out at once.
**For use with Pillsbury's Best Self-Rising Flour, omit salt.*

Chocolate Cherry Round

Senior Winner by Mrs. Norma Kohls, Ripon, Wisconsin

Chocolate yeast dough wound into interesting circular coffee cakes glazed and decorated with nuts and maraschino cherries.

BAKE at 350° for 25 to 35 minutes   MAKES two 8-inch coffee cakes

Soften . . . . 2 packets active dry **yeast** (or 2 cakes compressed) in
            ½ cup warm **water**
Melt . . . . 2 squares (2 oz.) unsweetened **chocolate** with
            3 tablespoons **butter** or margarine in saucepan. Cool.
Combine . . . . ½ cup **sugar**
            1 teaspoon **salt***
            1 unbeaten **egg**
            ¾ cup lukewarm scalded **buttermilk** or **milk** and
            ½ cup finely chopped **maraschino cherries** in large
            mixing bowl. Add chocolate mixture and softened
            yeast.
Add . . . . 4 to 4½ cups sifted **Pillsbury's Best All Purpose Flour***
            gradually to form a stiff dough, beating well after
            each addition. Cover.
Let rise . . . . in warm place (85°) until doubled, about 1½ hours.
Toss . . . . on well-floured surface until coated with flour and no
            longer sticky. Roll half of dough into 36-inch strip.
            Wind into flat coil in well-greased 8-inch round
            layer pan. Brush with melted **butter** and sprinkle with
            sugar. Repeat with remaining dough.
Let rise . . . . until light, about 1 hour.
Bake . . . . at 350° for 25 to 35 minutes. While warm, drizzle
            with **Vanilla Glaze**, page 326. Garnish with chopped
            nuts and **maraschino cherry pieces**.
**For use with Pillsbury's Best Self-Rising Flour, omit salt.*

Rich Butter Coffee Ring

Senior Winner by Mrs. Frank J. Lakota, Philadelphia, Pennsylvania

For variety add a hint of almond flavoring to the icing.

BAKE at 375° for 25 to 30 minutes   MAKES two 8-inch coffee rings

Soften.......1 packet active dry **yeast** (or 1 cake compressed) in
¼ cup warm **water**

Sift together..3 cups sifted **Pillsbury's Best All Purpose Flour***
2 tablespoons **sugar** and
1 teaspoon **salt** into large mixing bowl.

Cut in.......2 tablespoons **butter** or margarine and
2 tablespoons **shortening.** Make a well in center.

Add........2 beaten **eggs**
⅔ cup **sour cream** (thick or commercial) and softened
yeast. Blend well.

Tie..........dough in tea towel, allowing ample space for dough
to rise. Place in large bowl filled with water (about
80°). Let stand until dough rises to top of water,
1 to 1½ hours. Remove from water.**

Toss.........dough on well-floured surface until coated with
flour and no longer sticky. Cut into four pieces. Roll
each piece to about 14-inch strip.

Twist.........two strips together and seal ends to form a ring.
Repeat with remaining two strips. Place the rings
on large greased baking sheet or in two greased 8-
inch round layer pans. Brush with melted **butter.**

Let rise........in warm place (85°) until light, 30 to 45 minutes.

Bake.........at 375° for 25 to 30 minutes. While warm, frost with
Vanilla Glaze, page 326.

Pillsbury's Best Self-Rising Flour is not recommended for use in this recipe.
**Or place dough in covered bowl; let rise in warm place until doubled, about
1½ hours.*

Almond Marmalettes

Senior Winner by Mrs. Otto Aerne, Norfolk, Virginia

*Enticing, quick No-Knead coffee cake . . . with its rich marmalade
and almond topping sprinkled with cherries.*

BAKE at 350° for 30 to 35 minutes   MAKES one 15x10-inch
or two 9x9-inch coffee cakes

Soften.......1 packet active dry **yeast** (or 1 cake compressed) in
¼ cup warm **water**

Combine....⅓ cup **shortening,** melted
⅓ cup lukewarm scalded **milk**
2 tablespoons **sugar**
1 teaspoon **salt***
3 unbeaten **egg yolks** and softened yeast in large
mixing bowl.

Add........2 cups sifted **Pillsbury's Best All Purpose Flour***
gradually to form a dough; mix well after each
addition. Cover.

Let rise........in warm place (85°) until doubled, 45 to 60 minutes.

Spread.......dough in well-greased 15½x10½x1-inch jelly-roll pan
or two 9x9x2-inch pans. Cover.

Let rise........in warm place until light, 20 to 30 minutes.

Spread......1 cup (12-oz. jar) **orange marmalade** over dough.
Top with Almond Cream. Garnish with
10 **maraschino cherries,** cut in quarters

Bake.........at 350° for 30 to 35 minutes.

For use with Pillsbury's Best Self-Rising Flour, omit salt.

ALMOND CREAM

Cream ¼ cup butter or margarine and 1 cup sifted confectioners'
sugar. Add 1 cup almonds (chopped or ground), ¼ cup cream, ½ teaspoon vanilla and ¼ teaspoon almond extract. Blend thoroughly.

Kwik Peach Kuchen

Senior Winner by Mrs. Rae Judson, Chelsea, Michigan

A peach of a coffee cake . . . yeast-light with no rising period!

BAKE at 350° for 40 to 45 minutes   MAKES 13x9 or 12x8-inch coffee cake

Soften . . . . . . ½ packet active dry **yeast** (or ½ cake compressed) and
1 teaspoon **sugar** in
2 tablespoons warm **water**

Sift together . . 2 cups sifted **Pillsbury's Best All Purpose Flour***
3 teaspoons double-acting **baking powder** and
½ teaspoon **salt**

Cream . . . . . . ½ cup **butter** or margarine. Gradually add
½ cup **sugar,** creaming well.

Blend in . . . . . 2 unbeaten **eggs**
¼ teaspoon **lemon extract** and yeast mixture. Add
half the dry ingredients; beat until smooth.

Add . . . . ¼ cup **milk** and remaining dry ingredients. Beat well.

Kwik Peach Kuchen

(With mixer beat at low speed; beat 2 minutes.)

Spread . . . . half of batter in greased 13x9x2 or 12x8x2-inch pan.

Arrange . . . . 2½ cups (1 No. 2½ can) **peach slices,** well drained, on
top. Drop remaining dough by teaspoonfuls onto
peach slices. Sprinkle with Maple-Pecan Topping.

Bake . . . . at 350° for 40 to 45 minutes.

*For use with Pillsbury's Best Self-Rising Flour, omit baking powder and salt.

MAPLE-PECAN TOPPING

Combine ½ cup firmly packed brown sugar, ¼ cup Pillsbury's Best All Purpose Flour, ½ teaspoon cinnamon and ½ teaspoon maple flavoring. Cut in 3 tablespoons butter or margarine to make a crumb mixture. Add ¼ cup chopped pecans.

Fruit Tuck-In Coffee Cake

Senior Winner by Mrs. Joseph Lupfer, Denver, Colorado

You don't knead or shape. Just spread the dough in a pan.

BAKE at 375° for 25 to 30 minutes, then   MAKES 9x9-inch coffee cake
for 5 minutes

Soften . . . . 1 packet active dry **yeast** (or 1 cake compressed) in
½ cup warm **water** in large mixing bowl.

Blend in . . . . . 1 well-beaten **egg**
2 tablespoons **sugar**
¼ cup **shortening,** melted, or salad oil
1 teaspoon **salt*** and
½ teaspoon **mace** or nutmeg

Add . . . . 1½ cups sifted **Pillsbury's Best All Purpose Flour***
gradually; beat well after each addition.

Let rise . . . . in warm place (85°) until doubled, 1 to 1½ hours.

Stir down . . . . . . dough. Spread in well-greased 9x9x2-inch pan.

Arrange . . . . 16 cooked dried **apricot halves,** well drained (or 16
fresh plums, pitted), over batter.

Let rise . . . . in warm place until light, 45 to 60 minutes.

Combine . . . . ¼ cup **sugar** and
½ teaspoon **cinnamon**; sprinkle over batter.
Bake . . . . at 375° for 25 to 30 minutes. Sprinkle with
2 tablespoons **cream**. Bake 5 minutes. Serve warm.

For use with Pillsbury's Best Self-Rising Flour, omit salt.

Swedish Ripple Coffee Cake

Senior Third Prize Winner by Mrs. Kenneth Kennedy, Mahtomedi, Minnesota

Sour cream topping with caramel flavor ripples through this coffee cake.

BAKE at 350° for 30 to 35 minutes   MAKES 13x9-inch coffee cake

Combine . . . . . 2 tablespoons **shortening**
¼ cup **sugar**
½ teaspoon **salt** and
½ cup hot scalded **milk*** in large mixing bowl. Cool to
lukewarm.

Stir in . . . . 1 beaten **egg** and
½ cake compressed **yeast**, crumbled (or 1½ teaspoons
active dry yeast softened in ¼ cup warm water).*
Let stand 5 minutes. Mix well.

Add . . . . 2 to 2¼ cups sifted **Pillsbury's Best All Purpose Flour****
gradually to form a stiff dough; beat well after each
addition.

Spread . . . . in greased 13x9x2-inch pan. Brush with
1 tablespoon **butter**, melted. Cover.

Let rise . . . . in warm place (85°) until light, 1 to 1½ hours. Pour
Caramel-Sour Cream Topping over dough.

Bake . . . . at 350° for 30 to 35 minutes. Serve warm.

*If dry yeast is used, decrease milk to ¼ cup.
**Pillsbury's Best Self-Rising Flour is not recommended for use in this recipe.

CARAMEL-SOUR CREAM TOPPING

Combine 1 cup firmly packed brown sugar, ½ cup sour cream (thick
or commercial), 2 teaspoons cornstarch and ½ teaspoon vanilla.

Swedish Ripple Coffee Cake

Carioca Coffee Cake

Bride Winner by Mrs. Ann Guesman, Pittsburgh, Pennsylvania

For breakfast or brunch, a no-knead yeast coffee cake . . . unique cocoa-nut filling and rum-flavored glaze for novelty and goodness.

BAKE at 375° for 30 to 35 minutes   MAKES 9x9 or 11x7-inch coffee cake

Combine . . . . ⅓ cup firmly packed **brown sugar**
                ½ cup **nuts**, chopped
                1 tablespoon **flour**
                1 tablespoon **cocoa**
                2 tablespoons soft **butter** or margarine and
                1 teaspoon **rum flavoring**. Set aside.
Soften . . . . 1 packet active dry **yeast** (or 1 cake compressed) in
                ¼ cup warm **water**
Combine . . . . ¼ cup **butter** or margarine and
                ½ cup hot scalded **milk** in large mixing bowl; stir to
                melt butter. Cool to lukewarm.
Add . . . . 1 unbeaten **egg**
                1 cup sifted **Pillsbury's Best All Purpose Flour***
                ¼ cup **sugar**
                1 teaspoon **salt** and softened yeast. Mix well until
                smooth.
Stir in . . . . . 1¼ cups sifted **Pillsbury's Best All Purpose Flour**; blend
                thoroughly.
Spread . . . . half of dough in greased 9x9x2 or 11x7x2-inch pan.
                Sprinkle with cocoa-nut mixture. Drop remaining
                dough by teaspoonfuls on top.
Let rise . . . . in warm place (85°) until light, about 1 hour.
Bake . . . . at 375° for 30 to 35 minutes. While warm, drizzle
                with Rum Glaze.
For use with Pillsbury's Best Self-Rising Flour, omit salt.

RUM GLAZE

Brown 2 tablespoons butter in saucepan. Add ½ cup sifted confectioners' sugar, 1 tablespoon cream and 1 teaspoon rum flavoring; beat until smooth.

VARIETY YEAST BREADS include those unusual

breads that do not fall into any particular category. Here you will find suggestions for snacks, between-meal treats for those hungry teen-agers, and the ever-popular doughnut.

Shrimp Cocktail Rolls

Senior Winner by Mrs. Dorothy M. Proctor, Seymour, Indiana

Tucked inside each "sea-shell" roll is a shrimp with its own zesty sauce. Parmesan cheese and corn meal are sprinkled over before baking.

BAKE at 375° for 15 to 20 minutes   MAKES about 3 dozen

Combine . . . . . 1 cup lukewarm **buttermilk**, sour milk or sweet milk*
                1 tablespoon prepared **horse-radish**
                1 teaspoon **salt****
                1 teaspoon **sugar**
                ¼ teaspoon **soda** (omit with sweet milk) and
                3 tablespoons **shortening**, melted, in large mixing bowl.
Add . . . . 1 cake compressed **yeast**, crumbled (or 1 packet active
                dry yeast softened in ¼ cup warm water).* Let stand
                5 minutes; mix well.
Blend in . . . . 2½ cups sifted **Pillsbury's Best All Purpose Flour,****
                half at a time. Mix well after each addition. Cover;
                let stand 10 minutes. Prepare Shrimp Sauce.

Knead . . . . .dough on well-floured surface until smooth, about 2 minutes. Roll out to ¼-inch thickness. Cut with 2½-inch round cutter. Make a crease across each round slightly off center. Do not cut through dough. Place about ¼ teaspoon Sauce on each round.

Open . . . . . . .1 can (5 oz.) small **shrimp.** Place one shrimp on the larger side of each round. Fold over small side so back of shrimp shows. Press edges together well to seal. Twist each end once or twice. Place on greased baking sheets. Curve ends slightly to resemble a shell; press ends with floured fork.

Let rise . . . . .in warm place (85°) until light, 30 to 45 minutes. Brush with melted **butter** or margarine.

Combine . . . . .2 tablespoons grated **Parmesan cheese** and 1 tablespoon **corn meal.** Sprinkle over rolls.

Bake . . . . .at 375° for 15 to 20 minutes. Serve warm.

*If dry yeast is used, decrease buttermilk to ¾ cup.
**For use with Pillsbury's Best Self-Rising Flour, omit salt.

SHRIMP SAUCE

Combine 3 tablespoons catsup, 2 teaspoons prepared horse-radish and ¼ teaspoon Worcestershire sauce. Mix well.

Doughboys

Senior Winner by Ellen M. Ryynanen, Hancock, Michigan

These anise-flavored raised doughnuts look like "bear claws." They're easily shaped—with no re-rolling of dough.

FRY at 375° for 2 to 3 minutes   MAKES 2½ dozen

Soften . . . . . . .1 packet active dry **yeast** (or 1 cake compressed) in ⅛ cup warm **water**

Heat . . . . .2 cups **milk** and ⅛ cup **shortening** in saucepan until milk is scalded.

Combine . . . . .½ cup **sugar**

2 teaspoons **salt**
½ to 1 teaspoon **anise seed** and hot milk mixture in large mixing bowl. Cool to lukewarm.

Blend in . . . . .1 slightly beaten **egg** and softened yeast.

Add . . . . .6 to 6½ cups sifted **Pillsbury's Best All Purpose Flour*** gradually to form a stiff dough. Cover.

Let rise . . . . .in warm place (85°) until doubled, about 1 hour.

Divide . . . . .dough in half. Roll out each half on floured surface to a 12x10-inch rectangle. Cut into 4x2-inch strips. Cut each strip on a 4-inch side at two intervals about half way across. Place on ungreased baking sheet.

Let rise . . . . .in warm place until light, about 1 hour.

Fry . . . . .in hot deep fat (375°) until golden brown, 1 to 2 minutes on each side. Drain on absorbent paper. Roll in **sugar,** if desired.

*Pillsbury's Best Self-Rising Flour is not recommended for use in this recipe.

Doughboys

Coffee-Time Doughnuts

Senior Winner by Miss Loretto Yaeger, St. Louis, Missouri

This is an old family favorite and combines tenderness with tempting flavor. And no kneading is necessary!

FRY at 375° about 4 minutes　　　　　MAKES about 3 dozen

Soften . . . . 1 packet active dry **yeast** (or 1 cake compressed) in
　　　　　　　¼ cup warm **water**
Combine . . . . ½ cup **boiling water**
　　　　　　　2 tablespoons **shortening**
　　　　　　　¼ cup **sugar** and
　　　　　　　1½ teaspoons **salt.*** Cool to lukewarm by adding
　　　　　　　½ cup **milk**
Blend in . . . . . 1 unbeaten **egg**
　　　　　　　1 teaspoon **nutmeg** and softened yeast. Mix well.
Add . . . . 3¾ to 4 cups sifted **Pillsbury's Best All Purpose Flour***
　　　　　　　Mix to soft dough. Cover; chill 3 hours or overnight.
Roll out . . . . on floured surface to ¼-inch thickness.
Cut . . . . into 3x1-inch strips or cut with doughnut cutter.
Let rise . . . . in warm place (85°) until doubled, about 40 minutes.
Fry . . . . in hot deep fat (375°) about 2 minutes on each side.
　　　　　　　Drain on absorbent paper; sprinkle with **sugar.**
For use with Pillsbury's Best Self-Rising Flour, omit salt.

Cheese Snack Bread

Best of Class Winner by Mrs. Fredericka A. Vici, Ripley, Ohio

Cheese, a trace of onion and caraway or poppy seeds are baked right on top of this unusual bread! Equally good morning, noon or night.

BAKE at 425° for 15 to 20 minutes　　　MAKES one 15x10-inch or
　　　　　　　　　　　　　　　　two 9x9-inch coffee breads

Soften . . . . 1 packet active dry **yeast** (or 1 cake compressed) in
　　　　　　　¼ cup warm **water**

Combine . . . . . 1 tablespoon **sugar**
　　　　　　　2 tablespoons **shortening**
　　　　　　　1 teaspoon **salt*** and
　　　　　　　¾ cup hot scalded **milk** in large mixing bowl. Cool to
　　　　　　　lukewarm. Add softened yeast.
Add . . . . 2¼ to 2½ cups sifted **Pillsbury's Best All Purpose Flour;***
　　　　　　　mix well.
Knead . . . . on floured surface until smooth and satiny, about 3
　　　　　　　minutes. Place in greased bowl and cover.
Let rise . . . . in warm place (85°) until doubled, 1 to 1½ hours.
Press . . . . dough into greased 15½x10½x1-inch pan (or two
　　　　　　　9x9x2-inch pans).
Let rise . . . . in warm place until light, about 45 minutes.
Combine . . . . . 1 unbeaten **egg**
　　　　　　　⅓ cup **milk**
　　　　　　　1 teaspoon grated **onion**
　　　　　　　¼ teaspoon **salt** and
　　　　　　　½ pound (2 cups) shredded **American cheese** in small
　　　　　　　bowl. Spread over dough. Sprinkle with **caraway
　　　　　　　seeds** or poppy seeds, if desired.
Bake . . . . at 425° for 15 to 20 minutes. Serve warm.
For use with Pillsbury's Best Self-Rising Flour, omit salt.

Hey Gang Snack Buns

Senior Winner by Mrs. Edward E. Ronning, Columbus, North Dakota

These light, tender yeast buns are split, spread with a snappy mixture of grated cheese, tomato soup, onion and green pepper, then broiled.

BAKE at 400° for 12 to 15 minutes　　　　MAKES 16 buns

Soften . . . . 1 packet active dry **yeast** (or 1 cake compressed) in
　　　　　　　¼ cup warm **water**

Combine.....2 tablespoons **sugar**
              2 tablespoons **shortening**
              1 teaspoon **salt*** and
              1 cup hot scalded **milk** in large mixing bowl. Cool to
              lukewarm.
Add........1 unbeaten **egg** and softened yeast. Mix well.
Add.......3½ cups sifted **Pillsbury's Best All Purpose Flour***
              gradually; beat well after each addition. Cover.
Let rise........in warm place (85°) until doubled, about 2 hours.
Shape........into 16 buns. Place on greased baking sheet.
Let rise........in warm place until light, about 1 hour.
Bake.........at 400° for 12 to 15 minutes. Cool. Split buns and
              spread bottom halves with Cheese Filling. Place
              under broiler 3 to 5 minutes. Top with remaining
              halves.

For use with Pillsbury's Best Self-Rising Flour, omit salt.

CHEESE FILLING

Combine ½ pound (2 cups) shredded cheese, 3 tablespoons finely chopped onion, ¼ cup finely chopped green pepper, ½ cup (½ can) undiluted condensed tomato soup, ½ teaspoon salt and ⅛ teaspoon pepper. Mix well.

Hamwiches

Best of Class Winner by Mrs. Lillian Leonard, Guthrie Center, Iowa

You'll like these ham sandwiches at meals and for snacks. Roll up ham slices in wedges of yeast dough—then bake.

BAKE at 400° for 15 to 20 minutes   MAKES 1 dozen

Soften.......1 packet active dry **yeast** (or 1 cake compressed) in
              ¼ cup warm **water**
Combine.....1 beaten **egg**
              ½ cup lukewarm **tomato juice**
              1 tablespoon **brown sugar**

Hamwiches

              3 tablespoons **shortening,** melted
              1½ teaspoons **celery salt***
              1 tablespoon grated **onion** and softened yeast in large
              mixing bowl.
Add.......2½ cups sifted **Pillsbury's Best All Purpose Flour***
              gradually, beating well after each addition. Cover.
Let rise........in warm place (85°) until doubled, about 1 hour.
Divide........dough in half. Roll out each half on floured surface
              to 9-inch circle. Cut each circle into 6 wedges.
Place.......12 small slices **boiled ham** on wedges. Roll up each
              wedge, starting at wide end and rolling to point.
              Place on greased baking sheet, point-side down.
Let rise........in warm place until light, about 1 hour.
Bake.........at 400° for 15 to 20 minutes. Serve warm.

For use with Pillsbury's Best Self-Rising Flour, omit celery salt.

QUICK BREADS

Quick breads are so named because they may be mixed and baked quickly, without the rising periods necessary when making most yeast breads. Although quick breads are especially popular in the South, hot, flaky biscuits or moist, tender muffins are welcome additions to a meal anywhere!

Quick breads include loaves, biscuits and muffins, cake dough- *nuts, coffee cakes, pancakes and waffles, corn breads, popovers and dumplings.*

Nearly all quick breads are a combination of flour, liquid, shortening, salt and a leavening agent. Eggs and sugar are added to some quick breads, too. Because each type of quick bread is different, special hints are included with each section.

QUICK LOAVES

When including fruit or nuts in quick breads, chop them fine (unless otherwise directed in recipe) and coat with flour to prevent their sinking in the batter. For good banana bread, use only the ripest bananas with skins showing brown.

Although quick loaves and coffee cakes are often mixed by the muffin method (see Muffins, page 103), they require more mixing than muffins. The batter should appear almost smooth.

For a well-rounded loaf, spread batter to corners of pan (photo A) and let stand 20 minutes before baking.

Shiny metal pans are best for baking quick loaves. If dull-finished metal pans or glass baking dishes are used, reduce oven temperature 25 degrees, as these utensils absorb heat more readily.

Cracks appear in the top crust of a quick loaf because the crust browns and sets before the center has baked. The center continues to bake and rise, pushing through the top crust.

Remove bread from the pan 5 to 10 minutes after baking; cool on wire rack so air may reach all sides.

Quick loaves baked in 9x5x3-inch pans should be cooled thoroughly before slicing, then cut in thin slices with a sharp-bladed or serrated knife, using a sawing motion.

To store: Wrap breads in aluminum foil or plastic film, or place in airtight plastic bags, and store in a cool place. Most quick breads keep well; some improve with age.

A "druggist's wrap" is most often used for packaging. Place product in center of foil. Bring longest sides together on top of product; fold edges over one inch. Fold as many times as necessary to bring foil tight and flat against top (photo B). Turn over and fold corners toward each other; fold ends over and stretch tight.

Many quick breads may be sliced and toasted just like yeast breads. This is especially practical if the bread has dried out slightly.

To freshen: Place bread in top of double boiler and heat over boiling water until warm. Or heat bread in dampened brown paper bag in moderate oven until bag has dried out. Breads may also be wrapped in aluminum foil and reheated in a 350° oven.

Cornbread and gingerbread should be served hot. Gingerbread, of course, may also be served as a dessert.

A

B

Peppy Apple-Cheese Bread

Junior Winner by Jean Brt, Norfolk, Nebraska

Shredded fresh apples, nuts and sharp cheese are blended into this hearty quick bread.

BAKE at 350° for 50 to 60 minutes   MAKES 9x5-inch loaf

Sift together . . 2 cups sifted **Pillsbury's Best All Purpose Flour***
                  1 teaspoon double-acting **baking powder**
                  ½ teaspoon **soda** and
                  ½ teaspoon **salt**
Cream . . . . . . ½ cup **butter** or margarine. Gradually add
                  ⅔ cup **sugar**, creaming well.
Add . . . . ½ cup shredded **Cheddar cheese.** Mix until smooth and creamy.
Blend in . . . . . 2 slightly beaten **eggs**; beat well.
Add . . . . 1½ cups shredded raw **apples**; mix well.
Blend in . . . . the dry ingredients, half at a time, mixing well after each addition.
Stir in . . . . . . ½ cup **nuts**, chopped
Turn . . . . into well-greased 9x5x3-inch pan.
Bake . . . . at 350° for 50 to 60 minutes. Cool before slicing.
*For use with Pillsbury's Best Self-Rising Flour, omit baking powder, soda, salt.

Cheese Nut Loaf

Senior Winner by Mrs. Maude Dietrich, Wichita, Kansas

Chopped pecans and American cheese are the happy blend in this easily-prepared quick bread.

BAKE at 350° for 55 to 60 minutes   MAKES 9x5-inch loaf

Sift together . . 2 cups sifted **Pillsbury's Best All Purpose Flour***
                  2 tablespoons **sugar**
                  3 teaspoons double-acting **baking powder** and
                  1 teaspoon **salt** in large mixing bowl.

Add . . . . 1⅓ cups shredded **American cheese** and
                  ¼ cup **pecans**, chopped; mix well.
Combine . . . . . 1 beaten **egg**
                  ⅞ cup **milk** (¾ cup plus 2 tablespoons) and
                  3 tablespoons **shortening**, melted. Add to the dry ingredients; mix until all dry particles are moistened.
Turn . . . . into well-greased 9x5x3-inch pan.
Bake . . . . at 350° for 55 to 60 minutes. Cool before slicing.
*For use with Pillsbury's Best Self-Rising Flour, omit baking powder and salt; decrease milk to ¾ cup.

Pennsylvania Applesauce Bread

Senior Winner by Mrs. Merrill B. Hearn, Ridley Park, Pennsylvania

Stir up this apple bread in a hurry. It is made with walnuts and spice and will remind you of old-fashioned applesauce cake.

BAKE at 350° for 55 to 60 minutes   MAKES 9x5-inch loaf

Sift together . . 2 cups sifted **Pillsbury's Best All Purpose Flour***
                  1 teaspoon double-acting **baking powder**
                  1 teaspoon **soda**
                  1 teaspoon **salt**
                  1 teaspoon **cinnamon** and
                  ½ teaspoon **nutmeg.** Set aside.
Add . . . . ¾ cup **sugar** gradually to
                  ½ cup **shortening**, creaming well.
Blend in . . . . . 2 unbeaten **eggs** and
                  1 teaspoon **vanilla**; beat well.
Add . . . . the sifted dry ingredients gradually; mix well after each addition.
Stir in . . . . 1 cup sweetened **applesauce** and
                  ½ cup **walnuts**, chopped
Turn . . . . into well-greased 9x5x3-inch pan.
Bake . . . . at 350° for 55 to 60 minutes. Cool before slicing.
*For use with Pillsbury's Best Self-Rising Flour, omit baking powder, soda, salt.

Nutty Apricot Snack Loaf

Junior Winner by Antoinette Herout, Elm Grove, Wisconsin

Apricots give just the right amount of tartness to this quick bread. Nuts give it an interesting texture and flavor.

BAKE at 375° for 45 to 55 minutes   MAKES 9x5-inch loaf

Cover . . . . . . .1 cup dried **apricots** with warm water; soak 15 minutes. Drain; cut into pieces.

Sift together . .2 cups sifted **Pillsbury's Best All Purpose Flour***
2 teaspoons double-acting **baking powder**
1 teaspoon **salt** and
¼ teaspoon **soda;** set aside.

Add . . . . .1 cup **sugar** gradually to
¼ cup **shortening,** creaming well.

Blend in . . . . .1 unbeaten **egg;** beat well.

Add . . . . .half the dry ingredients; mix thoroughly.

Blend in . . . . .¼ cup **water** and
½ cup **orange juice,** then remaining dry ingredients; mix until well blended.

Stir in . . . . . .½ cup **walnuts,** chopped, and the apricots.

Turn . . . . .into well-greased 9x5x3-inch pan. Let stand 20 minutes.

Bake . . . . .at 375° for 45 to 55 minutes. Cool before slicing.

*For use with Pillsbury's Best Self-Rising Flour, omit baking powder, salt, soda.

English Honey Loaf

Senior Winner by Mrs. Harry A. Winer, Kansas City, Missouri

A quick bread with a cake-like texture, delicately flavored with lemon, honey and spices. Good sliced thin and buttered.

BAKE at 350° for 55 to 65 minutes   MAKES 9x5-inch loaf

Sift together 2¼ cups sifted **Pillsbury's Best All Purpose Flour***
1 teaspoon double-acting **baking powder**
1 teaspoon **salt**
¾ teaspoon **soda**
½ teaspoon **cinnamon**
½ teaspoon **cloves**
½ teaspoon **allspice** and
¼ teaspoon **ginger.** Set aside.

Add . . . . .1 cup **sugar** gradually to
⅓ cup **shortening,** creaming well.

Blend in . . . . .2 unbeaten **eggs,** beating well.

Add . . . . .⅓ cup **honey** and
1½ teaspoons grated **lemon rind;** mix until blended.

Add . . . . .½ cup strong, cooled **coffee** alternately with the dry ingredients. Blend well after each addition.

Stir in . . . . . .½ cup **raisins** and
½ cup **nuts,** chopped

Turn . . . . .into well-greased 9x5x3-inch pan.

Bake . . . . .at 350° for 55 to 65 minutes.

*For use with Pillsbury's Best Self-Rising Flour, omit baking powder, salt, soda.

Orange Prune Coffee Cake

Senior Winner by Mrs. William Greenbacker, Cromwell, Connecticut

A colorful quick coffee cake blends the flavors of orange and prune batters marbled together. Best sliced cold.

BAKE at 350° for 55 to 60 minutes*   MAKES 9x5-inch loaf

Sift together 2½ cups sifted **Pillsbury's Best All Purpose Flour***
¾ cup **sugar**
3 teaspoons double-acting **baking powder** and
1½ teaspoons **salt**

Combine . . . . .1 well-beaten **egg**

2 to 3 tablespoons grated **orange rind**
juice of 1 **orange** and **water** to measure ¾ cup
⅓ cup **milk** and
¼ cup **shortening,** melted, in large mixing bowl. Blend
in the dry ingredients.

Place . . . . half of batter in a second bowl. Blend in
1 cup finely cut, cooked **prunes,** (about 1½ cups
whole), well drained
1 tablespoon **molasses**
2 tablespoons **flour**
¼ teaspoon **soda** and
¼ teaspoon **cinnamon;** mix thoroughly.

Spoon . . . . light and dark batters alternately into 9x5x3-inch
pan, well greased and lightly floured on the bottom.

Combine . . . . ¼ cup firmly packed **brown sugar**
1 tablespoon **flour** and
2 tablespoons **butter,** melted. Spread over batter. Let
stand 20 minutes.

Bake . . . . at 350° for 55 to 60 minutes. Cool before slicing.

*For use with Pillsbury's Best Self-Rising Flour, omit baking powder and salt;
increase baking time to 65 to 70 minutes.*

Holiday Treat

Senior Winner by Mrs. Milton Wruble, Kalamazoo, Michigan

*Sweet raisins and tangy apricots give delightful flavor and color to
this quick-to-mix nut bread.*

BAKE at 350° for 50 to 60 minutes   MAKES four small loaves
or two 9x5-inch loaves

Combine . . . 1½ cups (12-oz. can) **apricot nectar**
1½ cups **raisins** and
⅓ cup cut dried **apricots** (about 12) in saucepan;
simmer 5 minutes.

Add . . . . 1 tablespoon grated **orange rind.** Cool.

Holiday Treat

Sift together 2¾ cups sifted **Pillsbury's Best All Purpose Flour***
2 teaspoons **soda** and
1 teaspoon **salt.** Add
½ cup **walnuts,** chopped

Blend . . . . 1 tablespoon **shortening** with
1 cup **sugar.** Add
1 unbeaten **egg** and
⅓ cup **cream;** beat well.

Add . . . . the dry ingredients alternately with fruit mixture to
creamed mixture. Blend well after each addition.

Turn . . . . into four greased No. 2 cans or two well-greased
9x5x3-inch pans.

Bake . . . . at 350° for 50 to 60 minutes. Cool before slicing.

*For use with Pillsbury's Best Self-Rising Flour, decrease soda to ½ teaspoon
and omit salt.*

Peachy Nut Bread

Junior Winner by Lucille Bonvouloir, Shoreham, Vermont

A moist fruit loaf . . . peaches, maraschino cherries, orange rind and nuts make a refreshing flavor combination. It stores well.

BAKE at 350° for 50 to 60 minutes   MAKES 9x5-inch loaf

Sift together . . 2 cups sifted **Pillsbury's Best All Purpose Flour***
          1 teaspoon double-acting **baking powder**
          ½ teaspoon **soda** and
          ½ teaspoon **salt.** Set aside.
Add . . . . .⅔ cup **sugar** gradually to
          ⅓ cup **shortening,** creaming well.
Blend in . . . . . 2 unbeaten **eggs;** beat well.
Stir in . . . . . . ¼ cup **buttermilk** or sour milk and
          1 cup mashed, drained canned **peaches**
Add . . . . .the dry ingredients, mixing until all dry particles are
          moistened.
Fold in . . . . . .1 tablespoon grated **orange rind**
          ¼ cup cut **maraschino cherries** and
          ½ cup **nuts,** chopped. Do not beat.
Turn . . . . .batter into greased 9x5x3-inch pan.
Bake . . . . .at 350° for 50 to 60 minutes.
**For use with Pillsbury's Best Self-Rising Flour, omit baking powder, soda, salt.*

Four Seasons Fruit Loaf

Senior Winner by Mrs. Philip Neef, Homedale, Idaho

Cottage cheese, dried prunes and apricots make this nutritious quick bread moist and colorful.

BAKE at 350° for 60 to 65 minutes   MAKES 9x5-inch loaf

Sift together . .2 cups sifted **Pillsbury's Best All Purpose Flour***
          1½ teaspoons double-acting **baking powder**
          ½ teaspoon **soda** and
          ½ teaspoon **salt**
Add . . . . .⅔ cup firmly packed **brown sugar** gradually to
          ½ cup **shortening,** creaming well.
Blend in . . . . .2 unbeaten **eggs,** beating well after each.
Add . . . . .the dry ingredients alternately with
          ½ cup **milk.** Blend well after each addition.
Stir in . . . . . .½ cup creamed small curd **cottage cheese**
          ½ cup uncooked dried **prunes,** cut fine, and
          ½ cup uncooked dried **apricots,** cut fine
Turn . . . . .into well-greased 9x5x3-inch pan.
Bake . . . . .at 350° for 60 to 65 minutes. Cool before slicing.
**For use with Pillsbury's Best Self-Rising Flour, omit baking powder, soda, salt.*

Toasted Almond Anise Loaf

Senior Winner by Mrs. N. S. Barranco, Birmingham, Alabama

An old Italian quick bread with the unique flavor combination of toasted almonds and anise seed. Rich and moist, too.

BAKE at 350° for 50 to 60 minutes   MAKES 9x5-inch loaf

Toast . . . . . . .¾ cup blanched **almonds,** chopped fine, at 450° for
          5 minutes until golden brown, stirring occasionally.
          Cool.
Sift together 2¼ cups sifted **Pillsbury's Best All Purpose Flour***
          2 teaspoons double-acting **baking powder** and
          ½ teaspoon **salt**
Cream . . . . . .½ cup **butter** or margarine. Gradually add
          1 cup **sugar,** creaming well.
Stir in . . . . . .½ to 1 teaspoon **anise seed** and
          ¼ teaspoon **almond extract**
Add . . . . .5 unbeaten **eggs,** beating well after each.
Blend in . . . . . . .the dry ingredients and toasted almonds. Mix well.
Turn . . . . .into 9x5x3-inch pan, well greased on the bottom.
Bake . . . . .at 350° for 50 to 60 minutes.
**For use with Pillsbury's Best Self-Rising Flour, omit baking powder and salt.*

Candied Orange Bread

Senior Winner by Mrs. Bess Atkinson, Brunswick, Georgia

Whole wheat adds flavor and texture to this quick bread . . . chock full of candied orange peel and chopped pecans.

BAKE at 350° for 55 to 65 minutes   MAKES 9x5-inch loaf

Sift together . . 2 cups sifted **Pillsbury's Best All Purpose Flour***
          ¾ cup **sugar**
          3½ teaspoons double-acting **baking powder** and
          1 teaspoon **salt** into large mixing bowl.
Add . . . . 1 cup unsifted **Pillsbury's Whole Wheat (Graham) Flour**
          ¾ cup (3 oz.) candied **orange peel,** thinly sliced, and
          ½ cup **pecans,** chopped. Set aside.
Combine . . . . . 1 well-beaten **egg**
          1¼ cups **milk** and
          ¼ cup **shortening,** melted, or salad oil
Add . . . . to the dry ingredients all at once; mix until all dry
          particles are moistened.
Turn . . . . into well-greased 9x5x3-inch pan.
Bake . . . . at 350° for 55 to 65 minutes. Cool before slicing.

**For use with Pillsbury's Best Self-Rising Flour, omit baking powder; decrease salt to ½ teaspoon.*

Holiday Cranberry Bread

Senior Winner by Mrs. Martin Stevlingson, Menomonie, Wisconsin

Besides being delicious, it is very colorful for the holiday season. And so fragrant when it comes from your oven!

BAKE at 350° for 55 to 65 minutes   MAKES 9x5-inch loaf

Sift together . . 2 cups sifted **Pillsbury's Best All Purpose Flour***
          1 cup **sugar**
          1½ teaspoons double-acting **baking powder**

Holiday Cranberry Bread

          1 teaspoon **salt** and
          ½ teaspoon **soda** into large mixing bowl.
Grate . . . . 1 **orange;** reserve 1 tablespoon rind.
Combine . . . . . . juice of 1 **orange** with enough **boiling water** to
          measure ¾ cup. Stir in
          2 tablespoons **shortening** and
          1 well-beaten **egg.** Add to the dry ingredients; mix
          until all dry particles are moistened.
Stir in . . . . 1 cup **nuts,** chopped
          1 cup raw **cranberries,** cut in half, and reserved
          orange rind.
Turn . . . . into greased 9x5x3-inch pan.
Bake . . . . at 350° for 55 to 65 minutes. Cool before slicing.

**For use with Pillsbury's Best Self-Rising Flour, omit baking powder, salt, soda.*

Banana Luncheon Bread

Junior Winner by Gracy Zeppenfeld, Ironwood, Michigan

Delicious banana-nut bread can be served plain, or with butter or cream cheese. Stays fresh for days.

BAKE at 350° for 60 to 70 minutes   MAKES 9x5-inch loaf

Sift together..2 cups sifted **Pillsbury's Best All Purpose Flour***
        1 teaspoon double-acting **baking powder**
        1 teaspoon **salt** and
        ½ teaspoon **soda**. Set aside.
Add........1 cup **sugar** gradually to
        ½ cup **shortening**, creaming well.
Blend in.....2 unbeaten **eggs**, beating well after each.
Stir in.......1 cup mashed ripe **bananas** (2 medium)
Blend in.......the sifted dry ingredients. Stir in
        ½ cup **nuts**, chopped
Turn..........into 9x5x3-inch pan, well greased on the bottom.
Bake........at 350° for 60 to 70 minutes. Cool before slicing.

For use with Pillsbury's Best Self-Rising Flour, omit baking powder and salt; decrease soda to ¼ teaspoon.

Peanut Banana Bread

Junior Winner by Genevieve George, Pemberville, Ohio

Chopped peanuts in the loaf and peanut butter frosting on top make this banana bread different.

BAKE at 350° for 60 to 70 minutes   MAKES 9x5-inch loaf

Sift together.. 2 cups sifted **Pillsbury's Best All Purpose Flour***
        2 teaspoons double-acting **baking powder**

        1 teaspoon **salt** and
        ¼ teaspoon **soda**. Set aside.
Add........½ cup **sugar** gradually to
        ⅓ cup **shortening**, creaming well.
Add........2 unbeaten **eggs**
        ¾ cup mashed ripe **banana** (1 large) and
        ⅓ cup **milk**; beat well.
Stir in.........the dry ingredients and
        ½ cup **peanuts**, chopped. Mix thoroughly. Turn into
        well-greased 9x5x3-inch pan.
Bake........at 350° for 60 to 70 minutes. Cool in pan 5 minutes.
        Frost with Peanut Butter Frosting while warm.

For use with Pillsbury's Best Self-Rising Flour, omit baking powder, salt, soda.

PEANUT BUTTER FROSTING

Combine ½ cup sifted confectioners' sugar, 2 tablespoons peanut butter and 2 tablespoons cream; beat well. Thin with cream, if necessary.

Old Country Raisin Loaf

Junior Winner by Ruth Lietz, Brownton, Minnesota

Slices of this moist quick raisin-nut bread are wonderful plain— or spread with butter or cream cheese.

BAKE at 350° for 40 to 50 minutes   MAKES one 9x5-inch
        and two small loaves

Sift together.. 3 cups sifted **Pillsbury's Best All Purpose Flour***
        2 teaspoons **soda**
        1½ teaspoons **salt**
        1 teaspoon **cinnamon** and
        ¼ teaspoon **cloves**
Grind.......1 cup **raisins** with
        ½ cup **walnuts**
Add........1 cup firmly packed **brown sugar** gradually to
        ½ cup **shortening**, creaming well. Add

1 unbeaten **egg;** beat well. Stir in the raisin mixture; mix well.

Add.......1½ cups **buttermilk** or sour milk alternately with the dry ingredients. Blend well after each addition.

Turn.........into two well-greased No. 2 cans, filling each half full; spread remaining batter in one well-greased 9x5x3-inch pan.

Bake.........at 350° for 40 to 50 minutes.

Pillsbury's Best Self-Rising Flour is not recommended for use in this recipe.

Magic Molasses Bread
Bride Winner by Mrs. William L. Lowell, East Cleveland, Ohio

A really quick bread for breakfast because it's made the day before! Walnuts, raisins and orange rind add zest to this molasses-buttermilk loaf.

BAKE at 350° for 50 to 60 minutes   MAKES 9x5-inch loaf

Sift together..2 cups sifted **Pillsbury's Best All Purpose Flour***
     1 teaspoon double-acting **baking powder**
     1 teaspoon **salt** and
     ½ teaspoon **soda**

Combine.....1 beaten **egg**
     ⅛ cup **sugar**
     ¼ cup **shortening,** melted
     ½ cup **molasses**
     1 tablespoon grated **orange rind**
     ½ cup **raisins** and
     ½ cup **walnuts,** chopped, in large mixing bowl.

Add........¾ cup **buttermilk** or sour milk alternately with the dry ingredients. Blend well after each addition.

Turn.........into 9x5x3-inch pan, well greased on the bottom. Let stand 15 minutes.

Bake.........at 350° for 50 to 60 minutes. Let stand at least 8 hours before slicing.

Pillsbury's Best Self-Rising Flour is not recommended for use in this recipe.

Magic Molasses Bread

Walnut Honey Loaf

Senior Winner by Mrs. B. J. Feeney, Los Angeles, California

This quick honey nut loaf looks like a yeast bread. Light in color when it goes into the oven, it turns a rich brown as it bakes.

BAKE at 325° for 1¼ to 1½ hours   MAKES 9x5-inch loaf

Combine . . . . . 1 cup **honey**
             1 cup **milk** and
             ½ cup **sugar** in 3-quart saucepan. Heat to lukewarm, stirring constantly, until sugar is dissolved. Cool.
Sift together 2½ cups sifted **Pillsbury's Best All Purpose Flour***
             1 teaspoon **soda** and
             1 teaspoon **salt**
Add . . . . the dry ingredients
             ½ cup **walnuts**, chopped
             ¼ cup **shortening** and
             2 unbeaten **egg yolks** (or 1 egg) to honey mixture.
Beat . . . . 2 minutes, until well blended. Turn into 9x5x3-inch pan, well greased on the bottom.
Bake . . . . at 325° for 1¼ to 1½ hours.
*Pillsbury's Best Self-Rising Flour is not recommended for use in this recipe.

Ginger Tea Bread

Senior Winner by Mrs. Ann R. Apple, Grosse Pointe Woods, Michigan

Made with dark molasses for old-fashioned flavor . . . and with just a subtle hint of spice. Especially good—and easy to prepare.

BAKE at 350° for 30 to 35 minutes   MAKES 8x8-inch gingerbread

Sift together 1¼ cups sifted **Pillsbury's Best All Purpose Flour***
             ¼ cup **sugar**
             1 teaspoon **soda**
             ½ teaspoon **salt**
             ½ teaspoon **ginger**

             ½ teaspoon **cinnamon** and
             ½ teaspoon **cloves** into large mixing bowl.
Add . . . . 1 unbeaten **egg**
             ¼ cup **shortening** and
             ½ cup **molasses**; beat well.
Blend in . . . . . ½ cup **boiling water**; mix thoroughly.
Pour . . . . into 8x8x2-inch pan, well greased and lightly floured on the bottom.
Bake . . . . at 350° for 30 to 35 minutes. Serve warm.
*For use with Pillsbury's Best Self-Rising Flour, omit soda and salt.

Graham Cracker Brown Bread

Senior Winner by Mrs. Grace M. Kain, West Boothbay Harbor, Maine

An old-fashioned brown bread, made "modern" with graham crackers.

BAKE at 375° for 35 to 45 minutes   MAKES four small or two 9x5-inch loaves or one 13x9-inch loaf

Sift together 1¾ cups sifted **Pillsbury's Best All Purpose Flour***
             2 teaspoons **soda**
             1½ teaspoons **salt** and
             ½ teaspoon **nutmeg**. Set aside.
Add . . . . 2 cups crushed **graham crackers** gradually to
             ½ cup **shortening**, blending well.
Stir in . . . . . . ¾ cup **molasses** and
             2 unbeaten **eggs**; beat well.
Add . . . . 1¾ cups **buttermilk** or sour milk alternately with the dry ingredients. Blend well after each addition.
Stir in . . . . . . 1 cup **raisins**
Turn . . . . batter into pans, well greased and lightly floured on the bottoms: two 9x5x3-inch pans, four No. 2 cans or 13x9x2-inch pan.
Bake . . . . at 375° for 35 to 45 minutes.
*For use with Pillsbury's Best Self-Rising Flour, decrease soda to 1 teaspoon and salt to ½ teaspoon.

Quick Whole Wheat Nut Bread

Senior Winner by Mrs. Irene M. Farnham, South Portland, Maine

Orange, whole wheat and molasses, a different flavor combination for a quick nut bread.

BAKE at 350° for 60 to 70 minutes   MAKES 9x5-inch loaf

Sift together 1¼ cups sifted **Pillsbury's Best All Purpose Flour***
      ¾ cup **sugar**
      1 teaspoon double-acting **baking powder**
      1 teaspoon **soda** and
      1 teaspoon **salt** into large mixing bowl.
Add . . . . . . .1¼ cups **Pillsbury's Whole Wheat (Graham) Flour**
      1 cup **nuts,** chopped, and
      2 tablespoons grated **orange rind**
Combine . . . . .1 beaten **egg**
      1¼ cups **milk**
      ½ cup **shortening**, melted, and
      ¼ cup **molasses**. Add to the dry ingredients; mix until well blended.
Turn . . . . .batter into greased 9x5x3-inch pan.
Bake . . . . .at 350° for 60 to 70 minutes. Cool before slicing.

*For use with Pillsbury's Best Self-Rising Flour, omit baking powder and salt; decrease soda to ½ teaspoon.

Merry Mince Brown Bread

Senior Winner by Lettie L. Spencer, East Greenwich, Rhode Island

Mincemeat and corn meal give old-fashioned brown bread a new-fashioned flavor. Delicious warm or cold, buttered or plain.

STEAM for 2 hours   MAKES 4 small loaves

Sift together 1½ cups sifted **Pillsbury's Best All Purpose Flour***
      2 teaspoons **soda** and
      1 teaspoon **salt** into large mixing bowl. Stir in

Blend in . . . . .2 cups **corn meal**
      2 cups **milk** and
      ¾ cup dark **molasses**; mix well.
Stir in . . . . . . .1 cup prepared **mincemeat**
Divide . . . . .batter into 4 well-greased No. 2 cans. (If desired, use a well-greased 1½-quart mold.) Cover tightly with aluminum foil. Place on rack in a large steamer or kettle; add boiling water to one-third height of cans. Cover tightly.
Steam . . . . .2 hours. Cool.

*Pillsbury's Best Self-Rising Flour is not recommended for use in this recipe.

Date-Rich Bran Bread

Senior Winner by Mrs. John A. Bolt, Chicago, Illinois

A tantalizing combination of crunchy bran cereal, with pecans and sweet, moist dates.

STEAM for 1½ hours   MAKES 3 small loaves

Sift together . .2 cups sifted **Pillsbury's Best All Purpose Flour***
      2 teaspoons **soda** and
      ½ teaspoon **salt** into large mixing bowl.
Add . . . . . . .1½ cups **bran flakes**
      ¾ cup firmly packed **brown sugar**
      1 cup **dates**, cut
      ½ cup **pecans** or other nuts, chopped, and
      1½ cups **buttermilk** or sour milk; mix until well combined.
Divide . . . . .into 3 well-greased No. 2 cans. Cover tightly with aluminum foil.
Place . . . . .pans on rack in steamer. Add boiling water to a depth of 1 inch above rack. Cover. Keep water at boiling point.
Steam . . . . .1½ hours.

*For use with Pillsbury's Best Self-Rising Flour, decrease soda to 1 teaspoon and omit salt.

BISCUITS and SWEET ROLLS

—Biscuits are a popular and easy quick bread. Shortening is cut into the flour mixture with a pastry blender or two knives until mixture is similar in texture to coarse crumbs. Add liquid all at once. Mix dough with a fork, as a spoon tends to pack the ingredients together. Handle dough lightly, mixing until it clings together.

Place on floured surface and knead 10 to 15 strokes to develop the gluten of the flour and build flaky, high biscuits. Overkneading, however, will toughen the biscuits.

Roll or pat dough to desired thickness (biscuits usually double in volume during baking). For crusty biscuits, roll dough ¼ inch thick; for high, fluffy biscuits, have dough ⅜ to ½ inch thick.

For even rolling of biscuit dough, prepare "sticks" the height and width of the desired thickness and about 12 inches long. (To roll dough to ½ inch thickness, for instance, the stick would measure ½x ½x12 inches.) Place a stick on either side of the dough and roll until rolling pin rests evenly on the sticks. Sticks may be washed and re-used.

Cut dough with sharp-edged floured cutter, pressing straight down to obtain even, straight-sided biscuits. Dough may be cut into any desired shapes, such as diamonds, squares, triangles, etc.

For biscuits with soft white sides, bake them close together, sides touching. For crisper brown sides, do not have sides touching.

Always serve biscuits hot. If you have leftover biscuits, slice in two and toast under the broiler. Serve with butter or jam.

Quick sweet rolls are an easy way to satisfy the family hunger for something different. When baking "sticky" rolls, invert pan onto serving plate or wire rack with waxed paper underneath. Allow syrup to drip over rolls before removing pan.

Teena's Luncheon Biscuits

Senior Winner by Mrs. John Angle, Santa Ana, California

You'll be pleased with the flavor of whole wheat and cheese in these buttermilk biscuits. And you can make them in minutes!

BAKE at 450° for 12 to 15 minutes   MAKES about 1½ dozen

Sift together 1⅔ cups sifted **Pillsbury's Best All Purpose Flour***
          3 teaspoons double-acting **baking powder**
          1 teaspoon **salt** and
          ½ teaspoon **soda** into large mixing bowl.
Add........½ cup **Pillsbury's Whole Wheat (Graham) Flour**
Cut in.....¼ cup **shortening** until particles are fine.
Stir in.....1 cup (¼ lb.) shredded **American cheese**; mix well.
Add........1 cup **buttermilk** or sour milk; mix until all dry
          particles are moistened. Knead on floured surface
          12 to 15 strokes.
Roll out.......to ½-inch thickness; cut with 2-inch round cutter.
          Place on ungreased baking sheet.
Bake.........at 450° for 12 to 15 minutes. Serve warm.
For use with Pillsbury's Best Self-Rising Flour, omit baking powder and salt.

Chipper Cheese Biscuits

Junior Winner by Molly Jo Hunter, Charleston, South Carolina

These colorful cheese biscuits have bits of red pimiento and green pepper baked right into them.

BAKE at 450° for 12 to 15 minutes   MAKES 1½ dozen

Sift together..2 cups sifted **Pillsbury's Best All Purpose Flour***
          3 teaspoons double-acting **baking powder** and
          1 teaspoon **salt** into large mixing bowl.
Cut in......⅓ cup **shortening** until particles are fine.
Blend in.....⅔ cup shredded **American cheese**
          1 tablespoon chopped **pimiento** and

2 tablespoons chopped **green pepper;** mix well.

Add . . . . ¾ cup **milk;** mix until all dry particles are moistened. Knead on floured surface 12 strokes.

Roll . . . . to ½-inch thickness and cut with floured 2-inch round cutter. Place on ungreased baking sheet.

Bake . . . . at 450° for 12 to 15 minutes. Serve hot.

For use with Pillsbury's Best Self-Rising Flour, omit baking powder and salt; decrease milk to ⅔ cup.

Speedy Cinnamon Fan Tans

Senior Winner by Mrs. H. H. Terrell, Richmond, Indiana

Cinnamon and nuts are baked between layers of tender baking powder biscuit. Make them quickly—serve them warm.

BAKE at 400° for 15 to 20 minutes   MAKES 1 dozen

Sift together . . 2 cups sifted **Pillsbury's Best All Purpose Flour***
   2 tablespoons **sugar**
   4 teaspoons double-acting **baking powder** and
   ½ teaspoon **salt** into large mixing bowl.

Cut in . . . . . . ¼ cup **shortening** until particles are fine.

Combine . . . . . 2 slightly beaten **eggs** and
   ⅛ cup **milk;** add to flour mixture, mixing until all dry particles are moistened.

Knead . . . . gently on floured surface 12 strokes.

Roll . . . . to 15x12-inch rectangle. Brush with melted **butter.**

Combine . . . . . ¼ cup **sugar**
   ½ teaspoon **cinnamon** and
   ¼ cup **nuts,** finely chopped; sprinkle over dough.

Cut . . . . rectangle into eight strips, 1½ inches wide, 15 inches long. Stack strips together; cut into twelve equal pieces. Place each stack, cut-side down, in greased muffin cup.

Bake . . . . at 400° for 15 to 20 minutes.

For use with Pillsbury's Best Self-Rising Flour, omit baking powder and salt.

Orange Upsidaisies

Senior Winner by Mrs. R. H. McCann, Annapolis, Maryland

A shiny orange glaze covers these quick cinnamon rolls when turned "upsidaisy" from the pan.

BAKE at 400° for 17 to 22 minutes   MAKES 1 dozen

Combine . . . . . 1 teaspoon grated **orange rind**
   ¾ cup **orange juice**
   ½ cup **sugar**
   ⅓ cup **butter** or margarine and
   ⅛ teaspoon **salt** in saucepan. Simmer over low heat 10 minutes. Divide into 12 well-greased muffin cups.

Sift together . . 2 cups sifted **Pillsbury's Best All Purpose Flour***
   3 teaspoons double-acting **baking powder** and
   1 teaspoon **salt** into large mixing bowl.

Combine . . . . ⅛ cup **salad oil** and
   ¾ cup **milk.** Add all at once to the dry ingredients; blend well.

Roll out . . . . on floured surface to 13x10-inch rectangle.

Combine . . . . . 2 tablespoons **sugar**
   1 teaspoon **cinnamon** and
   ⅛ teaspoon **salt;** sprinkle over dough.

Roll . . . . as for jelly roll, starting with 10-inch side. Cut into 12 slices. Place in prepared muffin cups.

Bake . . . . at 400° for 17 to 22 minutes. Loosen and invert.

For use with Pillsbury's Best Self-Rising Flour, omit baking powder and salt.

Cobblescones

Senior Winner by Mrs. Robert E. Neiman, Lakeside, California

A rich baking powder bread with cranberry-apple filling . . . easily cut to resemble cobblestones.

BAKE at 450° for 15 to 18 minutes   MAKES 12 to 16 squares

Sift together . . 2 cups sifted **Pillsbury's Best All Purpose Flour***
                  4 teaspoons double-acting **baking powder**
                  1 tablespoon **sugar** and
                  ½ teaspoon **salt** into large mixing bowl.
Cut in . . . . . . ¼ cup **butter** or margarine until particles are fine.
Combine . . . . . 2 unbeaten **eggs** with **cream** to measure ¾ cup. Add to flour mixture and stir until dough clings together.
Roll out . . . . on aluminum foil to a 16x8-inch rectangle. Spread Cranberry Filling over half of dough. Fold dough over Filling to make an 8-inch square. Remove foil

Cobblescones

from top crust. Seal edges. Brush with **milk;** then sprinkle with
                  2 tablespoons **sugar**
Transfer . . . . to ungreased baking sheet, lifting by foil. Cut into 2 or 3-inch squares (do not separate squares).
Bake . . . . at 450° for 15 to 18 minutes.
*For use with Pillsbury's Best Self-Rising Flour, omit baking powder and salt.

CRANBERRY FILLING

Combine ¾ cup whole cranberry sauce, ½ cup shredded apple, 2 tablespoons brown sugar and ½ teaspoon cinnamon.

Highland Griddle Scones

Senior Winner by Mrs. Albert G. Sharpe, Stockton, California

These rich, tender biscuits are given a corn meal coating, then "baked" on a hot griddle.

BAKE on hot griddle about 16 minutes   MAKES 1½ to 2 dozen

Sift together . . 2 cups sifted **Pillsbury's Best All Purpose Flour***
                  ¼ cup **sugar**
                  4 teaspoons double-acting **baking powder** and
                  ½ teaspoon **salt** into large mixing bowl.
Cut in . . . . . . ⅓ cup **shortening** until particles are fine.
Combine . . . . . 1 unbeaten **egg** with **milk** to measure ¾ cup. Blend together. Add all at once to flour mixture; stir just until all dry particles are moistened.
Roll out . . . . on surface sprinkled with
                  3 to 4 tablespoons **corn meal.** Roll to about ¼-inch thickness, turning dough over to coat both sides with corn meal. Cut with 2½-inch round cutter.
Bake . . . . on preheated, moderately hot griddle about 8 minutes on each side. Turn only once. Serve hot.
*For use with Pillsbury's Best Self-Rising Flour, omit baking powder and salt; decrease egg-milk mixture to ⅔ cup.

DOUGHNUTS

DOUGHNUTS are of two types—cake doughnuts, leavened by baking powder or soda, and raised doughnuts, leavened with yeast (see pages 85 and 86).

If dough for rolled doughnuts appears soft, chill it for several hours. Rolling the soft dough in flour will make doughnuts tough.

It is important to use hot fat while frying doughnuts to keep fat absorption low. Frying too many doughnuts at one time will lower the fat temperature. The fat should be 3 to 4 inches deep. A temperature of 375° is usually recommended. If you have an electric deep-fat fryer, watch the temperature indicator. If you are using a pan without temperature control, a deep-fat thermometer would be helpful. Be sure temperature is correct each time.

Doughnuts should be drained on absorbent paper immediately after frying.

Country Kitchen Doughnuts

Senior Winner by Mrs. Ren Lyon, Cumberland, Ohio

Really light and fine-textured cake doughnuts, crisp and tender crusted. And they're made with mashed potatoes!

FRY at 375° for 2 to 3 minutes   MAKES about 4 dozen

Sift together . . 5 cups sifted **Pillsbury's Best All Purpose Flour***
        4 teaspoons double-acting **baking powder**
        1½ teaspoons **salt**
        1 teaspoon **soda** and
        ½ teaspoon **cinnamon**. Set aside.
Add . . . . 1¼ cups **sugar** gradually to
        1 cup **mashed potatoes** in large mixing bowl, mixing thoroughly.
Blend in . . . . . 2 unbeaten **eggs** and
        ¼ cup **butter** or margarine, melted; beat thoroughly.

Combine . . . . ⅔ cup **buttermilk** or sour milk
        1 teaspoon **vanilla**
        ½ teaspoon **lemon extract** and
        ½ teaspoon grated **lemon rind**. Add alternately with the dry ingredients to potato mixture. Blend well. If desired, chill dough for easier handling.
Roll out . . . . on well-floured surface to about ¼-inch thickness.
Cut . . . . with 3-inch doughnut cutter.
Fry . . . . in hot deep fat (375°) 2 to 3 minutes or until golden brown on both sides. Drain on absorbent paper. Sprinkle with **granulated** or **confectioners' sugar**.

*For use with Pillsbury's Best Self-Rising Flour, omit baking powder, salt, soda.

Golden Apple Puffs

Senior Winner by Mrs. Helen Knoll, Houston, Texas

Apple fritters deluxe! Golden-crusted, apple-filled puffs, fried in deep fat and rolled in sugar.

FRY at 375° about 7 minutes   MAKES about 2 dozen

Sift together . . 2 cups sifted **Pillsbury's Best All Purpose Flour***
        1 tablespoon **sugar**
        3 teaspoons double-acting **baking powder**
        ½ teaspoon **salt** and
        ½ teaspoon **nutmeg**.
Beat . . . . 2 **eggs** until light. Add
        1 cup **milk** and
        ½ teaspoon **vanilla**.
Blend in . . . . the dry ingredients. Do not overmix.
Add . . . . 1¼ cups pared, diced **apple**
Drop . . . . by rounded tablespoonfuls into hot deep fat (375°); fry until both sides are golden brown.
Drain . . . . on absorbent paper. Roll in **granulated** or **confectioners' sugar**.

*For use with Pillsbury's Best Self-Rising Flour, omit baking powder and salt.

Taffy "Apple" Doughnuts

Senior Winner by Mrs. Albert Krauthamer, Indianapolis, Indiana

Doughnut balls are dipped into honey syrup coating, then sprinkled with nuts. Serve taffy-apple style—on skewers—with apple cider.

FRY at 350° for 3 to 4 minutes   MAKES 3½ dozen

Sift together 2¼ cups sifted **Pillsbury's Best All Purpose Flour***
2 teaspoons double-acting **baking powder**
1 teaspoon **salt** and
¼ teaspoon **nutmeg.** Set aside.

Add . . . . ½ cup **sugar** to
¼ cup **shortening,** creaming well. Blend in
2 well-beaten **eggs**

Combine . . . . ½ cup **milk** and
1 teaspoon **vanilla.** Add alternately with the dry ingredients to creamed mixture. Blend well after each addition.

Taffy "Apple" Doughnuts

Drop . . . . by rounded teaspoonfuls into hot deep fat (350°). Fry until golden brown, 3 to 4 minutes. Drain on absorbent paper.

Insert . . . . a wooden skewer or stick firmly into each doughnut. Dip each into hot Honey Syrup, then sprinkle with finely chopped **nuts.** Cool on wire rack.

**Pillsbury's Best Self-Rising Flour is not recommended for use in this recipe.*

HONEY SYRUP

Combine ¾ cup honey and ¾ cup firmly packed brown sugar in saucepan. Bring to boil. Reheat if syrup becomes too thick.

Bonbon Donut Drops

Junior Winner by Joan Downing, Anchorage, Alaska

Dainty little doughnut balls flecked with shredded semi-sweet chocolate.

FRY at 375° for about 3 minutes   MAKES 4 dozen

Sift together 2¼ cups sifted **Pillsbury's Best All Purpose Flour***
2½ teaspoons double-acting **baking powder** and
½ teaspoon **salt.** Set aside.

Add . . . . ½ cup **sugar** to
3 tablespoons **shortening,** creaming well.

Blend in . . . . . 2 well-beaten **eggs**

Combine . . . . ⅔ cup **milk** and
1 teaspoon **vanilla.** Add alternately with the dry ingredients to creamed mixture. Blend well after each addition.

Stir in . . . . . 1½ squares (1½ oz.) **semi-sweet chocolate,** shredded or shaved

Drop . . . . by teaspoonfuls into hot deep fat (375°). Fry until well browned on both sides, about 3 minutes. Drain on absorbent paper. Cool and roll in sifted **confectioners'** or **granulated sugar.**

**For use with Pillsbury's Best Self-Rising Flour, omit baking powder and salt.*

MUFFINS

—To produce tender muffins, the amount of mixing is very important. A well should be made in the center of the dry ingredients. Combine liquid ingredients and add all at once, stirring only until dry particles are moistened. The batter will be lumpy.

The bottoms of muffin cups should be well greased, the sides greased lightly. Place batter in pans with small measuring cup, filling cups one-half to two-thirds full. Add batter all in one step, otherwise peaks may result on baked muffins. Fill any empty muffin cups one-third full with water to prevent burning and discoloration of pan.

Little Miss Muffins

Bride Winner by Mrs. Richard Kent, Los Angeles, California

Banana muffins, so quick and easy, topped with colorful red jelly that bakes in.

BAKE at 375° for 18 to 20 minutes   MAKES 1 dozen

Sift together . . 2 cups sifted **Pillsbury's Best All Purpose Flour***
　　　　　　 2 teaspoons double-acting **baking powder**
　　　　　　 1 teaspoon **salt**
　　　　　　 ½ teaspoon **soda** and
　　　　　　 ¼ teaspoon **nutmeg** into large mixing bowl.

Combine . . . . . 1 slightly beaten **egg**
　　　　　　 1 cup mashed **bananas** (2 medium)
　　　　　　 ½ cup **sugar**
　　　　　　 ⅓ cup **shortening,** melted, or salad oil and
　　　　　　 ⅓ cup **milk.** Add all at once to the dry ingredients. Mix until all dry particles are moistened.
Fill . . . . well-greased muffin cups two-thirds full.
Make . . . . a slight indentation in center of dough with a teaspoon. Fill with
　　　　　　 1 teaspoon firm **red jelly**
Bake . . . . at 375° for 18 to 20 minutes. Serve warm.
For use with Pillsbury's Best Self-Rising Flour, omit baking powder, salt, soda.

Luncheon Muffins

Senior Winner by Mrs. Linda Flesh Born, Freeport, New York

These muffins have a color and seasoning all their own.

BAKE at 400° for 20 to 25 minutes   MAKES 1 dozen

Sift together 1¾ cups sifted **Pillsbury's Best All Purpose Flour***
　　　　　　 ¼ cup **sugar**
　　　　　　 3½ teaspoons double-acting **baking powder**
　　　　　　 1 teaspoon **celery salt** and
　　　　　　 ½ teaspoon **dry mustard** into large mixing bowl. Make a well in center.
Combine . . . . . 2 well-beaten **eggs**
　　　　　　 ⅔ cup **condensed tomato soup**
　　　　　　 ½ cup **milk**
　　　　　　 1 tablespoon **onion juice** or grated onion and
　　　　　　 ⅛ cup **salad oil.** Add to the dry ingredients; stir until all dry particles are moistened.
Fill . . . . well-greased muffin cups two-thirds full.
Bake . . . . at 400° for 20 to 25 minutes. Serve hot.
For use with Pillsbury's Best Self-Rising Flour, omit baking powder; decrease milk to ⅓ cup.

Jam-Dandy Muffins

Junior Winner by Mary Alice Tuttle, Fresno, California

A delightful apricot jam-nut mixture is spooned on the top, bakes right in.

BAKE at 400° for 20 to 25 minutes   MAKES 12 large muffins

Sift together 1⅔ cups sifted **Pillsbury's Best All Purpose Flour***
⅔ cup **sugar**
2 teaspoons double-acting **baking powder** and
1 teaspoon **salt** into large mixing bowl. Make a well in center.
Add . . . . 1 unbeaten **egg**
⅛ cup **salad oil**
⅔ cup **milk** and
⅛ cup drained **crushed pineapple;** mix until all dry particles are moistened.
Fill . . . . well-greased muffin cups half full.

Jam-Dandy Muffins

Combine . . . . ¼ cup **apricot preserves** and
2 tablespoons chopped **nuts.** Place a teaspoonful on top of each.
Bake . . . . at 400° for 20 to 25 minutes. Serve hot.
*For use with Pillsbury's Best Self-Rising Flour, omit baking powder and salt.

Mecca Muffins

Senior Winner by Marie D. Schreier, Chicago, Illinois

Very special corn meal muffins with added flavors of caraway, onion and green pepper. A cheese topping gives interesting glazed crust.

BAKE at 400° for 20 to 25 minutes   MAKES 1 dozen

Sift together . . 1 cup sifted **Pillsbury's Best All Purpose Flour***
2 tablespoons **sugar**
3 teaspoons double-acting **baking powder** and
1 teaspoon **salt** into large mixing bowl.
Stir in . . . . 1 cup **corn meal**
1½ cups shredded **Cheddar cheese**
1 tablespoon finely chopped **onion**
1 tablespoon chopped **green pepper** and
1 teaspoon **caraway seed**
Combine . . . . . 1 cup **milk**
1 beaten **egg** and
3 tablespoons **butter,** melted; add to the dry ingredients. Mix until all dry particles are moistened.
Fill . . . . well-greased muffin cups two-thirds full.
Combine . . . . . 1 well-beaten **egg**
1 tablespoon **cream**
1 teaspoon finely chopped **onion** and
¼ cup shredded **Cheddar cheese;** mix well. Place a teaspoonful of mixture over batter in each cup.
Bake . . . . at 400° for 20 to 25 minutes.
*For use with Pillsbury's Best Self-Rising Flour, decrease baking powder to 1 teaspoon and omit salt.

Pineapple Bake-Ins

Junior Winner by Judith Lynne Stockwell, Los Angeles, California

Pineapple and bacon flavor these golden corn meal muffins, which use bacon drippings for shortening.

BAKE at 425° for 15 to 20 minutes   MAKES 1 dozen

Fry . . . . .3 strips **bacon** until crisp. Reserve ¼ cup drippings. Crumble bacon.

Sift together . .1 cup sifted **Pillsbury's Best All Purpose Flour***
1 teaspoon double-acting **baking powder**
1 teaspoon **salt** and
¾ teaspoon **soda** into large mixing bowl. Stir in
1 cup **corn meal** and
2 tablespoons **brown sugar**

Combine . . . . .2 slightly beaten **eggs**
1½ cups **buttermilk** or sour milk
½ cup well-drained **crushed pineapple** and bacon drippings. Add all at once to the dry ingredients, mixing until all dry particles are moistened.

Fill . . . . .well-greased muffin cups two-thirds full. Top each with crumbled bacon.

Bake . . . . .at 425° for 15 to 20 minutes.

For use with Pillsbury's Best Self-Rising Flour, omit baking powder and salt.

Mince Crowned Muffins

Senior Winner by Mrs. Fred Avril, Tallahassee, Florida

Muffins with a double topping—mincemeat and a nut-crumb mixture.

BAKE at 375° for 25 to 30 minutes   MAKES 1 dozen

Combine . . . .¼ cup **Pillsbury's Best All Purpose Flour**
3 tablespoons **brown sugar**
¼ teaspoon **cinnamon**
2 tablespoons chopped **nuts** and

2 tablespoons **butter**, melted. Reserve for topping.

Sift together . .2 cups sifted **Pillsbury's Best All Purpose Flour***
⅓ cup **sugar**
3 teaspoons double-acting **baking powder** and
½ teaspoon **salt** into large mixing bowl.

Blend . . . . . . .1 beaten **egg** together with
1 cup **milk** and
¼ cup **shortening,** melted and cooled. Add all at once to the dry ingredients; mix until all dry particles are moistened.

Fill . . . . .muffin cups, well greased or lined with paper baking cups, half full.

Press . . . . .1 teaspoon prepared **mincemeat** into center of each with back of spoon. Sprinkle topping over centers of muffins.

Bake . . . . .at 375° for 25 to 30 minutes.

For use with Pillsbury's Best Self-Rising Flour, omit baking powder and salt.

Pineapple Bake-Ins

Cracklin' Bread

Senior Winner by Mrs. Herbert Leslie Evans, New Cumberland, West Virginia

A strictly Southern corn bread . . . tender, tasty. Make it with pork sausage or cracklings. Eat it hot, with or without butter.

BAKE at 400° for 12 to 15 minutes   MAKES 18 muffins or corn sticks

Brown . . . . . . ¾ pound (about 1½ cups) bulk **pork sausage.** Drain and reserve drippings. (Cracklings may be substituted for sausage.*)

Sift together . . 1 cup sifted **Pillsbury's Best All Purpose Flour****
3 tablespoons **sugar**
3 teaspoons double-acting **baking powder**
1½ teaspoons **salt** and
1 teaspoon **soda** into large mixing bowl. Stir in
2 cups **corn meal**

Add . . . . browned sausage or cracklings.

Combine . . . . . 2 well-beaten **eggs**
1 cup **buttermilk** or sour milk and ¼ cup sausage drippings.

Add . . . . to the dry ingredients all at once; stir quickly until all dry particles are moistened.

Fill . . . . well-greased muffin cups or corn-stick pans two-thirds full. (Heat pans for crusty bread.)

Bake . . . . at 400° for 12 to 15 minutes.

*Cracklings are the crisp, brown meat tissue left over after lard is rendered.
**For use with Pillsbury's Best Self-Rising Flour, decrease baking powder to 1 teaspoon and salt to 1 teaspoon.*

QUICK COFFEE CAKES may be of many attractive

types—tea rings, quickly-made batter breads with toppings, braided doughs with fillings, sweet doughs with fruits added and many novel-shaped breads.

Scissors are very convenient for cutting tea rings and similar filled coffee-cake doughs. Slice baked coffee cakes with very sharp or serrated knife.

Cinnamon Crunch Coffee Cake

Senior Winner by Mrs. W. L. Carpenter, San Antonio, Texas

A crunchy cinnamon-pecan topping is baked right on this exceptionally good coffee bread. Mix it up in just a few minutes.

BAKE at 350° for 30 to 40 minutes   MAKES 12x8 or 9x9-inch coffee cake

Sift together . . 2 cups sifted **Pillsbury's Best All Purpose Flour***
¾ cup **sugar**
3 teaspoons double-acting **baking powder**
1 teaspoon **cinnamon**
½ teaspoon **salt** and
¼ teaspoon **nutmeg** into large mixing bowl.

Add . . . . ⅓ cup **shortening** and
1 cup **milk.** Beat 1½ minutes.

Add . . . . 2 unbeaten **eggs.** Beat 1½ minutes.

Turn . . . . half of batter into 12x8x2 or 9x9x2-inch pan, well greased and lightly floured on the bottom.

Combine . . . . ⅔ cup firmly packed **brown sugar** and
2 tablespoons **flour** in small bowl.

Cut in . . . . 2 tablespoons **butter** until particles are fine.

Add . . . . 1 cup **pecans,** chopped

Sprinkle . . . . two-thirds of crumb mixture over batter in pan. Cover with remaining batter; top with remaining crumb mixture.

Bake . . . . at 350° for 30 to 40 minutes. Serve warm.

For use with Pillsbury's Best Self-Rising Flour, omit baking powder and salt.

Jiffy Mince Coffee Ring

Junior Winner by Barbara Biddy, Hendersonville, North Carolina

There's spicy mincemeat all through this coffee cake which can be made in minutes. Decorate with icing while it is still warm.

BAKE at 375° for 30 to 35 minutes   MAKES 9-inch coffee ring

Sift together . . 2 cups sifted **Pillsbury's Best All Purpose Flour***
            ¾ cup **sugar**
            2½ teaspoons double-acting **baking powder** and
            ½ teaspoon **salt** into large mixing bowl.
Cut in . . . . . . ⅓ cup **shortening** until particles are fine.
Combine . . . . . 1 slightly beaten **egg**
            ½ cup **milk** and
            ¾ cup prepared **mincemeat**
Add . . . . to the dry ingredients; mix until all dry particles are moistened.
Turn . . . . into well-greased 9-inch ring mold.
Bake . . . . at 375° for 30 to 35 minutes. While warm, frost with **Vanilla Glaze**, page 326. Garnish with **nuts,** if desired.

*For use with Pillsbury's Best Self-Rising Flour, omit baking powder and salt.

Crunchy Chocolate Kuchen

Senior Winner by Mrs. J. C. Bivin, Cleveland, Oklahoma

This unusual chocolate-sour cream coffee cake is topped with a streusel mixture of pecans, brown sugar and coffee.

BAKE at 350° for 45 to 50 minutes   MAKES 13x9-inch coffee cake

Combine . . . . ¾ cup firmly packed **brown sugar**
            ¾ cup **pecans,** chopped
            3 tablespoons **flour**
            1½ teaspoons **instant coffee** and
            3 tablespoons **butter,** melted. Reserve for topping.

Jiffy Mince Coffee Ring

Sift together 2¾ cups sifted **Pillsbury's Best All Purpose Flour***
            1½ teaspoons **soda** and
            1 teaspoon **salt** into large mixing bowl. Add
            2 cups firmly packed **brown sugar**; mix well.
Add . . . . 3 unbeaten **eggs**
            1½ cups **sour cream** (thick or commercial) and
            1½ teaspoons **vanilla.** Beat until smooth.
Melt . . . . 1½ squares (1½ oz.) unsweetened **chocolate** in
            ⅓ cup **boiling water.** Add to batter; mix well.
Turn . . . . into 13x9x2-inch pan, well greased and lightly floured on bottom. Sprinkle with reserved topping.
Bake . . . . at 350° for 45 to 50 minutes.

*For use with Pillsbury's Best Self-Rising Flour, decrease soda to ½ teaspoon and omit salt.

Royal Danish Kuchen

Royal Danish Kuchen

Junior Winner by Janet Sprenger, Genesee, Idaho

A breakfast or brunch sensation! Rich coffee cake, flavorful with raisins, orange rind and a crusty cinnamon-sugar topping.

BAKE at 350° for 35 to 40 minutes   MAKES 9x9-inch coffee cake

Sift together..2 cups sifted **Pillsbury's Best All Purpose Flour***
          1 cup **sugar**
          1½ teaspoons double-acting **baking powder**
          1 teaspoon **cinnamon**
          ½ teaspoon **soda**
          ½ teaspoon **salt** and
          ¼ teaspoon **nutmeg** into large mixing bowl.
Add........1 cup **buttermilk** or sour milk

          1 slightly beaten **egg** and
          ⅓ cup **shortening**, melted; mix until well blended.
Stir in.......1 cup **raisins**, chopped or whole, and
          1 tablespoon grated **orange rind**
Turn..........into 9x9x2-inch pan, well greased and lightly floured
          on the bottom.
Combine....½ cup **sugar**
          ½ cup **nuts**, chopped, and
          1 teaspoon **cinnamon**; sprinkle over batter.
Dot with.....2 tablespoons **butter**
Bake.........at 350° for 35 to 40 minutes.
*For use with Pillsbury's Best Self-Rising Flour, omit baking powder, soda, salt.

Company Apple Kuchen

Junior Winner by Francine Hafner, Delmar, New York

A spicy apple-raisin-nut mixture bakes right inside this tender coffee cake.

BAKE at 350° for 50 to 60 minutes   MAKES 9x9-inch coffee cake

Sift together 1½ cups sifted **Pillsbury's Best All Purpose Flour***
          1½ teaspoons double-acting **baking powder** and
          1 teaspoon **salt.** Set aside.
Add........¾ cup **sugar** to
          ⅓ cup **shortening**, creaming well.
Add........2 unbeaten **eggs**; beat well.
Combine....⅓ cup **milk** and
          1 teaspoon **vanilla**. Add alternately with the dry
          ingredients to creamed mixture. Blend well after
          each addition.
Combine.....3 cups pared, finely chopped **apples** (3 medium)
          ¼ cup **raisins**
          ¼ cup **nuts**, chopped
          2 tablespoons **sugar** and
          1 teaspoon **cinnamon**; toss lightly.
Spread........one-third of batter in well-greased 9x9x2-inch pan.

Cover with apple mixture. Spoon remaining batter over apples; spread to cover. Sprinkle with
¼ cup **coconut**

Bake . . . . at 350° for 50 to 60 minutes. Serve warm.

For use with Pillsbury's Best Self-Rising Flour, omit baking powder and salt.

Cheery Apple Brunch Bread

Bride Winner by Mrs. John H. Dekle, Jr., Richmond, Virginia

A spicy grated-apple mixture atop this orange-tangy coffee cake makes it more moist and flavorful . . . maraschino cherries make it festive.

BAKE at 400° for 30 to 40 minutes   MAKES 13x9-inch coffee cake

Sift together . . 2 cups sifted **Pillsbury's Best All Purpose Flour***
1 cup **sugar**
2½ teaspoons double-acting **baking powder** and
1 teaspoon **salt** into large mixing bowl. Make a well in center.

Add . . . . 1 slightly beaten **egg**
¾ cup **milk**
1 tablespoon grated **orange rind**
¼ cup **orange juice**
1 teaspoon **vanilla**
¼ cup **butter** or margarine, melted, and
¼ cup **shortening**, melted. Mix only until blended.

Spread . . . . in 13x9x2-inch pan, well greased on the bottom. Spoon Cherry Apple Topping evenly over batter.

Bake . . . . at 400° for 30 to 40 minutes. Serve warm or cold.

For use with Pillsbury's Best Self-Rising Flour, omit baking powder and salt.

CHERRY APPLE TOPPING

Prepare 2½ cups pared, coarsely shredded apples (about 3 medium). Add 1 tablespoon orange juice, ¼ cup firmly packed brown sugar, 1 teaspoon cinnamon, 10 maraschino cherries, cut fine and drained thoroughly, and 2 tablespoons melted butter. Stir to combine.

Apricot Laden Coffee Cake

Senior Winner by Mrs. Joseph M. Skura, Wilmington, Delaware

Batter, topped with an apricot-pineapple-coconut mixture, then more batter.

BAKE at 400° for 25 to 30 minutes   MAKES 9x9 or 11x7-inch coffee cake

Cook . . . . 18 to 20 large dried **apricot halves** in water to cover until tender. Drain and stir to mash.

Combine . . . . ¾ cup (9 oz. can) drained **crushed pineapple**
¼ cup **sugar** and ¾ cup of mashed apricot in saucepan. Boil 3 minutes.

Stir in . . . . 1 teaspoon grated **orange rind**
2 tablespoons **orange juice** and
⅓ cup **coconut**, coarsely chopped. Mix well. Set aside.

Sift together . . 2 cups sifted **Pillsbury's Best All Purpose Flour***
½ cup **sugar**
3 teaspoons double-acting **baking powder** and
½ teaspoon **salt** into large mixing bowl.

Cut in . . . . . . ⅓ cup **shortening** until particles are fine.

Combine . . . . ¾ cup **milk** and
1 unbeaten **egg**. Add to the dry ingredients; stir until all dry particles are moistened.

Spread . . . . two-thirds of batter in 9x9x2 or 11x7x2-inch pan, well greased on bottom. Spread apricot mixture over batter. Drop remaining batter in small spoonfuls over filling to form marble effect. Sprinkle with **sugar**.

Bake . . . . at 400° for 25 to 30 minutes. Serve warm as coffee cake or top with **plain** or **whipped cream** for dessert.

For use with Pillsbury's Best Self-Rising Flour, omit baking powder and salt.

Bohemian Almond Bread

Senior Winner by Mrs. P. J. Stephenson, Drumright, Oklahoma

This sweet, rich teacake is filled with raisins and almonds. Serve it for afternoon coffee or tea . . . or as a dessert.

BAKE at 350° for 20 to 25 minutes   MAKES 2 dozen bars

Sift together . . 1 cup sifted **Pillsbury's Best All Purpose Flour***
      1½ teaspoons double-acting **baking powder** and
      ½ teaspoon **salt**
Beat . . . . 2 **eggs** slightly; gradually add
      ⅔ cup **sugar.** Continue beating until light and ivory colored. Add
      1 teaspoon **vanilla**
Stir in . . . . . . ½ cup **raisins**
      ½ cup blanched **almond halves** and the dry ingredients; mix well.
Spread . . . . batter in well-greased 13x9x2-inch pan.
Combine . . . . . 2 tablespoons **sugar** and
      1 teaspoon **nutmeg;** sprinkle over batter.
Bake . . . . at 350° for 20 to 25 minutes. Cut into bars; serve warm.

*For use with Pillsbury's Best Self-Rising Flour, omit baking powder and salt.

Crunchy Caramel Pecan Loaf

Senior Winner by Mrs. Nelson Mammel, Warren, Michigan

This quick coffee cake, flavored with instant coffee, is rippled through with butterscotch and chopped pecans.

BAKE at 375° for 25 to 30 minutes   MAKES 9x9 or 12x8-inch coffee cake

Prepare . . . . Pecan Filling.
Sift together . . 2 cups sifted **Pillsbury's Best All Purpose Flour***
      ¾ cup **sugar**
      1 tablespoon **instant coffee**
      2½ teaspoons double-acting **baking powder** and
      1 teaspoon **salt** into large mixing bowl.
Combine . . . . . 2 beaten **eggs**
      ⅔ cup **milk** and
      ½ cup **shortening,** melted. Add to the dry ingredients; mix until all dry particles are moistened.
Turn . . . . into well-greased 9x9x2 or 12x8x2-inch pan. Spread Filling over top; cut through Filling and batter to marble.
Bake . . . . at 375° for 25 to 30 minutes.

*For use with Pillsbury's Best Self-Rising Flour, omit baking powder and salt.

PECAN FILLING

Combine 2 tablespoons soft butter and ¾ cup firmly packed brown sugar in saucepan. Add 1 slightly beaten egg; mix well. Blend in ⅛ cup milk. Cook over medium heat, stirring constantly, until thick and smooth. Remove from heat; stir in ⅓ cup chopped pecans. Cool.

Mock Apple Kuchen

Junior Winner by Duane Heyman, Berkey, Ohio

A square coffee cake with a streusel topping that's a spicy-rich mixture of nuts, cinnamon, sour cream and . . . toast cubes!

BAKE at 375° for 30 to 40 minutes   MAKES 9x9 or 11x7-inch coffee cake

Sift together 1½ cups sifted **Pillsbury's Best All Purpose Flour***
      2 teaspoons double-acting **baking powder** and
      ¼ teaspoon **salt.** Set aside.
Add . . . . ¾ cup firmly packed **brown sugar** gradually to
      ¼ cup **shortening,** creaming well.
Blend in . . . . . 1 unbeaten **egg** and
      1 teaspoon **vanilla;** beat well.
Add . . . . the dry ingredients alternately with
      ⅔ cup **milk.** Blend well after each addition.
Turn . . . . into 9x9x2 or 11x7x2-inch pan, well greased and

lightly floured on the bottom. Spread Mock Apple Topping over batter; press down lightly.

Bake . . . . at 375° for 30 to 40 minutes.

For use with Pillsbury's Best Self-Rising Flour, omit baking powder and salt.

MOCK APPLE TOPPING

Prepare 1½ cups toast cubes (about 3¼ slices bread, toasted and cut into ½-inch cubes). Combine with 1 tablespoon melted butter, 2 tablespoons sugar, ⅛ cup chopped nuts, ¾ teaspoon cinnamon and ½ cup sour cream. Mix well.

Honey Ambrosia Coffee Cake

Junior Winner by Jeanette Ziegler, Blue Earth, Minnesota

A quick coffee cake batter with an ambrosia-like topping of coconut, pineapple, butter, honey and sugar.

BAKE at 375° for 35 to 40 minutes   MAKES 8x8-inch coffee cake

Blend . . . . 3 tablespoons soft **butter** or margarine with
⅛ cup **honey** in small bowl.

Stir in . . . . . . ¼ cup **coconut**, coarsely cut
¼ cup sifted **confectioners' sugar** and
⅛ cup well-drained **crushed pineapple**. Set aside.

Sift together 1½ cups sifted **Pillsbury's Best All Purpose Flour***
1½ teaspoons double-acting **baking powder** and
½ teaspoon **salt**. Set aside.

Add . . . . ½ cup **sugar** gradually to
¼ cup **shortening**, creaming well.

Blend in . . . . . 1 unbeaten **egg**; beat well.

Add . . . . the dry ingredients alternately with
½ cup **milk**. Blend well after each addition.

Turn . . . . into 8x8x2-inch pan, well greased and lightly floured on bottom. Spoon pineapple mixture over batter.

Bake . . . . at 375° for 35 to 40 minutes. Serve warm.

For use with Pillsbury's Best Self-Rising Flour, omit baking powder and salt.

Plum Perfect Coffee Cake

Senior Winner by Mrs. Harold B. Shepard, Independence, Missouri

Strained "baby food" plums drizzled over the batter plus a sweet and spicy streusel nut topping make this coffee cake "plum perfect."

BAKE at 375° for 40 to 45 minutes   MAKES 8x8-inch coffee cake

Sift together 1½ cups sifted **Pillsbury's Best All Purpose Flour***
2 teaspoons double-acting **baking powder** and
1 teaspoon **salt**

Combine . . . . ⅛ cup **salad oil**
½ cup **sugar** and
1 unbeaten **egg** in large mixing bowl. Beat until well combined.

Add . . . . the dry ingredients alternately with
⅔ cup **milk**. Blend well after each addition.

Turn . . . . into well-greased and lightly floured 8x8x2-inch pan. Drizzle with
1 can (5 oz.) strained **plums** (baby food)

Combine . . . . ¼ cup **brown sugar**
1 tablespoon **flour**
½ teaspoon **cinnamon**
1 tablespoon melted **butter** or margarine and
½ cup **pecans**, finely chopped. Sprinkle over batter.

Bake . . . . at 375° for 40 to 45 minutes. Serve warm.

For use with Pillsbury's Best Self-Rising Flour, omit baking powder and salt.

Cranberry Crisscross Coffee Cake

Senior Winner by Mrs. Lane Misenheimer, Grand Rapids, Michigan

There's a layer of bright cranberry-orange mixture baked in this tender coffee cake. More cranberry-orange crisscrosses the top. Festive!

BAKE at 350° for 45 to 50 minutes   MAKES 8x8-inch coffee cake

Combine . . . . . 2 cups fresh **cranberries,** ground
⅛ cup **orange rind** (1 medium orange), ground
⅛ cup **walnuts,** ground
¾ cup firmly packed **brown sugar** and
1 tablespoon **flour.** Set aside.
Sift together 1½ cups sifted **Pillsbury's Best All Purpose Flour***
1½ teaspoons double-acting **baking powder** and
½ teaspoon **salt.** Set aside.
Add . . . . ½ cup **sugar** gradually to
⅓ cup **shortening,** creaming well.
Blend in . . . . . 1 unbeaten **egg** and

Cranberry Crisscross Coffee Cake

1 teaspoon **vanilla;** beat well.
Add . . . . ½ cup **milk** alternately with the dry ingredients to creamed mixture. Blend well after each addition.
Spread . . . . half of batter in 8x8x2-inch pan, well greased and lightly floured on bottom. Spread with half the cranberry mixture. Top with remaining batter. Decorate with remaining cranberry mixture, crisscrossing it to form a checked pattern.
Bake . . . . at 350° for 45 to 50 minutes.
*For use with Pillsbury's Best Self-Rising Flour, omit baking powder and salt.

Quick Lattice Coffee Cake

Senior Winner by Mrs. Vincent Masek, Ashtabula, Ohio

Strips of biscuit and red strawberry jam make this a colorful coffee cake.

BAKE at 350° for 25 to 35 minutes   MAKES 12x8-inch coffee cake

Sift together 2½ cups sifted **Pillsbury's Best All Purpose Flour***
⅓ cup **sugar**
3 teaspoons double-acting **baking powder** and
1 teaspoon **salt** into large mixing bowl.
Cut in . . . . . . ½ cup **shortening** until particles are fine.
Combine . . . . . 2 unbeaten **egg yolks** (or 1 egg)
1 cup **milk** and
1 teaspoon **vanilla.** Add to the dry ingredients; mix until all dry particles are moistened.
Spread . . . . three-fourths of dough on well-greased baking sheet, forming 12x8-inch rectangle.
Spread . . . . . . 1 cup **strawberry jam** or other jam over dough.
Blend . . . . ⅓ cup sifted **Pillsbury's Best All Purpose Flour** into remaining dough. Roll to about ⅛-inch thickness.
Cut . . . . into strips ½ inch wide. Place strips across jam, crisscross fashion.
Bake . . . . at 350° for 25 to 35 minutes. Serve warm.
*For use with Pillsbury's Best Self-Rising Flour, omit baking powder and salt.

Cranberry Crown Coffee Cake

Senior Winner by Mrs. John C. Bailar, Urbana, Illinois

This upside-down quick bread is baked in a ring mold. When turned out it reveals a crown of pecans and bright-colored cranberries.

BAKE at 400° for 25 to 30 minutes   MAKES 9-inch coffee cake

Melt . . . . 2 tablespoons **butter** in 9-inch ring mold. Spread
⅟₄ cup firmly packed **brown sugar** over bottom of pan.

Combine . . . . . 1 cup cooked or canned **cranberry sauce**
¼ cup **pecans**, chopped, and
1 tablespoon grated **orange rind;** spread over brown sugar in pan.

Sift together 1½ cups sifted **Pillsbury's Best All Purpose Flour***
¼ cup **sugar**
2 teaspoons double-acting **baking powder** and
½ teaspoon **salt** into large mixing bowl.

Cut in . . . . . . ⅓ cup **shortening** until particles are fine.

Combine . . . . . 1 slightly beaten **egg** and
½ cup **milk;** add all at once to the dry ingredients, mixing until all dry particles are moistened.

Turn . . . . into prepared pan.

Bake . . . . at 400° for 25 to 30 minutes. Cool 5 minutes, then invert on serving plate. Serve warm.

For use with Pillsbury's Best Self-Rising Flour, omit baking powder and salt.

Ruby Red Apple Cake

Junior Winner by Peggy Stewart Marks, Camden, New Jersey

Apple wedges on jellied cranberry slices form the attractive and refreshing topping for this quick coffee cake.

BAKE at 400° for 30 to 35 minutes   MAKES 9x9-inch coffee cake

Sift together . . 2 cups sifted **Pillsbury's Best All Purpose Flour***
3 tablespoons **sugar**
3 teaspoons double-acting **baking powder** and
½ teaspoon **salt** into large mixing bowl.

Beat . . . . 1 cup **whipping cream** until thick. Blend in
1 slightly beaten **egg.** Add to the dry ingredients, stirring until dough clings together.

Spread . . . . into well-greased 9x9x2-inch pan.

Cut . . . . **jellied cranberry sauce** into nine ¼-inch slices (about half of a 1-lb. can). Place slices on dough.

Prepare . . . . . . 3 **apples;** pare, core and quarter. Cut each quarter into three slices. Arrange apples in rows on cranberry sauce, pressing slices through sauce to dough.

Sprinkle . . . . with mixture of
¼ cup **sugar** and
½ teaspoon **cinnamon.** Drizzle with
2 tablespoons **butter** or margarine, melted

Bake . . . . at 400° for 30 to 35 minutes. Serve warm with **cream,** if desired.

For use with Pillsbury's Best Self-Rising Flour, omit baking powder and salt.

Ruby Red Apple Cake

Pecan Sunrise Bread

Bride Winner by Mrs. Edward B. Cogswell, Jr., Lubbock, Texas

Bake this coffee cake in a round or square cake pan and serve it hot. Orange rind and rolled oats in the batter—pecans in the crumb top.

BAKE at 375° for 30 to 35 minutes   MAKES 9-inch coffee cake

Sift together 1½ cups sifted **Pillsbury's Best All Purpose Flour***
            1½ teaspoons double-acting **baking powder**
            ½ teaspoon **soda** and
            ½ teaspoon **salt**. Stir in
            ½ cup quick-cooking **rolled oats**; set aside.
Add........¾ cup **sugar** gradually to
            ⅓ cup **shortening**, creaming well.
Blend in.....2 unbeaten **eggs**; beat well.
Add.........the dry ingredients alternately with
            ¾ cup **milk**. Blend well after each addition.
Turn.........into 9x9-inch pan or 9x1½-inch round layer pan,
            greased on bottom and lined with waxed paper.
            Arrange
            ¼ cup **pecan halves** on top of batter.
Blend.. .....⅓ cup **sugar**
            2 tablespoons **butter** or margarine, and
            1 tablespoon grated **orange rind** until the mixture
            resembles coarse crumbs. Sprinkle over batter.
Bake........at 375° for 30 to 35 minutes. Serve hot.

For use with Pillsbury's Best Self-Rising Flour, omit baking powder and salt; decrease soda to ¼ teaspoon.

Quick Cottage Cheese Stollen

Senior Winner by Mrs. Flora Voitel, Winchester, Virginia

A modern twist on an old-country favorite. Fruit and raisin-filled stollen made from a cottage cheese biscuit dough.

BAKE at 350° for 55 to 65 minutes   MAKES one stollen

Press.......¾ cup **cottage cheese** through a sieve.
Sift together ..3 cups sifted **Pillsbury's Best All Purpose Flour***
            ¾ cup **sugar**
            2 teaspoons double-acting **baking powder**
            ¾ teaspoon **salt** and
            ½ teaspoon **soda** into large mixing bowl.
Cut in......⅓ cup **shortening** and sieved cottage cheese until
            particles are fine.
Blend in.....2 slightly beaten **eggs**
            2 tablespoons **milk** and
            ¼ teaspoon **almond extract**
Stir in......½ cup **raisins** and
            ½ cup chopped mixed **candied fruit**
Knead........on floured surface until smooth, about 5 minutes.
Roll out.......to a 10-inch circle. Lift one side and fold over to
            within 2 inches of opposite edge for typical stollen
            shape. Place on ungreased baking sheet.
Bake.........at 350° for 55 to 65 minutes. While warm, sprinkle
            with **confectioners' sugar**.

For use with Pillsbury's Best Self-Rising Flour, omit baking powder, soda, salt; decrease baking time to 45 to 55 minutes.

SNACKS and CANAPÉS

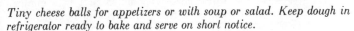

Cheese Nibblers

Junior Winner by Frank Burchfield, Riverside, California

Tiny cheese balls for appetizers or with soup or salad. Keep dough in refrigerator ready to bake and serve on short notice.

BAKE at 350° for 12 to 15 minutes   MAKES about 5 dozen puffs

Combine.....1 cup sifted **Pillsbury's Best All Purpose Flour***
    1 cup (¼ lb.) shredded **American** or **Cheddar cheese**
    ½ cup soft **butter** or margarine and
    ¼ teaspoon **salt.** Blend with pastry blender. Knead in
    bowl to form a dough.**

Shape........into balls, using 1 scant teaspoonful of dough for
    each. Place on ungreased baking sheets.

Bake........at 350° for 12 to 15 minutes.

Pillsbury's Best Self-Rising Flour is not recommended for use in this recipe.
**Dough may be stored in refrigerator and baked as needed.*

Dice o' Derv

Senior Winner by Rita W. Cherrington, Queenstown on the Eastern Shore, Md.

For peppy snacks, try these as tasty biscuits made with Parmesan cheese and dried beef. Or make as crackers and serve with soup.

BAKE at 425°   MAKES about 3 dozen biscuits
        or 10 dozen crackers

Sift together..3 cups sifted **Pillsbury's Best All Purpose Flour***
    2¼ teaspoons **cream of tartar**
    1¼ teaspoons **soda** and
    ¼ teaspoon **salt** into large mixing bowl.

Cut in......½ cup **shortening** until particles are fine.

Dice o' Derv

Mix in......½ cup (1½ oz.) grated **Parmesan cheese** and
    ¾ cup (2½-oz. jar) **dried beef,** cut fine

Add........1 cup **milk** and
    ⅓ cup **light cream*** all at once; mix until dough clings
    together. Divide in half.

Roll out.......one portion on floured surface to ¼-inch thickness
    for biscuits or ⅛-inch thickness for crackers. Cut
    with pastry wheel or knife into 2½x1½-inch strips.
    Place on ungreased baking sheets. Repeat with
    remaining dough.

Bake........at 425°: biscuits for 12 to 15 minutes; crackers
    for 8 to 10 minutes.**

For use with Pillsbury's Best Self-Rising Flour, omit cream of tartar, soda and salt; decrease cream to ¼ cup.
**Crackers or biscuits may be baked early, wrapped in aluminum foil and reheated in a 425° oven for 5 minutes just before serving.*

Cheese Caraway Nips

Senior Winner by Mr. Franklin D. Zook, San Francisco, California

Cheese, dry mustard and caraway seeds are put into these pastry strips. Serve them as appetizers or with soups or crisp salads.

BAKE at 450° for 7 to 9 minutes   MAKES 5 dozen crackers

Sift together . . 1 cup sifted **Pillsbury's Best All Purpose Flour***
          2 teaspoons **dry mustard** and
          1 teaspoon **salt** into mixing bowl.
Add . . . . ½ cup shredded **Cheddar cheese** and
          2 teaspoons **caraway seed**; mix well.
Cut in . . . . . . ⅛ cup **shortening** until the size of small peas.
Sprinkle . . . . . 3 to 4 tablespoons cold **water** over mixture, stirring with fork until dough clings together. Form into two balls.
Roll out . . . . on floured surface to 10x9-inch rectangles. Cut into 3x1-inch strips. Place on ungreased baking sheets.
Bake . . . . at 450° for 7 to 9 minutes.

*For use with Pillsbury's Best Self-Rising Flour, omit salt.

Cheesy Fiesta Squares

Senior Winner by Mrs. John J. Dutton, Algona, Iowa

Sour cream-herb biscuits with a smoky cheese topping.

BAKE at 450° for 12 to 15 minutes   MAKES 16 biscuits

Sift together . . 2 cups sifted **Pillsbury's Best All Purpose Flour***
          1 teaspoon **soda**
          1 teaspoon double-acting **baking powder** and
          ½ teaspoon **salt** into large mixing bowl.
Combine . . . 1¼ cups **sour cream** (thick or commercial)
          1 tablespoon chopped **pimiento** and
          1 tablespoon chopped **chives** (or 2 teaspoons finely chopped onion and 1 tablespoon minced parsley).

Add to the dry ingredients all at once and mix until all dry particles are moistened.
Roll out . . . . on floured surface to 10-inch square. Cut into sixteen 2½-inch squares. Place on greased baking sheet.
Bake . . . . at 450° for 12 to 15 minutes. Remove from oven; spread with Cheese Topping. Bake 1 to 3 minutes until topping melts and spreads over biscuits. Serve hot.

*For use with Pillsbury's Best Self-Rising Flour, decrease soda to ¼ teaspoon; omit baking powder and salt.

CHEESE TOPPING

Blend together one 5-oz. jar smoky cheese spread, 2 tablespoons sweet or sour cream and 1 teaspoon Worcestershire sauce.

Ham Chutney Canapés

Senior Winner by Mrs. Fred N. Kerwin, Grand Rapids, Michigan

A tantalizing ham, cheese and chutney mixture is spread on light, tender biscuit halves which are then broiled until piping hot and bubbly.

BAKE at 450° for 10 to 12 minutes   MAKES 4 dozen

Sift together . . 2 cups sifted **Pillsbury's Best All Purpose Flour***
          3 teaspoons double-acting **baking powder** and
          1 teaspoon **salt** into large mixing bowl.
Cut in . . . . . . ⅛ cup **shortening** until particles are fine.
Combine . . . . . 1 unbeaten **egg** with **water** to measure ¾ cup. Add to

flour mixture all at once; mix until all dry particles are moistened.

Roll out . . . . on floured surface to ¼-inch thickness. Cut with 2-inch round cutter. Place on ungreased baking sheets.

Bake . . . . at 450° for 10 to 12 minutes. Split in half; spread generously with Ham-Cheese Spread. Broil 2 to 3 minutes until hot and bubbly. Serve warm.

For use with Pillsbury's Best Self-Rising Flour, omit baking powder and salt.

HAM-CHEESE SPREAD

Combine ¼ cup soft butter or margarine, ½ cup shredded Cheddar cheese, 1 teaspoon grated onion, 1 cup ground cooked ham, ¼ cup finely chopped chutney or pickle relish, ⅟₁₆ teaspoon cloves, ¼ cup chopped parsley and ¼ cup cream. Mix thoroughly.

Sausage Snacks

Junior Winner by Phil Hooper, Minneapolis, Minnesota

Tiny sausages are wrapped in a savory biscuit dough, then rolled in grated Parmesan cheese. Bake early in day, then reheat before serving.

BAKE at 400° for 12 to 15 minutes   MAKES about 20 snacks

Sift together . . 1 cup sifted **Pillsbury's Best All Purpose Flour***
  2 teaspoons double-acting **baking powder**
  ½ teaspoon **onion salt**
  ¼ teaspoon **salt** and
  ¼ teaspoon **soda** into mixing bowl.

Cut in . . . . . . ¼ cup **shortening** until particles are fine. Add 1 teaspoon **parsley,** dried or chopped fresh

Add . . . . ⅛ cup **buttermilk** or sour milk; mix until all dry particles are moistened. Knead gently on floured surface 10 strokes.

Sprinkle . . . . . ¼ cup grated **Parmesan cheese** over kneading surface. Roll out dough to rectangle about ⅛ inch thick.

Open . . . . 1 can (9 oz.) **cocktail** or **Vienna sausages**

Cut . . . . rolled dough into squares ½ inch larger than length of sausages. Place a sausage on each square. Moisten edges of dough; wrap around sausage and pinch edges together. Place on greased baking sheet.

Bake . . . . at 400° for 12 to 15 minutes. (Snacks may be made ahead of time and reheated in a 350° oven for 5 minutes before serving.)

For use with Pillsbury's Best Self-Rising Flour, omit baking powder and salt.

Savory Snacks

Senior Winner by Mrs. W. S. Yuin, Freeport, Long Island, New York

These tangy little rolls with a touch of onion flavor go well with appetizers, soups or salads.

BAKE at 450° for 12 to 15 minutes   MAKES about 3 dozen rolls

Sift together . . 2 cups sifted **Pillsbury's Best All Purpose Flour***
  3 teaspoons double-acting **baking powder** and
  1 teaspoon **salt** into large mixing bowl.

Cut in . . . . . ½ cup **shortening** until particles are fine.

Add . . . . ⅔ cup **milk** all at once, mixing until all dry particles are moistened.

Divide . . . . in half. Roll each half on floured surface to a 20x12-inch rectangle. Brush with **butter** and sprinkle each with
  ¼ cup finely chopped **onion** (½ cup in all) and
  3 tablespoons **sesame seeds**.

Roll . . . . as for jelly roll, starting with 20-inch edge. Seal edge well.

Cut . . . . into 1-inch slices. Place on greased baking sheets; flatten slightly. Brush with **egg white** and sprinkle with **sesame seeds.**

Bake . . . . at 450° for 12 to 15 minutes. Serve hot.

For use with Pillsbury's Best Self-Rising Flour, omit baking powder and salt.

Olive Cheese Nuggets

Senior Winner by Mrs. Johnnie H. Williamson, Collins, Mississippi

A tangy cheese dough baked around a stuffed green olive.

BAKE at 400° for 12 to 15 minutes   MAKES 2 to 2½ dozen

Blend together 1 cup (¼ lb.) shredded **Cheddar cheese** and
⠀⠀⠀⠀⠀⠀⠀⠀⠀¼ cup soft **butter** or margarine in mixing bowl.
Sift . . . . ¾ cup sifted **Pillsbury's Best All Purpose Flour***
⠀⠀⠀⠀⠀⠀⠀⠀⠀⅛ teaspoon **salt** and
⠀⠀⠀⠀⠀⠀⠀⠀⠀½ teaspoon **paprika** into cheese mixture. Mix to form
⠀⠀⠀⠀⠀⠀⠀⠀⠀a dough.
Shape . . . . dough by teaspoonfuls around medium-sized **stuffed**
⠀⠀⠀⠀⠀⠀⠀⠀⠀**green olives.** Place on ungreased baking sheets.**
Bake . . . . at 400° for 12 to 15 minutes. Serve hot or cold.
⠀*For use with Pillsbury's Best Self-Rising Flour, omit salt.*
⠀***If desired, refrigerate 4 to 5 hours or overnight before baking.*

Olive Cheese Nuggets

VARIETY QUICK BREADS—Popover batter is
very thin and contains no leavening agent. Popovers
"pop" when liquid in the batter expands to form
steam during baking.

⠀⠀There is no danger of overbeating as in some quick
breads; in fact, popover batter should be beaten
vigorously.

⠀⠀The size of eggs varies during the year; if eggs
seem small, the number should be increased slightly,
perhaps adding one egg for every two in the recipe.

⠀⠀Pour batter into well-greased popover pans, custard cups or muffin pans, filling two-thirds to three-
fourths full.

⠀⠀Leftover cornbread may be reheated and used as
base for à la king toppings.

Cheese Popover Puffs

Senior Winner by Mrs. Nellie Knudson, Brooks, Wisconsin

Serve these peppy cheese popovers piping hot!

BAKE at 425° for 15 minutes, then   MAKES 8 to 10 popovers
⠀⠀⠀at 325° for 25 minutes

Sift together . . 1 cup sifted **Pillsbury's Best All Purpose Flour*** and
⠀⠀⠀⠀⠀⠀⠀⠀⠀½ teaspoon **salt** into mixing bowl.
Combine . . . . . 2 well-beaten **eggs** and
⠀⠀⠀⠀⠀⠀⠀⠀⠀1 cup **milk.** Add to the dry ingredients; beat until
⠀⠀⠀⠀⠀⠀⠀⠀⠀smooth with rotary beater or electric mixer.
Fold in . . . . . . ¼ cup shredded **Cheddar cheese**
Fill . . . . well-greased muffin cups or popover pans two-thirds
⠀⠀⠀⠀⠀⠀⠀⠀⠀full.
Bake . . . . at 425° for 15 minutes, then at 325° for 25 minutes.
⠀⠀⠀⠀⠀⠀⠀⠀⠀Prick with knife during last 5 minutes of baking to
⠀⠀⠀⠀⠀⠀⠀⠀⠀allow for escape of steam. Serve hot.
⠀**Pillsbury's Best Self-Rising Flour is not recommended for use in this recipe.*

Maryland Corn Bread

Senior Winner by Mrs. Lynn S. Strickler, Cantonsville, Maryland

Golden, fluffy corn bread . . . easy to make, and quick. Serve it hot.

BAKE at 400° for 25 to 30 minutes*   MAKES 9x9 or 11x7-inch loaf

Sift together . . 1 cup sifted **Pillsbury's Best All Purpose Flour****
          3 tablespoons **sugar**
          2 teaspoons double-acting **baking powder** and
          1 teaspoon **salt** into mixing bowl. Stir in
          1 cup **corn meal**
Beat . . . . 1 **egg** until light. Add
          1 cup **milk** and
          ¼ cup **shortening**, melted, or salad oil
Add . . . . to the dry ingredients all at once. Stir until all dry particles are moistened.
Pour . . . . into well-greased 9x9x2 or 11x7-inch pan.*
Bake . . . . at 400° for 25 to 30 minutes. Serve hot as bread or as main dish with à la king topping. Place in individual casseroles, top with hot sauce. Sprinkle with shredded cheese and buttered bread crumbs; broil until golden brown.

*Bread may be baked in a skillet on top of range. Pour into hot, well-greased, heavy 10-inch skillet. Cover tightly. Bake over low heat 25 to 30 minutes.
**For use with Pillsbury's Best Self-Rising Flour, omit baking powder and salt.

Creamy Smooth Corn Meal Bake

Senior Winner by Mrs. Wilford B. Isakson, Salt Lake City, Utah

A unique dish with corn bread on the bottom and rich custard on top.

BAKE at 375° for 10 minutes, then   SERVES 8 to 10
     for 45 to 50 minutes

Sift together . ¾ cup sifted **Pillsbury's Best All Purpose Flour***
          2 tablespoons **sugar**
          1½ teaspoons double-acting **baking powder** and
          ¾ teaspoon **salt**. Stir in
          ¾ cup **corn meal**
Beat . . . . ¾ cup **sour cream** (thick or commercial) with
          ⅛ teaspoon **soda** in mixing bowl until well blended.
Blend in . . . . . 2 unbeaten **eggs,** beating well after each.
Add . . . . the dry ingredients gradually, stirring until smooth. Blend in
          1½ cups **milk** gradually.
Melt . . . . 1½ tablespoons **butter** in heavy 10-inch skillet. Pour batter into skillet.
Bake . . . . at 375° for 10 minutes. Pour
          ¾ cup **sweet cream** in center of batter. Bake 45 to 50 minutes or until a knife inserted half way between center and edge comes out clean. Serve warm.

*For use with Pillsbury's Best Self-Rising Flour, decrease baking powder to ½ teaspoon and omit salt.

Maryland Corn Bread

Patio Skillet Bread

Senior Third Prize Winner by Mrs. Dorothy L. Ballard, Denver, Colorado

Cornbread flavored with onions, celery, pimiento and an added touch of sage . . . tasty as a hot bread, main dish or a dressing!

BAKE at 400° for 35 to 45 minutes   MAKES 10-inch round or 9x9-inch loaf

Sift together 1½ cups sifted **Pillsbury's Best All Purpose Flour***
 2 tablespoons **sugar**
 4 teaspoons double-acting **baking powder** and
 2½ teaspoons **salt** into large mixing bowl.
Add . . . . 2 teaspoons **sage**
 1 teaspoon **thyme**
 1½ cups **corn meal**
 1½ cups chopped **onion** (or ⅛ cup instant minced onion
 soaked in ⅛ cup water)
 1½ cups chopped **celery** and
 ¼ cup chopped **pimiento**; stir to blend.
Combine . . . . . 3 beaten **eggs**
 1½ cups **milk** and
 ⅓ cup **shortening**, melted. Add to the dry ingredients;
 stir only until blended.
Pour . . . . into 10 or 11-inch skillet or 9-inch square pan,
 lined with aluminum foil and greased.
Bake . . . . at 400° for 35 to 45 minutes. Serve hot with **butter**
 or as a main dish with a creamed meat or gravy. (May
 be crumbled and used as a poultry dressing.) To
 store, refrigerate.

**For use with Pillsbury's Best Self-Rising Flour, increase flour to 1¾ cups and
decrease baking powder and salt to 1½ teaspoons each.*

Patio Skillet Bread

MAIN DISHES

Don't get into a menu rut! With so many exciting foods and unusual ways of serving them at your finger tips, there is no reason for you to serve the same meals week after week.

On the following pages you will find many recipes that will be excellent to serve to guests, either formal or buffet style. There are recipes for simple economical main dishes using leftover meats . . . perfect for your own family! Many of these are one-dish meals . . . just serve salad and dessert with them.

Try some of these main dish recipes for Saturday and Sunday night suppers, picnics and backyard barbecues.

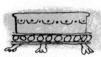   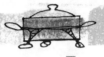 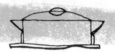 

GENERAL HINTS

- Plan your menus ahead of time, and make your food budget work for you.
- Study the recipe carefully, and prepare as much of it ahead of time as possible; then bake the recipe just before serving.
- Be sure to measure the basic ingredients in the recipe accurately; you can increase and decrease the amount of seasonings, spices and herbs to suit your family's tastes.
- Bake your main dishes in colorful casseroles . . . you can bring them to the table! Store leftovers, if there are any, right in the dish.

- For a "personal touch" to your meal, make individual casseroles or pies.
- For a smooth white sauce or gravy, melt the shortening, then add an equal amount of flour, and blend until smooth before gradually adding the liquid.
- If there is a cream sauce to be served over the main dish, cover pan containing sauce until serving time to prevent a skin layer from forming over top of sauce, and keep warm over hot water.

- For potluck suppers and picnics where your casserole must stay warm for two hours, just wrap it in newspaper immediately after baking.
- For biscuit-topped dishes, cut dough with diamond or doughnut cutters and arrange on hot filling in designs.

- Have ready a supply of bread crumbs in your refrigerator. Dry out leftover bread crusts and slices; roll to fine crumbs with rolling pin.
- Just before serving add a colorful touch to your main dish with fresh parsley, peppers, watercress, pimiento strips, sliced olives, mushrooms, or garnish with some ingredient used in the dish.

- To make smooth, round dumplings, dip the spoon in cold water before dropping each dumpling.
- Pressure saucepans make excellent heavy saucepans for browning meats.

MEAT DISHES

MEAT DISHES—Many of the recipes in this section are naturals for leftover meats. Plan your menu ahead of time and make good use of them.

Wild Rice Turnovers

Senior Winner by Andrew A. Wilson, St. Paul, Minnesota

A pastry turnover with a special filling—wild rice, beef, vegetables.

BAKE at 400° for 25 to 30 minutes   MAKES 8 turnovers

Soak . . . . ⅛ cup **wild rice** in cold **water** to cover, 30 minutes. Drain.

Boil . . . . 4 cups **water** in saucepan; add
2 teaspoons **salt** and the wild rice. Simmer until rice is tender. Drain.

Sauté . . . . ½ pound **ground beef** in
1 tablespoon **shortening** until lightly browned.

Add . . . . ¾ cup chopped **celery**
½ cup chopped **onion**
2 tablespoons chopped **green pepper**
1 cup drained cooked **tomatoes**
¾ cup (7-oz. can) chopped **mushrooms**, drained
1 teaspoon **salt**
⅛ teaspoon **pepper** and the rice. Set aside.

PASTRY

Sift together . . 3 cups sifted **Pillsbury's Best All Purpose Flour*** and
¾ teaspoon **salt** into large mixing bowl.

Cut in . . . . 1 cup **shortening** until the size of small peas.

Sprinkle . . . . . 8 to 9 tablespoons cold **water** over mixture, stirring with a fork until dough is moist enough to hold together.

Divide . . . . dough in half; form into two squares.

Roll out . . . . . . each half on floured surface to a 14-inch square; cut each into four 7-inch squares. Place on ungreased baking sheets. Place about ½ cup filling in center of each. Moisten edges and fold over to form triangle. Seal edges; cut slits in top of each. Brush with **milk** or cream.

Bake . . . . at 400° for 25 to 30 minutes. Meanwhile, sauté
½ cup blanched slivered **almonds** in
2 teaspoons **butter** over medium heat, stirring constantly, until golden brown. Serve turnovers hot with Quick Mushroom Sauce and browned almonds.

For use with Pillsbury's Best Self-Rising Flour, omit salt.

QUICK MUSHROOM SAUCE

Place 2 cans (10½ oz. each) condensed cream of mushroom soup in saucepan; stir until smooth. Gradually blend in 1⅛ cups cold milk, stirring constantly. Heat thoroughly.

Heirloom Meat Pie

Senior Winner by Mrs. A. J. Bofenkamp, Worthington, Minnesota

Serve this ground beef and pork filled pie with a hot vegetable sauce.

BAKE at 425° for 20 to 25 minutes   MAKES 9-inch pie

Prepare . . . . . . recipe for **Two-Crust Pastry**, page 460, using 9-inch pie pan.

Combine . . . . . 1 slightly beaten **egg**
⅛ cup **milk** and
2 tablespoons **water**. Add
½ cup **bread crumbs** (3 slices)

Sauté . . . . 1 pound **ground beef**
          ½ pound lean **ground pork**
          ½ cup sliced **onion** and
          2 tablespoons diced **green pepper** in skillet until meat is lightly browned, stirring occasionally.

Blend in . . . . . ¼ cup **tomato paste** or catsup
          1½ teaspoons **salt**
          ½ teaspoon **cinnamon**
          ¼ teaspoon **nutmeg** and the bread mixture. Turn into pie shell.

Roll out . . . . remaining dough; cut slits. Place over filling; seal and flute.

Bake . . . . at 425° for 20 to 25 minutes. Serve hot with Vegetable Cream Sauce.

VEGETABLE CREAM SAUCE

Melt ¼ cup butter or margarine in saucepan. Blend in ¼ cup Pillsbury's Best All Purpose Flour. Gradually add 2¼ cups milk; cook, stirring constantly, until thickened. Add 1½ teaspoons prepared mustard, 1½ cups cooked vegetables, and salt and pepper to taste. Heat thoroughly.

Pieburgers

Junior First Prize Winner by Karen Kay Folkmier, Battle Creek, Michigan

A pastry dough with cheese and caraway seed, plus a zesty ground beef filling.

BAKE at 425° for 10 to 15 minutes   MAKES 8

Brown lightly . . 1 pound lean **ground beef*** with
          1 package (1½ oz.) **dry onion soup** and
          ½ teaspoon **salt** in skillet. Add
          ⅓ cup **pickle relish** or chopped cucumber pickles and
          2 to 4 tablespoons **chili sauce**. Set aside.

Combine . . . . ½ cup undiluted **evaporated milk** or light cream and
          2 teaspoons **vinegar**

Sift together . . 2 cups sifted **Pillsbury's Best All Purpose Flour**** and
          1 teaspoon **salt** into mixing bowl. Stir in
          2 teaspoons **caraway seed** and
          ½ cup shredded sharp **Cheddar cheese**

Cut in . . . . . . ⅔ cup **shortening** until the size of small peas.

Add . . . . the milk mixture all at once; stir until moistened. Divide in half.**

Shape . . . . one portion into a square on floured surface.

Roll out . . . . to a 12-inch square; cut into four 6-inch squares. Place about ¼ cup of filling in center of each. Moisten edges and fold over to form triangles. Seal edges; prick 2 or 3 times. Place on ungreased baking sheet. Repeat with remaining dough.

Bake . . . . at 425° for 10 to 15 minutes. Serve hot with **chili sauce**.

*Or substitute 1½ pounds hamburger, draining off excess fat as it browns.
**For use with Pillsbury's Best Self-Rising Flour, omit salt and chill pastry.

Pieburgers

Tomato Cheeseburger Pie

Tomato Cheeseburger Pie

Junior Third Prize Winner by Trudy Roelle, Peetz, Colorado

Saturday night news! All the gang will love this variation.

BAKE at 400° for 20 to 25 minutes   MAKES 8 or 9-inch pie

Soak . . . . 2 teaspoons instant **minced onion** in
    ¼ cup cold **water**

Sift together . . 1 cup sifted **Pillsbury's Best All Purpose Flour*** and
    ½ teaspoon **salt** into mixing bowl.

Cut in . . . . . . ⅓ cup **shortening** until the size of small peas.

Sprinkle with . . 3 to 4 tablespoons of the onion-water mixture, stirring
    with a fork until dough is moist enough to hold
    together.

Form . . . . into a ball.

Roll out . . . . on floured surface to a circle 1½ inches larger than
    inverted 8 or 9-inch pie pan. Fit into pan. Fold edge
    to form a rim; flute.

**For use with Pillsbury's Best Self-Rising Flour, omit salt; decrease baking time to 15 to 20 minutes.*

HAMBURGER FILLING

Combine . . . . ¼ cup **catsup**
    2 teaspoons instant **minced onion**
    1 teaspoon **salt**
    ½ teaspoon **sweet basil**
    ¼ teaspoon **marjoram** and
    ⅛ teaspoon **pepper**

Brown . . . . 1 pound **ground beef** until it loses red color. Remove
    from heat.

Stir in . . . . 1 cup shredded **Cheddar** or **American cheese**
    1 beaten **egg**
    ½ cup **bread crumbs** and the catsup mixture.

Turn . . . . into pie shell.

Top with . . . . 6 fresh **tomato slices** (or 3 well-drained canned toma-
    toes, cut into halves)

Bake . . . . at 400° for 20 to 25 minutes. Top with
    6 wedge-shaped slices **Cheddar** or **American cheese**.
    Bake 1 minute longer. Serve hot.

Golden Nugget Meat Balls

Senior Winner by Mrs. Roland W. Giese, Loganville, Wisconsin

They'll remind you of cheeseburgers! Meat balls with cheese inside them are wrapped in biscuit dough, then baked.

BAKE at 450° for 15 to 20 minutes   SERVES 8

Combine . . . . . 1 slightly beaten **egg**
    ½ pound lean **ground beef**
    ¼ cup **bread crumbs**

½ teaspoon **salt** and
½ teaspoon **Worcestershire sauce**

Form . . . . into eight balls, enclosing a 1x1x¼-inch slice of **cheese** in each. Brown on all sides in
2 tablespoons **shortening**

Sift together 2¼ cups sifted **Pillsbury's Best All Purpose Flour*** and
4 teaspoons double-acting **baking powder**

Cut in . . . . . . ½ cup **shortening** until particles are fine.

Add . . . . 1 can (10½ oz.) **condensed cream of mushroom soup;** stir until dough clings together. Knead on floured surface for a few seconds.

Roll out . . . . to a 12-inch square. Cut into 3-inch squares.

Place . . . . meatballs in center of half the squares. Top with remaining squares. Seal edges; prick tops. Place on ungreased baking sheet.

Bake . . . . at 450° for 15 to 20 minutes. Serve hot with **tomato sauce** or **catsup.**

For use with Pillsbury's Best Self-Rising Flour, omit baking powder.

Yorkshire Burger

Junior Third Prize Winner by Paul C. Kellogg, Milwaukee, Wisconsin

Savory meat balls in custard-like pudding. Serve man-size portions.

BAKE at 350° for 50 to 60 minutes   SERVES 8 to 10

Combine . . . 1½ pounds **ground beef**
¼ cup **chili sauce**
1 package (1½ oz.) **dry onion soup**
2 tablespoons chopped **parsley**
¼ teaspoon **pepper** and
¼ teaspoon **poultry seasoning** in mixing bowl.

Blend . . . . 1 slightly beaten **egg** with
1 tablespoon **water.** Stir into meat mixture.

Form . . . . into 24 small meat balls. Place in well-greased 12x8x2-inch baking dish.

Sift together 1½ cups sifted **Pillsbury's Best All Purpose Flour***
1½ teaspoons double-acting **baking powder** and
1 teaspoon **salt**

Beat . . . . 4 **eggs** until foamy. Blend in
1½ cups **milk** and
3 tablespoons **butter,** melted

Add . . . . the dry ingredients all at once to egg mixture. Beat with rotary beater (or low speed on mixer) just until smooth. Pour over meat balls.

Bake . . . . at 350° for 50 to 60 minutes. Serve hot with Beef Gravy.

For use with Pillsbury's Best Self-Rising Flour, omit baking powder and salt.

BEEF GRAVY

Melt ¼ cup shortening or butter in saucepan. Blend in 3 tablespoons flour and 1 tablespoon beef extract. Add 2½ cups milk. Cook, stirring occasionally, until thickened.

Yorkshire Burger

Beef Tidbits

Senior Winner by Mrs. Morton M. Rayman, Chicago, Illinois

Hot and tasty . . . canapé treats! Rich, tender cream cheese pastry with a meat filling. Use your favorite meat sauce as a dip.

BAKE at 450° for 14 to 16 minutes   MAKES about 2½ dozen

Sift together . .1 cup sifted **Pillsbury's Best All Purpose Flour*** and
½ teaspoon **salt** into mixing bowl.

Cut in . . . . . .¼ cup **shortening** and
⅓ cup (3-oz. pkg.) **cream cheese** until the size of small peas.

Sprinkle . . . . .2 to 3 tablespoons cold **water** over mixture, stirring with a fork until dough is moist enough to hold together. Form into ball and chill at least 2 hours.

*For use with Pillsbury's Best Self-Rising Flour, omit salt.

MEAT FILLING

Sauté . . . . .in skillet
2 tablespoons finely chopped **onion** and
2 tablespoons finely chopped **green pepper** in
1 tablespoon **shortening** until tender.

Add . . . . .½ pound lean **ground beef;** cook only until red color disappears. Remove from heat. Stir in
¼ teaspoon **salt**
¼ teaspoon **seasoned salt**
⅛ teaspoon **monosodium glutamate**
1/16 teaspoon **pepper**
¼ teaspoon **Worcestershire sauce** and
2 tablespoons **chili sauce**

Roll out . . . . . . .half of dough on floured surface to a 15x6-inch rectangle. Spread with half of Filling. Roll as for jelly roll, starting with 15-inch side. Seal edges; place on ungreased baking sheet. Repeat with remaining dough.

Bake . . . . .at 450° for 14 to 16 minutes. Cut into 1-inch slices; serve hot.

Man-Cooked Meal

Senior Winner by Houston James Newman, St. Louis, Missouri

This meal-in-one has man appeal. It abounds in hearty flavor.

BAKE at 425° for 30 to 35 minutes   SERVES 6

Melt . . . . .2 tablespoons **shortening** in large skillet.

Add . . . . .⅓ cup chopped **celery**
⅓ cup chopped **green pepper**
½ cup chopped **onion**
1 clove **garlic,** finely chopped, and
1½ pounds **ground beef;** brown well.

Stir in . . . . . . .1 cup cooked **rice** (or 2 medium potatoes, boiled and diced)
2 cups (two 8-oz. cans) **tomato sauce**
2 teaspoons **chili powder**
1½ teaspoons **salt** and
⅛ teaspoon **pepper;** simmer while mixing topping.

Sift together . .1 cup sifted **Pillsbury's Best All Purpose Flour***
2 teaspoons double-acting **baking powder**
1 teaspoon **salt**
1 teaspoon **sugar** and
½ teaspoon **soda** into mixing bowl. Stir in
¾ cup yellow **corn meal**

Combine . . . . .1 cup **buttermilk** or sour milk
¼ cup **shortening,** melted, and
2 well-beaten **eggs.** Add all at once to the dry ingredients; stir until all dry particles are moistened.

Spread . . . . .meat mixture in 9x9x2-inch pan. Cover with batter.

Bake . . . . .at 425° for 30 to 35 minutes. Serve hot.

*For use with Pillsbury's Best Self-Rising Flour, omit baking powder and salt in topping.

Baked-In Beefburgers

Senior Winner by Mrs. Malcolm R. Wilson, Manchester, Connecticut

Tomato biscuits with meat rolled up inside. Economical and easy.

BAKE at 375° for 30 to 35 minutes   SERVES 6 to 8

Brown . . . . 1 pound **ground beef** (use 2 tablespoons shortening
          with lean ground beef)
          ¾ cup finely chopped **onion** and
          ½ cup diced **celery** lightly in skillet.

Add . . . . ⅓ cup **tomato sauce**
          1 teaspoon **salt** and
          ¼ teaspoon **pepper.** Cook, stirring occasionally, until
          thickened. Cool.

Sift together . . 2 cups sifted **Pillsbury's Best All Purpose Flour***
          3 teaspoons double-acting **baking powder**
          1 teaspoon **salt**
          ½ teaspoon **sage** and
          ⅛ teaspoon **marjoram** into large mixing bowl.

Cut in . . . . . . ¼ cup **shortening** until particles are fine.

Combine . . . . ½ cup **tomato sauce** and **water** to measure ¾ cup.
          Add to dry particles; stir until dough clings together.
          Knead gently on floured surface 12 to 15 strokes.

Roll out . . . . to a 12x9-inch rectangle. Spread with meat mixture.
          Roll as for jelly roll, starting with 9-inch edge. Seal
          edges; place on greased baking sheet.

Bake . . . . at 375° for 30 to 35 minutes.

Serve with . . . . . sauce made by heating
          1 can (10½ oz.) **condensed cream of mushroom soup**
          and
          ½ cup **milk** just to boiling.

*For use with Pillsbury's Best Self-Rising Flour, omit baking powder and salt
in biscuits.*

American Piece-a-Pie

Junior Winner by Jamie Marie Chisam, Oak Park, Illinois

*Peppy hamburger mixture and grated sharp cheese baked on top crisp
yeast dough flavored with tomato sauce and chili powder.*

BAKE at 425° for 15 to 18 minutes   SERVES 6

Soften . . . . 1 packet active dry **yeast** (or 1 cake compressed) in
          ¼ cup warm **water**

Add . . . . 1 unbeaten **egg**
          1 tablespoon **sugar**
          ¼ cup **tomato sauce** (¼ of 8-oz. can)
          3 tablespoons **shortening,** melted
          1 teaspoon **salt*** and
          ½ teaspoon **chili powder.** Blend thoroughly.

Add . . . . 2 to 2¼ cups sifted **Pillsbury's Best All Purpose Flour***
          gradually, blending thoroughly after each addition.

Knead . . . . on floured surface until smooth and satiny, 2 to 3
          minutes. Place in greased bowl and cover.

Let rise . . . . in warm place (85°) until light, about 1 hour. Mean-
          while prepare Hamburger Topping.

Pat . . . . or roll out dough to 14x9-inch rectangle on greased
          baking sheet. Brush with melted **butter.** Spread with
          Topping. Sprinkle with
          2 cups shredded **American cheese** or other sharp
          cheese

Bake . . . . at 425° for 15 to 18 minutes. Serve hot.

For use with Pillsbury's Best Self-Rising Flour, omit salt.

HAMBURGER TOPPING

Sauté . . . . ½ pound **ground beef** and
          ¼ cup chopped **onion** in skillet until meat loses red
          color. Drain off excess fat.

Stir in . . . . . . ¾ cup **tomato sauce** (remainder of can)
          ¼ to ½ teaspoon **chili powder**
          ½ teaspoon **salt** and
          ⅛ teaspoon **pepper**

Funny-Face Hamburgers

Funny-Face Hamburgers

Junior Third Prize Winner by Barbara Maddock, Los Angeles, California

*These hamburgers baked in buns are fun to make and fun to eat.
Easy to make ahead of time.*

BAKE at 400° for 12 to 15 minutes   MAKES 12 to 16

Dissolve . . . . . 1 packet active dry **yeast** (or 1 cake compressed) in
       ½ cup warm **water**

Combine . . . . ¼ cup **shortening**
       2 tablespoons **sugar**
       2 teaspoons **salt*** and
       ¾ cup hot scalded **milk.** Cool to lukewarm.

Blend in . . . . . 1 unbeaten **egg** and softened yeast.

Add . . . . 4 to 4½ cups sifted **Pillsbury's Best All Purpose Flour***
       to form a stiff dough. Knead dough on floured
       surface until smooth.

Roll out . . . . to ¼-inch thickness. Cut with 3-inch round cutter.
       Brush centers with melted **butter.**

Place . . . . 2 tablespoons Hamburger Filling in center of half of
       rounds. Top with remaining rounds; seal edges.
       Brush with **milk.** Cut gashes as eyes and mouth.

Combine . . . . ¼ cup **bread crumbs** (1 slice)
       2 tablespoons **brown sugar**
       1 teaspoon **cinnamon** and
       1 tablespoon **milk.** Shape mixture over one-third of
       bun for hair. (Or use ½ teaspoon shredded-type
       cereal for each.) Cut halves of **raisins** for eyes. Use
       small wedges of **tomato** or pimiento for mouth,
       making "faces." Place on ungreased baking sheet.

Let rise . . . . in warm place (85°) until doubled, about 45 minutes.

Bake . . . . at 400° for 12 to 15 minutes. Serve hot.

For use with Pillsbury's Best Self-Rising Flour, omit salt.

HAMBURGER FILLING

Brown . . . . . 1½ pounds **ground beef** and
       2 tablespoons chopped **onion** in
       2 tablespoons **shortening**

Add . . . . ⅓ cup chopped **parsley**
       ¼ cup grated **carrot**
       ¼ cup **catsup**
       3 tablespoons **flour**
       2 teaspoons **salt** and
       ¼ teaspoon **pepper;** cook 5 minutes, stirring constantly.
       Cool slightly.

Main-Dish Popovers

Senior Winner by Mrs. Wirt Downing, East St. Louis, Illinois

These popovers really pop! Split them hot from the oven, and serve with a meat-vegetable sauce.

BAKE at 425° for 15 minutes, then   SERVES 6 to 8
      at 325° for 30 to 35 minutes

Sift together . . 1 cup sifted **Pillsbury's Best All Purpose Flour*** and
           1 teaspoon **salt**
Combine . . . . . 3 well-beaten **eggs**
           1 cup **milk** and
           1 tablespoon **butter,** melted, in mixing bowl.
Blend in . . . . the dry ingredients gradually; beat well.
Fill . . . . well-greased muffin or popover pans two-thirds full.
Bake . . . . at 425° for 15 minutes. Decrease oven temperature to 325° and bake 30 to 35 minutes. Prick each with sharp knife and top with a 2-inch square of **cheese.** Heat 2 to 5 minutes until cheese melts. Split; serve with hot Vegetable-Meat Filling.

*Pillsbury's Best Self-Rising Flour is not recommended for use in this recipe.

VEGETABLE-MEAT FILLING

Sauté . . . . 1 pound **ground beef**
           2 tablespoons chopped **green pepper** and
           2 tablespoons chopped **onion** in skillet.
Blend in . . . . . 2 tablespoons **flour**
Add . . . . 1 can (10½ oz.) **condensed tomato soup**
           ½ cup finely diced **celery**
           ½ cup finely diced **carrots**
           ½ teaspoon **chili powder** and
           1 teaspoon **salt.** Cover and simmer 20 minutes.

Waffle Enchiladas

Junior Winner by David Ratzlaff, Wayne, Nebraska

Bake crisp corn meal waffles, fold them over like a sandwich, and serve a peppy meat sauce inside.

BAKE at medium heat for 5 to 7 minutes   SERVES 6

Sift together 1½ cups sifted **Pillsbury's Best All Purpose Flour***
           3 teaspoons double-acting **baking powder** and
           1½ teaspoons **salt** into mixing bowl. Stir in
           1 cup yellow **corn meal**
Combine . . . . . 3 slightly beaten **eggs**
           2 cups **milk** and
           ¾ cup **shortening,** melted. Add to the dry ingredients all at once; beat just until smooth.
Bake . . . . in preheated waffle iron at medium heat. Keep warm in oven until serving time. Serve waffles sandwich-style with hot Meat Filling between and on top. Sprinkle with **Parmesan cheese.**

*For use with Pillsbury's Best Self-Rising Flour, omit baking powder and salt.

MEAT FILLING

Brown . . . . 1 pound **ground beef** in
           1 tablespoon **shortening**
Add . . . . ½ cup chopped **onion**
           ½ cup chopped **green pepper**
           2 cups (No. 303 can) **tomatoes**
           1 cup (8-oz. can) **tomato sauce**
           1 teaspoon **chili powder**
           1 teaspoon **salt** and
           1 teaspoon **Worcestershire sauce.** Simmer for 1 hour, stirring occasionally.

Hot Ziggities

Junior Second Prize Winner by Jack Meili, Minneapolis, Minnesota

Ground wieners and a bit of mustard are inside a pastry jacket made with a dash of catsup. Try it with luncheon meat, too!

BAKE at 425° for 15 to 20 minutes   MAKES 8

Grind . . . . 1 pound **wieners;** blend in
       2 tablespoons **prepared mustard** and
       1 slightly beaten **egg.** Set aside.
Sift together . . 2 cups sifted **Pillsbury's Best All Purpose Flour*** and
       ½ teaspoon **salt** into mixing bowl.
Cut in . . . . . . ⅔ cup **shortening** until the size of small peas.
Combine . . . . ¼ cup **catsup** and
       3 tablespoons cold **water;** sprinkle over flour mixture, stirring with fork until dough is moist enough to hold together.
Divide . . . . dough in half. Roll out each half on floured surface to a 12x9-inch rectangle. Cut each into four 6x4½-inch rectangles.
Place . . . . meat mixture on rectangles. Fold over pastry so that 4½-inch edges are together; seal edges. Place on ungreased baking sheet.
Bake . . . . at 425° for 15 to 20 minutes. Serve hot.

*For use with Pillsbury's Best Self-Rising Flour, omit salt.

Chili Cheese Surprise

Senior Winner by Mrs. L. S. George, Cleburne, Texas

This ''stay-high'' cheese soufflé is baked on top of a chili-meat filling.

BAKE at 350° for 50 to 60 minutes   SERVES 4 to 6

Melt . . . . 3 tablespoons **shortening** in skillet.
Add . . . . ¼ cup chopped **onion**
       1 pound lean **ground beef**

       3 tablespoons **flour**
       1 teaspoon **salt** and
       1 teaspoon **chili powder;** brown well. Turn into ungreased 2-quart casserole.
Combine . . . . ⅓ cup **shortening,** melted
       ⅓ cup **Pillsbury's Best All Purpose Flour***
       1 teaspoon **salt**
       1 teaspoon **chili powder,** if desired, and
       ⅛ teaspoon **paprika** in saucepan.
Blend in . . . . 1½ cups **milk;** cook, stirring constantly, until thick.
Add . . . . 2 cups shredded **American cheese;** stir until melted. Remove from heat.
Blend . . . . a little of the hot mixture into
       4 slightly beaten **egg yolks.** Add to hot mixture; blend well.
Beat . . . . 4 **egg whites** until straight peaks form.
Fold . . . . cheese mixture into beaten egg whites. Pour over meat mixture in casserole.
Bake . . . . in pan of hot water at 350° for 50 to 60 minutes. Serve immediately.

*For use with Pillsbury's Best Self-Rising Flour, decrease salt in soufflé to ½ teaspoon.

Apple Lamb Casserole

Senior Winner by Mrs. Jamile Nahabedian, Brooklyn, New York

From Turkey . . . lamb flavored with apples and herbs, topped with tender egg biscuits delicately flavored with curry.

BAKE at 425° for 12 to 15 minutes   SERVES 4 to 6

Melt . . . . 2 tablespoons **shortening** in large skillet.
Add . . . . 1 pound cubed boneless **lamb shoulder.** Sprinkle with
       2 tablespoons **flour;** stir to coat. Brown well.
Stir in . . . . . . 2 cups **water**
       1 large **bay leaf**

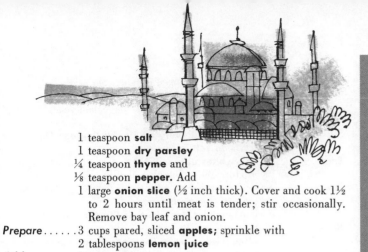

1 teaspoon **salt**
1 teaspoon **dry parsley**
¼ teaspoon **thyme** and
⅛ teaspoon **pepper.** Add
1 large **onion slice** (½ inch thick). Cover and cook 1½ to 2 hours until meat is tender; stir occasionally. Remove bay leaf and onion.

Prepare . . . . . . 3 cups pared, sliced **apples;** sprinkle with
2 tablespoons **lemon juice**

Add . . . . 1 cup **water**
2 to 4 tablespoons **sugar** and apples to meat mixture. Cook, stirring occasionally, until apples are tender, 15 to 20 minutes.

Turn . . . . into a 1½-quart casserole; top the hot mixture with Biscuit Topping.

Bake . . . . at 425° for 12 to 15 minutes.

BISCUIT TOPPING

Sift together 1½ cups sifted **Pillsbury's Best All Purpose Flour***
2 teaspoons double-acting **baking powder**
½ teaspoon **salt** and
⅛ teaspoon **curry powder** into mixing bowl.

Cut in . . . . . . ¼ cup **shortening** until particles are fine.

Combine . . . . . 1 unbeaten **egg**
3 tablespoons **milk** and
2 tablespoons **applesauce** (or omit applesauce and increase milk to ⅓ cup). Add to the dry ingredients; stir until dough clings together. Knead on floured surface 10 strokes.

Roll out . . . . to ½-inch thickness. Cut with 2-inch round cutter.

For use with Pillsbury's Best Self-Rising Flour, omit baking powder and salt in biscuits.

Top Hat Veal Pie

Senior Winner by Mrs. William Haeckel, Los Angeles, California

A ground veal filling with herbs and spices is baked in a tender crust . . . the "top hat" is a fluffy cheese soufflé.

BAKE at 425° for 15 minutes, then   MAKES 9-inch pie
at 375° for 20 to 25 minutes

Prepare . . . . . . recipe for **One-Crust Pastry,** page 460, using 9-inch pie pan. Do not prick crust; fill and bake as directed below.

Brown . . . . 1 medium **onion,** chopped fine, in
2 tablespoons **shortening** in large skillet.

Add . . . . 1½ pounds **ground veal** and
2 to 3 **bay leaves.** Cook, stirring occasionally, until lightly browned.

Stir in . . . . 2 cups **water;** bring to boil. Cover and simmer over low heat 45 minutes. Remove bay leaves; cook uncovered 15 minutes longer.

Combine . . . . . 1 beaten **egg**
1 tablespoon **flour**
1 tablespoon minced **parsley**
⅛ teaspoon **pepper**
⅛ teaspoon **thyme** and
1⁄16 teaspoon **ginger.** Add to the veal mixture; cook and stir until thickened. Add
1 to 1½ teaspoons **salt.** Turn into pie shell.

Bake . . . . at 425° for 15 minutes. Meanwhile prepare Cheese Soufflé; spread over pie, sealing to edge. Decrease oven temperature to 375°; bake for 20 to 25 minutes.

CHEESE SOUFFLÉ

Melt 2 tablespoons butter in saucepan. Blend in 2 tablespoons flour. Add ½ cup milk; cook and stir over medium heat until thickened. Blend in 1 cup (¼ lb.) shredded Cheddar cheese; stir until smooth. Remove from heat. Blend in 2 slightly beaten egg yolks. Beat 2 egg whites until straight peaks form. Fold in cheese mixture.

Veal Good Pie

Veal Good Pie

Senior Winner by Mrs. Cana Perisich, Wadsworth, Ohio

Delicately-seasoned ground veal between layers of soufflé . . . a garnish of cheese is the finishing touch.

BAKE at 400° for 10 minutes, then   SERVES 4 to 6
  for 10 to 15 minutes

Sauté . . . . . . .1 cup finely chopped **onions** (2 medium) in
    1 tablespoon **shortening** in large skillet.
Add . . . . .1 pound **ground veal** and
    1 tablespoon **flour;** cook until tender.
Stir in . . . . . . .1 cup **milk**
    1 teaspoon **salt** and
    1/16 teaspoon **pepper.** Simmer until thick, about 15

minutes. Stir in
  2 tablespoons chopped **parsley.** Set aside.
Blend . . . . . . .3 unbeaten **egg yolks** and
    1 cup **sour cream** (thick or commercial) in large
    mixing bowl; beat well.
Stir in . . . . . .2/3 cup sifted **Pillsbury's Best All Purpose Flour*** and
    1/2 teaspoon **salt**
Beat . . . . .3 **egg whites** until stiff but not dry; fold into egg-yolk
    mixture gently but thoroughly.
Pour . . . . .half of the egg mixture into well-greased 9-inch
    pie pan. Top with
    3/4 cup shredded **American** or **Cheddar cheese**
Bake . . . . .at 400° for 10 minutes. Remove from oven and
    place veal mixture on top. Pour remaining egg
    mixture over veal. Bake 10 to 15 minutes. Top with
    3/4 cup shredded **cheese.** Serve hot with **sour cream**.

*Pillsbury's Best Self-Rising Flour may be substituted.

Hearty Ham Corncake

Senior Winner by Mrs. Vaneta F. Hartman, Casey, Illinois

This corncake is baked in a ring and served with celery cream sauce.

BAKE at 400° for 25 to 30 minutes   SERVES 6

Sift together . .1 cup sifted **Pillsbury's Best All Purpose Flour***
    2 teaspoons double-acting **baking powder**
    1 teaspoon **celery salt** and
    1/2 teaspoon **soda** into mixing bowl. Stir in
    1 cup **corn meal**
Combine . . . . .2 well-beaten **eggs**
    1 cup **buttermilk** or sour milk and
    1/3 cup **shortening,** melted. Add to the dry ingredients
    all at once; mix only until all dry particles are
    moistened.
Add . . . . . . .1 1/2 cups ground **ham** to one cup of the corn meal

mixture. Spread in bottom of well-greased 9-inch ring mold.

Cover . . . . with remaining corn meal mixture.

Bake . . . . at 400° for 25 to 30 minutes. Serve hot with Celery Cream Sauce or your favorite vegetable sauce.

For use with Pillsbury's Best Self-Rising Flour, omit baking powder; decrease celery salt to ½ teaspoon and soda to ¼ teaspoon.

CELERY CREAM SAUCE

Combine in saucepan 1 can (10½ oz.) condensed cream of celery soup, ½ cup milk and 1 teaspoon chopped parsley. Heat thoroughly.

Ham-Somes

Senior Winner by Mrs. Arel W. Berrier, Daly City, California

Leftover ham? Try caraway biscuit pinwheels—with zippy ham filling and golden cheese sauce.

BAKE at 425° for 20 to 25 minutes   SERVES 8

Sift together . . 2 cups sifted **Pillsbury's Best All Purpose Flour***
3½ teaspoons double-acting **baking powder**
2 teaspoons **sugar** and
½ teaspoon **salt** into mixing bowl.

Cut in . . . . . . ½ cup **shortening** until particles are fine.

Stir in . . . . 2 teaspoons **caraway seed**

Combine . . . . . 1 unbeaten **egg** and **milk** to measure ⅔ cup. Add to the dry ingredients all at once; stir until dough clings together. Knead on floured surface 10 strokes. Roll out to a 12x10-inch rectangle.

For use with Pillsbury's Best Self-Rising Flour, omit baking powder and salt.

HAM FILLING

Combine . . . . . 1 well-beaten **egg**
2½ cups ground **ham**
1 medium **onion**, ground

Ham-Somes

2 tablespoons chopped **parsley**
1 tablespoon **prepared horse-radish**
2 teaspoons **prepared mustard** and
⅛ teaspoon **cayenne pepper**; mix well.

Spread . . . . over dough. Roll as for jelly roll, starting with 12-inch side; cut into 8 slices. Place cut-side down on ungreased baking sheet.

Bake . . . . at 425° for 20 to 25 minutes. Serve hot with Cheese Sauce. Garnish with **parsley**.

CHEESE SAUCE

Melt 3 tablespoons butter in saucepan over low heat. Blend in 3 tablespoons flour. Gradually add 2 cups milk; cook, stirring constantly, until thick. Add 1 cup shredded Cheddar cheese, 2 teaspoons Worcestershire sauce and salt to taste; cook until cheese melts.

Parmesan Puff Chops

Senior Winner by Mrs. Sara F. Reaves, Gadsden, Alabama

Savory Parmesan cheese and onion puffs baked atop browned pork chops.

BAKE at 350° for about 1 hour   SERVES 4

Brown . . . . . . .4 **pork chops** quickly on one side only in heavy 10-inch
skillet; drain off fat. Turn chops brown-side up.

Sift together . ½ cup sifted **Pillsbury's Best All Purpose Flour*** and
½ teaspoon double-acting **baking powder**

Melt . . . . .2 tablespoons **shortening.** Blend in the flour mixture.

Add . . . . .⅔ cup **milk** gradually. Cook over medium heat, stirring
constantly, until very thick. Remove from heat.

Blend in . . . . .2 unbeaten **eggs.** Cook over low heat, beating hard,
until very thick. Remove from heat.

Add . . . . .⅓ cup grated **Parmesan cheese**
2 tablespoons grated **onion**
½ teaspoon **salt*** and

¼ teaspoon **pepper;** blend thoroughly. Cover chops with
cheese batter. Sprinkle with **paprika.**

Bake . . . . .at 350° for about 1 hour.

*For use with Pillsbury's Best Self-Rising Flour, omit baking powder and salt.

Picnic Basket Bunwich

Senior Winner by Mrs. William E. Brebner, Des Moines, Iowa

A tangy ham and olive filling is baked inside these buns.

BAKE at 400° for 15 to 20 minutes   MAKES 1 dozen

Soften . . . . . . .1 packet active dry **yeast** (or 1 cake compressed) in
¼ cup warm **water**

Combine . . . .¼ cup **shortening**
1 tablespoon **sugar**
1 teaspoon **salt*** and
¾ cup hot scalded **milk** in large mixing bowl. Cool to
lukewarm. Add softened yeast.

Add . . . . . . .2½ to 2¾ cups sifted **Pillsbury's Best All Purpose Flour***
gradually to form a stiff dough.

Knead . . . . .on floured surface until smooth and satiny, 3 to 5
minutes.

Roll out . . . . . . .to an 18x12-inch rectangle. Cut into 3-inch squares;
brush centers with melted **butter.**

Place . . . . .2 tablespoonfuls Ham Filling in center of 12 squares;
top with remaining squares. Seal edges; prick tops.
Brush with **cream.** Place on greased baking sheet.

Let rise . . . . . . .in warm place (85°) until light, about 45 minutes.

Bake . . . . .at 400° for 15 to 20 minutes. Serve hot.

*For use with Pillsbury's Best Self-Rising Flour, omit salt.

HAM FILLING

Combine 3 cups (1 lb.) ground cooked ham, 2 tablespoons chopped
stuffed olives, 2 teaspoons prepared mustard, 1 well-beaten egg and
¼ cup cream. Mix well.

Picnic Basket Bunwich

MEAT and VEGETABLE DISHES

—Your meal is complete . . . right in one dish! Remember that the dish you bake in may go to the table, so select your prettiest. And you can dress up any dish with a garnish. Serve with salad, and add a dessert for the finishing touch.

One-Step Beef Pie

Bride Winner by Mrs. Joan Taraba, Chicago, Illinois

Meat 'n' potatoes with vegetables too . . . a flaky crust on a deep-dish pie for a wholesome meal.

BAKE at 400° for 30 minutes, then   SERVES 8
    at 350° for 1½ to 2 hours

Sift together . . 3 cups sifted **Pillsbury's Best All Purpose Flour*** and 1½ teaspoons **salt** into large mixing bowl.

Cut in . . . . 1 cup **shortening** until the size of small peas.

Sprinkle . . . . . ⅔ to ¾ cup **water** over mixture, stirring with fork until dough is moist enough to hold together.

Divide . . . . dough into two portions, one twice as large as the other.

Roll out . . . . larger portion on floured surface to fit 12x8x2-inch baking dish or 3-quart casserole; fit into baking dish.

For use with Pillsbury's Best Self-Rising Flour, omit salt; decrease water to 7 to 8 tablespoons.

MEAT 'N' VEGETABLE FILLING

Place . . . . . . 1½ pounds **round steak** (cut into 1-inch pieces) in bottom of pastry-lined dish.

Top with . . . . . 3 medium **onions,** sliced
    3 cups sliced **potatoes** and
    1½ cups diced **carrots**

Blend . . . . . . 1½ cups **water** with
    3 tablespoons **flour**
    2 teaspoons **salt**
    ½ teaspoon **pot herbs**
    ⅛ teaspoon **pepper**
    1½ teaspoons **meat extract** and
    1 teaspoon **Worcestershire sauce.** Pour over meat and vegetables.

Roll out . . . . remaining dough to fit top of baking dish; cut slits. Place over filling; seal and flute.

Bake . . . . at 400° for 30 minutes, then at 350° for 1½ to 2 hours until meat is tender.

One-Step Beef Pie

Deauville Dumplings with Beef Stew

Best of Class Winner by Mrs. Joseph F. Maley, Osborn, Ohio

Currants and onion are an unusual combination. And what fresh, original flavor they add to these prize dumplings!

STEAM for 20 minutes   SERVES 8 to 10

Prepare . . . . Beef Stew (or your favorite chicken stew).
Sift together . . 1 cup sifted **Pillsbury's Best All Purpose Flour***
           2 teaspoons double-acting **baking powder** and
           1 teaspoon **salt** into mixing bowl.
Cut in . . . . 1 tablespoon **butter** or margarine
Stir in . . . . . . ½ cup dried **currants** and
           ½ cup fine, dry **bread crumbs**
Combine . . . . . 1 well-beaten **egg**
           ⅔ cup **milk** and
           2 teaspoons grated **onion**. Add all at once to the dry ingredients; stir only until all dry particles are moistened.
Dip . . . . a tablespoon into cold water. Drop batter from spoon onto hot stew. Cover tightly.
Steam . . . . for 20 minutes. Serve immediately.
*For use with Pillsbury's Best Self-Rising Flour, omit baking powder and salt.

BEEF STEW

Brown 2 pounds cubed beef in 2 tablespoons shortening in large skillet or kettle. Stir in 6 cups boiling water, 1 teaspoon lemon juice, 2 onions, sliced, and 1 tablespoon salt. Cover and simmer 2 hours until meat is tender, stirring occasionally. Add 6 small whole carrots and 6 potatoes, cut into pieces. Cook 15 to 20 minutes until vegetables are almost tender. Blend together ½ cup sifted Pillsbury's Best All Purpose Flour and ½ cup cold water. Add to hot stew; stir constantly until thickened. Add 1 package frozen peas. Heat to boiling.

Deauville Dumplings with Beef Stew

Pork and 'Tater Pie

Senior Winner by Mrs. Loretta Secret, Monrovia, California

A new version of the typical English pork pie.

BAKE at 400° for 40 to 50 minutes   SERVES 4 to 6

Prepare . . . . recipe for **Two-Crust Pastry**, page 460, using 9-inch pie pan.
Cook . . . . 1 pound **ground pork*** in skillet until well browned. Drain off excess fat.
Add . . . . 2 cups diced cooked **potatoes**
           1 teaspoon **salt**
           ½ teaspoon **savory**
           ¼ teaspoon **sage**
           ⅛ teaspoon **cinnamon**
           ⅛ teaspoon **cloves**
           ⅛ teaspoon **pepper** and
           ½ cup **water****; mix well. Turn into pie shell.

Roll out . . . . remaining dough; cut slits. Moisten rim of bottom
crust. Place top crust over filling. Fold edge under
bottom crust; press to seal. Flute.

Bake . . . . at 400° for 40 to 50 minutes.

If desired, use 2 cups leftover cooked pork, diced. Increase liquid to ¾ cup.

**If desired, substitute 1 cup vegetable liquid for water and add 2 cups drained,
cooked vegetables.*

Teen Bean Bake

Junior Third Prize Winner by Barbara Maley, Shelby, Ohio

*Juicy frankfurters, canned baked beans and catsup sauce are com-
bined, then baked with an onion-flavored corn bread topping.*

BAKE at 400° for 35 to 40 minutes   SERVES 8 to 10

Combine . . . . ½ pound **frankfurters,** cut in ½-inch pieces
            3½ cups (two 1-lb. cans) **baked beans**
            ½ cup **catsup***
            ½ cup **water** and
            1 tablespoon **prepared mustard** in 12x8x2-inch baking
                dish.

Sift together . ¾ cup sifted **Pillsbury's Best All Purpose Flour****
            1 tablespoon **sugar**
            1½ teaspoons double-acting **baking powder** and
            1 teaspoon **salt** into large bowl. Stir in
            ⅔ cup **corn meal**

Add . . . . 1 slightly beaten **egg**
            ⅔ cup **milk**
            ¼ cup **shortening,** melted, or salad oil and
            ⅓ cup finely chopped **onion,** all at once, to the dry in-
                gredients; stir to combine. Spoon over beans.

Bake . . . . at 400° for 35 to 40 minutes.

For mild flavor, use 1 cup (8-oz. can) tomato sauce for catsup and water.

**For use with Pillsbury's Best Self-Rising Flour, decrease baking powder to
½ teaspoon and omit salt.*

Teen Bean Bake

Pork and Corn Bread Bake

Senior Winner by Mrs. Jack Meyer, Miami, Florida

A thrifty one-dish meal with tomato sauce, corn and cubes of pork.

BAKE at 400° for 25 to 30 minutes   SERVES 6 to 8

Brown. . . . . . .2 cups (1 lb.) cubed **pork** in
       1 tablespoon **shortening.** Cook until tender.
Simmer . . . . .¼ cup chopped **green pepper** in
       ½ cup **water** until tender. Drain and set aside.
Combine . . . . .2 cups (two 8-oz. cans) **tomato sauce**
       2 cups **whole-kernel corn** (frozen or canned) and the
       browned meat in 2-quart casserole.
Sift together. ½ cup sifted **Pillsbury's Best All Purpose Flour***
       1 tablespoon **sugar**
       2 teaspoons double-acting **baking powder** and
       ¾ teaspoon **salt** into mixing bowl. Stir in
       ½ cup **yellow corn meal**
Combine . . . . .1 well-beaten **egg**
       ½ cup **milk**
       2 tablespoons **shortening,** melted, and the green pepper.
       Add to the dry ingredients, mixing just until smooth.
       Pour over hot pork mixture.
Bake . . . . .at 400° for 25 to 30 minutes.
*For use with Pillsbury's Best Self-Rising Flour, omit baking powder and salt.

California Casserole

Grand Prize Winner by Mrs. Hildreth H. Hatheway, Santa Barbara, California

You'll know why this won top prize when you taste its crunchy dumplings, its chicken-seasoned veal, its sour cream-chicken soup sauce.

BAKE at 425° for 20 to 25 minutes   SERVES 8

Coat. . . . . . . .2 pounds **veal round steak** (cut into 2-inch pieces)
       with mixture of
       ⅓ cup **Pillsbury's Best All Purpose Flour** and
       1 teaspoon **paprika**
Brown. . . . . . . .veal thoroughly in
       ¼ cup **salad oil** or shortening
Add. . . . . . . .½ teaspoon **salt**
       ⅛ teaspoon **pepper** and
       1 cup **water** (part onion liquid may be used); cover
       and simmer 30 minutes or until tender.
Transfer. . . . . . .to large baking dish (14x10x2 or 13x9x2-inch) or 3-
       quart casserole, or 2 smaller casseroles.
Heat. . . . . . . .1 can **condensed cream of chicken soup** in skillet
       used for browning.
Blend in. . . .1¾ cups **water** gradually. Bring to boil, stirring constantly. Combine with meat and gravy.
Add. . . . . . .1¾ cups small cooked **onions** (1-lb. can, drained)
Top with . . . .14 to 16 Butter Crumb Dumplings
Bake. . . . .*uncovered* at 425° for 20 to 25 minutes.
Serve with . . . . .sauce made by heating
       1 can (10½ oz.) **condensed cream of chicken soup** and
       1 cup **sour cream** to boiling. (Add milk if thinner sauce
       is desired.)

BUTTER CRUMB DUMPLINGS

Sift together . .2 cups sifted **Pillsbury's Best All Purpose Flour***
       4 teaspoons double-acting **baking powder**
       ½ teaspoon **salt** and
       1 teaspoon **poultry seasoning** into mixing bowl. Stir in
       1 teaspoon **celery seed**
       1 teaspoon dry **onion flakes** and
       1 tablespoon **poppy seed,** if desired.
Add. . . . . . . .¼ cup **salad oil** and
       1 cup **milk.** Stir just until moistened.
Drop. . . . . . . .rounded tablespoonfuls of dough into a mixture of
       ¼ cup **butter,** melted, and
       1 cup **bread crumbs;** roll to coat well with crumbs.
*For use with Pillsbury's Best Self-Rising Flour, increase flour to 2⅓ cups; omit baking powder and salt.

BEST of the BAKE-OFF

California Casserole
Grand Prize Winner of the Eighth Grand National Bake-Off®

Cranberry Whirl Ham Dinner

Senior Winner by Mrs. Frank J. Neeley, Troy, New York

Ham, pineapple and sweet potatoes baked in a spicy pineapple sauce, then topped with cranberry-filled biscuits.

BAKE at 400° for 15 minutes, then   SERVES 6 to 8
        for 25 to 30 minutes

Drain . . . . 1 No. 2 can **pineapple chunks** or **tidbits**, reserving juice. Measure 1 cup pineapple; add 3 cups (2 lbs.) cubed cooked **ham**

Prepare . . . . . . 2 cups sliced cooked **sweet potatoes**

Alternate . . . . . layers of ham-pineapple mixture and sweet potato in greased 2-quart casserole, starting with ham mixture.

Combine . . . . ⅓ cup firmly packed **brown sugar**
        1½ tablespoons **cornstarch**
        ½ teaspoon **salt**
        ½ teaspoon **cinnamon** and
        ⅛ teaspoon ground **cloves** in saucepan.

Add . . . . 2 tablespoons **butter** and 1 cup of the reserved pineapple juice. Cook, stirring constantly, until thick. Pour over mixture in casserole.

Bake . . . . at 400° for 15 minutes. Meanwhile prepare Cranberry Whirl Biscuits.

CRANBERRY WHIRL BISCUITS

Combine . . . . ¾ cup fresh **cranberries**, ground or chopped fine
        3 tablespoons **sugar** and
        1 tablespoon **flour**. Set aside.

Sift together 1½ cups sifted **Pillsbury's Best All Purpose Flour***
        3 teaspoons double-acting **baking powder** and
        ½ teaspoon **salt** into mixing bowl.

Cut in . . . . . . ⅓ cup **shortening** until particles are fine.

Add . . . . 1 beaten **egg** and
        ⅓ cup **milk**. Stir until dough clings together. Knead on floured surface 10 strokes.

Roll out . . . . . . to a 12-inch square. Spread with the cranberry mixture. Roll as for jelly roll. Cut into 1¼-inch slices; arrange cut-side down on hot mixture in casserole. Bake 25 to 30 minutes.

**For use with Pillsbury's Best Self-Rising Flour, omit baking powder and salt.*

Porky Corn Bread

Junior Winner by Karen Brown, Cincinnati, Ohio

There's a hidden layer of pork sausage under this tender, light corn bread. Serve it with a gravy made from sausage drippings.

BAKE at 425° for 20 to 25 minutes   SERVES 6 to 9

Cook . . . . 1 pound bulk **pork sausage** in skillet until lightly browned; do not overcook. Drain sausage, reserving ¼ cup drippings for Gravy, if desired. Place sausage in bottom of greased 8x8x2-inch pan.

Sift together . ¾ cup sifted **Pillsbury's Best All Purpose Flour***
        1 tablespoon **sugar**
        3 teaspoons double-acting **baking powder** and
        ½ teaspoon **salt** into mixing bowl. Stir in
        ¾ cup **yellow corn meal**

Add . . . . ¾ cup **milk**
        1 slightly beaten **egg** and
        3 tablespoons **shortening**, melted. Stir until smooth. Spread over sausage in pan.

Bake . . . . at 425° for 20 to 25 minutes. Serve hot, with or without Gravy.

**For use with Pillsbury's Best Self-Rising Flour, decrease baking powder to 2 teaspoons and salt to ¼ teaspoon.*

GRAVY

Blend ¼ cup Pillsbury's Best All Purpose Flour into the reserved drippings in skillet. Add gradually 1¼ cups water and 1¼ cups milk. Cook, stirring constantly, until thick. Add 1½ teaspoons salt.

Cantonese Egg Roll

Senior Winner by Mrs. Robert Batchelor, Defiance, Ohio

Now you can make that famous specialty of Chinese restaurants!

FRY at 360° for 5 to 8 minutes   MAKES 24 egg rolls

Combine . . . . . 2 cups finely chopped cooked **pork**
1 cup finely chopped cooked **shrimp** or lobster
2 cups finely chopped **celery**
1 cup finely chopped green **onion** and
1 cup finely chopped **water chestnuts**

Blend in . . . . . 1 tablespoon **monosodium glutamate**
1 tablespoon **soy sauce**
2 teaspoons **sugar**
1 teaspoon **salt**
1 small **egg** and
¼ cup **shortening**, melted. Refrigerate.

EGG ROLL

Sift together 1⅓ cups sifted **Pillsbury's Best All Purpose Flour***
⅔ cup **cornstarch** and
½ teaspoon **salt** into mixing bowl.

Blend together 2 unbeaten **eggs** and
½ cup **water**. Add gradually to the dry ingredients; blend well.

Add . . . . 1 cup more **water** gradually, beating until smooth. Reserve ⅓ cup of batter.

Heat . . . . a skillet over medium high heat. Brush with **shortening.**

Pour . . . . batter, about 2 tablespoons at a time, into skillet. Tilt pan to make a 7-inch round, thin pancake. Cook until mixture looks dry and begins to curl around the edges. Do not turn. Remove from heat. Repeat with remaining batter, stacking pancakes until all are baked.

Place . . . . a scant ¼ cup filling in center of each pancake, then fold 2 sides over filling. Brush edges with reserved

Cantonese Egg Roll

batter. Beginning at one open end, roll up the pancake, pressing edges to seal. (Rolls may be stored in refrigerator until serving time.)

Fry . . . . in hot deep fat (360°) 5 to 8 minutes; turn only once. Serve hot with Apricot Sauce, Hot Mustard Sauce or both.

For use with Pillsbury's Best Self-Rising Flour, omit salt in Egg Roll.

APRICOT SAUCE

Combine 2 cups apricot preserves, ¼ cup finely chopped pimiento and 2 tablespoons vinegar in saucepan. Bring to boil; simmer for 2 minutes, stirring occasionally.

HOT MUSTARD SAUCE

Blend together dry mustard and water to form a paste.

Shanghai Casserole

Senior Winner by Mrs. Henry T. Vaughan, Youngstown, Ohio

Start out with an excellent chow mein dish, and cover it with onion-flavored drop biscuits.

BAKE at 400° for 25 to 30 minutes   SERVES 6 to 8

Sauté . . . . ¾ cup sliced **onions** in
2 tablespoons **shortening** in large skillet; * remove from pan and reserve.
Brown . . . . . . ½ pound boneless **pork**, cut into small thin strips, and
½ pound boneless **veal**, cut into small thin strips
Add . . . . 2 tablespoons **soy sauce**
½ teaspoon **onion salt** and
¼ teaspoon **monosodium glutamate**, if desired.
Pour . . . . 2 to 3 cups hot **water** over meat to cover; cover pan and simmer 30 to 45 minutes.
Add . . . . . . 1½ cups diced **celery**; simmer 15 minutes.
Stir in . . . . . . ½ cup (4-oz. can) **mushroom pieces**, undrained.
1 No. 2 can (2 cups) **chow mein vegetables**, undrained, and browned onions, reserving 1 tablespoon for Topping.
Combine . . . . . 2 tablespoons **cornstarch** and
3 tablespoons **water;** mix to a smooth paste. Blend into meat mixture, stirring constantly until thick and clear. Season with **pepper**. Pour into 2-quart casserole.

ONION BISCUIT TOPPING

Sift together . . 1 cup sifted **Pillsbury's Best All Purpose Flour****
1½ teaspoons double-acting **baking powder** and
½ teaspoon **salt**. Stir in
1 teaspoon **celery seed** and reserved onion.
Cut in . . . . . . ¼ cup **shortening** until particles are fine.
Add . . . . 1 slightly beaten **egg** and
⅛ cup **milk;** mix only until all dry particles are moistened. Drop by rounded teaspoonfuls onto hot

Shanghai Casserole

meat mixture in casserole.

Bake . . . . at 400° for 25 to 30 minutes. Serve hot.

If desired, onion-meat mixture may be prepared in pressure saucepan. Follow the directions given with saucepan.

**For use with Pillsbury's Best Self-Rising Flour, omit baking powder and salt.*

Liver and Onion Dinner

Senior Winner by Mrs. Robert Wellman, Kenosha, Wisconsin

A crusty biscuit-crescent filled with ground liver and onions is served with hot tomato sauce and crispy bacon slices.

BAKE at 425° for 20 to 25 minutes   SERVES 6

Simmer . . . . . . 1 pound **liver** in saucepan with
          1½ cups **water** for 15 minutes. Drain.

Grind . . . . 1 small **onion** and the cooked liver.

Add . . . . ½ teaspoon **salt**
          ½ teaspoon **celery salt**
          ⅛ teaspoon **marjoram**
          ⅛ teaspoon **pepper** and
          ¼ cup **catsup**. Blend thoroughly. Set aside.

Sift together . . 2 cups sifted **Pillsbury's Best All Purpose Flour***
          3 teaspoons double-acting **baking powder** and
          ½ teaspoon **salt** into mixing bowl.

Cut in . . . . . . ¼ cup **shortening** until mixture resembles coarse crumbs.

Add . . . . ¾ cup **milk**; mix until all dry particles are moistened. Knead gently on floured surface 20 strokes.

Roll out . . . . to a 12x10-inch rectangle. Spread with liver mixture. Roll as for jelly roll, starting with 12-inch edge. Seal edges. Place on ungreased baking sheet in crescent shape.

Bake . . . . at 425° for 20 to 25 minutes. Serve hot with
          1 can heated undiluted **tomato soup,** and crisp **bacon slices.**

For use with Pillsbury's Best Self-Rising Flour, omit baking powder and salt.

POULTRY DISHES—In recipes calling for chicken you can use leftover turkey as a substitute. Also, other shortenings may be substituted for chicken fat.

To prepare cooked chicken: Season ready-to-cook stewing hen, cut up, add hot water to cover, and simmer, covered, until tender. Refrigerate until ready to use. (For quicker cooking, use a pressure saucepan; follow directions.)

Crusty Sweet 'Tater Shortcake

Senior Winner by Mrs. Edith Lawson, White Haven, Pennsylvania

Sweet potato biscuits served piping hot with creamed chicken. Tempting and quick to make!

BAKE at 450° for 15 to 20 minutes   SERVES 4 to 6

Sift together 1½ cups sifted **Pillsbury's Best All Purpose Flour***
          1 tablespoon **sugar**
          2½ teaspoons double-acting **baking powder** and
          1½ teaspoons **salt** into mixing bowl.

Cut in . . . . . . ¼ cup **shortening** until particles are fine.

Combine . . . . ½ cup mashed **sweet potatoes** (canned or cooked) and
          ½ cup **milk**; add all at once to flour mixture, stirring only until all dry particles are moistened. Knead on floured surface about 10 strokes.

Roll out . . . . to ½-inch thickness; cut into rounds with 2-inch cutter (or into diamonds with knife). Place on ungreased baking sheet.

Bake . . . . at 450° for 15 to 20 minutes.

Serve with . . . . . sauce made by heating
          1 can (10½ oz.) **condensed cream of chicken soup** with
          ½ cup **milk or light cream** and
          1 cup cubed cooked **chicken**

For use with Pillsbury's Best Self-Rising Flour, omit baking powder and salt.

Chicken à la Cheese Pie

Bride Second Prize Winner by Mrs. Herman D. Baldner, Jr., Dallas Center, Iowa

Chicken or leftover turkey? Use it in a colorful pie filling made with carrots, green pepper and onion in broth, topped with sliced cheese.

BAKE at 425° for 8 minutes, then   SERVES 6
       at 400° for 20 to 25 minutes

Sift together . . 1 cup sifted **Pillsbury's Best All Purpose Flour*** and ½ teaspoon **salt** into mixing bowl.

Cut in . . . . . . ⅓ cup **shortening** until the size of small peas.

Beat . . . . 1 **egg** slightly. Combine 1 tablespoon of the beaten egg with
             2 tablespoons **water**. (Reserve remainder of egg for filling.)

Sprinkle . . . . combined egg and water over flour mixture, stirring with fork until dough is moist enough to hold together. Form into a ball.

Roll out . . . . on floured surface to a circle 1½ inches larger than inverted 9-inch pie pan. Fit loosely into pan. Fold edge to form standing rim; flute. Prick generously.

Bake . . . . at 425° for 8 minutes.

*For use with Pillsbury's Best Self-Rising Flour, omit salt.

CHICKEN FILLING

Sauté . . . . ½ cup chopped **onion** and
           2 tablespoons chopped **green pepper** in ¼ cup **chicken fat** or butter until tender.

Stir in . . . . 2 tablespoons **flour** and ½ cup **chicken broth.** Cook until thickened.

Add . . . . 3 cups cubed cooked **chicken**
          ¾ cup cooked **carrots** (diced or sticks)
          ½ teaspoon **monosodium glutamate** and the reserved egg.

Turn . . . . into partially baked pie shell. Top with 8 slices (½ lb.) **American cheese**

Bake . . . . at 400° for 20 to 25 minutes.

Chicken à la Cheese Pie

Chicken Almond Party Bake

Senior Winner by Mrs. Lynn Shurter, Omaha, Nebraska

Tender, golden almond biscuit rings baked atop a chicken-mushroom-almond casserole.

BAKE at 425° for 20 to 25 minutes   SERVES 6 to 8

Cook........1 large stewing **chicken,** or use 1 canned chicken; cut into bite-size pieces (3 to 4 cups).

Melt........3 tablespoons **chicken fat** in saucepan; blend in 3 tablespoons **flour**

Add........2 cups **chicken stock** gradually; cook over medium heat, stirring constantly, until thickened.

Stir in......½ cup (4-oz. can) chopped **mushrooms** 1 to 2 teaspoons grated **onion** ¼ cup chopped **pimiento** ½ teaspoon **monosodium glutamate** and **salt** to taste. Bring to boil.

Add........¼ cup blanched **almonds,** slivered, and the chicken.

Turn.........into 6 to 8 individual casseroles or a 12x8-inch baking pan. Top with Almond Biscuits while hot.

Bake.........at 425° for 20 to 25 minutes.

ALMOND BISCUITS

Sift together..2 cups sifted **Pillsbury's Best All Purpose Flour*** 4 teaspoons double-acting **baking powder** and ½ teaspoon **salt** into large mixing bowl.

Add........⅓ cup blanched **almonds,** ground

Cut in......¼ cup **shortening** until particles are fine.

Add........¾ cup **milk** and ⅛ teaspoon **almond extract** all at once; stir until dough clings together. Knead on floured surface 10 strokes. Roll out to ¼-inch thickness.

Cut...........circles to fit tops of casseroles; cut out 1-inch circle in center. (For large casserole, use doughnut cutter to cut out biscuits.)

*For use with Pillsbury's Best Self-Rising Flour, omit baking powder and salt.

Giant Chicken Turnover

Senior Winner by Miss Joanne Talley, Westminster, Maryland

More filling, less crust per serving because all the chicken filling is in one corn meal-crunchy crust . . . serve with mushroom-pimiento sauce.

BAKE at 425° for 25 to 30 minutes   SERVES 6

Sauté........½ cup finely chopped **onion** and ½ cup cut **celery** in ¼ cup **chicken fat** or butter until tender.

Add........1 tablespoon **flour** 3 cups finely chopped cooked **chicken** and ½ to 1 teaspoon **salt.** Set aside.

Sift together..2 cups sifted **Pillsbury's Best All Purpose Flour*** and 1 teaspoon **salt** into large mixing bowl. Stir in ⅓ cup **corn meal**

Cut in......¾ cup **shortening** until the size of small peas.

Sprinkle.....5 to 7 tablespoons cold **water** over mixture, stirring with fork until dough is moist enough to hold together. Form into a square.

Roll out.......to a 13-inch square on floured surface. Place on large ungreased baking sheet.

Spread........chicken mixture on half of dough. Moisten edges and fold other half over to form a rectangle. Seal edges with fork. Cut gashes to mark servings and allow steam to escape.

Bake.........at 425° for 25 to 30 minutes. Serve hot with Chicken-Mushroom Sauce.

*For use with Pillsbury's Best Self-Rising Flour, omit salt in pastry.

CHICKEN-MUSHROOM SAUCE

Sauté ½ cup mushroom pieces (fresh or 4-oz. can) in 3 tablespoons chicken fat. Add 3 tablespoons flour and 1½ cups chicken broth. Cook until thickened; add 2 tablespoons chopped pimiento, ⅛ teaspoon poultry seasoning and salt and pepper to taste. Blend a little of the hot mixture into 1 slightly beaten egg; add to hot mixture. Heat 1 minute, stirring constantly.

Chicken Party Pie

Chicken Party Pie

Senior Winner by Mrs. Peter DuBovy, Woodland Hills, California

Perfect for the ladies! Chicken chiffon pie that'll win applause at any luncheon.

BAKE at 425° for 10 to 12 minutes   MAKES 9-inch pie

Sift together . . 1 cup sifted **Pillsbury's Best All Purpose Flour***
      1 teaspoon **poppy seed** and
      ½ teaspoon **salt** into mixing bowl.
Combine . . . . . ¼ cup **salad oil** and
      2 tablespoons **milk** in measuring cup. Beat with fork
      until thick and creamy. Pour all at once over flour.
      Toss and cut with fork until blended. Form into ball.
Roll out . . . . on waxed paper to a circle 1½ inches larger than

inverted 9-inch pie pan. Fit loosely into pan; gently pat out air pockets. Fold edge to form a standing rim; flute. Prick generously.
Bake . . . . at 425° for 10 to 12 minutes.
**Pillsbury's Best Self-Rising Flour is not recommended for use in this recipe.*

CHICKEN CHIFFON FILLING

Soften . . . . 2 envelopes (2 tablespoons) unflavored **gelatin** in
      ¼ cup **milk**
Combine . . . . . 1 can (10½ oz.) **condensed cream of mushroom soup**
      2 beaten **egg yolks** and the softened gelatin; mix well.
Cook . . . . in top of double boiler over boiling water until
      gelatin dissolves, about 3 minutes.
Add . . . . 1 cup cubed cooked **chicken**
      ¼ cup chopped stuffed **olives**
      2 tablespoons chopped **water chestnuts**
      1 teaspoon chopped **onion** and
      ⅛ teaspoon **pepper**. Chill, stirring occasionally, until
      thickened but not set.
Fold in . . . . . . 2 stiffly beaten **egg whites**. Spoon into pie shell.
      Decorate with sliced **stuffed olives**. Chill until firm,
      at least 1 hour.

Log Cabin Chicken Pie

Senior Winner by Mrs. Mason Parker, Kenney, Illinois

Abraham Lincoln stopped at Mrs. Parker's great, great grandparents' log cabin. This tasty chicken pie was served.

BAKE at 425° for 10 minutes, then   MAKES 10-inch pie
   at 400° for 10 to 15 minutes

Sift together 1½ cups sifted **Pillsbury's Best All Purpose Flour*** and
      1 teaspoon **salt** into mixing bowl.
Cut in . . . . . . ½ cup **shortening** until the size of small peas.
Combine . . . . . 1 slightly beaten **egg** and

1 tablespoon **lemon juice;** sprinkle over flour mixture tossing lightly with fork.

Add........1 to 2 tablespoons cold **milk** or water, tossing until dough is moist enough to hold together. Form into a ball.

Roll out.......on floured surface to a circle 1½-inches larger than inverted 10-inch pie pan. Fit loosely into pan. Fold edge to form standing rim; flute. Prick generously.

Bake........at 425° for 10 minutes. Decrease oven temperature to 400°.

CHICKEN FILLING

Sauté.......½ cup chopped **celery**
¼ cup chopped **green pepper** and
2 tablespoons chopped **onion** in
3 tablespoons **chicken fat** in large skillet until tender, about 5 minutes.

Blend in.....3 tablespoons **flour**

Add.......1½ cups **chicken stock**
¼ teaspoon **poultry seasoning** and **salt** to taste. Cook, stirring constantly, until thickened.

Stir in.......3 cups cubed cooked **chicken;** simmer.

Combine.....1 cup **bread crumbs** (2 to 3 slices)
¼ cup melted **chicken fat** or butter
⅛ teaspoon **salt**
⅛ teaspoon **pepper** and
⅛ teaspoon **poultry seasoning**

Turn..........hot Chicken Filling into partially baked pie shell. Top with crumb mixture.

Bake........at 400° for 10 to 15 minutes.

For use with Pillsbury's Best Self-Rising Flour, omit salt.

Luncheon Chicken Puffs

Senior Winner by Mrs. Wm. A. Sutherland, Liberty Corner, New Jersey

These main dish cream puffs are flavored with onion, mustard and ham and filled with creamed chicken.

BAKE at 450° for 10 minutes, then   SERVES 6
at 375° for 20 minutes

Combine.....1 cup **water**
⅓ cup **shortening**
¼ cup **bacon** or ham fat, finely diced
1 teaspoon grated **onion**
1 teaspoon **dry mustard** and
¼ teaspoon **salt*** in saucepan. Heat to boiling.

Add........1 cup sifted **Pillsbury's Best All Purpose Flour*** all at once. Cook, stirring constantly, until mixture leaves sides of pan and is smooth and compact. Cool about 1 minute.

Blend in.....3 unbeaten **eggs,** one at a time, beating vigorously after each until mixture is smooth.

Stir in.......1 teaspoon chopped **parsley**
¼ cup finely-chopped cooked **ham**

Drop.........dough by heaping tablespoons in 6 or 8 mounds on greased baking sheet.

Bake.........at 450° for 10 minutes, then at 375° for 20 minutes. Turn off heat. Prick with sharp knife; leave in oven 10 minutes to dry out.

Fill...........puffs with Creamed Chicken or Ham. Sprinkle with **paprika.**

For use with Pillsbury's Best Self-Rising Flour, omit salt.

CREAMED CHICKEN OR HAM

In saucepan melt 2 tablespoons butter or margarine over low heat; blend in 2 tablespoons flour. Gradually add 1 cup milk, ¼ teaspoon salt and ⅛ teaspoon paprika; cook, stirring constantly, until thick. Blend a little of hot mixture into 1 slightly beaten egg yolk; add to hot mixture. Stir in 2 cups cubed cooked chicken or ham. Heat thoroughly.

Chicken Devil Puffs

Senior Winner by Mrs. Dorothy L. Ferguson, Pittsfield, Massachusetts

Deviled ham adds zest to the puffs and to the rich chicken-cheese filling.

BAKE at 425° for 20 to 25 minutes   MAKES 1 dozen

Melt . . . . ½ cup **shortening** in
1 cup **boiling water** in saucepan.
Add . . . . 1 cup sifted **Pillsbury's Best All Purpose Flour*** and
½ teaspoon **salt** all at once. Cook over medium heat, stirring constantly, until mixture leaves sides of pan and is smooth and compact, about 2 minutes. Cool about 1 minute.
Blend in . . . . 4 unbeaten **eggs,** one at a time, beating vigorously after each until mixture is smooth and glossy.
Stir in . . . . . . 3 tablespoons (½ of 3 oz. can) **deviled ham.** Drop by rounded tablespoons onto greased baking sheet.
Bake . . . . at 425° for 20 to 25 minutes. Turn off oven. Prick side of each with sharp knife. Leave puffs in oven for 10 minutes to dry out centers. Split and fill with hot Chicken Filling.

CHICKEN FILLING

Melt . . . . ¼ cup **chicken fat** or butter in saucepan. Blend in
¼ cup **Pillsbury's Best All Purpose Flour.*** Add
1½ cups **milk** or chicken stock and
1 cup **light cream** gradually. Cook over medium heat, stirring constantly, until thickened.
Stir in . . . . . . 1 cup shredded **Cheddar cheese**
¼ teaspoon **salt***
⅛ teaspoon **pepper**
1/16 teaspoon **cayenne pepper,** if desired
1 teaspoon **prepared mustard** and
3 tablespoons **deviled ham**
Add . . . . 3 to 4 cups cooked **chicken** or turkey, cut in bite-size pieces. Reheat if necessary.
*For use with Pillsbury's Best Self-Rising Flour, omit salt.

Onion Corn Puffs

Senior Winner by Mrs. James D. Buckelew, Baltimore, Maryland

Creamed chicken in little vegetable puffs made with packaged onion soup and whole kernel corn.

BAKE at 400° for 25 to 30 minutes   SERVES 8 to 12

Melt . . . . ½ cup **shortening** in
1 cup **boiling water** in saucepan.
Add . . . . 1 cup sifted **Pillsbury's Best All Purpose Flour*** and
⅛ teaspoon **soda,** all at once. Cook over medium heat, stirring constantly, until mixture leaves sides of pan and is smooth and compact, about 2 minutes. Cool about 1 minute.
Blend in . . . . 4 **eggs,** one at a time, beating vigorously after each until mixture is smooth.
Stir in . . . . . . 1 package (1½ oz.) dried **onion soup** and
1½ cups drained, cooked **whole-kernel corn**
Drop . . . . by rounded tablespoonfuls onto greased baking sheet.
Bake . . . . at 400° for 25 to 30 minutes. Do not underbake. Turn off oven. Prick with knife; leave in oven for 10 minutes to dry out. Split and fill with hot Creamed Chicken.
*For use with Pillsbury's Best Self-Rising Flour, omit soda.

CREAMED CHICKEN

Melt . . . . ¼ cup **chicken fat** or butter in top of double boiler.
Add . . . . ¼ cup chopped **green pepper;** cook over boiling water 10 minutes until tender.
Blend in . . . . . ⅓ cup **Pillsbury's Best All Purpose Flour**
Add . . . . 1 cup **milk** and
1 cup **chicken stock** gradually. Cook; stir until thick.
Stir in . . . . . . 2 cups cubed cooked **chicken**
2 tablespoons chopped **pimiento**
½ teaspoon **salt**
⅛ teaspoon **paprika** and
1/16 teaspoon **pepper.** Keep hot in double boiler.

Party Chicken Loaf

Senior Winner by Mrs. Victor Walker, St. Louis, Missouri

A new kind of one-dish chicken dinner—a mixture of cooked chicken, celery, pimiento and seasonings is baked in a blanket of flaky pastry. Just add a relish tray or simple salad for a festive meal.

BAKE at 425° for 30 to 40 minutes   SERVES 6 to 8

Combine.....3 to 4 cups cubed cooked **chicken**
½ cup chopped **celery**
1 unbeaten **egg**
2 tablespoons chopped **pimiento**
1 to 1½ teaspoons **salt**
½ teaspoon **Worcestershire sauce** and
⅛ teaspoon **pepper**

Melt........¼ cup **chicken fat** or butter in saucepan; blend in
¼ cup **Pillsbury's Best All Purpose Flour**

Add........⅔ cup **chicken stock** gradually; cook, stirring constantly, until thickened. Blend with the chicken mixture. Refrigerate.

PASTRY

Prepare.......recipe for **Two-Crust Pastry,** page 460; shape pastry as directed below.

Divide........into two portions, one twice as large as the other. Form into squares.

Roll out.......larger portion on floured surface to 15x10-inch rectangle. Fit loosely into 9x5x3-inch pan. Fill with the chicken mixture.

Roll out.......remaining dough to 10x6-inch rectangle; cut slits. Moisten rim of bottom crust. Place top crust over filling fold edge over bottom crust. Flute. Brush with **milk.**

Bake.........at 425° for 30 to 40 minutes. Cool 5 minutes. Gently turn out on wire rack; then place right side up on serving plate. Cut into 1½-inch slices; serve hot with Mushroom Sauce.

Party Chicken Loaf

MUSHROOM SAUCE

Melt 3 tablespoons chicken fat in saucepan. Blend in 3 tablespoons flour. Add gradually 1½ cups chicken stock, stirring constantly. Cook and stir until thickened. Add ½ cup (4-oz. can) chopped mushrooms and salt to taste.

Individual Tarts: Divide dough into two portions, one slightly larger. Roll out larger portion to ⅛-inch thickness. Cut out six 6-inch circles; fit loosely into 4-inch tart pans. Fill each with about ½ cup chicken filling. Roll out remaining dough to ⅛-inch thickness; cut six 5-inch circles. Cut slits in center of each. Moisten rims of bottom crusts. Place top crusts over filling; fold edge under bottom crust. Seal edge; flute. Bake at 425° for 20 to 25 minutes.

Chicken Salad Pie

Junior Winner by Marlyce Ann Snay, Haven, Kansas

A brand new luncheon dish! Fill a flaky pastry shell with a hearty salad of chicken, pineapple, cheese and almonds.

BAKE at 450° for 10 to 12 minutes   SERVES 6

Prepare . . . . recipe for **One-Crust Pastry,** page 460, using 9-inch pie pan. Bake as directed.

Combine . . . . . 2 cups cooked **chicken,** cut in bite-size pieces
¾ cup shredded **American cheese**
½ cup diced **celery**
½ cup (9-oz. can) **crushed pineapple,** well drained
⅓ cup blanched slivered **almonds** or chopped walnuts
½ teaspoon **paprika**
½ teaspoon **salt** and
½ cup **mayonnaise.** Toss lightly. Turn into pie shell.

Chicken Salad Pie

Beat . . . . ½ cup **whipping cream** until thick. Fold in
¼ cup **mayonnaise.** Spread over salad in pie shell. Garnish with shredded **cheese.** Chill 30 minutes.

Filled Luncheon Pancakes

Senior Winner by Mrs. Paul H. Weller, Los Angeles, California

Chicken-mushroom filling is rolled up in rich, delicate pancakes, baked with sour cream and cheese topping.

BAKE at 425° for 15 to 20 minutes   SERVES 6

Sift together 1½ cups sifted **Pillsbury's Best All Purpose Flour*** and ½ teaspoon **salt**

Beat . . . . 3 **eggs** until light and fluffy. Add
1½ cups **milk**

Blend in . . . . the dry ingredients. Stir until smooth. (With mixer use a low speed.)

Heat . . . . skillet over medium high heat. Brush with **shortening.**

Pour . . . . batter, 3 tablespoons at a time, into skillet. Tilt pan to make a 6-inch round thin pancake. Brown lightly, turn and brown other side.

Spread . . . . each pancake with a rounded tablespoonful of Chicken Filling. Roll up; place in 12x8-inch baking dish.

Spread with . . 1 cup thick **sour cream.** Sprinkle with
½ cup shredded **American cheese**

Bake . . . . at 425° for 15 to 20 minutes. Serve hot.

**For use with Pillsbury's Best Self-Rising Flour, omit salt.*

CHICKEN FILLING

Sauté ¼ cup chopped green pepper, 2 tablespoons chopped onion and ¼ cup chopped mushrooms in 2 tablespoons butter until tender. Add 1½ cups chopped cooked chicken or turkey and ½ cup chicken gravy. (If desired, ½ cup undiluted cream of chicken or mushroom soup may be substituted for gravy.)

Chicken-Filled Crepes

Senior Winner by Mrs. James Watson, New York, New York

Rich, tender pancakes rolled around a buttery chicken-mushroom filling and topped with an easy hollandaise sauce.

BAKE at 450° for 10 minutes   SERVES 6 to 8

Beat . . . . 1 cup **whipping cream** until thick.
Combine . . . . . 6 **eggs**
         1 tablespoon **sugar**
         ½ teaspoon **salt** and
         2 teaspoons grated **orange rind.** Beat until thick and ivory colored; fold into whipped cream.
Fold in . . . . . . 1 cup sifted **Pillsbury's Best All Purpose Flour,*** one-third at a time. Stir in
         3 tablespoons **butter,** melted
Bake . . . . on hot griddle until light brown on each side (use scant ¼ cup butter for each pancake; spread to make 6-inch cake).**

CHICKEN FILLING

Sauté . . . . ½ cup (4-oz. can) chopped **mushrooms** in
         5 tablespoons **butter** or margarine in skillet until tender.
Blend in . . . . . ⅓ cup sifted **Pillsbury's Best All Purpose Flour.*** Gradually add
         2 cups **milk.** Cook until thickened, stirring constantly.
Stir in . . . . 3 cups finely chopped cooked **chicken**
         1 teaspoon **salt*** and
         ⅛ teaspoon **pepper**
Spread . . . . each pancake with a heaping tablespoonful of Chicken Filling; roll up and place in greased 14x10x2-inch baking dish. Top with Easy Hollandaise Sauce.
Bake . . . . at 450° for 10 minutes.

For use with Pillsbury's Best Self-Rising Flour, omit salt in pancakes; decrease salt in filling to ½ teaspoon.
**If desired, prepare pancakes and filling ahead of time; refrigerate. Make Easy Hollandaise Sauce just before using.*

EASY HOLLANDAISE SAUCE

Cream 1 cup butter or margarine in mixing bowl; add 6 egg yolks, one at a time, beating well after each. Stir in 1 teaspoon salt, ⅛ teaspoon pepper and 3 tablespoons lemon juice. Gradually add 1 cup boiling water, beating well with rotary beater or electric mixer. Transfer to top of double boiler. Cook over boiling water, stirring constantly, for 5 minutes.

Chicken Corn-Bread Waffles

Senior Winner by Mrs. Otto S. Wagner, Merrimac, Massachusetts

Mrs. Wagner changed a corn muffin recipe into these tender waffles.

BAKE at medium heat 3 to 5 minutes   SERVES 4

Heat . . . . in top of double boiler over hot water
         1 can (10½ oz.) **condensed cream of chicken soup**
         1 cup cubed cooked **chicken** and
         3 tablespoons chopped **chives** or onion
Sift together . ¾ cup sifted **Pillsbury's Best All Purpose Flour***
         3 teaspoons double-acting **baking powder** and
         ¼ teaspoon **salt** into mixing bowl. Stir in
         ½ cup yellow **corn meal**
Combine . . . . . 1 slightly beaten **egg**
         1 cup **milk** and
         2 tablespoons **butter,** melted; add to the dry ingredients all at once. Mix well.
Bake . . . . in preheated waffle iron until steaming stops and waffle is golden brown. Top with chicken mixture.

For use with Pillsbury's Best Self-Rising Flour, omit baking powder and salt.

Savory Chicken-Bread Bake

Senior Winner by Mrs. Luther F. Anders, Roanoke, Virginia

*Different! A crusty-topped yeast bread—with chicken baked right into it!
You serve a mushroom-soup sauce with it . . and listen to the family's
exclamations.*

BAKE at 425° for 20 to 25 minutes   SERVES 8

Soften . . . . 1 packet active dry **yeast** (or 1 cake compressed) in
          ¼ cup warm **water**
Combine . . . . ½ cup hot scalded **milk**
          1 tablespoon **sugar** and
          1 teaspoon **salt*** in large mixing bowl. Cool to lukewarm.
Stir in . . . . 1 unbeaten **egg** and softened yeast. Gradually add
          2½ cups sifted **Pillsbury's Best All Purpose Flour*** to
          form a soft dough.
Let rise . . . . in warm place (85°) until light and doubled, 1 to

Savory Chicken-Bread Bake

1½ hours. Prepare Savory Chicken.
Add . . . . chicken to risen dough; mix well.
Turn . . . . into well-greased 9x9x2-inch pan or 2½-quart
          casserole. Cover; let rise until light, about 45 minutes.
Bake . . . . at 425° for 20 to 25 minutes.
Serve . . . . hot with sauce made by heating
          1 can **condensed cream of mushroom soup** with
          ½ cup **milk**
For use with Pillsbury's Best Self-Rising Flour, omit salt.

SAVORY CHICKEN

Simmer ½ cup chopped celery and ½ cup chopped onion in ¼ cup
water until tender; drain. Add ½ cup butter or margarine, ½ cup
(4-oz. can) chopped mushrooms and 2 tablespoons chopped pimiento;
heat until butter melts. Stir in 3 cups cubed cooked chicken, ½ teaspoon salt, ½ teaspoon poultry seasoning and ⅛ teaspoon pepper.

Crusty Chicken Casserole

Junior Winner by Virginia Maxwell, Gazelle, California

*A savory-rich batter is poured over cooked chicken. Like Yorkshire
pudding, it puffs up as it bakes to a golden brown.*

BAKE at 350° for 50 to 60 minutes   SERVES 6

Prepare . . . . . . 1 cooked **stewing chicken** by boning and cutting into
          bite-size pieces. Arrange in well-greased 12x8x2-
          inch baking dish.
Sift together 1½ cups sifted **Pillsbury's Best All Purpose Flour***
          1½ teaspoons double-acting **baking powder**
          1 teaspoon **salt** and
          ½ teaspoon **poultry seasoning**
Beat . . . . 4 **eggs** until light and fluffy. Stir in
          1½ cups **milk** and
          3 tablespoons **chicken fat,** melted
Add . . . . the dry ingredients gradually. Beat with rotary beater

until smooth. Pour over chicken. Sprinkle with
pepper.

Bake . . . . at 350° for 50 to 60 minutes. Serve hot with Giblet
Sauce.

For use with Pillsbury's Best Self-Rising Flour, omit baking powder and salt.

GIBLET SAUCE

Sauté ¼ cup chopped onion in ⅓ cup chicken fat or butter in saucepan
over medium heat until tender. Blend in ⅓ cup Pillsbury's Best All
Purpose Flour. Add 2½ cups chicken broth; bring to boil and simmer,
stirring constantly, until thickened. Season with salt and pepper. Add
the cooked chicken giblets, cut fine.

Chicken and Dressing Casserole

Senior Winner by Mrs. Michael M. Peterson, Denver, Colorado

*"This is one of my favorite luncheon or buffet casseroles because
you can serve a dozen people with one big chicken."*

BAKE at 350° for 20 to 25 minutes   SERVES 10 to 12

Cook . . . . 1 large stewing **chicken**; cube.* Set aside. (If desired,
grind the chicken skin for custard.)

Brown . . . . 1 cup dry **bread crumbs** (about 5 slices bread) in
2 tablespoons **butter** or margarine. Set aside.

Sauté . . . . ¾ cup chopped **celery**
½ cup chopped **onion** (1 medium) and
2 tablespoons chopped **parsley** in
½ cup **butter** or margarine in heavy skillet.

Prepare . . . . . 6 cups day-old **bread** (about 1-lb. loaf), cut into small
pieces. Add sautéed vegetables; toss with fork.

Add . . . . 1 teaspoon **salt**
½ to 1 teaspoon **poultry seasoning** and
1/16 teaspoon **pepper**

Sprinkle with . . 3 tablespoons **chicken broth**; toss lightly.

Turn . . . . into greased 14x10-inch or 2½-quart casserole. Cover

Chicken and Dressing Casserole

with half the Chicken Custard and then with the
cubed chicken. Pour remaining Custard over top.
Sprinkle with the bread crumbs.

Bake . . . . at 350° for 20 to 25 minutes.

CHICKEN CUSTARD

Melt 1 cup chicken fat (part butter may be used) in large saucepan.
Blend in 1 cup sifted Pillsbury's Best All Purpose Flour.** Gradually
add 4 cups chicken broth and 1 cup milk, stirring constantly. Add 2
teaspoons salt. Cook, stirring constantly, until thick. Blend a little of
the hot mixture into 4 slightly beaten eggs; add to hot mixture in
saucepan. Cook over low heat 3 to 4 minutes. Add ground chicken skin.

Cooked turkey may be substituted.

**For use with Pillsbury's Best Self-Rising Flour, decrease salt in custard to
1 teaspoon.*

Thrifty Giblet Supper

Senior Winner by Elizabeth Provencher, Ferrisburg, Vermont

Well-seasoned chicken giblet filling goes between two flaky biscuit crusts flavored with onion and poultry seasoning.

BAKE at 425° for 20 to 25 minutes   SERVES 4 to 6

Cover.......1 pound **chicken giblets** (all gizzards, if desired) and
           1 teaspoon **salt** with **water** in saucepan; cook until tender. Drain, reserving broth. Put through food grinder, using coarse blade.

Cook.......½ cup chopped **celery**
           ¼ cup chopped **green pepper** and
           2 tablespoons chopped **onion** in
           2 tablespoons **butter** until tender; stir occasionally.

Add.......¼ cup **giblet broth**
           2 tablespoons **flour**
           ½ teaspoon **salt**
           ¼ teaspoon **poultry seasoning** and the ground giblets.

ONION BISCUIT CRUST

Sift together 1½ cups sifted **Pillsbury's Best All Purpose Flour***
           2½ teaspoons double-acting **baking powder**
           1 teaspoon **salt** and
           ⅛ teaspoon **poultry seasoning** into mixing bowl.
Cut in......¼ cup **shortening** until mixture resembles coarse crumbs.
Add.......⅔ cup **milk** and

2 tablespoons chopped **onion;** mix only until all dry particles are moistened.

Roll out......two-thirds of dough on well-floured surface to a circle 3 inches larger than inverted 8 or 9-inch shallow baking dish. Fit into bottom and sides of dish. Fill with giblet mixture.

Roll out......remaining dough; cut slits. Place over filling. Seal edge. Brush with **cream.**

Bake.........at 425° for 20 to 25 minutes. Serve warm with
           1 can hot undiluted **tomato soup**

*For use with Pillsbury's Best Self-Rising Flour, omit baking powder and salt.

Turkey Oyster Triumph

Senior Winner by Mrs. V. F. Carlson, Portland, Oregon

Two holiday favorites, turkey and oysters, are delectable baked in sauce between tender pastry. A real dress-up for leftover turkey.

BAKE at 425° for 10 minutes, then   SERVES 4 to 6
      at 350° for 30 to 35 minutes

Prepare.......recipe for **Two-Crust Pastry,** page 460, using 9-inch pie pan.

Melt.........2 tablespoons **butter** in saucepan. Blend in
           2 tablespoons **flour.** Gradually add
           1 cup **milk**

Cook.........over medium heat, stirring constantly, until thick.

Add.........2 cups cubed cooked **turkey**
           ¼ cup finely chopped **celery**
           1 tablespoon chopped **parsley**
           1 teaspoon **salt** and
           ⅛ teaspoon **pepper.** Turn into pie shell.

Arrange.....½ cup fresh, frozen or canned whole **oysters** over filling.*

Roll out.......remaining dough; cut slits. Moisten rim of bottom crust. Place top crust over filling. Fold edge under bottom crust. Seal edge; flute.

Bake . . . . at 425° for 10 minutes, then at 350° for 30 to 35 minutes.

For a milder oyster flavor, cut oysters in small pieces and add to turkey filling.

Almond Turkey Puffs

Senior Winner by Lelia C. Houser, Knoxville, Tennessee

Turkey and almonds are blended with a muffin batter . . . puffs are deep fat fried and served with easy mushroom sauce.

FRY at 350° for 3 to 4 minutes   SERVES 8

Sift together 1½ cups sifted **Pillsbury's Best All Purpose Flour***
2 teaspoons double-acting **baking powder**
1½ teaspoons **salt**
½ teaspoon ground **sage** and
1⁄16 teaspoon **pepper** into mixing bowl. Stir in
½ teaspoon **celery seed**

Beat . . . . 2 **eggs** until light and fluffy. Blend in
½ cup **milk**
½ teaspoon **soy sauce** and
1 tablespoon **salad oil** or melted shortening. Add to dry ingredients; mix only until all dry particles are moistened.

Stir in . . . . 2 cups finely chopped cooked **turkey** and
½ cup blanched **almonds**, chopped

Drop . . . . by rounded teaspoonfuls into hot deep fat (350°) Fry for 3 to 4 minutes until golden brown. Serve hot with Mushroom-Celery Sauce.

For use with Pillsbury's Best Self-Rising Flour, omit baking powder and salt.

MUSHROOM-CELERY SAUCE

Combine 1 can cream of mushroom soup, 1 can cream of celery soup and ½ cup milk in saucepan. Mix well. Bring to boil and simmer for 2 minutes, stirring until smooth.

FISH DISHES have increased widely in popularity with the trend towards variety and foreign cookery.

Tuna, crab meat and other canned fish are easy to keep on hand and provide bases for tasty main dishes if unexpected guests arrive.

Down East Crab Meat Pie

Senior Winner by Mrs. Gladys Dole, Portland, Maine

Mrs. Dole calls this "a State-of-Maine dish" . . . zesty crab meat is covered with golden cheese sauce and baked in pastry.

BAKE at 450° for 10 minutes, then   SERVES 6
at 400° for 25 to 30 minutes

Prepare . . . . recipe for **One-Crust Pastry,** page 460, using 9-inch pie pan; bake as directed.

Combine . . . . . 2 cups (two 6½-oz. cans) **crab meat**
⅔ cup **chili sauce**
¼ to ½ cup chopped **green pepper**
½ cup chopped **celery**
¼ teaspoon **salt** and
1½ teaspoons grated **onion;** blend well. Turn into pie shell. Pour Cheese Sauce over top.

CHEESE SAUCE

Melt 3 tablespoons butter or margarine in top of double boiler over boiling water. Blend in 3 tablespoons flour, ¼ teaspoon salt, ½ teaspoon Worcestershire sauce and ½ cup milk. Cook, stirring constantly, until thickened. Blend in 1 cup shredded American cheese.

Cape Cod Crepes

Cape Cod Crepes

Bride Winner by Mrs. Arthur B. Pisula, Pittsburgh, Pennsylvania

Colorful luncheon pancakes . . . well-liked because of the mild crab meat filling rolled up inside and spicy tomato sauce on top.

BAKE at 350° for 20 minutes   MAKES 8 filled crepes

Mix together..1 can (6½ oz.) **crab meat,** boned and flaked
         1 slightly beaten **egg**
         1 tablespoon chopped **parsley**
         ¼ teaspoon **salt** and
         ¼ teaspoon **orégano**
Sift together . ½ cup sifted **Pillsbury's Best All Purpose Flour*** and
         ½ teaspoon **salt** into small mixing bowl.
Combine . . . . . 2 unbeaten **eggs**

         ⅔ cup **milk** and
         1 tablespoon **butter,** melted. Add to the dry ingredients; mix until smooth.
Heat . . . . .lightly-greased skillet over medium high heat.
Pour . . . . .batter, 2 tablespoons at a time, into skillet. Tilt pan to make a 6-inch round, thin pancake. Brown about 1 minute; turn and brown on other side.
Place . . . . .a tablespoonful of crab meat mixture on each; roll up and place in baking dish. Brush with melted **butter.**
Bake . . . . .at 350° for 20 minutes. Serve with hot Spicy Tomato Sauce and **Parmesan cheese.**
**For use with Pillsbury's Best Self-Rising Flour, omit salt.*

SPICY TOMATO SAUCE

In saucepan combine 1 cup (8-oz. can) tomato sauce, 1 teaspoon chopped parsley, 1/16 teaspoon orégano. Bring to boil over medium heat.

Creole Gumbo

Senior Winner by Mrs. H. T. Thornton, Long Beach, Mississippi

Crab meat and vegetables mingle flavors in this savory gumbo.

BAKE at 450° for 8 to 10 minutes   SERVES 6 to 8

Heat . . . . .3 tablespoons **olive oil** in 3-quart saucepan.
Add . . . . .2 cloves minced **garlic**
         ⅛ cup chopped **onion**
         ⅛ cup chopped **green pepper** and
         ¾ cup chopped **celery**; sauté 5 minutes.
Blend in . . . . . ¼ cup **Pillsbury's Best All Purpose Flour**; stir over medium heat until browned, about 10 minutes.
Add . . . . .1¼ cups **tomatoes** (½ No. 2 can) and
         4 cups **water** gradually, stirring constantly.
Add . . . . .1 cup diced **okra** (canned, frozen or fresh)
         1 can (6½ oz.) **crab meat,** boned
         1 tablespoon chopped **parsley**

1½ teaspoons **salt** and
⅛ teaspoon **pepper.** Cover; simmer 1 hour. Serve hot with Paprika Croutons.

PAPRIKA CROUTONS

Sift together . . 2 cups sifted **Pillsbury's Best All Purpose Flour***
1 tablespoon **paprika**
2¼ teaspoons double-acting **baking powder**
1 teaspoon **salt** and
¼ teaspoon **soda** into large mixing bowl.
Cut in . . . . . . ⅛ cup **shortening** until particles are fine.
Add . . . . ¾ cup **buttermilk** or sour milk all at once; stir until dough clings together.
Knead . . . . on floured surface 10 strokes. Roll out to ¼ to ⅜-inch thickness. Cut into ¾-inch squares or 1-inch circles. Place on ungreased baking sheet.
Bake . . . . at 450° for 8 to 10 minutes.

For use with Pillsbury's Best Self-Rising Flour, omit baking powder and salt in croutons.

Crab Meat Cobbler

Best of Class Winner by Mrs. G. Harold Kirk, Bar Harbor, Maine

Cheese biscuits baked atop flavorful crab meat, tomato and cheese sauce.

BAKE at 450° for 20 to 25 minutes   SERVES 6 to 8

Melt . . . . ½ cup **butter** or margarine in top of double boiler.
Add . . . . ½ cup chopped **green pepper** and
½ cup chopped **onion.** Cook over boiling water until tender, about 10 minutes.
Blend in . . . . . ½ cup sifted **Pillsbury's Best All Purpose Flour**
1 teaspoon **dry mustard**
½ teaspoon **monosodium glutamate**
1 cup **milk** and
1 cup shredded **American cheese.** Cook, stirring

constantly, until very thick.
Stir in . . . . 1 cup (6½-oz. can) **crab meat,** boned
1½ cups drained **tomatoes** (No. 2 can)
2 teaspoons **Worcestershire sauce** and
½ teaspoon **salt.** Pour into 2-quart casserole.

CHEESE BISCUIT TOPPING

Sift together . . 1 cup sifted **Pillsbury's Best All Purpose Flour***
2 teaspoons double-acting **baking powder** and
½ teaspoon **salt** into mixing bowl.
Add . . . . ¼ cup shredded **American cheese**
Cut in . . . . 2 tablespoons **shortening** until particles are fine.
Add . . . . ½ cup **milk;** mix only until all particles are moistened. Drop by teaspoonfuls on top of crab meat mixture.
Bake . . . . at 450° for 20 to 25 minutes.

For use with Pillsbury's Best Self-Rising Flour, omit baking powder and salt in biscuits.

Crab Meat Cobbler

Salmon-Cheese Pie

Junior Third Prize Winner by Lynn Fernald, St. Cloud, Minnesota

Salmon-onion filling and cheese slices are baked between biscuit crusts.

BAKE at 375° for 25 to 30 minutes   SERVES 6

Sift together . . 2 cups sifted **Pillsbury's Best All Purpose Flour***
      3 teaspoons double-acting **baking powder** and
      ½ teaspoon **salt** into large mixing bowl.
Cut in . . . . . . ⅓ cup **shortening** until particles are fine.
Combine . . . . . 2 unbeaten **eggs** and
      ⅓ cup **milk**; beat well. Add all at once to the dry
      ingredients; mix only until all particles are moistened.
Roll out . . . . . . two-thirds of dough on floured surface to 11-inch
      circle. Fit into 9-inch pie pan or layer cake pan.
Drain . . . . . . 1 can (1 lb.) **salmon,** reserving juice. Flake into bowl,
      removing skin and bones.

Salmon-Cheese Pie

Add . . . . 1 tablespoon grated **onion** and 2 tablespoons of the
      salmon juice.
Turn . . . . into pastry-lined pan. Cover with
      ¼ pound **American cheese,** thinly sliced
Roll out . . . . . . remaining dough to 7-inch circle. Place on top of
      cheese.
Bake . . . . at 375° for 25 to 30 minutes. Serve hot with Vege-
      table Sauce.

*For use with Pillsbury's Best Self-Rising Flour, omit baking powder and salt.

VEGETABLE SAUCE

Melt ¼ cup butter or margarine in saucepan. Blend in ¼ cup Pillsbury's Best All Purpose Flour and 1 teaspoon prepared mustard; mix well. Gradually add 2 cups milk. Cook over low heat, stirring constantly, until thick. Add ½ teaspoon salt and 2 cups cooked green vegetable. Or garnish with ¼ cup chopped parsley.

Simple Salmon Pie

Junior Winner by Fay Patterson, Leeds, North Dakota

Another colorful, hearty pie—filled with salmon, peas and pimiento.

BAKE at 450° for 10 minutes, then   MAKES 8 or 9-inch pie
   at 400° for 20 to 25 minutes

Prepare . . . . . . recipe for **Two-Crust Pastry,** page 460, using 8 or
      9-inch pie pan.
Melt . . . . 2 tablespoons **butter** in 2-quart saucepan. Blend in
      3 tablespoons **flour.** Gradually add
      1 cup **milk;** cook, stirring constantly, until thick.
Add . . . . 1 slightly beaten **egg yolk**
      1 teaspoon **salt**
      1/16 teaspoon **pepper**
      1 can (1 lb.) **salmon,** broken into large pieces
      1 can (4 oz.) coarsely chopped **pimiento,** and
      ¾ cup cooked **peas.** Turn into pie shell.

Roll out . . . . remaining dough; cut slits. Place over filling; seal and flute.

Bake . . . . at 450° for 10 minutes, then at 400° for 20 to 25 minutes.

Gourmet Salmon Pie

Senior Winner by Mrs. Margerey Mulkey, Colorado Springs, Colorado

Canned salmon with a gourmet touch—bake salmon-egg mixture in a flaky crust, then serve it with cucumber sauce.

BAKE at 425° for 20 to 25 minutes   SERVES 4 to 6

Prepare . . . . recipe for **One-Crust Pastry**, page 460, using 8-inch pie pan. Do not prick crust; fill and bake as directed below.

Slice . . . . 2 hard-cooked **eggs;*** arrange in bottom of pie shell.

Flake . . . . 1 can (1 lb.) **salmon**** into bowl, removing skin and bones.

Add . . . . 2 beaten **eggs**
    ¼ cup **butter** or margarine, melted
    2 teaspoons minced **parsley** (fresh or dried)
    ¼ teaspoon **salt** and
    ¼ teaspoon **sweet basil,** if desired; mix well. Pour over eggs in pie pan.

Bake . . . . at 425° for 20 to 25 minutes. Serve hot with Cucumber Sauce.

*Hard-cooked eggs may be omitted and beaten eggs increased to 3.

**Or 2½ cups flaked, cooked fresh salmon may be substituted; increase salt to 1 teaspoon.

CUCUMBER SAUCE

Grate 1 medium cucumber (⅓ cup) and ½ onion slice (1 teaspoon); press in strainer to remove juice. Add ¼ cup mayonnaise or salad dressing, 2 teaspoons vinegar, ½ cup thick sour cream, 2 teaspoons minced parsley, 1/16 teaspoon pepper and salt to taste.

Gourmet Salmon Pie

Shrimp Snack Puffs

Senior Winner by Mrs. E. E. Hardies, Santa Rosa, California

Use this shrimp cream puff recipe for hors d'oeuvres with olive-shrimp filling, or as a main dish with creamed shrimp.

BAKE at 425° for 18 to 20 minutes   MAKES about 4 dozen small puffs*

Sift together . ½ cup sifted **Pillsbury's Best All Purpose Flour**** and ¼ teaspoon **salt**

Melt . . . . ¼ cup **shortening** in
½ cup **water;** heat to boiling.

Add . . . . the dry ingredients all at once to boiling liquid, stirring constantly. Cook until mixture leaves sides of pan in smooth compact ball. Remove from heat; cool 1 minute.

Blend in . . . . . 2 **eggs,** one at a time, beating vigorously after each.

Add . . . . ¼ cup finely chopped cooked **shrimp**

Drop . . . . by teaspoonfuls onto greased baking sheets.

Bake . . . . at 425° for 18 to 20 minutes.

Turn . . . . off oven. Prick puffs with sharp knife for escape of steam; leave puffs in oven for 10 minutes to dry out centers. Cool and fill with Olive-Shrimp Filling.

*If desired, main-dish puffs may be made. Drop dough in eight portions on greased baking sheet; bake at 425° for 20 to 25 minutes. While hot, fill with Creamed Shrimp.

**For use with Pillsbury's Best Self-Rising Flour, omit salt.

OLIVE-SHRIMP FILLING

Combine 1 cup chopped cooked shrimp, 8 chopped ripe olives, ½ cup chopped celery, 1 chopped hard-cooked egg, 1 to 2 tablespoons mayonnaise, ¼ teaspoon Worcestershire sauce and, if desired, ½ teaspoon anchovy paste.

CREAMED SHRIMP

Melt ¼ cup butter or margarine over low heat; blend in ¼ cup Pillsbury's Best All Purpose Flour. Gradually add 1½ cups milk; cook, stirring constantly, until thickened. Stir in 1 teaspoon salt, 1 cup chopped cooked shrimp, 1 chopped hard-cooked egg, 2 tablespoons chopped pimiento and ⅛ teaspoon pepper.

Fancy Fish Soufflé

Senior Winner by Mrs. Anna Lindstrom, Highland Mills, New York

An easy-to-make luncheon delight . . . soufflé with a delicate fish flavor.

BAKE at 350° for 50 to 60 minutes   SERVES 4 to 6

Combine . . . . . 1 cup **bread crumbs** and
2 tablespoons **butter,** melted. Sprinkle half of mixture on bottom and sides of well-greased 9x9x2-inch baking dish or 2-quart casserole. Reserve remaining crumbs.

Sift together . ½ cup sifted **Pillsbury's Best All Purpose Flour***
1 teaspoon **salt** and
⅛ teaspoon **pepper**

Melt . . . . ⅓ cup **butter** or margarine in top of double boiler over boiling water. Blend in the dry ingredients.

Add . . . . 2 cups **milk** gradually. Cook, stirring occasionally, until thick.

Stir in . . . . 2 cups (1 lb.) cooked **white fish** boned and flaked**
Blend . . . . a little of hot mixture into
4 beaten **egg yolks.** Add to hot mixture; mix well.
Place over hot water.
Beat . . . . 4 **egg whites** until stiff. Fold into hot mixture.
Turn . . . . into prepared baking dish. Sprinkle with crumbs.
Bake . . . . at 350° for 50 to 60 minutes. Serve immediately with
hot Mustard Lemon Sauce.

*For use with Pillsbury's Best Self-Rising Flour, omit salt.
**Or substitute one 9¼-oz. can well-drained tuna.

MUSTARD LEMON SAUCE

Melt ¼ cup butter or margarine in saucepan. Add ¼ cup Pillsbury's
Best All Purpose Flour, 1 to 2 teaspoons prepared mustard and
1 teaspoon salt, blending well. Gradually add 2 cups hot water and
cook over low heat, stirring constantly, until thickened. Add 2 tablespoons lemon juice; cook 3 minutes.

Tun-au-Gratin

Bride Second Prize Winner by Mrs. Herbert Ward Whitney, Dallas, Texas

*Colorful and appetizing . . . creamy filling of tuna, mushrooms, peas
and pimiento with a cheese and pastry crumb topping.*

BAKE at 450° for 10 to 12 minutes, then   MAKES 9-inch pie
at 425° for 12 to 15 minutes

Prepare . . . . . . recipe for **Lattice Pastry,** page 461, using 9-inch
pie pan; roll out and trim pastry as directed below.
Form . . . . into a ball.
Roll out . . . . . . on floured surface to ⅛-inch thickness. Fit loosely
into pie pan. Trim pastry and place extra pieces in
small baking pan. Fold edge to form a standing rim;
flute. Prick generously.
Bake . . . . crust and pastry pieces at 450° for 10 to 12 minutes.
Crumble pastry pieces for crumb topping.

Tun-au-Gratin

TUNA FILLING

Combine . . . . . 1 can (10½ oz.) **condensed cream of mushroom soup**
¼ cup **milk**
2 tablespoons **flour** and
2 tablespoons **onion flakes** in saucepan. Cook until
thickened.
Add . . . . 1 package (1½ cups) frozen **peas,** thawed and drained
2 cans (6½ oz. each) **tuna** and
1 can (4 oz.) **pimiento,** chopped. Turn hot filling into
pie shell.
Sprinkle . . . . . 1 cup shredded **American cheese** (or 4 slices, halved)
over filling. Top with pastry crumbs.
Bake . . . . at 425° for 12 to 15 minutes.

Colorful Tuna Sandwiches

Junior Winner by La Vern Thompson, St. Joseph, Louisiana

Tuna salad baked between cheese biscuits, flecked with red and green.

BAKE at 450° for 12 to 15 minutes   MAKES 10

Combine . . . . . 1 can (6½ or 9¼ oz.) **tuna**
                ¼ cup **mayonnaise** or salad dressing
                2 hard-cooked **eggs,** diced
                2 tablespoons diced **sweet pickle** or stuffed olives
                2 tablespoons chopped **pimiento** and
                1 tablespoon chopped **green pepper**
Sift together . . 2 cups sifted **Pillsbury's Best All Purpose Flour***
                3 teaspoons double-acting **baking powder** and
                1 teaspoon **salt** into large mixing bowl.
Cut in . . . . . . ½ cup **shortening** until particles are fine.
Stir in . . . . 1 cup shredded **Cheddar cheese** and
                2 tablespoons chopped **pimiento**
Add . . . . ⅔ cup **milk;** stir until dough clings together. Knead on floured surface about 15 strokes.
Roll out . . . . . . to ⅛ to ¼-inch thickness. Cut into twenty 4-inch rounds. Top 10 rounds with a tablespoonful of tuna mixture. Moisten edges; cover with remaining rounds. Seal edges with fork; prick tops. Place on ungreased baking sheet.
Bake . . . . at 450° for 12 to 15 minutes. Serve hot with Pimiento Cheese Sauce.

*For use with Pillsbury's Best Self-Rising Flour, omit baking powder and salt.

PIMIENTO CHEESE SAUCE

Melt ¼ cup butter or margarine in top of double boiler. Add 3 tablespoons chopped green pepper; cook over boiling water until soft, about 2 minutes. Blend in ¼ cup Pillsbury's Best All Purpose Flour. Add 2 cups milk and cook, stirring occasionally, until thickened. Stir in 1½ cups shredded Cheddar cheese, ⅓ cup sliced mushrooms, if desired, 2 tablespoons chopped pimiento and ½ teaspoon salt; cook and stir just until cheese is melted.

Colorful Tuna Sandwiches

CHEESE and EGG DISHES

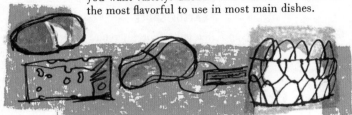

with their rich amount of protein are wonderful substitutes for meats when you want variety. Cheddar and American cheese are the most flavorful to use in most main dishes.

Cheesy Eggplant Pie

Senior Winner by Mrs. Carry Tom Smith, Fort Worth, Texas

Hiding between layers of cheese pastry is a medley of eggplant, tomatoes and cheese . . . a wonderful blend of flavors.

BAKE at 425° for 30 to 35 minutes   SERVES 6 to 8

Shred . . . . . . ½ pound sharp **Cheddar cheese**; set aside.

Prepare . . . . recipe for **Two-Crust Pastry,** page 460, cutting in ¼ cup of the cheese with the shortening. Shape and roll out pastry as directed below.

Divide . . . . into two portions, one twice as large as the other. Form into balls.

Roll out . . . . larger portion on floured surface to circle 1½ inches larger than inverted 10-inch pie pan; fit loosely into pan. (Or fit into 2-quart casserole.) Cover while preparing Eggplant Filling.

EGGPLANT FILLING

Pare . . . . 1 large **eggplant** (about 1¼ lbs.). Cut into slices ⅛ inch thick; quarter slices.

Sauté . . . . half of eggplant in ¼ cup **butter** or margarine in large skillet until tender. Repeat with remaining eggplant, using ¼ cup more **butter**. Drain on absorbent paper.

Melt . . . . 2 tablespoons **butter** in same skillet. Add ¼ cup chopped **green pepper** and 2 tablespoons chopped **onion**. Cook until tender. Add 1 cup (8-oz. can) **tomato sauce**; heat thoroughly.

Melt . . . . 2 tablespoons **butter** in small saucepan. Blend in 2 tablespoons **flour**. Gradually add 1 cup **milk**; cook, stirring constantly, until thick. Add ¾ teaspoon **salt** and 1/16 teaspoon **pepper**

Place . . . . half of eggplant, half of the remaining cheese and half of tomato sauce in pie shell. Repeat with remainder. Pour white sauce over top.*

Roll out . . . . . . remaining dough to fit top of pan; place over filling. Seal and flute.

Bake . . . . at 425° for 30 to 35 minutes. Let stand 5 minutes before serving.

If desired, white sauce may be omitted.

Cheesy Eggplant Pie

Luncheon Cheeseolettes

Junior Winner by Sharon Reny, Chicago, Illinois

Like individual cheese omelets, these tasty little cakes come piping hot off the griddle. Satisfying, yet light as a feather.

FRY about 3 minutes   SERVES 6 to 8

Sift together . ¾ cup sifted **Pillsbury's Best All Purpose Flour***
                1 teaspoon double-acting **baking powder** and
                ½ teaspoon **salt**
Sauté . . . . ½ cup finely chopped **onion** in
                2 tablespoons **shortening** until golden brown.
Beat . . . . 6 **eggs** until thick and ivory colored.
Fold in . . . . . 2½ cups shredded **Cheddar cheese** (½ pound). Add dry
                ingredients and onion, folding gently but thoroughly.
Drop . . . . by rounded teaspoonfuls onto hot greased griddle.

Luncheon Cheeseolettes

Bake until golden brown on both sides, turning only once. Serve hot with Catsup Sauce.

*For use with Pillsbury's Best Self-Rising Flour, omit baking powder and salt.

CATSUP SAUCE

Combine ½ cup catsup, 1 teaspoon Worcestershire sauce and ¼ cup water in saucepan; heat to simmering point.

French Original Sandwiches

Senior Winner by Mrs. A. F. Pulliam, Sullivan, Missouri

The family will love these for breakfast or lunch—sandwiches with cottage cheese, applesauce, brown sugar . . . dipped in batter, then fried.

FRY about 4 minutes   MAKES 2 dozen

Butter . . . . 6 slices day-old **bread**
Spread . . . . each slice with
                2 tablespoons small-curd **cottage cheese,** then with
                1 tablespoon sweetened **applesauce**
Sprinkle . . . . . 1 tablespoon **brown sugar** over each slice. Top with
                6 additional slices buttered **bread,** sandwich-style. Cut
                sandwiches into fourths.
Sift together 1¾ cups sifted **Pillsbury's Best All Purpose Flour***
                1½ teaspoons double-acting **baking powder** and
                ½ teaspoon **salt** into large mixing bowl.
Add . . . . 3 unbeaten **egg yolks**
                1⅓ cups **milk** and
                3 tablespoons **butter,** melted. Beat only until blended.
Beat . . . . 3 **egg whites** until stiff but not dry. Fold into batter.
Dip . . . . sandwiches into batter, coating completely.
Fry . . . . in skillet in ¾ inch of fat until golden brown, about
                2 minutes on each side. Turn only once. Serve plain
                or sprinkled with **confectioners' sugar** and topped
                with **jelly.**

*Pillsbury's Best Self-Rising Flour is not recommended for use in this recipe.

Egg Baskets

Best of Class Winner by Mrs. James Morrison Bridges, La Crescenta, California

Eggs baked inside tender cheese pastry in muffin cups. Serve plain for breakfast or with cheese sauce for lunch or supper.

BAKE at 450° for 20 to 22 minutes   SERVES 6

Prepare....... recipe for **Lattice Pastry,** page 461, cutting in ⅓ cup shredded **Cheddar cheese** with the shortening. Shape and roll out as directed below.

Form......... into a ball.

Roll out....... on floured surface to ⅛-inch thickness. Cut out six circles about 5 inches across. Fit each into a muffin cup or individual tart pan, forming a smooth lining. Let pastry edges extend ¼ inch above pan.

Cut out....... six more circles, about 4 inches across, re-rolling dough for last few circles. Cut slit in center of each.

Break....... 6 **eggs** in pastry-lined pans. Sprinkle with **salt** and **pepper.** Cover with circles. Seal edges; flute. Sprinkle with **paprika.**

Bake......... at 450°: in muffin cups for 20 to 22 minutes; in tart pans for 15 to 18 minutes. Serve hot with Cheese Dill Sauce.

CHEESE DILL SAUCE

Melt ⅓ cup butter or margarine in saucepan. Blend in ⅓ cup Pillsbury's Best All Purpose Flour. Gradually add 2½ cups milk; cook over medium heat, stirring constantly, until thickened. Remove from heat; stir in ½ cup shredded Cheddar cheese, 2 tablespoons chopped parsley, 2 teaspoons crushed dill seed and ½ teaspoon salt. Cover until serving time.

Egg Baskets

Lima Cheese Pie

Add . . . . 2½ cups (No. 2 can) **tomatoes,** undrained
  1 teaspoon **salt** and
  1 teaspoon **Worcestershire sauce.** Cook over medium
    heat, stirring constantly, until thickened. Set aside.
Place . . . . 2 cups cooked **lima beans** (1 pkg. frozen) alternately with
  1 cup shredded **cheese** and the tomato-onion mixture
    in pie shell, ending with tomato-onion mixture.
Roll out . . . . . . remaining dough; cut slits. Place over filling. Fold
    edge under bottom crust, pressing to seal. Flute.
Bake . . . . at 425° for 25 to 30 minutes.
  *Pie may be baked in a shallow casserole with just a top crust; divide pastry
  recipe in half, roll out and place over filling in casserole.*
  **For use with Pillsbury's Best Self-Rising Flour, decrease salt to ½ teaspoon.*

Yorkshire Cheese Puff

Senior Winner by Mrs. Margaret Leighton, Wichita, Kansas

*They'll say, "More, please," when you serve this English popover
with your meal.*

BAKE at 400° for 30 to 35 minutes   SERVES 4 to 6

Sift together . . 1 cup sifted **Pillsbury's Best All Purpose Flour***
  ½ teaspoon **salt** and
  1/16 teaspoon **pepper** into mixing bowl.
Add . . . . 2 unbeaten **eggs** and
  ½ cup **milk.** Beat with electric mixer or rotary beater
    until smooth.
Blend in . . . . . ½ cup **milk,** mixing thoroughly. Stir in
  ½ cup shredded **cheese** (Swiss, American or Cheddar)
Melt . . . . 2 tablespoons **butter** in 9-inch square pan.
Pour . . . . batter into pan. Sprinkle with
  ½ cup shredded **cheese**
Bake . . . . at 400° for 30 to 35 minutes. Serve hot with roast
    meat or chicken.
  Pillsbury's Best Self-Rising Flour is not recommended for use in this recipe.

Lima Cheese Pie

Senior Winner by Mrs. George H. Gitz, Jr., Corning, Iowa

*A succulent lima bean, cheese and tomato mixture is baked in a
double crust of tender cheese pastry.*

BAKE at 425° for 25 to 30 minutes   MAKES 9-inch pie*

Prepare . . . . recipe for **Lattice Pastry,** page 461, cutting in
  ½ cup shredded **Cheddar cheese** with the shortening.
    Use 9-inch pie pan.* Fill and roll out remaining
    pastry as directed below.
Sauté . . . . ½ cup chopped **onion** in
  ¼ cup **shortening** in saucepan until tender.
Blend in . . . . . ¼ cup **Pillsbury's Best All Purpose Flour****

Inflation Soufflé

Junior Winner by Betty Muller, Forest Hills, New York

This is a cheese soufflé with a special flavor. And it stays high and fluffy! One of the best we've ever eaten.

BAKE at 350° for 45 to 55 minutes   SERVES 6

Melt........½ cup **butter** or margarine in saucepan; remove from heat.

Sift together.¾ cup sifted **Pillsbury's Best All Purpose Flour***
   ½ teaspoon **salt**
   ¼ teaspoon **dry mustard** and
   ⅛ teaspoon **onion salt.** Add to melted butter in saucepan; mix thoroughly.

Add.......1½ cups **milk** gradually. Cook over low heat, stirring constantly, until very thick.

Add.......1½ cups shredded **Cheddar cheese** and
   ¼ teaspoon **Worcestershire sauce**; stir until cheese is melted.

Blend in.....6 unbeaten **egg yolks,** one at a time.

Beat........6 **egg whites** until stiff but not dry; fold into cheese mixture. Pour into ungreased 2-quart casserole.

Bake.........in pan of hot water at 350° for 45 to 55 minutes.

*For use with Pillsbury's Best Self-Rising Flour, omit salt.

PANCAKES, FRITTERS and WAFFLES

Pancakes or fritters make a good potato substitute; serve with roast meat and gravy. Waffles are ideal for Sunday-night suppers and breakfast variety.

To season a griddle or waffle iron: Preheat iron, brush with unsalted fat and let fat "smoke off" several times.

Pancakes should be baked on hot griddle or in a skillet. To test, drop water on griddle; if drops "dance," griddle should be ready for baking. Electric griddles and skillets have a special temperature setting for baking pancakes.

Overmixing of pancake batter should be avoided; the batter may appear slightly lumpy. (If pancake or waffle batter thickens upon standing, add more milk.)

Pour batter for each pancake onto skillet in one step; pancakes are ready to turn when the tops are full of holes and have lost their shiny surface. The bottom sides should be golden brown. Turn pancakes only once; do not press down with spatula.

Griddles need not be greased after the first pancake if batter contains two or more tablespoons of shortening for every cup of liquid.

While baking pancakes, griddle may be rubbed with a cloth bag filled with salt. Use bag after baking to clean the griddle.

The waffle iron must be hot before baking the first waffle. Do not wash a waffle iron after each use; steel brushes are available for cleaning. Cool the waffle iron with the cover open.

Banana Griddle Cakes

Banana Griddle Cakes

Senior Winner by Mrs. Clifford Moes, APO 10, New York, New York

A brunch favorite! Maple syrup will bring out the true banana flavor in these cakes.

BAKE on hot griddle   MAKES 8 to 10

Sift together..1 cup sifted **Pillsbury's Best All Purpose Flour***
               2 tablespoons **sugar**
               2 teaspoons double-acting **baking powder** and
               ½ teaspoon **salt** into mixing bowl.
Combine.....1 beaten **egg**
               ¾ cup **milk**
               2 tablespoons **butter** or margarine, melted, and

⅓ cup mashed **banana** (1 medium). Add to the dry
         ingredients all at once. Beat just until large lumps
         disappear. (With mixer use a low speed.)
Bake.........on hot griddle (375°), using 3 tablespoons batter for
         each. Turn when edges start to dry. Serve hot with
         butter and **maple syrup.**

*For use with Pillsbury's Best Self-Rising Flour, omit baking powder and salt.

Berry Brunch Cakes

Senior Winner by Mrs. Joan Whiteside, Kernville, California

Start the day off right with pancakes, tender and light . . . or top with berry cream for pancake supreme.

BAKE on hot griddle   SERVES 8 to 10

Sift together..1 cup sifted **Pillsbury's Best All Purpose Flour***
               2 tablespoons **sugar**
               4 teaspoons double-acting **baking powder** and
               1½ teaspoons **salt** into mixing bowl. Add
               ⅓ cup quick-cooking **rolled oats** and
               ¼ cup **yellow corn meal**
Combine.....4 unbeaten **egg yolks**
               1½ cups **milk** and
               2 tablespoons **salad oil**. Add to the dry ingredients
         all at once. Mix until smooth. (With mixer use a
         low speed.)
Beat.........4 **egg whites** until stiff but not dry. Fold half of
         beaten egg whites into batter. Save remainder for
         Topping.
Bake.........on hot griddle (375°), using 2 tablespoons batter for
         each**. Turn when edges start to dry. Serve with
         Berry Cream Topping.

*For use with Pillsbury's Best Self-Rising Flour, decrease baking powder to 2½ teaspoons and salt to 1 teaspoon.

**For larger pancakes, use ¼ cup batter.

BERRY CREAM TOPPING

Add 2 tablespoons sugar and ⅛ teaspoon salt to the reserved egg whites; beat until straight peaks form. Beat 1 cup whipping cream until thick. Fold in beaten egg whites, then 1 package (10 oz.) frozen raspberries or strawberries, well drained.

Cheese 'n' Herb Pancakes

Senior Winner by Mrs. Gertrude W. Ensign, Cleveland, Ohio

Hot, flavorful pancakes just off the griddle! Everyone will compliment you on this delicious potato substitute.

BAKE on hot griddle   MAKES 14 to 16

Sift together 1½ cups sifted **Pillsbury's Best All Purpose Flour***
       3 teaspoons double-acting **baking powder**
       1 teaspoon **sugar**
       ½ teaspoon **salt** and
       ¼ teaspoon **pot herbs** into mixing bowl.
Combine . . . . . 3 beaten **egg yolks**
       1½ cups **milk** and
       3 tablespoons **butter,** melted. Add to the dry ingredients all at once. Beat just until large lumps disappear. (With mixer use a low speed.)
Beat . . . . 3 **egg whites** until stiff but not dry. Fold into batter with
       1½ cups shredded **Cheddar cheese**
Bake . . . . on hot griddle (375°), using ¼ cup batter for each. Turn when edges start to dry. Serve hot with roast meat and gravy, if desired.

*For use with Pillsbury's Best Self-Rising Flour, omit baking powder and salt.

Ham 'n' Corn Fritters

Junior Winner by Louise Propst, New Brunswick, New Jersey

Fritters filled with nuggets of golden corn and bits of ham and topped with tangy cheese sauce.

FRY at 375° for 3 to 4 minutes   MAKES about 4 dozen

Sift together 1½ cups sifted **Pillsbury's Best All Purpose Flour***
       2 teaspoons double-acting **baking powder**
       1 teaspoon **salt** and
       1 teaspoon **dry mustard** into mixing bowl.
Combine . . . . . 2 slightly beaten **eggs**
       ½ cup **milk** and
       2 tablespoons **shortening,** melted. Add to the dry ingredients all at once; mix until all dry particles are moistened.
Stir in . . . . . 1½ cups finely chopped cooked **ham** and
       1½ cups (12-oz. pkg.) drained **whole kernel corn**
Drop . . . . by rounded teaspoonfuls into hot deep fat (375°), and fry on both sides until golden brown, 3 to 4 minutes. Serve hot with Cheese Sauce.

*For use with Pillsbury's Best Self-Rising Flour, omit baking powder and salt.

CHEESE SAUCE

Melt ¼ cup butter or margarine in saucepan. Blend in 3 tablespoons flour. Gradually add 2 cups milk; cook over low heat, stirring constantly, until thickened. Add 1 teaspoon salt, ½ teaspoon Worcestershire sauce and ¾ cup shredded cheese. Heat thoroughly.

Crispy Cream Waffles

Crispy Cream Waffles

Senior Winner by Mrs. Leroy W. Hall, Oklahoma City, Oklahoma

Mrs. Hall was searching for a really crisp waffle when she developed this recipe. They're quick to make—and delicious!

BAKE at medium heat 3 to 4 minutes   MAKES 3 four-section waffles

Sift together . . 1 cup sifted **Pillsbury's Best All Purpose Flour***
              1 tablespoon **sugar**
              1½ teaspoons double-acting **baking powder** and
              ½ teaspoon **salt**
Beat . . . . 2 **egg yolks** until thick and lemon colored.
Add . . . . 1 cup **whipping cream** to egg yolks; mix slightly.
Stir in . . . . the dry ingredients all at once, mixing only until smooth.

Blend in . . . . . 2 tablespoons **butter** or margarine, melted
Beat . . . . 2 **egg whites** until stiff but not dry. Fold gently into batter. (Batter will be stiff.)
Bake . . . . in preheated waffle iron until steaming stops and waffle is golden brown. Serve topped with **sour cream,** if desired.

*For use with Pillsbury's Best Self-Rising Flour, omit baking powder and salt.

Date Waffles

Senior Winner by Mrs. Lillis Engler, Utica, Michigan

Crispy date waffles! Serve as dessert with lemon topping or for breakfast with syrup.

BAKE at medium heat 5 to 6 minutes   MAKES 3 four-section waffles

Sift together . . 2 cups sifted **Pillsbury's Best All Purpose Flour***
              3 teaspoons double-acting **baking powder** and
              1 teaspoon **salt** into large mixing bowl. Stir in
              ¼ cup firmly packed **brown sugar** and
              1 cup **dates,** finely cut
Combine . . . . . 2 well-beaten **egg yolks**
              1¾ cups **milk** and
              ½ cup **shortening,** melted. Add to the dry ingredients all at once; mix until smooth.
Beat . . . . 2 **egg whites** until stiff but not dry. Fold into batter.
Bake . . . . in preheated waffle iron until steaming stops and waffle is golden brown. Serve as a dessert with Lemon Topping or lemon sauce and ice cream. Or serve as a breakfast waffle with **maple syrup.**

*For use with Pillsbury's Best Self-Rising Flour, omit baking powder and salt.

LEMON TOPPING

Combine 1 package (8 oz.) softened cream cheese, ¼ cup cream, 2 teaspoons grated lemon rind, 2 tablespoons lemon juice and ¼ cup sugar. Beat until light and fluffy.

VEGETABLE DISHES

VEGETABLE DISHES are perfect for a simple luncheon or a meatless meal. Include a crisp green salad or fruit gelatin mold with any of the recipes in this section.

Asparagus Cheese Pie

Senior Winner by Mrs. Paul M. Scheffer, Portland, Oregon

Rich cheese and asparagus filling in a biscuit crust. Easy!

BAKE at 350° for 35 to 40 minutes   MAKES 8-inch pie

Combine . . . . . 1 cup shredded **Cheddar cheese**
½ cup **mayonnaise** or salad dressing
1 teaspoon **lemon juice** and
1½ cups cut cooked **asparagus** (10-oz. pkg.). Set aside.

Sift together . . 1 cup sifted **Pillsbury's Best All Purpose Flour***
2 teaspoons double-acting **baking powder** and
¼ teaspoon **salt** into mixing bowl.

Cut in . . . . . . ¼ cup **shortening** until particles are fine.

Add . . . . ⅓ cup **milk**; stir until dough clings together. Form into a ball.

Roll out . . . . . . on floured surface to 9-inch circle. Fit into 8-inch pie pan. Dough should reach just to rim of pan. (Do not flute.)

Spread . . . . filling in biscuit-lined pan. Sprinkle with 2 tablespoons blanched, slivered **almonds** and **paprika**

Bake . . . . at 350° for 35 to 40 minutes. Serve hot.

For use with Pillsbury's Best Self-Rising Flour, omit baking powder and salt.

Dinner Bell Corn Pie

Senior Winner by Dorothy G. Kent, Sunbury, Pennsylvania

Two flaky crusts cradle a filling of bacon, green pepper, corn and celery soup. An economical, satisfying meal.

BAKE at 400° for 45 to 50 minutes   SERVES 4 to 6

Fry . . . . ½ pound **bacon** until crisp. Reserve drippings. Crumble bacon and set aside.

Sift together . . 2 cups sifted **Pillsbury's Best All Purpose Flour*** and ¼ teaspoon **salt** into large mixing bowl. Add ½ cup of bacon drippings; mix only until all dry particles are moistened.

Sprinkle . . . . . 6 to 7 tablespoons cold **milk** over mixture, stirring with fork until dough is moist enough to hold together.

Divide . . . . in half. Form into balls.

Roll out . . . . . . one portion on floured surface to a circle 1½ inches larger than inverted 9-inch pie pan. Fit into pan.

For use with Pillsbury's Best Self-Rising Flour, omit salt.

CORN-BACON FILLING

Combine . . . . . 1 package (10 oz.) frozen **whole-kernel corn,** thawed (or 2 cups canned corn)
¼ cup chopped **green pepper**
¼ cup chopped **onion**
3 hard-cooked **eggs,** chopped
1 can (10½ oz.) **condensed cream of celery soup**
salt to taste and the reserved crumbled bacon. Turn into pie shell.

Roll out . . . . . . remaining dough; cut slits. Moisten rim of bottom crust. Place top crust over filling. Fold edge under bottom crust. Seal edge; flute.

Bake . . . . at 400° for 45 to 50 minutes. If desired, sprinkle with **paprika.**

Corn Beanie Casserole

Corn Beanie Casserole

Senior Winner by Mrs. Charles N. Colstad, Portuguese Bend, California

Baked beans and bacon, with corn meal biscuits to boot! A wonderful western-style meal for patio or buffet.

BAKE at 350° for 45 minutes, then   SERVES 8 to 10
    at 425° for 15 to 20 minutes

Fry . . . . ½ pound **bacon** until crisp; crumble.
Sauté . . . . 1 cup (2 bunches) chopped **green onions,** including
         tops, in 2 tablespoons of bacon fat.
Combine . . . . . . in 2-quart casserole
         3 cans (15½ oz. each) **red kidney beans**

        ⅓ cup **chili sauce**
        ⅓ cup firmly packed **brown sugar**
        1 teaspoon **Worcestershire sauce**
        ¼ teaspoon **dry mustard**
        2 drops **Tabasco sauce,** crumbled bacon and sautéed
        onion.
Bake . . . . at 350° for 45 minutes, stirring occasionally. In-
        crease temperature to 425°.
Top . . . . with Corn Meal Biscuits. Bake for 15 to 20 minutes.

CORN MEAL BISCUITS

Sift together 1½ cups sifted **Pillsbury's Best All Purpose Flour*
        3 teaspoons double-acting **baking powder**
        2 teaspoons **sugar** and
        1 teaspoon **salt** into mixing bowl. Stir in
        ½ cup **corn meal**
Cut in . . . . . . ¼ cup **shortening** until particles are fine.
Add . . . . ¾ cup **milk;** stir until dough clings together. Knead on
        floured surface 10 strokes.
Roll out . . . . to ½-inch thickness. Cut with 2-inch round cutter.
*For use with Pillsbury's Best Self-Rising Flour, decrease baking powder to
  1 teaspoon and omit salt.

Succotash Supper

Senior Winner by Mrs. Helen Trotter, Paoli, Indiana

Rich egg biscuits filled with deviled ham top a creamy succotash and pimiento mixture.

BAKE at 425° for 25 to 30 minutes   SERVES 6 to 9

Sauté . . . . ¼ cup finely chopped **onion** in
        3 tablespoons **shortening** in saucepan until tender,
        about 5 minutes.
Blend in . . . . . 3 tablespoons **flour;** stir until smooth.
Add . . . . 2 cups **milk** gradually, stirring constantly. Cook and

stir until thickened.

Stir in	3 cups cooked drained **succotash** (two 12-oz. pkgs.)
	¼ cup finely chopped **pimiento** and
	1 to 1½ teaspoons **salt**. Heat to simmering point, stirring occasionally. Prepare Deviled Ham Biscuits.
Pour	succotash mixture into greased 9-inch square or 2-quart casserole. Top with Biscuits, cut-side down.
Bake	at 425° for 25 to 30 minutes.

DEVILED HAM BISCUITS

Sift together . .	1 cup sifted **Pillsbury's Best All Purpose Flour***
	2 teaspoons double-acting **baking powder**
	1 teaspoon **sugar** and
	½ teaspoon **salt** into mixing bowl.
Cut in	¼ cup **shortening** until particles are fine.
Combine	1 unbeaten **egg** and **milk** to measure ⅓ cup. Beat with fork. Add to the dry ingredients all at once; stir until dough clings together.
Roll out	on floured surface to 9-inch square. Spread with 2 cans (3¼ oz. each) **deviled ham**. Roll as for jelly roll; cut into 1-inch slices.

For use with Pillsbury's Best Self-Rising Flour, omit baking powder and salt in biscuits.

Savory Corn Bake

Senior Winner by Mrs. J. C. H. Ballentine, Columbia, South Carolina

A fluffy corn pudding made flavorful with bits of bacon and green pepper.

BAKE at 350° for about 1 hour   SERVES 4 to 6

Fry	½ pound **bacon** until crisp; drain. Crumble.*
Sift together .	¾ cup sifted **Pillsbury's Best All Purpose Flour****
	2 tablespoons **corn meal**
	1 teaspoon **salt** and
	1/16 teaspoon **pepper**

Savory Corn Bake

Combine	2 unbeaten **egg yolks** and
	1 cup **milk** in large mixing bowl. Beat thoroughly. Blend in the dry ingredients; beat until smooth.
Stir in	1¾ cups (16-oz. can) **cream-style corn**
	½ cup chopped **green pepper** and the bacon.
Beat	2 **egg whites** with
	3 teaspoons double-acting **baking powder** until stiff but not dry. Fold thoroughly into corn mixture. Turn into well-greased 2-quart casserole.
Bake	at 350° for about 1 hour.

If desired, 1 cup diced cooked ham may be substituted for the bacon.

***For use with Pillsbury's Best Self-Rising Flour, decrease baking powder to 1 teaspoon.*

Caraway Onion Pie

Caraway Onion Pie

Bride Winner by Mrs. Jakob Schor, San Luis Obispo, California

A hearty luncheon dish . . . onion and cheese custard in a caraway crust.

BAKE at 400° for 35 to 40 minutes   MAKES 9-inch pie

Prepare . . . . recipe for **One-Crust Pastry,** page 460, adding 1 tablespoon **caraway seed** to flour-salt mixture. Use 9-inch pie pan. Fill and bake as directed.

Steam . . . . 4 cups thinly sliced and quartered **onions** in 2 tablespoons **butter** in covered saucepan over *low heat* until tender, about 15 minutes. Place in pie shell.

Combine . . . . . 2 tablespoons **flour**
  1½ teaspoons **salt**

¼ teaspoon **paprika** and
½ cup grated **Parmesan cheese** in bowl. Add
3 unbeaten **eggs** and
1¼ cups **milk;** mix well. Pour mixture over onions.

Bake . . . . at 400° for 35 to 40 minutes.

Creamy-Onion Delish'

Senior Winner by Mrs. Melvin T. Lake, Madison, Wisconsin

Family-size vegetable dish . . . circles of pastry line this tasty casserole of creamed onions and mushrooms.

BAKE at 425° for 20 to 25 minutes   SERVES 6 to 8

Sift together 1½ cups sifted **Pillsbury's Best All Purpose Flour*** and ½ teaspoon **salt** into mixing bowl.

Cut in . . . . . . ½ cup **butter** or margarine until the size of small peas.

Blend . . . . 1 slightly beaten **egg** with 1 tablespoon **milk.** Sprinkle over mixture, stirring with fork until dough is moist enough to hold together.

Roll out . . . . to ⅛-inch thickness. Cut with 2½-inch round cutter. Arrange on bottom and sides of 8-inch or 1½-quart casserole. Reserve 8 circles for top.

Cook . . . . 4 cups sliced and quartered **onions** (5 medium) in boiling salted water for 10 minutes.** Drain.

Add . . . . ¼ cup **butter** or margarine and ½ cup **mushrooms,** chopped fresh or canned, to onions. Sauté 10 minutes.

Stir in . . . . . . ⅓ cup (3-oz. pkg.) **cream cheese,** stirring until cheese is softened.

Blend in . . . . . 1 cup **milk** and 1 tablespoon **flour.** Pour into baking dish and top with pastry circles.

Bake . . . . at 425° for 20 to 25 minutes. Serve hot.

*For use with Pillsbury's Best Self-Rising Flour, *omit salt in pastry.*
**Two No. 303 cans onions, drained, may be substituted; *omit the boiling step.*

Tomato Cheeserole Dinner

Best of Class Winner by Mrs. Verne E. Starke, Claremont, California

There's cheese in fluffy dumplings served with delicious tomato sauce.

STEAM 20 to 25 minutes   SERVES 4 to 6

Sauté . . . . 2 tablespoons chopped **onion** and
    1 tablespoon chopped **green pepper** in
    2 tablespoons **shortening** in wide, deep saucepan until tender.
Blend in . . . . . 2 tablespoons **flour;** stir until smooth.
Add . . . . 3½ cups (No. 2½ can) **tomatoes.** Stir.
Stir in . . . . 1 tablespoon chopped **celery tops** or parsley
    1 teaspoon **sugar**
    ½ teaspoon **salt** and
    ⅛ teaspoon **pepper.** Bring to boil, stirring constantly. Simmer over low heat 5 minutes, stirring occasionally.

CHEESE DUMPLINGS

Sift together . . 1 cup sifted **Pillsbury's Best All Purpose Flour***
    2 teaspoons double-acting **baking powder** and
    ½ teaspoon **salt** into mixing bowl.
Cut in . . . . 2 tablespoons **shortening** until particles are fine.
Blend in . . . . . ⅔ cup shredded **American** or **Cheddar cheese** and
    1 tablespoon chopped **parsley**
Add . . . . ½ cup **milk** all at once; stir only until all dry particles are moistened.
Dip . . . . a tablespoon into cold water. Drop batter from spoon onto hot tomato sauce. Cover tightly.
Steam . . . . for 20 to 25 minutes. Do not remove the cover during steaming process. Serve immediately.

For use with Pillsbury's Best Self-Rising Flour, omit baking powder and salt in dumplings.

Garden Medley Pie

Junior Winner by Joan Hunsberger, Manhattan, Kansas

Flavorful, colorful vegetables with a bacon biscuit topping.

BAKE at 425° for 20 to 25 minutes   SERVES 6 to 8

Fry . . . . 4 or 5 strips **bacon** until crisp. Reserve drippings. Crumble bacon and set aside.
Blend . . . . ¼ cup **Pillsbury's Best All Purpose Flour** with ¼ cup of bacon drippings in 3-quart saucepan.
Stir in . . . . 3 cups **milk.** Cook over medium heat, stirring constantly, until thickened.
Add . . . . 1 cup cooked small white **onions**
    2 cups cooked **green vegetable** (peas, green beans or lima beans)
    1 cup diced cooked **carrots** and
    1 cup diced cooked **potatoes.** Bring to boil, stirring constantly. Remove from heat.
Stir in . . . . 1 to 1½ teaspoons **salt**
    ½ teaspoon **celery salt** and
    ½ teaspoon **paprika.** Cover.

BACON BISCUIT TOPPING

Sift together 1½ cups sifted **Pillsbury's Best All Purpose Flour***
    2 teaspoons double-acting **baking powder** and
    ½ teaspoon **salt** into mixing bowl.
Cut in . . . . . . ⅓ cup **shortening** until particles are fine.
Crumble . . . . the bacon into the flour mixture. Add
    ½ cup plus 1 tablespoon **milk;** mix until dough clings together.
Knead . . . . on floured surface 10 strokes. Roll out to a 12x8-inch rectangle; cut slits.
Pour . . . . hot filling into 12x8x2-inch baking dish. Top with biscuit rectangle; brush with **cream** or **milk.**
Bake . . . . at 425° for 20 to 25 minutes. Serve hot.

For use with Pillsbury's Best Self-Rising Flour, omit baking powder and salt in topping.

Bacon Spinach Pie

Junior Winner by Linda Lee Bauman, Whitehouse, Ohio

Colorful spinach in a main-dish custard pie, flavored with crisp bacon and topped with shredded cheese. You'll like spinach this way.

BAKE at 400° for 25 to 30 minutes   SERVES 6

Prepare . . . . recipe for **One-Crust Pastry**, page 460, using 9-inch pie pan. Fill and bake as directed below.

Chop . . . . 3 cups washed and thoroughly drained fresh **spinach**. (Or substitute 12-oz. pkg. frozen chopped spinach, thawed and thoroughly drained.)

Fry . . . . 6 strips **bacon** until crisp; crumble into pie shell. Add spinach.

Combine . . . . . 3 slightly beaten **eggs**
2 teaspoons **sugar**

Bacon Spinach Pie

1 teaspoon **salt**
¼ teaspoon **onion salt**
⅛ teaspoon **pepper** and
1/16 teaspoon **cayenne pepper,** if desired, in large mixing bowl.

Stir in . . . . 2 cups hot **milk**

Pour . . . . over spinach in pie shell. Top with
1 cup (¼ lb.) shredded **American** or **Cheddar cheese**

Bake . . . . at 400° for 25 to 30 minutes. Let stand 5 minutes before serving.

Patio Picnic Casserole

Senior Winner by Mrs. Earl Raymond Broadwell, Santa Barbara, California

Spices and black olives add a real Western touch to this meatless main dish. It's inexpensive and easy to make.

BAKE at 350° for 1½ hours   SERVES 4 to 6

Sift together . ½ cup sifted **Pillsbury's Best All Purpose Flour***
2 teaspoons **salt**
1 teaspoon double-acting **baking powder**
2 teaspoons **chili powder** and
¼ teaspoon **pepper** into mixing bowl. Stir in
1 cup **corn meal**

Combine . . . 3½ cups (two 16-oz. cans) **cream-style corn**
1 cup (8-oz. can) **tomato sauce**
1 cup **milk**
½ cup **shortening**, melted, and
2 well-beaten **eggs**. Add to the dry ingredients; mix well.

Stir in . . . . 1 cup chopped **ripe** or **green olives** and
2 tablespoons grated **onion**. Pour into greased 2-quart casserole.

Bake . . . . at 350° for 1½ hours.

*For use with Pillsbury's Best Self-Rising Flour, omit baking powder.

CAKES

A glamourous cake is one of the most appealing of foods. How proud and satisfied you'll be to serve a delicate, moist, light-as-a feather, velvet-grained cake! It's fun to bake a delicious cake . . . even more fun to see the family enjoy it.

The number of cake recipes is limitless. However, nearly every cake contains the same basic ingredients; they are the framework on which a cake is "built." In the oven, these ingredients in the batter miraculously turn into light, tender and flavorful cakes.

KNOW YOUR INGREDIENTS—*For the BEST cakes, start with the BEST ingredients!*

Flour is the basic ingredient that gives body to your cake. The recipes in this book have been developed for use with Pillsbury's Best All Purpose Flour. Although special cake flours are available, very fine cakes may be made with all purpose flour. It is best to use the type of flour for which a recipe has been developed.

Sugar gives flavor and tenderness to your cake; it is necessary for browning and for good texture.

Shortening adds richness and makes your cake tender. Shortenings include butter, margarine, lard, hydrogenated vegetable and animal fats, and salad oil. Again, it is important to use the type of shortening recommended in the recipe. Some recipes require the use of a "quick-mix" or hydrogenated shortening (see Mixing Methods). Salad oil is used in certain types of cakes, but should not be substituted for solid shortenings.

Leavening increases volume and produces a light, tender cake. Baking powder, soda and air are all leavening agents. In sponge- and angel food cakes, the air beaten into the eggs is usually the only leavening. In shortening cakes, baking powder or soda is the chief leavening.

There are various types of baking powder, each varying in formula and speed of action. Recipes in this book specify double-acting baking powder; check the label on your baking-powder can if you're not sure which type you have. Baking powder should be tightly covered and

stored in a cool, dry place. Long storage may reduce its strength, so if you do little baking, purchase a small can; it is wise to date the can.

Soda is generally used in recipes calling for sour cream, buttermilk or molasses.

Eggs bind the other ingredients together and contribute to the framework of a cake. They add flavor and increase volume, especially in cakes where whites are beaten separately and folded into the batter.

Liquid, usually sweet milk or buttermilk, dissolves the sugar and salt and develops the starch and gluten in flour.

MIXING METHODS—*For Shortening Cakes*

Conventional Method—The sugar and shortening are creamed together first. Butter, margarine or lard should be at room temperature for easy creaming. Sugar should be added gradually to the shortening until the mixture is very light and fluffy. An electric mixer at high speed does this quickly. If creaming by hand, use wooden spoon.

Eggs are then added, unbeaten or beaten separately, according to the recipe. If unbeaten, add one at a time and beat thoroughly with other ingredients. If eggs are separated, fold the stiffly beaten whites into the batter just before pouring batter into pan.

To add the liquid and flour mixtures, always begin and end with dry ingredients; the batter may curdle if liquid is added first. Blend well after each addition, but *do not overbeat.* (With electric mixer use a low speed.) First add about ⅓ of the flour, then remainder of milk; complete mixing with remainder of flour.

Quick-Mix Method is relatively new, but very popular. As the name implies, these cakes may be made quickly. There's no creaming of shortening and sugar, no beating of eggs separately. All ingredients are mixed together in one bowl. Quick-mix batters are generally thinner than conventional-method batters.

Hydrogenated shortenings are recommended for cakes made by this method. If butter, lard or margarine is substituted, decrease each cup of milk by 2 tablespoons.

Beat the batter the full amount of time given in the recipe. If electric mixer is used, blend at lowest speed, then beat at a low speed. If beating by hand, allow 150 strokes per minute.

GENERAL HINTS

When mixing

- Choose a reliable, tested recipe. Read the recipe carefully; assemble all ingredients, utensils and baking pans. Have ingredients at room temperature unless otherwise directed. Use quality ingredients.
- Always preheat the oven before mixing your cake.
- Cake recipes are delicately balanced. For that reason, all ingredients must be measured accurately.
- Use an electric mixer for all mixing steps except folding; it does a better job than you can do by hand and does it so much easier!
- When using electric mixer, scrape the beaters with a rubber spatula, as shortening may cling there and not be mixed in completely.
- Use a timer when recipes recommend mixing time.
- Eggs separate easiest when cold, but allow them to come to room temperature before beating to obtain greatest volume.
- Roll lumpy brown sugar between two sheets of waxed paper with a rolling pin. If not removed, lumps will leave "holes" in baked cake.
- For shortening-type cakes, grease the bottom of the pan well and coat lightly with flour; shake out excess flour. *Do not* grease sides of pan. If desired, the bottom of the greased pan may be lined with waxed paper. For sponge- and angel food cakes, do not grease the pan (unless using a jelly-roll pan).

When baking

- For best results, use the pan size recommended in the recipe. If too small a pan is used, cake may hump, crack or fall. If pan is too large, cake will be thin. To measure cake pans, check top inside length and width and inside depth.
- The following pan sizes are equivalent and usually may be interchanged:
  Two 8-inch round layer pans = one 12x8x2-inch = one 13x9x2-inch
  Two 9-inch round layer pans = two 8x8-inch = one 13x9x2-inch
  One 9x9-inch pan = one 11x7-inch pan
- Place cakes in oven so center of cake is in center of oven. When baking cake layers, arrange pans so they do not touch each other or sides of oven. When using glass ovenware or dull-finished metal pans, decrease oven temperature 25° as these pans absorb heat readily.
- If your oven will not accommodate three layers, keep one layer in the refrigerator. Bake it immediately after the other two layers.
- A cake is baked if it springs back without leaving an impression when touched lightly in the center. Some cakes, when done, will pull slightly from the sides of the pan. If a wooden pick or metal cake tester inserted into the cake comes out clean, the cake is done.

After baking

- Cool cake layers on wire rack about 10 minutes before removing from pans unless otherwise directed in recipe. Then run spatula around sides of pan to release cake; turn out on wire rack to cool.
- Cool loaf cakes on wire rack; frost in the pan, then cover with cake cover, aluminum foil or place pan in large plastic bag.
- To split layers crosswise, cut with long sharp or serrated knife.
- To cut a frosted layer cake, use a long, thin, sharp knife rinsed in hot water. Cut through with a gentle sawing motion; don't press down. Rinse knife after each cut.
- To cut angel food and spongecakes, use a serrated knife; place end of knife in center of cake, then cut with gentle back and forth motion.
- Store layer cakes under "cake saver" with roomy cover that fits over the plate or tray. Or invert a large bowl over the plate. Covered cake may be stored in the refrigerator.
- Store cakes with custard or cream fillings in the refrigerator.

WHITE CAKES

Frosty Snow-berry Cake

Senior Winner by Mrs. Marguerite Marks, Camden, New Jersey

Cubes of cranberry sauce are baked right into these white cake layers.

BAKE at 375° for 30 to 35 minutes   MAKES two 8-inch layers

Sift together 2¼ cups sifted **Pillsbury's Best All Purpose Flour***
          3 teaspoons double-acting **baking powder** and
          1 teaspoon **salt**

Blend . . . . . . ⅔ cup **shortening** with
          1 cup **sugar** and
          1 teaspoon grated **lemon rind**; cream well.

Add . . . . the dry ingredients alternately with
          ¾ cup **milk.** Blend well after each addition.

Beat . . . . 4 **egg whites** until mounds form. Gradually add
          ½ cup **sugar**; continue beating until meringue stands
          in stiff peaks. Fold into batter.

Fold in . . . . . . 1 cup **jellied-cranberry sauce,** cut into ¼-inch cubes

Turn . . . . into two 8-inch round layer pans, well greased and
          lightly floured on the bottoms.

Bake . . . . at 375° for 30 to 35 minutes. Cool; fill and frost with
          Pink Fluffy Frosting, page 317.

*For use with Pillsbury's Best Self-Rising Flour, omit baking powder and salt.

Candlelight Cake

Senior Winner by Mrs. Thomas S. Hefley, Des Moines, Iowa

A beautiful, regal white cake frosted with mounds of fluffy icing!

BAKE at 350° for 30 to 35 minutes   MAKES two 8-inch layers

Sift together . . 2 cups sifted **Pillsbury's Best All Purpose Flour***

          ¼ cup sifted **cornstarch**
          3 teaspoons double-acting **baking powder** and
          1 teaspoon **salt**

Cream . . . . . . ½ cup **butter** or margarine; gradually add
          1⅓ cups **sugar,** creaming well.

Combine . . . . . 1 cup **milk**
          1 teaspoon **vanilla** and
          ¼ teaspoon **almond extract.** Add alternately with the
          dry ingredients to creamed mixture. Blend well after
          each addition.

Beat . . . . 5 **egg whites** (⅔ cup) until stiff but not dry. Fold
          into batter.

Turn . . . . into two 8-inch round layer pans, well greased and
          lightly floured on the bottoms.

Bake . . . . at 350° for 30 to 35 minutes. Cool; frost with **Fluffy**
          Marshmallow Frosting, page 317.

*For use with Pillsbury's Best Self-Rising Flour, omit baking powder and salt.

Frosty Snow-berry Cake

Grandmother's Almond Snow Cake

Senior Winner by Mrs. Elisabeth H. Tinkler, Maitland, Florida

High, light and creamy-white . . . a dainty old-fashioned cake with white fluffy frosting and delicate almond flavor.

BAKE at 350° for 30 to 35 minutes   MAKES two 8-inch layers

Sift together 2¼ cups sifted **Pillsbury's Best All Purpose Flour***
          2½ teaspoons double-acting **baking powder** and
          1 teaspoon **salt**
Beat . . . . 4 **egg whites** (½ cup) until soft mounds form. Add gradually
          ⅓ cup **sugar;** continue beating until stiff.
Cream . . . . . . ½ cup **butter** or margarine. Gradually add
          1 cup **sugar,** creaming well.
Combine . . . . . 1 cup **milk** and
          ½ teaspoon **almond extract.** Add alternately with the dry ingredients to creamed mixture. Blend well after each addition.
Fold in . . . . the beaten egg whites.
Turn . . . . into two 8-inch round layer pans, well greased and lightly floured on the bottoms.
Bake . . . . at 350° for 30 to 35 minutes. Cool; frost with **Seven-Minute Frosting,** page 318.

For use with Pillsbury's Best Self-Rising Flour, omit baking powder and salt.

Dutch Ridge Reception Cake

Senior Winner by Mrs. J. Vincent Orlett, West Portsmouth, Ohio

A favorite for birthdays, parties and church festivals, with an old-fashioned "something" that appeals.

BAKE at 350° for 30 to 35 minutes   MAKES two 8-inch layers

Sift together . . 2 cups sifted **Pillsbury's Best All Purpose Flour***
          2 teaspoons double-acting **baking powder**

          1 teaspoon **salt** and
          ½ teaspoon **soda.** Set aside.
Add . . . . 1 cup **sugar** gradually to
          ½ cup **shortening,** creaming well.
Combine . . . . ¾ cup **buttermilk** or sour milk
          ¼ cup **milk**
          1 teaspoon **vanilla** and
          1 teaspoon **almond extract.** Add alternately with the dry ingredients to creamed mixture. Blend well after each addition.
Beat . . . . 4 **egg whites** until stiff but not dry. Add
          ⅓ cup **sugar** gradually. Fold into batter.
Turn . . . . into two 8-inch round layer pans, well greased and lightly floured on the bottoms.
Bake . . . . at 350° for 30 to 35 minutes. Cool; frost with **Fluffy White Frosting,** page 317.

For use with Pillsbury's Best Self-Rising Flour, omit baking powder and salt.

Orange Sparkle Cake

Senior Winner by Frances Mathews, Council Bluffs, Iowa

The "sparkle" in this tender white cake comes from colorful orange rind.

BAKE at 375° for 25 to 30 minutes   MAKES two 8-inch layers

Sift together 2¼ cups sifted **Pillsbury's Best All Purpose Flour***
          3 teaspoons double-acting **baking powder**
          1 teaspoon **salt** and
          ¼ teaspoon **soda**
Beat . . . . 4 **egg whites** (½ cup) with
          ½ teaspoon **cream of tartar** until slight mounds form. Gradually add
          ¼ cup **sugar;** continue beating until stiff straight peaks form. Set aside.
Add . . . . 1 cup **sugar** gradually to
          ½ cup **shortening,** creaming well.

Combine....⅔ cup **milk**
        ½ cup **buttermilk** or sour milk and
        2 tablespoons grated **orange rind.** Add alternately with the dry ingredients to creamed mixture. Blend well after each addition.
Fold.........egg whites into batter. Turn into two 8-inch round layer pans, well greased and lightly floured on the bottoms.
Bake........at 375° for 25 to 30 minutes. Cool; frost with **Creamy Orange Frosting,** page 325.
For use with Pillsbury's Best Self-Rising Flour, omit baking powder and salt.

Poppy Seed Cream Cake

Senior Winner by Mrs. Melvin H. Wunsch, Chicago, Illinois

Heavy cream in this old-fashioned white cake makes it rich and moist. Poppy seeds give it delicate flavor.

BAKE at 375° for 25 to 30 minutes   MAKES two 8-inch layers

Soak.......¼ to ½ cup **poppy seeds** in
        ½ cup **milk**
Sift together..2 cups sifted **Pillsbury's Best All Purpose Flour***
        3 teaspoons double-acting **baking powder** and
        1 teaspoon **salt**
Beat.......3 **egg whites** until stiff but not dry.
Add.......1¼ cups **sugar** gradually to
        ⅓ cup **shortening,** creaming well.
Combine....½ cup **heavy cream** and
        1 teaspoon **vanilla;** add alternately with the dry ingredients to creamed mixture. Blend well after each addition.
Add.........poppy seed-milk mixture.
Fold in.......beaten egg whites gently but thoroughly.
Turn.........into two 8-inch round layer pans, well greased and lightly floured on the bottoms.

Bake........at 375° for 25 to 30 minutes. Cool; spread **Cream Filling,** page 328, between layers and sprinkle top with **confectioners' sugar.**
For use with Pillsbury's Best Self-Rising Flour, omit baking powder and salt.

Banquet Layer Cake

Senior Winner by Mrs. O. A. Ornburn, Moberly, Missouri

A truly regal white cake . . . with red cherries, coconut and nuts in the filling, and fluffy white frosting.

BAKE at 350° for 25 to 30 minutes   MAKES three 9-inch layers

Sift together..3 cups sifted **Pillsbury's Best All Purpose Flour***
        3½ teaspoons double-acting **baking powder** and
        1 teaspoon **salt**
Cream......¾ cup **butter** or margarine. Gradually add
        1½ cups **sugar,** creaming well.
Combine...1⅓ cups **milk**
        1 teaspoon **vanilla** and
        1 teaspoon **almond extract.** Add alternately with the dry ingredients to creamed mixture. Blend well after each addition.
Beat........7 **egg whites** (¾ cup) until stiff but not dry. Gradually add
        ½ cup **sugar,** beating until stiff. Fold into batter.
Turn.........into three 9-inch round layer pans, well greased and lightly floured on bottoms.
Bake........at 350° for 25 to 30 minutes. Cool; fill and frost with **De Luxe Fluffy White Frosting,** page 317.
For use with Pillsbury's Best Self-Rising Flour, omit baking powder and salt.

DE LUXE FILLING

Remove one-third of De Luxe Fluffy White Frosting to small bowl. Stir in ½ cup chopped nuts, ¼ cup maraschino cherries, drained and cut in small pieces, and ½ cup coconut.

Rippling Shadow Cake

Senior Winner by Mrs. W. A. Heschong, St. Joseph, Missouri

Chocolate-dipped coconut makes the delicious chewy shadow which ripples through this beautiful white cake.

BAKE at 350° for 35 to 40 minutes   MAKES two 9-inch layers

Combine . . . 1½ cups **coconut,** chopped, and
                         ¼ cup **water.** Stir in
                         2 squares (2 oz.) melted **semi-sweet chocolate** (or 1½ squares unsweetened chocolate). Reserve.

Sift together 2¾ cups sifted **Pillsbury's Best All Purpose Flour***
                         3½ teaspoons double-acting **baking powder** and
                         1 teaspoon **salt.** Set aside.

Add . . . . 1⅔ cups **sugar** gradually to
                         ⅔ cup **shortening,** creaming well.

Combine . . . 1⅓ cups **milk** or water and
                         1 teaspoon **vanilla.** Add alternately with the dry ingredients to creamed mixture. Blend well after each addition.

Beat . . . . 4 **egg whites** until stiff but not dry; fold into batter.

Spoon . . . . tablespoonfuls of the batter and small teaspoonfuls of the coconut mixture alternately into two 9-inch round layer pans, at least 1½ inches deep, well greased and lightly floured on the bottoms. Cut through with knife to marble.

Bake . . . . at 350° for 35 to 40 minutes. Cool; frost with **Seven-Minute Frosting,** page 318.

Combine . . . . ½ square (½ oz.) melted unsweetened **chocolate** and
                         1 teaspoon melted **butter.** Spoon around top edge of cake, allowing to drip down sides.

For use with Pillsbury's Best Self-Rising Flour, omit baking powder and salt.

Sour Cream Maple Cake

Junior Winner by Karen Collins, Indianapolis, Indiana

A sour-cream white cake frosted in its baking pan with the most luscious maple-sour cream frosting ever!

BAKE at 350° for 30 to 35 minutes   MAKES 8x8 or 11x7-inch cake

Sift together 1½ cups sifted **Pillsbury's Best All Purpose Flour***
                         2 teaspoons double-acting **baking powder**
                         ½ teaspoon **soda** and
                         ½ teaspoon **salt.**

Cream . . . . . . 3 tablespoons **butter** or margarine. Gradually add
                         ¾ cup **sugar,** creaming well.

Blend in . . . . . 2 unbeaten **egg whites** and
                         ½ teaspoon **vanilla.** Beat well.

Add . . . . the dry ingredients alternately with
                         1 cup **sour cream** (thick or commercial). Blend well after each addition.

Turn . . . . into 8x8x2 or 11x7x2-inch pan, well greased and lightly floured on the bottom.

Bake . . . . at 350° for 30 to 35 minutes. Cool; frost with **Maple Sour Cream Frosting,** page 315. Decorate with **pecan halves,** if desired.

For use with Pillsbury's Best Self-Rising Flour, omit baking power and salt; decrease soda to ¼ teaspoon.

Texas Hospitality Cake

Senior Winner by Mrs. Price Campbell, Houston, Texas

Perfect for church suppers and family reunions, this cake is easy to carry and cuts to advantage.

BAKE at 350° for 40 to 45 minutes   MAKES 13x9-inch cake

Sift together . . 3 cups sifted **Pillsbury's Best All Purpose Flour***
                         3 teaspoons double-acting **baking powder** and

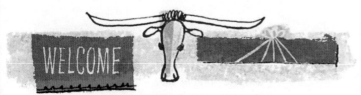

1 teaspoon **salt**

Cream......¾ cup **butter** or margarine. Gradually add
1⅜ cups **sugar,** creaming well.

Combine....½ cup **milk**
½ cup **water**
1 teaspoon **vanilla** and
¼ teaspoon **almond extract.** Add alternately with the
dry ingredients to creamed mixture. Blend well after
each addition.

Add........¾ cup **pecans,** finely chopped.

Beat.......3 **egg whites** until stiff but not dry. Fold into batter.

Turn.........into 13x9x2-inch pan, well greased and lightly
floured on the bottom.

Bake.........at 350° for 40 to 45 minutes. Cool; frost with
Pecan Fondant Frosting, page 315.

For use with Pillsbury's Best Self-Rising Flour, omit baking powder and salt.

Sugar 'n' Spice Cake

Senior Winner by Mrs. Lillian Ballenger, Chapel Hill, North Carolina

*A simple sugar-cinnamon syrup drizzled over the batter gives this
inexpensive loaf cake unique design.*

BAKE at 350° for 35 to 40 minutes   MAKES 9x9-inch cake

Combine....¼ cup **sugar**
2 teaspoons **cinnamon** and
3 tablespoons **water** in saucepan. Cook, stirring constantly, until mixture begins to boil. Remove from
heat; set aside.

Sift together 1¾ cups sifted **Pillsbury's Best All Purpose Flour***
2 teaspoons double-acting **baking powder** and
½ teaspoon **salt.**

Cream......⅓ cup **butter** or margarine. Gradually add
1 cup **sugar,** creaming well.

Combine....⅔ cup **milk** and
1 teaspoon **vanilla.** Add 2 tablespoons to creamed
mixture; beat well.

Add.........remaining milk mixture alternately with the dry
ingredients. Blend well after each addition.

Beat........2 **egg whites** until stiff but not dry; fold into batter.

Turn.........into 9x9x2-inch pan, well greased and lightly floured
on the bottom. Drizzle cinnamon syrup over top;
cut back and forth through batter with knife for
marbled effect.

Bake.........at 350° for 35 to 40 minutes. Serve plain or with
Cinnamon Whipped Cream, page 329.

For use with Pillsbury's Best Self-Rising Flour, omit baking powder and salt.

Sugar 'n' Spice Cake

Peanut Petit Fours

Senior Winner by Mrs. Frank Winderl, Milwaukee, Wisconsin

A delicate white cake is baked as a loaf, cut into small shapes, frosted with a creamy frosting and rolled in ground peanuts.

BAKE at 350° for 35 to 45 minutes   MAKES 2 dozen

Sift together 2¼ cups sifted **Pillsbury's Best All Purpose Flour***
    3 teaspoons double-acting **baking powder** and
    1 teaspoon **salt**. Set aside.
Add . . . . 1 cup **sugar** gradually to
    ½ cup **shortening**, creaming well.
Combine . . . . . 1 cup **milk** and
    1 teaspoon **vanilla**. Add alternately with the dry ingredients to creamed mixture. Blend well after each addition.
Beat . . . . 4 **egg whites** until mounds form. Gradually add
    ⅓ cup **sugar**; continue beating until stiff peaks form. Fold into batter.
Turn . . . . into 13x9x2 or 12x8x2-inch pan, well greased and lightly floured on the bottom.
Bake . . . . at 350° for 35 to 45 minutes. Cool; cut into 2-inch squares. Frost with **Petit Four Frosting**, page 321, and roll in ground **peanuts**.

*For use with Pillsbury's Best Self-Rising Flour, omit baking powder and salt.

Swing-Your-Partner Cake

Senior Winner by Mrs. Roger Slick, Waynesboro, Pennsylvania

Here is a really showy Quick-Mix cake with a fluffy white frosting and a special "Turkey-in-the-Straw" topping.

BAKE at 350° for 25 to 35 minutes   MAKES two 8-inch layers

Sift together . . 2 cups sifted **Pillsbury's Best All Purpose Flour***
    1¼ cups **sugar**

    3 teaspoons double-acting **baking powder** and
    1 teaspoon **salt** into large mixing bowl.
Add . . . . ½ cup **shortening**
    ⅞ cup **milk** (1 cup minus 2 tablespoons)
    1 teaspoon **vanilla** and
    1 teaspoon **almond extract**
Beat . . . . 1½ minutes. (With mixer use a low speed.)
Add . . . . 3 unbeaten **egg whites**. Beat 1½ minutes.
Turn . . . . into two 8-inch round layer pans, well greased and lightly floured on the bottoms.
Bake . . . . at 350° for 25 to 35 minutes. Cool; frost with **Fluffy White Frosting**, page 317. Top with Turkey-in-the-Straw Topping.

*For use with Pillsbury's Best Self-Rising Flour, omit baking powder and salt.

TURKEY-IN-THE-STRAW TOPPING

Toast ½ cup chopped coconut. Sprinkle over top of frosted cake. Cut a slit in each of 6 green maraschino cherries; cut 1 red maraschino cherry into 6 strips, inserting one strip into the slit in each green cherry to make "turkey." Stand "turkeys" in coconut "straw."

Royal Highness Cake

Junior Winner by Wanda Miller, Tonkawa, Oklahoma

A regal and delicate-textured white cake with shiny golden lemon filling and creamy lemon frosting. Bound to be a family favorite.

BAKE at 350° for 25 to 35 minutes   MAKES two 8 or 9-inch layers

Beat . . . . 4 **egg whites** (½ cup) until stiff but not dry.
Add . . . . ¼ cup **sugar** gradually, beating thoroughly after each addition.

Sift together 2¼ cups sifted **Pillsbury's Best All Purpose Flour***
          1¼ cups **sugar**
          3¼ teaspoons double-acting **baking powder** and
          1 teaspoon **salt** into large mixing bowl.
Add . . . . ½ cup **shortening**
          1 cup **milk** and
          ½ teaspoon **lemon extract**
Beat . . . . 3 minutes. (With mixer use a low speed.)
Fold . . . . egg whites into batter.
Turn . . . . into two 8 or 9-inch round layer pans, well greased
          and lightly floured on the bottoms.
Bake . . . . at 350° for 25 to 35 minutes. Cool; fill with **Lemon
          Filling**, page 330. Frost with **Creamy Lemon Frosting**,
          page 325.
For use with Pillsbury's Best Self-Rising Flour, omit baking powder and salt.

Square Dance Nut Cake

Best of Class Winner by Mrs. Clara E. Fischer, Weatherly, Pennsylvania

A simple Quick-Mix cake that looks fancy—just cut this cake into four squares; frost two with white frosting, two with chocolate.

BAKE at 350° for 40 to 50 minutes   MAKES 8x8-inch cake

Sift together 1⅔ cups sifted **Pillsbury's Best All Purpose Flour***
          1 cup **sugar**
          2 teaspoons double-acting **baking powder** and
          ½ teaspoon **salt** into large mixing bowl.
Add . . . . ¼ cup soft **butter** or margarine
          ¼ cup **shortening** and
          ¾ cup **milk**
Beat . . . . 1½ minutes. (With mixer use a low speed.)
Add . . . . 3 unbeaten **egg whites**
          ½ teaspoon **vanilla** and
          ¼ teaspoon **lemon extract**. Beat 1½ minutes.
Stir in . . . . . . ½ cup **walnuts**, chopped.

Square Dance Nut Cake

Turn . . . . into 8x8x2-inch pan, well greased and lightly floured
          on the bottom.
Bake . . . . at 350° for 40 to 50 minutes. Cool. Cut into four
          squares. Frost two cake squares with white frosting,
          two with chocolate. Arrange checkerboard fashion.
          Decorate with chopped **nuts**.
For use with Pillsbury's Best Self-Rising Flour, omit baking powder and salt.

CHECKERBOARD FROSTING

Blend together 2½ cups sifted confectioners' sugar, 2 tablespoons melted butter and 1 tablespoon warm milk. Stir in 1 egg yolk and ½ teaspoon vanilla. Beat until of spreading consistency, adding ¼ to ½ cup additional confectioners' sugar, if necessary. Add 1 square (1 oz.) melted unsweetened chocolate to one-third of the frosting; gradually stir in 1 to 3 teaspoons milk until of spreading consistency.

"*My Inspiration*"
Cake
**Grand Prize Winner
of the Fifth
Grand National
Bake-Off**®

"My Inspiration" Cake

Grand Prize Winner by Mrs. A. B. Kanago, Webster, South Dakota

A Quick-Mix white cake, with a chocolate surprise that gives two layers a four-layer look, was this winning inspiration.

BAKE at 350° for 35 to 40 minutes   MAKES two 9-inch layers

Sprinkle . . . . . 1 cup **pecans,** finely chopped, evenly over bottoms of two 9-inch round layer pans, well greased and lightly floured on the bottoms.

Grate . . . . 2 ounces **sweet** or **semi-sweet chocolate;** reserve.

Sift together 2½ cups sifted **Pillsbury's Best All Purpose Flour***
1½ cups **sugar**
4 teaspoons double-acting **baking powder** and
1 teaspoon **salt** into large mixing bowl.

Add . . . . ⅔ cup **shortening**
1¼ cups **milk** and
1 teaspoon **vanilla**

Beat . . . . 1½ minutes. (With mixer use a low speed.)

Add . . . . ⅔ cup unbeaten **egg whites.** Beat 1½ minutes.

Spoon . . . . one-fourth of batter carefully into each nut-lined pan. Sprinkle with the grated chocolate. Spoon remaining batter into pans; spread carefully.

Bake . . . . at 350° for 35 to 40 minutes. Cool 10 minutes. Remove from pans and cool. Frost layers, nut-side up, with Chocolate Frosting. Spread between and on sides of layers, but frost only ½ inch around top edge of cake. Decorate with reserved White Frosting, thinned with 1 to 2 teaspoons water.

*For use with Pillsbury's Best Self-Rising Flour, omit baking powder and salt.

CHOCOLATE AND WHITE FROSTINGS

Combine 2 squares (2 oz.) unsweetened chocolate, ½ cup sugar and ¼ cup water in saucepan. Cook over low heat, stirring constantly, until mixture is smooth and thickened. Remove from heat. Add 4 egg yolks; beat thoroughly. Cool. Cream ½ cup butter and 1 teaspoon vanilla. Gradually add 2 cups sifted confectioners' sugar, creaming

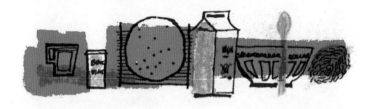

well. Reserve ⅓ cup of this frosting to decorate cake. Add the cool chocolate mixture to remaining white frosting; beat until smooth.

Dandy Candy Cake

Senior Winner by Mrs. E. O. Hatcher, Princeton, West Virginia

A white loaf cake made the Quick-Mix way with a caramel and coconut confection baked right on top.

BAKE at 350° for 30 to 35 minutes   MAKES 9x9-inch cake

Sift together 1½ cups sifted **Pillsbury's Best All Purpose Flour***
¾ cup **sugar**
2 teaspoons double-acting **baking powder** and
½ teaspoon **salt** into mixing bowl.

Add . . . . ⅓ cup **shortening**
½ cup **milk** and
1 teaspoon **vanilla**

Beat . . . . 1½ minutes. (With mixer use a low speed.)

Add . . . . 2 unbeaten **egg whites;** beat 1½ minutes.

Turn . . . . into 9x9x2-inch pan, well greased and lightly floured on the bottom. Sprinkle Dandy Topping over batter.

Bake . . . . at 350° for 30 to 35 minutes.

*For use with Pillsbury's Best Self-Rising Flour, omit baking powder and salt.

DANDY TOPPING

Combine ¼ cup Pillsbury's Best All Purpose Flour and ⅓ cup firmly packed brown sugar. Cut in ¼ cup butter until mixture resembles coarse crumbs. Stir in ½ cup flaked or chopped shredded coconut and 1½ teaspoons lemon juice.

YELLOW CAKES

Gold Rush Cake

Best of Class Winner by Mrs. Vava M. Blackburn, Walla Walla, Washington

An extra high, luscious and fine-textured gold cake with swirls of fluffy orange frosting.

BAKE at 350° for 30 to 35 minutes   MAKES two 8 or 9-inch layers

Sift together 1¾ cups sifted **Pillsbury's Best All Purpose Flour***
     1 teaspoon **salt** and
     ½ teaspoon **soda**
Beat . . . . ⅔ cup **egg yolks** (about 8) until thick and lemon colored, about 5 minutes. Set aside.
Add . . . . 1¼ cups **sugar** gradually to
     ½ cup **shortening**, creaming well. Blend in beaten yolks.
Combine . . . . ¾ cup **buttermilk** or sour milk
     ½ teaspoon **vanilla** and
     1 teaspoon grated **lemon rind**. Add alternately with the dry ingredients to creamed mixture. Blend well after each addition.
Turn . . . . into two 8 or 9-inch round layer pans, well greased and lightly floured on the bottoms.
Bake . . . . at 350° for 30 to 35 minutes. Cool; frost with **Fluffy Orange Frosting,** page 317.

*For use with Pillsbury's Best Self-Rising Flour, omit salt and soda.

Royal Orange Cake

Senior Winner by Mrs. Louise A. Hamrick, Kenmore, New York

A stately golden layer cake with fresh orange juice in the cake and frosting to give just the right amount of tartness.

BAKE at 350° for 25 to 30 minutes   MAKES two 8-inch layers

Sift together 2⅛ cups sifted **Pillsbury's Best All Purpose Flour***
     1 teaspoon double-acting **baking powder**
     1 teaspoon **salt** and
     ½ teaspoon **soda**. Set aside.
Add . . . . 1¼ cups **sugar** gradually to
     ½ cup **shortening**, creaming well.
Blend in . . . . . 1 unbeaten **egg** and
     2 unbeaten **egg yolks**, beating well after each.
Add . . . . 1 cup **orange juice** alternately with the dry ingredients. Blend well after each addition.
Turn . . . . into two 8-inch round layer pans well greased and lightly floured on the bottoms.
Bake . . . . at 350° for 25 to 30 minutes. Cool; frost with **Fluffy Orange Frosting,** page 317.

*For use with Pillsbury's Best Self-Rising Flour, omit baking powder, salt, soda.

Honey Almond Cake

Senior Winner by Mrs. George Miller, Mansfield, Ohio

The blend of honey, almond and orange gives an intriguing flavor.

BAKE at 375° for 25 to 30 minutes   MAKES two 8-inch layers

Sift together . . 2 cups sifted **Pillsbury's Best All Purpose Flour***
     2 teaspoons double-acting **baking powder** and
     ½ teaspoon **salt**. Set aside.
Add . . . . ⅔ cup **sugar** gradually to
     ½ cup **shortening**, creaming well. Add
     ⅓ cup **honey**; mix well.

Add . . . . 5 unbeaten **egg yolks,** beating well after each.
Blend in . . . . the dry ingredients alternately with
      ½ cup **milk.** Blend well after each addition.
Stir in . . . . . . ¼ cup **almonds,** ground or finely chopped
      1 tablespoon grated **orange rind** and
      2 tablespoons **orange juice**
Turn . . . . into two 8-inch round layer pans, well greased and
      lightly floured on the bottoms.
Bake . . . . at 375° for 25 to 30 minutes. Cool; frost with **Fluffy
      Honey Frosting,** page 317.

For use with Pillsbury's Best Self-Rising Flour, omit baking powder and salt.

Almond Coconut Party Cake

Senior Winner by Kenneth Stevens, Cambrian Park, California

*Rich in coconut, with true almond flavor, this layer cake has an almond-
butter icing with a lacy chocolate shadow.*

BAKE at 350° for 35 to 40 minutes   MAKES two 8-inch layers

Sift together 1¾ cups sifted **Pillsbury's Best All Purpose Flour***
      2 teaspoons double-acting **baking powder** and
      1 teaspoon **salt**
Cream . . . . . . ½ cup **shortening** with
      ½ cup **almond paste.** Gradually add
      1 cup **sugar,** creaming well. *Do not underbeat.*
Add . . . . 2 unbeaten **eggs,** beating well after each.
Combine . . . . ⅔ cup undiluted **evaporated milk** and
      ⅓ cup **water.** Add alternately with the dry ingredients
      to creamed mixture. Blend well after each addition.
Stir in . . . . . . ½ cup **coconut,** chopped.
Turn . . . . into two 8-inch round layer pans, well greased and
      lightly floured on the bottoms.
Bake . . . . at 350° for 35 to 40 minutes. Cool; frost with
      Almond Butter Cream Frosting. Drizzle top with a
      mixture of

½ square melted unsweetened **chocolate** and
1 teaspoon **butter**

For use with Pillsbury's Best Self-Rising Flour, omit baking powder and salt.

ALMOND BUTTER CREAM FROSTING

Combine ½ cup butter or margarine with ¼ cup almond paste; cream
thoroughly. Blend in 1 pound (4 to 4¼ cups) sifted confectioners'
sugar. Gradually add ⅓ to ½ cup undiluted evaporated milk, beating
until of spreading consistency.

Coconut Treasure Cake

Junior Winner by Peggy Lee Hoskins, Deerfield, Ohio

Coconut both inside and outside this lavish and moist golden cake.

BAKE at 375° for 25 to 30 minutes   MAKES two 8 or 9-inch layers

Combine . . . . ½ cup **coconut,** chopped
      1¼ cups **buttermilk** or sour milk
Sift together 2¼ cups sifted **Pillsbury's Best All Purpose Flour***
      1½ teaspoons double-acting **baking powder**
      1 teaspoon **salt** and
      ½ teaspoon **soda**
Cream . . . . . . ½ cup **butter** or margarine. Gradually add
      1½ cups **sugar,** creaming well.
Blend in . . . . . . 3 unbeaten **eggs,** beating well after each.
Add . . . . the dry ingredients alternately with coconut mixture.
      Blend well after each addition.
Stir in . . . . . 1½ teaspoons **vanilla.** Turn into two 8 or 9-inch round
      layer pans, well greased and lightly floured on the
      bottoms.
Bake . . . . at 375° for 25 to 30 minutes. Cool; frost with **White
      Mountain Frosting,** page 318. Decorate with shredded
      coconut.

*For use with Pillsbury's Best Self-Rising Flour, omit baking powder and salt;
decrease soda to ¼ teaspoon.*

Sweet Chocolate Cake

Senior Winner by V. Claire Nelson, Stamford, Connecticut

Flecks of grated chocolate are baked into this chocolate-frosted cake.

BAKE at 350° for 30 to 35 minutes   MAKES two 8-inch layers

Sift together . . 2 cups sifted **Pillsbury's Best All Purpose Flour***
3 teaspoons double-acting **baking powder** and
½ teaspoon **salt.** Set aside.
Add . . . . 1 cup **sugar** gradually to
½ cup **shortening,** creaming well.
Blend in . . . . . 3 unbeaten **egg yolks,** beating well after each.
Combine . . . . . 1 cup **milk** and
1 teaspoon **vanilla.** Add alternately with the dry
ingredients to creamed mixture. Blend well after
each addition.
Fold in . . . . . . 3 squares (3 oz.) coarsely grated **semi-sweet chocolate**
Beat . . . . 3 **egg whites** until stiff but not dry. Fold gently but
thoroughly into batter.
Pour . . . . into two 8-inch round layer pans, well greased and
lightly floured on the bottoms.
Bake . . . . at 350° for 30 to 35 minutes. Cool; frost with **Chocolate Cream Cheese Frosting,** page 322.

*For use with Pillsbury's Best Self-Rising Flour, omit baking powder and salt.

Ruth's Dotted Swiss Cake

Senior Winner

Flecks of chocolate in the batter make this cake really luscious.

BAKE at 350° for 30 to 40 minutes   MAKES two 8 or 9-inch layers

Sift together . . 2 cups sifted **Pillsbury's Best All Purpose Flour***
3 teaspoons double-acting **baking powder** and
1 teaspoon **salt.** Set aside.
Add . . . . 1¼ cups **sugar** gradually to

½ cup **shortening,** creaming well.
Blend in . . . . . 2 unbeaten **eggs,** beating well after each.
Combine . . . . . 1 cup **milk**
1 teaspoon **vanilla** and
½ teaspoon **orange extract.** Add alternately with the
dry ingredients to creamed mixture. Blend well after
each addition.
Blend in . . . . . 2 squares (2 oz.) shaved **semi-sweet** or **German's
sweet chocolate**
Turn . . . . into two 8 or 9-inch round layer pans, well greased
and lightly floured on the bottoms.
Bake . . . . at 350° for 30 to 40 minutes. Cool; frost with
Creamy Butter Frosting, page 320. Decorate with
melted **chocolate.**

*For use with Pillsbury's Best Self-Rising Flour, omit baking powder and salt.

Cashew Cream Cake

Senior Winner by Mrs. S. F. Barbaric, Clarksburg, West Virginia

There are sugared cashews in the layers and atop the fluffy meringue.

BAKE at 350° for 30 to 35 minutes, then   MAKES two 8-inch layers
for 12 to 15 minutes

Combine . . . . ½ cup firmly packed **brown sugar** and
¼ cup **water** in saucepan. Cook until a little syrup
dropped in cold water forms a firm soft ball (240°).
Remove from heat.
Add . . . . 1 cup **cashews** or other nuts, chopped; stir gently
until mixture sugars and becomes creamy. Pour onto
greased baking sheet. Cool; chop fine.
Sift together . . 2 cups sifted **Pillsbury's Best All Purpose Flour***
2½ teaspoons double-acting **baking powder** and
½ teaspoon **salt**
Cream . . . . . . ½ cup **butter** or margarine. Gradually add
1 cup **sugar,** creaming well.

Add . . . . 1 unbeaten **egg** and
2 unbeaten **egg yolks,** beating well after each.

Combine . . . . . 1 cup **milk** and
1 teaspoon **vanilla.** Add alternately with the dry ingredients to creamed mixture. Blend well after each addition.

Fold in . . . . sugared nuts, reserving ¼ cup.

Turn . . . . into two 8-inch round layer pans, well greased and lightly floured on the bottoms.

Bake . . . . at 350° for 30 to 35 minutes. Cool. Spread **Cream Filling,** page 328, between layers. Cover top and sides with Meringue. Sprinkle with the reserved nuts.

Brown . . . . at 350° for 12 to 15 minutes.

Pillsbury's Best Self-Rising Flour is not recommended for use in this recipe.

MERINGUE

Beat 3 egg whites, ¼ teaspoon salt and ¼ teaspoon cream of tartar until slight mounds form. Add 6 tablespoons sugar gradually, beating well after each addition. Continue beating until meringue stands in stiff, glossy peaks.

Duchess Cream Cake

Senior Winner by Mrs. Edgar E. Billings, New Windsor, Maryland

The creamy filling and fluffy meringue taste as good as they look!

BAKE at 350° for 25 to 30 minutes, then for 10 to 15 minutes   MAKES two 8-inch layers

Sift together . . 2 cups sifted **Pillsbury's Best All Purpose Flour***
2 teaspoons double-acting **baking powder** and
1 teaspoon **salt**

Cream . . . . . . ½ cup **butter** or margarine. Gradually add
1 cup **sugar,** creaming well.

Blend in . . . . . 1 unbeaten **egg** and
2 unbeaten **egg yolks,** beating well after each.

Combine . . . . . 1 cup **milk** and
1 teaspoon **vanilla.** Add alternately with the dry ingredients to creamed mixture. Blend well after each addition.

Turn . . . . into two 8-inch round layer pans, well greased and lightly floured on the bottoms.

Bake . . . . at 350° for 25 to 30 minutes. Cool; place on oven-proof plate. Spread cooled **Cream Filling,** page 328, between layers; spread Meringue on top and sides of cake.

Bake . . . . at 350° for 10 to 15 minutes.

For use with Pillsbury's Best Self-Rising Flour, omit baking powder and salt.

MERINGUE

Beat 3 egg whites until soft mounds form. Gradually add 6 tablespoons sugar, beating well after each. Blend in ½ teaspoon vanilla. Continue beating until meringue stands in stiff, glossy peaks.

Duchess Cream Cake

Strawberry Alaska

1 teaspoon **vanilla** and
¼ teaspoon **lemon extract;** beat well.

Add . . . . the dry ingredients alternately with
1 cup **milk.** Blend well after each addition.

Turn . . . . into two 8-inch round layer pans, well greased and
lightly floured on the bottoms.

Bake . . . . at 350° for 35 to 40 minutes. Cool. Arrange Strawberry Filling on one layer; top with second layer.
Frost with Meringue.

Bake . . . . at 325° for 20 minutes. Garnish with **strawberries.**
Serve warm.

*For use with Pillsbury's Best Self-Rising Flour, omit baking powder and salt.

STRAWBERRY FILLING

Combine 2½ cups sliced strawberries and ¼ cup sugar. Let stand 30
minutes. Drain well.

MERINGUE

Beat 4 egg whites and ¼ teaspoon double-acting baking powder until
soft mounds form. Gradually add ¾ cup sugar, beating until meringue
stands in stiff, glossy peaks.

Strawberry Alaska

Senior Winner by Mrs. R. H. Borth, Sr., Dearborn, Michigan

*Dessert deluxe . . . layers of rich yellow cake are filled with fresh
strawberries . . . meringue frosting is baked on just before serving.*

BAKE at 350° for 35 to 40 minutes, then   MAKES two 8-inch layers
    at 325° for 20 minutes

Sift together 2¼ cups sifted **Pillsbury's Best All Purpose Flour***
3 teaspoons double-acting **baking powder** and
1 teaspoon **salt.** Set aside.

Add . . . . . . 1¼ cups **sugar** gradually to
½ cup **shortening,** creaming well.

Blend in . . . . . 4 well-beaten **egg yolks**

Jelly Ripple Cake

Junior Winner by Robert Koran, Mingo Junction, Ohio

*Pretty pink swirls of jelly ripple all through this festive layer cake.
Attractive, with a fine, even texture.*

BAKE at 375° for 30 to 35 minutes   MAKES two 8-inch layers

Sift together 2⅛ cups sifted **Pillsbury's Best All Purpose Flour*** (2
cups plus 2 tablespoons)
2½ teaspoons double-acting **baking powder** and
½ teaspoon **salt**

Cream . . . . . . ½ cup **butter** or margarine. Gradually add
1¼ cups **sugar,** creaming well.

Add . . . . 2 unbeaten **eggs,** beating well after each.
Combine . . . . . 1 cup **evaporated milk** and
1½ teaspoons **vanilla.** Add alternately with the dry ingredients to creamed mixture. Blend well after each addition.
Turn . . . . into two 8-inch round layer pans, well greased and lightly floured on bottoms; reserve ¾ cup.
Combine . . . . ¼ cup **red jelly** and
⅛ teaspoon **red food coloring;** mix thoroughly. Stir into reserved batter. Drop by teaspoonfuls onto batter in pans. Cut through batters many times in both directions with spatula to marble.
Bake . . . . at 375° for 30 to 35 minutes. Cool; frost with **Creamy Butter Frosting,** page 320, stacking layers top-sides up.
Combine . . . . . 2 tablespoons **red jelly** and
1/16 teaspoon **red food coloring.** Drizzle over top.
For use with Pillsbury's Best Self-Rising Flour, omit baking powder and salt.

Chocolate Spangled Cake

Senior Winner by Mrs. Kenneth Brewer, Evanston, Illinois

Flecks of chocolate shot and chopped nuts are sprinkled all through this yellow cake. The frosting needs no cooking.

BAKE at 375° for 25 to 30 minutes   MAKES two 9-inch layers

Sift together 2¼ cups sifted **Pillsbury's Best All Purpose Flour***
3 teaspoons double-acting **baking powder** and
1 teaspoon **salt.** Set aside.
Add . . . . 1⅛ cups **sugar** gradually to
½ cup **shortening,** creaming well.
Blend in . . . . . 3 unbeaten **eggs,** beating well after each.
Combine . . . . . 1 cup **milk** and
1 teaspoon **vanilla.** Add alternately with the dry ingredients to creamed mixture. Blend well after

each addition.
Stir in . . . . . . ½ cup **chocolate cake decorations** and
½ cup **nuts,** chopped
Turn . . . . into two 9-inch round layer pans, well greased and lightly floured on the bottoms.
Bake . . . . at 375° for 25 to 30 minutes. Cool; frost with **Creamy Chocolate Frosting,** page 323.
For use with Pillsbury's Best Self-Rising Flour, omit baking powder and salt.

Apricot Queen Cake

Senior Winner by Mrs. Marion L. Bailey, Lebo, Kansas

Apricot nectar gives a unique flavor to the three layers and amber-colored filling of this impressive cake.

BAKE at 350°   MAKES two or three 9-inch layers

Sift together 2½ cups sifted **Pillsbury's Best All Purpose Flour***
2½ teaspoons double-acting **baking powder** and
1 teaspoon **salt.** Set aside.
Add . . . . . . 1¾ cups **sugar** gradually to
⅔ cup **shortening,** creaming well.
Blend in . . . . . 2 unbeaten **eggs** and
2 unbeaten **egg yolks,** beating well after each.
Add . . . . one-fourth of the dry ingredients; mix well. Blend in
¼ cup **milk**
Combine . . . . . 1 cup **apricot nectar** and
½ teaspoon **lemon extract.** Add alternately with the remaining dry ingredients to creamed mixture. Blend well after each addition.
Turn . . . . into two or three 9-inch round layer pans, well greased and lightly floured on the bottoms.
Bake . . . . at 350°: 25 to 30 minutes for three pans; 30 to 35 minutes for two pans. Cool; fill with **Apricot Filling,** page 329. Frost with **Fluffy White Frosting,** page 317.
For use with Pillsbury's Best Self-Rising Flour, omit baking powder and salt.

Royal Apricot Cake

Bride Winner by Mrs. Barbara L. Welch, Tracy, California

Its dried apricot-pineapple-coconut filling and beautiful apricot-tinted and flavored fluffy frosting make this large yellow cake really fit for a king.

BAKE at 350° for 35 to 40 minutes   MAKES two 9-inch layers

Sift together. . 3 cups sifted **Pillsbury's Best All Purpose Flour***
       3 teaspoons double-acting **baking powder** and
       1 teaspoon **salt**. Set aside.
Add. . . . . . 1¾ cups **sugar** gradually to
       ¾ cup **shortening**, creaming well.
Blend in . . . . . 4 unbeaten **egg yolks**, beating well after each.
Combine . . . 1¼ cups **milk** and
       1 teaspoon **vanilla**. Add alternately with the dry ingredients to creamed mixture. Blend well after each addition.
Beat. . . . . . . 3 **egg whites** until stiff. Fold into batter.
Turn. . . . . into two 9-inch round layer pans, at least 1½ inches deep, well greased and lightly floured on the bottoms.
Bake. . . . . at 350° for 35 to 40 minutes. Cool; fill with Apricot Filling. Frost with Royal Apricot Frosting.
For use with Pillsbury's Best Self-Rising Flour, omit baking powder and salt.

APRICOT FILLING

Cook dried apricots (about 1 cup) in water to cover; drain and mash. Reserve ⅓ cup of mashed apricot for Frosting. Combine ½ cup sugar, ½ cup mashed apricot and ½ cup drained crushed pineapple in saucepan. Cook until thick, about 10 minutes. Remove from heat. Stir in ¼ cup coconut; cool.

ROYAL APRICOT FROSTING

In top of double boiler combine ⅓ cup apricot pulp, ¾ cup sugar, 1 egg white and 2 tablespoons water. Cook over rapidly boiling water, beating with electric mixer or rotary beater until mixture stands in straight peaks and is of spreading consistency.

Coconut Kiss Cake

Senior Winner by Mrs. W. J. Caldwell, Lakewood, Ohio

Finely-chopped coconut is folded right into the three golden layers of this lofty and lovely cake. Wonderful for a party!

BAKE at 350° for 25 to 30 minutes   MAKES three 9-inch layers

Sift together. . 3 cups sifted **Pillsbury's Best All Purpose Flour***
       3 teaspoons double-acting **baking powder** and
       1 teaspoon **salt**. Set aside.
Add. . . . . 2 cups **sugar** gradually to
       1 cup **shortening**, creaming well.
Blend in . . . . . 4 unbeaten **eggs**, beating well after each.
Combine . . . . . 1 cup **milk** and
       1 teaspoon **vanilla**. Add alternately with the dry ingredients to creamed mixture. Blend well after each addition.
Stir in . . . . 1 cup **coconut**, chopped
Turn. . . . . into three 9-inch round layer pans, well greased and lightly floured on the bottoms.
Bake. . . . . at 350° for 25 to 30 minutes. Cool; frost with **De Luxe Fluffy White Frosting**, page 317.
For use with Pillsbury's Best Self-Rising Flour, omit baking powder and salt.

Elegant Fresh Coconut Cake

Senior Winner by Mr. Ray Sharp, Hopewell, Virginia

A cake for coconut lovers! The buttery layers have a fresh coconut sauce for extra moistness.

BAKE at 375° for 30 to 35 minutes   MAKES two 9-inch layers

Sift together. . 3 cups sifted **Pillsbury's Best All Purpose Flour***
       3 teaspoons double-acting **baking powder** and
       ½ teaspoon **salt**
Cream. . . . . . ¾ cup **butter** or margarine. Gradually add

1¾ cups **sugar**, creaming well.

Add . . . . 4 unbeaten **egg yolks;** beat well.

Combine . . . 1¼ cups **milk** and

½ teaspoon **almond extract.** Add alternately with the dry ingredients to creamed mixture. Blend well after each addition.

Beat . . . . 4 **egg whites** until stiff; fold into batter.

Turn . . . . into two 9-inch round layer pans, at least 1½ inches deep, well greased and lightly floured on the bottoms.

Bake . . . . at 375° for 30 to 35 minutes.

Prepare . . . . . . 1 **fresh coconut,** reserving the liquid and shredding coconut meat. Cover and set aside. Then prepare Fresh Coconut Sauce.

Cool . . . . layers 10 minutes; turn out on wire racks, top-sides up. Brush tops immediately with Fresh Coconut Sauce until all sauce is absorbed. Cool completely.

Frost . . . . with **White Mountain Frosting,** page 318, stacking layers top-sides up. Sprinkle with **coconut.**

For use with Pillsbury's Best Self-Rising Flour, omit baking powder and salt.

FRESH COCONUT SAUCE

Combine reserved coconut liquid (⅓ to ½ cup), ½ cup sugar, 1 teaspoon lemon juice and 1 teaspoon almond extract in saucepan. Simmer for 20 minutes.

Deep South Caramel Cake

Junior Winner by Nancy Jones, Birmingham, Alabama

A rich brown sugar caramel frosting completes this queenly cake. For company, you can bake it in three layers.

BAKE at 350° for 25 to 30 minutes   MAKES three 9-inch layers*

Sift together . . 3 cups sifted **Pillsbury's Best All Purpose Flour****
3½ teaspoons double-acting **baking powder** and
1 teaspoon **salt.** Set aside.

Deep South Caramel Cake

Add . . . . 2 cups **sugar** gradually to
⅔ cup **shortening,** creaming thoroughly.

Blend in . . . . . 4 unbeaten **eggs,** beating well after each.

Combine . . . 1¼ cups **water** and
1 teaspoon **vanilla.** Add alternately with the dry ingredients to creamed mixture. Blend well after each addition.

Turn . . . . into three 9-inch round layer pans, well greased and lightly floured on bottoms.

Bake . . . . at 350° for 25 to 30 minutes. Cool; frost with **Hasty Butterscotch Frosting,** page 315.

If desired, cake may be baked in 15x11-inch pan for 35 to 45 minutes. Or, ingredients may be cut in half and baked in 9x9x2-inch pan for 40 to 50 minutes.

**For use with Pillsbury's Best Self-Rising Flour, omit baking powder and salt.*

Sour Cream Walnut Cake

Senior Winner by Louise A. Drake, Battle Creek, Michigan

Quick smooth caramel frosting on a rich, moist cake, flavored with black walnut.

BAKE at 350° for 45 to 50 minutes   MAKES 12x8-inch cake

Sift together..2 cups sifted **Pillsbury's Best All Purpose Flour***
           3 teaspoons double-acting **baking powder**
           ½ teaspoon **soda** and
           ½ teaspoon **salt**

Blend.......3 tablespoons soft **butter** or margarine with
           1⅛ cups **sugar** (1 cup plus 2 tablespoons), creaming well.

Add.......1½ cups **sour cream** (thick or commercial) and
           ¼ teaspoon **black walnut flavoring**; mix well.

Blend in.....2 unbeaten **eggs**, beating well after each.

Add..........the dry ingredients all at once; mix thoroughly.

Turn..........into 12x8x2-inch pan, well greased and lightly floured on the bottom.

Bake.........at 350° for 45 to 50 minutes. Cool; frost with **Speedy Caramel Frosting,** page 314.

**For use with Pillsbury's Best Self-Rising Flour, omit baking powder and salt; decrease soda to ¼ teaspoon.*

Cranberry-Topped Cake

Senior Winner by Mrs. Joseph Serafino, Muskegon, Michigan

There's no extra icing for this easy loaf! Cranberry sauce and nuts bake right on top of the batter.

BAKE at 350° for 45 to 50 minutes   MAKES 8x8 or 9x9-inch cake

Combine.....3 tablespoons **sugar**
           1 teaspoon grated **lemon rind**
           ¼ teaspoon **cinnamon** and
           ⅓ cup **nuts,** chopped

Add........⅔ cup **jellied-cranberry sauce,** broken into pieces. Set aside.

Sift together..2 cups sifted **Pillsbury's Best All Purpose Flour***
           2 teaspoons double-acting **baking powder** and
           1 teaspoon **salt.** Set aside.

Add.........1 cup **sugar** gradually to
           ⅓ cup **shortening,** creaming well.

Blend in.....1 unbeaten **egg.** Beat well.

Combine....¾ cup **milk** and
           1 teaspoon **lemon extract.** Add alternately with the dry ingredients to creamed mixture. Blend well after each addition.

Turn..........into 8x8x2 or 9x9x2-inch pan, well greased and lightly floured on the bottom. Spread cranberry topping over batter.

Bake.........at 350° for 45 to 50 minutes.

**For use with Pillsbury's Best Self-Rising Flour, omit baking powder and salt.*

Candied Ginger Cake

Senior Winner by Mrs. E. F. Roberts, Cleveland, Ohio

A sour cream loaf cake made with candied ginger, grated semi-sweet chocolate and nuts.

BAKE at 350° for 30 to 35 minutes   MAKES 12x8 or 13x9-inch cake

Sift together..2 cups sifted **Pillsbury's Best All Purpose Flour***
           1 teaspoon **soda** and
           ½ teaspoon **salt**

Cream......½ cup **butter** or margarine. Gradually add
           ½ cup **sugar** and
           ½ cup firmly packed **brown sugar,** creaming well.

Add........2 unbeaten **eggs,** beating well after each. Stir in
           1 teaspoon **vanilla**

Blend in.......the dry ingredients alternately with
           1 cup **sour cream.** Blend well after each addition.

Fold in......2 tablespoons finely chopped **candied ginger**
        ½ cup **nuts**, chopped, and
        2 squares (2 oz.) grated **semi-sweet chocolate**
Turn..........into 12x8x2 or 13x9x2-inch pan, well greased and
        lightly floured on the bottom.
Bake.........at 350° for 30 to 35 minutes. Serve warm or cold
        with **whipped cream.**
For use with Pillsbury's Best Self-Rising Flour, omit soda and salt.

Chocolate Pecan Meringue Cake

Senior Winner by Mrs. Irma L. Yovanovich, Gary, Indiana

A chocolate-nut meringue topping is baked on this golden loaf cake.

BAKE at 350° for 25 to 35 minutes   MAKES 13x9-inch cake

Sift together..2 cups sifted **Pillsbury's Best All Purpose Flour***
        2 teaspoons double-acting **baking powder** and
        ½ teaspoon **salt.** Set aside.
Add.........⅔ cup **sugar** gradually to
        ½ cup **shortening,** creaming well.
Blend in.....3 unbeaten **egg yolks,** beating well after each.
Combine....⅔ cup **milk** and
        ½ teaspoon **vanilla.** Add alternately with the dry
        ingredients to creamed mixture. Blend well after
        each addition.
Turn..........into 13x9x2-inch pan, well greased and lightly
        floured on bottom. Spread with Chocolate-Nut
        Meringue.
Bake.........at 350° for 25 to 35 minutes.
For use with Pillsbury's Best Self-Rising Flour, omit baking powder and salt.

CHOCOLATE-NUT MERINGUE

Beat 3 egg whites until foamy. Gradually add ⅓ cup sugar. Beat until stiff, straight peaks form. Fold in 1 cup chopped pecans and 4 squares (4 oz.) grated semi-sweet chocolate.

Caramel-Nut Meringue Cake

Senior Winner by Mrs. George Allen Baird, Washington, D.C.

Here's a nut meringue torte that will soon be a favorite at your house. You'll like the easy, baked-on frosting.

BAKE at 325° for 50 to 55 minutes   MAKES 9x9-inch cake

Sift together 1¾ cups sifted **Pillsbury's Best All Purpose Flour***
        1 teaspoon double-acting **baking powder** and
        1 teaspoon **salt.** Set aside.
Add.........1 cup **sugar** gradually to
        ½ cup **shortening,** creaming well.
Blend in.....2 unbeaten **eggs** and
        1 unbeaten **egg yolk.** Beat well.
Combine....¼ cup **milk** and
        1 teaspoon **vanilla.** Add alternately with the dry
        ingredients to creamed mixture. Blend well after
        each addition.
Spread.......in 9x9x2-inch pan, well greased and lightly floured
        on the bottom. Sprinkle with
        ½ cup **nuts,** chopped
Beat.........1 **egg white** until stiff. Gradually add
        ½ cup firmly packed **brown sugar,** beating constantly
        until stiff. Blend in
        ½ teaspoon **vanilla.** Spread over batter.
Bake.........at 325° for 50 to 55 minutes.
For use with Pillsbury's Best Self-Rising Flour, omit baking powder and salt.

Take-to-Meeting Pecan Cake

Senior Winner by Mrs. Ralph Hallead, St. Johns, Michigan

Chopped pecans are scattered through the cake and the rich caramel frosting on top. It's delicious with hickory nuts, too!

BAKE at 350° for 50 to 55 minutes   MAKES 13x9-inch cake

Sift together 2½ cups sifted **Pillsbury's Best All Purpose Flour***
          2½ teaspoons double-acting **baking powder**
          1 teaspoon **salt** and
          ½ teaspoon **nutmeg**
Cream......¾ cup **butter** or margarine. Gradually add
          1¾ cups **sugar**, creaming well.
Blend in.....4 unbeaten **eggs**, beating well after each.
Combine.....1 cup **milk** and
          1 teaspoon **lemon extract.** Add alternately with the dry ingredients to creamed mixture. Blend well after each addition.
Add.........1 cup **pecans** or hickory nuts, chopped
Turn..........into 13x9x2-inch pan, well greased and lightly floured on the bottom.
Bake.........at 350° for 50 to 55 minutes. Cool; frost with Caramel Nut Frosting.

**For use with Pillsbury's Best Self-Rising Flour, omit baking powder and salt.*

CARAMEL NUT FROSTING

In large, heavy saucepan, combine 1½ cups firmly packed brown sugar, 1 cup chopped pecans or hickory nuts and 1 cup sour cream. Cook over direct heat until a little syrup dropped in cold water forms a very soft ball (230°). Spread immediately over cooled cake.

Little French Butter Cake

Senior Winner by Mrs. Irene J. Hackman, Westons Mills, New York

A simple butter cake, made in one layer and split in two, with a coffee-pecan filling and a creamy chocolate frosting.

BAKE at 350° for 40 to 45 minutes   MAKES 9-inch round cake*

Sift together 1½ cups sifted **Pillsbury's Best All Purpose Flour****
          1½ teaspoons double-acting **baking powder** and
          ¼ teaspoon **salt**
Cream......⅓ cup **butter** or margarine. Gradually add
          ⅞ cup **sugar** (¾ cup plus 2 tablespoons), creaming well.
Add........2 unbeaten **egg yolks** and
          1 teaspoon **vanilla.** Beat well.
Blend in.......the dry ingredients alternately with
          ⅔ cup **milk.** Blend well after each addition.
Beat........2 **egg whites** until stiff. Fold into batter.
Turn..........into 9-inch round layer pan,* at least 1½ inches deep, well greased and lightly floured on the bottom.
Bake.........at 350° for 40 to 45 minutes. Cool. Split in half, making two layers. Fill and frost.

  **Cake may also be baked in 8x8x2-inch pan.*
***For use with Pillsbury's Best Self-Rising Flour, omit baking powder and salt.*

FILLING AND FROSTING

Cream ½ cup butter or margarine thoroughly. Gradually add 1 teaspoon instant coffee and 3 cups sifted confectioners' sugar, creaming well. Add 1 egg and 1 teaspoon vanilla; beat well. Blend in 1 tablespoon cream. Measure ¾ cup of this mixture into second bowl; stir in ¼ cup pecans, ground or chopped fine. Spread between layers. Blend 1½

squares (1½ oz.) melted chocolate into the remaining mixture; frost top and sides.

Apricot Gooey Cake

Junior Second Prize Winner by LaVonn Jost, Stringtown, Oklahoma

An easy, one-egg loaf cake with a simple apricot and coconut topping . . . colorful and moist, a practical busy-day cake.

BAKE at 350° for 35 to 45 minutes   MAKES 9x9 or 11x7-inch cake

Cook.......18 large dried **apricot halves** in water to cover until tender. Drain and mash. Set aside.

Sift together 1⅔ cups sifted **Pillsbury's Best All Purpose Flour***
½ teaspoon double-acting **baking powder**
½ teaspoon **soda** and
½ teaspoon **salt**; set aside.

Add........1 cup **sugar** gradually to
⅓ cup **shortening**, creaming well.

Blend in.....1 unbeaten **egg**
½ teaspoon **vanilla** and
¼ teaspoon **lemon extract**; beat well.

Add..........the dry ingredients alternately with
¾ cup **water**. Blend well after each addition.

Blend in.....2 tablespoons of mashed apricots thoroughly.

Turn..........into 9x9x2 or 11x7x2-inch pan, well greased and lightly floured on the bottom.

Bake.........at 350° for 35 to 45 minutes. Cool; frost with Apricot Coconut Topping.

*For use with Pillsbury's Best Self-Rising Flour, omit baking powder, soda, salt.

APRICOT COCONUT TOPPING

Combine 2 tablespoons butter, ¼ cup firmly packed brown sugar and the ½ cup mashed apricots in saucepan. Cook over medium heat 3 minutes, stirring constantly. Remove from heat. Add ½ cup coarsely chopped coconut. Spread over cake while topping is warm.

Apricot Gooey Cake

Toasty Coconut-Orange Cake

Best of Class Winner by Mrs. W. C. Turley, Jr., Morgantown, West Virginia

*You bake this cake, spread while warm with orange-coconut topping,
then toast it under the broiler until the coconut browns.*

BAKE at 350° for 35 to 40 minutes   MAKES 13x9-inch cake

Sift together 2¼ cups sifted **Pillsbury's Best All Purpose Flour***
  2 teaspoons double-acting **baking powder**
  ½ teaspoon **salt** and
  ½ teaspoon **soda**. Set aside.
Add.......1⅛ cups **sugar** gradually to
  ¾ cup **shortening**, creaming well.
Blend in....4 unbeaten **egg yolks**, beating well after each.
Combine....¾ cup **buttermilk** or sour milk and
  1 teaspoon **orange extract**. Add alternately with the
  dry ingredients to creamed mixture. Blend well after
  each addition.
Beat........4 **egg whites** until stiff but not dry. Fold gently into
  batter.
Pour.........into 13x9x2-inch pan, well greased and lightly floured
  on the bottom.
Bake.........at 350° for 35 to 40 minutes. Remove from oven.
  Turn oven to "broil."
Spread........Orange-Coconut Topping over warm cake. Place 4
  to 5 inches below broiling unit. Broil 1 to 3 minutes.

**For use with Pillsbury's Best Self-Rising Flour, omit baking powder and salt;
decrease soda to ¼ teaspoon.*

ORANGE-COCONUT TOPPING

Cream together ¼ cup butter and ½ cup firmly packed brown sugar.
Blend in 3 tablespoons orange juice and ¾ cup coconut.

Candy Kisses Cake

Senior Winner by Mrs. Harold Hartman, West Bend, Wisconsin

Dates, nuts and candy kisses are the secret of this party cake!

BAKE at 350° for 60 to 70 minutes   MAKES 9 or 10-inch tube cake

Sift together 3½ cups sifted **Pillsbury's Best All Purpose Flour***
  3½ teaspoons double-acting **baking powder** and
  1 teaspoon **salt**
Combine.....1 cup **dates**, finely cut
  ½ cup **nuts**, chopped, and ¼ cup dry ingredients.
Cream......⅔ cup **butter** or margarine. Gradually add
  1½ cups **sugar**, creaming well.
Blend in.....3 unbeaten **egg yolks**, one at a time, beating well.
Combine.....1 cup **milk** and
  1 teaspoon **vanilla**. Add alternately with the dry
  ingredients to creamed mixture. Blend well after
  each addition. Add the dates and nuts.
Beat........3 **egg whites** until stiff but not dry. Fold gently but
  thoroughly into batter.
Turn.........into 9 or 10-inch tube pan, well greased on the bottom.
Arrange.....1 cup **milk chocolate candy kisses** over top of batter,
  pressing them down so tips show.
Bake.........at 350° for 60 to 70 minutes. Sprinkle with **confectioners' sugar** before serving.

*For use with Pillsbury's Best Self-Rising Flour, omit baking powder and salt.

Colonial Raisin Cake

Senior Winner by Mrs. Chester H. Burghoff, Yalesville, Connecticut

Creamy frosting makes this old-fashioned favorite a special treat.

BAKE at 350°   MAKES 9-inch tube or 12x8-inch cake

Sift together..2 cups sifted **Pillsbury's Best All Purpose Flour***
  3 teaspoons double-acting **baking powder**

1 teaspoon **salt** and
½ teaspoon **nutmeg**

Combine . . . . ⅔ cup **raisins**
¼ cup chopped **citron**, if desired, and 2 tablespoons dry ingredients. Set aside.

Add . . . . 1 cup **sugar** gradually to
⅔ cup **shortening**, creaming well.

Blend in . . . . 3 unbeaten **eggs**, beating well after each.

Combine . . . . ⅔ cup **milk** and
1 teaspoon **vanilla**. Add alternately with the dry ingredients to creamed mixture. Blend well after each addition.

Stir in . . . . floured fruit. Turn into 9-inch tube pan or 12x8x2-inch pan, well greased and lightly floured on the bottom.

Bake . . . . at 350°: 50 to 60 minutes for tube cake; 40 to 45 minutes for loaf cake. Cool; frost with **Creamy Vanilla Frosting**, page 321.

For use with Pillsbury's Best Self-Rising Flour, omit baking powder and salt.

Bavarian Guglhuph

Senior Winner by Mrs. Friederike Lehr, Montclair, New Jersey

Grated chocolate ripples prettily throughout this rich butter cake. A slivered almond topping is baked right on.

BAKE at 350° for 55 to 65 minutes   MAKES 10-inch tube cake

Sift together . . 2 cups sifted **Pillsbury's Best All Purpose Flour***
3 teaspoons double-acting **baking powder** and
1 teaspoon **salt**

Cream . . . . . . ⅓ cup **butter** or margarine with
⅓ cup **shortening**. Gradually add
1 cup **sugar**, creaming well.

Add . . . . 4 unbeaten **eggs**, beating well after each.

Combine . . . . ½ cup **milk** and

Bavarian Guglhuph

1 teaspoon **vanilla**. Add alternately with the dry ingredients to creamed mixture. Blend well after each addition.

Arrange . . . . 24 blanched **almonds**, slivered, over well-greased and lightly floured bottom of 10-inch fluted** or standard tube pan.

Grate . . . . 2 squares (2 oz.) **semi-sweet chocolate**

Spoon . . . . one-third of batter carefully into pan; spread evenly over nuts. Cover with half of grated chocolate; spoon in another one-third of batter and cover with remaining chocolate. Top with remaining batter.

Bake . . . . at 350° for 55 to 65 minutes. Cool in pan 15 minutes; turn out and sprinkle with **sugar**.

For use with Pillsbury's Best Self-Rising Flour, omit baking powder and salt.
**The fluted pan gives Guglhuph a characteristic design.*

Meringue Cradle Cake

Senior Third Prize Winner by Mrs. Stephen A. Hornung, New York, New York

Golden cake bakes inside the meringue "cradle." Turn cake upside down after baking—it's already "frosted."

BAKE at 325° for 1¼ to 1½ hours   MAKES 10-inch tube cake*

Beat . . . . 4 **egg whites** until soft mounds form. Gradually add
1 cup **sugar,** beating constantly until straight, glossy peaks form.

Fold in . . . . . . 1 cup **pecans** or filberts, finely chopped, and
1 square (1 oz.) grated unsweetened **chocolate**

Spread . . . . evenly over bottom and three-fourths up sides of 10-inch tube pan, well greased and lined with waxed paper on the bottom.*

Sift together . . 2 cups sifted **Pillsbury's Best All Purpose Flour****
2½ teaspoons double-acting **baking powder** and
1 teaspoon **salt**

Cream . . . . . . ½ cup **butter** or margarine. Gradually add
1 cup **sugar,** creaming well.

Add . . . . 4 unbeaten **egg yolks;** beat well.

Combine . . . . . 1 cup **milk** and
1 teaspoon **vanilla.** Add alternately with the dry ingredients to creamed mixture. Blend well after each addition.

Turn . . . . into meringue-lined pan.

Bake . . . . at 325° for 1¼ to 1½ hours. *Do not underbake.* Cool 20 minutes. Loosen cake with spatula; cool 30 minutes longer before removing from pan. Decorate top of cake with **pecan halves** dipped in melted **semi-sweet chocolate,** if desired.

*Cake may also be baked in two 9x5x3-inch pans for 50 to 60 minutes.
**For use with Pillsbury's Best Self-Rising Flour, omit baking powder and salt.

Meringue Cradle Cake

Yellow Daisy Cake

Senior Winner by Mrs. Chester C. Holloman, Saratoga Springs, New York

Make this with an angel food, utilizing the many egg yolks left over.

BAKE at 325° for 55 to 65 minutes   MAKES 9 or 10-inch tube cake

Sift together 2¼ cups sifted **Pillsbury's Best All Purpose Flour***
    2 teaspoons double-acting **baking powder** and
    ½ teaspoon **salt**
Beat........9 **egg yolks** until very thick and lemon colored.
Cream......½ cup **butter** or margarine. Gradually add
    1½ cups **sugar,** creaming well. Add beaten egg yolks and mix well.
Combine.....1 cup **milk** and
    1 teaspoon **lemon extract.** Add alternately with the dry ingredients to creamed mixture. Blend well after each addition.
Turn........into 9 or 10-inch tube pan, well greased and lightly floured on the bottom.
Bake........at 325° for 55 to 65 minutes. Cool. If desired, frost with **Lemon Butter Frosting,** page 324.
**For use with Pillsbury's Best Self-Rising Flour, omit baking powder and salt.*

Whipped Cream Lady Cake

Senior Winner by Mrs. William Berry, Kansas City, Missouri

There's no shortening in this simply prepared cake. Just blend all the ingredients into whipped cream and bake.

BAKE at 350° for 30 to 35 minutes   MAKES two 8-inch layers

Sift together..2 cups sifted **Pillsbury's Best All Purpose Flour***
    3 teaspoons double-acting **baking powder** and
    ½ teaspoon **salt**
Beat........1 cup **whipping cream** in large bowl until very stiff.
Add........3 **eggs,** one at a time; beat well after each.

Add........1¼ cups **sugar** gradually, beating until well blended.
Stir in.......1 teaspoon **vanilla**
Fold in........the dry ingredients, one-fourth at a time. Fold gently after each addition until dry particles disappear.
Turn.........into two 8-inch round layer pans, well greased and lightly floured on the bottoms.
Bake.........at 350° for 30 to 35 minutes. Cool; frost with **Tutti-Frutti Frosting,** page 318.
**For use with Pillsbury's Best Self-Rising Flour, omit baking powder and salt.*

Colony Cream Cake

Senior Winner by Mrs. John A. Kurz, Cheshire, Connecticut

This golden cake is baked in two layers, then cut into four. There's a smooth cream filling and an easy chocolate frosting.

BAKE at 350° for 25 to 30 minutes   MAKES two 8-inch layers

Sift together 1¼ cups sifted **Pillsbury's Best All Purpose Flour***
    1 teaspoon double-acting **baking powder**
    ½ teaspoon **salt** and
    ¼ teaspoon **cream of tartar**
Beat........3 **eggs** in mixing bowl until thick. Gradually add
    1 cup **sugar;** continue beating until thick and ivory colored. Do not underbeat.
Combine.....1 teaspoon **vanilla** and
    ⅓ cup cold **water.** Fold into egg mixture alternately with the dry ingredients. Blend well after each addition.
Turn.........into two 8-inch round layer pans, well greased and lightly floured on the bottoms.
Bake.........at 350° for 25 to 30 minutes. Cool; split to make four layers. Spread **Butter Cream Filling,** page 328, between layers; frost only top with **Velvet Chocolate Frosting,** page 326.
**For use with Pillsbury's Best Self-Rising Flour, omit baking powder and salt.*

Eggnog Cream Cake

Senior Winner by Mrs. W. R. McDaniel, Anchorage, Alaska

The light, tender layers of this whipped cream cake have a delicate blend of nutmeg and rum flavors.

BAKE at 350° for 25 to 35 minutes   MAKES two 9-inch layers

Sift together . . 2 cups sifted **Pillsbury's Best All Purpose Flour***
3 teaspoons double-acting **baking powder**
1 teaspoon **salt** and
½ teaspoon **nutmeg**

Beat . . . . 1½ cups **whipping cream** in large bowl until stiff.

Add . . . . 3 **eggs,** one at a time; beat well after each.

Add . . . . . 1½ cups **sugar** gradually, beating until well blended. Add
2 teaspoons **rum flavoring**

Fold in . . . . the dry ingredients gently, one-fourth at a time, until
all dry particles disappear.

Turn . . . . into two 9-inch round layer pans, well greased and
lightly floured on the bottoms.

Bake . . . . at 350° for 25 to 35 minutes. Cool. Spread Rum
Cream Frosting between layers and on top. Garnish
with **nutmeg**. Refrigerate until serving time.

For use with Pillsbury's Best Self-Rising Flour, omit baking powder and salt.

RUM CREAM FROSTING

Beat 1½ cups whipping cream until stiff. Set aside. Beat 2 eggs. Add ⅓ cup sugar and 1 teaspoon rum flavoring; continue beating until thick and ivory colored. Stir in ¼ cup melted and cooled (but not set) butter or margarine. Fold gently into whipped cream just until well blended.

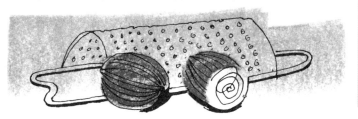

Princess Party Cake

Senior Winner by Mrs. Clayton Curtis, Winslow, Indiana

An elegant, three-layer Quick-Mix cake, using pineapple-orange juice in cake, fluffy frosting and filling.

BAKE at 350° for 25 to 30 minutes   MAKES three 9-inch layers

Sift together . . 3 cups sifted **Pillsbury's Best All Purpose Flour***
1¾ cups **sugar**
4 teaspoons double-acting **baking powder** and
1½ teaspoons **salt** into large mixing bowl.

Add . . . . 1 cup **milk**
¾ cup **shortening**

Beat . . . . 1½ minutes. (With mixer use a low speed.)

Add . . . . 2 unbeaten **eggs** and
3 unbeaten **egg yolks,** one at a time, beating well after
each.

Blend in . . . . . ¼ cup **milk**
⅓ cup frozen **pineapple-orange juice,** undiluted, and
1 teaspoon **vanilla**. Beat 1½ minutes.

Turn . . . . into three 9-inch round layer pans, well greased and
lightly floured on the bottoms.

Bake . . . . at 350° for 25 to 30 minutes. Cool; fill and frost
with Tangy Fluff Frosting.

For use with Pillsbury's Best Self-Rising Flour, omit baking powder and salt; increase baking time to 30 to 35 minutes.

TANGY FLUFF FROSTING

In top of double boiler combine 1 cup sugar, ⅛ cup light corn syrup, ¼ cup undiluted pineapple-orange juice, ¼ teaspoon cream of tartar, ¼ teaspoon salt and 3 egg whites. Cook over rapidly boiling water, beating with electric mixer or rotary beater until mixture stands in peaks. Remove from heat; continue beating until of spreading consistency.

Filling: To one-third of frosting add ¼ cup chopped coconut, ¼ cup chopped pecans and ½ cup well-drained crushed pineapple (drain pineapple thoroughly).

Chocolate Cherry Covered Cake

Senior Winner by Geneva J. McCollum, Washington, D.C.

Maraschino cherries hide in the frosting on this Quick-Mix cake.

BAKE at 375° for 30 to 35 minutes   MAKES 8x8 or 9x9-inch cake

Sift together 1½ cups sifted **Pillsbury's Best All Purpose Flour***
          1 cup **sugar**
          2½ teaspoons double-acting **baking powder** and
          ½ teaspoon **salt** into mixing bowl.
Add . . . . 1 cup **whipping cream**
          2 unbeaten **eggs** and
          1 teaspoon **vanilla**
Beat . . . . 2 minutes. (With mixer use a low speed.)
Turn . . . . into 8x8x2 or 9x9x2-inch pan, well greased and
          lightly floured on the bottom.
Bake . . . . at 375° for 30 to 35 minutes. Cool; frost with
          Chocolate Cherry Frosting, page 322.

*For use with Pillsbury's Best Self-Rising Flour, omit baking powder and salt.

Apple-Orange Sunburst Cake

Senior Winner by Mrs. F. R. Tait, Ocean Springs, Mississippi

An elegant party-sized orange cake that's quick to mix. The orange and grated apple filling adds extra moistness.

BAKE at 350° for 30 to 35 minutes   MAKES three 9-inch layers

Sift together . . 3 cups sifted **Pillsbury's Best All Purpose Flour***
          2 cups **sugar**
          5 teaspoons double-acting **baking powder** and
          1 teaspoon **salt** into large mixing bowl.
Add . . . . 1 tablespoon grated **orange rind**
          1 cup **milk** and
          ¾ cup **shortening**
Beat . . . . 1½ minutes. (With mixer use a low speed.)

Apple-Orange Sunburst Cake

Add . . . . 4 unbeaten **eggs,** beating well after each.
Stir in . . . . . . ½ cup **milk;** beat 1½ minutes.
Turn . . . . into three 9-inch round layer pans,** well greased
          and lightly floured on the bottoms. Use about 2⅔
          cups batter in each pan.
Bake . . . . at 350° for 30 to 35 minutes. Cool; fill with Orange
          Filling, stacking layers top-side up. Frost with
          Creamy Orange Frosting, page 325.

*For use with Pillsbury's Best Self-Rising Flour, omit baking powder and salt.
***If only two 9-inch layer pans are available, two layers may be baked first.
Refrigerate remaining batter and bake as soon as possible.*

ORANGE FILLING

Combine 3½ cups pared and coarsely grated apples (4 medium), 1 tablespoon grated orange rind, ⅓ cup orange juice, 2 egg yolks and 1¼ cups sugar in saucepan. Boil 3 minutes, stirring constantly. Cool.

Licorice Lemon Cake

Licorice Lemon Cake

Senior Winner by Mrs. Glenn Marsh, Seattle, Washington

Anise seed and lemon in a moist, tender Quick-Mix loaf cake. Combine all the ingredients in a bowl, beat—then bake.

BAKE at 375° for 30 to 35 minutes   MAKES 9x9-inch cake

Sift together 1¾ cups sifted **Pillsbury's Best All Purpose Flour***
     2½ teaspoons double-acting **baking powder** and
     ½ teaspoon **salt** into large mixing bowl.
Add . . . . .1 cup **sugar**
     ¾ cup **milk**
     ½ cup soft **butter** or margarine
     2 unbeaten **eggs**

     1 tablespoon **anise seed**
     1 tablespoon grated **lemon rind**
     1 teaspoon **vanilla** and
     1 teaspoon **lemon extract**
Beat . . . . .2 minutes. (With mixer use a low speed.)
Turn . . . . .into 9x9x2-inch pan, well greased and lightly floured
     on the bottom.
Bake . . . . .at 375° for 30 to 35 minutes. Cool; frost with **Lemon
     Butter Frosting,** page 324. Garnish with **lemon
     slices,** quartered, and **licorice candy,** if desired.
*For use with Pillsbury's Best Self-Rising Flour, omit baking powder and salt.

Sally's Hurry-Up Cake

Senior Winner by Mrs. Sally Clark, Santa Maria, California

No frosting needed—no fuss to make this Quick-Mix cake. Takes to lunchboxes, coffee parties or after-school snacks.

BAKE at 350° for 45 to 55 minutes MAKES 12x8 or 13x9-inch cake

Sift together 2¼ cups sifted **Pillsbury's Best All Purpose Flour***
     1½ cups **sugar**
     3 teaspoons double-acting **baking powder** and
     1 teaspoon **salt**
Add . . . . .½ cup **shortening**
     ½ cup **nuts,** chopped
     3 unbeaten **eggs**
     1 cup **milk**
     1 teaspoon **vanilla** and
     grated rind of 1 **orange**
Beat . . . . .2 minutes. (With mixer use a medium speed.)
Turn . . . . .into 12x8x2 or 13x9x2-inch pan, well greased and
     lightly floured on the bottom.
Sprinkle with . ¼ cup **nuts,** chopped
Bake . . . . .at 350° for 45 to 55 minutes.
*For use with Pillsbury's Best Self-Rising Flour, omit baking powder and salt.

French Whipped Cream Cake

Senior Winner by Mrs. Hilton S. Clifton, Philadelphia, Pennsylvania

No shortening in this delicate whipped cream cake. Smooth chocolate frosting goes on top—or serve with fresh fruit or sauce.

BAKE at 350° for 35 to 40 minutes   MAKES 12x8 or 13x9-inch cake

Combine.....3 unbeaten **eggs**
    1¼ cups **sugar**
    1 teaspoon **vanilla** and
    ½ teaspoon **almond extract** in mixing bowl. Beat until thick and ivory colored.
Sift together 1½ cups sifted **Pillsbury's Best All Purpose Flour***
    2 teaspoons double-acting **baking powder** and
    1 teaspoon **salt.** Add gradually to egg mixture; blend well.
Beat........1 cup **whipping cream** until thick; fold into batter.
Turn.........into 12x8x2 or 13x9x2-inch pan, well greased and lightly floured on the bottom.
Bake........at 350° for 35 to 40 minutes. Cool; frost with **Chocolate Butter Cream Frosting,** page 321.

For use with Pillsbury's Best Self-Rising Flour, omit baking powder and salt.

Creamy Apple Topped Cake

Senior Winner by Mrs. Ralph Whitmer, Pacific Palisades, California

An applesauce-brown sugar mixture forms a creamy layer that's baked on top of this cardamom-flavored nut cake.

BAKE at 350°   MAKES 8x8 or 9x9-inch cake

Sift together 1½ cups sifted **Pillsbury's Best All Purpose Flour***
    ½ cup **sugar**
    ¾ teaspoon ground **cardamom**
    ½ teaspoon **soda** and
    ½ teaspoon **salt** into mixing bowl. Add
    ½ cup firmly packed **brown sugar**
Cut in......⅓ cup **shortening** until particles are very fine.
Blend.......⅔ cup **buttermilk** or sour milk with
    1 unbeaten **egg.** Add to flour mixture; mix until thoroughly blended. Stir in
    ½ cup **nuts,** chopped
Turn.........into 8x8x2 or 9x9x2-inch pan, well greased and lightly floured on the bottom.
Bake........at 350°: 40 to 45 minutes in 8-inch pan; 35 to 40 minutes in 9-inch pan.**

APPLE-SOUR CREAM TOPPING

Combine.....1 cup thick sweetened **applesauce**
    1 tablespoon **brown sugar** and
    ¼ teaspoon **cinnamon.** Spread over top of partially baked cake.
Blend.......½ cup **sour cream** (thick or commercial) with
    2 tablespoons **brown sugar** and
    ½ teaspoon **vanilla.** Spoon carefully over applesauce mixture.
Bake........15 minutes longer at 350°. Then turn on broiler to brown slightly, 2 to 5 minutes. Serve warm.

For use with Pillsbury's Best Self-Rising Flour, omit soda and salt.

**If desired, cake may be prepared ahead of time and topping added just before serving.*

CHOCOLATE CAKES

Arabian Sour Cream Cake

Senior Winner by Mrs. Doris Hoopman, West Bend, Wisconsin

Chocolate and spices blend to give a unique flavor. Fluffy orange frosting is the refreshing topper.

BAKE at 350° for 35 to 40 minutes   MAKES two 8-inch layers

Melt . . . . 1 square (1 oz.) unsweetened **chocolate** in
½ cup hot **water** in saucepan over low heat. Cook, stirring constantly, until thickened. Remove from heat.

Sift together   2 cups sifted **Pillsbury's Best All Purpose Flour***
1 teaspoon **soda**
½ teaspoon **salt**
1½ teaspoons **cinnamon** and
½ teaspoon **cloves**. Set aside.

Add . . . . 1¼ cups **sugar** gradually to
⅓ cup **shortening**, creaming well.

Add . . . . 3 unbeaten **eggs**, beating well after each. Blend in the chocolate mixture.

Combine . . . . . 1 cup **sour cream** (thick or commercial) and
1 teaspoon **vanilla**. Add alternately with the dry ingredients to creamed mixture. Blend well after each addition.

Stir in . . . . 1 cup **nuts**, chopped. Turn into two 8-inch round layer pans, well greased and lightly floured on bottoms.

Bake . . . . at 350° for 35 to 40 minutes. Cool; frost with **Fluffy Orange Frosting**, page 317.

*For use with Pillsbury's Best Self-Rising Flour, decrease soda to ½ teaspoon and omit salt.

Apricot Surprise Fudge Cake

Senior Winner by Miss Florence C. Schoenleber, Lincoln, Nebraska

Apricots are blended into chocolate fudge cake batter to make a moist cake that's really special.

BAKE at 350° for 35 to 40 minutes   MAKES two 8-inch layers

Sift together . . 2 cups sifted **Pillsbury's Best All Purpose Flour***
2½ teaspoons double-acting **baking powder**
½ teaspoon **salt** and
¼ teaspoon **soda**

Cream . . . . . . ½ cup **butter** or margarine. Gradually add
1¼ cups **sugar**, creaming well.

Blend in . . . . . 2 unbeaten **eggs**, one at a time
3 squares (3 oz.) melted unsweetened **chocolate** and
1 teaspoon **vanilla**. Beat well.

Add . . . . the dry ingredients alternately with
¾ cup **milk**. Blend well after each addition.

Stir in . . . . . . ¾ cup cooked dried **apricots**, drained and cut.

Turn . . . . into two 8-inch round layer pans, well greased and lightly floured on the bottoms.

Bake . . . . at 350° for 35 to 40 minutes. Cool.

Beat . . . . 1 cup **whipping cream**. Sweeten to taste and spread between and on top of layers.

*For use with Pillsbury's Best Self-Rising Flour, omit baking powder and salt.

Cocoa Layer Cake

Senior Winner by Mrs. Peter Funcke, Cedar Rapids, Iowa

Cocoa-flavored layers frosted with glamorous snowy frosting.

BAKE at 350° for 30 to 35 minutes   MAKES two 8-inch layers

Sift together 1¾ cups sifted **Pillsbury's Best All Purpose Flour***
¼ cup **cocoa**
1 teaspoon **soda** and

1 teaspoon **salt**. Set aside.

Add . . . . 1¼ cups **sugar** gradually to
⅔ cup **shortening**, creaming well.

Blend in . . . . . 2 unbeaten **eggs**, beating well after each.

Combine . . . . ⅔ cup **evaporated milk**
½ cup **water** and
1 teaspoon **vanilla**. Add alternately with the dry ingredients to creamed mixture. Blend well after each
addition.

Turn . . . . into two 8-inch round layer pans, well greased and
lightly floured on the bottoms.

Bake . . . . at 350° for 30 to 35 minutes. Cool; frost with **White
Mountain Frosting**, page 318.

*For use with Pillsbury's Best Self-Rising Flour, decrease soda to ¼ teaspoon
and omit salt.*

French Chocolate Cake

Junior Winner by Deanne Froidcoeur, Gibson City, Illinois

*Rich brown sugar chocolate frosting complements this delicate and
tender cocoa cake, made with sour cream instead of shortening.*

BAKE at 350° for 25 to 30 minutes   MAKES two 8-inch layers

Sift together . . 2 cups sifted **Pillsbury's Best All Purpose Flour***
½ cup **cocoa**
1 teaspoon **soda** and
½ teaspoon **salt**

Cream . . . . . . ⅛ cup **butter** or margarine. Gradually add
1⅛ cups **sugar**, creaming well.

Add . . . . 3 unbeaten **egg whites;** beat 1 minute.

Combine . . . . ¾ cup **water**
¾ cup **sour cream** and

1 teaspoon **vanilla**. Add alternately with the dry ingredients to creamed mixture. Blend well after each
addition.

Turn . . . . into two 8-inch round layer pans, well greased and
lightly floured on the bottoms.

Bake . . . . at 350° for 25 to 30 minutes. Cool; fill and frost with
Brown Sugar Chocolate Frosting, page 316.

For use with Pillsbury's Best Self-Rising Flour, omit soda and salt.

Dream Devil's Food

Junior Winner by Patricia Tatka, Cleveland, Ohio

*This handsome and fine-textured cocoa cake contrasts the rich color of
devil's food with light-colored cocoa frosting.*

BAKE at 350° for 30 to 35 minutes   MAKES two 8 or 9-inch layers

Combine . . . . ¾ cup **milk** and
1 tablespoon **vinegar**

Sift together 1¾ cups sifted **Pillsbury's Best All Purpose Flour*** and
½ teaspoon **salt**. Set aside.

Add . . . . 1½ cups **sugar** gradually to
½ cup **shortening**, creaming well.

Blend in . . . . . 2 unbeaten **eggs,** beating well after each.

Combine . . . . . 1 teaspoon **vanilla** and the soured milk. Add alternately
with the dry ingredients to creamed mixture. Blend
well after each addition.

Blend . . . . 1 teaspoon **soda** and
½ cup **cocoa** with
½ cup warm **water**. Add to batter; mix well.

Turn . . . . into two 8 or 9-inch round layer pans, well greased
and lightly floured on the bottoms.

Bake . . . . at 350° for 30 to 35 minutes. Cool; frost with **Cocoa
Butter Frosting**, page 323.

*For use with Pillsbury's Best Self-Rising Flour, omit salt and decrease soda
to ¼ teaspoon.*

Aunt Carrie's Bonbon Cake

Senior Third Prize Winner by Mrs. Richard W. Sprague, San Marino, California

A high, delicate cake with a milk-chocolate color and flavor, frosted with swirls of fudge frosting.

BAKE at 350° for 30 to 35 minutes   MAKES two 8-inch layers

Sift together 1¾ cups sifted **Pillsbury's Best All Purpose Flour***
  2 teaspoons double-acting **baking powder** and
  ½ teaspoon **salt**
Combine . . . 2½ squares (2½ oz.) shaved unsweetened **chocolate** and
  ⅓ cup **boiling water.** Stir until smooth. Set aside.
Cream . . . . . . ½ cup **butter** or margarine. Gradually add
  1⅓ cups **sugar,** creaming well.
Add . . . . 1 teaspoon **vanilla** and the cooled chocolate.
Blend in . . . . . 4 unbeaten **egg yolks,** beating well after each.
Add . . . . the dry ingredients alternately with
  ½ cup **milk.** Blend well after each addition.
Beat . . . . 4 **egg whites** until stiff but not dry. Fold gently but
  thoroughly into batter.
Pour . . . . into two 8-inch round layer pans, well greased and
  lightly floured on the bottoms.
Bake . . . . at 350° for 30 to 35 minutes. Cool; fill with **Bonbon
  Filling,** page 328. Frost with **Fudge Frosting,** page
  316.
*For use with Pillsbury's Best Self-Rising Flour, omit baking powder and salt.

Midnight Magic Cake

Senior Winner by Mrs. Ernest M. Fisher, Scarsdale, New York

Dark chocolate layers, heaped with swirls of marshmallow frosting.

BAKE at 350° for 25 to 30 minutes   MAKES two 8-inch layers

Combine . . . . ⅓ cup **sugar**
  ½ cup **cocoa** and

Aunt Carrie's Bonbon Cake

½ cup **boiling water.** Cool.

Sift together . . 2 cups sifted **Pillsbury's Best All Purpose Flour***
3 teaspoons double-acting **baking powder** and
1 teaspoon **salt.** Set aside.

Add . . . . 1 cup **sugar** gradually to
⅔ cup **shortening,** creaming well.

Blend in . . . . . 3 unbeaten **eggs,** beating well after each. Stir in
cooled cocoa mixture.

Combine . . . . ½ cup **milk** and
1 teaspoon **vanilla.** Add alternately with the dry ingredients to creamed mixture. Blend well after each
addition.

Turn . . . . into two 8-inch round layer pans, well greased and
lightly floured on the bottoms.

Bake . . . . at 350° for 25 to 30 minutes. Cool; frost with
Marshmallow Fluff Frosting.

For use with Pillsbury's Best Self-Rising Flour, omit baking powder and salt.

MARSHMALLOW FLUFF FROSTING

In top of double boiler, combine 1 cup light corn syrup, ⅛ teaspoon
cream of tartar and 2 egg whites. Cook over rapidly boiling water, beating constantly with rotary beater or electric mixer until mixture stands
in peaks. Add 6 diced marshmallows and beat until dissolved. Remove
from heat. Add ½ teaspoon almond extract and ½ teaspoon vanilla;
continue beating until of spreading consistency.

Milk Chocolate Queen's Cake

Junior Winner by Virginia Lee Ford, Tulsa, Oklahoma

A delicate chocolate flavor and color make this cake truly special.

BAKE at 350° for 40 to 45 minutes   MAKES two 8-inch layers

Melt . . . . 1 bar (¼ lb.) **German's sweet chocolate** or 3 squares
(3 oz.) semi-sweet chocolate in
2 tablespoons **water** over hot water.

Milk Chocolate Queen's Cake

Sift together 2¼ cups sifted **Pillsbury's Best All Purpose Flour*** and
1 teaspoon **salt**

Cream . . . . . . ½ cup **butter** or margarine. Gradually add
1¼ cups **sugar,** creaming well.

Add . . . . 3 unbeaten **eggs,** beating well after each.

Stir in . . . . 1 teaspoon **vanilla** and the melted chocolate; mix well.

Dissolve . . . . . 1 teaspoon **soda** in
1 cup **buttermilk** or sour milk. Add alternately with
the dry ingredients to creamed mixture. Blend well
after each addition.

Turn . . . . into two 8-inch round layer pans, well greased and
lightly floured on the bottoms.

Bake . . . . at 350° for 40 to 45 minutes. Cool; frost with **Mocha
Butter Cream Frosting,** page 324.

For use with Pillsbury's Best Self-Rising Flour, omit salt and soda.

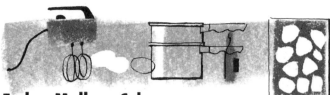

Fudge-Mallow Cake

Senior Winner by Mrs. William L. Coffey, Detroit, Michigan

Here's an unusual idea in fudge cakes. Marshmallows in the batter! Mounds of seven-minute white frosting go on top.

BAKE at 350° for 30 to 35 minutes   MAKES two 8 or 9-inch layers

Combine . . . . 16 **marshmallows** (¼ lb.)
  ½ cup **cocoa** and
  ½ cup hot **water** in top of double boiler; let stand over hot water until marshmallows melt. Do not cook. Stir until smooth. Cool.

Sift together . . 2 cups sifted **Pillsbury's Best All Purpose Flour***
  1 teaspoon double-acting **baking powder** and
  ½ teaspoon **salt**. Set aside.

Add . . . . 1 cup **sugar** gradually to
  ⅓ cup **shortening**, creaming well.

Blend in . . . . . 3 unbeaten **eggs**, beating well after each.

Combine . . . . . 1 cup **sour cream** (thick or commercial) and
  1 teaspoon **soda**. Add alternately with the dry ingredients to creamed mixture. Blend well after each addition.

Add . . . . 1 teaspoon **vanilla** and
  ½ teaspoon **red food coloring** to chocolate mixture; blend into batter.

Turn . . . . into two 8 or 9-inch round layer pans, well greased and lightly floured on the bottoms.

Bake . . . . at 350° for 30 to 35 minutes. Cool; frost with **Seven-Minute Frosting**, page 318.

*For use with Pillsbury's Best Self-Rising Flour, omit baking powder and salt; decrease soda to ¼ teaspoon.

Double Chocolate Delight

Junior Winner by Lois Evelyn Steiner, Louisville, Kentucky

A party hit! This rich chocolate cake, deep red brown in color, will be popular with its creamy chocolate butter frosting.

BAKE at 375° for 30 to 35 minutes   MAKES two 8 or 9-inch layers

Sift together . . 2 cups sifted **Pillsbury's Best All Purpose Flour*** and
  1 teaspoon **salt**. Set aside.

Add . . . . . . 1¾ cups **sugar** gradually to
  ½ cup **shortening**, creaming well.

Blend in . . . . . 2 unbeaten **eggs**; beat well.

Combine . . . . ½ cup **cocoa** and
  1 cup **hot coffee**; stir to dissolve cocoa. Add to creamed mixture. Add the dry ingredients gradually; blend thoroughly.

Dissolve . . . . . 1 teaspoon **soda** in
  ½ cup **boiling water**. Add to batter; mix well.

Pour . . . . into two 8 or 9-inch round layer pans, well greased and lightly floured on the bottoms.

Bake . . . . at 375° for 30 to 35 minutes. Cool; frost with **Chocolate Frosting**, page 322.

*For use with Pillsbury's Best Self-Rising Flour, omit salt; decrease soda to ¼ teaspoon.

Black Walnut Devil Cake

Junior Winner by Ermalea Roberson, Bushyhead, Oklahoma

Black walnuts add mellowness to this devil's food cake. It is high and moist and lavishly frosted with creamy chocolate butter frosting.

BAKE at 350° for 30 to 35 minutes   MAKES two 9-inch layers

Sift together . . 2 cups sifted **Pillsbury's Best All Purpose Flour***
  1 teaspoon **soda** and
  1 teaspoon **salt**. Set aside.

Add.......1¼ cups **sugar** gradually to
½ cup **shortening**, creaming well.
Blend in......2 squares (2 oz.) melted unsweetened **chocolate** and
2 unbeaten **eggs**, beating well after each.
Combine.....1 cup **buttermilk** or sour milk and
1 teaspoon **vanilla**. Add alternately with the dry ingredients to creamed mixture. Blend well after each
addition.
Add.......1 cup **black walnuts** or English walnuts, chopped
Turn.........into two 9-inch round layer pans, well greased and
lightly floured on the bottoms.
Bake.........at 350° for 30 to 35 minutes. Cool; frost with
Chocolate Butter Frosting, page 322.

*For use with Pillsbury's Best Self-Rising Flour, decrease soda to ¼ teaspoon
and omit salt.*

Double Chocolate Cake

Senior Winner by Mrs. D. J. Schindelholz, Racine, Wisconsin

*This deep "red" cocoa cake is moist and luscious and has a frosting
as smooth and chocolatey as chocolate pudding.*

BAKE at 350° for 30 to 35 minutes   MAKES two 9-inch layers

Sift together..2 cups sifted **Pillsbury's Best All Purpose Flour***
1½ teaspoons **soda** and
1 teaspoon **salt**. Set aside.
Add.........1 cup **sugar** gradually to
½ cup **shortening**, creaming thoroughly.
Blend in.....2 unbeaten **eggs**, beating well after each.
Combine....½ cup **sugar**
½ cup **cocoa**
1½ cups **buttermilk** or sour milk and
1 teaspoon **vanilla**. Add alternately with the dry ingredients to creamed mixture. Blend well after each
addition.

Pour.........into two 9-inch round layer pans, well greased and
lightly floured on the bottoms.
Bake.........at 350° for 30 to 35 minutes. Cool; frost with **Old
Smoothy Chocolate Frosting**, page 316.

*For use with Pillsbury's Best Self-Rising Flour, decrease soda to ½ teaspoon
and omit salt.*

New England Fudge Cake

Senior Winner by Mrs. Numa F. Pigeon, Springfield, Massachusetts

*Rich, moist chocolate fudge cake . . . with walnuts added for extra
good flavor. White fluffy frosting on top.*

BAKE at 350° for 30 to 35 minutes   MAKES two 9-inch layers

Sift together 1⅔ cups sifted **Pillsbury's Best All Purpose Flour***
2½ teaspoons double-acting **baking powder**
1 teaspoon **salt** and
¼ teaspoon **soda**. Set aside.
Add.......1½ cups **sugar** gradually to
⅔ cup **shortening**, creaming well.
Blend in.....4 unbeaten **egg yolks**, one at a time, beating well after
each.
Add.........3 squares (3 oz.) melted unsweetened **chocolate** and
1 cup **walnuts**, chopped; mix well.
Combine.....1 cup **milk** and
1 teaspoon **vanilla**. Add alternately with the dry ingredients to creamed mixture. Blend well after each
addition.
Beat.........4 **egg whites** until stiff but not dry. Fold into batter
gently but thoroughly.
Turn.........into two 9-inch round layer pans, well greased and
lightly floured on the bottoms.
Bake.........at 350° for 30 to 35 minutes. Cool; frost with **Fluffy
White Frosting**, page 317.

For use with Pillsbury's Best Self-Rising Flour, omit baking powder and salt.

Magic Fudge Cake

Senior Winner by Miss Marie Shahan, Weston, West Virginia

Prepare rich, smooth fudge, use part of it in the batter—and save the rest for frosting.

BAKE at 350° for 30 to 35 minutes   MAKES two 9-inch layers

Combine . . . 2½ cups **sugar** and
> 1 cup **evaporated milk** in heavy saucepan. Cook over medium heat, stirring occasionally, until a little syrup dropped in cold water forms a very soft ball (230°).

Place . . . . . . 1½ cups **semi-sweet chocolate pieces**
> ½ cup **butter** or margarine
> 1 cup (about 4 oz.) **marshmallow creme** and
> 1 teaspoon **vanilla** in large mixing bowl.

Add . . . . the cooked sugar mixture; blend well. Chill 1 cup of this mixture. Reserve remainder for frosting.

Sift together 2¼ cups sifted **Pillsbury's Best All Purpose Flour***
> 1½ teaspoons **soda** and
> 1 teaspoon **salt.** Set aside.

Add . . . . ½ cup firmly packed **brown sugar** gradually to
> ½ cup **shortening,** creaming well.

Add . . . . 3 unbeaten **eggs,** beating well after each.

Blend in . . . . the 1 cup chilled fudge gradually; beat well.

Combine . . . . ¾ cup **milk** and
> 1 teaspoon **vanilla;** add alternately with the dry ingredients to creamed mixture. Blend well after each addition.

Combine . . . . ½ cup **walnuts,** chopped, and
> 1 tablespoon **flour;** fold into batter.

Turn . . . . into two 9-inch round layer pans, well greased and lightly floured on the bottoms.

Bake . . . . at 350° for 30 to 35 minutes. Cool; frost with reserved fudge, thinned with 1 to 4 tablespoons **evaporated milk,** if necessary.

*Pillsbury's Best Self-Rising Flour is not recommended for use in this recipe.

Starlight Double-Delight Cake

Grand Prize Winner by Mrs. Samuel P. Weston, La Jolla, California

A bit of mint flavor is carried into this beautifully moist, fine chocolate cake from the frosting mixture.

BAKE at 350° for 30 to 40 minutes   MAKES two 9-inch layers

CHOCOLATE FROSTING

Cream . . . . . . 6 ounces (2 pkgs.) **cream cheese**
> ½ cup **shortening**
> ½ teaspoon **vanilla** and
> ½ teaspoon **mint flavoring;** blend well.

Add . . . . 6 cups (1½ lbs.) sifted **confectioners' sugar** alternately with
> ¼ cup hot **water** to cream cheese mixture.

Blend in . . . . . 4 squares (4 oz.) melted unsweetened **chocolate**

CHOCOLATE CAKE

Sift together 2¼ cups sifted **Pillsbury's Best All Purpose Flour***
> 1½ teaspoons **soda** and
> 1 teaspoon **salt.** Set aside.

Combine . . . . ¼ cup **shortening** and 2 cups of Chocolate Frosting; cream well.

Blend in . . . . . 3 unbeaten **eggs,** beating well after each.

Add . . . . the dry ingredients alternately with
> ¾ cup **milk.** Blend well after each addition.

Turn . . . . into two 9-inch round layer pans, well greased and lightly floured on the bottoms.

Bake . . . . at 350° for 30 to 40 minutes. Cool; frost with remaining Chocolate Frosting (thin with a few drops cream if necessary).

*For use with Pillsbury's Best Self-Rising Flour, omit soda and salt.

BEST of the BAKE-OFF

Starlight
Double-Delight
Cake
Grand Prize Winner
of the Third
Grand National
Bake-Off®

Double Date Devil's Food

Junior First Prize Winner by Mary Ann Wasylow, Grand Forks, North Dakota

Tune in to the sweet combination of old-fashioned devil's food, creamy date filling and luscious marshmallow frosting.

BAKE at 350° for 25 to 35 minutes   MAKES three 8 or 9-inch layers

Sift together 2¾ cups sifted **Pillsbury's Best All Purpose Flour***
1½ teaspoons **soda** and
1 teaspoon **salt**

Cream . . . . . . ¾ cup **butter** or margarine. Gradually add
2 cups **sugar,** creaming well.

Blend in . . . . 1 teaspoon **vanilla** and
3 unbeaten **eggs,** beating well after each.

Stir in . . . . 3 squares (3 oz.) melted unsweetened **chocolate**

Add . . . . the dry ingredients alternately with
1⅓ cups **water.** Blend well after each addition.

Turn . . . . into three 8 or 9-inch round layer pans, well greased
and lightly floured on the bottoms.

Bake . . . . at 350° for 25 to 35 minutes. Cool; fill with **Date Filling,** page 330. Frost with **Fluffy Marshmallow Frosting,** page 317.

For use with Pillsbury's Best Self-Rising Flour, omit soda and salt.

Dark Secret Chocolate Cake

Senior Winner by Mrs. W. Olon Wiginton, Birmingham, Alabama

Lots of rich, dark chocolate helps make this cake extra luscious and moist.

BAKE at 350° for 30 to 35 minutes   MAKES two 9-inch layers

Combine . . . . . 4 squares (4 oz.) unsweetened **chocolate**
½ cup **milk** and
¼ cup **sugar** in top of double boiler. Cook over hot
water until thick and smooth. Cool.

Sift together . . 2 cups sifted **Pillsbury's Best All Purpose Flour***

1¼ teaspoons **soda** and
1 teaspoon **salt.** Set aside.

Add . . . . 1¼ cups **sugar** gradually to
½ cup **shortening,** creaming well.

Blend in . . . . . 3 unbeaten **eggs,** beating well after each. Stir in
1 teaspoon **vanilla** and the chocolate mixture.

Add . . . . the dry ingredients alternately with
1 cup **milk.** Blend well after each addition.

Turn . . . . into two 9-inch round layer pans, well greased and
lightly floured on the bottoms.

Bake . . . . at 350° for 30 to 35 minutes. Cool; frost with **Fluffy White Frosting,** page 317. Let stand a few minutes.

Combine . . . . ½ square (½ oz.) melted unsweetened **chocolate** and
1 teaspoon **butter.** Pour slowly around top of cake,
allowing to drip down sides.

For use with Pillsbury's Best Self-Rising Flour, decrease soda to ¼ teaspoon and omit salt.

Dreambrosia Fudge Cake

Senior Winner by Mrs. Charles F. Lowman, Fountain City, Tennessee

This moist chocolate fudge cake has shredded coconut in the batter; toasted coconut tops the creamy butter icing.

BAKE at 350° for 30 to 40 minutes   MAKES two 9-inch layers

Sift together . . 2 cups sifted **Pillsbury's Best All Purpose Flour***
2½ teaspoons double-acting **baking powder**
1 teaspoon **salt** and
½ teaspoon **soda**

Cream......½ cup **butter** or margarine. Gradually add
1¼ cups **sugar,** creaming well.

Blend in.....3 unbeaten **egg yolks,** one at a time, and
3 squares (3 oz.) melted unsweetened **chocolate;** beat well.

Combine.....1 cup **milk** and
1 teaspoon **vanilla.** Add alternately with the dry ingredients to creamed mixture. Blend well after each addition.

Fold in......¾ cup **coconut,** chopped

Beat........3 **egg whites** until stiff but not dry. Fold into batter.

Turn..........into 9-inch round layer pans, well greased and lightly floured on the bottoms.

Bake.........at 350° for 30 to 40 minutes. Cool; frost with **Coconut Butter Frosting,** page 321. Sprinkle with toasted **coconut.**

For use with Pillsbury's Best Self-Rising Flour, omit baking powder and salt.

Vienna Two-Tone Cake

Senior Winner by Mrs. Malcolm Hankins, Vienna, Virginia

Extra-special party cake! Three layers in which chocolate batter is topped with a filbert spongecake batter.

BAKE at 350° for 35 to 40 minutes   MAKES three 9-inch layers

Sift together..2 cups sifted **Pillsbury's Best All Purpose Flour***
3 teaspoons double-acting **baking powder** and
½ teaspoon **salt.** Set aside.

Add.......1½ cups **sugar** gradually to
⅔ cup **shortening,** creaming well.

Blend in.....2 unbeaten **eggs,** beating well after each.

Add........3 squares (3 oz.) melted unsweetened **chocolate** and
1 teaspoon **vanilla;** mix thoroughly.

Blend in.......the dry ingredients alternately with
1 cup **milk.** Blend well after each addition.

Turn.........into three 9-inch round layer pans, well greased and lightly floured on the bottoms. Set aside.

Beat........5 **egg whites** (⅔ cup) until soft mounds form. Gradually add
⅓ cup **sugar,** beating until stiff, straight peaks form.

Beat........5 **egg yolks** with
1 teaspoon **vanilla** and
½ teaspoon **salt** in small bowl until blended. Add
⅓ cup **sugar;** beat until thick and lemon colored. Fold gently into egg white mixture.

Fold in......¾ cup **filberts,** ground, and
2 tablespoons **flour** until thoroughly blended. Spread over chocolate batter.

Bake........at 350° for 35 to 40 minutes. Cool; frost with **Cocoa Whipped Cream,** page 329. Chill.

For use with Pillsbury's Best Self-Rising Flour, omit baking powder and salt in chocolate batter.

Vienna Two-Tone Cake

Regency Ribbon Cake

Senior Second Prize Winner by Mrs. Claude E. Hughes, Orange, Virginia

A one-bowl, one-batter cake, with four layers made out of two to achieve an attractive ribbon effect . . . a really regal cake with a "luxury" chocolate frosting.

BAKE at 350° for 30 to 40 minutes   MAKES two 9-inch layers

Sift together 2½ cups sifted **Pillsbury's Best All Purpose Flour***
              3 teaspoons double-acting **baking powder** and
              1 teaspoon **salt.** Set aside.
Add . . . . 1⅔ cups **sugar** gradually to
              ⅔ cup **shortening,** creaming well.
Blend in . . . . . 3 unbeaten **eggs,** beating well after each.
Combine . . . 1¼ cups **milk** and
              ½ teaspoon **orange extract** or **vanilla.** Add alternately with the dry ingredients to creamed mixture. Blend well after each addition.
Turn . . . . half of batter into one 9-inch round layer pan, well greased and lightly floured on the bottom.
Combine . . . . . 1 tablespoon **instant coffee**
              1½ tablespoons **cocoa**
              1 tablespoon **water** and
              ¼ teaspoon **almond extract;** blend into remaining batter. Turn into a second 9-inch layer pan, well greased and lightly floured on the bottom.
Bake . . . . at 350° for 30 to 40 minutes. Cool. Split layers in half, making four thin layers. Frost with **Luxury Chocolate Frosting,** page 323, alternating light and dark layers, starting with dark layer (use ½ cup frosting on each).

For use with Pillsbury's Best Self-Rising Flour, omit baking powder and salt.

Regency Ribbon Cake

Choco-Truffle Layer Cake

Senior Winner by Mrs. Malvin H. Abrams, Seattle, Washington

A velvety, chocolate mixture fills and frosts this layer cake.

BAKE at 375° for 25 to 30 minutes   MAKES two 9-inch layers

Melt . . . . .2 squares (2 oz.) unsweetened **chocolate** in top of double boiler over hot water. Blend in
1 cup **sugar**
2 teaspoons **cornstarch** and
1 slightly beaten **egg yolk.** Mix well.

Add . . . . .½ cup **milk.** Cook until smooth, about 15 minutes. Cool.

Sift together . .2 cups sifted **Pillsbury's Best All Purpose Flour***
1 teaspoon **soda** and
½ teaspoon **salt**

Cream . . . . . .½ cup **butter** or margarine. Gradually add
1 cup firmly packed **brown sugar,** creaming well.

Blend in . . . . .2 unbeaten **egg yolks;** beat well.

Combine . . . .¾ cup **milk** and
1 teaspoon **vanilla.** Add alternately with the dry ingredients to creamed mixture. Blend well after each addition.

Blend in . . . . . . .the cooled chocolate mixture.

Beat . . . . .3 **egg whites** until stiff but not dry. Fold gently into batter.

Turn . . . . .into two 9-inch round layer pans, well greased and lightly floured on the bottoms.

Bake . . . . .at 375° for 25 to 30 minutes. Cool; frost with **French Frosting,** page 322.

*For use with Pillsbury's Best Self-Rising Flour, omit soda and salt.

Chocolate Encore Cake

Senior Winner by Lillian E. Schlueter, University City, Missouri

This four-layer, sour cream chocolate-nut cake—big and moist and fudgy—is the "special occasion" kind.

BAKE at 350° for 18 to 22 minutes   MAKES four 9-inch layers*

Sift together 2½ cups sifted **Pillsbury's Best All Purpose Flour****
1 teaspoon **soda** and
1 teaspoon **salt.** Add
1 cup **nuts,** chopped. Set aside.

Add . . . . .2 cups **sugar** gradually to
¾ cup **shortening** (half butter may be used), creaming well.

Blend in . . . . .5 unbeaten **eggs,** beating well after each. Stir in
4 squares (4 oz.) melted unsweetened **chocolate**

Combine . . . . .1 cup **sour cream** (thick or commercial)
⅓ cup **water** and
1 teaspoon **vanilla.** Add alternately with the dry ingredients to creamed mixture. Blend well after each addition.

Turn . . . . .into four 9-inch round layer pans*, well greased and lightly floured on the bottoms (two layers may be baked at a time).

Bake . . . . .at 350° for 18 to 22 minutes. Cool; fill and frost with **Creamy Chocolate Frosting,** page 323. Garnish with **walnut** or **pecan halves.**

*If desired, cake may be baked in two 9x9x2-inch pans at 350° for 40 to 45 minutes. Cool and split each layer, making four thin layers.

**For use with Pillsbury's Best Self-Rising Flour, omit soda and salt.

Mission Sunday Fudge Cake

Mission Sunday Fudge Cake

Senior Winner by Mrs. Albert G. Plagens, St. Paul, Minnesota

A rich chocolate fudge loaf cake, with nuts and coconut in the batter . . . and a special chocolate frosting.

BAKE at 325° for 45 to 55 minutes   MAKES 8x8 or 9x9-inch cake*

Sift together . . 1 cup sifted **Pillsbury's Best All Purpose Flour****
      ½ teaspoon **soda** and
      ¼ teaspoon **salt**

Cream . . . . . . ½ cup **butter** or margarine. Gradually add
      1 cup firmly packed **brown sugar,** creaming well.

Blend in . . . . . 3 **eggs,** beating well after each.

Add . . . . 1½ squares (1½ oz.) melted unsweetened **chocolate**

Combine . . . . ½ cup **buttermilk** or sour milk and
      1 teaspoon **vanilla.** Add alternately with the dry ingredients to creamed mixture. Blend well after each addition.

Fold in . . . . . . ¼ cup **nuts,** finely chopped, and
      ½ cup **coconut,** chopped, if desired.

Turn . . . . into 8x8x2 or 9x9x2-inch pan, well greased and lightly floured on the bottom.

Bake . . . . at 325° for 45 to 55 minutes. Cool; frost with **Chocolate Mallow Frosting,** page 323.

*If desired, recipe may be doubled and baked in a 15x10x2-inch pan for 1 hour.
**For use with Pillsbury's Best Self-Rising Flour, decrease soda to ¼ teaspoon and omit salt.

Chocolate Chipper Cake

Senior Winner by Mrs. Bert Copeland, Irondale, Alabama

This chocolate date cake will be a prize at your picnic . . . the topping of chocolate chips and nuts is baked right on.

BAKE at 350° for 45 to 50 minutes   MAKES 13x9-inch cake

Combine . . . 1¼ cups (8 oz.) **dates,** cut
      1 teaspoon **soda*** and
      1¼ cups **boiling water.** Cool.

Sift together 2¼ cups sifted **Pillsbury's Best All Purpose Flour*** and
      1 teaspoon **salt;** set aside.

Add . . . . 1½ cups **sugar** gradually to
      ¾ cup **shortening,** creaming well.

Blend in . . . . 3 unbeaten **eggs,** beating well. Stir in
      2 squares (2 oz.) melted unsweetened **chocolate** and
      1 teaspoon **vanilla**

Add . . . . the dry ingredients alternately with the date mixture. Blend well after each addition.

Turn . . . . into 13x9x2-inch pan, well greased and lightly floured on the bottom.

Sprinkle with . . 1 cup **semi-sweet chocolate pieces.** Arrange
½ cup **pecan halves** on batter, two per serving.

Bake . . . . at 350° for 45 to 50 minutes. If desired, sprinkle with
confectioners' sugar.

For use with Pillsbury's Best Self-Rising Flour, omit soda and salt.

Chocolate Date Cake

Senior Winner by Mrs. Carl Garilli, Newington, Connecticut

There's a pleasant surprise in this moist, dark fudge cake—dates and nuts throughout.

BAKE at 350° for 35 to 45 minutes   MAKES 12x8 or 13x9-inch cake

Sift together 1½ cups sifted **Pillsbury's Best All Purpose Flour***
1 teaspoon **soda** and
1 teaspoon **salt**

Combine . . . . ½ cup **dates,** finely cut
½ cup **nuts,** chopped, and 2 tablespoons dry ingredients. Set aside.

Add . . . . . . 1¼ cups **sugar** gradually to
½ cup **shortening,** creaming well.

Blend in . . . . . 2 unbeaten **egg yolks,** beating well after each.

Add . . . . 2 squares (2 oz.) melted unsweetened **chocolate**

Combine . . . . . 1 cup **buttermilk** or sour milk and
1 teaspoon **vanilla.** Add alternately with the dry ingredients to creamed mixture. Blend well after each addition.

Beat . . . . 2 **egg whites** until stiff but not dry. Fold into batter.

Fold in . . . . the floured dates and nuts.

Turn . . . . into 12x8x2 or 13x9x2-inch pan, well greased and lightly floured on the bottom.

Bake . . . . at 350° for 35 to 45 minutes. Cool; frost with
Chocolate Butter Cream Frosting, page 321.

For use with Pillsbury's Best Self-Rising Flour, decrease soda to ½ teaspoon and omit salt.

Cheese Cocoa Cake

Senior Winner by Mrs. Guy Best, Dearborn, Missouri

Cottage cheese and buttermilk give this cocoa loaf cake its wonderful moistness. Walnuts contribute crunchy texture.

BAKE at 350° for 45 to 50 minutes   MAKES 13x9-inch cake

Sieve . . . . ¾ cup (8 oz.) creamed **cottage cheese;** reserve.

Sift together 2⅔ cups sifted **Pillsbury's Best All Purpose Flour***
¼ cup **cocoa**
1 teaspoon **soda**
1 teaspoon **salt** and
½ teaspoon double-acting **baking powder.** Set aside.

Add . . . . 1 cup **sugar** and
1 cup firmly packed **brown sugar** gradually to
½ cup **shortening,** creaming well.

Blend in . . . . the sieved cottage cheese; mix thoroughly.

Add . . . . 2 unbeaten **eggs,** beating well after each.

Add . . . . 1¼ cups **buttermilk** or sour milk alternately with the dry ingredients. Blend well after each addition.

Stir in . . . . 1 cup **walnuts,** chopped. Turn into 13x9x2-inch pan, well greased and lightly floured on the bottom.

Bake . . . . at 350° for 45 to 50 minutes. Cool; frost with
Creamy Chocolate Frosting, page 323.

For use with Pillsbury's Best Self-Rising Flour, decrease soda to ½ teaspoon; omit salt and baking powder.

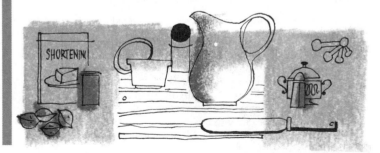

Orange Cocoa Cake

Orange Cocoa Cake

Senior Winner by Mrs. Jack S. Webster, Columbia, South Carolina

This light cocoa loaf cake is delicately flavored with orange. A quick broiled icing goes on while the cake is still warm.

BAKE at 350° for 35 to 40 minutes   MAKES 13x9-inch cake

Sift together 2½ cups sifted **Pillsbury's Best All Purpose Flour***
          ½ cup **cocoa**
          3 teaspoons double-acting **baking powder** and
          1 teaspoon **salt**. Set aside.
Add . . . . . . 1½ cups **sugar** gradually to
          ⅔ cup **shortening**, creaming well.
Blend in . . . . . 3 unbeaten **eggs**, beating well after each.
Add . . . . one-third of the dry ingredients; mix well.

Blend in . . . . . ½ cup undiluted **evaporated milk**
Combine . . . . ½ cup **orange juice** and
          1 tablespoon grated **orange rind**. Add alternately with the remaining dry ingredients to creamed mixture. Blend well after each addition.
Turn . . . . into 13x9x2-inch pan, well greased and lightly floured on the bottom.
Bake . . . . at 350° for 35 to 40 minutes. Spread with **Broiled Frosting**, page 324; place under broiler 2 to 3 minutes.

*For use with Pillsbury's Best Self-Rising Flour, omit baking powder and salt.

Limelight Fudge Cake

Junior Winner by Clifford T. Pacenta, Jr., Hawthorne, New York

The chocolate is melted in an unusual way to make this beautiful fudgy tube cake.

BAKE at 350° for 55 to 65 minutes   MAKES 10-inch tube cake

Pour . . . . 2 cups **boiling water** over
          4 squares (4 oz.) unsweetened **chocolate**. Cool to lukewarm.
Sift together . . 3 cups sifted **Pillsbury's Best All Purpose Flour***
          1 teaspoon double-acting **baking powder**
          1½ teaspoons **soda** and
          1 teaspoon **salt**. Set aside.
Add . . . . 2 cups **sugar** gradually to
          ⅔ cup **shortening**, creaming well.
Blend in . . . . . 2 unbeaten **eggs** and
          1 teaspoon **vanilla**; beat well. Pour off and reserve water from chocolate. Blend chocolate into creamed mixture.
Add . . . . the dry ingredients alternately with reserved water. Blend well after each addition.
Turn . . . . into 10-inch tube pan, well greased on the bottom.
Bake . . . . at 350° for 55 to 65 minutes. Cool; frost with **Lime**

Frosting, page 326. (Or split cake in half, making two layers. Fill; frost.)

For use with Pillsbury's Best Self-Rising Flour, omit baking powder and salt; decrease soda to ½ teaspoon.

Family Treat Cake

Best of Class Winner by Mrs. Morris Avery, Greybull, Wyoming

An easily-mixed cake that's surprisingly moist, yet light, topped with a very special frosting.

BAKE at 350° for 40 to 45 minutes   **MAKES 13x9-inch cake**

Sift together 2¼ cups sifted **Pillsbury's Best All Purpose Flour***
3 tablespoons **cocoa** and
1 teaspoon **salt.** Set aside.

Add . . . . 2 cups **sugar** gradually to
½ cup **shortening,** creaming well.

Blend in . . . . . 3 unbeaten **eggs,** beating well after each.

Combine . . . . . 1 teaspoon **soda** with
½ cup **milk.** Add gradually to creamed mixture, beating well. Add the dry ingredients all at once; mix until blended.

Stir in . . . . 1 cup **boiling water** until well blended.

Pour . . . . into 13x9x2-inch pan, well greased and lightly floured on the bottom.

Bake . . . . at 350° for 40 to 45 minutes. Cool; frost with Special Fruit-Nut Frosting.

For use with Pillsbury's Best Self-Rising Flour, omit salt and soda.

SPECIAL FRUIT-NUT FROSTING

Combine 3 egg yolks and ⅔ cup sugar; beat until thick and lemon colored. Pour into heavy saucepan. Add ½ cup soft butter or margarine and ½ cup white raisins. Bring to boil and cook over medium heat, stirring constantly, until thickened, 5 to 7 minutes. Add ½ cup coconut, chopped, and ½ cup nuts, chopped. Spread immediately.

Family Treat Cake

Lemon Layer Chocolate Meringue

Senior Winner by Mrs. R. L. Thibodeau, Hastings, Nebraska

Lemon filling between chocolate cake and meringue layers. Impressive . . . yet so easy to make.

BAKE at 350° for 35 to 40 minutes, then   MAKES 13x9-inch cake
    at 425° for 6 to 8 minutes

Melt . . . . 1½ squares (1½ oz.) unsweetened **chocolate** in 1¼ cups hot **coffee** in saucepan over low heat. Cool to lukewarm.

Sift together . . 2 cups sifted **Pillsbury's Best All Purpose Flour***
    1 teaspoon **soda**
    1 teaspoon **salt** and
    ½ teaspoon double-acting **baking powder.** Set aside.

Add . . . . 1½ cups **sugar** gradually to ⅔ cup **shortening,** creaming well.

Lemon Layer Chocolate Meringue

Blend in . . . . . 1 unbeaten **egg** and
    3 unbeaten **egg yolks,** beating well after each.

Add . . . . the dry ingredients alternately with chocolate-coffee mixture. Blend well after each addition.

Turn . . . . into 13x9x2-inch pan, well greased and lightly floured on the bottom.

Bake . . . . at 350° for 35 to 40 minutes. Cool.

Prepare . . . . . . 1 package **lemon pudding** as directed on package. Cool. (A lemon pie filling recipe may also be used.) Spread over cake; cover with Meringue.

Bake . . . . at 425° for 6 to 8 minutes until golden brown.

*For use with Pillsbury's Best Self-Rising Flour, decrease soda to ¼ teaspoon; omit salt and baking powder.

MERINGUE

Beat 4 egg whites with ¼ teaspoon salt until soft mounds form. Add gradually ½ cup sugar, beating well after each addition. Continue beating until meringue stands in stiff, glossy peaks.

Peanut Butter Fudge Cake

Senior Winner by Mary Jane Lowery, Akron, Ohio

A moist chocolate cake with subtle peanut butter flavor . . . cooked fudge frosting makes a double chocolate treat.

BAKE at 350° for 35 to 40 minutes   MAKES two 8-inch layers

Sift together 1¾ cups sifted **Pillsbury's Best All Purpose Flour***
    1 teaspoon **soda** and
    1 teaspoon **salt.** Set aside.

Combine . . . 1¼ cups **sugar**
    ½ cup **water**
    ⅓ cup **shortening** and
    2 squares (2 oz.) unsweetened **chocolate** in saucepan.

Cook . . . . over medium heat, stirring constantly, until smooth. Stir in

2 tablespoons **peanut butter**; cool.

Add . . . . 2 unbeaten **eggs**, beating well after each.

Blend in . . . . . 1 cup **sour cream** (thick or commercial) alternately with the dry ingredients. Blend well after each addition.

Turn . . . . into two 8-inch round layer pans, well greased and lightly floured on the bottoms.

Bake . . . . at 350° for 35 to 40 minutes. Cool; frost with **Fudge Frosting**, page 316.

For use with Pillsbury's Best Self-Rising Flour, decrease soda to ½ teaspoon and omit salt.

Chocolate Cola Cake

Senior Winner by Mrs. Clyde Holden, Lantana, Florida

Cola beverage adds a bit of mystery to the flavor of this chocolate cake.

BAKE at 350° for 30 to 35 minutes   MAKES two 8 or 9-inch layers

Sift together . . 2 cups sifted **Pillsbury's Best All Purpose Flour***
       1⅓ cups **sugar**
       ½ cup **cocoa**
       1½ teaspoons **soda** and
       1 teaspoon **salt** into large mixing bowl.

Add . . . . ½ cup **shortening**
       ⅔ cup **buttermilk** or sour milk and
       ⅔ cup **cola beverage**

Beat . . . . 1½ minutes. (With mixer use a low speed.)

Add . . . . 1 unbeaten **egg** and
       2 **egg yolks**. Beat 1½ minutes.

Turn . . . . into two 8 or 9-inch round layer pans, well greased and lightly floured on the bottoms.

Bake . . . . at 350° for 30 to 35 minutes. Cool; frost with **Cola Frosting**, page 317.

For use with Pillsbury's Best Self-Rising Flour, decrease soda to ¼ teaspoon and omit salt.

Dark-Magic Mocha Cake

Senior Winner by Mrs. James H. White, Cumberland, Maryland

The "dark-magic" ingredient is a strong coffee "syrup" which flavors both cake and frosting.

BAKE at 350° for 30 to 40 minutes   MAKES two 8-inch square or 9-inch round layers

Combine . . . 1½ cups **water** and
       3 tablespoons **sugar**. Bring to boil; pour over
       ¾ cup ground **coffee**. Let stand 10 minutes. Strain.

Sift together . . 2 cups sifted **Pillsbury's Best All Purpose Flour***
       1 teaspoon **soda** and
       1 teaspoon **salt**. Set aside.

Combine . . . . ½ cup **shortening**
       2 squares (2 oz.) unsweetened **chocolate** and ½ cup of the coffee syrup in 3-quart saucepan. (Reserve remaining syrup for Frosting.) Cook, stirring constantly, until chocolate melts. Cool.

Add . . . . 1⅔ cups **sugar** to chocolate mixture; beat well.

Blend in . . . . . 2 unbeaten **eggs**, beating well after each.

Combine . . . . . 1 cup **buttermilk** or sour milk and
       2 teaspoons **vanilla**. Add alternately with the dry ingredients to creamed mixture. Blend well after each addition.

Turn . . . . into two 8-inch square or 9-inch round layer pans, well greased and lightly floured on the bottoms.

Bake . . . . at 350° for 30 to 40 minutes. Cool; frost with Coffee Frosting. Garnish with chopped **nuts**.

For use with Pillsbury's Best Self-Rising Flour, increase flour to 2⅛ cups (2 cups plus 2 tablespoons); omit soda and salt.

COFFEE FROSTING

Cream ½ cup butter or margarine. Blend in 1 pound (4 to 4¼ cups) sifted confectioners' sugar alternately with 4 to 5 tablespoons reserved hot coffee syrup until of spreading consistency. Stir in ½ teaspoon vanilla.

Choc-o-Cherry Cake

Bride Winner by Mrs. Keith W. Miller, Eskridge, Kansas

Elegant three-layer Quick-Mix chocolate cake with luscious chocolate icing . . . maraschino cherries add flavor and interest.

BAKE at 350° for 30 to 35 minutes   MAKES three 9-inch layers

Sift together..3 cups sifted **Pillsbury's Best All Purpose Flour***
     2 cups **sugar**
     1½ teaspoons **soda** and
     1 teaspoon **salt** into large mixing bowl.
Add........¾ cup **butter** or margarine
     1½ cups **milk**
Beat..........1½ minutes. (With mixer use a low speed.)
Add........3 unbeaten **eggs**
     ¼ cup **maraschino cherry juice**
     3 squares (3 oz.) melted unsweetened **chocolate** and
     12 **maraschino cherries**, sliced. Beat 1½ minutes.
Turn..........into three 9-inch round layer pans, well greased and
     lightly floured on the bottoms.
Bake........at 350° for 30 to 35 minutes. Cool; frost with
     Creamy Chocolate Frosting, page 323.
*Pillsbury's Best Self-Rising Flour is not recommended for use in this recipe.

Midnight Mallow Cake

Senior Winner by Ethel Wittenberg, Orange County, New York

Dark, moist bittersweet chocolate cake with marshmallows and sour cream in the batter and a fluffy white marshmallow frosting.

BAKE at 375° for 25 to 30 minutes   MAKES two 9-inch layers

Melt.......16 **marshmallows** (¼ lb.) and
     3 squares (3 oz.) unsweetened **chocolate** in top of
     double boiler over hot water.
Add........¾ cup **boiling water;** stir until smooth. Cool.

Sift together 2¼ cups sifted **Pillsbury's Best All Purpose Flour***
     1½ teaspoons **soda** and
     1½ teaspoons **salt**
Beat........3 **eggs** until foamy. Gradually add
     1¼ cups **sugar;** beat until thick and ivory colored.
Add........1 teaspoon **vanilla** and the chocolate mixture. Mix
     thoroughly.
Blend in....1½ cups **sour cream;** mix well. Add the dry ingredients
     gradually. Mix thoroughly.
Turn..........into two 9-inch round layer pans, well greased and
     lightly floured on the bottoms.
Bake........at 375° for 25 to 30 minutes. Cool; frost with **Fluffy**
     Marshmallow Frosting, page 317.
*For use with Pillsbury's Best Self-Rising Flour, decrease soda to ½ teaspoon and omit salt.

Boston Tea Party Cake

Senior Winner by Mrs. Arnold C. Anderson, Cleveland, Ohio

Boston cream pie with a party touch—the Quick-Mix cake is chocolate, the filling is butterscotch.

BAKE at 350° for 30 to 35 minutes   MAKES 9-inch round cake

Sift together..1 cup sifted **Pillsbury's Best All Purpose Flour***
     ¾ cup **sugar**
     ⅓ cup **cocoa**
     ¾ teaspoon **soda** and
     ½ teaspoon **salt** into mixing bowl.
Add........¼ cup **shortening** and
     ⅔ cup **milk**
Beat..........1½ minutes. (With mixer use a low speed.)
Add........1 unbeaten **egg** and
     ½ teaspoon **vanilla.** Beat 1½ minutes.
Turn..........into one 9-inch round layer pan, well greased and
     lightly floured on the bottom.

Bake . . . . at 350° for 30 to 35 minutes. Cool. Split into two layers. Fill with **Butterscotch Filling**, page 329. Top with Sweetened Whipped Cream; drizzle with 1 tablespoon **butterscotch sauce,** if desired.

For use with Pillsbury's Best Self-Rising Flour, omit soda and salt.

SWEETENED WHIPPED CREAM

Beat ½ cup whipping cream until thick. Fold in 1 tablespoon sugar and ½ teaspoon vanilla.

Maple Hi-Light Fudge Cake

Junior First Prize Winner by Irene Korrell, Frederick, Maryland

A velvety Quick-Mix cocoa layer cake with fluffy maple-nut frosting that makes it elegant enough for a party.

BAKE at 350° for 30 to 40 minutes   MAKES two 9-inch layers

Sift together . . 2 cups sifted **Pillsbury's Best All Purpose Flour***
          1 cup **sugar**
          ⅔ cup **cocoa**
          1 teaspoon double-acting **baking powder**
          1 teaspoon **salt** and
          ¾ teaspoon **soda** into large mixing bowl. Add
          1 cup firmly packed **brown sugar**
Add . . . . ⅔ cup **shortening** and
          1 cup **milk**
Beat . . . . 1½ minutes. (With mixer use a low speed.)
Add . . . . 3 unbeaten **eggs**
          ¼ cup **milk** and
          1 teaspoon **vanilla.** Beat 1½ minutes.
Turn . . . . into two 9-inch round layer pans, well greased and lightly floured on the bottoms.
Bake . . . . at 350° for 30 to 40 minutes. Cool; frost with **Fluffy Maple Frosting,** page 320.

Pillsbury's Best Self-Rising Flour is not recommended for use in this recipe.

Maple Hi-Light Fudge Cake

Cocorama Cake

Senior Winner by Mrs. Emma Seefelt, Trenton, New Jersey

No shortening in this moist chocolate and coconut cake . . . luscious pink frosting is flavored with cinnamon candies.

BAKE at 350° for 30 to 35 minutes   MAKES two 8-inch layers

Sift together . . 2 cups sifted **Pillsbury's Best All Purpose Flour*** and
1 teaspoon **salt**
Combine . . . 1¾ cups firmly packed **brown sugar** and
2 unbeaten **eggs** in mixing bowl. Beat well.
Blend in . . . . . 2 squares (2 oz.) melted unsweetened **chocolate**
1 cup **light cream** and
2 teaspoons **vanilla**. Add the dry ingredients gradually;
mix thoroughly.
Dissolve . . . . . 2 teaspoons **soda*** in

½ cup **boiling water**; stir into batter.
Combine . . . . . 2 tablespoons **vinegar** and
¼ cup hot **water**; blend into batter. Stir in
1 cup **coconut**, finely chopped
Pour . . . . into two 8-inch round layer pans, well greased and
lightly floured on the bottoms.
Bake . . . . at 350° for 30 to 35 minutes. Cool; frost with
Cinnarama Frosting, page 319. Sprinkle with **coconut**.

*For use with Pillsbury's Best Self-Rising Flour, omit salt and decrease soda
to ½ teaspoon.

Cocorama Cake

Beat 'n' Bake Cocoa Cake

Senior Winner by Mrs. Robert H. Knapp, Grosse Pointe Woods, Michigan

A single layer cake mixed right in the baking pan . . . a sprinkle of peanuts adds crunchiness and flavor.

BAKE at 350° for 25 to 30 minutes   MAKES 9-inch round cake
or 8-inch square

Sift together . . . into greased 9-inch round or 8x8x2-inch pan
1½ cups sifted **Pillsbury's Best All Purpose Flour***
¾ cup **sugar**
¼ cup **cocoa**
1 teaspoon **soda** and
½ teaspoon **salt**. Combine ingredients with fork.
Add . . . . ¼ cup **salad oil**
1 tablespoon **vinegar**
1 teaspoon **vanilla** and
¾ cup cold **water**; mix well with fork. Blend in
¼ cup additional **water**
Sprinkle with ¼ cup **salted peanuts**, coarsely chopped
Bake . . . . at 350° for 25 to 30 minutes. Serve with **ice cream**
or whipped cream, if desired.

*For use with Pillsbury's Best Self-Rising Flour, decrease soda to ¼ teaspoon
and omit salt.

Cream-Filled Chocolate Cake

Junior Winner by Priscilla Senning, Tucson, Arizona

There's a creamy filling between the layers of this luscious chocolate cake, and an easy mocha frosting on top.

BAKE at 350° for 30 to 35 minutes   MAKES two 9-inch layers

Sift together 2½ cups sifted **Pillsbury's Best All Purpose Flour***
                    1½ cups **sugar**
                    ½ cup **cocoa**
                    2 teaspoons **soda** and
                    1 teaspoon **salt** into large mixing bowl.
Add . . . . ⅔ cup **shortening**
                    2 unbeaten **eggs**
                    1 cup **buttermilk** or sour milk
                    ½ cup **water** and
                    1 teaspoon **vanilla**
Beat . . . . 3 minutes. (With mixer use a low speed.)
Turn . . . . into two 9-inch round layer pans, well greased and
                    lightly floured on the bottoms.
Bake . . . . at 350° for 30 to 35 minutes. Cool. Spread **Cream
                    Filling,** page 328, between layers; frost top and sides
                    with **Speedy Mocha Frosting,** page 324.

*For use with Pillsbury's Best Self-Rising Flour, decrease soda to 1 teaspoon and omit salt.

De Luxe Choco-Cream Cake

Senior Winner by Mabel A. Yarian, Phoenix, Arizona

You'll want to serve this American favorite often . . . moist chocolate cake made with whipped cream . . . delectable with its fudge frosting.

BAKE at 350° for 30 to 35 minutes   MAKES two 8 or 9-inch layers

Sift together . . 2 cups sifted **Pillsbury's Best All Purpose Flour*** and
                    1 teaspoon **salt**

De Luxe Choco-Cream Cake

Beat . . . . 1 cup **whipping cream** and
                    1 teaspoon **vanilla** until very thick.
Blend in . . . . . 3 **eggs,** one at a time, beating well after each.
Add . . . . 1½ cups **sugar** gradually, mixing thoroughly.
Combine . . . . . 1 teaspoon **soda** and
                    ½ cup **sour cream;** stir into cream mixture.
Add . . . . the dry ingredients. Fold in gradually; mix well.
Blend in . . . . . 2 squares (2 oz.) melted unsweetened **chocolate** until
                    well blended.
Turn . . . . into two 8 or 9-inch round layer pans, well greased
                    and lightly floured on the bottoms.
Bake . . . . at 350° for 30 to 35 minutes. Cool; frost with
                    Marshmallow Fudge Frosting, page 316.

*For use with Pillsbury's Best Self-Rising Flour, omit salt and soda.

Chocolate Skillet Cake

Senior Winner by Mrs. A. C. Hornbaker, Neosho, Missouri

A Quick-Mix skillet cake with double-chocolate flavor . . . cocoa in the batter, milk chocolate candy baked on top.

BAKE at 350° for 50 to 55 minutes*   MAKES 10-inch round cake

Add . . . . ½ cup cold **water** gradually to
½ cup **cocoa,** mixing well after each addition. Set aside.

Sift together 1½ cups sifted **Pillsbury's Best All Purpose Flour***
1 teaspoon **soda** and
½ teaspoon **salt** into mixing bowl.

Add . . . . .1 cup firmly packed **brown sugar**
½ cup **shortening**
3 unbeaten **eggs** and
¼ cup **buttermilk** or sour milk. Beat 3 minutes. (With
mixer use a low speed.)

Blend in . . . . .1 teaspoon **vanilla**
¼ cup **buttermilk** and the cocoa mixture. Beat 2 minutes.

Turn . . . . .into well-greased heavy skillet measuring 10 inches
across top.*

Divide . . . . . . .4 thin **milk chocolate bars** (4 oz.) into small squares
and arrange on top of batter. Cover.

Bake . . . . .at 350° for 50 to 55 minutes.* Serve plain, with
whipped cream, ice cream, a hard sauce or your
favorite chocolate frosting.

*Cake may be baked in 10½-inch electric skillet. Pour batter into cold well-
greased skillet. Open steam vents; bake at 275° for 50 to 60 minutes.*

**For use with Pillsbury's Best Self-Rising Flour, decrease soda to ¼ teaspoon
and omit salt.*

Chocolate Skillet Cake

Dutch Supper Cake

Senior Winner by Miss Irene Herdtner, Huntington, West Virginia

Chocolate, applesauce and pecans combine to make an extra moist chocolate cake which keeps well four to five days.

BAKE at 350° for 35 to 40 minutes   MAKES 8x8-inch cake

Melt . . . . 2 squares (2 oz.) unsweetened **chocolate** and
½ cup **shortening** in large saucepan over low heat, stirring constantly. Cool.

Sift together . . 1 cup sifted **Pillsbury's Best All Purpose Flour***
½ teaspoon **soda** and
½ teaspoon **salt**. Set aside.

Stir . . . . 1 cup **sugar**
2 well-beaten **eggs**
½ cup thick **applesauce**
½ cup **pecans** or other nuts, chopped, and
1 teaspoon **vanilla** into the chocolate mixture.

Add . . . . the dry ingredients; blend thoroughly. Turn into 8x8x2-inch pan, well greased and lightly floured on the bottom.

Bake . . . . at 350° for 35 to 40 minutes. Serve plain or with whipped cream.

For use with Pillsbury's Best Self-Rising Flour, omit soda and salt.

Quick Malted Milk Cake

Senior Winner by Mrs. Leona Kroupa, Cedar, Michigan

A subtle flavor of chocolate malted milk powder makes this quick and easy loaf cake outstanding.

BAKE at 350° for 40 to 45 minutes   MAKES 8x8-inch cake

Sift together . . 1 cup sifted **Pillsbury's Best All Purpose Flour***
1½ cups **chocolate malted milk powder**
1 teaspoon **soda** and

½ teaspoon **salt** into mixing bowl.

Add . . . . 1 cup **sour cream** (thick or commercial)

Beat . . . . 1½ minutes. (With mixer use a low speed.)

Add . . . . 2 unbeaten **eggs** and
1 teaspoon **vanilla**. Beat 1½ minutes.

Turn . . . . into 8x8x2-inch pan, well greased and lightly floured on the bottom.

Bake . . . . at 350° for 40 to 45 minutes. Cool; frost with **Honey Nougat Frosting,** page 319.

For use with Pillsbury's Best Self-Rising Flour, decrease soda to ¼ teaspoon; omit salt.

Busy Day Chocolate Cake

Senior Winner by Mrs. Stanley L. Smith, Kansas City, Missouri

This is a hurry-up cake. The time from lighting the oven to serving is only one hour!

BAKE at 350° for 40 to 45 minutes   MAKES 8x8, 9x9 or 11x7-inch cake

Sift together 1⅓ cups sifted **Pillsbury's Best All Purpose Flour***
1 cup **sugar**
1 teaspoon **soda** and
½ teaspoon **salt** into mixing bowl.

Add . . . . ¼ cup **shortening**
1 cup **buttermilk** or sour milk
1 unbeaten **egg**
1 teaspoon **vanilla** and
2 squares (2 oz.) melted unsweetened **chocolate**

Beat . . . . 3 minutes. (With mixer use a low speed.)

Turn . . . . into 8x8x2, 9x9x2 or 11x7-inch pan, well greased and lightly floured on the bottom.

Bake . . . . at 350° for 40 to 45 minutes. Frost or serve warm with **whipped cream.**

For use with Pillsbury's Best Self-Rising Flour, decrease soda to ½ teaspoon and omit salt.

Choco-Dot Fudge Cakes

Choco-Dot Fudge Cakes

Junior Winner by Leah Mae Sanders, Port Arthur, Texas

So simple to make and no frosting required; chocolate chips partially bake in and provide tasty topping.

BAKE at 350° for 25 to 30 minutes   MAKES 13x9x2-inch cake or 2 dozen brownies

Melt........½ cup **butter** or margarine and
      2 squares (2 oz.) unsweetened **chocolate*** in sauce-pan over low heat, stirring constantly. Cool.

Sift together.¾ cup sifted **Pillsbury's Best All Purpose Flour****
      ½ teaspoon **salt** and
      ¼ teaspoon **soda**. Set aside.

Add........1 cup **sugar**
      3 slightly beaten **eggs** and
      1 teaspoon **vanilla** to chocolate mixture; mix well.

Blend in.......the dry ingredients and
      ½ cup **pecans,** chopped. Mix well.

Turn.........into greased 13x9x2-inch pan. Sprinkle with
      ½ cup **semi-sweet chocolate pieces**

Bake........at 350° for 25 to 30 minutes. Cool and cut into bars. If desired, roll bars in **confectioners' sugar** before serving.

**For a mild milk chocolate brownie, substitute ¼ cup cocoa for the chocolate.*
***For use with Pillsbury's Best Self-Rising Flour, omit salt and soda.*

Sweet Cherry Chocolate Cake

Senior Winner by Mrs. W. Jay Smart, Springville, Utah

This is no ordinary cocoa cake. It's a Quick-Mix cake made with sour cream, walnuts, sweet cherries and spices.

BAKE at 350° for 45 to 55 minutes   MAKES 13x9-inch cake

Sift together..2 cups sifted **Pillsbury's Best All Purpose Flour***
      1 cup **sugar**
      ¼ cup **cocoa**
      1 teaspoon double-acting **baking powder**
      1 teaspoon **soda**
      1 teaspoon **salt**
      ½ teaspoon **cinnamon** and
      ½ teaspoon **nutmeg** into large mixing bowl.

Add........½ cup **shortening**
      ½ cup **cherry juice,** drained from a No. 2 can Royal Anne or sweet Bing cherries, and
      ⅔ cup **sour cream.** Beat 1½ minutes. (With mixer use a low speed.)

Add........2 unbeaten **eggs** and
      1 unbeaten **egg yolk.** Beat 1½ minutes.

Turn . . . . into 13x9x2-inch pan, well greased and lightly floured on the bottom.

Combine . . . . . 1 cup **walnuts,** chopped

1 cup **Royal Anne** or **sweet Bing cherries,** drained, pitted and halved, and

2 tablespoons **flour.** Sprinkle mixture over batter and blend with fork into top of batter.

Bake . . . . at 350° for 45 to 55 minutes. Cool; frost with **Snowy White Frosting,** page 318.

For use with Pillsbury's Best Self-Rising Flour, omit baking powder and salt; decrease soda to ½ teaspoon.

Fudgy Chocolate Loaf

Junior Winner by George R. Palen, Schenectady, New York

Chocolate lovers—especially those teen-agers—will go for this brownie-like, nut-filled loaf cake.

BAKE at 350° for 35 to 40 minutes   MAKES 13x9-inch cake

Sift together . . 2 cups sifted **Pillsbury's Best All Purpose Flour***

3 teaspoons double-acting **baking powder** and

½ teaspoon **salt.** Set aside.

Add . . . . 1¾ cups **sugar** gradually to

¼ cup **shortening,** mixing thoroughly.

Add . . . . 2 unbeaten **eggs,** beating well after each.

Blend in . . . . . 4 squares (4 oz.) melted unsweetened **chocolate** and

1 teaspoon **vanilla**

Add . . . . the dry ingredients alternately with

1½ cups **milk.** Blend well after each addition. (With mixer use a low speed.)

Stir in . . . . 1 cup **nuts,** chopped. Turn into 13x9x2-inch pan, well greased and lightly floured on the bottom.

Bake . . . . at 350° for 35 to 40 minutes. Cool; frost with **Chocolate Butter Cream Frosting,** page 321.

For use with Pillsbury's Best Self-Rising Flour, omit baking powder and salt.

BUTTERSCOTCH, COFFEE and MAPLE CAKES

Black Walnut Butterscotch Cake

Junior Winner by Arnita Braschler, Doniphan, Missouri

Brown sugar and buttermilk give this cake wonderful butterscotch flavor—black walnuts add flavor and crunchiness.

BAKE at 350° for 30 to 35 minutes   MAKES two 9-inch layers

Sift together 2⅓ cups sifted **Pillsbury's Best All Purpose Flour***

1 teaspoon double-acting **baking powder**

1 teaspoon **soda** and

½ teaspoon **salt**

Cream . . . . . . ½ cup **butter** or margarine. Gradually add

1½ cups firmly packed **brown sugar,** creaming well.

Add . . . . 3 unbeaten **eggs,** beating well after each.

Combine . . . . . 1 cup **buttermilk** or sour milk and

1 teaspoon **vanilla.** Add alternately with the dry ingredients to creamed mixture. Blend well after each addition.

Stir in . . . . . . ½ cup **black walnuts,** finely chopped

Turn . . . . into two 9-inch round layer pans, well greased and lightly floured on the bottoms.

Bake . . . . at 350° for 30 to 35 minutes. Cool. Spread **Sea-Foam Frosting,** page 318, on bottom layer; sprinkle with ½ cup **black walnuts,** chopped, if desired. Cover with top layer; frost top and sides.

For use with Pillsbury's Best Self-Rising Flour, omit baking powder, soda, salt.

Toffee-Turvy Cake

Senior Winner by Mrs. Joseph Blodgett, Kenosha, Wisconsin

A caramelized condensed milk mixture lines the pans that this almond-rich cake is baked in, to give an upside-down topping.

BAKE at 350° for 35 to 40 minutes   MAKES two 8-inch layers

TURVY-TOPPING

Melt . . . . ¼ cup **sugar** in heavy skillet over low heat, stirring constantly, just until sugar melts and turns light golden brown. Add very slowly
⅓ cup **boiling water**, stirring constantly until sugar dissolves completely.

Add . . . . . . 1⅓ cups (15-oz. can) **sweetened condensed milk** gradually; stir constantly over low heat until mixture comes to a boil.

Pour . . . . into two 8-inch round layer pans, greased on the bottom, lined with waxed paper, then greased again.

CAKE

Chop . . . . ½ cup **almonds** very fine.

Sift together 1½ cups sifted **Pillsbury's Best All Purpose Flour***
2 teaspoons double-acting **baking powder**
½ teaspoon **salt** and
1½ teaspoons **instant coffee**. Set aside.

Add . . . . ½ cup **sugar** and
½ cup firmly packed **brown sugar** gradually to
⅓ cup **shortening**, creaming well.

Blend in . . . . .3 unbeaten **egg yolks** and
1 teaspoon **vanilla**. Beat thoroughly.

Add . . . . the dry ingredients alternately with
⅔ cup **milk**. Blend well after each addition. Stir in the almonds (reserve 3 tablespoons and toast them for topping).

Beat . . . . .3 **egg whites** until stiff. Fold into batter.

Spoon . . . . batter carefully over caramel mixture in pans.

Bake . . . . at 350° for 35 to 40 minutes. Turn out immediately;

remove waxed paper.

Sprinkle . . . . . . bottom of one layer with the reserved toasted almonds, pressing gently into topping. Cool. Spread other layer with Sweetened Whipped Cream, top with nut-covered layer, and frost sides with Sweetened Whipped Cream.

For use with Pillsbury's Best Self-Rising Flour, omit baking powder and salt.

SWEETENED WHIPPED CREAM

Beat 1 cup whipping cream until stiff. Fold in 2 tablespoons sugar and ½ teaspoon vanilla.

Maple Fluff Cake

Junior Winner by Bernadette Ann Schott, Lafayette, Colorado

Just made for the small family is this tender cake with maple flavor.

BAKE at 350° for 40 to 45 minutes   MAKES 9-inch tube cake*

Sift together 1⅓ cups sifted **Pillsbury's Best All Purpose Flour****
2 teaspoons double-acting **baking powder** and
¾ teaspoon **salt**. Set aside.

Add . . . . 1 cup firmly packed **brown sugar** to
½ cup **shortening**, creaming well.

Blend in . . . . .2 unbeaten **eggs**
1 teaspoon **vanilla** and
¼ teaspoon **maple flavoring**. Beat well.

Add . . . . the dry ingredients alternately with
⅔ cup **milk**. Blend well after each addition. Stir in
½ cup **walnuts**, chopped

Turn . . . . into 9-inch tube pan, well greased on the bottom.*

Bake . . . . at 350° for 40 to 45 minutes. Cool; frost with **Maple Fluff Frosting**, page 320. Sprinkle with chopped **walnuts**.

If desired, cake may be baked in a 9x5x3-inch pan for 50 to 55 minutes.
**For use with Pillsbury's Best Self-Rising Flour, omit baking powder and salt.*

Double Caramel Cake

Senior Winner by Mrs. Arthur A. George, Stroudsburg, Pennsylvania

Caramel sauce in the layers and in the frosting gives this unique cake a wonderful candy-like flavor.

BAKE at 350° for 35 to 40 minutes   MAKES two 9-inch layers

Combine.....2 cups firmly packed **brown sugar**
    ¼ cup **butter** or margarine
    2 tablespoons **water** and
    ¼ teaspoon **salt** in saucepan. Cook over medium heat, stirring constantly, until a little syrup dropped in cold water forms a soft ball (234°). Remove from heat.

Add . . . . .1 cup undiluted **evaporated milk** and
    2 teaspoons **vanilla.** Cool thoroughly.

Sift together 2¼ cups sifted **Pillsbury's Best All Purpose Flour***
    1 teaspoon double-acting **baking powder**
    1 teaspoon **soda** and
    1 teaspoon **salt** into large mixing bowl.

Add . . . . .½ cup **shortening**
    ½ cup **milk** and 2 cups of the caramel sauce. (Reserve remaining sauce, about ⅓ cup.)

Beat . . . . .1½ minutes. (With mixer use a low speed.)

Add . . . . .3 unbeaten **eggs;** beat 1½ minutes.

Turn . . . . .into two 9-inch round layer pans, well greased and lightly floured on the bottoms.

Bake . . . . .at 350° for 35 to 40 minutes. Cool; frost with Caramel Cheese Frosting.

For use with Pillsbury's Best Self-Rising Flour, omit baking powder and salt; decrease soda to ¼ teaspoon.

CARAMEL CHEESE FROSTING

Cream the reserved caramel sauce with ⅓ cup (3-oz. pkg.) softened cream cheese. Gradually blend in 3 cups sifted confectioners' sugar and 1 teaspoon vanilla. Beat until smooth and of spreading consistency. Thin with cream, if necessary.

Double Caramel Cake

Maple Syrup Layer Cake

Senior Winner by Mrs. Warren C. Meeker, Rochester, New York

Maple syrup gives a wonderfully different flavor to the high layers and the fluffy frosting of this attractive cake.

BAKE at 350° for 30 to 35 minutes   MAKES two 8-inch layers

Sift together 2½ cups sifted **Pillsbury's Best All Purpose Flour***
               2 teaspoons double-acting **baking powder**
               ¾ teaspoon **soda**
               ½ teaspoon **salt** and
               ¼ teaspoon **ginger**
Cream......½ cup **butter** or margarine. Gradually add
               ¼ cup **sugar**, creaming well.
Add........2 unbeaten **eggs**, beating well after each.
Blend in......1 cup **maple syrup** gradually.
Add.........the dry ingredients alternately with

½ cup hot **water.** Blend well after each addition.
Turn.........into two 8-inch round layer pans, well greased and
               lightly floured on the bottoms.
Bake.........at 350° for 30 to 35 minutes. Cool; frost with
               Fluffy Maple Frosting, page 320.
For use with Pillsbury's Best Self-Rising Flour, omit baking powder, soda, salt.

Maple Syrup Layer Cake

Bonny Tweed Cake

Junior Winner by Diana Junker, Fairbury, Nebraska

This is an impressive company cake with walnuts, grated orange rind and flecks of chocolate folded into the batter.

BAKE at 350° for 25 to 35 minutes   MAKES two 8 or 9-inch layers

Sift together..2 cups sifted **Pillsbury's Best All Purpose Flour***
               1 teaspoon **soda** and
               1 teaspoon **salt.** Set aside.
Add........1 cup firmly packed **brown sugar** gradually to
               ½ cup **shortening,** creaming well.
Blend in.....2 unbeaten **eggs,** beating well after each.
Add.......3½ squares (3½ oz.) **semi-sweet chocolate,** coarsely
               grated
               2 tablespoons grated **orange rind** and
               ⅓ cup **walnuts,** chopped
Combine.....1 cup **buttermilk** or sour milk and
               1 teaspoon **vanilla.** Add alternately with the dry
               ingredients to creamed mixture. Blend well after
               each addition.
Turn.........into two 8 or 9-inch round layer pans, well greased
               and lightly floured on the bottoms.
Bake.........at 350°: 30 to 35 minutes for 8-inch layers; 25 to
               30 minutes for 9-inch layers. Cool; frost with
               Fluffy Orange Frosting, page 317.
*For use with Pillsbury's Best Self-Rising Flour, decrease soda to ½ teaspoon
and omit salt.*

Mocha Fleck Cake

Bride Winner by Mrs. Wm. C. Kaegy, Greenville, Illinois

A layer cake with chocolate cake decorations giving a "tweed" effect. The soft mocha-butter frosting is a perfect accompaniment.

BAKE at 375° for 30 to 40 minutes   MAKES two 8 or 9-inch layers

Sift together . . 2 cups sifted **Pillsbury's Best All Purpose Flour***
2½ teaspoons double-acting **baking powder** and
1 teaspoon **salt.** Set aside.

Add . . . . 2½ cups sifted **confectioners' sugar** gradually to
¾ cup **shortening,** creaming well.

Blend in . . . . . 3 unbeaten **eggs,** beating well after each.

Combine . . . . . 1 cup strong **coffee** and
1 teaspoon **vanilla.** Add alternately with the dry ingredients to creamed mixture. Blend well after each addition.

Stir in . . . . . . ½ cup **nuts,** finely chopped, and
⅓ to ⅔ cup **chocolate cake decorations**

Turn . . . . into two 8 or 9-inch round layer pans, well greased and lightly floured on the bottoms.

Bake . . . . at 375° for 30 to 40 minutes. Cool; frost with **Mocha Butter Cream Frosting,** page 324.

*For use with Pillsbury's Best Self-Rising Flour, omit baking powder and salt.

Butterscotch Dandy Cake

Senior Winner by Mrs. Walter Spracklen, Nokomis, Illinois

A "double-butterscotch" cake, with butterscotch sauce in the cake and creamy butterscotch frosting.

BAKE at 375° for 25 to 30 minutes   MAKES two 9-inch layers

Combine . . . . . 1 cup firmly packed **brown sugar**
¼ cup **butter** or margarine and
¼ cup **milk** in saucepan. Cook over medium heat, stir-ring constantly, until a little syrup dropped in cold water forms a hard ball (250°). Remove from heat.

Add . . . . 1¼ cups hot **milk** slowly; blend until smooth. Cool.

Sift together 2¾ cups sifted **Pillsbury's Best All Purpose Flour***
3 teaspoons double-acting **baking powder** and
1 teaspoon **salt.** Set aside.

Add . . . . ¾ cup **sugar** gradually to
⅔ cup **shortening,** creaming well.

Blend in . . . . . 1 teaspoon **vanilla** and
3 unbeaten **eggs,** beating well after each.

Add . . . . the dry ingredients alternately with the cooled syrup. Blend well after each addition.

Turn . . . . into two 9-inch round or square layer pans, well greased and lightly floured on the bottoms.

Bake . . . . at 375° for 25 to 30 minutes. Cool; frost with **Hasty Butterscotch Frosting,** page 315.

*For use with Pillsbury's Best Self-Rising Flour, omit baking powder and salt.

Mocha Fleck Cake

Southern Belle Butterscotch Cake

Senior Winner by Mrs. John Cirino, Pascagoula, Mississippi

A regal brown sugar cake, with coffee lending an intriguing flavor. Billows of pale green fluffy frosting top it.

BAKE at 350° for 30 to 35 minutes   MAKES two 8-inch layers

Sift together 2⅓ cups sifted **Pillsbury's Best All Purpose Flour***
  2½ teaspoons double-acting **baking powder** and
  ½ teaspoon **salt**
Cream . . . . . . ½ cup **butter** or margarine. Gradually add
  1⅓ cups firmly packed **brown sugar,** creaming well.
Add . . . . 3 unbeaten **eggs,** beating well after each.
Combine . . . . ¾ cup cold, double-strength **coffee** and
  1½ teaspoons **vanilla.** Add alternately with the dry ingredients to creamed mixture. Blend well after each addition.

Turn . . . . into two 8-inch round layer pans, well greased and lightly floured on the bottoms.
Bake . . . . at 350° for 30 to 35 minutes. Cool; frost with **Pastel Green Frosting,** page 319.
Combine . . . . ½ square (½ oz.) melted unsweetened **chocolate** and 1 teaspoon melted **butter.** Spoon around top edge of cake, allowing to drip down sides.
For use with Pillsbury's Best Self-Rising Flour, omit baking powder and salt.

Toffee Nut Filled Cake

Senior Winner by Mrs. Russell N. Farr, Bath, Michigan

A flavor surprise! This Quick-Mix brown sugar cake has an unusual sour cream-nut filling and a sea-foam frosting.

BAKE at 350° for 35 to 40 minutes   MAKES two 8 or 9-inch layers

Sift together 2¼ cups sifted **Pillsbury's Best All Purpose Flour***
  2½ teaspoons double-acting **baking powder** and
  1 teaspoon **salt** into large mixing bowl.
Add . . . . 1½ cups firmly packed **brown sugar**
  ½ cup **shortening** and
  1 cup **milk**
Beat . . . . 1½ minutes. (With mixer use a low speed.)
Add . . . . 2 unbeaten **eggs**
  1 **egg yolk** and
  1 teaspoon **vanilla.** Beat 1½ minutes.
Turn . . . . into two 8 or 9-inch round layer pans, well greased and lightly floured on the bottoms.
Bake . . . . at 350° for 35 to 40 minutes. Cool; fill with Nut Filling. Frost with **Toffee Frosting,** page 319.
For use with Pillsbury's Best Self-Rising Flour, omit baking powder and salt.

NUT FILLING

In saucepan combine ½ cup firmly packed brown sugar, 2 tablespoons flour and ½ cup nuts, ground (hickory nuts, filberts or black walnuts).

Southern Belle Butterscotch Cake

Add ⅓ cup cream, ⅓ cup sour cream and 2 tablespoons butter; mix well. Cook over medium heat, stirring constantly, until very thick. Add ½ teaspoon vanilla. Cool to lukewarm.

Praline Crunch Cake

Senior Second Prize Winner by Mrs. Helen L. Pentleton, Mattapoisett, Mass.

Quick to make and easy to take! Flavored with coffee, molasses and a toasty brown sugar topping.

BAKE at 350° for 35 to 45 minutes   MAKES 12x8 or 13x9-inch cake

Sift together . . 2 cups sifted **Pillsbury's Best All Purpose Flour***
             1¼ cups **sugar**
             2 teaspoons double-acting **baking powder**
             1 teaspoon **salt** and
             2 teaspoons **instant coffee** into large mixing bowl.
Add . . . . ¾ cup **milk**
             ½ cup **shortening** and
             2 tablespoons **molasses**
Beat . . . . 1½ minutes. (With mixer use a low speed.)
Add . . . . ¼ cup **milk**
             2 unbeaten **eggs** and
             1 teaspoon **vanilla**. Beat 1½ minutes.
Turn . . . . into 12x8x2 or 13x9x2-inch pan, well greased and
             lightly floured on the bottom.
Bake . . . . at 350° for 35 to 45 minutes. Cool; frost with
             Butter Cream Frosting, page 314. Top with Praline
             Crunch.
*For use with Pillsbury's Best Self-Rising Flour, omit baking powder and salt.

PRALINE CRUNCH

Cut 2 tablespoons butter into ¼ cup Pillsbury's Best All Purpose Flour and 2 tablespoons brown sugar to make a crumb mixture. Add ¼ cup chopped pecans. Place in a small pan. Bake at 350° for 15 minutes. Cool; break into small pieces.

Praline Crunch Cake

Caramel-Rich Date Cake

Senior Winner by Mrs. Budd O. Jackson, South Bend, Indiana

Dates and nuts in a burnt sugar layer cake, with marmalade in the date-nut filling and caramel fudge frosting on top.

BAKE at 350° for 35 to 45 minutes　　　　　MAKES two 9-inch layers

Cover. . . . . . .1 cup **dates,** cut in small pieces, with
　　　　　　1¼ cups **boiling water.** Cool.

Melt. . . . . . . .¼ cup **sugar** in heavy skillet over low heat, stirring
　　　　　　constantly, just until sugar melts and turns dark
　　　　　　golden brown. Add very slowly
　　　　　　¼ cup hot **water,** a few drops at a time at first, stirring
　　　　　　constantly, until sugar is completely dissolved. Cool.

Sift together. .3 cups sifted **Pillsbury's Best All Purpose Flour***
　　　　　　1½ teaspoons **soda** and
　　　　　　1 teaspoon **salt.** Set aside.

Add. . . . . . .1½ cups **sugar** gradually to
　　　　　　¾ cup **shortening** (half butter may be used), creaming
　　　　　　well.

Blend in . . . . .2 unbeaten **eggs** and
　　　　　　2 teaspoons **vanilla;** beat well.

Combine. . . . . .the date and burnt sugar mixtures. Add alternately
　　　　　　with the dry ingredients to creamed mixture. Blend
　　　　　　well after each addition. Stir in

½ cup **nuts,** chopped

Turn. . . . . .into two 9-inch round layer pans, at least 1½ inches
　　　　　　deep, well greased and lightly floured on the bottoms.

Bake. . . . . . . .at 350° for 35 to 45 minutes. Cool; fill with Date-Nut
　　　　　　Filling. Frost with **Caramel Frosting,** page 314.

**For use with Pillsbury's Best Self-Rising Flour, omit soda and salt.*

DATE-NUT FILLING

Combine ½ cup cut dates, ½ cup chopped nuts, 2 tablespoons butter, 3 tablespoons orange marmalade or apricot jam and 3 tablespoons water in saucepan. Bring to boil over medium heat, stirring constantly. Cook until thickened.

Maple Nut Luscious Cake

Senior Winner by Mrs. Harry Kupsch, Cato, Wisconsin

Brown sugar and maple give old-fashioned flavor to this truly luscious Quick-Mix cake filled with pecans.

BAKE at 375° for 25 to 30 minutes　　　　　MAKES two 8-inch layers

Sift together 2¼ cups sifted **Pillsbury's Best All Purpose Flour***
　　　　　　3 teaspoons double-acting **baking powder** and
　　　　　　1 teaspoon **salt** into large mixing bowl.

Add. . . . . . .1¼ cups firmly packed **brown sugar**
　　　　　　½ cup **shortening**
　　　　　　1 cup **milk** and
　　　　　　1 teaspoon **maple flavoring**

Beat. . . . . .1½ minutes. (With mixer use a low speed.)

Add. . . . . . .2 unbeaten **eggs;** beat 1½ minutes.

Stir in . . . . . .½ cup **pecans,** chopped

Turn. . . . . .into two 8-inch round layer pans, well greased and
　　　　　　lightly floured on the bottoms.

Bake. . . . . . . .at 375° for 25 to 30 minutes. Cool; frost with
　　　　　　Browned Butter Frosting, page 321.

**For use with Pillsbury's Best Self-Rising Flour, omit baking powder and salt.*

Golden Burnt Sugar Cake

Junior Winner by Dolores H. Schlesser, Maurice, Iowa

There is a good, old-fashioned, burnt sugar caramel flavor in this cake—and more caramel flavor in the fluffy frosting on top.

BAKE at 350° for 30 to 35 minutes   MAKES two 8-inch layers

Melt. . . . . . . .¾ cup **sugar** in heavy skillet over low heat until medium dark brown, stirring constantly. Gradually add

½ cup **boiling water**, a few drops at a time, stirring until caramel mixture dissolves. Cool. Reserve 2 tablespoons for frosting.

Pour. . . . . .the remaining syrup into a measuring cup; add enough **milk** to measure 1 cup.

Sift together. .2 cups sifted **Pillsbury's Best All Purpose Flour***

¾ cup **sugar**

3 teaspoons double-acting **baking powder** and

1 teaspoon **salt** into large mixing bowl.

Add. . . . . . . .½ cup **shortening** and the caramel-milk mixture.

Beat. . . . . .1½ minutes. (With mixer use a low speed.)

Add. . . . . . .2 unbeaten **eggs** and

1 teaspoon **vanilla**. Beat 1½ minutes.

Turn. . . . . .into two 8-inch round layer pans, well greased and lightly floured on the bottoms.

Bake. . . . . .at 350° for 30 to 35 minutes. Cool; frost with **Fluffy Caramel Frosting**, page 317.

*For use with Pillsbury's Best Self-Rising Flour, omit baking powder and salt.

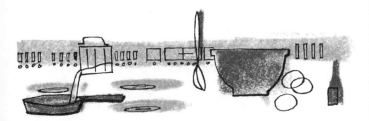

Burnt Sugar Cream Cake

Senior Winner by Bess Klabbatz, Akron, Ohio

Caramelized sugar gives both cake and frosting a luscious flavor.

BAKE at 350° for 45 to 55 minutes   MAKES 9-inch tube cake

Prepare. . . . . . .Caramelized Sugar; see below

Sift together. .2 cups sifted **Pillsbury's Best All Purpose Flour***

1¼ cups **sugar**

2½ teaspoons double-acting **baking powder** and

½ teaspoon **salt**

Beat. . . . . . . .3 **egg whites** until stiff but not dry.

Beat. . . . . . . .1 cup **whipping cream** in large mixing bowl until very thick. Fold in the beaten egg whites.

Combine. . . .¼ cup of the Caramelized Sugar (reserve remainder)

¼ cup cold **water** and

1 teaspoon **vanilla**. Add gradually to the whipped-cream mixture, folding gently.

Add. . . . . .the dry ingredients, one-third at a time, folding gently until dry particles disappear.

Turn. . . . . .into 9-inch tube pan, well greased and lightly floured on the bottom.

Bake. . . . . .at 350° for 45 to 55 minutes. Cool; frost with Burnt Sugar Frosting.

*For use with Pillsbury's Best Self-Rising Flour, omit baking powder and salt.

CARAMELIZED SUGAR

Melt ½ cup sugar in heavy skillet over low heat, stirring constantly, just until sugar melts and turns dark golden brown. Add very slowly ½ cup hot water, a few drops at a time at first, stirring constantly, until sugar is completely dissolved. Cool.

BURNT SUGAR FROSTING

Cream ¼ cup butter or margarine. Add 2 unbeaten egg yolks, 1½ tablespoons Caramelized Sugar, ½ teaspoon vanilla, and ⅛ teaspoon salt; beat well. Blend in 2 to 2½ cups sifted confectioners' sugar until of spreading consistency.

Butterscotch Chewy Cake

Butterscotch Chewy Cake

Senior Second Prize Winner by Mrs. Richard Enloe, Atlanta, Georgia

A chewy, brownie-type cake, quickly mixed in one pan. It'll remind you of date bars, although there are no dates in it.

BAKE at 350° for 25 to 30 minutes   MAKES 13x9-inch cake

Beat . . . . .4 medium **eggs** (about ¾ cup) with rotary beater in top of double boiler just until blended.

Blend in . . . . .2 cups firmly packed **brown sugar** and
1 tablespoon **butter.** Place over rapidly boiling water, stirring constantly, just until hot, about 5 minutes. Remove from heat.

Sift together 1½ cups sifted **Pillsbury's Best All Purpose Flour*** and

1½ teaspoons double-acting **baking powder.** Add all at once to cooked mixture; blend well.

Stir in . . . . .1½ cups **pecans,** chopped, and
1 teaspoon **vanilla**

Turn . . . . .into 13x9x2-inch pan, well greased and lightly floured on the bottom.

Bake . . . . .at 350° for 25 to 30 minutes. Serve with **ice cream** or whipped cream, or sprinkle with sifted confectioners' sugar.

*For use with Pillsbury's Best Self-Rising Flour, omit baking powder.

Tasty Cake

Senior Winner by Mrs. Charles P. Collins, Burlington, Vermont

A delicate blend of coffee and maple complemented by banana-butter icing will make this loaf cake a sure bet.

BAKE at 350° for 30 to 35 minutes   MAKES 12x8 or 13x9-inch cake

Sift together . .2 cups sifted **Pillsbury's Best All Purpose Flour***
1⅓ cups **sugar**
1 teaspoon double-acting **baking powder**
1 teaspoon **soda**
1 teaspoon **salt** and
2 teaspoons **instant coffee** into large mixing bowl.

Add . . . . .½ cup **shortening**
1 cup **milk** and
1 teaspoon **maple flavoring**

Beat . . . . .1½ minutes. (With mixer use a low speed.)

Add . . . . .2 unbeaten **eggs;** beat 1½ minutes. Stir in ⅛ cup **walnuts,** chopped

Turn . . . . .into 12x8x2 or 13x9x2-inch pan, well greased and lightly floured on the bottom.

Bake . . . . .at 350° for 30 to 35 minutes. Cool; frost with **Banana Nut Frosting,** page 324.

*For use with Pillsbury's Best Self-Rising Flour, omit baking powder, soda, salt.

SPICE CAKES

NUT MEG — GIN GER — CLO VES

Smorgasbord Spice Cake

Senior Winner by Mrs. Ellis O. Carlson, Rockford, Illinois

This old Swedish recipe makes a glamorous "company" layer cake, topped with sea-foam frosting.

BAKE at 350° for 30 to 35 minutes*   MAKES two 9-inch layers*

Sift together . 2¼ cups sifted **Pillsbury's Best All Purpose Flour****
        1½ teaspoons double-acting **baking powder**
        1 teaspoon **salt**
        1 teaspoon **cinnamon**
        ½ teaspoon **soda**
        ½ teaspoon **cloves** and
        ½ teaspoon **ginger**
Cream . . . . . . ½ cup **butter** or margarine. Gradually add
        1 cup **sugar** and
        ⅓ cup firmly packed **brown sugar**, creaming well.
Blend in . . . . . 2 unbeaten **eggs**, beating well after each.
Combine . . . . . 1 cup **milk** and
        1 teaspoon **vanilla**. Add alternately with the dry ingredients to creamed mixture. Blend well after each addition.
Turn . . . . into two 9-inch round layer pans, well greased and lightly floured on the bottoms.*
Bake . . . . at 350° for 30 to 35 minutes.* Cool; frost with **Sea-Foam Frosting**, page 318.

If desired, cake may be baked in 12x8x2-inch pan for 40 to 50 minutes.
**For use with Pillsbury's Best Self-Rising Flour, omit baking powder and salt.*

Gypsy Jamboree Cake

Senior Winner by Mrs. James M. Hepner, Harlingen, Texas

Lemon, spices, walnuts and a hint of cocoa make this cake very special. The "two-in-one" mocha frosting is cinnamon flavored.

BAKE at 350° for 30 to 35 minutes   MAKES two 8-inch layers

Sift together 1½ cups sifted **Pillsbury's Best All Purpose Flour***
        2 tablespoons **cocoa**
        1 teaspoon **cinnamon**
        ½ teaspoon double-acting **baking powder**
        ½ teaspoon **soda**
        ½ teaspoon **salt** and
        ½ teaspoon **nutmeg** or mace. Set aside.
Add . . . . 1¼ cups **sugar** gradually to
        ½ cup **shortening**, creaming well.
Blend in . . . . . 3 unbeaten **eggs**, beating well after each.
Add . . . . ¾ cup **buttermilk** or sour milk alternately with the dry ingredients. Blend well after each addition. (With mixer use a low speed.)
Blend in . . . . . 1 teaspoon **vanilla**
        ½ to 1 teaspoon **lemon extract** and
        ½ cup **walnuts**, chopped.
Turn . . . . into two 8-inch round layer pans, well greased and lightly floured on the bottoms.
Bake . . . . at 350° for 30 to 35 minutes. Cool; frost with Mocha Cinnamon Frosting.

**For use with Pillsbury's Best Self-Rising Flour, omit baking powder and salt.*

MOCHA CINNAMON FROSTING

Cream ⅓ cup butter. Blend in 1 egg yolk, ½ teaspoon cinnamon and ⅛ teaspoon salt. Add gradually 4 cups (about 1 lb.) sifted confectioners' sugar alternately with 2 tablespoons hot coffee. Beat until of spreading consistency. If necessary, thin with a few teaspoons of hot coffee. Spread ⅔ cup of frosting between layers. Add 2 tablespoons cocoa to remainder of frosting. Beat well, thinning with a few drops more coffee, if necessary.

Molasses Whisper Cake

Junior Winner by Margaret Mary Flesse, Youngstown, Ohio

A hint of molasses flavor in a moist, tender spice cake, with a luscious raisin and nut filling.

BAKE at 350° for 25 to 35 minutes   MAKES two 8 or 9-inch layers

Sift together 1¾ cups sifted **Pillsbury's Best All Purpose Flour***
                1 teaspoon **soda**
                ½ teaspoon **salt**
                ½ teaspoon **cinnamon** and
                ½ teaspoon **cloves**. Set aside.
Add . . . . 1 cup **sugar** gradually to
                ½ cup **shortening,** creaming well.
Blend in . . . . . 3 unbeaten **eggs,** beating well after each.
Stir in . . . . . . ¼ cup **molasses**
Add . . . . ¾ cup **buttermilk** or sour milk alternately with the dry

Molasses Whisper Cake

ingredients. Blend well after each addition.
Turn . . . . into two 8 or 9-inch round layer pans, well greased and lightly floured on the bottoms.
Bake . . . . at 350° for 25 to 35 minutes. Cool; fill with **Raisin Nut Filling,** page 330. Frost with **Toffee Frosting,** page 319.

For use with Pillsbury's Best Self-Rising Flour, decrease soda to ½ teaspoon and omit salt.

Aunt Lou's Dixie Spice Cake

Senior Winner by Mrs. Lona Rosemary Gibson, Latonia, Kentucky

An old family favorite recipe—a delicious brown sugar spice cake with a complementary cream filling.

BAKE at 350°   MAKES two 9-inch layers
                                or 13x9-inch cake

Sift together 2¾ cups sifted **Pillsbury's Best All Purpose Flour***
                1 teaspoon **soda**
                1 teaspoon **salt**
                ½ teaspoon **nutmeg** and
                ½ teaspoon **allspice**. Set aside.
Add . . . . ½ cup **sugar** and
                1½ cups firmly packed **brown sugar** gradually to
                1 cup **shortening,** creaming well.
Blend in . . . . . 3 unbeaten **eggs,** beating well after each.
Add . . . . the dry ingredients alternately with
                1¼ cups **buttermilk** or sour milk. Blend well after each addition.
Stir in . . . . . . 1 teaspoon **vanilla** and
                1 cup **black walnuts** or English walnuts, chopped
Turn . . . . into pans (see sizes below), well greased and lightly floured on the bottoms.
Bake . . . . at 350°: 40 to 45 minutes in two 9-inch round layer pans; 45 to 55 minutes in one 13x9x2-inch pan.

Cool; fill with **Vanilla Cream Filling**, page 328. Top with **whipped cream**.

For use with Pillsbury's Best Self-Rising Flour, decrease soda to ¼ teaspoon and omit salt.

Granddear's Spice Cake

Senior Winner by Mrs. A. L. Orsen, Portland, Oregon

A good cake to bake with leftover egg yolks—flecks of chocolate are added to an old-fashioned spice cake.

BAKE at 325° for 50 to 60 minutes, or   MAKES 9-inch tube cake
at 350° for 25 to 30 minutes   or two 8-inch layers

Sift together 1⅔ cups sifted **Pillsbury's Best All Purpose Flour***
    2 teaspoons double-acting **baking powder**
    1 teaspoon **salt**
    ½ teaspoon **cinnamon** and
    ¼ teaspoon **allspice**
Beat . . . . . . 10 **egg yolks** in small mixing bowl until thick and lemon colored.
Cream . . . . . . ½ cup **butter** or margarine. Gradually add
    1 cup **sugar**, creaming well.
Blend in . . . . . . the egg yolks; mix well.
Combine . . . . ½ cup **milk** and
    1 teaspoon **vanilla**. Add alternately with the dry ingredients to creamed mixture. Blend well after each addition.
Stir in . . . . 1 square (1 oz.) grated **semi-sweet** or **unsweetened chocolate**
Turn . . . . into 9-inch tube pan or two 8-inch round layer pans, greased and lightly floured on bottoms.
Bake . . . . at 325° for 50 to 60 minutes for tube cake, or at 350° for 25 to 30 minutes for 8-inch layers. Cool; frost with **Caramel Frosting**, page 314.

For use with Pillsbury's Best Self-Rising Flour, omit baking powder and salt.

Raspberry-Nut Cake

Senior Winner by Mrs. Loay Wilshire, Wichita, Kansas

Fresh raspberries make this spice cake colorful and refreshing.

BAKE at 350° for 30 to 40 minutes   MAKES two 8-inch layers

Sift together . . 2 cups sifted **Pillsbury's Best All Purpose Flour***
    1½ teaspoons double-acting **baking powder**
    1 teaspoon **salt**
    1 teaspoon **cinnamon** and
    ½ teaspoon **soda**. Set aside.
Add . . . . 1¼ cups **sugar** gradually to
    ½ cup **shortening**, creaming well.
Blend in . . . . . 3 unbeaten **eggs**, beating well after each.
Combine . . . . ¾ cup **buttermilk** or sour milk and
    1 teaspoon **vanilla**. Add alternately with the dry ingredients to creamed mixture. Blend well after each addition.
Stir in . . . . . . ½ cup **nuts**, chopped. Fold in
    1 cup fresh **raspberries**
Turn . . . . into two 8-inch round layer pans, well greased and lightly floured on the bottoms.
Bake . . . . at 350° for 30 to 40 minutes. Cool; frost with Pink Raspberry Frosting.

For use with Pillsbury's Best Self-Rising Flour, omit baking powder, salt, soda.

PINK RASPBERRY FROSTING

Cream ⅓ cup butter or margarine, 1 teaspoon vanilla and ¼ teaspoon salt. Blend in 3 cups sifted confectioners' sugar, 2 tablespoons puréed raspberries and 2 to 3 tablespoons hot cream, beating until of spreading consistency.

Scotch Spice Cake

Scotch Spice Cake

Senior Winner by Mrs. Charles J. Suckle, San Marcos, Texas

A moist brown sugar-spice cake with nuts and raisins. Its unusual texture comes from rolled oats.

BAKE at 350° for 50 to 60 minutes   MAKES 9x9-inch cake

Pour . . . . ⅓ cup **boiling water** over
     ½ cup quick-cooking **rolled oats.** Stir in
     ¾ cup undiluted **evaporated milk;** cool.
Sift together 1¼ cups sifted **Pillsbury's Best All Purpose Flour***
     1 teaspoon **salt**
     ½ teaspoon **soda**
     ½ teaspoon **cinnamon** and
     ½ teaspoon **cloves**

Mix . . . . ½ cup **raisins** and
     ½ cup **nuts,** chopped, into flour mixture. Set aside.
Add . . . . 1 cup firmly packed **brown sugar** and
     ¼ cup **sugar** gradually to
     ½ cup **shortening,** creaming well.
Blend in . . . . . 2 unbeaten **eggs,** beating well after each. Stir in the
     cooled oatmeal.
Add . . . . the dry ingredients gradually. Mix thoroughly.
Turn . . . . into 9x9x2-inch pan, well greased and lightly floured
     on the bottom.
Bake . . . . at 350° for 50 to 60 minutes. Cool; frost with
     Coffee Icing, page 326, or sprinkle with confection-
     ers' sugar.

*For use with Pillsbury's Best Self-Rising Flour, omit salt and soda.

Londonderry Spice Cake

Senior Winner by Mrs. Rhoda Marquart, Beaverdam, Ohio

Spices and coffee make this cake outstanding in flavor. Raisins and brown sugar help keep it moist. Stays fresh for days.

BAKE at 350° for 40 to 50 minutes   MAKES 8x8 or 9x9-inch cake

Sift together 1½ cups sifted **Pillsbury's Best All Purpose Flour***
     1 teaspoon double-acting **baking powder**
     1 teaspoon **salt**
     ½ teaspoon **soda**
     ½ teaspoon **cinnamon**
     ½ teaspoon **nutmeg** and
     ½ teaspoon **cloves**
Combine . . . . . ½ cup cooked **raisins** and 2 tablespoons dry ingredients.
Cream . . . . . . ½ cup **butter** or margarine. Gradually add
     ½ cup **sugar** and
     ½ cup firmly packed **brown sugar,** creaming well.
Blend in . . . . . 2 unbeaten **eggs,** beating well after each.
Add . . . . ½ cup strong cold **coffee** alternately with the dry

ingredients. Blend well after each addition.

Stir in . . . . the floured raisins. Turn into 8x8x2 or 9x9x2-inch pan, well greased and lightly floured on the bottom.

Bake . . . . at 350° for 40 to 50 minutes. Cool; frost with **Speedy Caramel Frosting,** page 314, or serve warm with whipped cream.

*For use with Pillsbury's Best Self-Rising Flour, omit baking powder, salt, soda.

Cottage Apple-Spice Cake

Junior Winner by Felicia Schroetel, Portland, Maine

Cottage cheese and apples add unusual flavor and texture to this moist spice loaf cake.

BAKE at 350° for 35 to 40 minutes   MAKES 9x9 or 11x7-inch cake

Sift together 1½ cups sifted **Pillsbury's Best All Purpose Flour***
          1½ teaspoons double-acting **baking powder**
          ½ teaspoon **salt**
          ¼ teaspoon **cloves**
          ¼ teaspoon **cinnamon** and
          ¼ teaspoon **ginger.** Set aside.

Add . . . . ¾ cup **sugar** gradually to
          ⅓ cup **shortening,** creaming well.

Blend in . . . . . 2 tablespoons **molasses** and
          2 unbeaten **eggs,** beating well after each.

Add . . . . ½ cup (4 oz.) creamed **cottage cheese**
          ¼ cup **milk**
          1 teaspoon grated **lemon rind** and

1½ teaspoons **lemon juice;** beat well.

Blend in . . . . the dry ingredients gradually. Stir in
          1 cup (1 medium) pared, cubed **apples**

Turn . . . . into 9x9x2 or 11x7x2-inch pan, well greased and lightly floured on the bottom.

Bake . . . . at 350° for 35 to 40 minutes. Serve warm, cut into squares and topped with **Cinnamon Whipped Cream,** page 329.

*For use with Pillsbury's Best Self-Rising Flour, omit baking powder and salt.

Tip Top Molasses Cake

Senior Winner by Mrs. Robert C. Ambrose, San Antonio, Texas

This simple old-fashioned molasses cake has spices to give it flavor— fresh apples to give it extra moistness.

BAKE at 350° for 35 to 45 minutes   MAKES 9x9 or 11x7-inch cake

Sift together 1¾ cups sifted **Pillsbury's Best All Purpose Flour***
          1 teaspoon **soda**
          ½ teaspoon **salt**
          ½ teaspoon **cinnamon** and
          ¼ teaspoon **cloves.** Set aside.

Add . . . . ½ cup **sugar** gradually to
          ⅓ cup **shortening,** creaming well.

Blend in . . . . . 2 unbeaten **eggs,** one at a time, and
          ⅓ cup **molasses.** Beat well.

Add . . . . ½ cup **buttermilk** or sour milk alternately with the dry ingredients. Blend well after each addition.

Fold in . . . . . . 1 cup **apples,** pared, cored and sliced very thin

Turn . . . . into 9x9x2 or 11x7x2-inch pan, well greased and lightly floured on the bottom.

Bake . . . . at 350° for 35 to 45 minutes. Serve warm with **whipped cream.**

*For use with Pillsbury's Best Self-Rising Flour, decrease soda to ¼ teaspoon and omit salt.

Apple Butter Spice Cake

Senior Winner by Mrs. Arthur L. Eads, Meade, Kansas

A spicy brown sugar-nut mixture ripples through this moist rich cake, and forms the baked-on topping, too.

BAKE at 350° for 40 to 45 minutes   MAKES 12x8 or 13x9-inch cake

Sift together 2¼ cups sifted **Pillsbury's Best All Purpose Flour***
    1 teaspoon double-acting **baking powder**
    1 teaspoon **soda** and
    ½ teaspoon **salt**
Cream......½ cup **butter** or margarine. Gradually add
    1 cup **sugar,** creaming well.
Add........2 unbeaten **eggs**; beat well.
Blend in.....¾ cup **apple butter** and
    1 teaspoon **vanilla**
Add........1 cup **sour cream** (thick or commercial) alternately with
    the dry ingredients. Blend well after each addition.
Turn.........half of batter into 12x8x2 or 13x9x2-inch pan, well
    greased and lightly floured on the bottom. Sprinkle
    with half of Topping. Spoon remaining batter into
    pan; spread evenly. Sprinkle with remaining Topping.
Bake.........at 350° for 40 to 45 minutes. Serve warm or cold,
    plain or with whipped cream.

For use with Pillsbury's Best Self-Rising Flour, omit baking powder and salt; decrease soda to ¼ teaspoon.

TOPPING

Combine ½ cup firmly packed brown sugar, 1 teaspoon cinnamon, ½ teaspoon nutmeg and ½ cup chopped nuts.

Toasted Meringue Spice Cake

Senior Winner by Mrs. Peter Paris, Milwaukee, Wisconsin

An ideal take-to-the picnic cake . . . self-frosted with a brown sugar-nut meringue.

BAKE at 325° for 50 to 60 minutes   MAKES 13x9-inch cake

Sift together 2⅓ cups sifted **Pillsbury's Best All Purpose Flour***
    1 teaspoon double-acting **baking powder**
    ½ teaspoon **salt**
    1 teaspoon **cinnamon**
    ¼ teaspoon **allspice**
    ¼ teaspoon **cloves** and
    ¼ teaspoon **nutmeg**
Cream......½ cup **butter** or margarine. Gradually add
    ½ cup **sugar** and
    ½ cup firmly packed **brown sugar,** creaming well.
Blend in.....1 teaspoon **vanilla** and
    2 unbeaten **egg yolks** (reserve whites for Meringue);
    beat well.
Dissolve.....1 teaspoon **soda** in
    1 cup **sour cream** (thick or commercial) and
    ¼ cup **milk.** Add to batter; mix thoroughly.
Add.........the dry ingredients gradually; blend well.
Turn.........into 13x9x2-inch pan, well greased and lightly
    floured on the bottom.
Spread.......Sea-Foam Meringue over batter; sprinkle with
    ½ cup **pecans,** chopped
Bake.........at 325° for 50 to 60 minutes. Cool thoroughly before
    serving.

For use with Pillsbury's Best Self-Rising Flour, omit baking powder and salt.

SEA-FOAM MERINGUE

Beat 2 egg whites until stiff but not dry. Gradually add 1 cup firmly packed brown sugar, beating well after each addition. Continue beating until meringue stands in stiff, straight peaks. Fold in ½ cup chopped pecans.

Picnic Special Cake

Senior Winner by Mrs. R. N. Willson, Elko, Nevada

*There's cottage cheese for moistness—coffee, spices and nuts for flavor.
Coconut gives a delightful crunchy crust.*

BAKE at 350° for 35 to 45 minutes   MAKES 12x8 or 13x9-inch cake

Sift together 1½ cups sifted **Pillsbury's Best All Purpose Flour***
    2 teaspoons double-acting **baking powder**
    ½ teaspoon **soda**
    ½ teaspoon **salt**
    ½ teaspoon **allspice**
    ½ teaspoon **cloves** and
    ½ teaspoon **cinnamon.** Set aside.
Add . . . . 1 cup **sugar** gradually to
    ½ cup **shortening,** creaming well.
Stir in . . . . . ½ cup creamed **cottage cheese** and
    1 teaspoon **vanilla**
Blend in . . . . 3 unbeaten **eggs,** beating well after each.
Add . . . . ⅓ cup cool, strong **coffee** alternately with the dry
    ingredients. Blend well after each addition.
Stir in . . . . . ½ cup **nuts,** chopped. Turn into 12x8x2 or 13x9x2-inch
    pan, well greased and lightly floured on the bottom.
    Sprinkle top with
    ¼ cup **coconut,** chopped
Bake . . . . at 350° for 35 to 45 minutes. Cool; frost with
    Caramel Icing, page 315.

**For use with Pillsbury's Best Self-Rising Flour, omit baking powder and salt.*

Hurry-Up Spice Cake

Senior Winner by Mrs. Bessie R. Kent, Los Angeles, California

*A layer of sugar, pecans and spice bakes inside and on top of this cake.
A simple cinnamon icing completes the cake.*

BAKE at 350° for 50 to 60 minutes   MAKES 13x9-inch cake

Combine . . . . ¾ cup **pecans,** chopped
    ½ cup firmly packed **brown sugar**
    2 tablespoons **flour**
    1 teaspoon **cinnamon** and
    2 tablespoons **butter;** mix well. Set aside.
Sift together . .3 cups sifted **Pillsbury's Best All Purpose Flour***
    3 teaspoons double-acting **baking powder**
    1 teaspoon **salt**
    1 teaspoon **cinnamon**
    ½ teaspoon **allspice** and
    ½ teaspoon **nutmeg.** Set aside.
Add . . . . 1 cup **sugar** and
    ¾ cup firmly packed **brown sugar** gradually to
    ½ cup **shortening,** creaming well.
Blend in . . . . 3 unbeaten **eggs,** beating well after each.
Combine . . . . 1 cup **milk** and
    1 teaspoon **vanilla.** Add alternately with the dry
    ingredients to creamed mixture. Blend well after
    each addition.
Pour . . . . half of batter in 13x9x2-inch pan, well greased and
    lightly floured on bottom. Sprinkle with pecan
    mixture, reserving ¼ cup. Top with remaining batter
    and the pecan mixture.
Bake . . . . at 350° for 50 to 60 minutes. While hot, drizzle with
    Cinnamon Icing.

**Pillsbury's Best Self-Rising Flour is not recommended for use in this recipe.*

CINNAMON ICING

Combine 1 cup sifted confectioners' sugar, ¼ teaspoon cinnamon,
¼ teaspoon vanilla and 3 tablespoons cream. Mix thoroughly.

Prune Whip Spice Cake

Prune Whip Spice Cake

Best of Class Winner by Mrs. Harold Johnston, Homer City, Pennsylvania

Prune juice gives this even-textured spice cake its delicious flavor. A fluffy frosting contains prunes, prune juice and almonds.

BAKE at 375° for 25 to 30 minutes   MAKES two 8 or 9-inch layers

Sift together 2¼ cups sifted **Pillsbury's Best All Purpose Flour***
    1⅓ cups **sugar**
    2 teaspoons double-acting **baking powder**
    1 teaspoon **salt**
    ½ teaspoon **cinnamon**
    ¼ teaspoon **soda**
    ¼ teaspoon **nutmeg** and
    ¼ teaspoon **allspice** into large mixing bowl.

Add . . . . ½ cup **shortening**
    ½ cup **prune juice** and
    ½ cup **milk**
Beat . . . . 1½ minutes. (With mixer use a low speed.)
Add . . . . 2 unbeaten **eggs** and
    1 teaspoon **vanilla.** Beat 1½ minutes.
Turn . . . . into two 8 or 9-inch round layer pans, well greased and lightly floured on the bottoms.
Bake . . . . at 375° for 25 to 30 minutes. Cool; frost with **Fluffy Prune Frosting,** page 320.
For use with Pillsbury's Best Self-Rising Flour, omit baking powder, salt, soda.

Mardi Gras Spice Cake

Senior Winner by Mrs. William Sonnenburg, Oak Lawn, Illinois

There's cream and spice and everything nice in this elegant Quick-Mix cake, filled and frosted with whipped cream.

BAKE at 350° for 30 to 35 minutes   MAKES two 9-inch layers

Sift together 2½ cups sifted **Pillsbury's Best All Purpose Flour***
    1½ cups **sugar**
    2 teaspoons double-acting **baking powder**
    1 teaspoon **salt**
    1 teaspoon **cinnamon**
    ½ teaspoon **soda**
    ½ teaspoon **allspice** and
    ½ teaspoon **nutmeg** into large mixing bowl.
Add . . . . ½ cup **shortening**
    1 cup **milk**
    ¼ cup **molasses** and
    1 teaspoon **vanilla**
Beat . . . . 1½ minutes. (With mixer use a low speed.)
Blend in . . . . . 3 unbeaten **eggs.** Beat 1½ minutes.
Turn . . . . into two 9-inch round layer pans, well greased and lightly floured on the bottoms.

Bake . . . . at 350° for 30 to 35 minutes. Cool. Split layers in half, making four thin layers. Fill and frost with Sweetened Whipped Cream. Sprinkle with chopped **pecans.** Chill until serving time.

For use with Pillsbury's Best Self-Rising Flour, omit baking powder and salt; decrease soda to ¼ teaspoon.

SWEETENED WHIPPED CREAM

Beat 1 pint (2 cups) whipping cream until stiff. Fold in ¼ cup sugar and 1 teaspoon vanilla.

Mocha Apple Cake

Junior Winner by Rose Marie Pullar, International Falls, Minnesota

This spice cake is filled with fresh apples and raisins. The coffee flavor in the cake and frosting make it a little bit different.

BAKE at 375° for 30 to 40 minutes   MAKES 9x9 or 12x8-inch cake

Sift together 1¼ cups sifted **Pillsbury's Best All Purpose Flour***
⅞ cup **sugar** (¾ cup plus 2 tablespoons)
1 teaspoon **salt**
1 teaspoon **cinnamon** and
¼ teaspoon **cloves**

Combine . . . . . 1 cup pared, finely chopped **apple** (about 1 medium)
½ cup **raisins** and
¼ cup sifted **Pillsbury's Best All Purpose Flour;** set aside.

Add . . . . 2 unbeaten **eggs,** one at a time, to
½ cup **shortening,** beating well after each.

Combine . . . . . 1 teaspoon **soda** and
½ cup cold **coffee.** Add alternately with the dry

ingredients to shortening mixture. Blend well after each addition.

Stir in . . . . the floured fruit.

Turn . . . . into 9x9x2 or 12x8x2-inch pan, well greased and lightly floured on the bottom.

Bake . . . . at 375° for 30 to 40 minutes. Cool; frost with **Mocha Frosting,** page 323.

For use with Pillsbury's Best Self-Rising Flour, omit salt and decrease soda to ½ teaspoon.

By Ginger Crumb Cake

Junior Winner by Ruth Magney, Mound, Minnesota

Mild, light gingerbread, perky with dates, is a variation of an old English gingerbread.

BAKE at 350° for 30 to 35 minutes   MAKES 9x9 or 11x7-inch cake

Sift together . . 2 cups sifted **Pillsbury's Best All Purpose Flour***
1 cup **sugar**
1 teaspoon **cinnamon**
½ teaspoon **salt**
½ teaspoon **ginger** and
½ teaspoon **nutmeg** into large mixing bowl.

Cut in . . . . . . ½ cup **butter** or margarine until particles are fine. Reserve 1 cup of crumbs for topping.

Blend in . . . . . 1 unbeaten **egg** to remaining crumb mixture.

Add . . . . 1 teaspoon double-acting **baking powder**
½ teaspoon **soda**
¾ cup **buttermilk** or sour milk and
1 cup **dates,** cut. Mix thoroughly.

Press . . . . half of the reserved crumbs on the bottom of well-greased 9x9x2 or 11x7x2-inch pan.

Pour . . . . batter into pan. Sprinkle with remaining crumbs.

Bake . . . . at 350° for 30 to 35 minutes.

For use with Pillsbury's Best Self-Rising Flour, omit baking powder, salt, soda.

Suppertime Ginger Cake

Senior Winner by Mrs. William T. Mooney, Petaluma, California

Mellow molasses flavor and the tang of spices make this a truly luscious ginger cake.

BAKE at 350° for 45 to 50 minutes   MAKES 12x8 or 13x9-inch cake

Sift together 2½ cups sifted **Pillsbury's Best All Purpose Flour***
1½ teaspoons double-acting **baking powder**
1 teaspoon **soda**
1 teaspoon **salt**
2 teaspoons **cinnamon**
1½ teaspoons **ginger**
½ teaspoon **nutmeg** and
½ teaspoon **cloves**

Combine . . . . ½ cup **raisins**
½ cup **nuts**, chopped, and ¼ cup dry ingredients.

Blend . . . . 1 cup firmly packed **brown sugar** with
⅔ cup dark **molasses** and
2 **eggs** in large bowl. Beat well.

Add . . . . ⅔ cup **shortening** and the dry ingredients. Beat thoroughly.

Blend in . . . . . 1 cup **boiling water** gradually. Fold in floured raisins and nuts.

Pour . . . . into 12x8x2 or 13x9x2-inch pan, well greased and lightly floured on the bottom.

Bake . . . . at 350° for 45 to 50 minutes. Sprinkle with **confectioners' sugar,** or top with butter frosting. May be served warm as gingerbread.

**For use with Pillsbury's Best Self-Rising Flour, omit baking powder, soda, salt.*

Honey Harmony Cake

Senior Winner by Mrs. J. O. Foltz, Ponca City, Oklahoma

A spicy orange and honey loaf cake made the Quick-Mix way. The nut-crumb topping is baked on.

BAKE at 350° for 35 to 45 minutes   MAKES 12x8 or 13x9-inch cake

Sift together 2½ cups sifted **Pillsbury's Best All Purpose Flour***
2 teaspoons double-acting **baking powder**
1 teaspoon **cinnamon**
1 teaspoon **mace**
½ teaspoon **salt** and
¼ teaspoon **soda.** Set aside.

Add . . . . ¾ cup **sugar** gradually to
½ cup **shortening** and
1 teaspoon grated **orange rind**, creaming well.

Blend in . . . . the dry ingredients, making a crumb mixture. Reserve ¾ cup for topping.

Add . . . . ⅔ cup **milk**
½ cup **honey** and
1 teaspoon **vanilla** to remaining crumb mixture.

Beat . . . . 1½ minutes. (With mixer use a low speed.)

Add . . . . 2 unbeaten **eggs**; beat 1 minute.

Turn . . . . into 12x8x2 or 13x9x2-inch pan, well greased and lightly floured on the bottom.

Combine . . . . . . reserved crumb mixture
½ cup **pecans**, chopped, and
2 tablespoons **honey.** Sprinkle over batter.

Bake . . . . at 350° for 35 to 45 minutes.

**For use with Pillsbury's Best Self-Rising Flour, omit baking powder, salt, soda.*

MARBLE CAKES

Malted Coconut Marble Cake

Senior Winner by Mrs. Erwin Kleine, St. Louis, Missouri

The light part is creamy yellow—chocolate malted flavors the dark part.

BAKE at 350° for 60 to 70 minutes   MAKES 10-inch tube cake

Sift together . . 3 cups sifted **Pillsbury's Best All Purpose Flour***
    2 teaspoons double-acting **baking powder** and
    1 teaspoon **salt.** Set aside.
Add . . . . 2 cups **sugar** gradually to
    1 cup **shortening,** creaming well.
Blend in . . . . . 4 well-beaten **eggs**
Combine . . . . . 1 cup **milk** and
    1 teaspoon **vanilla.** Add alternately with the dry ingredients to creamed mixture. Blend well after each addition.
Place . . . . two cups of batter in a second bowl. Add
    ½ cup **chocolate malted milk powder.** Blend well.
Spoon . . . . yellow and malted batters alternately into 10-inch tube pan, well greased on the bottom.
Bake . . . . at 350° for 60 to 70 minutes. Spread with **Broiled Frosting,** page 324. Broil 2 to 5 minutes.

Pillsbury's Best Self-Rising Flour is not recommended for use in this recipe.

Chocolate Intrigue

Bride Winner by Mrs. S. Martin Goldman, Forest Hills, Long Island, New York

The chocolate sinks during baking to give this cake an intriguing design.

BAKE at 350° for 65 to 70 minutes   MAKES 10-inch tube cake

Sift together . . 3 cups sifted **Pillsbury's Best All Purpose Flour***
    2 teaspoons double-acting **baking powder** and
    ½ teaspoon **salt**
Cream . . . . 1 cup **butter** or margarine. Gradually add
    2 cups **sugar,** creaming until light and fluffy.
Blend in . . . . . 3 **eggs,** one at a time; beat well after each.
Combine . . . . . 1 cup **milk** and
    1½ teaspoons **vanilla.** Add alternately with the dry ingredients to creamed mixture. Blend well after each addition.
Turn . . . . two-thirds of batter into 10-inch tube pan, greased on the bottom.
Add . . . . to remaining batter
    ¾ cup **chocolate syrup**
    ¼ teaspoon **soda** and
    ¼ teaspoon **peppermint extract,** if desired. Mix well.
Pour . . . . over white batter. *Do not mix.*
Bake . . . . at 350° for 65 to 70 minutes. Cool in pan.

Pillsbury's Best Self-Rising Flour is not recommended for use in this recipe.

Chocolate Intrigue

Mystery Marble Cake

Senior Winner by Mrs. Joseph Francis Frewer, Savannah, Georgia

Here's an unusually delicious blending of maple and lemon flavors.

BAKE at 350° for 55 to 65 minutes   MAKES 9 or 10-inch tube cake

Sift together . . 2 cups sifted **Pillsbury's Best All Purpose Flour***
2 teaspoons double-acting **baking powder** and
½ teaspoon **salt**

Cream . . . . . . ⅔ cup **butter** or margarine. Gradually add
1¾ cups **sugar,** creaming well.

Add . . . . the dry ingredients alternately with
¾ cup **milk.** Blend well after each addition.

Beat . . . . 6 **egg whites** until stiff but not dry. Fold gently but thoroughly into batter.

Place . . . . about 1 cup of batter in a small bowl. Add
1 tablespoon **cocoa** and
½ teaspoon **maple extract.** Mix well.

Blend . . . . ½ teaspoon **lemon extract** into remainder of light batter.

Pour . . . . ½ inch of light batter into 9 or 10-inch greased tube pan; then dot with 3 teaspoons dark batter. Continue alternating light and dark batters.

Bake . . . . at 350° for 55 to 65 minutes.

*For use with Pillsbury's Best Self-Rising Flour, omit baking powder and salt.

Golden Marble Cake

Senior Winner by Mrs. Peggy Inman, North Vernon, Indiana

White and gold batters marbled together, then baked in a tube pan. Black walnut flavoring adds the final touch.

BAKE at 325° for 60 to 65 minutes   MAKES 10-inch tube cake

Sift together 2¾ cups sifted **Pillsbury's Best All Purpose Flour***
3 teaspoons double-acting **baking powder** and

---

1 teaspoon **salt**

Cream . . . . . . ½ cup **butter** or margarine with
¼ cup **shortening.** Gradually add
1½ cups **sugar,** creaming well.

Add . . . . the dry ingredients alternately with
¾ cup **milk.** Blend well after each addition.

Place . . . . half of batter in a second bowl.

Add . . . . 3 unbeaten **egg whites** and
¼ teaspoon **black walnut flavoring** to half of batter. Beat 1½ minutes.

Add . . . . 3 unbeaten **egg yolks**
1 teaspoon **vanilla** and
4 to 6 drops **yellow food coloring** to remaining batter. Beat 1½ minutes.

Spoon . . . . white and yellow batters alternately into 10-inch tube pan, well greased on the bottom.

Bake . . . . at 325° for 60 to 65 minutes. Cool; frost with **Creamy Vanilla Frosting,** page 321.

*For use with Pillsbury's Best Self-Rising Flour, omit baking powder and salt.

Fudge Marvel Cake

Senior Winner by Mrs. Genevieve E. Canfield, Newington, Connecticut

Plain yellow cake batter topped with a fudgy cocoa-rich batter gives a really different cake. No frosting to make!

BAKE at 350° for 35 to 40 minutes   MAKES 9x9-inch cake

Sift together 1½ cups sifted **Pillsbury's Best All Purpose Flour***
2 teaspoons double-acting **baking powder** and

½ teaspoon **salt**

Cream . . . . . . ⅓ cup **butter** or margarine. Gradually add
½ cup **sugar,** creaming well.

Add . . . . 2 unbeaten **eggs,** beating well after each.

Combine . . . . ⅔ cup **milk** and
½ teaspoon **vanilla.** Add alternately with the dry ingredients to creamed mixture. Blend well after each addition.

Turn . . . . into 9x9x2-inch pan, well greased and lightly floured on the bottom.

Pour . . . . Fudge Topping over batter in pan. Sprinkle with
½ cup **nuts,** chopped

Bake . . . . at 350° for 35 to 40 minutes.

Pillsbury's Best Self-Rising Flour is not recommended for use in this recipe.

FUDGE TOPPING

Beat 2 eggs until light and fluffy. Gradually add 1 cup sugar; continue beating until thick and ivory colored. Stir in ⅓ cup cocoa and ⅓ cup melted butter or margarine. Add ½ cup sifted Pillsbury's Best All Purpose Flour, ½ teaspoon salt, ¼ cup milk and 1 teaspoon vanilla. Blend thoroughly. (With mixer use lowest speed.)

Molasses Zigzag Cake

Senior Winner by Mrs. Shirley Poyer, Ithaca, New York

Molasses and yellow batters are swirled together to give this attractive zigzag effect.

BAKE at 350° for 65 to 70 minutes   MAKES 9x5-inch cake

Sift together . . 2 cups sifted **Pillsbury's Best All Purpose Flour***
2 teaspoons double-acting **baking powder** and
¼ teaspoon **salt.** Set aside.

Add . . . . 1 cup **sugar** gradually to
½ cup **shortening,** creaming well.

Add . . . . 2 unbeaten **eggs,** beating well after each.

Molasses Zigzag Cake

Combine . . . . ⅔ cup **milk** and
1 teaspoon **black walnut flavoring.** Add alternately with the dry ingredients to creamed mixture. Blend well after each addition.

Place . . . . one-third of batter in a second bowl. Add
2 tablespoons dark **molasses** and
1 teaspoon **allspice**

Spoon . . . . light and dark batters alternately into 9x5x3-inch pan, well greased on the bottom. Run a fork through the batter several times in both directions to marble.

Bake . . . . at 350° for 65 to 70 minutes. Cool; frost with **Cinnamon Glaze,** page 326. Sprinkle with chopped **nuts.**

Pillsbury's Best Self-Rising Flour is not recommended for use in this recipe.

Gold 'n' Spice Marble Cake

Gold 'n' Spice Marble Cake

Senior Winner by Mrs. Therese Tercek, Wausaukee, Wisconsin

A spicy molasses batter and a delicate yellow batter are marbled together to make this unusual loaf cake.

BAKE at 350° for 35 to 40 minutes   MAKES 12x8-inch cake

Sift together..2 cups sifted **Pillsbury's Best All Purpose Flour***
           2 teaspoons double-acting **baking powder** and
           1 teaspoon **salt**. Set aside.
Add.......1¼ cups **sugar** gradually to
           ½ cup **shortening**, creaming well.
Blend in.....2 unbeaten **eggs,** beating well after each.

Combine.....1 cup **milk** and
           1 teaspoon **vanilla.** Add alternately with the dry ingredients to creamed mixture. Blend well after each addition.
Place.........one-third of batter in a second bowl; blend in
           2 tablespoons **molasses**
           1 teaspoon **cinnamon**
           ½ teaspoon **nutmeg** and
           ¼ teaspoon **cloves**
Spoon........plain and spice batters alternately into 12x8x2-inch pan, well greased and lightly floured on the bottom.
Bake.........at 350° for 35 to 40 minutes. Cool; frost with **Lemon Butter Frosting,** page 324.

*For use with Pillsbury's Best Self-Rising Flour, omit baking powder and salt.

Skip-to-My-Lou Marble Cake

Junior Winner by Irma C. Purdy, Georgetown, Ohio

Here is a chocolate-and-white Quick-Mix marble cake that uses just one bowl and one basic batter—wonderful for a party.

BAKE at 350° for 35 to 40 minutes   MAKES two 9-inch layers

Sift together 2½ cups sifted **Pillsbury's Best All Purpose Flour***
           1⅔ cups **sugar**
           4 teaspoons double-acting **baking powder** and
           1 teaspoon **salt** into large mixing bowl.
Add........⅔ cup **shortening**
           1 cup **milk**
Beat..........1½ minutes. (With mixer use a low speed.)
Add........5 unbeaten **egg whites** (⅔ cup)
           ¼ cup **milk** and
           1½ teaspoons **vanilla.** Beat 1½ minutes.
Divide........two-thirds of batter into two 9-inch round layer pans, well greased and lightly floured on the bottoms.
Combine.....1 square (1 oz.) melted unsweetened **chocolate**

2 tablespoons **warm water**

¼ teaspoon **soda** and

¼ teaspoon **red food coloring.** Blend into remaining batter.

Spoon . . . . chocolate batter evenly over white batter. Spread carefully; cut through batter with knife in both directions to give marble effect.

Bake . . . . at 350° for 35 to 40 minutes. Cool; frost with **Rich Chocolate Frosting,** page 322.

For use with Pillsbury's Best Self-Rising Flour, omit baking powder and salt.

Mocha-Nut Marble Cake

Senior Winner by Mrs. Alfred Bennyworth, St. Louis, Missouri

Two distinctly different cakes in one! Almond-flavored white cake and mocha-flavored nut cake marbled together.

BAKE at 350° for 35 to 40 minutes   MAKES two 9-inch layers

WHITE BATTER

Sift together 1½ cups sifted **Pillsbury's Best All Purpose Flour***

1 cup **sugar**

2 teaspoons double-acting **baking powder** and

½ teaspoon **salt** into mixing bowl.

Add . . . . ⅓ cup **shortening**

½ cup **water** and

1 teaspoon **almond extract**

Beat . . . . 1½ minutes. (With mixer use a low speed.)

Add . . . . 4 unbeaten **egg whites.** Beat 1½ minutes.

MOCHA-NUT BATTER

Sift together 1½ cups sifted **Pillsbury's Best All Purpose Flour***

1 cup firmly packed **brown sugar**

2 teaspoons double-acting **baking powder** and

½ teaspoon **salt** into mixing bowl.

Mocha-Nut Marble Cake

Add . . . . ⅓ cup **shortening**

½ cup cold strong **coffee** and

½ teaspoon **lemon extract**

Beat . . . . 1½ minutes.

Add . . . . 4 unbeaten **egg yolks.** Beat 1½ minutes.

Stir in . . . . . . ½ cup **nuts,** chopped

Spoon . . . . light and dark batters alternately into two 9-inch round layer pans, at least 1½ inches deep, well greased and lightly floured on the bottoms. Cut through batters gently with spatula to marble.

Bake . . . . at 350° for 35 to 40 minutes. Cool; frost with **Mocha Sea-Foam Frosting,** page 318.

For use with Pillsbury's Best Self-Rising Flour, omit baking powder and salt.

Gold-In-Shadows Cake

Senior Winner by Mrs. Elizabeth M. Baird, St. Joseph, Missouri

Gold and spice batters are combined in this heavenly light Quick-Mix marble cake.

BAKE at 350° for 35 to 40 minutes   MAKES two 9-inch layers

Sift together 2⅓ cups sifted **Pillsbury's Best All Purpose Flour***
　　　　　　3 teaspoons double-acting **baking powder** and
　　　　　　1 teaspoon **salt.** Set aside.
Add . . . . 1½ cups **sugar** gradually to
　　　　　　½ cup **shortening,** creaming well.
Add . . . . 1¼ cups **milk**
　　　　　　1½ teaspoons **vanilla** and sifted dry ingredients.
Beat . . . . 1½ minutes. (With mixer use a low speed.)
Add . . . . 5 unbeaten **egg yolks;** beat 1½ minutes.
Place . . . . half of batter in another bowl. Add

Viennese Marble Cake

　　　　　　2 tablespoons **dark corn syrup**
　　　　　　1 teaspoon **cinnamon**
　　　　　　½ teaspoon **nutmeg** and
　　　　　　½ teaspoon **cloves;** mix thoroughly.
Spoon . . . . light and dark batters alternately into two 9-inch
　　　　　　round layer pans, well greased and lightly floured
　　　　　　on the bottoms.
Bake . . . . at 350° for 35 to 40 minutes. Cool; frost with
　　　　　　Fluffy Marshmallow Frosting, page 317.

**For use with Pillsbury's Best Self-Rising Flour, omit baking powder and salt.*

Viennese Marble Cake

Senior Winner by Mrs. Louis O. Stanchfield, Mansfield, Ohio

See and taste an appealing combination—soft yellow cake, apricot preserves, small mounds of chocolate cake—all baked together.

BAKE at 350° for 30 to 35 minutes   MAKES 13x9-inch cake

Sift together 2¼ cups sifted **Pillsbury's Best All Purpose Flour***
　　　　　　1 cup **sugar**
　　　　　　1 teaspoon **soda** and
　　　　　　½ teaspoon **salt** into large mixing bowl.
Cut in . . . . . . ½ cup **butter** or margarine until particles are fine.
Add . . . . 2 unbeaten **eggs**
　　　　　　1 cup **sour cream** (thick or commercial) and
　　　　　　1 teaspoon **vanilla.** Beat 2 minutes. (With mixer use
　　　　　　a low speed.)
Turn . . . . into 13x9x2-inch pan, well greased and lightly floured
　　　　　　on bottom; reserve 1 cup for topping.
Spread with . . ⅔ cup **apricot preserves.** Sprinkle with
　　　　　　½ cup **nuts,** chopped
Add . . . . 3 tablespoons **cocoa**
　　　　　　1 tablespoon **milk** and
　　　　　　¼ teaspoon **soda** to reserved batter; mix well. Drop
　　　　　　by teaspoonfuls over preserves.

Bake........at 350° for 30 to 35 minutes. Serve warm or cold,
plain or with whipped cream.

For use with Pillsbury's Best Self-Rising Flour, omit soda and salt.

Caramel Marble Cake

Senior Winner by Mrs. T. J. Cruickshank, Coos Bay, Oregon

Melted candy caramels are marbled into the yellow cake batter.

BAKE at 350° for 45 to 50 minutes   MAKES 9x9-inch cake

Melt........5 ounces **candy caramels** (18 to 20) with
¼ cup **cream** in top of double boiler over hot water.
Keep warm but not hot.
Sift together..2 cups sifted **Pillsbury's Best All Purpose Flour***
3 teaspoons double-acting **baking powder** and
½ teaspoon **salt**. Set aside.
Combine.....1 cup **sugar**
½ cup **shortening**
2 unbeaten **eggs** and
1 teaspoon **vanilla** in mixing bowl. Beat 2 minutes.
Add..........the dry ingredients alternately with
1 cup **milk**. Blend well after each addition.
Pour..........one-third of batter into a second bowl. Fold in the
melted caramel mixture.
Spoon........white and caramel batters alternately into 9x9x2-
inch pan, well greased and lightly floured on the
bottom.
Bake........at 350° for 45 to 50 minutes. Cool; frost with
Maple Fluff Frosting, page 320.

For use with Pillsbury's Best Self-Rising Flour, omit baking powder and salt.

CUPCAKES

—You will find a variety of "little cakes" in this
section . . . from simple cupcakes for the lunchbox
to dainty cakes suitable for parties and wedding
receptions.

For best results, bake in muffin cups lined with
paper baking cups. Cups are usually filled one-half
to two-thirds full. Use a small round ice cream scoop
to fill muffin cups or paper liners. It's handy to use
and insures even-sized cupcakes.

For special occasions, make each cupcake different
by varying icings and decorations. Cakes may be
split crosswise or lengthwise and filled before they
are frosted.

Little Miss Muffet Cakes

Senior Winner by Mrs. Marie C. Slater, Baltimore, Maryland

Quick and easy to make—these little cakes are good served warm.

BAKE at 350° for 30 to 35 minutes   MAKES 2 dozen

Sift together 2¼ cups sifted **Pillsbury's Best All Purpose Flour***
1 teaspoon **salt** and
½ teaspoon **soda**. Set aside.
Add......1½ cups firmly packed **brown sugar** gradually to
½ cup **shortening**, creaming well.
Stir in......1 unbeaten **egg**; beat well.
Blend in....1½ cups (12 oz.) creamed **cottage cheese** and
2 tablespoons **cream**
Add..........the dry ingredients gradually; mix well.
Stir in......1 cup **raisins,** chopped, and
1 teaspoon grated **lemon rind**
Fill..........muffin cups, lined with paper baking cups, half full.
Bake........at 350° for 30 to 35 minutes. Serve warm, or cool
and frost with **Lemon Icing,** page 327.

For use with Pillsbury's Best Self-Rising Flour, omit salt and soda.

Swift Currant Cakes

Swift Currant Cakes

Senior First Prize Winner by Mrs. Osborne C. Phelan, Miami Shores, Florida

Refreshing currant flavor highlights these basic yellow cupcakes. Fruit baba sauce spooned over after baking adds sparkle, too!

BAKE at 350° for 20 to 25 minutes   MAKES about 2 dozen

Combine . . . . ½ cup **sugar**
          ¼ cup **water** and
          1 tablespoon grated **orange rind** in saucepan. Bring to a boil and remove from heat.
Add . . . . 1 cup dried **currants** and
          1 tablespoon **rum extract.** Let stand 30 minutes. Drain thoroughly, reserving syrup.
Sift together . . 2 cups sifted **Pillsbury's Best All Purpose Flour***

          3 teaspoons double-acting **baking powder** and
          ½ teaspoon **salt**
Cream . . . . . . ½ cup **butter** or margarine. Gradually add
          ¾ cup **sugar,** creaming well.
Blend in . . . . . 2 unbeaten **eggs** and
          1 teaspoon **vanilla**
Add . . . . the dry ingredients alternately with
          ¾ cup **milk.** Blend well after each addition.
Blend in . . . . drained currants. Fill muffin cups, lined with paper baking cups, half full.
Bake . . . . at 350° for 20 to 25 minutes. Prick tops.
Heat . . . . reserved syrup. Spoon ½ teaspoon over each hot cupcake. When cool, sprinkle with **confectioners' sugar,** frost with **Orange Frosting,** page 327, or serve plain.

*For use with Pillsbury's Best Self-Rising Flour, omit baking powder and salt.

Gang-Way Ginger Gems

Junior Winner by Walter John Rapp, Oaklawn, Illinois

Spicy ginger cupcakes dressed up with marmalade-flavored whipped cream and a cake "top hat."

BAKE at 350° for 15 to 20 minutes   MAKES 1 dozen

Sift together 1¼ cups sifted **Pillsbury's Best All Purpose Flour***
          1 teaspoon **cinnamon**
          ¾ teaspoon **soda**
          ½ teaspoon **salt**
          ½ teaspoon **ginger** and
          ¼ teaspoon **nutmeg.** Set aside.
Add . . . . ½ cup **sugar** gradually to
          ⅓ cup **shortening,** creaming well.
Blend in . . . . . ⅓ cup **molasses** and
          1 unbeaten **egg.** Add the dry ingredients; mix well.
Blend in . . . . . ½ cup **boiling water,** stirring until smooth.

Fill . . . . .muffin cups, lined with paper baking cups, one-third to one-half full.

Bake . . . . .at 350° for 15 to 20 minutes. Cool. Cut cone-shaped piece from center of each; fill hollow with Orange Fluff Cream. Top with cut-outs.

*For use with Pillsbury's Best Self-Rising Flour, decrease soda to ¼ teaspoon and omit salt.

ORANGE FLUFF CREAM

Beat ½ cup whipping cream until thick. Fold in ¼ cup orange marmalade.

Sugar 'n' Spice Gems

Junior Winner by Mona Benn, Linden, Pennsylvania

These spicy brown sugar cupcakes have nuts and raisins folded into them.

BAKE at 350° for 20 to 25 minutes   MAKES 2 dozen

Sift together . .2 cups sifted **Pillsbury's Best All Purpose Flour***
1 teaspoon **soda**
1 teaspoon **salt**
½ teaspoon **nutmeg**
½ teaspoon **cinnamon** and
¼ teaspoon **cloves**

Mix in . . . . . . .1 cup **raisins** and
½ cup **walnuts**, chopped. Set aside.

Add . . . . .1 cup firmly packed **brown sugar** gradually to
½ cup **shortening**, creaming thoroughly.

Blend in . . . . .2 unbeaten **eggs**, beating well after each.

Add . . . . .1 cup **buttermilk** or sour milk alternately with the dry ingredients. Blend well after each addition.

Fill . . . . .muffin cups, lined with paper baking cups, half full.

Bake . . . . .at 350° for 20 to 25 minutes. Cool; frost with **Lemon Butter Frosting,** page 324.

*For use with Pillsbury's Best Self-Rising Flour, decrease soda to ½ teaspoon and omit salt.

Peachy Date Cakes

Senior Winner by Mrs. Emil Christensen, Sharon, Massachusetts

Wonderful addition to a buffet party . . . tender cupcakes dotted with bits of dates and peaches.

BAKE at 350° for 30 to 35 minutes   MAKES about 20

Combine . . . . .1 cup **dates,** finely cut
½ cup finely cut canned **peaches**
1 teaspoon **soda*** and
¾ cup **boiling peach juice.** Cool.

Sift together 1½ cups sifted **Pillsbury's Best All Purpose Flour*** and
½ teaspoon **salt**

Cream . . . . . .½ cup **butter** or margarine. Gradually add
1 cup **sugar,** creaming well.

Blend in . . . . .2 unbeaten **eggs** and
1 teaspoon **vanilla.** Beat well.

Add . . . . .the dry ingredients; blend thoroughly. Stir in the fruit mixture; mix well.

Fill . . . . .muffin cups, lined with paper baking cups, two-thirds full.

Bake . . . . .at 350° for 30 to 35 minutes. Serve sprinkled with **confectioners' sugar,** frosted with **Brown-Butter Icing,** page 327, or as a dessert with whipped cream.

*For use with Pillsbury's Best Self-Rising Flour, omit soda and salt.

Cocoa-Pink Cuplets

Cocoa-Pink Cuplets

Senior Winner by Mrs. Robert Hoefer, Brookfield, Wisconsin

Lunch box treats! Delicately-flavored cupcakes with built-in frosting will disappear fast.

BAKE at 375° for 20 to 25 minutes   MAKES about 2 dozen

Sift together . . 2 cups sifted **Pillsbury's Best All Purpose Flour***
          1 tablespoon **cocoa** and
          1 teaspoon **salt.** Set aside.
Add . . . . 1¼ cups **sugar** gradually to
          ¾ cup **shortening,** creaming well.
Blend in . . . . . 2 unbeaten **eggs** and
          1 teaspoon **vanilla**
Combine . . . . . 1 teaspoon **soda** and

1 cup cold **water.** Add alternately with the dry ingredients to creamed mixture. Blend well after each addition.
Fill . . . . muffin cups, lined with paper baking cups, half full.
Sprinkle . . . . . 1 cup (6 oz.) **semi-sweet chocolate pieces** and
          ½ cup **nuts,** chopped, over cupcake batter.
Bake . . . . at 375° for 20 to 25 minutes.
For use with Pillsbury's Best Self-Rising Flour, omit salt and decrease soda to ¼ teaspoon.

Parisian Sophisticates

Senior Winner by Mrs. Warren H. Thorpe, Macon, Georgia

Almond cupcakes with a dark and satiny French chocolate filling and a sprinkling of toasted cupcake crumbs.

BAKE at 375° for 20 to 25 minutes   MAKES 1½ dozen

Sift together . . 2 cups sifted **Pillsbury's Best All Purpose Flour***
          1 teaspoon double-acting **baking powder**
          ½ teaspoon **soda** and
          ¼ teaspoon **salt**
Cream . . . . . . ½ cup **butter** or margarine. Gradually add
          1 cup **sugar,** creaming well.
Add . . . . 2 unbeaten **eggs,** beating well after each.
Combine . . . . ⅔ cup **buttermilk** or sour milk
          1 teaspoon **vanilla** and
          ½ teaspoon **almond extract.** Add alternately with the dry ingredients to creamed mixture. Blend well after each addition.
Fill . . . . muffin cups, lined with paper baking cups, half full.
Bake . . . . at 375° for 20 to 25 minutes. Cool.
Cut . . . . a cone from center of cupcakes; fill with Truffle Filling. Crumble centers and toast under broiler. Sprinkle over Filling in cupcakes.
For use with Pillsbury's Best Self-Rising Flour, omit baking powder, soda, salt.

TRUFFLE FILLING

Combine ¼ cup sugar, 3 tablespoons water and 2 squares (2 oz.) unsweetened chocolate in saucepan. Cook over low heat, stirring constantly, until chocolate melts. Remove from heat and blend in 3 egg yolks, one at a time, beating well after each. Stir in 1 teaspoon vanilla. Beat 3 egg whites until soft mounds form. Gradually add ¼ cup sugar; continue beating until stiff peaks form. Fold chocolate mixture into egg whites gently but thoroughly.

Festive Prune Cakes

Senior Winner by Mrs. Evan H. Lewis, Akron, Ohio

The spicy flavor is the big thing about these moist cupcakes.

BAKE at 350° for 20 to 25 minutes   MAKES 2 dozen

Sift together . . 2 cups sifted **Pillsbury's Best All Purpose Flour***
    1 teaspoon **soda**
    1 teaspoon **salt**
    1 teaspoon **cinnamon**
    ¼ teaspoon **nutmeg** and
    ¼ teaspoon **allspice.** Set aside.

Add . . . . 1 cup **sugar** gradually to
    ½ cup **shortening,** creaming well.
Blend in . . . . . 2 unbeaten **eggs,** beating well after each.
Add . . . . the dry ingredients alternately with
    1 cup **prune juice.** Blend well after each addition.
Fold in . . . . . . 1 cup cooked **prunes,** chopped, and
    ¾ cup **nuts,** chopped
Fill . . . . muffin cups, lined with paper baking cups, half full.
Bake . . . . at 350° for 20 to 25 minutes. Cool; frost with
    Orange Frosting, page 327.
*For use with Pillsbury's Best Self-Rising Flour, omit soda and salt.

Pineapple Tea Cakes

Senior Winner by Mrs. William Kretchman, Atkinson, Nebraska

Featuring pineapple and chocolate bits! These cakes stay fresh for days.

BAKE at 350° for 20 to 25 minutes   MAKES about 1½ dozen

Sift together . . 2 cups sifted **Pillsbury's Best All Purpose Flour***
    1 teaspoon double-acting **baking powder**
    1 teaspoon **salt** and
    ½ teaspoon **soda.** Set aside.
Add . . . . ½ cup **sugar** and
    ½ cup firmly packed **brown sugar** gradually to
    ½ cup **shortening,** creaming well.
Blend in . . . . . 2 unbeaten **eggs,** beating well after each.
Add . . . . ½ cup undrained, **crushed pineapple**
Add . . . . the dry ingredients alternately with
    ½ cup **water.** Blend well after each addition.
Stir in . . . . 1 teaspoon **vanilla** and
    1 cup (6 oz.) **semi-sweet chocolate pieces**
Fill . . . . muffin cups, lined with paper baking cups, half full.
Bake . . . . at 350° for 20 to 25 minutes. Cool; frost with
    Pineapple Butter Frosting, page 327.
*For use with Pillsbury's Best Self-Rising Flour, omit baking powder and salt.

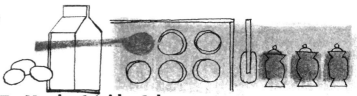

Trio Cupcakes

Junior Winner by Mary Ruddick, Washington, D. C.

Three-layer cupcakes made from one simple Quick-Mix batter divided in three and flavored with orange, spices and vanilla.

BAKE at 375° for 20 to 25 minutes   MAKES 2 dozen

Sift together . . 2 cups sifted **Pillsbury's Best All Purpose Flour***
            1½ cups **sugar**
            3 teaspoons double-acting **baking powder** and
            1 teaspoon **salt** into large mixing bowl.
Add . . . . ½ cup **shortening** and
            ¾ cup **milk**.
Beat . . . . 1½ minutes. (With mixer, use a low speed.)
Add . . . . ¼ cup **milk** and
            ½ cup **egg whites**. Beat 1½ minutes.
Divide . . . . batter into 3 parts.
Add . . . . 1 tablespoon grated **orange rind**
            1 teaspoon **orange juice** and
            4 drops **yellow food coloring** to first part.
Blend . . . . . . ¾ teaspoon **cinnamon**
            ¼ teaspoon **cloves** and
            ¼ teaspoon **allspice** into second part.
Add . . . . ½ teaspoon **vanilla** to third part.
Place . . . . one level tablespoonful of each batter into muffin
            cups, lined with paper baking cups.
Bake . . . . at 375° for 20 to 25 minutes. Cool; frost with
            Orange Frosting, page 327.

For use with Pillsbury's Best Self-Rising Flour, omit baking powder and salt.

Maple Crinkle Cakes

Bride Winner by Mrs. August A. Linse, Jr., Eau Claire, Wisconsin

Maple syrup flavors these Quick-Mix cupcakes and their "lazy daisy" broiled-on topping.

BAKE at 375° for 20 to 25 minutes   MAKES 2 to 2½ dozen

Sift together 2¼ cups sifted **Pillsbury's Best All Purpose Flour***
            ½ cup **sugar**
            3 teaspoons double-acting **baking powder** and
            1 teaspoon **salt** into large mixing bowl.
Add . . . . ½ cup **shortening**
            ½ cup **milk**
            1 cup **maple syrup**
Beat . . . . 1½ minutes. (With mixer use a low speed.)
Add . . . . 2 unbeaten **eggs;** beat 1½ minutes.
Fill . . . . muffin cups, lined with paper baking cups, half full.
Bake . . . . at 375° for 20 to 25 minutes. Remove from oven.
            Turn oven to "broil."
Spread . . . . Coconut Topping over each cupcake, covering completely. Place 4 to 5 inches below broiling unit.
Broil . . . . 1 to 3 minutes until golden brown, watching carefully. Remove from pans immediately.

For use with Pillsbury's Best Self-Rising Flour, omit baking powder and salt.

COCONUT TOPPING

Cream together ¼ cup butter and ½ cup firmly packed brown sugar. Blend in 2 tablespoons light cream, 1 tablespoon maple syrup and 1 cup coconut, chopped.

Cloud-Topped Cakettes

Senior Winner by Ruth Roitman, Chicago, Illinois

Deep red devil's food cupcakes, topped with a chocolate rum candy wafer and a "cloud" of meringue.

BAKE at 350° for 25 to 30 minutes   MAKES 1 dozen

Combine.....1 square (1 oz.) unsweetened **chocolate**
½ cup **water** and
⅓ cup **shortening** in saucepan. Heat until chocolate is melted, stirring constantly. Cool.

Sift together..1 cup sifted **Pillsbury's Best All Purpose Flour***
⅔ cup **sugar**
¾ teaspoon **soda** and
¼ teaspoon **salt**. Add to chocolate mixture. Mix well.

Add........2 unbeaten **egg yolks**
¼ cup **sour cream** and
1 teaspoon **vanilla**. Blend until smooth.

Fill..........muffin cups, lined with paper baking cups, half full.

Bake........at 350° for 25 to 30 minutes. Remove from oven. Turn oven to 450°.

Place........1 solid **chocolate rum candy wafer** on each hot cupcake. Top with rounded tablespoon of Meringue.

Bake........at 450° for 2 to 5 minutes until golden brown.

For use with Pillsbury's Best Self-Rising Flour, decrease soda to ¼ teaspoon and omit salt.

MERINGUE

Beat 2 egg whites until soft mounds form. Gradually add ¼ cup firmly packed brown sugar and ¼ teaspoon cream of tartar, beating well after each addition. Continue beating until meringue stands in stiff peaks.

Turnover Cupcakes

Senior Winner by Mrs. Joseph A. Melanson, Attleboro, Massachusetts

A spicy crumb topping, a cherry and peach slice go into these upside-down Quick-Mix cupcakes.

BAKE at 375° for 20 to 25 minutes   MAKES 1 dozen

Combine.....3 tablespoons soft **butter** or margarine
¼ cup **sugar**
¼ cup dry **bread crumbs**
2 tablespoons **flour**
¼ teaspoon **salt** and
½ teaspoon **cinnamon**

Prepare.......muffin cups; grease well and place a **maraschino cherry half** in each cup. Cover with about 2 teaspoonfuls of the crumb mixture; top with a well-drained **peach slice.**

Sift together 1¼ cups sifted **Pillsbury's Best All Purpose Flour***
⅔ cup **sugar**
2 teaspoons double-acting **baking powder** and
½ teaspoon **salt** into mixing bowl.

Add........½ cup **milk**
¼ cup **shortening**
1 unbeaten **egg** and
1 teaspoon **vanilla**. Beat 2 minutes. (With mixer use medium speed.)

Fill..........muffin cups one-third to one-half full.

Bake........at 375° for 20 to 25 minutes. Cool 3 to 5 minutes before turning out. Serve warm with **whipped cream** or ice cream.

For use with Pillsbury's Best Self-Rising Flour, omit baking powder and salt.

Watermelon Tea-Ettes

Senior Winner by Mrs. Milo D. Lucas, Enid, Oklahoma

Chopped watermelon pickles give a delightful flavor pick-up to these moist, spicy little cupcakes.

BAKE at 350° for 25 to 30 minutes   MAKES 1½ dozen

Combine.....1 cup **sugar**
1 cup **water**
1 cup (10-oz. jar) **watermelon pickles**, finely chopped
½ cup **butter** or margarine
1 teaspoon **cinnamon** and
½ teaspoon **cloves** in large saucepan; bring to boil. Cool at least 30 minutes.
Sift together..2 cups sifted **Pillsbury's Best All Purpose Flour***
1 teaspoon **soda** and
¼ teaspoon **salt** into mixture in saucepan.
Add........1 cup **pecans**, chopped, and
1 teaspoon **vanilla.** Mix thoroughly.
Fill..........muffin cups, lined with paper baking cups, about half full.
Bake........at 350° for 25 to 30 minutes. Cool; frost with **Creamy Cinnamon Frosting**, page 325.

For use with Pillsbury's Best Self-Rising Flour, omit salt and soda.

Spicy Oatmeal Cakes

Senior Winner by Mrs. Roy Slingerland, Davison, Michigan

Spices, oatmeal and molasses give unusual flavor and texture to these moist little cupcakes.

BAKE at 350° for 25 to 30 minutes   MAKES 1½ dozen

Sift together..2 cups sifted **Pillsbury's Best All Purpose Flour***
2 teaspoons double-acting **baking powder**
1 teaspoon **cinnamon**
¼ teaspoon **cloves** and
¼ teaspoon **nutmeg.** Set aside.
Blend.......2 unbeaten **eggs** with
1½ cups **sugar** in large saucepan.
Add......1½ cups **milk** and
½ cup **butter** or margarine. Cook over high heat, stirring occasionally, until mixture boils. Cool to lukewarm, about 30 minutes.
Stir in......¼ cup quick-cooking **rolled oats** and
3 tablespoons **molasses**
Add..........the dry ingredients. Blend, then beat 1 minute.
Fill..........muffin cups, lined with paper baking cups, about half full.
Bake........at 350° for 25 to 30 minutes. Cool; frost with **Quick Molasses Icing,** page 327.

For use with Pillsbury's Best Self-Rising Flour, omit baking powder.

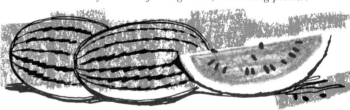

Little Almond Secrets

Senior Winner by Mrs. Charles Lickton, La Belle, Florida

There's hidden marzipan filling in each of these tender lemon sponge cupcakes, topped with buttery almond glaze.

BAKE at 350° for 15 to 20 minutes   MAKES 1½ dozen

Prepare.......Marzipan Cookies; see below.
Sift together..1 cup sifted **Pillsbury's Best All Purpose Flour***
1 teaspoon double-acting **baking powder** and
¼ teaspoon **salt**
Beat........2 **eggs** until thick and ivory colored.

Add . . . . 1 cup **sugar** gradually, beating constantly. Stir in
1 teaspoon **lemon extract**

Blend in . . . . the dry ingredients gradually. Add
½ cup **hot milk** and
1 tablespoon **soft butter;** blend well.

Fill . . . . muffin cups, lined with paper baking cups, about
half full. Place Marzipan Cookie in each cup; push
into batter until almost covered.

Bake . . . . at 350° for 15 to 20 minutes. Remove from oven.
Turn oven to "broil." Spread Almond Topping over
each cupcake. Broil until golden brown, 2 to 3
minutes.

For use with Pillsbury's Best Self-Rising Flour, omit baking powder and salt.

MARZIPAN COOKIES

Combine ½ cup almonds, ground, ¼ cup confectioners' sugar, ¼ teaspoon almond extract, 1 tablespoon egg white and ⅛ teaspoon salt; mix well. Drop by teaspoonfuls onto greased baking sheets, making 18. Bake at 350° for 10 minutes. Remove from baking sheet; cool. (For a more moist filling, do not bake marzipan.)

ALMOND TOPPING

Combine ½ cup sugar, ¼ cup flour, ⅓ cup butter or margarine and 2 tablespoons cream in saucepan. Heat, stirring constantly, to boiling. Remove from heat; stir in ⅓ cup slivered almonds.

Macaroon Angel Cakes

Senior Winner by Mrs. B. William Warren, Asheville, North Carolina

These tempting little cupcakes remind you of coconut macaroons. They're made of angel food batter—wonderful at teatime.

BAKE at 300° for 40 to 45 minutes   MAKES 2 to 2½ dozen

Sift together   ¾ cup sifted **Pillsbury's Best All Purpose Flour***
1 cup **sugar**

Macaroon Angel Cakes

½ teaspoon double-acting **baking powder** and
½ teaspoon **salt**

Beat . . . . 6 **egg whites** (¾ cup) with
½ teaspoon **cream of tartar**
½ teaspoon **vanilla** and
½ teaspoon **almond extract** until soft mounds form.

Add . . . . ⅓ cup **sugar** gradually, beating well after each addition.
Continue beating until stiff peaks form.

Fold in . . . . the dry ingredients gently but thoroughly; add
1 cup **coconut**

Fill . . . . paper baking cups about half full. Place in muffin
cups or on baking sheets.

Bake . . . . at 300° for 40 to 45 minutes.

For use with Pillsbury's Best Self-Rising Flour, omit baking powder and salt.

FOAM CAKES

include angel food cakes and spongecakes. The main difference between angel food and spongecakes is that angel foods use egg whites only, while spongecakes are made with egg yolks or both yolks and whites.

These cakes depend mainly upon the air beaten into the batter for leavening. (Air expands during baking to make the cake light.) That is why it is important to beat the eggs sufficiently and to handle the batter carefully when the beaten eggs are combined with dry ingredients.

An electric mixer may be used for beating egg whites and yolks. For most efficient mixing, use the small mixer bowl for egg yolks and for 4 or fewer egg whites.

The folding process must be done by hand. Folding is a gentle mixing motion that combines ingredients without losing the air that has been beaten into the yolks or whites. To fold properly, use a wire whisk or rubber spatula; cut down through batter on the far side of the bowl, bring the utensil across bottom of the bowl, up on the near side and over the top to the far side again. Repeat, turning the bowl with each fold, until dry particles disappear.

Foam cakes are usually baked in ungreased 9 or 10-inch tube pans; the center tube gives more support to the delicate batter. The batter clings to the sides and center tube of the pan during rising; greasing would result in an undersized cake.

Angel food and spongecakes are very delicate when taken from the oven and will shrink unless inverted in the pan and allowed to cool thoroughly. Allow space between cooling surface and cake for air to circulate. When cooled, carefully release cake from pan by cutting with a narrow knife or metal spatula with straight motions down and up between cake and pan. Continue around outer edge and center tube, then tap pan to release cake.

Jelly-roll cakes are usually foam-type cakes. For jelly rolls, spread foam-cake batter into a 15½x10½x1-inch pan, greased and lined with waxed paper. (If you do not have a jelly-roll pan, place an 18x12-inch sheet of heavy-duty aluminum foil on baking sheet; fold sides to make a 15x10x1-inch pan; grease bottom.) Jelly-roll cakes bake quickly and must be removed from pan immediately after baking.

When filling a jelly roll, leave one end uncovered; begin rolling with opposite end. Place filled jelly roll on serving plate, seam-side down. Slice to serve.

Quick-Trick Angel Cake

Senior Winner by Mrs. Virgil Hogdal, Constance, Minnesota

This angel food bakes in less than half the usual time, is moist and has a dark golden-brown crust.

BAKE at 475° for 10 minutes, then   MAKES 9 or 10-inch tube cake
at 425° for 15 minutes

Sift together ..1 cup sifted **Pillsbury's Best All Purpose Flour*** and
½ cup sifted **confectioners' sugar** three times.

Beat .... 1½ cups **egg whites** (10 to 12 eggs) with
1 teaspoon **salt*** and
1½ teaspoons **cream of tartar** in large mixing bowl until
soft mounds form.

Add ....1 cup **sugar** gradually, beating well after each addition.
Add
1 teaspoon **vanilla** and
½ teaspoon **almond extract;** continue beating until
stiff, straight peaks form.

Sift .... the dry ingredients gradually over beaten egg whites,
folding gently but thoroughly.

Turn .... into ungreased 9 or 10-inch tube pan. Cut gently
through batter with knife. Cover pan tightly with
aluminum foil.

Bake ....at 475° for 10 minutes; remove foil and bake at 425°
for 15 minutes.* Invert; cool. Serve plain or with
whipped cream.

**For use with Pillsbury's Best Self-Rising Flour, decrease salt to ½ teaspoon.
Bake at 475° for 15 minutes; remove foil and bake at 425° for 10 to 15 minutes.*

Pink Lemonade Angel Cake

Senior Winner by Mrs. Robert L. Kain, Wheeling, West Virginia

A pink angel food—high, light, delicate—with a refreshing lemon flavor.

BAKE at 325° for 50 to 60 minutes   MAKES 9 or 10-inch tube cake

Sift together . ¾ cup sifted **Pillsbury's Best All Purpose Flour***
            ¾ cup **sugar** and
            ¼ cup **cornstarch** three times.
Beat . . . . 1½ cups **egg whites** (10 to 12 eggs) with
            1½ teaspoons **cream of tartar**
            ¼ teaspoon **salt** and
            1¼ teaspoons **lemon extract** in large mixing bowl until soft mounds form.
Add . . . . ¾ cup **sugar** gradually, beating well after each addition.
Add . . . . 4 to 6 drops **red food coloring**. Continue beating until stiff, straight peaks form.
Sift . . . . the dry ingredients gradually over beaten egg whites, folding gently but thoroughly.
Turn . . . . into ungreased 9 or 10-inch tube pan. Cut gently through batter with knife.
Bake . . . . at 325° for 50 to 60 minutes. Invert; cool. Serve plain or with whipped cream.

For use with Pillsbury's Best Self-Rising Flour, omit salt.

Pecan-Chocolate Angel Cake

Senior Winner by Mrs. James Walch, Camp Carson, Colorado

A delicate chocolate angel food, filled with chopped pecans.

BAKE at 325° for 50 to 60 minutes*   MAKES 9 or 10-inch tube cake

Sift together . ¾ cup sifted **Pillsbury's Best All Purpose Flour***
            ¾ cup **sugar** and
            ¼ cup **cocoa** three times.
Beat . . . . 1½ cups **egg whites** (10 to 12 eggs) with

            1½ teaspoons **cream of tartar**
            ½ teaspoon **salt** and
            1½ teaspoons **vanilla** in large mixing bowl until soft mounds form.
Add . . . . ¾ cup **sugar** gradually; continue beating until stiff, straight peaks form.
Sift . . . . the dry ingredients, about 2 tablespoons at a time, over beaten egg whites. Fold gently but thoroughly.
Fold in . . . . . . 1 cup **pecans**, finely chopped
Turn . . . . into ungreased 9 or 10-inch tube pan. Cut gently through batter with knife.
Bake . . . . at 325° for 50 to 60 minutes. Invert; cool.

For use with Pillsbury's Best Self-Rising Flour, omit salt; increase baking time to 60 to 70 minutes.

Mother's Sponge Cake

Senior Winner by Miss Margaret M. Sullivan, Newport, New Hampshire

Hot-milk sponge cake is an old-time favorite. Economical and easy.

BAKE at 350° for 30 to 35 minutes   MAKES 8x8-inch cake

Sift together . . 1 cup sifted **Pillsbury's Best All Purpose Flour***
            1 teaspoon double-acting **baking powder** and
            ¼ teaspoon **salt**
Beat . . . . 2 **eggs** until thick and ivory colored.
Add . . . . 1 cup **sugar** gradually; beat well after each addition.
Stir in . . . . the dry ingredients all at once, gently but quickly.
Add . . . . 1 teaspoon **vanilla** and
            ½ cup hot scalded **milk** all at once. Mix thoroughly, blending as quickly as possible.
Turn . . . . into 8x8x2-inch pan, well greased and lightly floured on the bottom.
Bake . . . . at 350° for 30 to 35 minutes. If desired, spread with **Broiled Frosting**, page 324.

For use with Pillsbury's Best Self-Rising Flour, omit baking powder and salt.

Danish Wonder Cake

Senior Winner by Mrs. Helen J. Kliesrath, Huntington, Long Island, New York

Rich butter-sponge layers, split and filled with a mocha-nut filling, iced with a simple frosting. (Prepare it ahead of time for parties!)

BAKE at 350° for 25 to 30 minutes   MAKES two 8-inch layers

Sift together 1½ cups sifted **Pillsbury's Best All Purpose Flour*** and
1 teaspoon double-acting **baking powder**

Beat . . . . 5 **eggs** (1 cup) until thick. Gradually add
½ cup **sugar**; continue beating until thick and ivory colored.

Cream . . . . . . ¾ cup **butter** or margarine. Gradually add
¾ cup **sugar**, creaming well. Blend in
1 teaspoon **vanilla** and egg mixture; beat well.

Add . . . . the dry ingredients gradually. Mix thoroughly.

Turn . . . . into two 8-inch round layer pans, well greased and lightly floured on the bottoms.

Bake . . . . at 350° for 25 to 30 minutes. Cool. Split layers in half, making four thin layers. Fill with **Chocolate Coffee Filling**, page 329. Spread top and sides thinly with **Creamy Vanilla Frosting**, page 321. Sprinkle with chopped **pecans**. Chill.

*Pillsbury's Best Self-Rising Flour is not recommended for use in this recipe.

Happy Apple Sponge Cake

Senior Winner by Mrs. Grace England, Winlock, Washington

Salad oil gives moistness and sheen and apple juice lends flavor. More juice in the frosting . . . and applesauce in the filling.

BAKE at 325° for 30 to 35 minutes   MAKES two 8-inch square or 9-inch round layers

Sift together 1½ cups sifted **Pillsbury's Best All Purpose Flour***
¾ cup **sugar**
1½ teaspoons double-acting **baking powder**
½ teaspoon **nutmeg**
½ teaspoon **cinnamon**
¼ teaspoon **soda** and
¼ teaspoon **salt**

Beat . . . . 4 **egg whites** (½ cup) with
¼ teaspoon **cream of tartar** in large mixing bowl until soft mounds form.

Add . . . . ½ cup **sugar** gradually. Continue beating until very stiff, straight peaks form. *Do not underbeat.*

Beat . . . . 4 **egg yolks** until thick and lemon colored. Add
2 tablespoons **salad oil** and
½ cup **apple juice**; continue beating until well blended.

Blend in . . . . . . the dry ingredients gradually. (With mixer use lowest speed.)

Fold . . . . into beaten egg whites, one-third at a time, gently but thoroughly.

Turn . . . . into two 8x8x2-inch square or 9-inch round layer pans, greased on the bottoms and lined with waxed paper.

Bake . . . . at 325° for 30 to 35 minutes. Remove from pans immediately; cool. Fill with Apple Filling; frost with Nutty Apple Juice Frosting.

*For use with Pillsbury's Best Self-Rising Flour, omit baking powder, soda, salt.

APPLE FILLING

Combine ⅓ cup firmly packed brown sugar, 2 tablespoons flour, ½ teaspoon nutmeg, ½ teaspoon cinnamon, 1 egg yolk and 1¾ cups (17-oz. can) sweetened applesauce in saucepan. Cook over medium heat, stirring constantly, until thick, 10 to 12 minutes. Cool.

NUTTY APPLE JUICE FROSTING

Combine ¾ cup firmly packed brown sugar, 2 tablespoons light corn syrup, 1 egg white and 3 tablespoons apple juice in top of double boiler. Cook over rapidly boiling water, beating with electric mixer or rotary beater, until mixture stands in peaks. Remove from heat. Fold in ⅓ cup chopped walnuts.

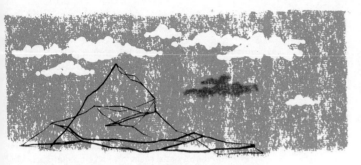

Chocolate Speckled Sponge Cake

Senior Winner by Mrs. Norman R. Hogue, Bismarck, North Dakota

Grated chocolate and ground walnuts give a novel appearance and pleasing flavor to this two-layer sponge cake.

BAKE at 375° for 25 to 30 minutes   MAKES two 9-inch layers

Sift together 1½ cups sifted **Pillsbury's Best All Purpose Flour***
          ½ teaspoon double-acting **baking powder** and
          ¼ teaspoon **salt**
Grind . . . . ⅔ cup **walnuts.** Reserve.
Beat . . . . 6 egg **yolks** and
          1⅓ cups **sugar** in large mixing bowl until thick and
          lemon colored (about 10 minutes with mixer at high
          speed).
Add . . . . ½ cup cold **water;** beat at low speed 1 minute.
Fold in . . . . the dry ingredients, one-third at a time,
          1 square (1 oz.) unsweetened **chocolate,** coarsely
          grated, and ⅓ cup of the ground walnuts. Fold gently
          but thoroughly.
Beat . . . . 6 egg **whites** with
          1 teaspoon **vanilla** until stiff but not dry. Fold into
          batter.
Turn . . . . batter into two 9-inch round layer pans, lined on the
          bottoms with waxed paper.

Bake . . . . at 375° for 25 to 30 minutes. Remove from pans
          immediately. Cool; frost with **Butter Cream Frosting,**
          page 314, and sprinkle with remaining walnuts.
*For use with Pillsbury's Best Self-Rising Flour, omit baking powder and salt.

Chocolate Cloud Cake

Senior Winner by Mrs. Robert L. Mayer, Miami, Florida

A double chocolate dream—milk chocolate candy in this tender sponge cake, with a fluffy chocolate frosting between layers and on top.

BAKE at 350° for 45 to 50 minutes   MAKES 9-inch cake*

Melt . . . . 4 or 5 ounces **milk chocolate candy**** in
          ¼ cup **water** over boiling water. Remove from heat;
          stir until smooth. Cool.
Sift together . ¾ cup sifted **Pillsbury's Best All Purpose Flour***** and
          ½ teaspoon **salt**
Beat . . . . 5 **egg whites** in mixing bowl until soft mounds form.
          Gradually add
          ⅔ cup **sugar;** beat until stiff, straight peaks form.
Beat . . . . 5 **egg yolks** until thick and lemon colored. Add
          ½ teaspoon **vanilla** and the cooled chocolate mixture.
          Beat until well blended and thick.
Fold . . . . the egg yolk mixture gently into egg whites, then
          fold in the dry ingredients carefully.
Turn . . . . into 9-inch spring-form pan, 3 inches deep, greased
          and lined with waxed paper on bottom.*
Bake . . . . at 350° for 45 to 50 minutes. Cool in pan at least 1
          hour. Cut crosswise into two layers. Fill and frost
          with **Chocolate Fluff Frosting,** page 316. Chill 1
          hour before serving.
          *Cake may be baked in two 8-inch round layer pans for 25 to 30 minutes, or in 9 or 10-inch tube pan for 45 to 50 minutes.
          **German's sweet chocolate may be substituted; increase water to ⅓ cup.
          ***For use with Pillsbury's Best Self-Rising Flour, omit salt.

Apricot Layers Supreme

Apricot Layers Supreme

Senior Winner by Mrs. Dora Balos, Newton, Massachusetts

Amaze your friends with this unique party cake . . . praiseworthy flavor combination and shaping.

BAKE at 375° for 15 to 20 minutes   MAKES 8-inch cake

Make . . . . a 15x12x1-inch pan from heavy-duty aluminum foil. Place on baking sheet.
Sift together 1¾ cups sifted **Pillsbury's Best All Purpose Flour** and
        ¼ teaspoon **salt**
Beat . . . . 7 **eggs** (1½ cups) until foamy. Gradually add
        1½ cups **sugar** and
        1 tablespoon grated **lemon rind.** Continue beating until thick and ivory colored.

Fold in . . . . the dry ingredients, one-fourth at a time, alternately with
        ½ cup **salad oil.** Fold gently but thoroughly.
Spread . . . . 1¾ cups of batter into each of two 8-inch round layer pans, greased on bottom, lined with waxed paper, greased again and floured. Spread remaining batter into foil pan.
Bake . . . . at 375° for 15 to 20 minutes. (Cakes do not have to be baked all at once.) Cool round layers 10 minutes; remove from pans. Remove foil from rectangular layer immediately and place on waxed paper sprinkled with **confectioners' sugar.** Trim edges. Spread with ¾ cup **apricot preserves** (break large pieces with fork).
Cut . . . . into six 15x2-inch strips. Roll one strip as for jelly roll, starting with 2-inch end. Wind remaining strips around the roll to form an 8-inch round layer. Place cut-side down. Cover and cool.
Place . . . . one round layer on serving plate; spread with **Coffee Cream Frosting,** page 324. Place rolled cake on top, spread with frosting and top with remaining layer. Frost top and sides.

*For use with Pillsbury's Best Self-Rising Flour, omit salt.

Frosty Sponge Layers

Senior Winner by Mrs. Gene Walden, Sparta, Wisconsin

An elegant torte . . . layer cake filled and frosted with a smooth French chocolate frosting.

BAKE at 350° for 30 to 35 minutes   MAKES two 9-inch layers

Combine . . . . . 1 cup hot scalded **milk** and
        ¼ cup **butter** or margarine
Sift together . . 2 cups sifted **Pillsbury's Best All Purpose Flour***
        2 teaspoons double-acting **baking powder** and
        ½ teaspoon **salt**

Beat . . . . 4 **eggs** until light and fluffy. Gradually add
1¾ cups **sugar** and
½ teaspoon **orange extract.** With mixer beat at high
speed 1 to 2 minutes.
Stir in . . . . the dry ingredients, then the milk-butter mixture.
Turn . . . . into two 9-inch round layer pans, greased on the
bottom, lined with waxed paper, then greased again
and floured lightly.
Bake . . . . at 350° for 30 to 35 minutes. Cool. Split layers in
half, making 4 thin layers. Fill and frost with
Butter Fleck Frosting. Garnish with chopped **nuts.**
Chill at least 2 hours before serving.

Pillsbury's Best Self-Rising Flour is not recommended for use in this recipe.

BUTTER FLECK FROSTING

Combine ½ cup sifted Pillsbury's Best All Purpose Flour, ½ cup sugar,
¼ cup cocoa and ¼ teaspoon salt with ⅓ cup cold milk. Add mixture to
2 cups hot milk. Cook over medium heat, stirring constantly, until
thick. Remove from heat. Cover and cool to room temperature. Cream
¾ cup butter or margarine. Blend in 1 cup sifted confectioners' sugar
and 2 teaspoons vanilla, creaming well. Add the cooled chocolate
mixture, blending well. Chill frosting until of spreading consistency.

Buttercup Sponge Cake

Senior Winner by Mrs. Sylvan Eisenstein, Doniphan, Missouri

*Old-fashioned sponge cake made in a way that is out of the ordinary . . .
a very versatile cake.*

BAKE at 325° for 50 to 60 minutes   MAKES 10-inch tube cake

Combine . . . 1½ cups **sugar** and
½ cup **water** in saucepan. Place over low heat and stir
until dissolved. Boil gently, stirring occasionally,
until a little syrup dropped in cold water forms a
soft ball (234°).

Frosty Sponge Layers

Beat . . . . 7 **egg whites** and
1 teaspoon **cream of tartar** until stiff but not dry.
Pour . . . . hot syrup slowly over egg whites, beating constantly.
Continue beating 2 minutes. Cool slightly.
Beat . . . . 7 **egg yolks** and
1 teaspoon **almond extract** until thick and lemon
colored. Fold gently but thoroughly into egg white
mixture.
Sift . . . . 1 cup sifted **Pillsbury's Best All Purpose Flour*** and
1 teaspoon **salt,** one-third at a time over batter,
folding gently but thoroughly.
Turn . . . . into ungreased 10-inch tube pan.
Bake . . . . at 325° for 50 to 60 minutes. Invert; cool in pan.
Frost or serve with fruit or ice cream.

For use with Pillsbury's Best Self-Rising Flour, omit salt.

Jonquil Sponge Cake

Jonquil Sponge Cake

Best of Class Winner by Mrs. Estella Worley, Los Angeles, California

There's an airy lightness about this cake and a tender melt-in-your-mouth delicacy; lemon gives a fresh flavor.

BAKE at 350° for 40 to 45 minutes   MAKES 10-inch tube cake

Sift together 1½ cups sifted **Pillsbury's Best All Purpose Flour*** and
1 teaspoon **salt**

Combine . . . 1½ cups **sugar** and
½ cup **water** in saucepan. Place over low heat and stir until dissolved. Boil gently, stirring occasionally, until a little syrup dropped in cold water forms a soft ball (234°).

Beat . . . . 8 **egg yolks** until thick and lemon colored. Pour hot syrup slowly over egg yolks, beating constantly.

Add . . . . 1 teaspoon **vanilla**
1 teaspoon grated **lemon rind**
1 tablespoon **lemon juice** and the dry ingredients gradually. Blend well after each addition.

Beat . . . . 8 **egg whites** with
1 teaspoon **cream of tartar** until stiff but not dry. Fold in egg yolk mixture gently but thoroughly.

Turn . . . . into ungreased 10-inch tube pan.

Bake . . . . at 350° for 40 to 45 minutes. Invert; cool. Serve topped with **whipped cream,** if desired.

*For use with Pillsbury's Best Self-Rising Flour, omit salt.

Old-Time Butter Sponge Cake

Senior Winner by Mrs. Thomas W. Wolfe, Hagerstown, Maryland

Extra egg yolks in the refrigerator? Then try this dainty butter-sponge cake. Serve it plain or with fresh fruits.

BAKE at 350° for 50 to 60 minutes   MAKES 9 or 10-inch tube cake

Sift together 2¼ cups sifted **Pillsbury's Best All Purpose Flour***
2 teaspoons double-acting **baking powder** and
1 teaspoon **salt**

Beat . . . . ¾ cup **egg yolks** (about 11) until thick and lemon colored. Gradually add
1¾ cups **sugar,** beating thoroughly.

Combine . . . . . 1 cup hot scalded **milk**
1 teaspoon **vanilla** and
½ teaspoon **lemon extract.** Gradually add to beaten egg yolks, beating well after each addition.

Fold in . . . . the dry ingredients, one-third at a time.

Fold in . . . . . ½ cup melted **butter,** blending well.

Turn . . . . into ungreased 9 or 10-inch tube pan.

Bake . . . . at 350° for 50 to 60 minutes. Invert; cool.

*For use with Pillsbury's Best Self-Rising Flour, omit baking powder and salt.

Hidden Treasure Cake

Senior Winner by Jean Colarusso, Philadelphia, Pennsylvania

Party-time sponge cake! High and light, with yummy apricot filling and snowy white frosting.

BAKE at 350° for 45 to 50 minutes   MAKES 10-inch tube cake

Sift together 1½ cups sifted **Pillsbury's Best All Purpose Flour***
        ¾ cup **sugar** and
        ½ teaspoon **salt**

Beat . . . . 6 **egg whites** (¾ cup) with
        ¾ teaspoon **cream of tartar** in large mixing bowl until soft mounds form. Gradually add
        ¾ cup **sugar;** continue beating until very stiff, straight peaks form. *Do not underbeat.*

Combine . . . . . 6 **egg yolks** (⅓ to ½ cup)
        ½ cup **apricot nectar**
        1 teaspoon **rum flavoring**
        1 tablespoon grated **orange rind** and the dry ingredients in mixing bowl. Beat 1 minute. (With mixer use medium speed.)

Add . . . . one-third at a time to egg whites, folding gently but thoroughly.

Turn . . . . into ungreased 10-inch tube pan.

Bake . . . . at 350° for 45 to 50 minutes. Invert; cool.

Cut . . . . into three layers. Spread **Apricot-Orange Filling,** page 330, between layers. Frost top and sides with **Snowy White Frosting,** page 318.

*For use with Pillsbury's Best Self-Rising Flour, omit salt.

Hidden Treasure Cake

Chocolate Mocha Sponge Cake

Senior Winner by Mrs. Marian Splet, Philadelphia, Pennsylvania

Slice this tender cocoa sponge cake into three layers, then fill and top with packaged vanilla pudding, flavored with instant coffee.

BAKE at 325° for 35 to 40 minutes   MAKES 9-inch tube cake

Sift together . ¾ cup sifted **Pillsbury's Best All Purpose Flour*** and
            ¼ cup **cocoa**

Combine . . . . . 3 tablespoons **water**
            1 tablespoon **lemon juice**
            ½ teaspoon **salt**
            ¾ cup **sugar** and
            5 unbeaten **egg yolks** in mixing bowl. Beat until thick and ivory colored. *Do not underbeat.*

Fold . . . . the dry ingredients, one-third at a time, into egg yolk mixture.

Beat . . . . 5 **egg whites** until stiff but not dry. Fold carefully into batter.

Turn . . . . into ungreased 9-inch tube or spring-form pan.

Bake . . . . at 325° for 35 to 40 minutes. Cool. Cut crosswise into three layers. Spread **Mocha Filling**, page 329, between layers and on top.

*Pillsbury's Best Self-Rising Flour is not recommended for use in this recipe.

Mocha Ring Sponge Cake

Senior Winner by Mrs. Robert S. Lyons, Coral Gables, Florida

Instant coffee and cocoa are the tricks to this sponge cake.

BAKE at 350° for 45 to 55 minutes   MAKES 9 or 10-inch tube cake

Sift together . . 1 cup sifted **Pillsbury's Best All Purpose Flour***
            ⅔ cup **sugar**
            2 tablespoons **cocoa**
            1 tablespoon instant **coffee**

            1 teaspoon double-acting **baking powder** and
            ½ teaspoon **salt**

Beat . . . . 4 **egg whites** (½ cup) with
            ½ teaspoon **cream of tartar** in large mixing bowl until soft mounds form.

Add . . . . ⅓ cup **sugar** gradually. Continue beating until stiff, straight peaks form. *Do not underbeat.*

Combine . . . . . 4 **egg yolks** (about ⅓ cup)
            ¼ cup **water**
            1 teaspoon **vanilla** and the dry ingredients in small bowl. Beat 1 minute. (With mixer use medium speed.)

Fold . . . . into beaten egg whites, gently but thoroughly.

Turn . . . . into ungreased 9 to 10-inch tube pan. Cut gently through batter with knife.

Bake . . . . at 350° for 45 to 55 minutes. Invert; cool. Frost with **Mocha Drift Frosting**, page 318.

*For use with Pillsbury's Best Self-Rising Flour, omit baking powder and salt.

Apple-Harvest Fluff Cake

Senior Winner by Miss Helen Ross, Columbus, Ohio

A Quick-Mix sponge cake made with apple juice. Apple juice, grated apple and nuts add freshness to the fluffy frosting.

BAKE at 350° for 45 to 50 minutes   MAKES 10-inch tube cake

Sift together 1½ cups sifted **Pillsbury's Best All Purpose Flour***
            ¾ cup **sugar**
            1 teaspoon double-acting **baking powder** and
            ½ teaspoon **salt**

Beat . . . . 6 **egg whites** (¾ cup) until soft mounds form. Add ¾ cup **sugar** gradually; continue beating until very stiff, straight peaks form. *Do not underbeat.*

Combine . . . . . 6 **egg yolks** (⅓ to ½ cup)
            ½ cup **apple juice**
            1 tablespoon **lemon juice** and the dry ingredients in

small mixing bowl. Beat 1 minute. (With mixer use medium speed.)

Fold.........into egg whites, one-third at a time, gently but thoroughly.

Turn.........into ungreased 10-inch tube pan.

Bake.........at 350° for 45 to 50 minutes. Invert; cool. Frost with Harvest Frosting.

For use with Pillsbury's Best Self-Rising Flour, omit baking powder and salt.

HARVEST FROSTING

In top of double boiler combine 1 cup sugar, ⅓ cup apple juice, 1 tablespoon light corn syrup and 2 unbeaten egg whites. Cook over boiling water, beating constantly with electric mixer or rotary beater, until mixture stands in peaks. Remove from heat. Add 2 tablespoons grated apple and 3 to 4 drops yellow food coloring; continue beating until of spreading consistency. Fold in ½ cup chopped nuts.

Applesauce Cake Roll

Bride Third Prize Winner by Jill Kully, Berkeley, California

Applesauce, raisins and spice baked right into a jelly-roll sponge cake with a fluffy orange-cream cheese filling.

BAKE at 375° for 15 to 20 minutes   MAKES one cake roll

Sift together..1 cup sifted **Pillsbury's Best All Purpose Flour***
    ½ teaspoon double-acting **baking powder**
    ½ teaspoon **soda**
    ½ teaspoon **cinnamon**
    ¼ teaspoon **salt** and
    ¼ teaspoon **cloves**

Beat.........3 **eggs** in large mixing bowl until thick. Gradually add ¾ cup **sugar**, beating constantly until thick and ivory colored. *Do not underbeat.*

Fold in......½ cup sweetened **applesauce** and
    ½ cup **raisins**

Add.........the dry ingredients, one-third at a time, folding gently but thoroughly.

Spread.......in 15½x10½x1-inch jelly-roll pan, greased on bottom, lined with waxed paper, then greased again and floured lightly.

Bake.........at 375° for 15 to 20 minutes. Turn out immediately onto towel sprinkled with **confectioners' sugar**. Remove paper.

Roll.........cake immediately in towel, starting with an end. Cool 10 minutes; unroll. Spread with Cream Cheese Filling. Roll again; chill.

For use with Pillsbury's Best Self-Rising Flour, omit baking powder, soda, salt.

CREAM CHEESE FILLING

Combine ⅔ cup (two 3-oz. pkgs.) softened cream cheese, 3 tablespoons light cream, 1 tablespoon grated orange rind and ¼ cup sugar. Beat until of spreading consistency.

Applesauce Cake Roll

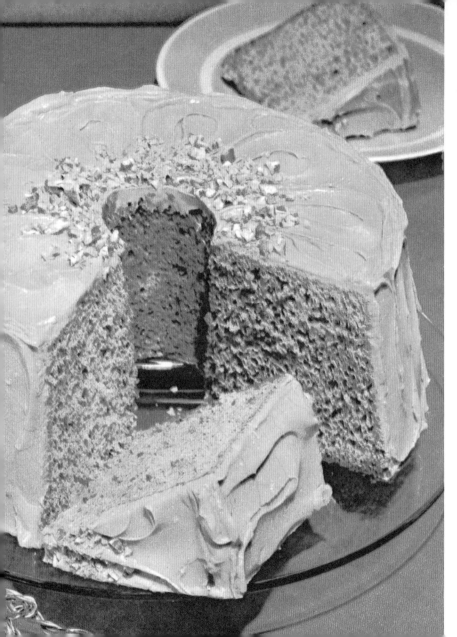

Coffee Cloud Sponge Cake

Best of Class Winner by Mrs. John Matyola, Manville, New Jersey

A surprising discovery in a sponge cake . . . delicate coffee flavor combined with crunchy pecans.

BAKE at 350° for 60 to 70 minutes   MAKES 10-inch tube cake

Dissolve . . . . . 1 tablespoon **instant coffee** in
          1 cup **boiling water.** Cool.

Sift together . . 2 cups sifted **Pillsbury's Best All Purpose Flour***
          3 teaspoons double-acting **baking powder** and
          ½ teaspoon **salt**

Beat . . . . 6 **egg whites** with
          ½ teaspoon **cream of tartar** in a large mixing bowl until very soft mounds begin to form.

Add . . . . ½ cup **sugar** to egg whites, 2 tablespoons at a time; continue beating until very stiff, straight peaks are formed. *Do not underbeat.* Set aside.

Beat . . . . 6 **egg yolks** in large mixing bowl until blended; gradually add
          1½ cups **sugar** and
          1 teaspoon **vanilla.** Beat at high speed until thick and lemon colored, 4 to 5 minutes.

Add . . . . the dry ingredients alternately with the coffee to egg yolk mixture. Blend well after each addition.

Fold in . . . . . . 1 cup **pecans** or other nuts, finely ground. Fold egg yolk mixture, one-fourth at a time, into the stiffly-beaten egg whites. Fold gently but thoroughly.

Turn . . . . into ungreased 10-inch tube pan.

Bake . . . . at 350° for 60 to 70 minutes. Invert; cool. Frost with **Coffee Icing,** page 326.

For use with Pillsbury's Best Self-Rising Flour, omit baking powder and salt.

Coffee Cloud Sponge Cake

Luscious Maple Log

Senior Winner by Mrs. Gloria A. Roden, Baldwinsville, New York

Maple syrup in the subtly spiced jelly-roll sponge cake and whipped cream filling. Quick and easy for a party dessert.

BAKE at 350° for 14 to 17 minutes   MAKES one cake roll

Sift together..1 cup sifted **Pillsbury's Best All Purpose Flour***
          1 teaspoon double-acting **baking powder**
          ½ teaspoon **cinnamon**
          ¼ teaspoon **salt** and
          ¼ teaspoon **nutmeg**

Beat........3 **egg whites** with
          ⅛ teaspoon **cream of tartar** in large mixing bowl until soft mounds form. Gradually add
          ⅓ cup **sugar**; beat until stiff, straight peaks form.

Beat........3 **egg yolks** until well blended; add
          ⅔ cup **maple syrup** and
          1 teaspoon **vanilla**. Continue beating until very thick. Fold into beaten egg whites.

Add..........the dry ingredients, one-third at a time; fold gently after each addition.

Spread........in 15½x10½x1-inch jelly-roll pan, greased and lined with waxed paper.

Bake.........at 350° for 14 to 17 minutes.

Turn out......immediately onto towel sprinkled with **confectioners' sugar**. Remove paper.

Roll..........immediately in towel. Cool; unroll. Spread with about ⅔ Maple Whipped Cream. Roll again. Place on serving plate.

Spread with....remaining whipped cream; sprinkle with ½ cup **nuts,** chopped. Chill.

For use with Pillsbury's Best Self-Rising Flour, omit baking powder and salt.

MAPLE WHIPPED CREAM

Beat 1½ cups whipping cream until thick; add ½ cup maple syrup and continue beating until of spreading consistency.

Pineapple Roll-Up

Senior Winner by Mrs. Edward Pogacnik, Lorain, Ohio

A jelly roll cake with the brown sugar-pineapple filling baked with it. A fluffy pineapple whipped cream tops each serving.

BAKE at 375° for 15 to 20 minutes   MAKES one cake roll

Melt........2 tablespoons **butter** in 15½x10½x1-inch jelly-roll pan.

Drain.......1 No. 2½ can **crushed pineapple** thoroughly, reserving 1 cup of juice. Spread fruit in pan. Sprinkle with ½ cup firmly packed **brown sugar**

Sift together.¾ cup sifted **Pillsbury's Best All Purpose Flour***
          1 teaspoon double-acting **baking powder** and
          ½ teaspoon **salt**

Beat........4 **egg whites** (½ cup) in large mixing bowl until soft mounds form.

Add.........½ cup **sugar** gradually. Continue beating until stiff, straight peaks form.

Combine.....4 **egg yolks** (about ⅓ cup)
          ½ teaspoon **vanilla** and
          ¼ cup **sugar**; beat until thick and lemon colored.

Fold..........into egg whites. *Do not stir.*

Add..........the dry ingredients, one-third at a time; fold gently but thoroughly. Pour batter over pineapple mixture.

Bake.........at 375° for 15 to 20 minutes. Loosen edges.

Turn out......immediately onto towel sprinkled with **confectioners' sugar**.

Roll..........cake immediately, starting with end. Cool. Slice and serve with Pineapple Fluff.

For use with Pillsbury's Best Self-Rising Flour, omit baking powder and salt.

PINEAPPLE FLUFF

Combine ⅓ cup sugar and 1½ tablespoons cornstarch in saucepan. Blend in 1 cup pineapple juice. Cook, stirring constantly, until thick and clear. Remove from heat. Add 1 tablespoon lemon juice and 2 teaspoons grated lemon rind. Cool. Beat 1 cup whipping cream until stiff; fold into pineapple mixture.

Chocolate Crunch Log

Senior Winner by Mrs. Robert L. Evans, Denver, Colorado

A chocolate jelly roll with a peanut brittle-whipped cream filling and a honey-chocolate glaze. Make early and have ready for guests.

BAKE at 375° for 14 to 16 minutes   MAKES one cake roll

Sift together . ¾ cup sifted **Pillsbury's Best All Purpose Flour***
　　　　　　　¼ teaspoon **soda** and
　　　　　　　¼ teaspoon **salt**
Beat . . . . 4 **eggs** and
　　　　　　　1 teaspoon **vanilla** until thick. Gradually add
　　　　　　　¾ cup **sugar;** beat until thick and ivory colored.
Fold in . . . . the dry ingredients, gently but thoroughly.
Combine . . . . . 2 squares (2 oz.) melted unsweetened **chocolate**
　　　　　　　¼ teaspoon **soda**
　　　　　　　2 tablespoons **sugar** and

Chocolate Crunch Log

3 tablespoons **water.** Fold gently into batter.
Spread . . . . in 15½x10½x1-inch jelly-roll pan, greased on the bottom, lined with waxed paper, then greased again and floured.
Bake . . . . at 375° for 14 to 16 minutes.
Turn out . . . . immediately onto towel sprinkled with **confectioners' sugar.** Remove paper.
Roll . . . . in towel, starting with a 10-inch end. Cool. Unroll and spread with Coffee Cream Crunch Filling. Roll again; drizzle with Honey Chocolate Glaze. Chill.

*For use with Pillsbury's Best Self-Rising Flour, omit soda and salt.

COFFEE CRUNCH CREAM FILLING

Beat 1 cup whipping cream with 1 teaspoon instant coffee until thick. Stir in 1 cup crushed peanut brittle or peanut crunch.

HONEY CHOCOLATE GLAZE

In top of double boiler over boiling water melt ½ cup semi-sweet chocolate pieces, 2 tablespoons butter and 2 tablespoons honey. Stir until smooth.

Nugget Surprise Cake Roll

Senior Winner by Jean Herbster, Indianapolis, Indiana

A candy-like mixture adds texture and flavor to delicate cake roll.

BAKE at 375° for 15 to 18 minutes   MAKES one cake roll

NUGGET SURPRISE FILLING

Melt . . . . 2 tablespoons **butter** in heavy skillet. Add
　　　　　　　2 slices **bread,** cut in ¼-inch cubes (1 cup), and
　　　　　　　½ teaspoon **vanilla.** Stir constantly over medium heat until butter is absorbed and cubes are light golden brown, 4 to 5 minutes.
Add . . . . ½ cup **sugar;** cook and stir about 5 minutes until sugar

melts and mixture is golden brown. Remove from heat.

Blend in . . . . . 2 tablespoons **light corn syrup**; mix thoroughly.

Turn out . . . . on greased pan; cool. Crush slightly.

Melt . . . . ¼ cup **butter** in heavy skillet. Blend in
⅓ cup **Pillsbury's Best All Purpose Flour** and
¾ cup firmly packed **brown sugar**; mix well.

Stir in . . . . . 1½ cups **milk**; cook, stirring constantly, until thick. Cool.

Add . . . . 1 teaspoon **vanilla**
2 teaspoons grated **orange rind** and caramelized cubes just before spreading on cake.

CAKE ROLL

Sift together . . 1 cup sifted **Pillsbury's Best All Purpose Flour***
1 teaspoon double-acting **baking powder** and
½ teaspoon **salt**

Beat . . . . 3 **egg whites** until stiff but not dry. Set aside.

Beat . . . . 3 **egg yolks** in large mixing bowl until blended. Gradually add
1 cup **sugar** and
½ teaspoon **almond extract,** beating constantly until thick and lemon colored.

Combine . . . . . 3 tablespoons **orange juice** and
3 tablespoons **water.** Add alternately with the dry ingredients to egg yolk mixture. Blend well after each addition. Gently fold egg whites into batter.

Pour . . . . into 15½x10½x1-inch jelly-roll pan, greased, lined with waxed paper, then greased again and floured lightly.

Bake . . . . at 375° for 15 to 18 minutes. Turn out immediately onto towel sprinkled with **confectioners' sugar.** Remove paper.

Roll . . . . cake immediately in towel. Cool 10 minutes. Unroll. Spread with Nugget Surprise Filling; roll again, starting with 10-inch edge. Chill.

*For use with Pillsbury's Best Self-Rising Flour, omit baking powder and salt.

FRUIT and NUT CAKES

include date-nut cakes, banana cakes and fruit-flavored cakes, as well as Christmas fruitcakes. All these cakes are moist and store very well. They make excellent picnic cakes— or bake one to take along on your vacation.

Fruitcakes vary; some are nearly solid with fruit, while others have a more cake-like texture with less fruit.

In order to keep fruit and nuts suspended in the batter, cut or chop them fine and coat with flour. For easier chopping of raisins and candied fruits, coat the fruit with a small amount of flour or grease the knife. (A French knife is preferred for chopping fruits and nuts.) Nuts and candied fruits may be purchased already chopped for your cake.

Drain maraschino cherries, crushed pineapple or other moist fruit thoroughly on absorbent paper such as paper toweling.

In recipes calling for nuts, you can use pecans, walnuts or any other kind you desire. If a specific kind is called for, it definitely gives a special flavor to the cake.

For the best flavor in banana cakes, use bananas that are very ripe. The skins should be well browned and show no signs of green.

Fruitcakes may be baked in a variety of pans— coffee cans, ring molds, casseroles, tube pans, loaf pans. When making a fruitcake in a loaf pan, line the pan with aluminum foil, allowing extra foil on all sides; fold extra foil down sides of pan during baking. When cake is cool, bring foil up around top of cake to wrap for storage.

Most fruitcakes keep well over a period of time. Fruitcake is often baked 3 to 4 weeks beforehand, especially at holiday time.

Fruitcakes should be thoroughly cooled before slicing and serving.

Swiss Banana Cake

Senior Winner by Mrs. Elizabeth Bolander, Indianapolis, Indiana

Brown sugar sea-foam frosting is perfect for this moist, light, old-fashioned banana cake.

BAKE at 350° for 30 to 35 minutes   MAKES two 8-inch layers

Sift together . . 2 cups sifted **Pillsbury's Best All Purpose Flour***
    1 teaspoon double-acting **baking powder**
    ½ teaspoon **soda** and
    ½ teaspoon **salt.** Set aside.
Add . . . . 1½ cups **sugar** gradually to
    ½ cup **shortening,** creaming well.
Blend in . . . . . 2 unbeaten **eggs,** one at a time, and
    1 cup mashed **bananas** (2 medium). Blend thoroughly.
Combine . . . . ⅓ cup **buttermilk** or sour milk and
    1 teaspoon **vanilla.** Add alternately with the dry ingredients to creamed mixture. Blend well after each addition.
Stir in . . . . . . ¾ cup **walnuts,** chopped
Turn . . . . into two 8-inch round layer pans, well greased and lightly floured on the bottoms.
Bake . . . . at 350° for 30 to 35 minutes. Cool; frost with **Sea-Foam Frosting,** page 318.

For use with Pillsbury's Best Self-Rising Flour, omit baking powder and salt; decrease soda to ¼ teaspoon.

Lemon Wonder Cake

Senior Winner by Mrs. Edward E. Olson, Baldwin, Michigan

Dates and a whole lemon are ground up for the batter of this unusual sweet-and-tart cake.

BAKE at 350° for 30 to 35 minutes   MAKES two 8-inch layers

Sift together 2¼ cups sifted **Pillsbury's Best All Purpose Flour***
    2 teaspoons double-acting **baking powder** and
    ½ teaspoon **soda**
Grind . . . . 1 **lemon** (rind only) together with
    1 cup **dates.** Add ¼ cup dry ingredients.
Cream . . . . . . ½ cup **butter** or margarine. Gradually add
    ⅔ cup **sugar** and
    ½ cup firmly packed **brown sugar,** creaming well.
Blend in . . . . . 2 unbeaten **eggs,** beating well after each.
Add . . . . fruit mixture; mix well.
Add . . . . 1 cup **buttermilk** or sour milk alternately with the dry ingredients to creamed mixture. Blend well after each addition.
Turn . . . . into two 8-inch round layer pans, well greased and lightly floured on the bottoms.
Bake . . . . at 350° for 30 to 35 minutes. Cool; frost with **Caramel Frosting,** page 314.

Pillsbury's Best Self-Rising Flour is not recommended for use in this recipe.

Best Black Walnut Cake

Senior Winner by Mrs. LeRoy Hedges, Hickman Mills, Missouri

The distinctive flavor of black walnuts is combined with coconut in a really tender, fine-textured buttermilk cake.

BAKE at 375°   MAKES two 8 or 9-inch layers

Grind . . . . 1 cup **coconut** together with
    ⅓ cup **black walnuts**
Sift together . . 2 cups sifted **Pillsbury's Best All Purpose Flour***
    1 teaspoon double-acting **baking powder**
    1 teaspoon **soda** and
    1 teaspoon **salt.** Set aside.
Add . . . . 1½ cups **sugar** gradually to
    ½ cup **shortening,** creaming well.
Blend in . . . . . 1 teaspoon **vanilla** and
    2 unbeaten **eggs,** beating well after each.

Add . . . . .1 cup **buttermilk** or sour milk alternately with the dry ingredients. Blend well after each addition.

Blend in . . . . .⅓ cup hot **coffee**

Stir in . . . . .the coconut mixture, reserving 2 tablespoons for topping.

Turn . . . . .into two 8 or 9-inch round layer pans, well greased and lightly floured on the bottoms.

Bake . . . . .at 375°: 30 to 35 minutes for 8-inch layers; 25 to 30 minutes for 9-inch layers. Cool and spread Coffee Frosting between layers and on top of cake; garnish with reserved coconut mixture. (To frost sides of cake, double frosting recipe.)

Pillsbury's Best Self-Rising Flour is not recommended for use in this recipe.

COFFEE FROSTING

Combine 2 cups sifted confectioners' sugar, 2 tablespoons shortening, 1 teaspoon vanilla and ⅛ teaspoon salt. Add 1 tablespoon melted butter and 1 to 2 tablespoons hot strong coffee. Beat to spreading consistency.

Date Jamboree Cake

Bride Winner by Mrs. William Cooper Harton, Hopkinsville, Kentucky

For a church social make this large jam cake with dates and pecans . . . spicy and rich with a cooked speedy butterscotch frosting.

BAKE at 325° for 60 to 65 minutes   MAKES two 9-inch square layers*

Sift together . .3 cups sifted **Pillsbury's Best All Purpose Flour****
        1 teaspoon **soda**
        1 teaspoon **salt**
        1 teaspoon **cinnamon**
        1 teaspoon **allspice** and
        ½ teaspoon **cloves**

Combine . . . . .1 cup **dates,** finely cut
        1 cup **pecans,** chopped, and 2 tablespoons of the dry ingredients; mix to coat fruit. Set aside.

Date Jamboree Cake

Add . . . . . . .1¾ cups **sugar** gradually to
        1 cup **shortening,** creaming well.

Blend in . . . . .4 unbeaten **eggs,** beating well after each.

Add . . . . .the dry ingredients alternately with
        1¼ cups **buttermilk** or sour milk. Blend well after each addition.

Stir in . . . . . . .1 cup **blackberry, cherry** or **plum preserves** and the date-nut mixture; blend thoroughly.

Turn . . . . .into two 9-inch square layer pans, well greased and lightly floured on the bottoms.

Bake . . . . .at 325° for 60 to 65 minutes. Cool; frost with **Hasty Butterscotch Frosting,** page 315.

If desired, one 9-inch square loaf cake may be made by dividing the ingredients in half. Frost with half the frosting recipe.

**For use with Pillsbury's Best Self-Rising Flour, omit soda and salt.*

Mince Pecan Cake

Senior Winner by Mrs. J. W. Hamilton, Altus, Oklahoma

Mincemeat and chopped pecans give this cake a rich, mellow flavor.

BAKE at 350° for 30 to 35 minutes   MAKES three 9-inch layers

Sift together 2½ cups sifted **Pillsbury's Best All Purpose Flour***
          2 teaspoons double-acting **baking powder**
          1 teaspoon **soda** and
          1 teaspoon **salt.** Set aside.
Add . . . . 1½ cups **sugar** gradually to
          ½ cup **shortening,** creaming well.
Blend in . . . . . 3 unbeaten **eggs,** beating well after each.
Combine . . . . . 1 cup **milk** and
          1 teaspoon **vanilla.** Add alternately with the dry
          ingredients to creamed mixture. Blend well after
          each addition.

Mince Pecan Cake

Blend in . . . . . ½ cup **pecans,** chopped, and
          1½ cups prepared **mincemeat**
Turn . . . . into three 9-inch round layer pans, well greased and
          lightly floured on the bottoms.
Bake . . . . at 350° for 30 to 35 minutes. Cool; frost with **De Luxe
          Fluffy White Frosting,** page 317, or **Hasty Butter-
          scotch Frosting,** page 315.
*For use with Pillsbury's Best Self-Rising Flour, omit baking powder, soda, salt.

Tropical Prune Cake

Bride Winner by Mrs. J. R. Nesbit, Evansville, Indiana

*Large buttery rich layer cake . . . luscious with pineapple filling and
fluffy toffee frosting.*

BAKE at 350° for 35 to 40 minutes   MAKES two 9-inch layers

Sift together . . 3 cups sifted **Pillsbury's Best All Purpose Flour***
          2 teaspoons **soda**
          1½ teaspoons **salt**
          1½ teaspoons **cinnamon** and
          ¾ teaspoon **cloves**
Cream . . . . . . ¾ cup **butter** or margarine. Gradually add
          1½ cups **sugar,** creaming well.
Blend in . . . . . 3 unbeaten **eggs** and
          ⅓ cup light **molasses;** mix well.
Add . . . . 1⅓ cups **buttermilk** or sour milk alternately with the
          dry ingredients. Blend well after each addition.
Stir in . . . . . 1½ cups uncooked tenderized **prunes,** very finely cut.
          Turn into two 9-inch round layer pans, at least 1½
          inches deep, well greased and lightly floured on the
          bottoms.
Bake . . . . at 350° for 35 to 40 minutes. Cool; fill with **Pineapple
          Filling,** page 330, and frost with **Toffee Frosting,**
          page 319.
*For use with Pillsbury's Best Self-Rising Flour, omit soda and salt.

Black Walnut Treasure Cake

Senior Winner by Mrs. Letty D. Johnson, LaGrange, Illinois

A sparkly orange-sugar top conceals raisins, dates, coconut and orange rind, as well as nuts, in this moist cake.

BAKE at 350° for 40 to 45 minutes   MAKES 12x8-inch cake*

Combine . . . . ½ cup **raisins**
          ½ cup **dates**, finely cut
          1 tablespoon grated **orange rind**
          ¼ cup **coconut**, chopped
          ¾ cup **black walnuts**, chopped, and
          ½ cup sifted **Pillsbury's Best All Purpose Flour**. Stir to coat with flour.

Sift together 1½ cups sifted **Pillsbury's Best All Purpose Flour****
          1 teaspoon **soda** and
          ½ teaspoon **salt**

Cream . . . . . . ½ cup **butter** or margarine. Gradually add
          1 cup **sugar**, creaming well.

Blend in . . . . . 2 unbeaten **eggs**, beating well after each.

Add . . . . the dry ingredients alternately with
          1 cup **buttermilk** or sour milk. Blend well after each addition. Stir in the fruit mixture.

Turn . . . . into 12x8x2-inch pan, well greased and lightly floured on the bottom.*

Bake . . . . at 350° for 40 to 45 minutes.* Brush hot cake with a mixture of

---

½ cup **sugar** and
¼ cup **orange juice** (do not combine ahead of time). Serve warm or cold.

Cake may be baked in two 9x5x3-inch loaf pans for 45 to 50 minutes.
**For use with Pillsbury's Best Self-Rising Flour, omit soda and salt.*

Banana Choco-Bit Cake

Junior Winner by Mary Furdek, Kenosha, Wisconsin

Moist, rich banana cake flecked with bits of chocolate and walnuts—a flavor combination reminiscent of banana split.

BAKE at 350° for 45 to 55 minutes   MAKES 9x9-inch cake

Sift together . . 2 cups sifted **Pillsbury's Best All Purpose Flour***
          1 teaspoon double-acting **baking powder**
          1 teaspoon **soda** and
          ¼ teaspoon **salt**. Set aside.

Add . . . . 1 cup **sugar** gradually to
          ½ cup **shortening**, creaming well.

Blend in . . . . . 2 unbeaten **eggs**; beat well.

Add . . . . 1 cup mashed ripe **bananas** (about 2 medium) and
          1 teaspoon **vanilla**. Mix well.

Combine . . . . ½ cup **milk** and
          1 tablespoon **vinegar**. Add alternately with the dry ingredients to creamed mixture. Blend well after each addition.

Stir in . . . . 1 square (1 oz.) coarsely shaved **semi-sweet chocolate** and
          ½ cup **walnuts**, chopped

Turn . . . . into 9x9x2-inch pan, well greased and lightly floured on the bottom.

Bake . . . . at 350° for 45 to 55 minutes. Cool; frost with **Creamy Vanilla Frosting**, page 321.

For use with Pillsbury's Best Self-Rising Flour, omit baking powder and salt; decrease soda to ¾ teaspoon.

Touch o' Lemon Tea Cake

Senior Winner by Mrs. Barbara B. Constant, Culver City, California

A moist cake made with tea and chopped raisins, with a delicate lemon flavor that is repeated in the icing.

BAKE at 350° for 40 to 45 minutes   MAKES 9x9-inch cake

Combine . . . . ½ cup golden or seedless **raisins**, chopped
               1½ teaspoons grated **lemon rind** and
               ⅔ cup hot strong **black tea**. Cool. Drain; reserve liquid.

Sift together 1¾ cups sifted **Pillsbury's Best All Purpose Flour***
               1 teaspoon **salt** and
               ¾ teaspoon **soda**. Add drained raisins. Set aside.

Add . . . . 1 cup **sugar** gradually to
               ½ cup **shortening**, creaming well.

Blend in . . . . . 2 unbeaten **eggs**; beat well.

Add . . . . the dry ingredients alternately with reserved liquid. Blend well after each addition.

Turn . . . . into 9x9x2-inch pan, well greased and lightly floured on the bottom.

Bake . . . . at 350° for 40 to 45 minutes. Cool; frost with **Lemon Butter Frosting,** page 324.

*For use with Pillsbury's Best Self-Rising Flour, omit salt and soda.

Scotch Prune Cake

Senior Winner by Mrs. Mary Larkin, Oak Ridge, Tennessee

Cocoa-spice prune cake with broiled-on topping . . . perfect for a picnic.

BAKE at 350° for 35 to 40 minutes   MAKES 12x8 or 13x9-inch cake

Sift together . . 2 cups sifted **Pillsbury's Best All Purpose Flour***
               1 tablespoon **cocoa**
               1 teaspoon **soda**
               1 teaspoon **salt**

Touch o' Lemon Tea Cake

½ teaspoon **cinnamon**
¼ teaspoon **nutmeg** and
¼ teaspoon **cloves.** Set aside.
Add........1 cup **sugar** gradually to
½ cup **shortening,** creaming well.
Blend in.....2 unbeaten **eggs,** beating well after each.
Combine....½ cup **prune juice** and
½ cup **water.** Add alternately with the dry ingredients to creamed mixture. Blend well after each addition.
Stir in.......1 cup cooked **prunes,** cut into small pieces
Turn..........into 12x8x2 or 13x9x2-inch pan, well greased and lightly floured on the bottom.
Bake........at 350° for 35 to 40 minutes. Top with **Broiled Frosting,** page 324.
For use with Pillsbury's Best Self-Rising Flour, omit soda and salt.

Date Nut Scotch Cake

Senior Winner by Mrs. Frank P. Gross, San Antonio, Texas

A spicy butterscotch-oatmeal loaf just filled with dates and nuts.

BAKE at 350° for 40 to 45 minutes   MAKES 12x8 or 13x9-inch cake

Pour.......1¼ cups **boiling water** over
1 cup quick-cooking **rolled oats;** stir. Set aside.
Sift together..1 cup sifted **Pillsbury's Best All Purpose Flour***
1 teaspoon **soda**
1 teaspoon **cream of tartar**
1 teaspoon **salt**
1 teaspoon **cinnamon** and
½ teaspoon **cloves.** Set aside.
Add.......1½ cups firmly packed **brown sugar** gradually to
½ cup **shortening,** creaming well.
Blend in.....2 unbeaten **eggs,** beating well after each. Stir in the rolled-oats mixture.
Add..........the dry ingredients gradually, mixing thoroughly.

Stir in.......1 cup **dates,** cut in small pieces, and
½ cup **pecans** or other nuts, finely chopped
Turn..........into 12x8x2 or 13x9x2-inch pan, well greased and lightly floured on the bottom.
Bake........at 350° for 40 to 45 minutes. Cool; frost with **Speedy Caramel Frosting,** page 314.
For use with Pillsbury's Best Self-Rising Flour, omit soda, cream of tartar, salt.

Marmalade Mixup

Senior Winner by Mrs. Caryol Coryell, Scottsbluff, Nebraska

Apricot marmalade in this banana-nut cake gives a fresh flavor. A wonderful family cake—stores well, too.

BAKE at 350° for 40 to 50 minutes   MAKES 13x9-inch cake

Sift together 2½ cups sifted **Pillsbury's Best All Purpose Flour***
1 teaspoon **soda**
1 teaspoon **salt**
1 teaspoon **cinnamon**
1 teaspoon **nutmeg**
½ teaspoon double-acting **baking powder** and
½ teaspoon **allspice.** Set aside.
Add........1 cup **sugar** gradually to
⅔ cup **shortening,** creaming well.
Stir in.......1 cup **apricot marmalade** and
½ cup mashed **banana** (1 medium). Mix well.
Blend in.....3 unbeaten **eggs,** beating well after each.
Add..........the dry ingredients alternately with
⅓ cup **buttermilk** or sour milk. Blend well after each addition.
Stir in.....½ cup **nuts,** chopped. Turn into 13x9x2-inch pan, well greased and lightly floured on bottom.
Bake........at 350° for 40 to 50 minutes. Cool; frost with **Marmalade Frosting,** page 325.
For use with Pillsbury's Best Self-Rising Flour, omit soda, salt, baking powder.

Frosted Date Loaf

Senior Winner by Mrs. Gladys B. Burger, Tucson, Arizona

A good lunchbox cake . . . with a baked-on brown sugar meringue.

BAKE at 350° for 35 to 40 minutes   MAKES 12x8 or 13x9-inch cake

Combine . . . . . 1 cup **dates,** cut
               1 teaspoon **soda*** and
               1 cup **boiling water**
Sift together 1¾ cups sifted **Pillsbury's Best All Purpose Flour*** and
               ½ teaspoon **salt;** set aside.
Add . . . . 1 cup **sugar** gradually to
               ½ cup **shortening,** creaming well.
Blend in . . . . 1 unbeaten **egg** and
               1 unbeaten **egg yolk;** beat well.
Add . . . . the dry ingredients alternately with date mixture. Blend well after each addition.
Stir in . . . . . . 1 teaspoon **vanilla** and
               ¾ cup **pecans,** chopped
Turn . . . . batter into 12x8x2 or 13x9x2-inch pan, well greased and lightly floured on the bottom.
Drop . . . . Praline Meringue by teaspoonfuls onto batter; spread carefully to cover.
Bake . . . . at 350° for 35 to 40 minutes.

*For use with Pillsbury's Best Self-Rising Flour, decrease soda to ¼ teaspoon and omit salt.

PRALINE MERINGUE

Beat 1 egg white until stiff but not dry. Gradually add ½ cup firmly packed brown sugar, beating well after each addition. Continue beating until meringue stands in stiff, straight peaks. Fold in ¼ cup chopped pecans and ½ teaspoon vanilla.

Honey-Top Graham Date Cake

Senior Winner by Mrs. Blanche Robb, Brunswick, Ohio

Whole wheat flour in a big rich date-nut cake—glazed right in the pan with a simple honey-orange mixture.

BAKE at 350° for 50 to 55 minutes   MAKES 13x9-inch cake

Sift together . . 1 cup **Pillsbury's Whole Wheat (Graham) Flour**
               ½ cup sifted **Pillsbury's Best All Purpose Flour***
               2 teaspoons double-acting **baking powder** and
               1 teaspoon **salt**
Mix in . . . . . . ½ cup **nuts,** chopped, and
               1 cup **dates,** finely cut. Set aside.
Add . . . . . . 1½ cups **sugar** gradually to
               1 cup **shortening,** creaming well. Blend in
               6 **egg yolks** and
               1 teaspoon **vanilla.** Beat well.
Add . . . . the dry ingredients alternately with
               ⅓ cup **milk.** Blend well after each addition.
Beat . . . . 6 **egg whites** until stiff but not dry. Fold into batter.
Spread . . . . in 13x9x2-inch pan, well greased and lightly floured on the bottom. Sprinkle with
               ½ cup **nuts,** chopped
Bake . . . . at 350° for 50 to 55 minutes. Pour Orange Honey Glaze over top while warm.

*For use with Pillsbury's Best Self-Rising Flour, decrease baking powder to 1½ teaspoons and salt to ½ teaspoon.

ORANGE HONEY GLAZE

Blend together 1 teaspoon cornstarch, ⅓ cup orange juice and 3 tablespoons honey in saucepan. Cook, stirring constantly, until clear and slightly thickened.

Tropicana Treats

Junior Winner by Paul Coon, Milwaukie, Oregon

Rolled oats and chocolate pieces in the cake and a coconut-nut baked-in filling and topping.

BAKE at 350° for 50 to 55 minutes   MAKES 13x9-inch cake

Toast . . . . ¼ cup **coconut** in 350° oven about 10 minutes until golden brown; stir occasionally.

Sift together . . 2 cups sifted **Pillsbury's Best All Purpose Flour***
1 teaspoon double-acting **baking powder**
1 teaspoon **salt** and
½ teaspoon **soda**. Set aside.

Add . . . . 1⅓ cups **sugar** gradually to
¾ cup **shortening**, creaming well.

Blend in . . . . . 2 unbeaten **eggs**, beating well after each.

Combine . . . . . 1 cup **milk** and
1 teaspoon **vanilla**. Add alternately with the dry ingredients to creamed mixture. Blend well after each addition.

Stir in . . . . 1 cup quick-cooking **rolled oats** and
1 cup (6-oz. pkg.) **semi-sweet chocolate pieces**

Turn . . . . half of batter into 13x9x2-inch pan, well greased and lightly floured on the bottom. Top with mixture of
¼ cup melted **butter** or margarine
1 cup **pecans**, chopped, and
½ cup **coconut**, chopped. Cover with remaining batter.

Bake . . . . at 350° for 50 to 55 minutes. Pour Pineapple Glaze

over top immediately; sprinkle with toasted coconut.

For use with Pillsbury's Best Self-Rising Flour, omit baking powder, soda, salt.

PINEAPPLE GLAZE

Combine 1 cup (No. 1 can) undrained crushed pineapple and ¼ cup sugar in saucepan. Boil 10 minutes over low heat.

Pantry Shelf Cake

Senior Winner by Mrs. F. M. Buesinger, Elmhurst, Illinois

A festive yet simple loaf cake just full of spices, fruits and nuts.

BAKE at 325° for 80 to 90 minutes   MAKES 13x9-inch cake

Cover . . . . 1 cup **raisins** with **boiling water**. Let stand 5 minutes; drain thoroughly.

Sift together . . 3 cups sifted **Pillsbury's Best All Purpose Flour***
1 teaspoon **soda**
1 teaspoon **salt**
1 teaspoon **cinnamon**
1 teaspoon **nutmeg** and
1 teaspoon **cloves**. Set aside.

Add . . . . 1½ cups **sugar** gradually to
⅔ cup **shortening**, creaming well.

Blend in . . . . . 3 unbeaten **eggs**, beating well after each.

Stir in . . . . 1 cup sweetened **applesauce**
1 cup **cherry preserves** and
1 cup **watermelon pickles**, finely chopped

Add . . . . the dry ingredients gradually.

Stir in . . . . 1 cup **black walnuts** or other nuts, finely chopped, and the drained raisins.

Turn . . . . into 13x9x2-inch pan, well greased and lightly floured on the bottom.

Bake . . . . at 325° for 80 to 90 minutes. Cool; frost with **Creamy Cinnamon Frosting**, page 325.

For use with Pillsbury's Best Self-Rising Flour, omit soda and salt.

Cranberry Date Cake

Senior Winner by Mrs. W. A. Gale, Whittier, California

Fresh cranberries and dates give a calico look to this festive cake.

BAKE at 350° for 80 to 85 minutes   MAKES 10-inch tube cake

Sift together . . 3 cups sifted **Pillsbury's Best All Purpose Flour***
              2½ teaspoons double-acting **baking powder** and
              ½ teaspoon **salt**
Cream . . . . . . ½ cup **butter** or margarine with
              ½ cup **shortening.** Gradually add
              1½ cups **sugar,** creaming well.
Add . . . . 4 unbeaten **eggs,** beating well after each.
Combine . . . . ¼ cup **milk** and
              ¼ cup **orange juice.** Add alternately with the dry in-
              gredients to creamed mixture. Blend well after each
              addition.
Fold in . . . . . . 1 cup **dates,** cut fine, and
              2 cups (½ lb.) fresh **cranberries,** sliced
Turn . . . . into 10-inch tube pan, well greased on bottom.
Bake . . . . at 350° for 80 to 85 minutes. Cool; frost with
              Orange Frosting, page 327.

*Pillsbury's Best Self-Rising Flour is not recommended for use in this recipe.

Raisin Nut Round

Junior Winner by Mary P. Evans, Washington, D.C.

Moist, tender raisin cake to keep on hand for afternoon coffee.

BAKE at 350° for 60 to 70 minutes   MAKES 9 or 10-inch tube cake

Sift together . . 2 cups sifted **Pillsbury's Best All Purpose Flour***
              1 teaspoon double-acting **baking powder**
              1 teaspoon **salt**
              ½ teaspoon **soda**
              ¾ teaspoon **mace**

              ¾ teaspoon **cinnamon** and
              ¼ teaspoon **cloves**
Coat . . . . 1 cup seedless **raisins,** chopped, and
              1 cup **nuts,** chopped, with ¼ cup dry ingredients.
Cream . . . . . . ½ cup **butter** or margarine. Gradually add
              1 cup **sugar,** creaming well.
Blend in . . . . . 2 unbeaten **eggs**
              1 teaspoon **almond extract** and
              1 teaspoon **vanilla.** Beat well.
Combine . . . . ¾ cup undiluted **evaporated milk** and
              ¼ cup **water.** Add alternately with the dry ingredients
              to creamed mixture. Blend well after each addition.
Stir in . . . . the fruit-nut mixture. Turn into 9 or 10-inch tube
              pan, well greased on bottom.
Bake . . . . at 350° for 60 to 70 minutes. Cool; frost with
              Lemon Icing, page 327.

*For use with Pillsbury's Best Self-Rising Flour, omit baking powder, salt, soda.

Good Moist Date Cake

Senior Winner by Mrs. H. W. Smiley, San Bernardino, California

Lots of dates and nuts are featured in this rich, lightly spiced cake.

BAKE at 350° for 55 to 65 minutes   MAKES 10-inch tube cake

Cook . . . . 1 cup **dates,** cut in small pieces, in
              ½ cup **water** in saucepan over medium heat, stirring
              occasionally, until thick. Cool.
Sift together 2¼ cups sifted **Pillsbury's Best All Purpose Flour***
              1½ teaspoons **soda**
              ½ teaspoon **salt**
              ½ teaspoon **cinnamon** and
              ½ teaspoon **cloves.** Set aside.
Add . . . . ¾ cup **sugar** gradually to
              ¾ cup **shortening,** creaming well.
Add . . . . 2 unbeaten **eggs,** beating well after each.

Stir in . . . . the cooled date mixture.

Combine . . . . ⅔ cup **buttermilk** or sour milk and
1 teaspoon **vanilla.** Add alternately with the dry ingredients to creamed mixture. Blend well after each addition.

Stir in . . . . . . ½ cup **nuts,** chopped. Turn into 10-inch tube pan, well greased on the bottom.

Bake . . . . at 350° for 55 to 65 minutes. Cool. Using a spoon or pastry tube, make a border of **Lemon Cheese Frosting,** page 325, on top of cake around center and outer rims; spread frosting part-way down sides.

*For use with Pillsbury's Best Self-Rising Flour, decrease soda to ½ teaspoon and omit salt.

Fantasy Fruit Cake

Junior Winner by Mrs. Frank L. Pantuso, San Antonio, Texas

You'll appreciate the economy of this spicy, high fruit cake filled with raisins, apples and nuts.

BAKE at 350° for 75 to 85 minutes   MAKES 10-inch tube cake

Cover . . . . 2 cups **raisins** with **water** in saucepan. Bring to boil and simmer 5 minutes. Drain.

Sift together 3¼ cups sifted **Pillsbury's Best All Purpose Flour***
2 tablespoons **cocoa**
1 teaspoon double-acting **baking powder**
1 teaspoon **soda**
1 teaspoon **salt**
1 teaspoon **cinnamon**
½ teaspoon **nutmeg** and
½ teaspoon **ginger.** Set aside.

Add . . . . 1½ cups **sugar** gradually to
1 cup **shortening,** creaming well.

Add . . . . 2 unbeaten **eggs;** beat well after each. Stir in
1 tablespoon **lemon juice**

Blend . . . . ½ cup **dark corn syrup** with
½ cup cool strong **coffee.** Add alternately with the dry ingredients to creamed mixture. Blend well after each addition.

Combine . . . . . 2 cups grated raw **apple**
1 cup **nuts,** chopped
½ cup sifted **Pillsbury's Best All Purpose Flour** and the drained raisins. Mix well. Stir into batter. Turn into 10-inch tube pan, well greased and lightly floured on the bottom.

Bake . . . . at 350° for 75 to 85 minutes. Cool thoroughly.

*For use with Pillsbury's Best Self-Rising Flour, omit baking powder, soda, salt.

Citron Jewel Cake

Senior Winner by Mrs. Alice Hartsuyker, El Monte, California

Citron, nutmeg and nuts give a piquant flavor to this fruit cake.

BAKE at 350° for 60 to 70 minutes   MAKES 9x5-inch cake

Sift together . . 2 cups sifted **Pillsbury's Best All Purpose Flour***
2 teaspoons double-acting **baking powder**
1 teaspoon **salt** and
½ teaspoon **nutmeg.** Set aside.

Add . . . . 1 cup firmly packed **brown sugar** gradually to
½ cup **shortening,** creaming well.

Blend in . . . . . 2 unbeaten **eggs** and
1 teaspoon **vanilla.** Beat well.

Add . . . . the dry ingredients alternately with
¾ cup **water.** Blend well after each addition.

Blend in . . . . . ½ cup finely chopped **citron** or candied fruit and
½ cup **nuts,** chopped. Mix thoroughly.

Turn . . . . into 9x5x3-inch pan, well greased on bottom.

Bake . . . . at 350° for 60 to 70 minutes. Cool; frost top with **Nutmeg Frosting,** page 327.

*Pillsbury's Best Self-Rising Flour is not recommended for use in this recipe.

Banana Fruit Cake

Banana Fruit Cake

Senior Winner by Mrs. Audrey Durey, Manchester, Connecticut

This cake makes you think of a rich banana bread, made with walnuts and candied fruit. No frosting is needed.

BAKE at 350° for 60 to 70 minutes   MAKES 9x5-inch cake

Sift together . . 2 cups sifted **Pillsbury's Best All Purpose Flour***
                3 teaspoons double-acting **baking powder** and
                ½ teaspoon **salt**
Combine . . . . ¾ cup chopped **candied fruit**
                ½ cup **nuts**, chopped, and ¼ cup dry ingredients.
Cream . . . . . . ¼ cup **butter** with
                ¼ cup **shortening**. Gradually add

                1 cup **sugar,** creaming well.
Add . . . . 2 unbeaten **eggs;** beat well.
Combine . . . . . 1 cup mashed ripe **bananas** (2 medium) and
                1 teaspoon **lemon juice;** blend into creamed mixture.
Blend in . . . . . . .the dry ingredients gradually; mix well. Stir in the
                floured fruit and nuts.
Turn . . . . .into 9x5x3-inch pan, well greased on the bottom.
Bake . . . . .at 350° for 60 to 70 minutes. Cool 10 minutes in pan,
                then turn out on rack.
**Pillsbury's Best Self-Rising Flour is not recommended for use in this recipe.*

Brown-Butter Nut Loaf

Senior Winner by Mrs. H. E. Thompson, Kress, Texas

Browned butter delicately tints and flavors a fine-textured pound cake-like nut loaf . . . more browned butter in the icing.

BAKE at 350° for 55 to 65 minutes   MAKES 9x5-inch cake

Brown . . . . . . ½ cup **butter** until deep brown. Chill until firm.
Sift together . . 2 cups sifted **Pillsbury's Best All Purpose Flour***
                2½ teaspoons double-acting **baking powder** and
                ½ teaspoon **salt.** Add
                ½ cup **nuts,** chopped
Cream . . . . .the browned butter. Gradually add
                1 cup **sugar,** creaming well.
Combine . . . . ⅔ cup **milk** and
                1 teaspoon **vanilla.** Add alternately with dry in-
                gredients to creamed mixture. Blend well after each
                addition.
Beat . . . . 3 **egg whites** until stiff but not dry. Fold into batter.
Turn . . . . .into 9x5x3-inch pan, well greased on the bottom.
Bake . . . . .at 350° for 55 to 65 minutes. Cool; frost with
                Browned Butter Frosting, page 321. Sprinkle with
                chopped **nuts,** if desired.
**For use with Pillsbury's Best Self-Rising Flour, omit baking powder and salt.*

Plum Nutty Cake

Senior Winner by Mrs. Elmer Arndt, Kenosha, Wisconsin

Plum jam makes this Quick-Mix loaf cake extra moist. Orange, cinnamon and nuts give it a delightful flavor.

BAKE at 350° for 40 to 50 minutes   MAKES 12x8 or 13x9-inch cake

Sift together . . 2 cups sifted **Pillsbury's Best All Purpose Flour***
              1¼ cups **sugar**
              1 teaspoon **soda**
              1 teaspoon **salt** and
              1 teaspoon **cinnamon** into large mixing bowl.
Add . . . . ½ cup **shortening** (half butter may be used)
              ½ cup **plum jam** or other red jam
              ½ cup **orange juice** and
              ¼ cup **water**
Beat . . . . 1½ minutes. (With mixer use a low speed.)
Add . . . . 2 unbeaten **eggs** and
              1 teaspoon grated **orange rind**. Beat 1½ minutes.
Stir in . . . . . . ½ cup **nuts,** chopped. Turn into 12x8x2 or 13x9x2-inch
              pan, well greased and lightly floured on the bottom.
Bake . . . . at 350° for 40 to 50 minutes. Cool; frost with
              Orange Butter Frosting, page 325.

For use with Pillsbury's Best Self-Rising Flour, decrease soda to ¼ teaspoon; omit salt.

Fruit Cake Layers

Senior Winner by Mrs. Regina R. Jones, Panama City, Florida

Fruit-filled layers—an attractive new way to bake a fruit cake. Pineapple filling between layers and on top adds refreshing flavor.

BAKE at 350° for 40 to 50 minutes   MAKES three 9-inch round
                         or two 9-inch square layers*

Sift together . . 3 cups sifted **Pillsbury's Best All Purpose Flour****
              2 teaspoons double-acting **baking powder**
              1 teaspoon **salt**
              1 teaspoon **cinnamon**
              ½ teaspoon **allspice** and
              ½ teaspoon **cloves** into large mixing bowl.
Add . . . . 1 pound chopped **candied fruit**
              1 cup **dates,** cut
              1 cup **currants** or raisins and
              1 cup **nuts,** chopped. Mix well.
Beat . . . . 4 **eggs** until light and fluffy. Blend in
              2 cups **sugar**
              ¾ cup melted **shortening** and
              1 cup **milk**. Add to flour-fruit mixture. Mix well.
Turn . . . . into three 9-inch round layer pans or two 9-inch
              square pans, well greased on the bottoms.
Bake . . . . at 350° for 40 to 50 minutes. Cool. Spread Pineapple
              Filling between and on top of layers. Decorate top
              with **pecan halves** and **candied cherries**. Cover; let
              stand in cool place 3 days before serving.

Cake may also be baked in two 9x5x3-inch pans for 60 to 75 minutes; omit filling.

**Pillsbury's Best Self-Rising Flour is not recommended for use in this recipe.*

PINEAPPLE FILLING

Combine 1½ cups sugar and 2 tablespoons cornstarch in saucepan. Add 1 No. 2 can (2¼ cups) crushed pineapple, ¼ cup grated orange rind and 1 tablespoon butter. Cook over medium heat for 20 minutes. Remove from heat. Stir in 1 cup chopped nuts. Cool to lukewarm.

Orleans Fruit Cake

Senior Winner by Mrs. E. L. Fortson, Shreveport, Louisiana

Watermelon pickles with pecans and maraschino cherries for flavor contrast in this colorful holiday fruit cake.

BAKE at 300° for 1½ to 2 hours   MAKES 9x5-inch cake

Sift together . . 1 cup sifted **Pillsbury's Best All Purpose Flour***
¾ cup **sugar**
1 teaspoon double-acting **baking powder** and
½ teaspoon **salt** into large mixing bowl.

Add . . . . 3 cups **pecan halves**
1½ cups **watermelon pickles,** cut in pieces, and
1 cup well-drained **maraschino cherries,** cut in quarters. Coat with the dry ingredients.

Blend in . . . . . 3 slightly beaten **eggs** and
1 teaspoon **vanilla.** Stir until well combined.

Turn . . . . batter into 9x5x3-inch pan, lined with aluminum foil or waxed paper, then greased.

Bake . . . . at 300° for 1½ to 2 hours.

**For use with Pillsbury's Best Self-Rising Flour, increase flour to 1⅛ cups (1 cup plus 2 tablespoons); omit baking powder and salt.*

Orleans Fruit Cake

Orange Kiss-Me Cake

Grand Prize Winner by Mrs. Peter Wuebel, Redwood City, California

Ground nuts, raisins and orange go into this Quick-Mix cake with easy orange juice and cinnamon-sugar topping. Cake stays moist for days.

BAKE at 350° for 40 to 50 minutes   MAKES 12x8 or 13x9-inch cake

Squeeze . . . . . 1 large **orange.** Reserve juice.

Grind . . . . pulp and rind of orange together with
1 cup seedless **raisins** and
⅓ cup **walnuts,** using coarse blade of food chopper.

Sift together . . 2 cups sifted **Pillsbury's Best All Purpose Flour***
1 cup **sugar**
1 teaspoon **soda** and
1 teaspoon **salt** into large mixing bowl.

Add . . . . ½ cup **shortening** and
¾ cup **milk**

Beat . . . . 1½ minutes. (With mixer use a low speed.)

Add . . . . 2 unbeaten **eggs** and
¼ cup **milk.** Beat 1½ minutes.

Fold . . . . orange-raisin mixture into batter. Turn into 12x8x2 or 13x9x2-inch pan, well greased and lightly floured on the bottom.

Bake . . . . at 350° for 40 to 50 minutes. Drip ⅓ cup orange juice over warm cake. Sprinkle with mixture of
⅓ cup **sugar**
1 teaspoon **cinnamon** and
¼ cup **walnuts,** chopped

**For use with Pillsbury's Best Self-Rising Flour, decrease soda to ¼ teaspoon and omit salt.*

BEST of the BAKE-OFF

Orange Kiss-Me
Cake
Grand Prize Winner
of the Second
Grand National
Bake-Off®

Orange Marmo Cake

Senior Winner by Anna J. Kendrick, Torrance, California

Spicy marmalade cake with orange butter icing . . . an all-occasion Quick-Mix cake that stores well.

BAKE at 350° for 45 to 55 minutes   MAKES two 9-inch layers

Sift together 2¾ cups sifted **Pillsbury's Best All Purpose Flour***
          1½ cups **sugar**
          1¼ teaspoons **soda**
          1 teaspoon **salt**
          1 teaspoon **cinnamon** and
          ½ teaspoon **cloves** into large mixing bowl.
Add . . . . ¾ cup **shortening** and
          1¼ cups **buttermilk** or sour milk
Beat . . . . 1½ minutes. (With mixer use a low speed.)
Add . . . . 4 unbeaten **eggs**; beat 1½ minutes.

Orange Marmo Cake

Stir in . . . . 1 cup sweet **orange marmalade**
          1 cup **nuts**, chopped, and
          1 tablespoon grated **orange rind**; mix thoroughly.
Turn . . . . into two 9-inch round layer pans, at least 1½ inches deep, well greased and floured on bottoms.
Bake . . . . at 350° for 45 to 55 minutes. Cool; frost with **Creamy Orange Frosting**, page 325.

*For use with Pillsbury's Best Self-Rising Flour, decrease soda to ½ teaspoon and buttermilk to 1 cup; omit salt.

Apricot Custard Cake

Senior Winner by Mrs. Frank J. Felder, San Francisco, California

Apricot halves and a creamy custard layer form a novel topping on this easy one-egg butter cake.

BAKE at 350° for 30 minutes, then   MAKES 8x8-inch cake
     for 12 to 15 minutes

Sift together . . 1 cup sifted **Pillsbury's Best All Purpose Flour***
          1 teaspoon double-acting **baking powder** and
          ½ teaspoon **salt**
Beat . . . . 1 **egg** until light and fluffy. Gradually add
          ½ cup **sugar**, beating until thick and ivory colored. Stir in
          1 teaspoon **vanilla** and
          ½ teaspoon **lemon extract**, if desired.
Blend in . . . . the dry ingredients alternately with
          ⅓ cup **milk**. Blend well after each addition.
Stir in . . . . . . ¼ cup melted **butter** or margarine
Turn . . . . into 8x8x2-inch pan, well greased and lightly floured on the bottom. Arrange
          16 fresh or well-drained canned **apricot halves** on the batter, cut-side up.
Bake . . . . at 350° for 30 minutes. Meanwhile, beat together
          1 **egg**

⅓ cup **cream** and

¼ teaspoon **vanilla**; pour over partially-baked cake. Sprinkle with mixture of

1 tablespoon **sugar** and

⅛ teaspoon **cinnamon**

Bake . . . . 12 to 15 minutes until custard is set. Serve warm.

For use with Pillsbury's Best Self-Rising Flour, omit baking powder and salt; decrease milk to ¼ cup.

Apple Filled Crumb Cake

Senior Winner by Mrs. Jos. A. Caputo, Palatka, Florida

"Company's a'coming," and this crumb topped cake-dessert rich with apples will score a big hit.

BAKE at 350° for 35 to 40 minutes   **MAKES 13x9-inch cake**

Combine . . . . . 4 cups **apples,** pared, cored and sliced

½ cup **sugar**

1 teaspoon **cinnamon**

1 tablespoon **butter** and

1 tablespoon **lemon juice** in saucepan. Cover; simmer over medium heat, stirring occasionally, just until tender. Cool; drain thoroughly.

Sift together 1¼ cups sifted **Pillsbury's Best All Purpose Flour***

¾ cup **sugar**

1 teaspoon double-acting **baking powder**

¾ teaspoon **salt** and

¼ teaspoon **cloves** into mixing bowl.

Add . . . . ⅓ cup **butter** or margarine and

⅓ cup **milk**

Beat . . . . 1½ minutes. (With mixer use a low speed.)

Add . . . . 2 unbeaten **eggs** and

½ teaspoon **vanilla**; beat 1½ minutes.

Spread . . . . half of batter into 13x9x2-inch pan, well greased and lightly floured on the bottom. Top with half the

apples. Cover with remaining batter, then remaining apples. Sprinkle Crumb Topping over apples.

Bake . . . . at 350° for 35 to 40 minutes. Serve warm or cold, plain or with whipped cream.

For use with Pillsbury's Best Self-Rising Flour, omit baking powder and salt.

CRUMB TOPPING

Combine ¾ cup firmly packed brown sugar, ½ cup sifted Pillsbury's Best All Purpose Flour, ¼ cup butter and ½ cup chopped pecans.

Johnny Appleseed Cake

Junior Winner by Kathleen Frazee, Western Springs, Illinois

A loaf cake moist with applesauce and raisins, with added flavor from nuts and spices.

BAKE at 350° for 40 to 50 minutes   **MAKES 9x9-inch cake**

Sift together . . 2 cups sifted **Pillsbury's Best All Purpose Flour***

1 cup **sugar**

1 teaspoon **salt**

1 teaspoon **cinnamon**

½ teaspoon **nutmeg** and

¼ teaspoon **cloves**

Add . . . . 1 cup **raisins**

1 cup **walnuts,** chopped, and

½ cup melted **butter** or margarine

Combine . . . 1½ cups hot **applesauce** and

2 teaspoons **soda**; add to the dry ingredients. Beat until well blended.

Turn . . . . into 9x9x2 or 11x7x2-inch pan, well greased and lightly floured on the bottom.

Bake . . . . at 350° for 40 to 50 minutes. Serve warm or cold with **whipped cream** or hard sauce.

For use with Pillsbury's Best Self-Rising Flour, omit salt and decrease soda to 1 teaspoon.

Molasses Orange Sugar Squares

Senior Winner by Mrs. Joseph Manners, Atlantic City, New Jersey

Similar to bar cookies, but with the tenderness and delicacy of cake.

BAKE at 350° for 30 to 35 minutes   MAKES 13x9-inch cake

Sift together 1¾ cups sifted **Pillsbury's Best All Purpose Flour***
    1 teaspoon double-acting **baking powder**
    ½ teaspoon **soda** and
    ½ teaspoon **salt** into large mixing bowl.
Add........½ cup **sugar**
    ½ cup **milk**
    ½ cup **molasses**
    ⅓ cup **shortening**
    2 unbeaten **eggs**
    1 tablespoon grated **orange rind** and

Molasses Orange Sugar Squares

    1 teaspoon **vanilla**
Beat..........2 minutes. (With mixer use a low speed.)
Turn..........into 13x9x2-inch pan, well greased and lightly floured
    on the bottom.
Combine.....⅓ cup finely crushed **loaf sugar** or granulated sugar and
    2 tablespoons grated **orange rind.** Sprinkle over batter.
Bake.........at 350° for 30 to 35 minutes. Serve warm or cool,
    cut into squares. Top with **whipped cream,** if desired.
For use with Pillsbury's Best Self-Rising Flour, omit baking powder, soda, salt.

Alaska Mincemeat Cake

Junior Winner by Patricia Wilcox, Sitka, Alaska

An inexpensive fruit cake mixed in a saucepan! A big moist cake that keeps well.

BAKE at 375°   MAKES 9 or 10-inch tube cake

Combine.....2 cups **water**
    1¾ cups **sugar**
    ¾ cup **shortening** and
    1 package (9 oz.) dry **mincemeat,** broken in pieces, in
    large saucepan. Bring to a rolling boil; boil 3 minutes,
    stirring occasionally. Cool.
Sift together..3 cups sifted **Pillsbury's Best All Purpose Flour***
    2 teaspoons **soda** and
    1 teaspoon **salt.** Add to mincemeat mixture; mix well.
Stir in......½ cup **nuts,** chopped
Turn..........into 9 or 10-inch tube pan, well greased and lightly
    floured on the bottom.**
Bake.........at 375°: 60 to 70 minutes for 9-inch cake; 55 to 65
    minutes for 10-inch cake.** Cool thoroughly;
    sprinkle with sifted **confectioners' sugar** before
    slicing.
Pillsbury's Best Self-Rising Flour is not recommended for use in this recipe.
**Cake may also be baked in two 9x5x3-inch loaf pans for 40 to 50 minutes.*

POUND CAKES

POUND CAKES—The authentic old-fashioned pound cake contains a pound each of sugar, butter, flour and eggs. A true pound cake has no liquid and little, if any, leavening agent. Of course, there are many variations of the basic pound cake.

It is important to cream the butter and sugar well—until very light and fluffy. The batter must be beaten well after the addition of eggs also.

Cool pound cake at least 30 minutes before removing from pan. *Do not invert.*

Although pound cake may be eaten while fresh, the flavor improves after 24 hours; it is usually sliced fairly thin and served plain, with a simple glaze, or sprinkled with confectioners' sugar.

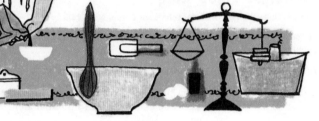

Golden Glory Ring Cake

Senior Winner by Helen Flynn, Glendale, New York

This high, pound-type cake is rich in butter and eggs. It's a generous cake—fine for a party.

BAKE at 350° for 60 to 65 minutes   MAKES 9-inch tube cake*

Sift together . . 3 cups sifted **Pillsbury's Best All Purpose Flour****
          2½ teaspoons double-acting **baking powder** and
          ¼ teaspoon **salt**
Cream . . . . 1 cup **butter** or margarine. Gradually add
          1½ cups **sugar,** creaming well.

Blend in . . . . . 2 unbeaten **eggs** and
          2 unbeaten **egg yolks,** beating well after each.
Combine . . . . . 1 cup **milk** and
          1 teaspoon **vanilla.** Add alternately with the dry ingredients to creamed mixture. Blend well after each addition.
Turn . . . . into 9-inch tube pan, well greased and lightly floured on the bottom.
Bake . . . . at 350° for 60 to 65 minutes. Serve plain, or frost with **Lemon Icing,** page 327.

  **Cake may be baked in two 9x5x3-inch pans for 40 to 50 minutes.*
***For use with Pillsbury's Best Self-Rising Flour, omit baking powder and salt.*

Sunburst Cake

Senior Winner by Mrs. Nolan Harris, Columbia, Tennessee

This fine-textured golden pound cake has such a good, buttery flavor; it needs no frosting.

BAKE at 350° for 30 minutes, then   MAKES 9 or 10-inch tube cake*
at 300° for 40 to 50 minutes

Sift together . . 2 cups sifted **Pillsbury's Best All Purpose Flour**** and
          ½ teaspoon double-acting **baking powder**
Cream . . . . . . ¾ cup **butter** or margarine. Add
          ⅓ cup (3-oz. pkg.) **cream cheese;** beat well. Add
          1½ cups **sugar** gradually, creaming well.
Add . . . . 5 **eggs,** one at a time; beat well after each.
Blend in . . . . the dry ingredients; stir just until blended.
Turn . . . . into 9 or 10-inch tube pan*, well greased on the bottom.
Bake . . . . at 350° for 30 minutes, then at 300° for 40 to 50 minutes.

  **Cake may also be baked in two 9x5x3-inch pans at 350° for 30 minutes, then at 300° for 25 to 30 minutes.*
***Pillsbury's Best Self-Rising Flour is not recommended for use in this recipe.*

Sunny Butter Cake

Junior Winner by Miriam Ruth Velez, Caguas, Puerto Rico

A big, easy butter cake . . . this handsome golden ring is so rich, so appetizing, it needs no frosting.

BAKE at 350° for 60 to 70 minutes   MAKES 10-inch tube cake

Sift together 2½ cups sifted **Pillsbury's Best All Purpose Flour***
2 teaspoons double-acting **baking powder** and
1 teaspoon **salt**

Cream . . . . 1 cup **butter** or margarine. Gradually add
1½ cups **sugar,** creaming well.

Add . . . . 3 unbeaten **eggs** and
3 unbeaten **egg yolks,** ** beating well after each.

Combine . . . . . 1 cup **milk** and
1 teaspoon **vanilla.** Add alternately with the dry ingredients to creamed mixture. Blend well after each
addition.

Turn . . . . into 10-inch tube pan, well greased on the bottom.

Bake . . . . at 350° for 60 to 70 minutes. Cool. Serve plain or
with a favorite frosting.

*Pillsbury's Best Self-Rising Flour is not recommended for use in this recipe.
**If desired, 5 eggs may be substituted for the 3 eggs and 3 egg yolks.

Tea Time in Paris Cake

Senior Winner by Mrs. Philip W. Peters, East Orange, New Jersey

A bit of lemon goes into this fine, rich pound cake. Almonds may be sprinkled over the top to take the place of frosting.

BAKE at 325° for 55 to 65 minutes   MAKES 9 or 10-inch tube cake

Sift together 2¼ cups sifted **Pillsbury's Best All Purpose Flour***
2 teaspoons double-acting **baking powder** and
½ teaspoon **salt**

Cream . . . . 1 cup **butter** or margarine. Gradually add
1¼ cups **sugar,** creaming well.

Blend in . . . . . 4 unbeaten **egg yolks,** beating well after each.

Add . . . . ¼ cup **lemon juice** and
1 to 2 tablespoons grated **lemon rind.** Add the dry
ingredients gradually. Blend well.

Beat . . . . 4 **egg whites** until soft peaks form. Fold into batter.

Turn . . . . into 9 or 10-inch tube pan, well greased on the
bottom. If desired, sprinkle ½ cup slivered blanched
almonds over top of cake.

Bake . . . . at 325° for 55 to 65 minutes.

*For use with Pillsbury's Best Self-Rising Flour, omit baking powder and salt.

Buttercot Filled Ring

Senior Winner by Mrs. Kate M. Lohmann, Olean, New York

A pound cake-type tube cake, split into three layers and filled with apricot preserves and buttery frosting.

BAKE at 350° for 55 to 65 minutes   MAKES 9 or 10-inch tube cake

Sift together 2½ cups sifted **Pillsbury's Best All Purpose Flour***
3 teaspoons double-acting **baking powder** and
1 teaspoon **salt.** Add
1 tablespoon grated **lemon rind.** Set aside.

Add . . . . 1⅓ cups **sugar** gradually to
¾ cup **shortening,** creaming well.

Blend in . . . . . 3 unbeaten **eggs,** beating well after each.

Add . . . . the dry ingredients alternately with
1 cup **milk.** Blend well after each addition.

Turn . . . . into 9 or 10-inch tube pan, well greased and lightly
floured on the bottom.

Bake . . . . at 350° for 55 to 65 minutes. Cool. Split into 3 layers.

Spread . . . . bottom layer of cake with
⅓ cup **apricot preserves;** cover with about ½ cup
Butter Cream Frosting, page 314. Place second layer
over first; spread with

⅓ cup **apricot preserves** and ½ cup frosting. Top with remaining layer of cake; frost sides and top with remaining frosting. Sprinkle Sugared-Nut Topping over top and sides.

*For use with Pillsbury's Best Self-Rising Flour, omit baking powder and salt.

SUGARED-NUT TOPPING

Melt 1 tablespoon butter and 3 tablespoons sugar in heavy saucepan over low heat, stirring constantly, until mixture is light brown. Add ¾ cup finely chopped pecans; cook and stir until golden brown. Cool; crumble into small pieces.

Cherry Confetti Cake

Senior Winner by Anne V. Allcock, Morris Plains, New Jersey

Lots of almonds and bright red cherries inside this pound cake, and butter, sugar and cinnamon on top.

BAKE at 350° for 55 to 65 minutes   MAKES 10-inch tube cake

Sift together . . 3 cups sifted **Pillsbury's Best All Purpose Flour***
2 teaspoons double-acting **baking powder** and
1 teaspoon **salt**. Set aside.

Add . . . . 4 cups (1 lb.) sifted **confectioners' sugar** gradually to
1 cup **shortening** (half butter may be used); cream
well.

Blend in . . . . . 1 teaspoon **almond extract** and
4 **eggs**, one at a time; beat well after each.

Add . . . . the dry ingredients alternately with
1 cup **milk**. Blend well after each addition.

Fold in . . . . . . ½ cup **almonds**, chopped, and
1 cup **maraschino cherries**, finely chopped

Turn . . . . into 10-inch tube pan, well greased on the bottom.

Bake . . . . at 350° for 55 to 65 minutes. While warm, brush
with **butter**; sprinkle with **cinnamon** and **sugar**.

*Pillsbury's Best Self-Rising Flour is not recommended for use in this recipe.

Candied Cherry Cake

Senior Winner by Mrs. L. G. Wietor, Chicago, Illinois

A really festive pound cake! Candied cherries sprinkled throughout give it a colorful, gay and attractive appearance.

BAKE at 350°   MAKES two 9x5-inch cakes
or one 10-inch tube cake

Grease . . . . generously the bottoms and sides of two 9x5x3-inch
pans or one 10-inch tube pan. Coat with mixture of
½ cup **nuts**, finely chopped, and
¼ cup **bread** or **cake crumbs** (or use ¼ cup more nuts)

Sift together . . 3 cups sifted **Pillsbury's Best All Purpose Flour*** and
2 teaspoons double-acting **baking powder**

Combine . . . . . ½ cup **candied cherries**
1 teaspoon grated **lemon rind** and ¼ cup of the dry
ingredients. Chop cherries very fine.

Cream . . . . 1 cup **butter** or margarine. Gradually add
1 cup **sugar**, creaming well.

Add . . . . 5 **eggs**, one at a time; beat well after each.

Combine . . . . . 1 cup **sweetened condensed milk** and
1 teaspoon **vanilla**. Add alternately with the dry ingredients to creamed mixture. Blend well after each
addition.

Stir in . . . . the cherry mixture. Turn into prepared pans.

Bake . . . . at 350°: 50 to 60 minutes for loaf pans; 65 to 75
minutes for tube pan. Cool 15 minutes. Remove
from pan.

*For use with Pillsbury's Best Self-Rising Flour, omit baking powder.

Cinnamon Nut Ring

Junior Winner by Kathy Tsamopoulos, Astoria, New York

A tall, cinnamon-flavored pound cake, filled with nuts.

BAKE at 350° for 75 to 85 minutes   MAKES 10-inch tube cake

Sift together . . 3 cups sifted **Pillsbury's Best All Purpose Flour***
           2 teaspoons double-acting **baking powder**
           2 teaspoons **cinnamon** and
           ½ teaspoon **salt.** Set aside.
Add . . . . 2 cups **sugar** gradually to
           1 cup **shortening,** creaming well.
Blend in . . . . . 4 **eggs,** one at a time; beat well after each.
Add . . . . the dry ingredients alternately with
           1 cup **milk.** Blend well after each addition.
Stir in . . . . . . ½ cup **almonds,** finely chopped, and
           ½ cup **walnuts,** finely chopped
Turn . . . . into 10-inch tube pan, well greased on the bottom.
Bake . . . . at 350° for 75 to 85 minutes. Serve plain, or ice with
           a simple glaze.

*For use with Pillsbury's Best Self-Rising Flour, omit baking powder and salt.

Hawaiian Pound Cake

Senior Winner by Mrs. Charles W. Braswell, Birmingham, Alabama

A rich, butter pound cake with candied pineapple and ginger inside and toasted sesame seeds sprinkled on top.

BAKE at 350° for 55 to 60 minutes   MAKES 9 or 10-inch tube cake

Toast . . . . 3 tablespoons **sesame seeds** at 350° for 8 to 10
           minutes until golden brown. Reserve.
Sift together 2¼ cups sifted **Pillsbury's Best All Purpose Flour***
           ½ teaspoon double-acting **baking powder** and
           ¼ teaspoon **salt**
Combine . . . . ½ cup chopped **candied pineapple** and
           2 to 4 tablespoons chopped **candied ginger** with 2
           tablespoons dry ingredients. Chop very fine.
Cream . . . . 1 cup **butter** or margarine. Gradually add
           1½ cups **sugar,** creaming well. *Do not underbeat.*
Add . . . . 6 **eggs,** one at a time; beat well after each.
Blend in . . . . . . .the dry ingredients; mix well. Stir in the candied
           fruit.
Turn . . . . into 9 or 10-inch tube pan, well greased on the bottom.
Bake . . . . at 350° for 55 to 60 minutes. While warm, frost with
           Creamy Vanilla Frosting, page 321. Sprinkle with
           the toasted sesame seeds, pressing them lightly into
           the frosting.

*Pillsbury's Best Self-Rising Flour is not recommended for use in this recipe.

Old-Time Fruit Pound Cake

Senior Winner by Mrs. Jean E. Smith, Blackstone, Virginia

Citron and a hint of mace are added to the batter of this high cake baked in a tube pan. Nice for large parties.

BAKE at 325° for 60 to 70 minutes   MAKES 10-inch tube cake

Sift together 2½ cups sifted **Pillsbury's Best All Purpose Flour***

2 teaspoons double-acting **baking powder**

1 teaspoon **salt** and

½ teaspoon **mace**

Combine.....1 cup **candied citron**, very finely chopped, and ½ cup dry ingredients. Set aside.

Add.......1½ cups **sugar** gradually to

⅔ cup **shortening** or butter, creaming well.

Blend in.....3 **eggs**, one at a time; beat well after each.

Add.........the dry ingredients alternately with

1 cup **milk.** Blend well after each addition.

Stir in.........the floured citron.

Turn..........into 10-inch tube pan, well greased on the bottom.

Bake.........at 325° for 60 to 70 minutes. Cool. Serve topped with **peach slices** and Orange Sauce.

For use with Pillsbury's Best Self-Rising Flour, omit baking powder and salt.

ORANGE SAUCE

Combine 1 cup sugar and ½ cup water in saucepan. Cook over low heat until a little syrup dropped in cold water forms a soft ball (238°). Add ½ cup orange juice and cool slightly.

Triple Seed Cake

Senior Winner by Anna D. Ellmer, Hillsdale, New York

Caraway seed, poppy seed and anise seed are sprinkled through this high pound cake.

BAKE at 350° for 75 to 80 minutes   MAKES 10-inch tube cake

Sift together..3 cups sifted **Pillsbury's Best All Purpose Flour***

2½ teaspoons double-acting **baking powder**

1 teaspoon **salt** and

¾ teaspoon **nutmeg.** Set aside.

Add........2 cups **sugar** gradually to

⅔ cup **shortening,** creaming well.

Add........4 unbeaten **eggs,** beating well after each.

Blend in.....2 tablespoons grated **orange rind** and

1 tablespoon grated **lemon rind;** mix thoroughly.

Add.........the dry ingredients alternately with

1 cup **milk.** Blend well after each addition.

Spread........one-fourth of batter in 10-inch tube pan, well greased on the bottom. Sprinkle with

1 tablespoon **caraway seed.** Alternate remaining batter with

1 tablespoon **poppy seed** and

1 tablespoon **anise seed,** ending with batter on top.

Bake.........at 350° for 75 to 80 minutes. Cool in pan 15 minutes. Pour Fruit Juice Glaze over top while slightly warm.

Pillsbury's Best Self-Rising Flour is not recommended for use in this recipe.

FRUIT JUICE GLAZE

Combine 1¼ cups sifted confectioners' sugar, 2 tablespoons orange juice and 1 teaspoon lemon juice. Blend well.

Triple Seed Cake

Mari-Gold Cake

Bride Winner by Mrs. Vincent DeMarco, Chicago, Illinois

Moist butter cake with subtle flavors of coconut and orange.

BAKE at 350° for 60 to 65 minutes   MAKES 9 or 10-inch tube cake*

Sift together . . 2 cups sifted **Pillsbury's Best All Purpose Flour****
         ¾ teaspoon **soda** and
         ½ teaspoon **salt**
Cream . . . . 1 cup **butter** or margarine. Gradually add
         1¼ cups **sugar,** creaming well.
Stir in . . . . 1 cup **coconut,** chopped
         1 tablespoon grated **orange rind** and
         1 teaspoon **orange extract**
Blend in . . . . . 4 unbeaten **eggs,** beating well after each.
Add . . . . ½ cup **sour cream** alternately with the dry ingredients.
         Blend well after each addition.

Turn . . . . into ungreased 9 or 10-inch tube pan.*
Bake . . . . at 350° for 60 to 65 minutes. Cool; frost with
         Orange Frosting, page 327.

*If desired, cake may be baked in two 9x5x3-inch pans for 30 to 35 minutes.
**For use with Pillsbury's Best Self-Rising Flour, omit soda and salt.

Hot Fudge Sundae Cake

Senior Winner by Mrs. A. P. Tillery, Pahokee, Florida

A simple hot fudge sauce is alternated with cake batter to give an intriguing rippled effect when the cake is sliced.

BAKE at 350° for 70 to 80 minutes   MAKES 10-inch tube cake

Sift together . . 3 cups sifted **Pillsbury's Best All Purpose Flour***
         3 teaspoons double-acting **baking powder** and
         1 teaspoon **salt**
Cream . . . . . . ½ cup **butter** or margarine with
         ½ cup **shortening.** Gradually add
         1½ cups **sugar,** creaming well, at least 5 minutes.
Add . . . . 4 unbeaten **eggs,** beating 1 minute after each.
Combine . . . . . 1 cup **milk** and
         1 teaspoon **vanilla.** Add alternately with the dry ingredients to creamed mixture. Blend well after each addition.
Turn . . . . one-fourth of batter into 10-inch tube pan, well greased on the bottom. Drizzle with Chocolate Sauce, alternating layers of batter and sauce to make three layers of sauce with batter on top.
Bake . . . . at 350° for 70 to 80 minutes. Cool; frost with
         Chocolate Glaze, page 326.

*Pillsbury's Best Self-Rising Flour is not recommended for use in this recipe.

CHOCOLATE SAUCE

Melt 4 ounces German's sweet chocolate with 2 tablespoons water over hot water. Remove from heat. Blend in 2 tablespoons cream.

Hot Fudge Sundae Cake

Caraway Ring Cake

Senior Winner by Mrs. Lorraine M. Horst, Westbury, New York

Cinnamon and caraway seeds in a butter-rich pound cake.

BAKE at 375° for 45 to 50 minutes   MAKES 9-inch tube cake

Sift together..2 cups sifted **Pillsbury's Best All Purpose Flour***
           2 teaspoons double-acting **baking powder** and
           2 teaspoons **cinnamon**
Cream.......1 cup **butter** or margarine. Gradually add
           1½ cups **sugar** and
           3 teaspoons **caraway seed,** creaming well.
Beat.......5 **egg yolks** until thick and lemon colored. Add to creamed mixture; blend well.
Add.........the dry ingredients alternately with
           ⅓ cup **milk.** Blend well after each addition. (With mixer use a low speed.)
Beat.......5 **egg whites** until stiff but not dry. Fold gently into batter.
Turn.........into 9-inch tube pan, well greased on the bottom.
Bake.........at 375° for 45 to 50 minutes. Cool; frost with **Cinnamon Glaze,** page 326.

*Pillsbury's Best Self-Rising Flour is not recommended for use in this recipe.

Spicy Pound Cake

Senior Winner by Mrs. John M. Lieser, Dover, Ohio

For a different pound-type cake try this Quick-Mix cake, flavored just right with brown sugar and spices.

BAKE at 350° for 50 to 60 minutes   MAKES 9 or 10-inch tube cake

Sift together..2 cups sifted **Pillsbury's Best All Purpose Flour***
           1 teaspoon **soda**
           1 teaspoon **salt**
           1 teaspoon **cinnamon**
           ¼ teaspoon **nutmeg** and
           ¼ teaspoon **cloves** into large mixing bowl.
Add.......1¼ cups firmly packed **brown sugar**
           ¾ cup **shortening** and
           ¾ cup **buttermilk** or sour milk
Beat.........1½ minutes. (With mixer use a low speed.)
Add.........3 unbeaten **eggs;** beat 1½ minutes.
Turn.........into 9 or 10-inch tube pan, well greased on the bottom.
Bake.........at 350° for 50 to 60 minutes. Cool; frost with **Brown-Butter Icing,** page 327.

*For use with Pillsbury's Best Self Rising Flour, omit soda and salt; increase cinnamon to 1½ teaspoons and cloves to ½ teaspoon.

Sugar 'n' Spice Pound Cake

Sugar 'n' Spice Pound Cake

Senior Winner by Mrs. Ernest Huscher, Concordia, Kansas

Confectioners' sugar gives fine texture to this tube pound cake—caraway and cinnamon spice it.

BAKE at 325°   MAKES 9 or 10-inch tube cake

Sift together . . 3 cups sifted **Pillsbury's Best All Purpose Flour***
               2 teaspoons double-acting **baking powder**
               1 teaspoon **cinnamon** and
               ½ teaspoon **salt**

Cream . . . . 1 cup **butter** or margarine. Gradually add
               2½ cups sifted **confectioners' sugar,** creaming well.

Add . . . . 2 unbeaten **eggs,** beating well after each.

Blend in . . . . . 3 unbeaten **egg yolks,** one at a time

               1 tablespoon **caraway seed** and
               1 teaspoon **vanilla.** Beat well.

Add . . . . the dry ingredients alternately with
               1 cup **milk.** Blend well after each addition.

Turn . . . . into 9 or 10-inch tube pan, well greased and lightly floured on the bottom.

Bake . . . . at 325°: 1½ to 1¾ hours for 9-inch cake; 1¼ to 1½ hours for 10-inch cake.

*For use with Pillsbury's Best Self-Rising Flour, omit baking powder and salt.

X-tra Fancy Pound Cake

Senior Winner by Mrs. Sophie Radcliffe, Philadelphia, Pennsylvania

A high, fine-textured variation of the old-fashioned pound cake, delicately flavored with nuts and just a little spice.

BAKE at 325° for 1¼ to 1½ hours   MAKES 10-inch tube cake

Sift together . . 4 cups sifted **Pillsbury's Best All Purpose Flour***
               2 teaspoons double-acting **baking powder**
               1 teaspoon **salt** and
               ¼ teaspoon **mace**

Cream . . . . . . 1 pound (2 cups) **butter** or margarine thoroughly. Gradually add
               1 pound (4 to 4¼ cups) sifted **confectioners' sugar,** creaming until light and fluffy.

Blend in . . . . . 1 teaspoon **vanilla**
               ½ teaspoon **lemon extract** and
               6 **eggs,** one at a time; beat well after each.

Add . . . . the dry ingredients alternately with
               ¾ cup **milk.** Blend well after each addition.

Stir in . . . . . 1½ cups **nuts,** chopped

Turn . . . . into 10-inch tube pan, well greased on the bottom.

Bake . . . . at 325° for 1¼ to 1½ hours. Cool; frost, if desired, with **Creamy Vanilla Frosting,** page 321.

*Pillsbury's Best Self-Rising Flour is not recommended for use in this recipe.

Co-Co Pound Cake

Senior Winner by Mrs. John W. Greene, Gibsonville, North Carolina

A "show-off" cake! Bake in a tube pan; glaze with chocolate icing.

BAKE at 325° for 1¼ to 1½ hours   MAKES 10-inch tube cake

Sift together . . 3 cups sifted **Pillsbury's Best All Purpose Flour***
         ½ cup **cocoa**
         1 teaspoon **salt** and
         ½ teaspoon double-acting **baking powder**

Cream . . . . 1 cup **butter** or margarine with
         ½ cup **shortening.** Gradually add
         2¼ cups **sugar,** creaming well.

Blend in . . . . . 1 teaspoon **vanilla** and
         5 **eggs,** one at a time; beat well after each.

Add . . . . the dry ingredients alternately with
         1 cup **milk.** Blend well after each addition. (With mixer use a low speed.)

Turn . . . . into 10-inch tube pan, well greased on the bottom.

Bake . . . . at 325° for 1¼ to 1½ hours. Cool; if desired, frost with **Chocolate Glaze,** page 326.

**Pillsbury's Best Self-Rising Flour is not recommended for use in this recipe.*

Chocolate Swirl Mocha Cake

Senior Winner by Mrs. W. H. Conley, Sacramento, California

Grated semi-sweet chocolate ripples through the coffee-flavored batter of this rich pound cake.

BAKE at 350° for 60 to 70 minutes   MAKES 9 or 10-inch tube cake

Grate . . . . 3 squares (3 oz.) **semi-sweet chocolate.** Set aside.

Sift together . . 2 cups sifted **Pillsbury's Best All Purpose Flour***
         1 teaspoon double-acting **baking powder**
         1 teaspoon **salt** and
         4 teaspoons **instant coffee.** Set aside.

Chocolate Swirl Mocha Cake

Add . . . . 1¼ cups **sugar** gradually to
         ⅔ cup **shortening,** creaming until light and fluffy.

Blend in . . . . . 3 unbeaten **eggs,** beating well after each.

Combine . . . . ⅔ cup cold **water** and
         1 teaspoon **vanilla.** Add alternately with the dry ingredients to creamed mixture. Blend well after each addition.

Turn . . . . half the batter into 9 or 10-inch tube pan, well greased on the bottom. Sprinkle with half the grated chocolate. Add remaining batter and sprinkle with remaining chocolate. Marble the chocolate into batter by folding with a rubber spatula or spoon.

Bake . . . . at 350° for 60 to 70 minutes. Cool; sprinkle with sifted **confectioners' sugar.**

**For use with Pillsbury's Best Self-Rising Flour, omit baking powder and salt.*

UPSIDE-DOWN CAKES

make delicious and simple desserts—slip one out of the oven at the last minute and serve warm. For an extra treat, serve with whipped cream or ice cream.

Drain the fruits well for an upside-down cake.

Let an upside-down cake cool in the pan 5 minutes unless otherwise directed in recipe, then invert on serving plate or wire rack.

Apricot Turnover Cake

Senior Winner by Mrs. Joseph Arena, Forest Hills, New York

There's old-fashioned goodness in this upside-down cake. Apricots in brown sugar on top, apricot juice in the cake!

BAKE at 350° for 40 to 45 minutes   MAKES 8x8-inch cake

Melt . . . . ¼ cup **butter** or margarine in 8x8x2-inch pan; sprinkle with
½ cup firmly packed **brown sugar**

Drain . . . . 1 No. 2 can **apricot halves**; reserve juice. (Cooked, dried apricots may be used.) Arrange 16 halves in pan.

Sift together 1¼ cups sifted **Pillsbury's Best All Purpose Flour***
1½ teaspoons double-acting **baking powder** and

¼ teaspoon **salt**. Set aside.

Add . . . . ½ cup **sugar** gradually to
⅓ cup **shortening,** creaming well.

Blend in . . . . . 1 unbeaten **egg** and
1 teaspoon **vanilla.** Beat well.

Add . . . . ½ cup **apricot juice** alternately with the dry ingredients. Blend well after each addition. Pour over apricot halves.

Bake . . . . at 350° for 40 to 45 minutes. Cool slightly; invert on serving plate. Serve with **whipped cream.**

**For use with Pillsbury's Best Self-Rising Flour, omit baking powder and salt.*

Virginia Reel Apple Cake

Junior Winner by Helen Hundley, Anawalt, West Virginia

A wonderful spicy fragrance when you take this apple cake out of the oven! An upside-down cake that needs no frosting.

BAKE at 350° for 35 to 40 minutes   MAKES 12x8 or 13x9-inch cake

Combine . . . . . 4 cups cooking **apples** (4 to 6), pared, cored and sliced
1 cup **sugar**
2 tablespoons **butter** and
1 teaspoon **cinnamon** in saucepan. Cook over low heat until tender. Pour into 12x8x2 or 13x9x2-inch pan, well greased on the bottom.

Sift together . . 2 cups sifted **Pillsbury's Best All Purpose Flour***
2½ teaspoons double-acting **baking powder** and
1 teaspoon **salt**. Set aside.

Add . . . . 1 cup **sugar** gradually to
½ cup **shortening,** creaming well.

Blend in . . . . . 2 unbeaten **eggs,** beating well after each.

Combine . . . . . 1 cup **milk** and
1 teaspoon **vanilla.** Add alternately with the dry ingredients to creamed mixture. Blend well after each addition.

Pour . . . . batter over apples in pan.
Bake . . . . at 350° for 35 to 40 minutes. Cool 5 minutes; invert on plate. Serve warm with **whipped cream.**
For use with Pillsbury's Best Self-Rising Flour, omit baking powder and salt.

Cranberry Skillet Cake

Senior Winner by Mrs. Mary Henson, Jacksonville, Florida

Bright cranberry sauce and nuts are the "upside down" of this unusual cake which is baked right in a skillet.

BAKE at 350° for 50 to 60 minutes   MAKES 9 or 10-inch round cake*

Line . . . . 9 or 10-inch skillet with aluminum foil.* Spread
1 can (1 lb.) **whole cranberry sauce** in bottom of skillet. Sprinkle with
1 tablespoon **lemon juice**
⅓ cup **sugar** and
¼ cup chopped **nuts,** if desired. Dot with
1 tablespoon **butter**
Sift together 1¼ cups sifted **Pillsbury's Best All Purpose Flour****
1½ teaspoons double-acting **baking powder** and
½ teaspoon **salt.** Set aside.
Add . . . . ¾ cup **sugar** gradually to
⅓ cup **shortening,** creaming well.
Stir in . . . . 1 unbeaten **egg;** beat well.
Combine . . . . ½ cup **milk** and
½ teaspoon **vanilla.** Add alternately with the dry ingredients to creamed mixture. Blend well after each addition.
Spoon . . . . over cranberry mixture; spread carefully.
Bake . . . . at 350° for 50 to 60 minutes. Cool in pan 30 minutes; invert on serving plate. Serve warm with **whipped cream.**

Or bake in 9x9x2-inch pan, well greased and lightly floured on bottom.
**For use with Pillsbury's Best Self-Rising Flour, omit baking powder and salt.*

Caramel Pear Upside-Down Cake

Senior Winner by Mrs. C. C. Faxon, Palmyra, Missouri

Pears and candy caramels combine to make the upside-down layer for this sponge cake.

BAKE at 350° for 35 to 40 minutes   MAKES 13x9-inch cake

Drain . . . . 1 No. 2½ can **pear halves,** reserving juice. Slice pear halves; arrange in well-greased 13x9x2-inch pan.
Combine . . . . ½ pound (about 28) light **candy caramels** and ½ cup pear juice in saucepan. Cook over medium heat, stirring frequently, until smooth.
Blend in . . . . . 2 tablespoons **butter.** Pour evenly over pears.
Sift together . . 1 cup sifted **Pillsbury's Best All Purpose Flour***
1 teaspoon double-acting **baking powder** and
¼ teaspoon **salt**
Beat . . . . 3 **eggs** until light and fluffy. Gradually add
¾ cup **sugar,** beating until thick and ivory colored. *Do not underbeat.*
Add . . . . 1 teaspoon **vanilla** and ⅓ cup pear juice; beat well.
Fold in . . . . the dry ingredients one-third at a time. Fold gently but thoroughly. Pour over pears.
Bake . . . . at 350° for 35 to 40 minutes. Cool 5 minutes; invert on serving plate. Sprinkle with chopped **nuts.** Serve warm or cold, plain or with whipped cream.

For use with Pillsbury's Best Self-Rising Flour, omit baking powder and salt.

Marbapple Ginger Cake

Marbapple Ginger Cake

Junior First Prize Winner by Joanne L. Littley, Bluff Point, New York

Creamy yellow and molasses-spice batters are marbled over a spicy cooked apple mixture.

BAKE at 350° for 50 to 60 minutes MAKES 13x9-inch cake

Combine......4 cups cooking **apples,** pared and sliced
1 cup **sugar**
1 tablespoon **flour**
1 teaspoon **cinnamon**
2 tablespoons **butter** or margarine
2 tablespoons **water** and
1 tablespoon **lemon juice** in saucepan. Cook over medium heat, stirring occasionally, until apples are tender. Pour into 13x9x2-inch pan, well greased on the bottom.

Sift together 2¼ cups sifted **Pillsbury's Best All Purpose Flour***
2 teaspoons double-acting **baking powder**
1 teaspoon **ginger** and
½ teaspoon **salt.** Set aside.
Add........1 cup **sugar** gradually to
½ cup **shortening,** creaming well.
Blend in.....2 unbeaten **eggs,** beating well after each.
Add........⅔ cup **milk** alternately with the dry ingredients to creamed mixture. Blend well after each addition.
Place........half of batter in second bowl. Blend in
¼ cup **molasses**
1 teaspoon **cinnamon**
¼ teaspoon **soda**
¼ teaspoon **cloves** and
¼ teaspoon **nutmeg**
Spoon........light and dark batters alternately over apples.
Bake........at 350° for 50 to 60 minutes. Cool 15 minutes, then invert on serving plate. Serve warm or cold, plain or with whipped cream.

**For use with Pillsbury's Best Self-Rising Flour, omit baking powder, salt, soda.*

Sunny-Side Up Cake

Senior Winner by Mrs. Arnold C. Johnson, Lansing, Michigan

A square Quick-Mix cocoa upside-down cake, using sunshiny orange sections or apricot halves as the fruit.

BAKE at 350° for 50 to 55 minutes MAKES 9x9-inch cake

Peel........3 medium **oranges** with sharp knife, removing all white membrane. Section and drain. (Or drain 1 No. 303 can apricot halves thoroughly.)
Combine....¼ cup **light corn syrup** and

2 tablespoons **sugar**; spread in well-greased 9x9x2-inch pan. Arrange fruit in pan. Add

⅓ cup **pecan halves**

Sift together 1½ cups sifted **Pillsbury's Best All Purpose Flour***

½ cup **sugar**

½ cup **cocoa**

1 teaspoon **soda** and

1 teaspoon **salt** into mixing bowl.

Add . . . . ½ cup firmly packed **brown sugar**

⅓ cup **shortening** and

¾ cup **buttermilk** or sour milk

Beat . . . . 1½ minutes. (With mixer use a low speed.)

Add . . . . 2 unbeaten **eggs**

¼ cup **buttermilk** and

1 teaspoon **vanilla**. Beat 1½ minutes.

Pour . . . . batter over fruit.

Bake . . . . at 350° for 50 to 55 minutes. Turn out immediately.

*For use with Pillsbury's Best Self-Rising Flour, decrease soda to ¼ teaspoon and omit salt.

Festive Upside-Down Cake

Senior Winner by Mrs. L. W. Willis, Portsmouth, Virginia

Candied fruit and chopped nuts are scattered through this high, upside-down Quick-Mix fruit cake.

BAKE at 350° for 65 to 75 minutes   MAKES 10-inch tube cake*

Spread . . . . . . 2 tablespoons soft **butter** over bottom of 10-inch tube pan (with stationary center tube). Sprinkle with

⅓ cup firmly packed **brown sugar**

Drain . . . . 1 No. 2 can sliced **pineapple** (reserve juice); arrange 5 pineapple slices on sugar. Place a **maraschino cherry** or nut in center of each.

Combine . . . . ½ cup sifted **Pillsbury's Best All Purpose Flour**

1½ cups chopped mixed **candied fruit** and

Festive Upside-Down Cake

½ cup **nuts,** chopped

Sift together . . 2 cups sifted **Pillsbury's Best All Purpose Flour****

1⅓ cups **sugar**

3 teaspoons double-acting **baking powder** and

1 teaspoon **salt** into large mixing bowl.

Add . . . . ½ cup **shortening** and ¾ cup of pineapple juice.

Beat . . . . 1½ minutes. (With mixer use a low speed.)

Add . . . . 3 unbeaten **eggs,** beating well after each.

Stir in . . . . floured fruit. Pour over pineapple slices.

Bake . . . . at 350° for 65 to 75 minutes. Cool 5 minutes. Turn out on serving plate. Serve with **whipped cream** or hard sauce.

*If desired, cake may be baked in 13x9x2-inch pan for 50 to 60 minutes.

**For use with Pillsbury's Best Self-Rising Flour, omit baking powder and salt.

FROSTINGS, FILLINGS AND TOPPINGS

A beautiful frosting does so much for a cake! It gives glamour and appeal; it complements the flavor of the cake, increasing the eating pleasure. It helps keep the cake moist and fresh. Frosting gives you the opportunity to show off your artistic and creative talents, as you give a cake your "personal touch." In fact, small children (and some adults) will tell you that frosting is more important than the cake!

There are many different types of frostings, each with its own special advantage. Cooked frostings are delicious and candy-like. They store well and dress up a cake beautifully.

Fluffy egg white frostings are ever so elegant; they are economical and quick to make. Fluffy frosting is easy to manage and can be coaxed into deep ripples and swirls.

Smooth, creamy butter frosting is a wise choice if you are in a hurry and want a simple, failure-proof frosting—or if you want a frosting that keeps fresh over a period of time and packs well.

In this section you will find numerous recipes for all these types; you may "juggle" cakes and frostings for different flavor experiences. Your cake and its frosting should team up to give you and your family a true taste treat!

A double boiler (or similar utensil) is necessary when making a fluffy frosting such as this. A mixer does the beating thoroughly, quickly and easily. Beat constantly until stiff peaks form when the beater is raised. *Do not underbeat*. (Corn syrup keeps frosting soft, reducing the danger of overbeating.)

Always cool cake thoroughly before frosting. Brush loose crumbs from sides. To keep cake plate clean while frosting, place strips of waxed paper under edges of cake; when cake is frosted, paper will slip out easily. Place first layer top-side down; spread frosting or filling completely to edge. Allow to set.

Place top layer on filling, bottom-side down. sides with "base coat" of frosting to seal in c Then apply more frosting to cake with a metal s using free, easy strokes. Spread with upward s leaving a ridge of frosting around top of cake sides straight.

TIPS ON FROSTING CAKES

- Loaf cakes are usually frosted in the pan, spreading frosting to all edges.
- To frost angel food or spongecakes, place top-side down and spread glaze over cake, allowing it to drip down sides—or frost entire cake with confectioners' sugar icing or fluffy frosting.
- When frosting the sides of a layer cake, always move spatula in same direction with same pressure, to keep sides straight. The fewer the strokes used, the more attractive the cake; using too many strokes and going back over the frosting gives the cakes a "worked over" appearance.
- The best time to frost a cake is just as soon as it is cool; the cake is still moist and frosting will help retain this moistness.

read frosting on top, making swirls or ripples with tula or the back of a spoon. Avoid smooth, flat es or top. The frosting should give the cake height d make it as good to look at as it is to eat. Use your n imagination for decorating touches (see Decorat-; Hints on this page).

DECORATING HINTS

- Part or all the frosting may be tinted with a few drops of food coloring.
- Decorate, repeating a food found in the cake; for instance, sliced bananas on a frosted banana cake, chocolate curls or grated chocolate over the icing of a chocolate cake. (To make chocolate curls, let square of unsweetened chocolate stand at room temperature. With sharp knife or vegetable parer, cut off thin shavings from back of square. Chocolate curls as you shave it.)

- Shadow frostings may be made by drizzling melted chocolate around the edges of a frosted cake, allowing it to drip down sides. Or drizzle chocolate across the top, cutting through with a knife to give desired design.
- Cut stencil from waxed paper—lay on cake; sprinkle with colored sugar or confectioners' sugar. Remove stencil and design remains.

- Make paper decorating tube, see page 321, for writing on cakes and making flowers.
- Check your nearest candy counter for ideas; a few colorful or seasonal candies can dress up your cake.
- Decorate with toasted or tinted coconut, cinnamon candies, maraschino cherries, whole or chopped nuts or marshmallows.

- Insert candles in gum drops or life savers for a quickly decorated birthday cake.
- Mark off individual pieces of a loaf cake, then decorate each piece with nuts, candies or your choice of decorations.

- Animal crackers can be used to make a clever circus cake for a children's party. Or make a "balloon cake" with colored mint patties.

COOKED FROSTINGS

COOKED FROSTINGS—Proper cooking temperatures are very important when making cooked frostings; a candy thermometer is very helpful. The thermometer should be placed well below the surface of the frosting, but should not touch the bottom of the pan. Allow the thermometer to heat up with the frosting, rather than placing it in boiling frosting.

Whether you use a candy thermometer or not, it is important to be familiar with other tests for doneness. The cold water tests are often used; a few drops of boiling frosting are placed in a cup of cold water. Remove the pan of frosting from heat while testing.

TEST	TEMPERATURE	DESCRIPTION
Thread	230° to 234°	Syrup spins 2-inch thread when dropped from fork or spoon.
Soft Ball	234° to 240°	Syrup dropped into very cold water forms soft ball which flattens when removed from water.
Firm Ball	244° to 248°	Syrup dropped into very cold water forms a firm ball which does not flatten when removed from water.

If necessary, spread a cooked frosting with a wet spatula to give a smooth appearance. If frosting appears thick enough to spread when pan is still hot, it may be overcooked and should be thinned with cream or milk before spreading. If frosting becomes too thick during spreading, thin it slightly before continuing.

BUTTER CREAM FROSTING

FROSTS two 8 or 9-inch layers or 13x9-inch cake

Combine . . . . ⅛ cup **Pillsbury's Best All Purpose Flour**
⅔ cup **sugar** and
2 tablespoons **cornstarch** in saucepan.

Blend in . . . 2¼ cups cold **milk.** Cook until thick, stirring constantly. Blend a little of the hot mixture into
3 slightly beaten **egg yolks;** add to remaining hot mixture. Cook over low heat, stirring constantly, 2 minutes.

Stir in . . . . . . 2 teaspoons **vanilla.** Cover; cool to lukewarm. Add to
¾ cup well-creamed **butter** or margarine. Cool completely.

CARAMEL FROSTING

FROSTS two 8 or 9-inch layers or 13x9-inch cake

Combine . . . . . 1 cup **sugar**
1 cup firmly packed **brown sugar** and
⅔ cup **sweet** or **sour cream** in saucepan. Cook to soft-ball stage (236°). Remove from heat and cool to lukewarm.

Add . . . . 1 teaspoon **vanilla;** beat until of spreading consistency. Thin with **cream,** if necessary.

SPEEDY CARAMEL FROSTING

FROSTS 12x8 or 13x9-inch cake

Melt . . . . ¼ cup **butter** or margarine in saucepan. Add
½ cup firmly packed **brown sugar;** cook over medium heat for 2 minutes, stirring constantly.

Add . . . . ¼ cup **light cream;** continue stirring and bring to a boil. Remove from heat. Blend in
1½ cups sifted **confectioners' sugar** and

⅛ cup **nuts**, chopped, if desired. Mix well.

Add . . . . ½ teaspoon **vanilla**; beat until of spreading consistency. Thin with **cream**, if necessary.

CARAMEL ICING

FROSTS 12x8 or 13x9-inch cake

Combine . . . . ⅛ cup **butter** or margarine and
1 cup firmly packed **brown sugar** in saucepan.

Stir in . . . . . . ¼ cup **milk**. Bring to boil and simmer 3 minutes. Remove from heat, cool 10 minutes.

Creamy Frosting: Cool Caramel Icing 10 minutes, then blend in 1 cup sifted confectioners' sugar.

HASTY BUTTERSCOTCH FROSTING

FROSTS two or three 8 or 9-inch layers

Melt . . . . ⅔ cup **butter** or margarine in saucepan over low heat. Blend in
1½ cups firmly packed **brown sugar**. Boil over low heat 2 minutes, stirring constantly.

Stir in . . . . . . ⅓ cup **milk**; cook until mixture comes to a boil. Gradually add
1 pound (4 to 4¼ cups) sifted **confectioners' sugar** and
1 teaspoon **vanilla**; beat until of spreading consistency. Thin with **milk**, if necessary.

MAPLE SOUR CREAM FROSTING

FROSTS 9x9, 11x7 or 12x8-inch cake

Combine . . . . ¼ cup **sugar**
¼ cup firmly packed **brown sugar**
1½ teaspoons **cornstarch** and

¼ teaspoon **salt** in heavy saucepan.

Blend in . . . . . ½ cup **sour cream** and
2 unbeaten **egg yolks**. Cook over low heat, stirring constantly, until thickened. Remove from heat.

Add . . . . ¼ teaspoon **maple flavoring** and
1 tablespoon **butter**. Chill until of spreading consistency.

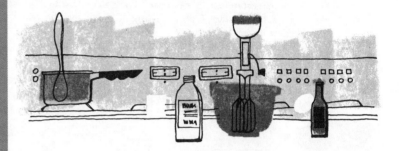

PECAN FONDANT FROSTING

FROSTS 13x9-inch cake

Combine . . . 1½ cups **sugar**
¼ cup **light corn syrup** and
¼ cup plus 2 tablespoons **water** in saucepan; cook over low heat, stirring constantly, until sugar dissolves. Cover pan 2 to 3 minutes. Uncover and continue cooking to firm-ball stage (244°). Remove from heat.

Beat . . . . 1 **egg white** with
½ teaspoon **vanilla**
¼ teaspoon **salt** and
⅛ teaspoon **almond extract** until stiff but not dry.

Pour . . . . hot syrup over egg white, beating constantly at high speed. Continue beating until frosting stands in peaks and begins to lose its gloss, 8 to 10 minutes. Add
¼ cup **pecans**, chopped. Thin with **cream**, if necessary.

FUDGE FROSTING

FROSTS two 8 or 9-inch layers or 13x9-inch cake

Combine.....2 cups **sugar**
¾ cup **milk**
2 squares (2 oz.) unsweetened **chocolate**
2 tablespoons **light corn syrup** and
⅛ teaspoon **salt** in saucepan. Cook over low heat to soft-ball stage (236°), stirring occasionally. Remove from heat.

Add........2 tablespoons **butter** or margarine;* cool to lukewarm (110°). Add
1 teaspoon **vanilla**; beat until thick and creamy. Thin with **cream,** if necessary.

If desired, add 2 teaspoons peanut butter with the butter.

BROWN SUGAR CHOCOLATE FROSTING

FROSTS two 8 or 9-inch layers or 13x9-inch cake

Combine....½ cup firmly packed **brown sugar**
½ cup **water** and
2 tablespoons **butter** or margarine. Cook to soft-ball stage (236°). Remove from heat.

Add........2 squares (2 oz.) unsweetened **chocolate;** stir until melted.

Blend in......2 cups sifted **confectioners' sugar** and
⅛ teaspoon **salt** alternately with

¼ cup **cream,** beating well. Add
1 teaspoon **vanilla.** Thin with **cream,** if necessary.

Marshmallow Fudge Frosting: Prepare Brown Sugar Chocolate Frosting, adding 1 cup miniature marshmallows (or 12 marshmallows, quartered) with the chocolate.

OLD SMOOTHY CHOCOLATE FROSTING

FROSTS two 8 or 9-inch layers

Combine.....1 cup **sugar** and
½ cup **Pillsbury's Best All Purpose Flour** in saucepan.

Blend in....1½ cups **milk** and
1 tablespoon **light corn syrup;** add
2 squares (2 oz.) unsweetened **chocolate.** Bring to boil, stirring constantly; cook over medium heat until very thick and smooth. Remove from heat.

Add........2 tablespoons **butter** or margarine
1 teaspoon **vanilla** and
½ teaspoon **salt.** Cool to lukewarm, stirring occasionally.

Fold in......1 stiffly beaten **egg white**

CHOCOLATE FLUFF FROSTING

FROSTS two or three 8 or 9-inch layers

Melt........1 cup (6-oz. pkg.) **semi-sweet chocolate pieces** in
¼ cup **water** in top of double boiler. Remove from heat; stir until smooth. Cool.

Cook.......¾ cup **light corn syrup** until it spins a thread (230°). Add slowly to
3 well-beaten **egg yolks,** beating constantly. Continue beating until stiff and creamy.

Blend in.....1 cup soft **butter** or margarine, well creamed
2 teaspoons **vanilla** and the cooled chocolate. Beat until fluffy.

FLUFFY FROSTINGS

—Use utensils free from grease when beating egg whites. Plastic bowls may be unsatisfactory since they absorb fat which may interfere with the beating of egg whites.

On a very damp day, the amount of water in a fluffy frosting may be reduced slightly, as the frosting may absorb moisture from the air.

Remove the head from your standard mixer and take it to the range with you. Beat fluffy frostings until stiff peaks form. *Do not underbeat.* After removing frosting from heat, blend flavoring in with rubber spatula, then beat with mixer until straight lustrous peaks form. Deep, definite swirls should remain as frosting is spread. (If underbeaten, frosting will not keep pattern or store as well.) Allow a cake frosted with a fluffy frosting to set about one hour before covering.

Vanilla is used as flavoring in most of the frostings in this section; however, you may substitute almond or rum flavoring, or any other that you might prefer.

FLUFFY WHITE FROSTING

FROSTS two 8 or 9-inch layers

Combine.... ¾ cup **sugar**
¼ cup **light corn syrup**
2 **egg whites**
2 tablespoons **water**
¼ teaspoon **salt** and
¼ teaspoon **cream of tartar** in top of double boiler.
Cook......... over rapidly boiling water, beating with electric mixer or rotary beater until mixture stands in peaks. Remove from heat.
Add........ 1 teaspoon **vanilla;** beat until of spreading consistency.

Fluffy Caramel Frosting: Prepare Fluffy White Frosting, substituting 2 tablespoons **Caramelized Sugar,** page 241, for half the corn syrup.

Fluffy Orange Frosting: Prepare Fluffy White Frosting, substituting 2 tablespoons orange juice and 1 teaspoon grated orange rind for the water; omit vanilla.

Fluffy Honey Frosting: Prepare Fluffy White Frosting, substituting 2 tablespoons honey for the light corn syrup; omit vanilla.

Cola Frosting: Prepare Fluffy White Frosting, substituting 2 tablespoons cola beverage for the water; omit vanilla.

Pink Fluffy Frosting: Prepare Fluffy White Frosting, adding 4 to 6 drops red food coloring with the vanilla.

Fluffy Marshmallow Frosting: Prepare Fluffy White Frosting, adding 6 marshmallows, cut in pieces, to the hot frosting; beat until dissolved. Remove from heat and add vanilla.

DE LUXE FLUFFY WHITE FROSTING

FROSTS three 8 or 9-inch layers

Combine..... 1 cup **sugar**
½ cup **light corn syrup**
3 **egg whites**
3 tablespoons **water**
¼ teaspoon **salt** and
¼ teaspoon **cream of tartar** in top of double boiler.
Cook......... over rapidly boiling water, beating with electric mixer or rotary beater until mixture stands in peaks. Remove from heat.
Add....... 1½ teaspoons **vanilla;** continue beating until of spreading consistency.

SEVEN-MINUTE FROSTING

FROSTS two 8 or 9-inch layers

Combine. . .1½ cups **sugar**
    1½ teaspoons **light corn syrup**
    2 **egg whites**
    5 tablespoons cold **water** and
    ¼ teaspoon **salt** in top of double boiler.

Cook. . . . . . . .over rapidly boiling water, beating with electric mixer or rotary beater until mixture stands in peaks. Remove from heat.

Add. . . . . . . .1 teaspoon **vanilla**; blend thoroughly.

WHITE MOUNTAIN FROSTING

FROSTS two 8 or 9-inch layers

Combine. . . . .2 cups **sugar**
    ½ cup **water** and
    1 tablespoon **light corn syrup** in saucepan.

Cook. . . . . . . .over low heat, stirring until sugar dissolves. Cover pan 2 to 3 minutes; uncover and continue cooking to firm soft-ball stage (240°).

Beat. . . . . . .2 **egg whites** with
    ⅛ teaspoon **salt** and
    ⅛ teaspoon **cream of tartar** until stiff but not dry.

Pour. . . . . .hot syrup over beaten egg whites in a slow, steady stream, beating constantly. Blend in
    1 teaspoon **vanilla**; continue beating until of spreading consistency.

Tutti-Frutti Frosting: Prepare White Mountain Frosting, folding in ½ cup chopped candied pineapple and ½ cup chopped candied cherries just before spreading.

SNOWY WHITE FROSTING

FROSTS 12x8, 13x9-inch cake or two 8-inch layers

Combine. . . . .⅔ cup **sugar**
    3 tablespoons **light corn syrup**
    1 **egg white**
    2 tablespoons **water**
    ¼ teaspoon **cream of tartar** and
    ⅛ teaspoon **salt** in top of double boiler.

Cook. . . . . . . .over rapidly boiling water, beating with electric mixer or rotary beater until mixture stands in peaks. Remove from heat.

Add. . . . . . . .½ teaspoon **rum** or **vanilla flavoring**; continue beating until of spreading consistency.

Mocha Drift Frosting: Prepare Snowy White Frosting, combining 1 teaspoon instant coffee with other ingredients.

SEA-FOAM FROSTING

FROSTS two 8 or 9-inch layers

Combine. . . . . .in top of double boiler
    ¾ cup firmly packed **brown sugar**
    ¼ cup **light corn syrup**
    2 **egg whites**
    2 tablespoons **water**
    ¼ teaspoon **salt** and
    ¼ teaspoon **cream of tartar**

Cook. . . . . . . .over rapidly boiling water, beating with electric mixer or rotary beater until mixture stands in peaks. Remove from heat.

Add. . . . . . . .½ teaspoon **vanilla**; continue beating until of spreading consistency.

Mocha Sea-Foam Frosting: Prepare Sea-Foam Frosting, substituting 2 tablespoons strong coffee for the water.

PASTEL GREEN FROSTING

FROSTS two 8-inch layers

Combine.....1 cup sifted **confectioners' sugar**
⅓ cup **water**
¼ teaspoon **salt** and
¼ teaspoon **cream of tartar** in saucepan. Bring to boil over medium heat; simmer 1 minute.

Pour.........hot syrup in thin steady stream over
1 unbeaten **egg white**, beating constantly with an electric mixer or rotary beater until mixture stands in peaks. Remove from heat.

Stir in.......1 teaspoon **vanilla** and
3 drops **green food coloring**

CINNARAMA FROSTING

FROSTS two 8 or 9-inch layers

Combine.....¾ cup **sugar**
⅓ cup **water**
2 to 3 tablespoons **red cinnamon candies**
1 tablespoon **light corn syrup** and
¼ teaspoon **cream of tartar** in saucepan. Cook to soft-ball stage (236°).

Beat.........2 **egg whites** with
¼ teaspoon **cream of tartar** and
⅛ teaspoon **salt** until stiff peaks form. Add hot syrup in slow, steady stream, beating constantly until of spreading consistency.

HONEY NOUGAT FROSTING

FROSTS 12x8 or 13x9-inch cake

Combine.....½ cup **sugar**
2 tablespoons **honey**
2 tablespoons **water**
1 **egg white** and
⅛ teaspoon **salt** in top of double boiler.

Cook.........over rapidly boiling water, beating with electric mixer or rotary beater until mixture stands in peaks. Remove from heat.

Add.........½ teaspoon **vanilla**; continue beating until of spreading consistency. Fold in
¼ cup **walnuts**, chopped

TOFFEE FROSTING

FROSTS 12x8 or 13x9-inch cake or two 8-inch layers

Combine.....⅔ cup firmly packed **brown sugar**
2 tablespoons **light corn syrup**
1 **egg white**
2 tablespoons **water**
¼ teaspoon **salt** and
¼ teaspoon **cream of tartar** in top of double boiler.

Cook.........over rapidly boiling water, beating with electric mixer or rotary beater until mixture stands in peaks. Remove from heat.

Add.........½ teaspoon **vanilla**; continue beating until of spreading consistency.

FLUFFY MAPLE FROSTING

FROSTS two 8 or 9-inch layers

Combine . . . . ⅔ cup **sugar**
⅓ cup **maple syrup**
1 tablespoon **light corn syrup**
2 **egg whites**
¼ teaspoon **salt** and
¼ teaspoon **cream of tartar** in top of double boiler.
Cook . . . . over rapidly boiling water, beating with electric mixer or rotary beater until mixture stands in peaks. Remove from heat.
Add . . . . 1 teaspoon **vanilla;** continue beating until of spreading consistency.

MAPLE FLUFF FROSTING

FROSTS 12x8 or 13x9-inch cake

Combine . . . . ⅔ cup **sugar**
3 tablespoons **light corn syrup**
1 large **egg white**
2 tablespoons **water**
⅛ teaspoon **salt** and
⅛ teaspoon **cream of tartar** in top of double boiler.
Cook . . . . over rapidly boiling water, beating with electric mixer or rotary beater until mixture stands in peaks. Remove from heat.
Add . . . . 1 teaspoon **maple flavoring;** continue beating until of spreading consistency.

FLUFFY PRUNE FROSTING

FROSTS two 8 or 9-inch layers

Combine . . . . . 1 cup firmly packed **brown sugar***
¼ cup **light corn syrup**

¼ cup **prune juice***
2 **egg whites**
2 teaspoons **lemon juice** and
¼ teaspoon **salt** in top of double boiler.
Cook . . . . over rapidly boiling water, beating with electric mixer or rotary beater until mixture stands in peaks. Remove from heat; continue beating until of spreading consistency.
Fold in . . . . . . ½ cup well-drained cooked **prunes,** cut fine, and
2 tablespoons **nuts,** chopped

*Or substitute ¾ cup granulated sugar and decrease prune juice to 2 tablespoons.

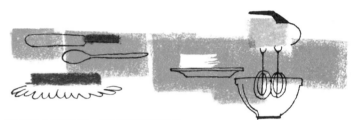

UNCOOKED FROSTINGS—Use butter at room temperature
for best results and easiest mixing. If frosting thickens upon standing, thin to spreading consistency with a few drops cream. Uncooked frostings may be made with electric mixer.

CREAMY BUTTER FROSTING

FROSTS two 8 or 9-inch layers

Cream . . . . . . ½ cup **butter** or margarine. Gradually add
3 cups sifted **confectioners' sugar,** creaming well.
Blend in . . . . . 1 unbeaten **egg**
1 teaspoon **vanilla** and
1 to 2 tablespoons **cream;** beat until of spreading consistency.

CREAMY VANILLA FROSTING

FROSTS 8x8, 9x9, 12x8, or 13x9-inch cake

Cream......¼ cup **butter** or margarine with
⅛ teaspoon **salt**
Blend in.....2 cups sifted **confectioners' sugar** alternately with
2 to 3 tablespoons hot **cream**. Add
1 teaspoon **vanilla**; beat until of spreading consistency.

COCONUT BUTTER FROSTING

FROSTS two 8 or 9-inch layers

Cream......½ cup **butter** or margarine. Gradually add
3 cups sifted **confectioners' sugar**, creaming well.
Blend in.....4 to 5 tablespoons **cream** until of spreading consistency.
Add........1 teaspoon **vanilla**; beat well.

BROWNED BUTTER FROSTING

FROSTS two 8 or 9-inch layers

Brown......½ cup **butter** or margarine in saucepan over medium heat until deep brown. Remove from heat.
Blend in.....1 pound (4 to 4¼ cups) sifted **confectioners' sugar**
¼ cup **cream** and
2 teaspoons **vanilla**; beat until of spreading consistency. Thin with **cream**, if necessary.

PETIT FOUR FROSTING

FROSTS 24 petit fours

Brown......¼ cup **butter** or margarine over medium heat until deep brown. Remove from heat.
Blend in.....3 cups sifted **confectioners' sugar**
2 unbeaten **egg yolks**

1 teaspoon **vanilla** and
2 to 4 teaspoons **cream**; beat until of spreading consistency.

DECORATOR FROSTING

Blend.......2 cups sifted **confectioners' sugar** with
2 to 3 tablespoons **milk** and
½ teaspoon **vanilla** until of spreading consistency.

To make paper decorating tube: Fold a 12-inch square of waxed paper in half to form a triangle. Place triangle on table with point opposite long side toward you. Bring left hand corner down to point forming a cone. Wind remaining part around cone bringing third corner to meet the first two. Fold corners down inside cone. Fill with Frosting. Then fold together top edges of cone toward bottom, forcing Frosting through the point. If necessary, cut off tip.

CHOCOLATE BUTTER CREAM FROSTING

FROSTS 12x8 or 13x9-inch cake

Combine....¼ cup **butter** or margarine
1 unbeaten **egg**
1 to 2 squares (1 to 2 oz.) melted, cooled unsweetened **chocolate** and
½ teaspoon **vanilla**
Blend in.....2 to 2½ cups sifted **confectioners' sugar** until of spreading consistency. Thin with **cream**, if necessary.

CHOCOLATE BUTTER FROSTING

FROSTS two 8 or 9-inch layers

Cream......¼ cup **butter** or margarine with
¼ teaspoon **salt**
Blend in.....3 cups sifted **confectioners' sugar** alternately with
4 to 5 tablespoons hot scalded **cream** or milk. Add
1 teaspoon **vanilla** and
1½ squares (1½ oz.) melted unsweetened **chocolate**;
beat until of spreading consistency. Thin with
cream, if necessary.

CHOCOLATE FROSTING

FROSTS two 8 or 9-inch layers or 13x9-inch cake

Melt........4 squares (4 oz.) unsweetened **chocolate** and
¼ cup **butter** or margarine in top of double boiler.
Combine.....3 cups sifted **confectioners' sugar**
⅓ cup hot **milk** and
⅛ teaspoon **salt;** beat until smooth. Add the hot chocolate mixture; beat until of spreading consistency.
Stir in
1 teaspoon **vanilla.** Thin with **milk,** if necessary.

RICH CHOCOLATE FROSTING

FROSTS two 8 or 9-inch layers

Cream......¼ cup **butter** or margarine. Gradually add
2½ cups sifted **confectioners' sugar,** creaming well.
Add........3 **egg yolks,** beating well after each. Stir in
3 squares (3 oz.) melted unsweetened **chocolate,**
cooled, and
1 teaspoon **vanilla.** Blend in
1 to 2 tablespoons hot **water;** beat until of spreading
consistency.

FRENCH FROSTING

FROSTS two 8 or 9-inch layers or 13x9-inch cake

Cream......½ cup **butter** or margarine. Gradually add
2½ cups sifted **confectioners' sugar,** creaming well.
Add........1 well-beaten **egg;** mix thoroughly. Blend in
3 squares (3 oz.) melted unsweetened **chocolate,**
cooled, and
1 teaspoon **vanilla;** beat until of spreading consistency.
Thin with **milk,** if necessary.

CHOCOLATE CREAM CHEESE FROSTING

FROSTS two 8-inch layers or 13x9-inch cake

Blend.......⅓ cup (3-oz. pkg.) **cream cheese** with
3 tablespoons **milk** and
⅛ teaspoon **salt.** Gradually add
2½ cups sifted **confectioners' sugar,** creaming well.
Blend in.....2 squares (2 oz.) melted unsweetened **chocolate** and
1 teaspoon **vanilla;** beat until of spreading consistency.
Thin with **milk,** if necessary.

CHOCOLATE CHERRY FROSTING

FROSTS 8x8 or 9x9-inch cake or 2 dozen cupcakes

Melt........1 square (1 oz.) unsweetened **chocolate** and
2 tablespoons **butter** or margarine with
3 tablespoons **cream** in top of double boiler. Remove
from heat.
Blend in.....2 cups sifted **confectioners' sugar**
½ teaspoon **vanilla** and
⅛ teaspoon **salt;** beat until of spreading consistency.
Stir in
¼ cup drained **maraschino cherries,** chopped. Thin
with **cherry juice,** if necessary.

CHOCOLATE MALLOW FROSTING

FROSTS 8x8 or 9x9-inch cake

Melt . . . . 1 square (1 oz.) unsweetened **chocolate** and
2 tablespoons **butter** in top of double boiler. Remove from heat.

Blend in . . . . 1½ cups sifted **confectioners' sugar**
1 teaspoon **vanilla** and
2 to 3 tablespoons **cream**; beat until of spreading consistency. Add
6 **marshmallows**, cut into eighths

CREAMY CHOCOLATE FROSTING

FROSTS two 8 or 9-inch layers

Melt . . . . 4 squares (4 oz.) unsweetened **chocolate** and
¼ cup **butter** or margarine in top of double boiler.

Combine . . . . . 1 pound (4 to 4¼ cups) sifted **confectioners' sugar**
½ cup **milk**
1 teaspoon **vanilla** and
¼ teaspoon **salt**; mix well. Add hot chocolate mixture; blend thoroughly. Chill 10 minutes. Beat until of spreading consistency, about 3 to 5 minutes. Stir in
6 **maraschino cherries**, chopped. Thin with **milk**, if necessary.

LUXURY CHOCOLATE FROSTING

FROSTS two 8 or 9-inch layers

Melt . . . . 2 cups (12-oz. pkg.) **semi-sweet chocolate pieces** in top of double boiler over hot water. *Cool completely* at room temperature (about 1 hour).

Cream . . . . . . ½ cup **butter** or margarine.* Gradually add
1 cup sifted **confectioners' sugar,** creaming well.

Add . . . . 3 unbeaten **eggs,** beating well after each. Blend in
1 teaspoon **vanilla** and the cooled chocolate; beat until smooth.

For a luscious bitter frosting, omit sugar and increase butter to ¾ cup.

COCOA BUTTER FROSTING

FROSTS two 8 or 9-inch layers

Sift together 3½ cups sifted **confectioners' sugar**
⅓ cup **cocoa** and
⅛ teaspoon **salt**

Cream . . . . . . ⅓ cup **butter** or margarine. Blend in
1 unbeaten **egg** and
1 teaspoon **vanilla**

Add . . . . the sugar-cocoa mixture alternately with
4 to 5 tablespoons hot **cream**; beat until of spreading consistency.

MOCHA FROSTING

FROSTS 8x8, 9x9 or 12x8-inch cake

Cream . . . . 3 tablespoons **butter** or margarine with
¼ teaspoon **salt** and
½ teaspoon **vanilla.**

Add . . . . 1½ cups sifted **confectioners' sugar** alternately with
1½ to 2 tablespoons hot **coffee;** beat until of spreading consistency.

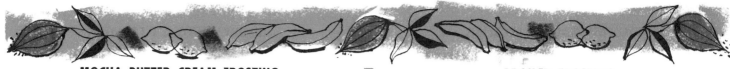

MOCHA BUTTER CREAM FROSTING

FROSTS two 8 or 9-inch layers

Cream......⅓ cup **butter** or margarine. Blend in
　　　　　¼ cup **cocoa**
　　　　　1 teaspoon **instant coffee**
　　　　　1 teaspoon **vanilla** and
　　　　　¼ teaspoon **salt**
Add........1 pound (4 to 4¼ cups) sifted **confectioners' sugar**
　　　　　alternately with
　　　　　7 to 8 tablespoons hot **milk;** beat until of spreading
　　　　　consistency. Thin with **milk,** if necessary.

COFFEE-CREAM FROSTING

FROSTS two 8-inch layers or 12x8 or 13x9-inch cake

Dissolve.....1 tablespoon **instant coffee** in
　　　　　1 tablespoon hot **water**
Cream......½ cup **butter** or margarine with
　　　　　¹⁄₁₆ teaspoon **salt.** Gradually add
　　　　　3 cups sifted **confectioners' sugar**
Blend in.....1 unbeaten **egg** and the coffee; beat until smooth.
　　　　　Thin with **water,** if necessary.

SPEEDY MOCHA FROSTING

FROSTS two 8 or 9-inch layers

Combine.....3 cups sifted **confectioners' sugar** and
　　　　　⅓ cup **cocoa**
Blend in.....¼ cup melted **butter** or margarine
　　　　　3 tablespoons warm **coffee** and
　　　　　1 teaspoon **vanilla;** beat until of spreading consistency.

BROILED FROSTING

FROSTS 12x8 or 13x9-inch cake

Combine....¼ cup melted **butter** or margarine
　　　　　½ cup firmly packed **brown sugar**
　　　　　3 tablespoons **cream** and
　　　　　1 cup **pecans** or coconut, chopped. Mix well.
Spread........over cake, covering completely. Place 4 to 5 inches
　　　　　below broiler unit.
Broil.........1 to 3 minutes until golden brown, watching closely.

BANANA NUT FROSTING

FROSTS 12x8 or 13x9-inch cake

Cream......¼ cup **butter** or margarine with
　　　　　¼ cup mashed **banana** and
　　　　　1 teaspoon **lemon juice**
Add......2½ cups sifted **confectioners' sugar;** blend well. Stir in
　　　　　⅓ cup **walnuts,** chopped

LEMON BUTTER FROSTING

FROSTS 9x9, 12x8 or 13x9-inch cake

Cream......¼ cup **butter** or margarine. Add
　　　　　2 tablespoons **milk**
　　　　　1 teaspoon grated **lemon rind**
　　　　　1 tablespoon **lemon juice**
　　　　　¼ teaspoon **vanilla** and
　　　　　⅛ teaspoon **salt.** Mix well.
Blend in.....2 cups sifted **confectioners' sugar;** beat until smooth
　　　　　and of spreading consistency. Thin with **milk,** if
　　　　　necessary.

CREAMY LEMON FROSTING

FROSTS two 8 or 9-inch layers

Cream . . . . . . ¼ cup **butter** or margarine with
¼ teaspoon **salt**. Blend in
3 cups sifted **confectioners' sugar** alternately with
3 tablespoons hot **cream**

Add . . . . 1 unbeaten **egg yolk**
1 tablespoon grated **lemon rind** and
1 teaspoon **lemon juice;** beat until smooth and creamy.
Thin with **cream,** if necessary.

LEMON CHEESE FROSTING

FROSTS 8x8 or 9x9-inch cake

Cream . . . . . . ⅓ cup (3-oz. pkg.) **cream cheese** until fluffy. Gradually add
1 cup sifted **confectioners' sugar,** creaming well.

Blend in . . . . . 1 teaspoon grated **lemon rind.** Thin with
1 to 2 teaspoons **cream** until of spreading consistency.

ORANGE BUTTER FROSTING

FROSTS 12x8 or 13x9-inch cake

Melt . . . . ⅓ cup **butter** or margarine. Remove from heat.

Blend in . . . . . 3 cups sifted **confectioners' sugar** alternately with
3 tablespoons **orange juice** until of spreading consistency.

CREAMY ORANGE FROSTING

FROSTS two 8 or 9-inch layers

Cream . . . . . . ¼ cup **butter** or margarine. Gradually add
1 pound (4 to 4¼ cups) sifted **confectioners' sugar**

Blend in . . . . . 1 unbeaten **egg**
½ teaspoon **vanilla**
¼ teaspoon **salt** and
1 tablespoon grated **orange rind**

Add . . . . 1 to 2 tablespoons **orange juice** until of spreading consistency. Stir in
2 to 4 drops **orange food coloring;** mix well.

MARMALADE FROSTING

FROSTS 12x8 or 13x9-inch cake

Cream . . . . 2 tablespoons **butter** or margarine with
2 tablespoons **apricot marmalade**

Blend in . . . . . 3 cups sifted **confectioners' sugar** and
3 tablespoons **cream;** beat well. Add more cream, a teaspoon at a time, until of spreading consistency.

CREAMY CINNAMON FROSTING

FROSTS 12x8 or 13x9-inch cake or 2 dozen cupcakes

Cream . . . . . . ¼ cup **butter** or margarine. Blend in
¼ teaspoon **cinnamon**
1 teaspoon **vanilla** and
2 cups sifted **confectioners' sugar**

Add . . . . 2 to 3 tablespoons hot **cream;** beat until of spreading consistency.

GLAZES are thin icings, usually drizzled or spread casually over cakes, cookies or breads. Confectioners' sugar glazes are commonly used with foam cakes and are spread slightly, then allowed to drip down sides of cake.

VANILLA GLAZE

Blend . . . . 1 cup sifted **confectioners' sugar** with
2 tablespoons **cream** and
½ teaspoon **vanilla**; beat until of spreading consistency.

CINNAMON GLAZE

FROSTS 9 or 10-inch tube cake or 8x8 or 9x9-inch cake

Blend . . . . 4 to 5 tablespoons hot **cream** into
2 cups sifted **confectioners' sugar** and
1 teaspoon **cinnamon**; beat until of spreading consistency.

COFFEE ICING

FROSTS 9x9, 12x8 or 13x9-inch cake

Cream . . . . 2 tablespoons **butter**. Add
2 cups sifted **confectioners' sugar** and
1 to 2 teaspoons **instant coffee**
Blend in . . . . . 2 to 3 tablespoons **milk** until of spreading consistency.

CHOCOLATE GLAZE

FROSTS 9 or 10-inch tube cake or 1 dozen cupcakes

Melt . . . . 1 square (1 oz.) unsweetened **chocolate** in top of double boiler. Blend in
2 tablespoons **butter** or margarine and
2 tablespoons **milk**. Remove from heat.
Add . . . . 1 cup sifted **confectioners' sugar**
¼ teaspoon **vanilla** and
⅛ teaspoon **salt**; beat until smooth. Thin with **cream**, if necessary.

VELVET CHOCOLATE FROSTING

FROSTS one 8 or 9-inch layer or 8x8-inch cake

Combine . . . . ½ cup **sugar** and
1½ tablespoons **cornstarch** in saucepan. Blend in
2 tablespoons **butter** or margarine and
1 cup **boiling water**
Add . . . . 1 square (1 oz.) unsweetened **chocolate**. Cook, stirring constantly, until chocolate melts and mixture becomes thick and smooth. Remove from heat. Blend in
½ teaspoon **vanilla**. Cool to lukewarm.

LIME FROSTING

FROSTS two 8 or 9-inch layers or 10-inch tube cake

Blend . . . . . . 1½ cups sifted **confectioners' sugar** with
⅓ cup **shortening**
1 unbeaten **egg** and
1 tablespoon grated **lime rind**; beat until fluffy.
Combine . . . . . juice of 2 **limes** with enough **water** to make ⅓ cup. Add to sugar mixture alternately with
2 cups sifted **confectioners' sugar**. Blend in
1 drop **green food coloring**, if desired.

LEMON ICING

FROSTS 9 or 10-inch tube cake or 2 dozen cupcakes

Blend . . . . 2 cups sifted **confectioners' sugar** with
3 to 4 tablespoons **cream** until of spreading consistency.
Stir in . . . . . . 1 teaspoon grated **lemon rind** and
1 teaspoon **lemon juice**

ORANGE FROSTING

FROSTS 9 or 10-inch tube cake, 2 dozen cupcakes
or 9x9 or 12x8-inch cake

Cream . . . . 2 tablespoons **butter** or margarine with
2 teaspoons grated **orange rind** and
⅛ teaspoon **salt**
Add . . . . 2 cups sifted **confectioners' sugar** alternately with
2 tablespoons **orange juice,** creaming well.

PINEAPPLE BUTTER FROSTING

FROSTS 8x8 or 9x9-inch cake or 1½ dozen cupcakes

Combine . . . . . 2 tablespoons **butter** or margarine, melted, and
½ cup sifted **confectioners' sugar;** mix well.
Blend in . . . . . 2 tablespoons undrained **crushed pineapple** alternately with
1 cup sifted **confectioners' sugar;** beat well. Thin with **cream,** if necessary.

NUTMEG FROSTING

FROSTS 9x5-inch cake or 1 dozen cupcakes

Combine . . . . . . 1 cup sifted **confectioners' sugar**
1 tablespoon **butter** or margarine
¼ teaspoon **nutmeg**
¼ teaspoon **vanilla**
2 tablespoons hot **cream** and
1⁄16 teaspoon **salt;** beat until of spreading consistency.

QUICK MOLASSES ICING

FROSTS 1 to 1½ dozen cupcakes

Combine . . . . . 1 tablespoon **butter,** melted, and
1 teaspoon **molasses**
Blend in . . . . 1½ cups sifted **confectioners' sugar** and
1 tablespoon **milk;** beat until smooth.

BROWN-BUTTER ICING

FROSTS 8x8 or 9x5-inch cake or 1 dozen cupcakes

Brown . . . . 2 tablespoons **butter** over medium heat until deep brown. Remove from heat.
Blend in . . . . . 1 cup sifted **confectioners' sugar** and
½ teaspoon **vanilla.** Add
2 to 3 tablespoons **cream;** beat until of spreading consistency.

FILLINGS and TOPPINGS

FILLINGS and TOPPINGS—When making a thickened filling, bring mixture to boil over high heat, then reduce heat to low. Do not undercook, or the filling will be thin and have a raw taste and unpleasant texture.

Whipped cream toppings are tasty, quick and easy; whip the cream just before serving. If using whipped cream as a frosting, whip it very thick; cake may be stored in refrigerator.

VANILLA CREAM FILLING

Heat . . . . 1 cup **milk** and
2 tablespoons **butter** or margarine in saucepan.
Combine . . . . ⅓ cup **Pillsbury's Best All Purpose Flour**
⅓ cup **sugar** and
¼ teaspoon **salt.** Add
½ cup cold **milk;** stir until smooth. Add to hot milk and cook over medium heat, stirring constantly, until thick.
Blend . . . . a little of the hot mixture into
2 slightly beaten **egg yolks.** Add to hot mixture; cook 2 minutes, stirring constantly. Cool; add
1 teaspoon **vanilla**

BUTTER CREAM FILLING

Heat . . . . 2 cups **milk** and
⅓ cup **butter** or margarine in saucepan.
Combine . . . . . 1 cup **sugar**
¼ cup **cornstarch** and
1 cup cold **milk.** Add to hot milk and cook over medium heat, stirring constantly, until thick.
Blend . . . . a little of the hot mixture into
2 slightly beaten **eggs.** Add to hot mixture; cook 2 minutes, stirring constantly. Cool; add
1 teaspoon **vanilla**

CREAM FILLING

Heat . . . . ⅔ cup **milk** and
2 tablespoons **butter** in saucepan.
Combine . . . . ⅓ cup **sugar**
2 tablespoons **flour** and
¼ teaspoon **salt.** Add
⅓ cup cold **milk;** stir until smooth. Add to hot milk and cook over medium heat, stirring constantly, until thick.
Blend . . . . a little of the hot mixture into
1 slightly beaten **egg.** Add to hot mixture; cook 2 minutes, stirring constantly. Cool; add
½ teaspoon **vanilla**

BONBON FILLING

Combine . . . . . 1 cup **sugar**
6 tablespoons **water**
1½ teaspoons **light corn syrup** and
⅛ teaspoon **salt** in saucepan. Cook over low heat, stirring until sugar is dissolved. Cover pan 2 to 3 minutes. Uncover and continue cooking to soft-ball stage (236°). Remove from heat.
Add . . . . hot syrup slowly to
1 beaten **egg white,** beating constantly. Blend in
½ teaspoon **vanilla.** Continue beating until of spreading consistency.

BUTTERSCOTCH FILLING

Combine . . . . ½ cup firmly packed **brown sugar**
1½ tablespoons **cornstarch** and
¼ teaspoon **salt** in saucepan. Blend in
1 unbeaten **egg yolk** and
1 cup **milk,** mixing thoroughly.
Cook . . . . over medium heat, stirring constantly, until thick. Remove from heat. Stir in
1 tablespoon **butter** and
½ teaspoon **vanilla.** Cover and cool.

MOCHA FILLING

Combine . . . . . 1 package **vanilla pudding mix**
1 tablespoon **instant coffee** and
1½ cups **milk** in saucepan. Cook over medium heat, stirring constantly, until thick. Cool to lukewarm.
Cream . . . . . . ½ cup **butter** or margarine; add lukewarm pudding, beating until smooth and fluffy. Blend in
⅓ cup sifted **confectioners' sugar** and
1 teaspoon **vanilla**

CINNAMON WHIPPED CREAM

Beat . . . . ¾ cup **whipping cream** until thick. Stir in
3 tablespoons **sugar**
½ teaspoon **vanilla** and
¼ teaspoon **cinnamon**

Applesauce Whipped Cream: Fold in ½ cup thick applesauce to which 1 teaspoon lemon juice has been added.

CHOCOLATE COFFEE FILLING

Combine . . . . ⅓ cup **Pillsbury's Best All Purpose Flour** and
1 tablespoon **instant coffee** in saucepan. Gradually add
1 cup **milk,** blending well.
Add . . . . 1 square (1 oz.) unsweetened **chocolate.** Cook over medium heat, stirring constantly, until thick. Cool to lukewarm.
Cream . . . . . . ¾ cup **butter** or margarine. Gradually add
1 cup **sugar,** creaming well. Stir in
1 teaspoon **vanilla**
1 cup **pecans,** finely chopped or ground, and the chocolate mixture. Beat until well blended. Chill until of spreading consistency.

COCOA WHIPPED CREAM

Combine . . . . . 2 cups **whipping cream**
⅔ cup **sugar**
⅓ cup **cocoa** and
⅛ teaspoon **salt.** Beat until thick.

APRICOT FILLING

Combine . . . . ¼ cup **sugar**
3 tablespoons **cornstarch**
⅛ teaspoon **salt** and
¼ cup **apricot nectar** in saucepan. Add
1¾ cups **apricot nectar;** blend well.
Cook . . . . over medium heat, stirring constantly, until thick and clear. Add
2 tablespoons **lemon juice;** cool.

APRICOT-ORANGE FILLING

Combine. . . . ½ cup **sugar**
¼ cup **cornstarch** and
⅛ teaspoon **salt** in saucepan. Add
1 cup **apricot nectar**
½ cup **orange juice** and
½ cup **water**; blend well. Cook over medium heat, stirring constantly, until very thick. Remove from heat.

Stir in. . . . . . . 2 tablespoons **butter** or margarine and
1 tablespoon grated **orange rind**

LEMON FILLING

Combine. . . . ½ cup **sugar**
1½ tablespoons **cornstarch**
⅔ cup **water**
3 unbeaten **egg yolks**
2 tablespoons **butter** or margarine
1 tablespoon grated **lemon rind**
2 tablespoons **lemon juice** and
⅛ teaspoon **salt** in saucepan. Cook over medium heat, stirring constantly, until thick. Remove from heat. Cool.

PINEAPPLE FILLING

Combine. . . . ½ cup **sugar**
2 tablespoons **cornstarch**
1 cup (9-oz. can) undrained **crushed pineapple**
¼ cup **water**
1 unbeaten **egg yolk**
1 teaspoon grated **lemon rind**
1 tablespoon **lemon juice** and
1 tablespoon **butter.** Cook over low heat, stirring constantly, until thick. Cool.

DATE FILLING

Combine. . . . ½ cup **sugar**
2 tablespoons **flour** and
⅛ teaspoon **salt** in saucepan. Gradually add
2 cups **milk**

Stir in . . . . . 1¼ cups (8-oz. pkg.) **dates,** cut fine. Bring to boil; cook over medium heat, stirring constantly, until very thick.

Blend. . . . . a little of the hot mixture into
2 slightly beaten **egg yolks**; add to hot mixture. Cook 2 minutes, stirring constantly. Stir in
1 teaspoon **vanilla.** Cool.

RAISIN NUT FILLING

Combine. . . . ⅓ cup **sugar**
3 tablespoons **flour** and
⅛ teaspoon **salt** in saucepan. Add
1 cup **milk.** Cook over medium heat, stirring constantly, until thick. Remove from heat.

Blend. . . . . a little of the hot mixture into
1 beaten **egg yolk** or 1 egg. Add to hot mixture; cook 2 minutes, stirring constantly.

Stir in . . . . . . ½ cup **raisins,** chopped
½ cup **nuts,** chopped
1 tablespoon **butter** or margarine
1 teaspoon **lemon rind**
1 tablespoon **lemon juice** and
1 teaspoon **vanilla**

COOKIES

Homemade cookies by the dozens can be found in most homes today. School's out! The kids immediately come home to that full cookie jar. Cookies with a glass of milk make perfect between-meal snacks. Cookies make good lunchbox fillers, too! Served with fruit or ice cream they make a complete dessert, and they are right on hand when friends stop in for a chat.

In this section the recipes have been divided by types of cookies: bar, drop, molded and shaped, rolled, refrigerator, press, and variety cookies. Special hints have been included with each section; read them carefully to make your baking easy and quick!

Here are some general baking hints for all cookie recipes, to help you turn out perfect cookies every time.

BEFORE BAKING

- Read the recipe carefully. Assemble the ingredients and utensils before you start.
- All ingredients should be at room temperature.
- Cream butter and sugar together well with electric mixer.
- When adding the dry ingredients to creamed mixture in rich butter cookies, mix thoroughly or the dough will be crumbly.

- Mixing bowls and baking sheets will not slip if a wet paper towel or cloth is placed underneath.
- Chill dough before shaping for easier handling, especially refrigerator, rolled, and molded and shaped cookie doughs.
- Chilled doughs may be refrigerated up to a week and baked as needed. Always cover dough before placing it in refrigerator.
- Use a kitchen spoon, not a measuring spoon, to measure correct amount of dough.
- To flatten drop or molded cookies, use palm of hand, floured or wet fork, or bottom of glass greased, then dipped in sugar or flour.
- Place cookies 2 inches apart on baking sheets unless otherwise directed in recipe.
- Use baking sheet with little or no sides. (Pans with deep sides prevent browning.) You can invert and use the bottom of large cake or jelly-roll pan.
- Use shiny baking sheets. Dark sheets absorb heat readily and cookies may burn on the bottom.
- Grease baking sheets lightly. Excessive greasing causes cookies to spread and burn on the bottom and edges.
- There should be 2 inches space between oven wall and baking sheet for good circulation.
- When making sticky cookies, line baking sheets with aluminum foil before baking. (Sheets will then be easy to clean.)

- If you bake 2 sheets of cookies at a time, place one on each rack; reverse the sheets in the oven during baking for better browning.
- Cool baking sheet before placing more unbaked cookies on it. Hot baking sheets melt shortening in the dough, causing cookies to spread too much during baking.

- If you do not have a 15½x10½x1-inch jelly-roll pan, make one out of an 18x12-inch piece of heavy-duty aluminum foil and place on baking sheet.

AFTER BAKING

- Remove cookies from baking sheets immediately after baking unless otherwise directed in recipe.
- To remove cookies from baking sheets easily, clean spatula when it becomes sticky.
- Cool cookies on wire rack; if there's a frosting or glaze, place waxed paper under rack.
- Confectioners' sugar glazes and frostings tend to thicken upon standing; just thin to spreading consistency with a few drops of cream.
- Keep cookie frostings or glazes in double boiler over hot water (not on range) while spreading. This will keep them the proper consistency.
- Glazes must set before storing or cookies will stick together.
- Never stack warm cookies or they will lose their shape.
- Make extra cookies in your spare time and freeze them. All cookies in this book are excellent for freezing (see Freezing Tips, page 10).

- Store soft cookies and crisp cookies in separate containers with tight-fitting covers. Keep soft cookies moist by putting a slice of bread in the container. If crisp cookies soften in storage, heat in 300° oven about 5 minutes before serving.
- Store bar cookies right in their baking pans, tightly covered with aluminum foil.
- Store frosted, fragile or large cookies in a flat pan covered with aluminum foil.
- Coffee and shortening cans make good storage containers for cookies. Seal lids tight with tape.

A

B

BAR COOKIES—Be sure to use pan size recommended.

If pan is too large, cookies will be dry. If pan is too small, cookies may not bake through properly. Spread batter evenly in pan with spatula (photo A).

Cut bar cookies when cool unless otherwise directed in the recipe (photo B).

Store cooled cookies in pan covered with aluminum foil till serving time; transfer to serving plate with wide spatula.

Bonbon Brownies

Senior Winner by Mrs. O. C. Jack, Jr., New Orleans, Louisiana

A pecan meringue makes the crinkly topping for these chewy chocolate brownies. No bother with frosting—it's already baked on.

BAKE at 350° for 30 to 35 minutes   MAKES about 1½ dozen

Sift together . ⅔ cup sifted **Pillsbury's Best All Purpose Flour***
 ¼ cup **cocoa**
 ½ teaspoon double-acting **baking powder** and
 ¼ teaspoon **salt**. Set aside.
Add . . . . ¾ cup **sugar** gradually to

½ cup **shortening**, creaming well.

Blend in . . . . . 1 unbeaten **egg**
1 **egg yolk** and
1 teaspoon **vanilla**. Beat well.

Add . . . . the dry ingredients and
¼ cup **pecans**, chopped; mix well. Spread in well-greased 8x8x2-inch pan.

Beat . . . . 1 **egg white** with
¼ teaspoon **cream of tartar** until foamy.

Add . . . . ¼ cup **sugar** gradually, beating until mixture stands in stiff, straight peaks.

Fold . . . . ¼ cup **pecans**, chopped, into meringue. Spread over batter.

Bake . . . . at 350° for 30 to 35 minutes.

For use with Pillsbury's Best Self-Rising Flour, omit baking powder and salt. Increase baking time to 35 to 40 minutes.

Marshmallow Fudge Bars

Senior Winner by Mrs. Elmer Ellis Mooring, Dallas, Texas

These chocolate pecan bars are topped with a fudge frosting made with marshmallows.

BAKE at 350° for 25 to 30 minutes   MAKES 1½ dozen

Sift together . ¾ cup sifted **Pillsbury's Best All Purpose Flour***
2 tablespoons **cocoa**
¼ teaspoon double-acting **baking powder** and
¼ teaspoon **salt**.

Melt . . . . ½ cup **shortening**. Stir in
¾ cup **sugar**. Cool to lukewarm.

Blend in . . . . . 2 unbeaten **eggs,** beating well after each. Add the dry ingredients; mix thoroughly.

Stir in . . . . 1 teaspoon **vanilla** and
½ cup **nuts**, chopped. Spread in well-greased 9x9x2 or 11x7x2-inch pan.

Bake . . . . at 350° for 25 to 30 minutes. Cool; frost with Rocky Road Chocolate Frosting.

For use with Pillsbury's Best Self-Rising Flour, omit baking powder and salt.

ROCKY ROAD CHOCOLATE FROSTING

Combine ⅓ cup firmly packed brown sugar, 2 tablespoons water and 1½ squares (1½ oz.) unsweetened chocolate in saucepan. Bring to boil; cook 3 minutes. Blend in 2 tablespoons butter, 1 teaspoon vanilla and 1 cup sifted confectioners' sugar. Add 8 marshmallows, cut in eighths. If necessary, thin with few drops of cream.

Beaucatcher Brownies

Junior Winner by Jo Anda Osgood, State College, Mississippi

This is a 'quickie' recipe, for it requires only one bowl and can be mixed in minutes.

BAKE at 350° for 30 to 35 minutes   MAKES 1½ dozen

Sift together . ¾ cup sifted **Pillsbury's Best All Purpose Flour***
½ cup **cocoa**
⅓ cup **dried skim milk,** if desired
½ teaspoon double-acting **baking powder** and
½ teaspoon **salt**. Set aside.

Add . . . . 1 cup **sugar** gradually to
½ cup **shortening**, creaming well.

Blend in . . . . . 2 unbeaten **eggs** and
1 teaspoon **vanilla**. Add the dry ingredients gradually; mix thoroughly.

Stir in . . . . . . ½ cup **nuts**, chopped

Spread . . . . in greased 9x9x2 or 11x7x2-inch pan.

Bake . . . . at 350° for 30 to 35 minutes. While warm, cut into bars or squares.

For use with Pillsbury's Best Self-Rising Flour, omit baking powder and salt.

Fudge Nut Thins

Bride Winner by Mrs. H. A. Comeskey, Albany, California

Favorite of all—very thin frosted fudge bars with a hint of almond.

BAKE at 375° for 17 to 20 minutes   MAKES about 3 dozen

Sift together . ¾ cup sifted **Pillsbury's Best All Purpose Flour***
                    1 teaspoon double-acting **baking powder** and
                    ¼ teaspoon **salt**
Melt . . . . ½ cup **butter** or margarine and
                    2 squares (2 oz.) unsweetened **chocolate** in saucepan
                    over low heat, stirring constantly. Remove from heat.
Blend in . . . . . 1 cup **sugar**
                    2 unbeaten **eggs** and
                    ½ teaspoon **vanilla**
Stir in . . . . the dry ingredients and
                    ½ cup **nuts**, chopped; mix thoroughly.
Spread . . . . into 15½x10½x1-inch jelly-roll pan, greased on the
                    bottom, lined with waxed paper and greased.
Bake . . . . at 375° for 17 to 20 minutes. Cool. Frost with
                    Almond Fudge Frosting, then sprinkle with
                    ½ cup **nuts**, chopped
For use with Pillsbury's Best Self-Rising Flour, omit baking powder and salt.

ALMOND FUDGE FROSTING

In small saucepan melt 1 tablespoon butter and 1 square unsweetened chocolate in ¼ cup water. Remove from heat; add 1½ cups sifted confectioners' sugar and ½ teaspoon almond extract. If necessary, thin with a few drops of milk.

Jumble Brownies

Junior Winner by Alice Radkowski, Clifton Heights, Pennsylvania

Coconut and walnuts give a wonderful chewy texture to these light chocolate bars. Prunes add moistness and a "different" flavor.

BAKE at 350° for 40 to 45 minutes*   MAKES about 3 dozen

Sift together 1¼ cups sifted **Pillsbury's Best All Purpose Flour***
                    1¼ cups **sugar**
                    ⅓ cup **cocoa**
                    ½ teaspoon double-acting **baking powder** and
                    ½ teaspoon **salt** into mixing bowl.
Add . . . . ⅔ cup **shortening**
                    2 unbeaten **eggs**
                    1 tablespoon **corn syrup**
                    1 teaspoon **vanilla** and
                    1 can (5 oz.) strained **prunes** (baby food)
Beat . . . . 2 minutes.
Stir in . . . . . . ½ cup **walnuts**, chopped, and
                    ½ cup flaked or chopped shredded **coconut**
Turn . . . . into well-greased 12x8x2 or 13x9x2-inch pan. Ar-
                    range **walnut halves** over top, one for each bar.
Bake . . . . at 350° for 40 to 45 minutes.* While warm, cut into
                    bars or squares.
For use with Pillsbury's Best Self-Rising Flour, omit baking powder and salt. Increase baking time to 50 to 55 minutes.

Banana Fudgies

Junior Winner by Roslinda Zaludek, Thrall, Texas

Chocolate fudge and banana flavor in these coconut topped squares.

BAKE at 400° for 15 minutes, then   MAKES 4 dozen
for 5 to 8 minutes

Sift together . . 2 cups sifted **Pillsbury's Best All Purpose Flour***

¼ cup **sugar**
¼ cup **cocoa** and
½ teaspoon **salt** into large mixing bowl.
Cut in . . . . . . ½ cup **shortening** and
¼ cup **butter** until particles are fine.
Combine . . . . ¼ cup **milk** and
1 teaspoon **vanilla**; sprinkle over mixture, stirring
with fork until all dry particles are moistened.
Press . . . . mixture firmly into greased 13x9-inch pan.
Bake . . . . at 400° for 15 minutes. Sprinkle with
1 cup flaked or chopped shredded **coconut**; drizzle with
Sugar Glaze. Bake 5 to 8 minutes longer.
For use with Pillsbury's Best Self-Rising Flour, omit salt.

SUGAR GLAZE

Combine ¾ cup sugar and ⅓ cup cream in saucepan. Bring to a boil;
cook for 1 minute. Remove from heat. Add 1 tablespoon butter and
¼ teaspoon banana extract.

Split Levels

Senior Winner by Janet K. Goodspeed, Ballston Spa, New York

Sugar cookie cutouts, baked on top, decorate these fudge-filled bars.

BAKE at 375° for 17 to 20 minutes*   MAKES 1½ dozen

Combine . . . . ⅓ cup undiluted **evaporated milk**
1 cup (6-oz. pkg.) **semi-sweet chocolate pieces** and
⅓ cup (3-oz. pkg.) **cream cheese** in top of double
boiler; cook over boiling water until chocolate melts;
blend thoroughly.
Add . . . . ½ cup **nuts**, chopped
¼ cup **sesame seed** and
¼ teaspoon **almond** or **orange extract**. Set aside.
Sift together 1½ cups sifted **Pillsbury's Best All Purpose Flour*****
½ teaspoon double-acting **baking powder** and

Split Levels

¼ teaspoon **salt**
Cream . . . . . . ½ cup **butter** or margarine. Gradually add
¾ cup **sugar**, creaming well.
Blend in . . . . . 1 unbeaten **egg**
¼ teaspoon **almond** or **orange extract** and the dry
ingredients; mix thoroughly.
Spread . . . . half of dough in a 13x9x2-inch pan, lightly greased
on the bottom. Cover dough with cooled filling.
Roll out . . . . . . remaining dough on floured surface to ¼-inch thickness; cut with small cookie cutters. Place cut-out
pieces on top of chocolate, one for each bar. Top
each with a **pecan half.**
Bake . . . . at 375° for 17 to 20 minutes*.

*For use with Pillsbury's Best Self-Rising Flour, omit baking powder and salt;
decrease baking time to 15 to 18 minutes.*

Waverly Fudge Squares

Senior Winner by Mrs. Milton C. Ohlemacher, Sandusky, Ohio

Chewy chocolate brownies with orange rind inside, orange frosting on top.

BAKE at 350° for 25 to 30 minutes   MAKES about 1½ dozen

Sift together . ⅔ cup sifted **Pillsbury's Best All Purpose Flour***
     ½ teaspoon double-acting **baking powder** and
     ¼ teaspoon **salt.** Set aside.

Add . . . . .¾ cup **sugar** gradually to
     ¼ cup **shortening,** creaming well.

Blend in . . . . .2 unbeaten **eggs,**
     1 tablespoon grated **orange rind** and
     2 squares (2 oz.) melted unsweetened **chocolate;** beat well.

Stir in . . . . .the dry ingredients; mix thoroughly. Spread in well-greased 8x8x2 or 9x9x2-inch pan.

Bake . . . . .at 350° for 25 to 30 minutes. Cool; frost with Orange Frosting. Sprinkle with
     ½ cup **nuts,** chopped

*For use with Pillsbury's Best Self-Rising Flour, omit baking powder and salt.

ORANGE FROSTING

Combine 1 tablespoon melted butter, 1 cup sifted confectioners' sugar, ½ teaspoon grated orange rind and 2 to 4 teaspoons orange juice. Beat until smooth and creamy.

Pineapple Brownies

Senior Winner by Josephine Demarco, Chicago, Illinois

Chewy and rich chocolate squares chock full of nuts, with a surprise layer of crushed pineapple.

BAKE at 375°   MAKES 2½ dozen

Sift together 1½ cups sifted **Pillsbury's Best All Purpose Flour***

     1 teaspoon double-acting **baking powder**
     ½ teaspoon **salt** and
     ½ teaspoon **cinnamon**

Cream . . . . . .¾ cup **butter** or margarine. Gradually add
     1½ cups **sugar,** creaming well.

Blend in . . . . .3 unbeaten **eggs,** one at a time, and
     1 teaspoon **vanilla;** beat well. Add the dry ingredients gradually; mix thoroughly.

Place . . . . .one cup of dough in second bowl. Stir in
     1 cup **crushed pineapple,** well drained. Set aside.

Add . . . . .2 squares (2 oz.) melted unsweetened **chocolate** and
     ½ cup **nuts,** chopped, to remaining dough; mix well.

Spread . . . . . . .1½ cups chocolate dough in well-greased 12x8x2 or 13x9x2-inch pan. Cover with pineapple dough. Drop remaining chocolate dough by spoonfuls over pineapple dough; spread carefully to cover.

Bake . . . . .at 375°: 40 to 45 minutes for 12x8x2-inch pan; 35 to 40 minutes for 13x9x2-inch pan.

*For use with Pillsbury's Best Self-Rising Flour, omit baking powder and salt.

Missouri Waltz Brownies

Best of Class Winner by Mrs. Natalie Townes, Kirksville, Missouri

The double frosting of creamy peppermint and melted chocolate makes these brownies as rich and good as candy. Children love them!

BAKE at 350° for 25 to 35 minutes   MAKES about 1½ dozen

Sift together . ¾ cup sifted **Pillsbury's Best All Purpose Flour***
     ½ teaspoon double-acting **baking powder** and

½ teaspoon **salt.** Set aside.

Add . . . . 1 cup **sugar** gradually to
½ cup **shortening,** creaming well.

Blend in . . . . . 2 unbeaten **eggs**
2½ squares (2½ oz.) melted unsweetened **chocolate** and
1 teaspoon **vanilla;** beat well.

Stir in . . . . the dry ingredients and
½ cup **nuts,** chopped. Mix thoroughly.

Spread . . . . into well-greased 9x9x2 or 11x7x2-inch pan.

Bake . . . . at 350° for 25 to 35 minutes. Cool. Frost with Mint
Cream Frosting; spread
2 squares (2 oz.) melted **unsweetened** or **semi-sweet
chocolate** over frosting. Let stand until set; cut into
bars.

For use with Pillsbury's Best Self-Rising Flour, omit baking powder and salt.

MINT CREAM FROSTING

Combine 1½ cups sifted confectioners' sugar and ½ cup light cream
in saucepan. Cook until a little syrup dropped in cold water forms a
soft ball (236°). Remove from heat. Add 1 tablespoon butter. Cool to
lukewarm (110°). Add ¼ teaspoon peppermint extract and 1 drop
green food coloring; beat until thick.

Snowcap Brownies

Senior Winner by Mrs. Judith A. Harper, Los Angeles, California

*The prettiest brownies ever, and so easy to make—fudge brownies with
meringue swirls baked on.*

BAKE at 325° for 25 to 30 minutes   MAKES about 2 dozen

Sift together . ¾ cup sifted **Pillsbury's Best All Purpose Flour***
1 teaspoon double-acting **baking powder** and
½ teaspoon **salt**

Melt . . . . ½ cup **butter** or margarine and
2½ squares (2½ oz.) unsweetened **chocolate** in 2-quart
saucepan over low heat. Cool.

Blend in . . . . 1¼ cups **sugar**
1 teaspoon **vanilla** and
½ teaspoon **red food coloring;** mix well.

Add . . . . 2 unbeaten **eggs** and
1 **egg yolk;** beat well.

Stir in . . . . the dry ingredients and
1 cup **nuts,** chopped. Mix thoroughly.

Spread . . . . in well-greased 15½x10½x1-inch jelly-roll pan.

Beat . . . . 1 **egg white** until stiff peaks form. Blend in
½ cup **sugar** and
½ teaspoon **vanilla**

Drop . . . . meringue by teaspoonfuls onto batter. Draw tip of
knife through batter lengthwise, then crosswise to
give meringue a design.

Bake . . . . at 325° for 25 to 30 minutes.

For use with Pillsbury's Best Self-Rising Flour, omit baking powder and salt.

Snowcap Brownies

By Cracky Bars

Junior Second Prize Winner by Yvonne M. Whyte, New Bedford, Massachusetts

Three layer cookies! Nuts and chocolate in bottom layer, graham crackers in between, and chocolate chip dough on top.

BAKE at 375° for 20 to 25 minutes*   MAKES about 3 dozen

Sift together 1¾ cups sifted **Pillsbury's Best All Purpose Flour***
        ½ teaspoon **salt** and
        ¼ teaspoon **soda**
Cream . . . . . ¾ cup **butter** (or use half shortening). Gradually add
        1 cup **sugar,** creaming well.
Add . . . . 2 unbeaten **eggs**; beat well.
Combine . . . . ⅛ cup **milk** and
        1 teaspoon **vanilla.** Add alternately with the dry ingredients to creamed mixture. Blend thoroughly after each addition.

By Cracky Bars

Place . . . . one-third of batter in a second bowl. Add
        1 square (1 oz.) melted unsweetened **chocolate** and
        ¾ cup **walnuts** or pecans, chopped. Spread in two well-greased 8x8x2-inch pans or one 13x9x2-inch pan.
Arrange . . . . . 9 double **graham crackers** over batter in pans.
Add . . . . ¾ cup **semi-sweet chocolate pieces** to remaining two-thirds of batter. Drop by spoonfuls over graham crackers and spread to cover.
Bake . . . . at 375° for 20 to 25 minutes.*

*For use with Pillsbury's Best Self-Rising Flour, omit salt and soda. Increase baking time to 30 to 35 minutes.

Chocolate Marble Bars

Senior Second Prize Winner by Mrs. William Sawdo, Sturgeon Bay, Wisconsin

Dark rich chocolate is swirled through these butterscotch-flavored coconut bars. A wonderful flavor combination.

BAKE at 375° for 25 to 30 minutes   MAKES about 4 dozen

Melt . . . . 2 squares (2 oz.) unsweetened **chocolate** with
        ¼ cup **sugar** and
        ¼ cup hot **water** over boiling water. Cool.
Sift together . . 2 cups sifted **Pillsbury's Best All Purpose Flour***
        1 teaspoon double-acting **baking powder** and
        ½ teaspoon **salt.** Set aside.
Add . . . . ½ cup **sugar** and
        1 cup firmly packed **brown sugar** gradually to
        ¾ cup **shortening** (half butter may be used), creaming well.
Blend in . . . . . 3 unbeaten **eggs**
        2 tablespoons **milk** and
        1 teaspoon **vanilla**; beat well.
Add . . . . the dry ingredients gradually; mix well.
Stir in . . . . . . 1 cup **coconut,** finely chopped
Spread . . . . in greased 15½x10½x1-inch jelly-roll pan or two

9x9x2-inch pans. Drizzle chocolate mixture over batter in pan in a diagonal pattern. Cut through batter with knife in opposite direction to give marbled effect.

Bake . . . . at 375° for 25 to 30 minutes.

*For use with Pillsbury's Best Self-Rising Flour, omit baking powder and salt.

Hoosier Peanut Bars

Senior Winner by Mrs. Edgar L. Bleeke, Fort Wayne, Indiana

Children will love these brown sugar bars with a layer of semi-sweet chocolate and a meringue topping sprinkled with peanuts.

BAKE at 325° for 40 to 45 minutes   MAKES about 2½ dozen

Sift together . . 2 cups sifted **Pillsbury's Best All Purpose Flour***
          1 teaspoon **soda** and
          ½ teaspoon **salt**
Cream . . . . . . ½ cup **butter** or shortening. Gradually add
          ½ cup **sugar** and
          ½ cup firmly packed **brown sugar,** creaming well.
Blend in . . . . . 2 unbeaten **egg yolks** and
          1 teaspoon **vanilla.** Stir in the dry ingredients gradually to form a crumb mixture.
Press . . . . into greased 13x9x2 or two 8x8x2-inch pans.
Sprinkle . . . . . 1 cup (6-oz. pkg.) **semi-sweet chocolate pieces** and
          ½ cup **salted peanuts,** chopped, over dough; pat in gently.
Beat . . . . 2 **egg whites** until slight mounds form. Gradually add
          1 cup firmly packed **brown sugar;** beat until stiff, straight peaks form. Spread over chocolate pieces.
Sprinkle with . ¼ cup **salted peanuts,** chopped; press into meringue slightly.
Bake . . . . at 325° for 40 to 45 minutes. While warm, cut into bars.

*For use with Pillsbury's Best Self-Rising Flour, omit soda and salt.

Hoosier Peanut Bars

Malted Milk Date Bars

Senior Winner by Katharine M. Adams, Auburndale, Massachusetts

An old favorite—chewy date-nut bars—with malted milk flavor.

BAKE at 350° for 25 to 30 minutes   MAKES about 16

Sift together . ⅔ cup sifted **Pillsbury's Best All Purpose Flour***
                ¾ cup **chocolate** or **vanilla malted milk powder** and
                ½ teaspoon double-acting **baking powder**
Melt . . . . ⅓ cup **butter** or margarine in medium saucepan.
Add . . . . ¾ cup firmly packed **brown sugar**; mix well.
Blend in . . . . . 2 unbeaten **eggs** and
                ½ teaspoon **vanilla**. Add the dry ingredients, mixing thoroughly.
Stir in . . . . 1 cup finely cut **dates** and
                ¾ cup **nuts**, chopped
Turn . . . . into greased 9x9x2 or 11x7x2-inch pan.

Malted Milk Date Bars

Bake . . . . at 350° for 25 to 30 minutes.
For use with Pillsbury's Best Self-Rising Flour, omit baking powder.

Malted Mocha Dreams

Senior Winner by Mrs. Benjamin A. Votava, Omaha, Nebraska

A brown sugar base, a chocolate-malted top and coffee-malted frosting.

BAKE at 350° for 10 minutes, then   MAKES about 3 dozen
        for 25 to 30 minutes

Combine . . . 1¾ cups sifted **Pillsbury's Best All Purpose Flour***
              ¾ cup **butter** or margarine and
              ⅔ cup firmly packed **brown sugar** with pastry blender or fork until particles are fine.
Press . . . . firmly into ungreased 13x9x2-inch pan.
Bake . . . . at 350° for 10 minutes.
Beat . . . . 3 **eggs** until foamy. Gradually add
              ½ cup **sugar**, beating until thick.
Add . . . . ¼ cup **Pillsbury's Best All Purpose Flour***
              1 teaspoon double-acting **baking powder**
              ¼ teaspoon **salt** and
              ¾ cup **chocolate malted milk powder**; blend well.
Stir in . . . . 2 teaspoons **vanilla**
              1 cup **coconut** and
              1 cup **nuts**, chopped. Spread over crust.
Bake . . . . at 350° for 25 to 30 minutes. Cool; frost with Mocha-Malt Frosting.
For use with Pillsbury's Best Self-Rising Flour, omit salt.

MOCHA-MALT FROSTING

Blend together 3 tablespoons chocolate malted milk powder, ½ teaspoon instant coffee and 2 tablespoons boiling water; beat well. Add 2 tablespoons melted butter, 1 teaspoon vanilla and 1½ cups sifted confectioners' sugar. Beat until of spreading consistency. Thin with a few drops of water if necessary.

Butterscotch Fudge Bars

Senior Winner by Georgia Dotson, Washington, D.C.

This rich, chewy butterscotch brownie is flavored with chocolate.

BAKE at 350° for 25 to 35 minutes   MAKES about 3 dozen

Sift together 1½ cups sifted **Pillsbury's Best All Purpose Flour*** and
      ½ teaspoon **soda**

Beat . . . . 2 **eggs** until foamy. Gradually add
      2 cups firmly packed **brown sugar;** beat until well
      blended.

Stir in . . . . . . ½ cup melted **butter** or margarine
      1 square (1 oz.) melted unsweetened **chocolate** and
      1 teaspoon **vanilla**

Add . . . . the dry ingredients and
      ¾ cup **nuts,** chopped; mix thoroughly. Turn into
      greased 13x9x2-inch pan.

Bake . . . . at 350° for 25 to 35 minutes. Cool. Drizzle with
      mixture of
      1 square melted **chocolate** and
      1 teaspoon melted **butter**

*For use with Pillsbury's Best Self-Rising Flour, omit soda.

Candy Bar Brownies

Senior Winner by Mrs. John Sedensky, Cleveland, Ohio

The luscious chocolate and coconut flavor in these easy cookies comes from melted candy bars. Moist and chewy.

BAKE at 350° for 25 to 30 minutes   MAKES 3 dozen

Sift together 1⅛ cups (1 cup plus 2 tablespoons) sifted **Pillsbury's
      Best All Purpose Flour*** and
      ½ teaspoon **salt**

Melt . . . . 2 **chocolate-covered coconut candy bars** (4 sections)
      with

½ cup **shortening** in top of double boiler over hot
      water; stir occasionally.

Blend in . . . . . 1 cup **sugar**
      1 teaspoon **vanilla** and
      2 unbeaten **eggs,** one at a time, beating well after each.

Add . . . . the dry ingredients gradually; mix thoroughly.

Stir in . . . . . . ½ cup **nuts,** chopped. Turn into well-greased 9x9x2-
      inch pan.

Bake . . . . at 350° for 25 to 30 minutes.

*Pillsbury's Best Self-Rising Flour is not recommended for use in this recipe.

Choconut Bars

Junior Winner by Mary Ann Cannon, Elwood, Indiana

There are semi-sweet chocolate pieces and pecans in this cake-like bar cookie.

BAKE at 350° for 35 to 40 minutes   MAKES 16

Sift together 1⅓ cups sifted **Pillsbury's Best All Purpose Flour***
      ½ teaspoon **soda** and
      ½ teaspoon **salt**

Blend . . . . ⅓ cup **shortening** with
      ¾ cup **sugar,** creaming well.

Add . . . . 1 slightly beaten **egg** and
      1½ teaspoons **vanilla;** beat well.

Blend in . . . . . . the dry ingredients. Add
      ¼ cup hot **water;** blend well.

Stir in . . . . . . ½ cup **semi-sweet chocolate pieces** and
      ½ cup **pecans,** chopped.

Spread . . . . in 8x8x2-inch pan, well greased and lightly floured
      on the bottom.

Bake . . . . at 350° for 35 to 40 minutes. Cool; cut into sixteen
      4x1-inch strips. Serve as a cookie, or as a dessert
      with whipped cream.

*Pillsbury's Best Self-Rising Flour is not recommended for use in this recipe.

Dreamy Chocolate Peanut Bars

Senior Winner by Mrs. Ernest P. Fletcher, Winchendon, Massachusetts

Peanut butter and chocolate layers on a butterscotch cookie base—a rich, candy-like bar cookie.

BAKE at 375° for 15 to 18 minutes*   MAKES about 3 dozen

Sift together 1⅛ cups sifted **Pillsbury's Best All Purpose Flour***
          1 teaspoon double-acting **baking powder** and
          ½ teaspoon **salt**
Melt........⅓ cup **shortening** in top of double boiler over hot
          water. Remove from heat. Blend in
          1 cup firmly packed **brown sugar;** cool slightly.
Add........1 teaspoon **vanilla** and
          2 unbeaten **eggs,** one at a time, beating well. Add the
          dry ingredients; blend well.
Spread........into well-greased 9x9x2 or 11x7x2-inch pan.
Bake.........at 375° for 15 to 18 minutes.* Cool slightly.

Spread........with Peanut Butter Topping, then with Chocolate
          Topping. If desired, sprinkle with
          ¼ cup **peanuts,** chopped
For use with Pillsbury's Best Self-Rising Flour, omit baking powder and salt; increase baking time to 18 to 20 minutes.

PEANUT BUTTER TOPPING

Heat ½ cup peanut butter and 1 tablespoon cream in top of double boiler over hot water, stirring to blend well. Do not cook.

CHOCOLATE TOPPING

Melt 1 cup (6-oz. pkg.) semi-sweet chocolate pieces and 1 tablespoon shortening over boiling water.

Chocodiles

Chocodiles

Junior First Prize Winner by Elizabeth Wickersham, Ft. Lauderdale, Florida

Like a butter-crunch candy bar . . . these cookies have a peanut butter base and a chocolate-cereal topping. The kids will love them!

BAKE at 350° for 25 to 30 minutes   MAKES 3 to 4 dozen

Combine.....3 cups sifted **Pillsbury's Best All Purpose Flour***
          1¼ cups firmly packed **brown sugar**
          ½ cup **butter** or margarine
          ½ cup **shortening**
          ⅓ cup crunchy **peanut butter** and
          ¼ teaspoon **salt.** Mix with low speed of mixer (or with
          pastry blender) until mixture is like coarse crumbs.
Add........1 beaten **egg yolk** and
          1 teaspoon **vanilla.** Mix well.
Press.........mixture firmly into ungreased 15½x10½x1-inch
          jelly-roll pan.
Bake.........at 350° for 25 to 30 minutes. Cool slightly. Spread
          with Chocolate Crunch. While warm, cut into squares.
For use with Pillsbury's Best Self-Rising Flour, omit salt.

CHOCOLATE CRUNCH

Melt 1 cup (6-oz. pkg.) semi-sweet chocolate pieces in top of double boiler over boiling water. Stir in ½ cup crunchy peanut butter and 1½ cups corn soya cereal

Southern Pecan Bars

Best of Class Winner by Mrs. Kenneth Pope, Aberdeen, South Dakota

Here's a triple treat! A chewy pecan pie mixture over a pecan cookie "crust," then topped with additional pecan halves.

BAKE at 350° for 10 minutes, then   MAKES about 2½ dozen
           for 25 to 30 minutes

Sift together 1⅓ cups sifted **Pillsbury's Best All Purpose Flour*** and
              ½ teaspoon double-acting **baking powder**
Cream......⅓ cup **butter** or margarine. Gradually add
              ½ cup firmly packed **brown sugar,** creaming well.
Add.........the dry ingredients; mix until particles are fine.
Stir in......¼ cup **pecans,** chopped fine. Press firmly into bottom
              of greased 12x8x2 or 13x9x2-inch pan.
Bake.........at 350° for 10 minutes.

PECAN TOPPING

Beat........2 **eggs** until foamy.
Add........¾ cup dark **corn syrup**
           ¼ cup firmly packed **brown sugar**
           3 tablespoons **flour**
           ½ teaspoon **salt**
           1 teaspoon **vanilla** and
           ¾ cup **pecans,** coarsely chopped; mix well. Pour over
           crust. Place **pecan halves** on top, one for each bar.
Bake.........at 350° for 25 to 30 minutes. Cool in pan.

*For use with Pillsbury's Best Self-Rising Flour, omit baking powder and salt.

Southern Pecan Bars

Chocolate Cherry Cheers

Chocolate Cherry Cheers

Senior Winner by Mrs. Howard Nestingen, La Crosse, Wisconsin

The cookie version of chocolate-covered cherries. Extra special the year 'round.

BAKE at 350° for 15 to 20 minutes   MAKES 3 dozen

Combine . . . . . 1 cup sifted **Pillsbury's Best All Purpose Flour*** and
⅓ cup firmly packed **brown sugar**

Cut in . . . . . ½ cup **butter** or margarine until particles are fine.

Press . . . . into ungreased 8x8x2-inch pan.

Bake . . . . at 350° for 15 to 20 minutes. While warm, cut into
36 squares.

Melt . . . . 6 squares (6 oz.) **semi-sweet chocolate** in top of

double boiler over boiling water. Blend until smooth.

Arrange . . . . squares on waxed paper. Place a well-drained
maraschino cherry on each. Top with teaspoonful
of melted chocolate. (Glaze should partially coat
cherry and cookie.)

*Pillsbury's Best Self-Rising Flour may be substituted.

Cashew Fudge

Senior Winner by Mrs. Harold Lina, Hibbing, Minnesota

Orange marmalade adds flavor to smooth chocolate fudge which needs no cooking. Coating top and bottom is a crunchy cashew mixture.

BAKE at 400° for 10 to 12 minutes   MAKES about 2½ dozen

Sift together . ¾ cup sifted **Pillsbury's Best All Purpose Flour*** and
¼ teaspoon **salt** into mixing bowl. Add
⅓ cup firmly packed **brown sugar**; mix well.

Cut in . . . . . . ⅓ cup **butter** or margarine until particles are fine.

Stir in . . . . 1 cup **cashew nuts** or pecans, chopped. Spread evenly
in jelly-roll pan or baking sheet.

Toast . . . . at 400° for 10 to 12 minutes. Cool.

FUDGE FILLING

Melt . . . . 2½ squares (2½ oz.) unsweetened **chocolate** in top of
double boiler over hot water.

Blend in . . . . . ¼ cup **orange** or **apricot marmalade** and
1 teaspoon **vanilla**

Add . . . . 2 cups sifted **confectioners' sugar** alternately with
¼ cup **cream**. Beat until smooth.

Spread . . . . half of nut mixture in ungreased 11x7x2 or 9x9x2-
inch pan. Spoon in Fudge Filling evenly; spread with
well-buttered spatula. Sprinkle with remaining nut
mixture; press firmly into fudge.

Chill . . . . at least ½ hour. Cut into squares. Store in refrigerator.

*For use with Pillsbury's Best Self-Rising Flour, omit salt.

Peanut Brittle Cookies

Best of Class Winner by Mrs. John Hamlon, Fergus Falls, Minnesota

*Just spread brown sugar cookie dough in a pan and bake. Then break
into irregular pieces. That's all there is to it!*

BAKE at 325° for 20 to 25 minutes   MAKES about 2 dozen

Sift together..1 cup sifted **Pillsbury's Best All Purpose Flour***
    ½ teaspoon **cinnamon** and
    ¼ teaspoon **soda**
Cream......½ cup **butter** or shortening. Gradually add
    ½ cup firmly packed **brown sugar,** creaming well.
Blend in.....2 tablespoons beaten **egg** (save remaining egg) and
    1 teaspoon **vanilla**; beat well.
Add........½ cup **salted peanuts,** finely chopped, and the dry
    ingredients. Mix well.
Spread........or pat dough on greased baking sheet to a 14x10-
    inch rectangle. Brush with reserved egg.
Sprinkle with.½ cup **salted peanuts,** coarsely chopped
Bake.........at 325° for 20 to 25 minutes. While warm, cut or
    break into pieces.

**For use with Pillsbury's Best Self-Rising Flour, omit soda.*

Cashew Caramel Yummies

Senior Winner by Ella Pauline Schulz, Racine, Wisconsin

*Rich and chewy caramel bars—there are cashews inside and in the
creamy brown sugar mixture that's broiled on top.*

BAKE at 350° for 20 to 25 minutes   MAKES about 3 dozen

Sift together.¾ cup sifted **Pillsbury's Best All Purpose Flour***
    ½ teaspoon double-acting **baking powder** and
    ¼ teaspoon **salt**
Combine.....2 slightly beaten **eggs**
    ½ cup **sugar** and

Peanut Brittle Cookies

    ½ cup firmly packed **brown sugar**; mix until just
    combined. (With mixer use a low speed.)
Stir in......½ cup salted **cashews,** chopped, and the dry ingredients.
Turn..........into greased 9x9x2-inch pan.
Bake.........at 350° for 20 to 25 minutes.
Spread........immediately with Cashew Topping, covering com-
    pletely. Place under broiler until Topping bubbles
    and is lightly browned, 1 to 3 minutes. While warm,
    cut into bars. Cool in pan.

**Pillsbury's Best Self-Rising Flour is not recommended for use in this recipe.*

CASHEW TOPPING

Melt 2 tablespoons butter. Add ¼ cup brown sugar, 1½ tablespoons
cream and ⅛ cup chopped salted cashews.

Chocolate Crumble Bars

Junior Winner by Peter Parent, Richmond, Vermont

There's a rich filling of chocolate and nuts hiding between two butterscotch layers in these moist bar cookies.

BAKE at 375° for 25 to 30 minutes   MAKES 1½ dozen

Sift together 1½ cups sifted **Pillsbury's Best All Purpose Flour***
          1 teaspoon **cream of tartar**
          ½ teaspoon **soda** and
          ½ teaspoon **salt** into large mixing bowl.
Add........½ cup firmly packed **brown sugar**
          ½ cup **shortening**
          1 unbeaten **egg** and
          ½ teaspoon **vanilla.** Blend until mixture resembles coarse crumbs. Press three-fourths of mixture into greased 8x8x2-inch pan.
Spread........with Chocolate Filling; sprinkle with remaining crumb mixture. Top with **pecan halves.**
Bake........at 375° for 25 to 30 minutes.
*For use with Pillsbury's Best Self-Rising Flour, omit cream of tartar, soda, salt.

CHOCOLATE FILLING

Melt 1 square (1 oz.) unsweetened chocolate and 2 tablespoons butter in 2 tablespoons cream. Blend in ¾ cup sifted confectioners' sugar. Stir in ½ teaspoon vanilla and ½ cup pecans, chopped.

Butterscotch Goody Bars

Senior Winner by Mrs. W. M. Decker, Lansing, Michigan

Rich, chewy bars, full of nuts and coconut and sprinkled with confectioners' sugar. No frosting is needed.

BAKE at 350° for 25 to 30 minutes   MAKES 2 dozen

Sift together 1½ cups sifted **Pillsbury's Best All Purpose Flour***

          1½ teaspoons double-acting **baking powder** and
          ½ teaspoon **salt.** Set aside.
Add.......1¼ cups firmly packed **brown sugar** gradually to
          ½ cup **shortening,** creaming well.
Blend in.....2 unbeaten **eggs** and
          ½ teaspoon **vanilla.** Add the dry ingredients gradually; mix thoroughly.
Stir in......½ cup **nuts,** chopped, and
          ½ cup **coconut**
Spread........in well-greased 9x9x2 or 12x8x2-inch pan.
Bake.........at 350° for 25 to 30 minutes. Sprinkle with **confectioners' sugar.** While warm, cut into bars.
*For use with Pillsbury's Best Self-Rising Flour, omit baking powder and salt.

Brazil Squares

Senior Winner by Mrs. Herman Johnson, Jr., Keokuk, Iowa

Simple-to-make, thin, rich brown sugar bars. Semi-sweet chocolate pieces melt to form a frosting as they are spread over hot cookies.

BAKE at 350° for 20 to 22 minutes   MAKES about 4 dozen

Sift together..2 cups sifted **Pillsbury's Best All Purpose Flour***
          ½ teaspoon double-acting **baking powder** and

½ teaspoon **salt**

*Cream......*½ cup **butter** or margarine and
½ cup **shortening.** Gradually add
1 cup firmly packed **brown sugar,** creaming well.

*Blend in.....*1 unbeaten **egg** and
1 teaspoon **vanilla.** Add the dry ingredients gradually;
mix thoroughly.

*Spread........*in ungreased 15½x10½x1-inch jelly-roll pan.

*Bake.........*at 350° for 20 to 22 minutes.

*Top with.....*1 cup (6-oz. pkg.) **semi-sweet chocolate pieces,**
spreading as chocolate melts.

*Sprinkle with.*¾ cup **Brazil nuts,** chopped, and, if desired,
¼ cup very finely chopped **candied orange peel.** Cut
into squares while warm.

*Pillsbury's Best Self-Rising Flour is not recommended for use in this recipe.

Sea-Foam Nut Squares

Best of Class Winner by Mrs. Eddie R. Wagoner, Bryan, Texas

*These nut squares have a delicious "chewiness" all their own and a
rich, brown sugar candy flavor. Wonderful for a party!*

BAKE at 350°, then   MAKES about 4 dozen
at 325° for 25 to 30 minutes

*Sift together..*2 cups sifted **Pillsbury's Best All Purpose Flour***
1 teaspoon double-acting **baking powder**
½ teaspoon **salt** and
⅛ teaspoon **soda.** Set aside.

*Add........*¼ cup **sugar** and
½ cup firmly packed **brown sugar** gradually to
½ cup **shortening,** creaming well.

*Blend in.....*2 unbeaten **egg yolks**
2 tablespoons **water** and
½ teaspoon **vanilla;** beat well.

*Stir in........*half of the dry ingredients. Add

Sea-Foam Nut Squares

¼ cup **milk,** then remaining dry ingredients. Blend
thoroughly.

*Spread........*in 15½x10½x1-inch jelly-roll pan or two 9x9x2-inch
pans, well greased on the bottoms.

*Bake........*at 350°: 15 to 18 minutes for jelly-roll pan; 12 to 15
minutes for 9x9x2-inch pans. Decrease oven tem-
perature to 325°.

*Beat........*2 **egg whites** until slight mounds form. Add
1¼ cups firmly packed **brown sugar** gradually, beating
until mixture stands in stiff, glossy peaks. Fold in
½ teaspoon **vanilla** and
½ cup **nuts,** chopped. Spread over baked layer.

*Sprinkle with.*½ cup chopped **nuts**

*Bake.........*at 325° for 25 to 30 minutes.

*For use with Pillsbury's Best Self-Rising Flour, omit baking powder and salt.

Peanut Meringue Bars

Senior Winner by Mrs. Michael J. Ingelido, Falls Church, Virginia

Brown sugar meringue and peanuts top these chewy bars—rich in candy-like flavor.

BAKE at 350° for 15 minutes, then   MAKES 2 dozen
for 10 to 15 minutes

Combine . . . 1½ cups sifted **Pillsbury's Best All Purpose Flour*** and
¾ cup firmly packed **brown sugar**
Cut in . . . . . . ½ cup **shortening** until particles are fine.
Blend in . . . . 2 unbeaten **egg yolks.** Press into ungreased 12x8x2 or
13x9x2-inch pan.
Bake . . . . at 350° for 15 minutes.
Beat . . . . 2 **egg whites** and
⅛ teaspoon **cream of tartar** until soft mounds form.
Add . . . . ⅓ cup **sugar** and
⅓ cup firmly packed **brown sugar** gradually, beating
until mixture stands in stiff, glossy peaks.
Fold in . . . . . . ½ teaspoon **vanilla**
2 tablespoons **flour** and
½ cup **salted peanuts,** chopped. Spread over crust.
Bake . . . . at 350° for 10 to 15 minutes. While warm, cut into
bars.

*Pillsbury's Best Self-Rising Flour may be substituted.

Saucy Black Walnut Bars

Senior Winner by Mrs. Robert O'Connell, Hartford City, Indiana

Black walnut is the outstanding flavor of these chewy coconut bars, drizzled with brown sugar sauce before baking.

BAKE at 350° for 25 to 30 minutes   MAKES 4½ dozen

Sift together . . 2 cups sifted **Pillsbury's Best All Purpose Flour*** and
½ teaspoon **salt.** Set aside.

Add . . . . 1½ cups firmly packed **brown sugar** gradually to
¾ cup **shortening,** creaming well.
Blend in . . . . . 3 unbeaten **eggs**
2 tablespoons **milk** and
1 teaspoon **vanilla;** beat well.
Add . . . . the dry ingredients gradually; mix thoroughly.
Stir in . . . . 1 cup **coconut,** ground, and
1 cup **black walnuts,** chopped fine
Turn . . . . into well-greased and lightly floured 15½x10½x1-
inch jelly-roll pan. Prepare Brown Sugar Sauce;
drizzle while hot over batter.
Bake . . . . at 350° for 25 to 30 minutes. Cool; cut into bars.

*Pillsbury's Best Self-Rising Flour is not recommended for use in this recipe.

BROWN SUGAR SAUCE

Blend together in saucepan ¾ cup firmly packed brown sugar, 2 tablespoons butter, ¼ cup cream and 1 teaspoon corn syrup. Cook, stirring occasionally, until a little syrup dropped in cold water forms a soft ball (236°). Stir in 1 teaspoon vanilla.

Molasses Orange Gingerlades

Senior Winner by Mrs. W. S. Hooper, Minneapolis, Minnesota

Double-decker bars with a spicy molasses flavor. Orange marmalade helps keep them moist; orange icing goes between the layers.

BAKE at 400° for 12 to 15 minutes   MAKES 4 dozen

Sift together 2½ cups sifted **Pillsbury's Best All Purpose Flour***
½ teaspoon **salt**
¼ teaspoon **soda**
½ teaspoon **ginger**
½ teaspoon **cinnamon** and
¼ teaspoon **nutmeg**
Blend . . . . . . ½ cup **shortening** with
⅓ cup **molasses** and

½ cup firmly packed **brown sugar,** creaming well.

Stir in . . . . . ½ cup **orange marmalade**

Add . . . . the dry ingredients alternately with
¼ cup cool strong **coffee.** Blend thoroughly after each addition. Spread into two well-greased 13x9x2-inch pans.**

Bake . . . . at 400° for 12 to 15 minutes. Cool in pans for 10 minutes; cut into 2x1-inch bars. Remove from pans; cool thoroughly. Place bars together sandwich-style with **Orange Frosting,** page 327.

**For use with Pillsbury's Best Self-Rising Flour, omit soda and salt.*

***If only one 13x9x2-inch pan is available, dough may be baked half at a time. Cover remaining dough.*

Crunchy Currant Events

Senior Winner by Mrs. L. A. Steele, Livonia, Michigan

Simple to mix and shape—a cinnamon-flavored currant filling is baked between layers of a crunchy oatmeal mixture.

BAKE at 350° for 30 to 35 minutes*   MAKES about 3 dozen

Blend . . . . . . 1 tablespoon **cornstarch** with
½ teaspoon **cinnamon** in saucepan. Gradually add 1 cup **water,** stirring until smooth.

Add . . . . . . 1½ cups (8-oz. pkg.) dried **currants** or chopped raisins. Bring to boil; cook for 5 minutes, stirring occasionally. Remove from heat.

Stir in . . . . . . 1 teaspoon grated **lemon rind** and
1 tablespoon **lemon juice.** Reserve.

Combine . . . 1½ cups sifted **Pillsbury's Best All Purpose Flour***
1 cup quick-cooking **rolled oats**
¾ cup firmly packed **brown sugar** and
½ teaspoon **salt** in mixing bowl.

Cut in . . . . . ¾ cup **shortening** until particles are fine. Press half of mixture in bottom of greased 13x9x2-inch pan.

Spread with currant filling.

Combine . . . . ½ cup **nuts,** chopped, with remaining crumb mixture; sprinkle over filling. Pat down firmly.

Bake . . . . at 350° for 30 to 35 minutes.* Cool; cut into small bars. Or, cut into large squares, top with whipped cream and serve as a dessert.

**For use with Pillsbury's Best Self-Rising Flour, omit salt; increase baking time to 35 to 40 minutes.*

Chewy Scotch Squares

Senior Winner by Mrs. Cecil Ginanni, Carlsbad, New Mexico

Fruit jam in cookies that taste like English toffee.

BAKE at 300° for 25 to 30 minutes   MAKES 3 dozen

Sift together . ¾ cup sifted **Pillsbury's Best All Purpose Flour***
1 teaspoon double-acting **baking powder** and
½ teaspoon **salt**

Melt . . . . ½ cup **butter** or margarine in saucepan. Add 1 cup firmly packed **brown sugar;** stir until dissolved.

Stir in . . . . . . ⅓ cup **peach** or **apricot preserves**

Add . . . . 1½ cups quick-cooking **rolled oats** and the dry ingredients; mix thoroughly.

Cover . . . . baking sheet with aluminum foil; turn up edges about ½ inch. Spread dough in center to a 6-inch square.

Bake . . . . at 300° for 25 to 30 minutes. Dough will spread during baking. Cool 15 minutes, then sprinkle with **confectioners' sugar** and cut into squares.

**For use with Pillsbury's Best Self-Rising Flour, omit baking powder and salt.*

Caramel Oatmeal Brownies

Junior Winner by Carol Ann Markford, Upper Darby, Pennsylvania

Caramel and chocolate—combined in a bar cookie. There's an oatmeal-brown sugar mixture on the bottom, a brownie layer on top.

BAKE at 350° for 10 minutes, then   MAKES 1½ dozen
       for 30 to 35 minutes

Sift together . ⅓ cup sifted **Pillsbury's Best All Purpose Flour***
       ¼ teaspoon **soda** and
       ⅛ teaspoon **salt** into mixing bowl.
Add . . . . ½ cup firmly packed **brown sugar** and
       1 cup quick-cooking **rolled oats**; stir to combine.
Blend in . . . . . ⅓ cup melted **butter** or margarine until mixture is
       crumbly. Press into ungreased 8x8x2-inch pan.
Bake . . . . at 350° for 10 minutes.

CHOCOLATE BROWNIES

Sift together . ⅔ cup sifted **Pillsbury's Best All Purpose Flour***
       ¼ teaspoon **soda** and
       ¼ teaspoon **salt**
Melt together . 1 square (1 oz.) unsweetened **chocolate** and
       ¼ cup **butter** or margarine in top of double boiler over
       hot water. Remove from heat.
Blend in . . . . . ¾ cup **sugar** gradually. Add
       1 unbeaten **egg**; beat well.
Add . . . . the dry ingredients; mix thoroughly.
Blend in . . . . . 2 tablespoons **milk** and
       1 teaspoon **vanilla**. Spread over crust.
Bake . . . . at 350° for 30 to 35 minutes.

*For use with Pillsbury's Best Self-Rising Flour, omit soda and salt.

Date Carnival Squares

Senior Winner by Mrs. George D. Henry, Jonesboro, Arkansas

Sweet, tender and chewy—a layer bar cookie made with a spicy brown sugar and oatmeal batter and a cooked date and lemon filling.

BAKE at 350° for 35 to 40 minutes   MAKES 1½ dozen

Combine . . . . . 1 cup **dates**, finely cut
       ⅓ cup **water**
       2 tablespoons **sugar** and
       2 tablespoons **lemon juice** in saucepan. Simmer over
       low heat, stirring occasionally, until thick, 8 to 10
       minutes. Cool.
Sift together 1½ cups sifted **Pillsbury's Best All Purpose Flour***
       1 teaspoon double-acting **baking powder**
       1 teaspoon **cinnamon**
       ¼ teaspoon **soda**
       ¼ teaspoon **salt** and
       ¼ teaspoon **nutmeg**
Cream . . . . . . ½ cup **butter** or margarine. Gradually add
       1 cup firmly packed **brown sugar,** creaming well.
Blend in . . . . . 1 unbeaten **egg** and
       2 tablespoons **milk**. Add the dry ingredients; mix
       thoroughly.
Stir in . . . . 1 cup quick-cooking **rolled oats**
Spread . . . . half the batter in 9x9x2 or 11x7x2-inch pan, well
       greased on the bottom. Cover with the date filling;
       spread with remaining batter.
Bake . . . . at 350° for 35 to 40 minutes. Cool. Sprinkle with
       sifted **confectioners' sugar.**

*For use with Pillsbury's Best Self-Rising Flour, omit baking powder, soda, salt.

Vernie's Date-Nut Bars

Senior Winner by Mrs. Vernon Ellington, Milwaukee, Wisconsin

These rich date-nut bars are especially good at coffee time.

BAKE at 350° for 35 to 40 minutes   MAKES about 2 dozen

Sift together 1½ cups sifted **Pillsbury's Best All Purpose Flour***
              1 tablespoon **cocoa**
              ½ teaspoon **soda** and
              ½ teaspoon **salt**
Combine.....1 cup **dates,** cut in pieces, and
              ¾ cup **boiling water.** Set aside to cool.
Add.......1¼ cups **sugar** gradually to
              ½ cup **shortening,** creaming well.
Blend in.....2 unbeaten **eggs** and
              ½ cup **pecans,** chopped; beat well.
Add.........the dry ingredients and date mixture alternately,
              mixing thoroughly.
Turn.........into greased and floured 13x9x2-inch pan. Sprinkle
              ½ cup **pecans,** chopped, over batter.
Bake.........at 350° for 35 to 40 minutes. Sprinkle with **con-
              fectioners' sugar.**

*For use with Pillsbury's Best Self-Rising Flour, omit soda and salt.

Lemon Mardi Gras Squares

Senior Winner by Mrs. Joseph Negrotto, New Orleans, Louisiana

These bright-gold bars taste tart and lemony. They pack and keep well.

BAKE at 400° for 25 to 30 minutes   MAKES 2 dozen

Sift together 1½ cups sifted **Pillsbury's Best All Purpose Flour***
              ½ teaspoon **salt** and
              ¼ teaspoon double-acting **baking powder**
Beat........3 **egg whites** until soft mounds form. Add
              1 cup sifted **confectioners' sugar** gradually, beating

Lemon Mardi Gras Squares

              until stiff, straight peaks form.
Cream......½ cup **butter** or margarine. Gradually add
              1 cup **sugar,** creaming well.
Add........3 **egg yolks,** one at a time, beating well.
Add.........the dry ingredients alternately with
              ⅓ cup **lemon juice** to creamed mixture. Blend thoroughly
              after each addition.
Stir in.......2 tablespoons grated **lemon rind** and
              ½ cup **pecans,** chopped
Fold in.......beaten egg whites gently but thoroughly. Pour into
              well-greased 13x9x2-inch pan.
Bake.........at 400° for 25 to 30 minutes. While warm, frost with
              Vanilla Glaze, page 326. Sprinkle with chopped
              pecans.

*Pillsbury's Best Self-Rising Flour is not recommended for use in this recipe.

Norwegian Almond Bars

Senior Winner by Nora Sagen, Aberdeen, Washington

These bars have the buttery richness so typical of Scandinavian cookies.

BAKE at 375° for 10 minutes, then MAKES about 2 dozen
for 20 to 25 minutes

Sift together . . 2 cups sifted **Pillsbury's Best All Purpose Flour***
¾ cup **sugar**
1 teaspoon double-acting **baking powder** and
1 teaspoon **salt** into large mixing bowl.

Cut in . . . . . . ¾ cup soft **butter** until particles are fine.

Press . . . . three-fourths of mixture into ungreased 13x9x2 or
12x8x2-inch pan. Reserve remainder for topping.

Bake . . . . at 375° for 10 minutes.

Blend . . . . . . ½ cup cold **mashed potatoes** with
1¼ cups sifted **confectioners' sugar**

Norwegian Almond Bars

1½ cups **almonds,** ground
1 teaspoon **cinnamon**
½ teaspoon **cardamom**
1 tablespoon **water** and
1 **egg white;** mix well. Spread over crust.

Combine . . . . . . remaining crumb mixture with
1 **egg yolk.** Roll out on floured surface to a 10x6-inch
rectangle. Cut into strips ½ inch wide. Place across
filling, crisscross fashion.

Bake . . . . at 375° for 20 to 25 minutes.

For use with Pillsbury's Best Self-Rising Flour, omit baking powder and salt.

Old World Almond Bars

Senior Winner by Mrs. Sophie Kaas, Chicago, Illinois

*A buttery cookie base, then layers of almond paste and jam. A chocolate
glaze gives the final touch to these luscious cookies.*

BAKE at 375° for 10 minutes, then MAKES 2 dozen
for 20 to 25 minutes

Sift together . . 1 cup sifted **Pillsbury's Best All Purpose Flour*** and
½ teaspoon double-acting **baking powder**

Cream . . . . . . ⅓ cup **butter** or margarine. Add
¼ cup **sugar,** creaming well.

Add . . . . 1 **egg yolk;** beat well. Stir in the dry ingredients until
particles are fine.

Blend in . . . . . 1 tablespoon **milk** to form a dough. Press into bottom
of greased 8x8x2-inch pan.

Bake . . . . at 375° for 10 minutes.

Combine . . . . ¾ cup blanched **almonds,** ground**
⅔ cup **sugar**
½ teaspoon **salt**
1 unbeaten **egg**
1 unbeaten **egg white**
½ teaspoon **vanilla** and

¼ teaspoon **almond extract**

Spread . . . . . ¼ cup **strawberry** or **raspberry jam** over hot baked base. Top with the almond mixture.

Bake . . . . at 375° for 20 to 25 minutes. Cool; frost with Shiny Chocolate Frosting. Let stand ½ hour; cut into bars.

*For use with Pillsbury's Best Self-Rising Flour, omit baking powder.

**If desired, substitute ½ cup almond paste; decrease sugar to ⅓ cup and omit almond extract.

SHINY CHOCOLATE FROSTING

Melt ½ square (½ oz.) unsweetened chocolate and 1 tablespoon butter over hot water. Blend in ½ cup sifted confectioners' sugar and ½ teaspoon vanilla. Gradually add 2 to 3 teaspoons boiling water to form a smooth, thin frosting.

Orange Almond Bars

Bride Winner by Mrs. Alice Lacher, Los Angeles, California

For an afternoon coffee hour, golden rich cookie bars with ground almond filling and zippy orange glaze.

BAKE at 375° for 25 to 30 minutes   MAKES about 2 dozen

Sift together . . 2 cups sifted **Pillsbury's Best All Purpose Flour***
⅓ cup **sugar**
1½ teaspoons double-acting **baking powder** and
½ teaspoon **salt** into large mixing bowl.

Cut in . . . . . . ⅔ cup **butter** or margarine until particles are fine.

Combine . . . . . 1 slightly beaten **egg** and
1 teaspoon **vanilla**. Add to flour mixture, stirring with fork until dough is moist enough to hold together.

Roll out . . . . half of dough on 13x9-inch piece of waxed paper; roll to edges of paper. Invert into 13x9-inch pan, greased on the bottom; remove paper. Roll out remainder of dough on waxed paper to a 13x9-inch rectangle; set aside.

Orange Almond Bars

Combine . . . . . 2 cups **almonds**, ground
⅔ cup **sugar**
1 tablespoon grated **orange rind**
½ cup **orange juice** and
1 tablespoon **lemon juice**. Spread over dough in pan.

Place . . . . remaining dough over filling; remove paper. Prick generously with fork.

Bake . . . . at 375° for 25 to 30 minutes. Frost immediately with Orange Icing.

*For use with Pillsbury's Best Self-Rising Flour, omit baking powder and salt; decrease butter to ½ cup.

ORANGE ICING

Combine 1½ cups sifted confectioners' sugar, 1 teaspoon grated orange rind and 2½ tablespoons orange juice.

Spicy Banana Bars

Senior Winner by Mrs. Byard Cummings, Enderlin, North Dakota

Mashed banana, spices and pecans blend in these cake-like cookies; tangy lemon frosting adds just the right contrast in flavor.

BAKE at 350° for 22 to 25 minutes   MAKES about 3 dozen

Sift together . . 1 cup sifted **Pillsbury's Best All Purpose Flour***
⅔ cup **sugar**
½ teaspoon double-acting **baking powder**
½ teaspoon **salt**
¼ teaspoon **soda**
¾ teaspoon **cinnamon**
¼ teaspoon **cloves** and
¼ teaspoon **allspice**
Combine . . . . ¼ cup **shortening** and
⅓ cup mashed ripe **banana** (1 small) in mixing bowl;

Spicy Banana Bars

beat 2 minutes.
Add . . . . 1 unbeaten **egg**; beat well.
Blend in . . . . . . the dry ingredients alternately with
¼ cup **milk.** Blend thoroughly after each addition.
Stir in . . . . . . ⅓ cup **pecans**, chopped
Spread . . . . in well-greased 13x9x2-inch pan.
Bake . . . . at 350° for 22 to 25 minutes. While warm, frost with Lemon Frosting.

*For use with Pillsbury's Best Self-Rising Flour, omit baking powder, salt, soda.

LEMON FROSTING

Combine 2 tablespoons melted butter, 1 tablespoon hot water and 2 teaspoons lemon juice. Blend in 1 cup sifted confectioners' sugar. Thin with hot water, a few drops at a time, if necessary.

Quicky Fruitcakes

Senior Winner by Mrs. John F. Ryan, Arlington, Virginia

Fruitcake made in a shallow pan . . . cut into bars—you'll like them too!

BAKE at 325° for 30 to 35 minutes   MAKES about 4 dozen

Sift together . . 1 cup sifted **Pillsbury's Best All Purpose Flour*** and
1½ teaspoons **salt**
Combine . . . . . 1 cup **nuts,** coarsely chopped
1 cup **golden raisins**
1 cup **seedless raisins** (or currants)
1 cup chopped **candied fruit**
1 cup **dates,** cut in large pieces, and
½ cup dried **figs,** cut in large pieces. Coat with ¼ cup dry ingredients.
Beat . . . . 4 **eggs** until foamy in large mixing bowl. Add
1 cup firmly packed **brown sugar**
1 tablespoon grated **orange rind** and
1 teaspoon **vanilla.** Beat just until blended.
Stir in . . . . dry ingredients and fruit mixture; mix well.

Spread . . . . in greased 15½x10½x1-inch jelly-roll pan.
Bake . . . . at 325° for 30 to 35 minutes. If desired, brush with
Orange Glaze while warm.

*For use with Pillsbury's Best Self-Rising Flour, omit salt.

ORANGE GLAZE

Combine ½ cup sugar and ¼ cup orange juice in small saucepan.
Heat, stirring constantly, just until sugar dissolves.

Fireside Fruit Bars

Senior Winner by Miss Jenifer Trace, Wilmington, Delaware

*These bars are filled with nuts and candied fruit. Spices add dash;
orange juice and rind add flavor.*

BAKE at 350° for 20 to 25 minutes   MAKES about 2½ dozen

Sift together . . 2 cups sifted **Pillsbury's Best All Purpose Flour***
        ½ teaspoon **soda**
        ½ teaspoon **salt**
        ½ teaspoon **cinnamon** and
        ¼ teaspoon **nutmeg**
Stir in . . . . 2 teaspoons grated **orange rind**
        ⅔ cup mixed chopped **candied fruit** and
        ¼ cup **nuts,** chopped. Set aside.
Add . . . . ¾ cup **sugar** gradually to
        ⅔ cup **shortening,** creaming well.
Combine . . . . ½ cup undiluted **evaporated milk** and
        ¼ cup **orange juice.** Add alternately with the dry in-
        gredients to creamed mixture, beginning and ending
        with dry ingredients.
Spread . . . . in well-greased 15x10½x1-inch jelly-roll pan or two
        9x9x2-inch pans.
Bake . . . . at 350° for 20 to 25 minutes. While warm, frost with
        Orange Frosting, page 327.

*For use with Pillsbury's Best Self-Rising Flour, omit soda and salt.

Hawaiian Fruit Squares

Junior Winner by Dorothy Ann Tetzlaff, De Pere, Wisconsin

*Moist fruity cookies chock full of pineapple, coconut, dates and nuts.
Serve as squares—or crush into balls—and roll in sugar.*

BAKE at 350° for 30 to 35 minutes   MAKES about 3 dozen

Sift together . ¾ cup sifted **Pillsbury's Best All Purpose Flour***
        1 teaspoon double-acting **baking powder** and
        ¼ teaspoon **salt**
Drain . . . . ½ cup **crushed pineapple;** spread on absorbent paper
        to drain thoroughly.
Beat . . . . 2 **eggs** until light and fluffy. Gradually add
        ¾ cup **sugar,** beating well.
Stir in . . . . the dry ingredients; mix well.
Fold in . . . . . . ½ cup **dates,** cut into pieces
        ½ cup **nuts,** chopped
        ½ cup **coconut,** cut, and the drained pineapple.
Spread . . . . in well-greased 9x9x2-inch pan.
Bake . . . . at 350° for 30 to 35 minutes. While warm, cut into
        squares. Roll in **confectioners'** or **granulated sugar.**
        If desired, squares may be pressed into balls before
        rolling in sugar.

*For use with Pillsbury's Best Self-Rising Flour, omit baking powder and salt.

Charmin' Cherry Bars

Junior Winner by Deanna Thompson, Alexandria, Minnesota

These cookies have a rich, buttery, cream-colored layer below, and scarlet cherries, coconut and walnuts in the layer on top.

BAKE at 350° for 10 minutes, then   MAKES 3 dozen
     for 30 to 40 minutes

Sift together . . 1 cup sifted **Pillsbury's Best All Purpose Flour*** and
             ¼ cup **confectioners' sugar** into mixing bowl.
Cut in . . . . . . ½ cup **butter** or margarine until particles are fine. Press mixture into ungreased 11x7x2 or 9x9x2-inch pan.
Bake . . . . at 350° for 10 minutes.
Sift together . ¼ cup sifted **Pillsbury's Best All Purpose Flour***
             ¾ cup **sugar**
             ½ teaspoon double-acting **baking powder** and
             ¼ teaspoon **salt** into mixing bowl.

Charmin' Cherry Bars

Stir in . . . . 2 slightly beaten **eggs**
             ½ cup **maraschino cherries,** finely cut
             ½ cup **coconut** and
             ½ cup **walnuts,** chopped. Spread over baked mixture.
Bake . . . . at 350° for 30 to 40 minutes.
*For use with Pillsbury's Best Self-Rising Flour, omit baking powder and salt.

Frosted Figeroos

Senior Winner by Mrs. Charlotte B. Bruce, Albuquerque, New Mexico

A chewy orange-fig bar that is perfect for school lunches and picnics.

BAKE at 375° for 25 to 30 minutes*   MAKES 4 dozen

Sift together 2½ cups sifted **Pillsbury's Best All Purpose Flour***
             ½ teaspoon **salt**
             ¼ teaspoon **soda**
             1 teaspoon **cinnamon**
             ½ teaspoon **nutmeg** and
             ¼ teaspoon **cloves.** Set aside.
Add . . . . 1½ cups firmly packed **brown sugar** gradually to
             ¾ cup **shortening,** creaming well.
Blend in . . . . . 3 unbeaten **eggs.** Add
             ½ cup **orange marmalade;** blend thoroughly.
Add . . . . the dry ingredients gradually and
             1½ cups dried **figs,** cut fine; mix well.
Spread . . . . in a greased 15½x10½x1-inch jelly-roll pan.
Bake . . . . at 375° for 25 to 30 minutes.* While warm, spread with Orange Glaze.
*For use with Pillsbury's Best Self-Rising Flour, omit salt and soda. Decrease baking temperature to 350°; increase baking time to 30 to 35 minutes.

ORANGE GLAZE

Cream together 2 tablespoons butter, 1½ cups sifted confectioners' sugar and 1 tablespoon grated orange rind. Blend in 1 to 2 tablespoons milk until of spreading consistency.

Prune-In-Between Squares

Junior Winner by Virginia Luzzi, Sebastopol, California

Sandwich a tangy prune filling between layers of rich tender pastry to make these cookies. Sprinkle them with cinnamon and sugar.

BAKE at 375° for 30 to 35 minutes   MAKES about 2 dozen

Sift together 2¾ cups sifted **Pillsbury's Best All Purpose Flour***
          ¼ cup **sugar**
          3 teaspoons double-acting **baking powder** and
          1¼ teaspoons **salt** into large mixing bowl.

Cut in . . . . . . ⅓ cup **butter** or margarine and
          ⅓ cup **shortening** until mixture is like coarse crumbs.

Combine . . . . . 1 slightly beaten **egg** and
          ⅓ cup **milk**; blend into dry ingredients.

Roll out . . . . half of dough on floured surface to a 13x9-inch rectangle. Fit into ungreased 13x9x2-inch pan. Spread with Spicy Prune Filling.

Roll out . . . . . . remaining dough; place over filling in pan. Cut slits.

Combine . . . . . 2 tablespoons **sugar** and
          ½ teaspoon **cinnamon**; sprinkle over top.

Bake . . . . at 375° for 30 to 35 minutes.

*For use with Pillsbury's Best Self-Rising Flour, omit baking powder and salt.

SPICY PRUNE FILLING

Combine in saucepan 1 pound (2 cups) prunes, cooked and chopped, ¼ cup prune juice, 1 tablespoon grated lemon rind, ¼ cup lemon juice, 1 teaspoon cinnamon, 1 teaspoon nutmeg, ⅛ teaspoon salt and ½ cup sugar. Cook until thickened, stirring occasionally. Cool.

Cornish Raisin Crisps

Senior Winner by Mrs. Edward Durant, Anna Maria City, Florida

Something novel for a coffee party—pastry wafers filled with raisins.

BAKE at 375° for 15 to 20 minutes   MAKES 3 dozen

Combine . . . . . 1 cup seedless **raisins**, chopped
          ¼ cup **sugar** and
          2 teaspoons grated **lemon rind**. Set aside.

Sift together . . 2 cups sifted **Pillsbury's Best All Purpose Flour***
          1 tablespoon **sugar**
          ¾ teaspoon **salt** and
          ½ teaspoon **soda** into large mixing bowl.

Cut in . . . . . . ⅓ cup **shortening** and
          ¼ cup **butter** or margarine until particles are fine.

Combine . . . . ½ teaspoon **lemon extract** with
          6 to 7 tablespoons cold **water**. Sprinkle over mixture, stirring with fork until dough clings together.

Place . . . . half of dough on greased baking sheet. Cover with waxed paper and roll out to a 14x10-inch rectangle. Remove paper and sprinkle with raisin mixture.

Roll out . . . . . . remaining dough between sheets of waxed paper to a 14x10-inch rectangle. Remove top sheet and invert over filling. Press down lightly with rolling pin. Remove paper and seal edges. Mark into 2-inch squares with pastry wheel or by pricking with fork. Brush with **cream**.

Bake . . . . at 375° for 15 to 20 minutes.

*For use with Pillsbury's Best Self-Rising Flour, omit salt and soda.

Minnesota Harvest Bars

Minnesota Harvest Bars

Senior Winner by Aquina G. Shea, Glyndon, Minnesota

Dates, nuts, spices and a hint of pumpkin give these bars special flavor. Serve as a cooky, or top with whipped cream for dessert.

BAKE at 350° for 30 to 35 minutes   MAKES about 1 dozen

Combine . . . . ½ cup **dates,** cut in small pieces
       ½ cup **walnuts,** chopped, and
       2 tablespoons **flour**
Sift together . ½ cup sifted **Pillsbury's Best All Purpose Flour***
       ½ teaspoon double-acting **baking powder**
       ½ teaspoon **salt**
       ¼ teaspoon **soda**
       ½ teaspoon **cinnamon**

       ½ teaspoon **nutmeg** and
       ½ teaspoon **ginger**
Melt . . . . ¼ cup **shortening** in saucepan. Stir in
       1 cup firmly packed **brown sugar.** Remove from heat.
Blend in . . . . ⅔ cup canned **pumpkin**
       ½ teaspoon **vanilla** and
       2 unbeaten **eggs,** one at a time; beat well.
Add . . . . the dry ingredients; mix well. Stir in the date-nut
       mixture.
Pour . . . . into well-greased 9x9x2-inch pan.
Bake . . . . at 350° for 30 to 35 minutes. Cool: cut into bars.
       Sprinkle with **confectioners' sugar.**
**For use with Pillsbury's Best Self-Rising Flour, omit baking powder and salt.*

Spicy Coconut Bars

Senior Winner by Mrs. Albert P. Kimball, New York, New York

A spicy tea-cake type cookie with a brown sugar-coconut topping.

BAKE at 350° for 25 to 30 minutes   MAKES 3 dozen

Toast . . . . ¾ cup **coconut** at 375° for 5 to 7 minutes, stirring
       occasionally.
Sift together . . 2 cups sifted **Pillsbury's Best All Purpose Flour***
       1 teaspoon double-acting **baking powder**
       1 teaspoon **salt**
       1 teaspoon **cinnamon**
       ½ teaspoon **nutmeg** and
       ¼ teaspoon **soda.** Set aside.
Add . . . . 1 cup firmly packed **brown sugar** gradually to
       ½ cup **shortening,** creaming well.
Blend in . . . . . . 1 unbeaten **egg**
       ¾ cup cooked **pumpkin** (fresh or canned)
       2 tablespoons **molasses** and
       1 teaspoon **vanilla;** beat well.
Add . . . . the dry ingredients gradually; mix well.

Spread........in greased 15½x10½x1-inch jelly-roll pan or two
9x9x2-inch pans.

Beat........1 **egg** until very thick. Gradually add
½ cup firmly packed **brown sugar;** beat until very
thick. Stir in toasted coconut. Spread over batter
in pan.

Bake........at 350° for 25 to 30 minutes.

*For use with Pillsbury's Best Self-Rising Flour, omit baking powder and salt.

Merry Mincemeaters

Bride Third Prize Winner by Mrs. Richard Hotze, Elk Grove Village, Illinois

*Like the wonderful flavor of mincemeat? Make these filled bar cookies
any time of the year for scrumptious eating.*

BAKE at 350° for 25 to 35 minutes   MAKES about 2 dozen

Sift together 2½ cups sifted **Pillsbury's Best All Purpose Flour***
½ teaspoon **cinnamon** and
¼ teaspoon **salt**

Cream......¾ cup **butter** or margarine. Add
⅔ cup **sugar,** creaming well.

Blend in.....1 unbeaten **egg** (reserve 1 tablespoon egg white) and
1 teaspoon **almond extract.** Beat well.

Stir in.........the dry ingredients; mix thoroughly.

Roll out......half of dough on greased baking sheet to a 10x8-inch
rectangle.

Spread with.1½ cups prepared **mincemeat**

Roll out.......remaining dough between sheets of waxed paper to a

10x8-inch rectangle. Remove top sheet; invert dough
over mincemeat. Remove paper. Brush with egg
white, slightly beaten. Sprinkle with
⅓ cup blanched **almonds,** chopped, if desired.

Bake.........at 350° for 25 to 35 minutes.

*Pillsbury's Best Self-Rising Flour is not recommended for use in this recipe.

Mince Mix-Up Bars

Senior Winner by Mrs. Neut Fagg, Grand Prairie, Texas

*These cookies have mincemeat, pineapple and walnuts inside and pine-
apple icing on top. You'll find them interesting and good.*

BAKE at 350° for 20 to 25 minutes   MAKES about 4 dozen

Sift together 1½ cups sifted **Pillsbury's Best All Purpose Flour***
½ teaspoon **salt**
½ teaspoon **cinnamon** and
¼ teaspoon **soda.** Set aside.

Add........¾ cup **sugar** gradually to
¼ cup **shortening,** creaming well.

Blend in.....2 unbeaten **eggs;** beat well.

Stir in......¾ cup prepared **mincemeat**
½ cup **crushed pineapple,** undrained, and
½ cup **walnuts,** chopped; mix thoroughly.

Add..........the dry ingredients gradually; mix well. Turn into
well-greased 15½x10½x1-inch jelly-roll pan or two
9x9x2-inch pans.

Bake.........at 350° for 20 to 25 minutes. While warm, frost with
Pineapple Icing, or sprinkle with confectioners'
sugar before serving.

*For use with Pillsbury's Best Self-Rising Flour, omit salt and soda.

PINEAPPLE ICING

Blend together 2 cups sifted confectioners' sugar and 2 to 3 tablespoons pineapple juice.

DROP COOKIES are second only to bar cookies in popularity because they are easily and quickly made. Drop dough onto baking sheets using a kitchen teaspoon, not a measuring spoon, to measure correct amount. Push dough from spoon with rubber spatula. Allow ample space, 2 to 3 inches, between cookies for spreading unless otherwise directed in recipe.

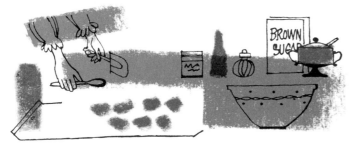

Chocolate-Peanut Cookies

Junior Winner by Jackie Rossow, Reno, Nevada

A peanut butter cooky is sandwiched between two chocolate cookies, then they're baked together.

BAKE at 325° for 12 to 15 minutes   MAKES about 3½ dozen

CHOCOLATE DOUGH

Sift together . . 1 cup sifted **Pillsbury's Best All Purpose Flour*** and 1 teaspoon **salt.** Set aside.

Add . . . . ¾ cup **sugar** gradually to ½ cup **shortening,** creaming well.

Blend in . . . . . 1 unbeaten **egg.**
2 squares (2 oz.) melted unsweetened **chocolate** and

1 teaspoon **vanilla;** beat well.

Add . . . . the dry ingredients; mix thoroughly.

PEANUT BUTTER DOUGH

Cream . . . . . . 2 tablespoons **butter** and ¼ cup **peanut butter.** Gradually add ½ cup firmly packed **brown sugar,** creaming well.

Blend in . . . . . 2 tablespoons **flour;** mix thoroughly.

Drop . . . . half of chocolate dough by scant teaspoonfuls onto ungreased baking sheets. Top each with the same amount of peanut butter dough, then with the same amount of chocolate dough, forming a sandwich. Press with fork dipped in flour.

Bake . . . . at 325° for 12 to 15 minutes.

*For use with Pillsbury's Best Self-Rising Flour, omit salt.

Double Chocolate Malteds

Senior Winner by Mr. Charles R. Kinison, Athens, Ohio

Chocolate malted milk powder, cream cheese and nuts flavor these easy cookies. They're sandwiched together with an icing.

BAKE at 350° for 12 to 15 minutes   MAKES 4 dozen sandwich cookies

Sift together . . 3 cups sifted **Pillsbury's Best All Purpose Flour***
1 cup **chocolate malted milk powder**
1½ teaspoons double-acting **baking powder**
½ teaspoon **soda** and
½ teaspoon **salt**

Cream . . . . . . 1 cup **butter** or margarine and 3 ounces (1 pkg.) **cream cheese.** Gradually add 1 cup **sugar,** creaming well.

Blend in . . . . . ⅓ cup **buttermilk** or sour milk 1 teaspoon **vanilla** and 1 unbeaten **egg.** Gradually add the dry ingredients; beat well.

Stir in . . . . . . ¾ cup **nuts,** chopped (pecans or hickory nuts)
Drop . . . . by scant teaspoonfuls onto ungreased baking sheets.**
Flatten to ¼-inch thickness (use bottom of glass, greased and dipped in **sugar**).
Bake . . . . at 350° for 12 to 15 minutes. Place flat sides of two cookies together with Icing, sandwich-style.

For use with Pillsbury's Best Self-Rising Flour, omit baking powder, soda, salt.

**For larger individual cookies, drop by rounded teaspoonfuls onto ungreased baking sheets.*

ICING

Combine ¼ cup butter, ½ cup chocolate malted milk powder and ¼ cup milk in saucepan. Cook over low heat, stirring constantly, until thickened. Remove from heat. Blend in 1 teaspoon vanilla and 2 to 2¼ cups sifted confectioners' sugar, beating until of spreading consistency.

Jim Dandies

Junior Winner by James Petersen, Withee, Wisconsin

The whole family's choice . . . a chocolate-cherry cookie with a surprise under the frosting.

BAKE at 350° for 12 to 15 minutes   MAKES about 3 dozen

Sift together 1½ cups sifted **Pillsbury's Best All Purpose Flour***
½ teaspoon **soda** and
½ teaspoon **salt.** Set aside.
Add . . . . ⅔ cup firmly packed **brown sugar** gradually to
½ cup **shortening,** creaming well.
Blend in . . . . . 1 unbeaten **egg.** Beat well.
Stir in . . . . half the dry ingredients. Add
¼ cup **maraschino cherry juice** and
2 tablespoons **milk,** then stir in the remaining dry ingredients. Mix well.
Blend in . . . . . 2 squares (2 oz.) melted unsweetened **chocolate**

½ cup **walnuts,** chopped, and
¼ cup chopped **maraschino cherries**
Drop . . . . by rounded teaspoonfuls onto ungreased baking sheets.
Bake . . . . at 350° for 12 to 15 minutes. Cut
18 **marshmallows** in half. Place cut-side down on hot cookies. Cool on rack. Frost with Chocolate Frosting; top each with a **nut half.**

For use with Pillsbury's Best Self-Rising Flour, omit soda and salt.

CHOCOLATE FROSTING

In top of double boiler over boiling water, cook ⅓ cup milk, ¼ cup butter or margarine, 2 squares (2 oz.) unsweetened chocolate and ⅛ teaspoon salt until thick. Remove from heat. Stir in 1 teaspoon vanilla and 2 to 2½ cups sifted confectioners' sugar until of spreading consistency.

Jim Dandies

Peanut Brownie Drops

Peanut Brownie Drops

Bride Second Prize Winner by Mrs. Frank Hills, Port Allegany, Pennsylvania

Made with only six ingredients . . . all mixing is done in a saucepan!

BAKE at 350° for 12 to 16 minutes   MAKES about 4 dozen

Melt . . . . ½ cup **butter** or margarine and
3 squares (3 oz.) unsweetened **chocolate** in saucepan over low heat, stirring constantly. Remove from heat.

Stir in . . . . . 1½ cups **sugar.** Add
3 unbeaten **eggs,** one at a time, beating thoroughly after each.

Blend in . . . . 1½ cups sifted **Pillsbury's Best All Purpose Flour*** and
1 cup whole **salted peanuts,** toasted almonds or other

nuts. Chill dough 2 hours or overnight.

Drop . . . . by rounded teaspoonfuls onto greased baking sheets.

Bake . . . . at 350° for 12 to 16 minutes until cookies spring back when touched lightly.

*Pillsbury's Best Self-Rising Flour is not recommended for use in this recipe.

Chocomint Cookies

Senior Winner by Mrs. Doris E. Williams, Hartford, Connecticut

Rich chocolate drop cookies are spread with creamy mint frosting. Nice for lunch boxes.

BAKE at 350° for 12 to 15 minutes   MAKES 4 dozen

Sift together . . 2 cups sifted **Pillsbury's Best All Purpose Flour***
2 teaspoons double-acting **baking powder** and
½ teaspoon **salt.** Set aside.

Add . . . . 1 cup **sugar** gradually to
¾ cup **shortening,** creaming well.

Blend in . . . . . 1 unbeaten **egg**
1 teaspoon **vanilla** and
3 squares (3 oz.) melted unsweetened **chocolate;** beat well.

Add . . . . ⅓ cup **milk** alternately with the dry ingredients; mix thoroughly. Stir in
½ cup **nuts,** chopped

Drop . . . . by rounded teaspoonfuls onto greased baking sheets.

Bake . . . . at 350° for 12 to 15 minutes. Cool; frost with Mint Frosting.

*For use with Pillsbury's Best Self-Rising Flour, omit baking powder and salt.

MINT FROSTING

Soften 4 wintergreen candy wafers (or use ⅛ teaspoon mint extract) and 1 tablespoon butter. Blend in 2 cups sifted confectioners' sugar and 3 tablespoons cream. Add 1 drop red food coloring; beat until smooth.

Coconut Islands

Senior Third Prize Winner by Sister Maria Jose Cannon, Honolulu, Hawaii

An easy-to-make cookie—moist, tender, good! There's chocolate in the cookie and frosting and a snowy cap of coconut on top.

BAKE at 375° for 12 to 15 minutes   MAKES about 3½ dozen

Sift together . . 2 cups sifted **Pillsbury's Best All Purpose Flour***
    ½ teaspoon **soda** and
    ½ teaspoon **salt**
Melt . . . . 3 squares (3 oz.) unsweetened **chocolate** in
    ¼ cup hot strong **coffee.** Cool.
Cream . . . . . . ½ cup **butter** or margarine. Gradually add
    1 cup firmly packed **brown sugar,** creaming well.
Blend in . . . . . 1 unbeaten **egg** and chocolate mixture. Beat well.
Add . . . . the dry ingredients alternately with
    ½ cup **sour cream** (thick or commercial) to creamed
    mixture. Blend well after each addition.
Stir in . . . . . . ⅓ cup chopped **coconut**
Drop . . . . by rounded teaspoonfuls onto greased baking sheets.
Bake . . . . at 375° for 12 to 15 minutes. Frost with Chocolate
    Frosting while warm. Sprinkle tops with **coconut.**
For use with Pillsbury's Best Self-Rising Flour, omit soda and salt.

CHOCOLATE FROSTING

In top of double boiler over boiling water melt 1½ squares (1½ oz.) unsweetened chocolate and 1 tablespoon butter in ¼ cup sour cream. Remove from heat. Gradually blend in 1½ to 2 cups sifted confectioners' sugar until of spreading consistency.

Coconut Islands

Cherry Malted Cookies

Senior Winner by Mrs. Walter A. Yaeger, Racine, Wisconsin

Enjoy the flavors of maraschino cherries and chocolate malted milk!

BAKE at 375° for 12 to 15 minutes   MAKES 3½ dozen

Sift together 1½ cups sifted **Pillsbury's Best All Purpose Flour***
　　　　　　　½ cup **chocolate malted milk powder**
　　　　　　　½ teaspoon **salt**
　　　　　　　½ teaspoon **cinnamon**, if desired, and
　　　　　　　¼ teaspoon **soda.** Set aside.
Add . . . . ⅔ cup firmly packed **brown sugar** to
　　　　　　　½ cup **shortening**, creaming well.
Blend in . . . . . 1 unbeaten **egg**
　　　　　　　2 tablespoons **maraschino cherry juice** and
　　　　　　　1 teaspoon **vanilla;** beat well.
Add . . . . the dry ingredients; mix thoroughly.
Stir in . . . . . . ¼ cup **maraschino cherries,** finely chopped.
Drop . . . . by rounded teaspoonfuls onto ungreased baking sheets.
Bake . . . . at 375° for 12 to 15 minutes.
*For use with Pillsbury's Best Self-Rising Flour, omit salt and soda.

Pineapple Masquerades

Senior Winner by Mrs. D. P. Newquist, Nashville, Tennessee

Simple to make with pineapple inside and out. Inexpensive, too!

BAKE at 350° for 18 to 20 minutes   MAKES about 4 dozen

Sift together 1½ cups sifted **Pillsbury's Best All Purpose Flour***
　　　　　　　¼ cup **cocoa**
　　　　　　　¼ teaspoon **soda** and
　　　　　　　¼ teaspoon **salt.** Set aside.
Add . . . . 1 cup firmly packed **brown sugar** gradually to
　　　　　　　½ cup **shortening**, creaming well.

Blend in . . . . . 1 unbeaten **egg** and
　　　　　　　1 teaspoon **vanilla;** beat well.
Add . . . . ½ cup **buttermilk** or sour milk alternately with the dry ingredients, blending well.
Stir in . . . . . . ½ cup well-drained **crushed pineapple**
Drop . . . . by teaspoonfuls onto greased baking sheets.
Bake . . . . at 350° for 18 to 20 minutes. While warm, top with Pineapple Glaze.
*For use with Pillsbury's Best Self-Rising Flour, omit salt.

PINEAPPLE GLAZE

Blend together 1 cup sifted confectioners' sugar and 2 tablespoons pineapple juice.

Apricot Thins

Senior Winner by Ellen Halstead, Somerville, New Jersey

Ground dried apricots give these tender wafers a golden "confetti" look. No rolling needed—just press them paper thin.

BAKE at 375° for 4 to 6 minutes   MAKES about 8 dozen

Soak . . . . 1 cup dried **apricots** in water at least 15 minutes. Drain well; grind.
Sift together 1¼ cups sifted **Pillsbury's Best All Purpose Flour*** and
　　　　　　　½ teaspoon double-acting **baking powder**
Cream . . . . . . ½ cup **butter** or margarine. Gradually add
　　　　　　　½ cup sifted **confectioners' sugar,** creaming well.
Add . . . . 1 **egg white** and
　　　　　　　½ teaspoon **vanilla;** beat well.
Blend in . . . . . . the ground apricots (¾ cup) and the dry ingredients.
Drop . . . . by half teaspoonfuls onto greased baking sheets. Press with floured hands to flatten as thin as possible. Score with fork.
Bake . . . . at 375° for 4 to 6 minutes. *Do not brown.*
*For use with Pillsbury's Best Self-Rising Flour, omit baking powder.

Spicy Fig Drops

Senior Winner by Catherine Ratcliffe, Spiceland, Indiana

Figs and a blend of spices go into these easy, soft drop cookies.

BAKE at 375° for 10 to 12 minutes   MAKES about 4 dozen

Cook........1 cup (6 oz.) dried **figs**, cut fine, in
         ½ cup **water** in saucepan about 5 minutes, stirring occasionally, until tender. Cool.

Sift together 2½ cups sifted **Pillsbury's Best All Purpose Flour***
         1 teaspoon **soda**
         1 teaspoon **salt**
         1 teaspoon **cinnamon**
         ¼ teaspoon **nutmeg** and
         ¼ teaspoon **ginger**. Set aside.

Add........½ cup firmly packed **brown sugar** gradually to
         ⅔ cup **shortening**, creaming well. Stir in
         ½ cup dark **corn syrup**; mix thoroughly.

Blend in.....1 unbeaten **egg**
         1 teaspoon **vanilla** and
         ½ teaspoon **lemon extract**; beat well.

Add..........the dry ingredients gradually; mix well. Stir in fig mixture.

Drop.........by teaspoonfuls onto greased baking sheets.
Bake.........at 375° for 10 to 12 minutes.

For use with Pillsbury's Best Self-Rising Flour, omit soda and salt.

Chewy Date Drops

Bride Winner by Mrs. Cynthia C. Anderson, Contoocook, New Hampshire

Fill up your favorite cookie jar with these chewy family-size brown sugar date drops.

BAKE at 375° for 12 to 15 minutes   MAKES about 7 dozen

Cook........2 cups cut **dates**

Chewy Date Drops

         ½ cup **sugar** and
         ½ cup **water** in saucepan until thickened. Cool.

Sift together..4 cups sifted **Pillsbury's Best All Purpose Flour***
         1 teaspoon **soda** and
         1 teaspoon **salt**

Cream.......1 cup **butter** or margarine. Gradually add
         1 cup **sugar** and
         1 cup firmly packed **brown sugar**, creaming well.

Blend in.....3 unbeaten **eggs** and
         1 teaspoon **vanilla**; beat well. Add the dry ingredients gradually; mix thoroughly.

Stir in.......1 cup **nuts**, chopped, and the date mixture.

Drop.........by rounded teaspoonfuls onto greased baking sheets.

Bake.........at 375° for 12 to 15 minutes.

For use with Pillsbury's Best Self-Rising Flour, omit soda and salt.

Date Jewel Drops

Senior Winner by Mrs. Gerard E. Krug, Swormville, New York

The bright golden apricots and flavorful dates make these cookies a lunchbox favorite.

BAKE at 375° for 10 to 12 minutes   MAKES 4½ dozen

Soak . . . . 1 cup dried **apricots** in boiling water at least 5 minutes. Drain well; cut in small pieces.

Sift together 2¼ cups sifted **Pillsbury's Best All Purpose Flour*** 1 teaspoon **salt** and ½ teaspoon **soda.** Set aside.

Add . . . . 1¼ cups firmly packed **brown sugar** gradually to ¾ cup **shortening,** creaming well.

Blend in . . . . . 2 unbeaten **eggs** and 1 teaspoon **vanilla;** beat well. Add the dry ingredients gradually; mix thoroughly.

Stir in . . . . 1 cup **dates,** cut, and the apricots.

Drop . . . . by rounded teaspoonfuls onto greased baking sheets.

Bake . . . . at 375° for 10 to 12 minutes.

*For use with Pillsbury's Best Self-Rising Flour, omit salt and soda.

Date Cashew Honeys

Senior Winner by Mrs. Sibyl Schneller, Mill Valley, California

Dates and honey in a cakey cookie with a crunchy coating of cashews.

BAKE at 400° for 10 to 12 minutes   MAKES 4 dozen

Grind . . . . 1 cup (¼ lb.) **cashews;** set aside.

Grind . . . . 1 cup **dates;** set aside.

Date Jewel Drops

Sift together 1½ cups sifted **Pillsbury's Best All Purpose Flour***
        ½ teaspoon double-acting **baking powder** and
        ½ teaspoon **salt**
Cream . . . . . . ½ cup **butter** or margarine. Gradually add
        ½ cup firmly packed **brown sugar,** creaming well.
Add . . . . ¼ cup **honey**
        1 unbeaten **egg**
        1 teaspoon **vanilla** and the ground dates; beat well.
Stir in . . . . the dry ingredients, mixing thoroughly.
Drop . . . . by rounded teaspoonfuls into ground cashews; coat
        thoroughly. Place on greased baking sheets; flatten
        slightly. Top each with a **cashew half.**
Bake . . . . at 400° for 10 to 12 minutes.
For use with Pillsbury's Best Self-Rising Flour, omit baking powder and salt;
decrease baking time to 8 to 10 minutes.

Hawaiian Moon Drops

Senior Winner by Mrs. Lyell Roberts, Chisholm, Minnesota

Tender cake-like cookies full of nuts and pineapple, topped with a
tangy glaze and toasted coconut.

BAKE at 375° for 12 to 15 minutes   MAKES about 4 dozen

Sift together . . 3 cups sifted **Pillsbury's Best All Purpose Flour***
        1 teaspoon double-acting **baking powder**
        1 teaspoon **soda** and
        1 teaspoon **salt.** Set aside.
Add . . . . ¾ cup firmly packed **brown sugar** and
        ½ cup **sugar** gradually to
        ⅔ cup **shortening,** creaming well.
Blend in . . . . . 2 unbeaten **eggs**
        1 teaspoon **vanilla** and
        ¼ teaspoon **lemon extract.** Beat well.
Stir in . . . . . . ⅔ cup (No. 1 can) drained **crushed pineapple,** re-
        serving juice for Icing.

Hawaiian Moon Drops

Add . . . . the dry ingredients gradually and
        1 cup **walnuts,** chopped. Blend thoroughly.
Drop . . . . by rounded teaspoonfuls onto greased baking sheets.
Bake . . . . at 375° for 12 to 15 minutes. Cool. Frost with
        Lemon Icing and dip tops in
        1½ cups toasted **coconut**
For use with Pillsbury's Best Self-Rising Flour, omit baking powder, soda, salt.

LEMON ICING

Combine in saucepan ½ cup pineapple juice and ½ cup water with
¼ cup cornstarch. Cook over medium heat, stirring constantly, until
thickened. Add 2 tablespoons lemon juice, 1 tablespoon butter, 1
teaspoon vanilla and 2 drops yellow food coloring. Blend in 1½ cups
sifted confectioners' sugar.

Lemon Drop Wafers

Senior Winner by Mrs. Marguerite Balbach, Verdugo City, California

These honey-lemon cookies will remind you of candy lemon drops—the delight of childhood.

BAKE at 350° for 10 to 12 minutes   MAKES about 5 dozen

Sift together . . 2 cups sifted **Pillsbury's Best All Purpose Flour***
        1 teaspoon double-acting **baking powder** and
        1 teaspoon **salt**
Add . . . . ½ cup **sugar** and
        1 teaspoon grated **lemon rind** to
        ½ cup **shortening**, creaming well.
Blend in . . . . . 1 unbeaten **egg** and
        ⅓ cup **honey**; beat well. Add the dry ingredients
        gradually; mix thoroughly.

Lemon Drop Wafers

Drop . . . . by teaspoonfuls onto greased baking sheets.
        Flatten with fork. Decorate with grated **lemon rind**
        or candied lemon peel.
Bake . . . . at 350° for 10 to 12 minutes.
*For use with Pillsbury's Best Self-Rising Flour, omit baking powder and salt.

Lemon Larks

Senior Winner by Mrs. W. J. Bellerose, West Roxbury, Massachusetts

Lemon and orange flavors perk up these easy-to-make cookies. A cloud of light meringue gives each one a party touch.

BAKE at 350° for 15 to 18 minutes   MAKES about 3 dozen

Sift together . . 2 cups sifted **Pillsbury's Best All Purpose Flour***
        1 teaspoon double-acting **baking powder** and
        1 teaspoon **salt**. Set aside.
Add . . . . ⅔ cup **sugar** gradually to
        ⅔ cup **shortening**, creaming well.
Stir in . . . . 2 unbeaten **egg yolks**
        1 teaspoon grated **lemon rind**
        1 teaspoon grated **orange rind** and
        1 tablespoon **lemon juice**. Beat well.
Add . . . . ⅔ cup light **cream** alternately with the dry ingredients;
        mix thoroughly.
Drop . . . . by rounded teaspoonfuls onto lightly greased baking
        sheets. Flatten cookies with greased bottom of glass
        which has been dipped into **sugar**. Decorate with
        Meringue.
Bake . . . . at 350° for 15 to 18 minutes.
*Pillsbury's Best Self-Rising Flour is not recommended for use in this recipe.

MERINGUE

Beat 2 egg whites with ¼ teaspoon cream of tartar until soft mounds form. Gradually add ½ cup sugar, beating well after each addition. Continue beating until meringue stands in stiff, glossy peaks.

Pistachio Orange Drops

Senior Winner by Mary Frances Buck, Somerville, Indiana

Cardamom and pistachio nuts are added to these tender, cakey orange drop cookies.

BAKE at 375° for 15 to 17 minutes   MAKES about 3 dozen

Sift together . . 2 cups sifted **Pillsbury's Best All Purpose Flour***
      1 teaspoon double-acting **baking powder**
      ½ teaspoon **soda**
      ½ teaspoon **salt** and
      1 teaspoon ground **cardamom**

Cream . . . . . . ½ cup **butter** or margarine. Gradually add
      ⅓ cup **sugar** and
      ⅓ cup firmly packed **brown sugar,** creaming well.

Blend in . . . . . 1 unbeaten **egg**
      2 tablespoons grated **orange rind** and
      1 teaspoon **almond extract;** beat well. Add half the dry ingredients, mixing thoroughly.

Combine . . . . . 2 tablespoons **orange juice** with enough **water** to measure ⅓ cup. Stir into creamed mixture.

Blend in . . . . the remaining dry ingredients and
      ½ cup **pistachio nuts** or other nuts, chopped

Drop . . . . by rounded teaspoonfuls onto greased baking sheets.

Bake . . . . at 375° for 15 to 17 minutes.

*For use with Pillsbury's Best Self-Rising Flour, omit baking powder, soda, salt.

Nut-Dip Orange Drops

Senior Winner by Theodora N. Lourekas, Queens Village, Long Island, New York

These crisp honey cookies have a bit of orange rind inside. And they're rolled in nuts just before baking.

BAKE at 375° for 10 to 12 minutes   MAKES 4½ dozen

Sift together . . 2 cups sifted **Pillsbury's Best All Purpose Flour***
      1 teaspoon **soda** and
      1 teaspoon **salt**

Cream . . . . . ½ cup **butter** and
      ½ cup **shortening.** Add
      ½ cup **sugar,** creaming well.

Add . . . . ½ cup **honey**
      1 unbeaten **egg**
      1 tablespoon grated **orange rind** and
      1 tablespoon **orange juice;** beat well.

Blend in . . . . the dry ingredients; mix thoroughly.

Add . . . . ½ cup **walnuts,** chopped. Chill at least 1 hour.

Drop . . . . by rounded teaspoonfuls into
      1 cup **nuts,** finely chopped; coat thoroughly. Place on greased baking sheets.

Bake . . . . at 375° for 10 to 12 minutes. Cool; remove from baking sheets.

*For use with Pillsbury's Best Self-Rising Flour, decrease soda to ½ teaspoon and omit salt.

Brazil Nut Melts

Senior Winner by Mrs. W. P. Lanier, Atlanta, Georgia

Brazil nuts and orange in a tender, rich drop cookie.

BAKE at 350° for 9 to 12 minutes   MAKES 3 dozen

Prepare.....¼ pound shelled **Brazil nuts.** Chop ½ cup nuts. Cover remaining ¼ cup nuts with hot **water** and let stand 10 minutes; drain and slice thin.

Sift together..1 cup sifted **Pillsbury's Best All Purpose Flour*** and ½ teaspoon **salt.** Add ½ teaspoon grated **orange rind** and the ½ cup chopped Brazil nuts.

Add........⅓ cup **sugar** gradually to ½ cup **shortening,** creaming well.

Blend in.....1 unbeaten **egg.** Beat well.

Add.........half the dry ingredients, mixing well. Add 3 tablespoons **orange juice** and the remaining dry ingredients. Blend thoroughly.

Fold in........the ¼ cup sliced Brazil nuts.

Drop.........by rounded teaspoonfuls onto ungreased baking sheets.

Bake........at 350° for 9 to 12 minutes. While hot, roll in sifted **confectioners' sugar.**

For use with Pillsbury's Best Self-Rising Flour, omit salt.

Pineapple Cherry Drops

Senior Winner by Mrs. Robert Bennetts, Davison, Michigan

A bit of cooked rice, crushed pineapple and candied cherries make these cookies unusual. They keep fresh a long time, too.

BAKE at 375° for 8 to 10 minutes   MAKES 5½ dozen

Sift together..2 cups sifted **Pillsbury's Best All Purpose Flour***
2 teaspoons double-acting **baking powder** and
½ teaspoon **salt**

Coat.......¼ cup chopped **candied cherries** with 1 tablespoon **flour**

Add........1 cup firmly packed **brown sugar** gradually to ½ cup **shortening,** creaming well.

Blend in.....2 unbeaten **eggs;** beat well.

Add........¼ cup well-drained **crushed pineapple** and 1 teaspoon **vanilla.** Add the dry ingredients; mix thoroughly.

Stir in........floured cherries and, if desired, ¼ cup cooked **rice,** mashed or sieved

Drop........by rounded teaspoonfuls onto greased baking sheets.

Bake........at 375° for 8 to 10 minutes.

For use with Pillsbury's Best Self-Rising Flour, omit baking powder and salt.

Golden Nut Drops

Junior Winner by Mary Janssen, Oak Park, Illinois

The color and moistness of these simple cookies comes from "baby food" carrots blended into the dough. Orange icing completes cookie.

BAKE at 400° for 12 to 15 minutes   MAKES about 4 dozen

Sift together..2 cups sifted **Pillsbury's Best All Purpose Flour***
1½ teaspoons double-acting **baking powder**
½ teaspoon **soda** and
¼ teaspoon **salt.** Set aside.

Add........½ cup **sugar** and ¼ cup firmly packed **brown sugar** gradually to ¾ cup **shortening,** creaming well.

Blend in.....1 unbeaten **egg;** beat well.

Add.........the dry ingredients alternately with 1 can (4¾ oz.) strained **carrots** (baby food) and 1 teaspoon **vanilla.** Mix thoroughly.

Stir in.......1 cup **walnuts,** chopped

Drop........by rounded teaspoonfuls onto greased baking sheets.

Bake . . . . at 400° for 12 to 15 minutes. Frost while warm with
Orange Icing.

For use with Pillsbury's Best Self-Rising Flour, omit baking powder, soda, salt.

ORANGE ICING

Combine 1 cup sifted confectioners' sugar, 2 teaspoons grated orange
rind and 1 to 2 tablespoons orange juice. Mix until smooth.

Chewy Coconut Macaroons

Senior Winner by Mrs. Marshall O'Rourke, Chicago, Illinois

*A moist, really good and chewy coconut macaroon. Delicious plain, or
drizzle with a simple semi-sweet chocolate icing.*

BAKE at 325° for 20 to 25 minutes   MAKES about 3½ dozen

Beat . . . . ½ cup **egg whites** (4 medium) until stiff but not dry.
Gradually add
¼ cup **sugar** and
½ teaspoon **vanilla**, beating constantly until very stiff,
straight peaks form.
Sift together . ½ cup sifted **Pillsbury's Best All Purpose Flour***
¼ teaspoon **salt** and
1 cup **sugar** into mixing bowl; add
2½ cups (6 to 8 oz.) **coconut**. Mix well; fold into meringue, half at a time, with spoon or rubber spatula.
Drop . . . . by rounded teaspoonfuls onto baking sheet covered
with *heavy brown wrapping paper.*
Bake . . . . at 325° for 20 to 25 minutes. Place brown paper on
wet cloth for 2 minutes, then remove cookies care-
fully. Cool. If desired, drizzle with Chocolate Icing.

For use with Pillsbury's Best Self-Rising Flour, omit salt.

CHOCOLATE ICING

Melt ⅓ cup semi-sweet chocolate pieces with 1 tablespoon milk over
hot water.

Strawberry Buttons

Senior Winner by Mrs. Fred T. Rogers, Palatine, Illinois

*Tiny, button-sized cookies, flavored with frozen strawberries and topped
with a glaze made from the strawberry juice.*

BAKE at 350° for 15 to 18 minutes*   MAKES 6 dozen

Drain . . . . 1 package (10 oz.) thawed frozen **strawberries**
Sift together 1⅓ cups sifted **Pillsbury's Best All Purpose Flour***
1 teaspoon double-acting **baking powder** and
¼ teaspoon **salt**. Set aside.
Add . . . . ⅔ cup **sugar** gradually to
½ cup **shortening**, creaming well.
Blend in . . . . . 1 **egg yolk**
1 teaspoon **lemon juice** and
½ teaspoon **vanilla**; beat well.
Add . . . . the dry ingredients alternately with ½ cup of the
drained strawberries to creamed mixture.
Drop . . . . by half teaspoonfuls onto greased baking sheets.
Bake . . . . at 350° for 15 to 18 minutes.* Brush with Strawberry
Glaze while warm.

*For use with Pillsbury's Best Self-Rising Flour, omit baking powder and salt;
decrease baking time to 12 to 15 minutes.*

STRAWBERRY GLAZE

Combine 2 tablespoons strawberry juice, ¼ cup sugar and 1 teaspoon
lemon juice. Stir until sugar is dissolved.

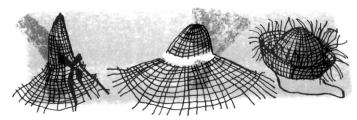

Coconut Straw Hats

Senior Winner by Mrs. L. R. Schweitzerhof, Jr., Honolulu, Hawaii

A brown sugar cookie forms the "brim;" the "crown" is a marsh-mallow half spread with melted caramels and sprinkled with coconut.

BAKE at 375° for 7 to 10 minutes   MAKES 2½ dozen

Sift together 1¼ cups sifted **Pillsbury's Best All Purpose Flour***
      ½ teaspoon double-acting **baking powder** and
      ¼ teaspoon **salt**
Cream . . . . . ½ cup **butter** or margarine. Gradually add
      ⅓ cup firmly packed **brown sugar,** creaming well.
Add . . . . 1 unbeaten **egg** and
      ½ teaspoon **vanilla;** beat well. Blend in the dry in-gredients gradually.
Drop . . . . by rounded teaspoonfuls onto ungreased baking sheets. Flatten slightly.
Bake . . . . at 375° for 7 to 10 minutes. Cut
    16 **marshmallows** (¼ lb.) in half. Place cut-side down on hot cookies. Cool on rack.
Toast . . . . 1 cup **coconut** in shallow pan at 375° about 5 minutes, stirring occasionally.
Melt . . . . . . 25 **caramels** (about ½ lb.) with
    3 tablespoons **cream** in top of double boiler over hot water; stir frequently until smooth. Spread caramel mixture quickly over marshmallows; dip tops im-mediately in toasted coconut. (If caramel mixture becomes stiff while spreading, thin with cream.)

*For use with Pillsbury's Best Self-Rising Flour, omit baking powder and salt.

Almond-Coconut Twinkles

Senior Winner by Mrs. John E. Matthews, Charlotte, North Carolina

Macaroon-like cookies with an almond and coconut flavor.

BAKE at 375° for 10 to 12 minutes   MAKES about 3 dozen

Sift together 1¼ cups sifted **Pillsbury's Best All Purpose Flour***
      1 teaspoon double-acting **baking powder** and
      ¼ teaspoon **salt.** Set aside.
Add . . . . ⅔ cup **sugar** gradually to
      ½ cup **shortening,** creaming well.
Blend in . . . . . 2 unbeaten **egg whites**
      ½ teaspoon **vanilla** and
      ¼ teaspoon **almond extract;** beat well.
Add . . . . 1 cup **coconut** and the dry ingredients. Mix well.
Drop . . . . by rounded teaspoonfuls onto greased baking sheets.
Bake . . . . at 375° for 10 to 12 minutes. If desired, frost with **Chocolate Glaze,** page 326.

*For use with Pillsbury's Best Self-Rising Flour, omit baking powder and salt.

Toasted Coconut Drops

Senior Winner by Mrs. J. C. Wilkinson, Des Moines, Iowa

Almonds and toasted coconut go into these tender, cake-like brown sugar cookies; more almonds and a simple frosting go on top.

BAKE at 375° for 10 to 12 minutes   MAKES about 5 dozen

Toast . . . . . . 1½ cups (4 oz.) **coconut** at 375° about 5 minutes, stirring occasionally.
Combine . . . . . 1 cup **evaporated milk** and
      1 tablespoon **vinegar.** Set aside to sour.
Sift together 2½ cups sifted **Pillsbury's Best All Purpose Flour***
      1 teaspoon **soda**
      ½ teaspoon double-acting **baking powder** and
      ½ teaspoon **salt.** Set aside.

Add . . . . 1½ cups firmly packed **brown sugar** gradually to
¾ cup **shortening**, creaming well.
Blend in . . . . . 2 unbeaten **eggs**
1 teaspoon **vanilla** and
¼ teaspoon **almond extract**. Stir in half of the dry
ingredients.
Add . . . . the soured milk; mix well. Stir in remaining dry
ingredients.
Stir in . . . . . . ¾ cup unblanched **almonds,** chopped, and the toasted
coconut. Chill 15 minutes.
Drop . . . . by teaspoonfuls onto greased baking sheets.
Bake . . . . at 375° for 10 to 12 minutes. Cool. Dip tops of cookies
into Butter Frosting; sprinkle with
¼ cup chopped **almonds**

*For use with Pillsbury's Best Self-Rising Flour, omit baking powder and salt;
decrease soda to ¼ teaspoon.*

BUTTER FROSTING

Add ½ cup melted butter or margarine slowly to 2 cups sifted confectioners' sugar in mixing bowl. Blend in ¼ cup boiling water and
¼ teaspoon almond extract.

Orange Sparklers

Senior Winner by Mrs. Loren Mattson, Minneapolis, Minnesota

*The attractive lacy sparkle on these orange coconut cookies comes from
the crushed loaf sugar they're rolled in before baking.*

BAKE at 400° for 10 to 12 minutes   MAKES about 3 dozen

Sift together 2½ cups sifted **Pillsbury's Best All Purpose Flour***
½ teaspoon **soda** and
¼ teaspoon **salt**
Cream . . . . . . ¾ cup **butter** or margarine. Gradually add
1 cup **sugar**, creaming well.
Add . . . . 2 unbeaten **eggs**; beat well.

Combine . . . . . 1 tablespoon grated **orange rind** and
½ cup **orange juice**. Add alternately with the dry
ingredients to the creamed mixture; mix well.
Stir in . . . . . . ½ cup **coconut**, cut. Chill 4 hours or overnight.
Drop . . . . dough by rounded teaspoonfuls into
1 cup **loaf sugar**, finely crushed;** coat thoroughly.
Place on greased baking sheets.
Bake . . . . at 400° for 10 to 12 minutes.

For use with Pillsbury's Best Self-Rising Flour, omit soda and salt.
***Granulated sugar may be substituted.*

Tangy Orange Drops

Junior Winner by Susan Johnson, West Jordan, Utah

Fresh orange flavor and coconut in quick, tender drop cookie.

BAKE at 350° for 12 to 15 minutes   MAKES about 4 dozen

Sift together 1½ cups sifted **Pillsbury's Best All Purpose Flour***
1 teaspoon double-acting **baking powder** and
½ teaspoon **salt**
Cream . . . . . ¼ cup **butter** or margarine and
¼ cup **shortening**. Gradually add
¾ cup **sugar**, creaming well.
Blend in . . . . . 1 unbeaten **egg**; beat well. Add the dry ingredients;
mix thoroughly.
Add . . . . 3 tablespoons **orange juice** and
¾ cup **coconut**; mix well.
Drop . . . . by rounded teaspoonfuls onto greased baking sheets.
Bake . . . . at 350° for 12 to 15 minutes. Frost while warm with
Orange Frosting.

For use with Pillsbury's Best Self-Rising Flour, omit baking powder and salt.

ORANGE FROSTING

Blend together 1 tablespoon orange juice, 1 tablespoon water and
1 cup sifted confectioners' sugar.

Ambrosia Spice Drops

Ambrosia Spice Drops

Senior Winner by Mrs. Neill D. Zuber, Jr., Denver, Colorado

Crisp rich nut-crunchy drop cookies . . . a special trick keeps their coconut topping from burning.

BAKE at 350° for 15 to 18 minutes   MAKES about 3 dozen

Soak . . . . .1 cup **coconut** in
⅛ cup **fruit juice** (apricot, orange or apple). Let stand 1 hour; drain thoroughly.

Sift together 1¾ cups sifted **Pillsbury's Best All Purpose Flour***
1 teaspoon **salt** and
2 teaspoons **cinnamon**. Set aside.

Add . . . . .1 cup **sugar** gradually to

1 cup **shortening,** creaming well.
Blend in . . . . .2 unbeaten **eggs** and
1 teaspoon **vanilla**; beat well. Add the dry ingredients, mixing thoroughly.
Stir in . . . . . . .1 cup **walnuts,** finely chopped
Drop . . . . .by rounded teaspoonfuls onto ungreased baking sheets. Top with ½ to 1 teaspoon drained soaked coconut, pressing ends into dough.
Bake . . . . .at 350° for 15 to 18 minutes.
For use with Pillsbury's Best Self-Rising Flour, omit salt.

Coconut Cherry Drops

Senior Winner by Miss Adele Guerin, St. Paul, Minnesota

These cookies are flavored with almond. Coconut and pecans make them chewy. A cherry in center of each gives a touch of color.

BAKE at 375° for 10 to 12 minutes   MAKES about 3 dozen

Sift together 1¼ cups sifted **Pillsbury's Best All Purpose Flour***
½ teaspoon double-acting **baking powder** and
½ teaspoon **salt**
Cream . . . . . .¼ cup **butter** and
¼ cup **shortening**. Gradually add
½ cup **sugar,** creaming well.
Blend in . . . . .1 unbeaten **egg** and
½ teaspoon **almond extract**; beat well. Add the dry ingredients; mix thoroughly.
Stir in . . . . . .¼ cup chopped **maraschino cherries**
1 cup flaked or chopped shredded **coconut** and
½ cup **pecans,** chopped
Drop . . . . .by rounded teaspoonfuls onto greased baking sheets. Top each with ¼ **maraschino cherry**. (For a crisper cookie, flatten slightly.)
Bake . . . . .at 375° for 10 to 12 minutes.
For use with Pillsbury's Best Self-Rising Flour, omit baking powder and salt.

Cherry-Chocolate Honeys

Bride Winner by Mrs. George Njaa, Gazelle, California

Oh boy! Chocolate chips and cherries in these honey-flavored cookies.

BAKE at 375° for 10 to 12 minutes   MAKES about 3½ dozen

Sift together . . 2 cups sifted **Pillsbury's Best All Purpose Flour***
       1 teaspoon **soda** and
       1 teaspoon **salt**
Cream . . . . 1 cup **shortening** with
       ¾ cup **honey** and
       1 teaspoon **vanilla**
Blend in . . . . the dry ingredients and
       1 cup quick-cooking **rolled oats**
Stir in . . . . . . ½ cup **filberts** or other nuts, chopped
       ½ cup **semi-sweet chocolate pieces** and
       ¼ cup chopped **maraschino cherries**
Drop . . . . by rounded teaspoonfuls onto ungreased baking
       sheets.
Bake . . . . at 375° for 10 to 12 minutes.
*For use with Pillsbury's Best Self-Rising Flour, omit soda and salt.

Cherry Winks

Junior First Prize Winner by Ruth Derousseau, Rice Lake, Wisconsin

Crunchy cookies filled with pecans, dates and cherries. Each is rolled in cornflakes and topped with a cherry.

BAKE at 375° for 12 to 15 minutes   MAKES 5 dozen

Sift together 2¼ cups sifted **Pillsbury's Best All Purpose Flour***
       1 teaspoon double-acting **baking powder**
       ½ teaspoon **soda** and
       ½ teaspoon **salt**. Set aside.
Add . . . . 1 cup **sugar** gradually to
       ¾ cup **shortening**, creaming well.

Blend in . . . . . 2 unbeaten **eggs**
       2 tablespoons **milk** and
       1 teaspoon **vanilla**; beat well.
Add . . . . the dry ingredients; mix thoroughly.
Stir in . . . . 1 cup **pecans**, chopped
       1 cup cut **dates,** and
       ⅓ cup **maraschino cherries,** drained and chopped. If
       desired, chill dough for easier handling.
Drop . . . . by rounded teaspoonfuls into
       2½ cups coarsely crushed **cornflakes;** coat thoroughly.
       Form into balls.
Place . . . . on greased baking sheets. Top each with ¼ **mara-**
       schino cherry
Bake . . . . at 375° for 12 to 15 minutes.
*For use with Pillsbury's Best Self-Rising Flour, omit baking powder and salt; decrease soda to ¼ teaspoon.

Cherry-Chocolate Honeys

Mocha Mambos

Senior Winner by Mrs. Ben Hager, Wasco, California

Easy drop cookies are made with coconut and brown sugar. Then they're double-frosted with simple chocolate and coffee frostings.

BAKE at 400° for 7 to 10 minutes   MAKES about 3 dozen

Sift together 1¾ cups sifted **Pillsbury's Best All Purpose Flour***
       ½ teaspoon **soda** and
       ½ teaspoon **salt**
Cream . . . . . . ¼ cup **shortening** with
       ¼ cup **butter** or margarine. Gradually add
       1 cup firmly packed **brown sugar,** creaming well.
Add . . . . 1 unbeaten **egg** and
       ½ teaspoon **vanilla;** beat well.
Blend in . . . . . ¼ cup **buttermilk** or sour milk alternately with the dry ingredients. Mix well after each addition.

Java Crunch Cookies

Stir in . . . . . . ½ cup **coconut.** Cover and chill for 1 hour.
Drop . . . . by rounded teaspoonfuls onto ungreased baking sheets.
Bake . . . . at 400° for 7 to 10 minutes. Cool; frost with Chocolate Frosting. Drizzle with Coffee Glaze in zigzag pattern.

*For use with Pillsbury's Best Self-Rising Flour, omit soda and salt.

CHOCOLATE FROSTING

Melt together 1 tablespoon butter with 1 square (1 oz.) unsweetened chocolate. Blend in 1½ cups sifted confectioners' sugar. Add ½ teaspoon vanilla and 3 to 4 tablespoons cream, beating until of spreading consistency.

COFFEE GLAZE

Blend 1 teaspoon soft butter with ½ teaspoon instant coffee. Blend in ½ cup sifted confectioners' sugar. Gradually add 4 to 5 teaspoons hot water until the consistency of a glaze.

Java Crunch Cookies

Senior Winner by Joann Gambaro, St. Louis, Missouri

A crisp coconut drop cookie . . . so different with the coffee flavor.

BAKE at 350° for 10 to 13 minutes   MAKES about 3½ dozen

Sift together 1½ cups sifted **Pillsbury's Best All Purpose Flour***
       1 teaspoon double-acting **baking powder** and
       ½ teaspoon **salt.** Set aside.
Add . . . . ½ cup **sugar** and
       ¼ cup firmly packed **brown sugar** to
       ¾ cup **shortening,** creaming well.
Dissolve . . . . . 1 tablespoon **instant coffee** in
       2 tablespoons hot **water**
Blend . . . . 1 unbeaten **egg** and the coffee into the creamed mixture; beat well.

Stir in . . . . . 1½ cups **coconut** and the dry ingredients.
Drop . . . . by rounded teaspoonfuls onto ungreased baking sheets.
Bake . . . . at 350° for 10 to 13 minutes.
*For use with Pillsbury's Best Self-Rising Flour, omit baking powder and salt.

Fruitaroons

Junior Winner by Margaret Borner, Lincoln, Nebraska

A most colorful cookie . . . real fruit flavor from fruit cocktail.

BAKE at 375° for 14 to 17 minutes   MAKES about 3 dozen

Sift together 1½ cups sifted **Pillsbury's Best All Purpose Flour***
    ½ teaspoon double-acting **baking powder**
    ½ teaspoon **soda** and
    ½ teaspoon **salt**. Set aside.
Add . . . . 1 cup firmly packed **brown sugar** gradually to
    ⅓ cup **shortening,** creaming well.
Blend in . . . . . 1 unbeaten **egg** and
    2 tablespoons **sour** or **sweet cream**. Add the dry ingredients.
Stir in . . . . . 1½ cups toasted **coconut**
    1 cup quick-cooking **rolled oats**
    1 cup (1-lb. can) well-drained **fruit cocktail**
    ½ cup **nuts,** chopped, and
    ¼ cup chopped **maraschino cherries**
Drop . . . . by rounded teaspoonfuls onto ungreased baking sheets.
Bake . . . . at 375° for 14 to 17 minutes.
*For use with Pillsbury's Best Self-Rising Flour, omit baking powder, soda, salt.

Scottish Reels

Senior Winner by Mrs. J. Edwin Estes, Ponca City, Oklahoma

These easy-to-make cookies feature a unique flavor combination of chocolate, brown sugar, cream cheese and pecans.

BAKE at 350° for 12 to 15 minutes   MAKES about 4 dozen

Sift together . . 2 cups sifted **Pillsbury's Best All Purpose Flour***
    1 teaspoon double-acting **baking powder**
    ½ teaspoon **soda** and
    ½ teaspoon **salt**
Cream . . . . . 1½ ounces (3 tablespoons) **cream cheese**
    ½ cup **shortening** and
    ½ cup **butter** or margarine. Gradually add
    1 cup firmly packed **brown sugar** and
    ½ cup sifted **confectioners' sugar,** creaming well.
Add . . . . 2 unbeaten **eggs**
    2 squares (2 oz.) melted unsweetened **chocolate** and
    2 teaspoons **vanilla;** beat well. Blend in the dry ingredients gradually.
Stir in . . . . 1 cup **pecans** or other nuts, chopped. Chill at least 1 hour.
Combine . . . . . 1 cup quick-cooking **rolled oats** and
    ¼ cup sifted **confectioners' sugar**
Drop . . . . dough by rounded teaspoonfuls into oatmeal mixture; coat thoroughly. Place on greased baking sheets; flatten to about ½ inch.
Bake . . . . at 350° for 12 to 15 minutes. Cool; frost with Chocolate Cream Cheese Frosting.
*For use with Pillsbury's Best Self-Rising Flour, omit baking powder, soda and salt; decrease baking time to 10 to 12 minutes.

CHOCOLATE CREAM CHEESE FROSTING

Melt 1 cup (6-oz. pkg.) semi-sweet chocolate pieces in top of double boiler over hot water. Blend in 1½ ounces cream cheese and 1½ cups sifted confectioners' sugar. Add 5 to 6 tablespoons cream, beating until of spreading consistency.

Crisp Lemon Thins

Bride Winner by Mrs. Joe E. McGinty, Austin, Texas

Here's a speedy brown sugar-rolled oat cookie. It's real lemony for good eating and wafer thin because it spreads during baking.

BAKE at 350° for 7 to 10 minutes   MAKES 3 dozen

Cream . . . . . . ½ cup **butter** or margarine. Gradually add
                 ¾ cup firmly packed **brown sugar,** creaming well.
Blend in . . . . . 1 unbeaten **egg.** Stir in
                 ¾ cup sifted **Pillsbury's Best All Purpose Flour***
Add . . . . ½ cup **almonds,** finely chopped
                 ¼ cup quick-cooking **rolled oats**
                 1 tablespoon grated **lemon rind** and
                 ½ teaspoon **lemon extract.** Mix well.
Drop . . . . by scant teaspoonfuls at least 3 inches apart onto
                 greased baking sheets.

Crisp Lemon Thins

Bake . . . . at 350° for 7 to 10 minutes until edges are golden
                 brown. Remove from baking sheets immediately.
*Pillsbury's Best Self-Rising Flour may be substituted.

Boutonnieres

Senior Winner by Mrs. B. Ziegler, Culver City, California

For a party-time touch, top basic brown sugar-oatmeal drop cookies with tinted or plain coconut!

BAKE at 350° for 10 minutes, then   MAKES about 6 dozen
          for 3 to 5 minutes

Sift together . . 2 cups sifted **Pillsbury's Best All Purpose Flour***
                 2 teaspoons double-acting **baking powder** and
                 ¾ teaspoon **salt**
Cream . . . . 1 cup **butter** or margarine. Gradually add
                 1½ cups firmly packed **brown sugar,** creaming well.
Add . . . . 1 unbeaten **egg** and
                 1 teaspoon **vanilla**; beat well. Blend in the dry in-
                 gredients. Mix thoroughly.
Stir in . . . . . 1½ cups quick-cooking **rolled oats** and
                 1 cup **nuts,** chopped
Drop . . . . by teaspoonfuls onto ungreased baking sheets.
Bake . . . . at 350° for 10 minutes. Remove from oven; cool 1
                 minute. Brush tops with slightly beaten **egg white.**
                 Press
                 1 cup chopped **coconut,** plain or tinted, onto cookies,
                 using ½ teaspoonful for each. Bake 3 to 5 minutes
                 longer.

*For use with Pillsbury's Best Self-Rising Flour, omit baking powder and salt.

Orange Raisin Drops

Senior Winner by Mrs. Park S. Avery, Grand Rapids, Michigan

Orange juice and raisins go into these soft oatmeal drop cookies.

BAKE at 375° for 10 to 12 minutes   MAKES about 4 dozen

Sift together . . 2 cups sifted **Pillsbury's Best All Purpose Flour***
  1 teaspoon **soda**
  1 teaspoon **cinnamon**
  1 teaspoon **nutmeg** and
  ½ teaspoon **salt**. Set aside.
Add . . . . 1 cup firmly packed **brown sugar** gradually to
  ¾ cup **shortening**, creaming well.
Blend in . . . . . 2 unbeaten **eggs**
  1 tablespoon grated **orange rind** and
  2 tablespoons **orange juice**
Stir in . . . . the dry ingredients; mix thoroughly.
Add . . . . 1 cup quick-cooking **rolled oats**
  1 cup **raisins** or currants and
  ½ cup **nuts**, chopped; mix well.
Drop . . . . by rounded teaspoonfuls onto greased baking sheets.
  Flatten slightly with fork.
Bake . . . . at 375° for 10 to 12 minutes.
For use with Pillsbury's Best Self-Rising Flour, omit soda and salt.

Peekaberry Boos

Bride Winner by Mrs. Robert Gregg, Spokane, Washington

Tasty oatmeal cookies . . . an easy way to make jam-filled cookies.

BAKE at 400° for 10 to 12 minutes   MAKES about 4½ dozen

Sift together 2½ cups sifted **Pillsbury's Best All Purpose Flour***
  1 teaspoon **soda**
  1 teaspoon **salt** and
  ½ teaspoon **cinnamon**

Peekaberry Boos

Cream . . . . . . ½ cup **butter** or margarine with
  ½ cup **shortening**. Gradually add
  1 cup firmly packed **brown sugar** and
  ¾ cup **sugar**, creaming well.
Add . . . . 2 unbeaten **eggs**
  ½ cup **water** and
  1 teaspoon **almond extract**; beat well.
Blend in . . . . the dry ingredients and
  2 cups quick-cooking **rolled oats**; mix thoroughly.
Drop . . . . by rounded teaspoonfuls onto ungreased baking
  sheets. Place
  ½ teaspoon firm **red raspberry preserves** on each
  cookie; press jam lightly into dough with back of
  spoon. Top with a level teaspoonful of dough.
Bake . . . . at 400° for 10 to 12 minutes.
Pillsbury's Best Self-Rising Flour is not recommended for use in this recipe.

Chocolate-Filled Tea Cookies

Senior Winner by Mrs. Carroll C. Harrison, Lima, Ohio

Each cookie is really two rich, buttery drop cookies in one . . . sand-wiched together with creamy chocolate filling.

BAKE at 375° for 9 to 12 minutes   MAKES about 3 dozen

Sift together 1¾ cups sifted **Pillsbury's Best All Purpose Flour***
             1½ teaspoons double-acting **baking powder** and
             1 teaspoon **salt**
Cream . . . . . . ⅓ cup **butter** or shortening. Gradually add
             ¾ cup **sugar,** creaming well.
Blend in . . . . . 3 unbeaten **eggs** and
             1 teaspoon **vanilla**; beat well.
Stir in . . . . the dry ingredients; mix thoroughly.
Drop . . . . by level teaspoonfuls onto greased baking sheet.
Bake . . . . at 375° for 9 to 12 minutes. Place flat sides of two
             cookies together with **Chocolate Butter Cream
             Frosting,** page 321, sandwich-style.

For use with Pillsbury's Best Self-Rising Flour, omit baking powder and salt.

Candy Lasses

Senior Winner by Mrs. Milton C. Olson, Elsmere, New York

Spicy molasses cookies filled with crushed peppermint stick candy.

BAKE at 350° for 12 to 15 minutes   MAKES about 3 dozen

Sift together 1½ cups sifted **Pillsbury's Best All Purpose Flour***
             ½ teaspoon double-acting **baking powder**
             ½ teaspoon **salt**

½ teaspoon **cinnamon**
½ teaspoon **nutmeg** and
¼ teaspoon **ginger.** Set aside.
Add . . . . ¼ cup **sugar** and
             ¼ cup firmly packed **brown sugar** to
             ⅔ cup **shortening,** creaming well.
Blend in . . . . . 1 unbeaten **egg** and
             2 tablespoons **molasses**; beat well.
Stir in . . . . . . ½ cup crushed **peppermint stick candy** and the dry
             ingredients.
Drop . . . . by teaspoonfuls onto greased baking sheets.
Bake . . . . at 350° for 12 to 15 minutes. Cool 5 minutes; remove
             from baking sheets.

For use with Pillsbury's Best Self-Rising Flour, omit baking powder and salt.

Peanut Ginger Crisps

Senior Winner by Mrs. Francis Charlton, Williams, Minnesota

Salted peanuts give extra zip to these spicy ginger snaps.

BAKE at 350° for 12 to 15 minutes   MAKES 4½ dozen

Sift together . . 3 cups sifted **Pillsbury's Best All Purpose Flour***
             1 teaspoon **soda**
             1 teaspoon **ginger**
             1 teaspoon **cinnamon** and
             ½ teaspoon ground **cloves.** Set aside.
Add . . . . 1 cup **sugar** gradually into
             ⅔ cup **shortening,** creaming well.
Blend in . . . . . 2 unbeaten **eggs** and
             ½ cup **molasses**; beat well. Add the dry ingredients
             gradually; mix thoroughly.
Stir in . . . . . . 1 cup **salted peanuts,** chopped
Drop . . . . by rounded teaspoonfuls onto greased baking sheets.
Bake . . . . at 350° for 12 to 15 minutes.

For use with Pillsbury's Best Self-Rising Flour, omit soda.

Snack Time Molasses Cookies

Junior Winner by Renee Marie DeMillar, Framingham, Massachusetts

It's simple to prepare these molasses cookies. Coconut and walnuts make them crunchy and chewy.

BAKE at 375° for 8 to 10 minutes   MAKES about 3 dozen

Sift together 1½ cups sifted **Pillsbury's Best All Purpose Flour***
    ¾ teaspoon **soda** and
    ½ teaspoon **salt**. Set aside.
Add........¾ cup **sugar** gradually to
    ½ cup **shortening**, creaming well.
Blend in.....1 unbeaten **egg** and
    ¼ cup **molasses**. Add dry ingredients; mix well.
Stir in......½ cup flaked or chopped shredded **coconut** and
    ½ cup **walnuts**, chopped
Drop.........by rounded teaspoonfuls onto greased baking sheets.
Bake.........at 375° for 8 to 10 minutes.
*For use with Pillsbury's Best Self-Rising Flour, decrease soda to ¼ teaspoon and omit salt.

Triplets

Junior Winner by Gloria Jean Ailie, New York Mills, Minnesota

There's a trio of flavors in each novel cookie!

BAKE at 400° for 10 to 13 minutes   MAKES about 4 dozen

Sift together 2½ cups sifted **Pillsbury's Best All Purpose Flour***
    2 teaspoons double-acting **baking powder** and
    1 teaspoon **salt**
Add........½ cup **sugar** and
    ½ cup firmly packed **brown sugar** gradually to
    1 cup **shortening**, creaming well.
Stir in.......2 unbeaten **eggs** and
    1 teaspoon **vanilla**; beat well.

Triplets

Blend in.......half of the dry ingredients, then
    ½ cup **milk**, then remaining dry ingredients.
Divide........dough into three parts.
Add........1 teaspoon **cinnamon** and
    ½ cup finely cut **dates** to first part.
Blend.......1 teaspoon **almond extract** into second part.
Add........1 square (1 oz.) melted unsweetened **chocolate**
    1 tablespoon **water** and
    ½ cup cut **coconut** to third part.
Drop.........a small teaspoonful of each dough onto greased
    baking sheet so balls of dough just touch, forming
    a triangle. Top almond-flavored balls with a sliver
    of **maraschino cherry**.
Bake.........at 400° for 10 to 13 minutes.
*For use with Pillsbury's Best Self-Rising Flour, omit baking powder and salt.

Maple Memory Cookies

Senior Winner by Mrs. Charles Hutton, Walled Lake, Michigan

There is a real, old-time maple syrup flavor in these walnut cookies! Keen reminders of sugar-gathering time in New England!

BAKE at 400° for 8 to 10 minutes   MAKES 5 dozen

Sift together 2¼ cups sifted **Pillsbury's Best All Purpose Flour***
       2 teaspoons double-acting **baking powder**
       ½ teaspoon **soda** and
       ½ teaspoon **salt**
Add . . . . ½ cup firmly packed **brown sugar** to
       ¾ cup **shortening,** creaming well.
Blend in . . . . . 1 unbeaten **egg** and
       1 teaspoon **maple flavoring;** beat well.
Add . . . . ½ cup **maple syrup** alternately with the dry ingredients, blending well after each addition.
Stir in . . . . . . ½ cup **walnuts,** chopped
Drop . . . . by rounded teaspoonfuls onto ungreased baking sheets; top each with a **walnut half.**
Bake . . . . at 400° for 8 to 10 minutes.

For use with Pillsbury's Best Self-Rising Flour, omit baking powder, soda, salt.

Toffee Nut Cookies

Senior Winner by Mrs. John S. Moore, Savannah, Georgia

There are bits of English toffee throughout these delicious cookies.

BAKE at 400° for 9 to 12 minutes   MAKES 3 dozen

Sift together 1¾ cups sifted **Pillsbury's Best All Purpose Flour***
       ½ teaspoon double-acting **baking powder**
       ½ teaspoon **salt** and
       ¼ teaspoon **soda.** Set aside.
Add . . . . 1 cup firmly packed **brown sugar** gradually to
       ½ cup **shortening,** creaming well.
Blend in . . . . . 1 unbeaten **egg** and
       1 teaspoon **vanilla;** beat well.
Add . . . . 2 tablespoons **milk** and the dry ingredients; mix thoroughly.
Blend in . . . . . 3 ounces (¾ cup) brittle **English toffee,** coarsely crushed
Drop . . . . by rounded teaspoonfuls onto greased baking sheets.
Bake . . . . at 400° for 9 to 12 minutes.

For use with Pillsbury's Best Self-Rising Flour, omit baking powder and salt; decrease baking time to 8 to 10 minutes.

Sour Cream Walnutties

Junior Winner by Philip Marion Delham, Salt Lake City, Utah

Rich, crisp cookies with definite black walnut flavor. So easy you can whisk a batch together in practically no time.

BAKE at 375° for 9 to 12 minutes   MAKES about 5 dozen

Sift together . . 2 cups sifted **Pillsbury's Best All Purpose Flour***
       1 teaspoon double-acting **baking powder**
       ½ teaspoon **salt** and
       ¼ teaspoon **soda.** Set aside.
Add . . . . ¾ cup **sugar** gradually to
       ½ cup **shortening,** creaming well.
Blend in . . . . . 1 unbeaten **egg** and
       ½ teaspoon **vanilla;** beat well.
Add . . . . ½ cup **sour cream** (thick or commercial) alternately with dry ingredients, blending thoroughly.
Stir in . . . . . . ½ cup **black** or **English walnuts,** chopped
Drop . . . . by teaspoonfuls onto greased baking sheets. Dip greased bottom of glass into mixture of
       1 tablespoon **sugar** and

½ teaspoon **cinnamon.** Flatten each cookie.

Bake. . . . . at 375° for 9 to 12 minutes.

For use with Pillsbury's Best Self-Rising Flour, omit baking powder, salt, soda.

Cashew Crunch Cookies

Senior Winner by Alma Berenato, Wilmington, Delaware

Treat your family to delicious cookies made crunchy with candy.

BAKE at 350° for 12 to 15 minutes   MAKES about 5 dozen

Sift together 2¼ cups sifted **Pillsbury's Best All Purpose Flour***
          ½ teaspoon **soda** and
          ½ teaspoon **cream of tartar**

Cream. . . . . . . 1 cup **butter** or margarine. Gradually add
          ¾ cup firmly packed **brown sugar** and
          ½ cup **sugar,** creaming well.

Blend in. . . . . 1 unbeaten **egg** and
          1 teaspoon **vanilla;** beat well. Add the dry ingredients
          gradually; mix thoroughly.

Stir in. . . . . 1½ cups (7 oz.) **cashew** or **peanut crunch candy,**
          finely crushed

Drop. . . . . by rounded teaspoonfuls onto greased baking sheets.

Bake. . . . . at 350° for 12 to 15 minutes.

For use with Pillsbury's Best Self-Rising Flour, omit soda and cream of tartar.

Mother's Mint Mist Cookies

Senior Winner by Mrs. Murray S. Goodfellow, Hanover, Pennsylvania

These delicate peppermint cookies are delicious with afternoon tea.

BAKE at 375° for 8 to 10 minutes   MAKES about 4 dozen

Sift together. .2 cups sifted **Pillsbury's Best All Purpose Flour***
          ½ teaspoon **soda**

Cashew Crunch Cookies

          ¼ teaspoon **cream of tartar** and
          ¼ teaspoon **salt**

Cream. . . . . . ½ cup **butter** or margarine (half shortening may be
          used). Gradually add
          1 cup **sugar,** creaming well.

Blend in. . . . . 1 unbeaten **egg**
          ½ teaspoon **vanilla** and
          ¼ teaspoon **peppermint extract;** beat well.

Add. . . . . ⅓ cup **buttermilk** or sour milk alternately with the dry
          ingredients, blending well after each addition.

Drop. . . . . by rounded teaspoonfuls onto greased baking sheets.
          Flatten to ¼-inch thickness (use bottom of glass,
          greased and dipped in **sugar**).

Bake. . . . . at 375° for 8 to 10 minutes.

For use with Pillsbury's Best Self-Rising Flour, omit soda, cream of tartar, salt.

Maple Nut Drops

Senior Winner by Mrs. Frank Kelso, New Castle, Pennsylvania

Maple syrup teams up with dates, pecans and coconut for a new flavor in a tender, cake-like drop cookie.

BAKE at 350° for 13 to 16 minutes.　　　MAKES 5 to 6 dozen

Sift together . . 3 cups sifted **Pillsbury's Best All Purpose Flour***
　　　　　　　　1 teaspoon double-acting **baking powder**
　　　　　　　　1 teaspoon **soda** and
　　　　　　　　1 teaspoon **salt**
Blend . . . . ½ cup **shortening** with
　　　　　　　　½ cup **butter** or margarine, creaming well.
Add . . . . 3 unbeaten **eggs**
　　　　　　　　1 cup **maple syrup** and
　　　　　　　　¼ teaspoon **maple flavoring**; beat well.
Blend in . . . . . . the dry ingredients gradually, mixing thoroughly.
Add . . . . ¼ cup **boiling water**; mix well.
Stir in . . . . 1 cup cut **dates**
　　　　　　　　1 cup **pecans**, chopped, and
　　　　　　　　¾ cup **coconut**, if desired. Chill at least 1 hour.
Drop . . . . by rounded teaspoonfuls onto ungreased baking sheets.
Bake . . . . at 350° for 13 to 16 minutes. Cool; frost with Maple Frosting, then top each with a **pecan half**, if desired.

For use with Pillsbury's Best Self-Rising Flour, omit baking powder and salt; decrease soda to ¼ teaspoon.

MAPLE FROSTING

Combine ¼ cup melted butter, 2 tablespoons cream, 1 teaspoon vanilla and 1 tablespoon maple syrup. Blend in 2 cups sifted confectioners' sugar. Beat until of spreading consistency.

A

B

MOLDED and SHAPED COOKIES—Chill

dough if it is too soft to mold into balls. Shape dough with palm of hand into balls, cylinders, or other shapes (photo A). Place cookies 2 to 3 inches apart on baking sheets unless otherwise directed in recipe.
To make thin crisp cookies: Dip greased bottom of glass into flour or sugar and flatten balls on baking sheet. Or flatten cookies with a floured fork (photo B).
To coat baked cookies with sugar: Place sugar and about one dozen cookies in paper bag; shake carefully until coated.

Chocolate Almond Bonbons

Senior Winner by Mrs. Jesse Rosoff, Pasadena, California

Delicious milk chocolate cookies with almond filling.

BAKE at 350° for 12 to 15 minutes　　　MAKES 3½ dozen

Sift together . . 2 cups sifted **Pillsbury's Best All Purpose Flour*** and
　　　　　　　　½ teaspoon **salt**
Melt . . . . 4 ounces **milk chocolate candy** or German's sweet chocolate with
　　　　　　　　2 tablespoons **milk** over hot water. Cool.
Cream . . . . . . ¾ cup **butter** or margarine. Add

¼ cup **sugar** and
2 teaspoons **vanilla,** creaming well. Blend in the chocolate mixture.

Add . . . . the dry ingredients gradually; mix thoroughly.

Shape . . . . by rounded teaspoonfuls into balls. Make dent in center of each and fill with ¼ teaspoon Almond Filling; seal. Roll in **granulated sugar** (or in confectioners' sugar after baking). Place on ungreased baking sheets.

Bake . . . . at 350° for 12 to 15 minutes.

For use with Pillsbury's Best Self-Rising Flour, omit salt.

ALMOND FILLING

Combine ½ cup ground almonds, 1 unbeaten egg white, 1 tablespoon water and ½ teaspoon almond extract. Mix well.

Chocolate-Shell Peanuts

Senior Winner by Mrs. R. W. Fantz, Seattle, Washington

Candy-like cookies shaped to resemble peanuts—chocolate cookie around a peanut butter filling.

BAKE at 325° for 13 to 15 minutes   MAKES 6 dozen

Combine . . . . ¾ cup **peanut butter** and
½ cup sifted **confectioners' sugar.** Set aside.

Sift together . . 2 cups sifted **Pillsbury's Best All Purpose Flour***
⅓ cup **cocoa** and
½ teaspoon **salt**

Cream . . . . . . ½ cup **butter** or margarine. Gradually add
¾ cup **sugar,** creaming well.

Blend in . . . . . 1 unbeaten **egg** and
1 teaspoon **vanilla;** beat well. Add the dry ingredients; mix thoroughly.

Shape . . . . dough by half teaspoonfuls into balls. Flatten each ball; place ¼ teaspoonful peanut butter mixture in

center. Shape dough around filling; press to seal. Pinch ends and centers to form "peanuts." Place on ungreased baking sheets.

Bake . . . . at 325° for 13 to 15 minutes. Roll warm cookies in **confectioners'** or **granulated sugar.**

For use with Pillsbury's Best Self-Rising Flour, omit salt.

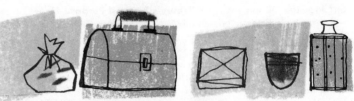

Chocolate Nutbutter Cookies

Senior Winner by Mrs. Marvin J. Duncan, Washington, D.C.

These quickly-prepared cookies combine cocoa and peanut butter. They're sure to make a hit with the family. Perfect for lunchboxes!

BAKE at 400° for 8 to 10 minutes   MAKES about 4 dozen

Sift together . . 2 cups sifted **Pillsbury's Best All Purpose Flour***
½ cup **cocoa**
2 teaspoons double-acting **baking powder** and
½ teaspoon **salt**

Blend . . . . ½ cup **shortening** with
½ cup **peanut butter.** Gradually add
1¼ cups **sugar,** creaming well.

Add . . . . 2 unbeaten **eggs** and
1½ teaspoons **vanilla;** beat well.

Blend in . . . . . . the dry ingredients alternately with
⅓ cup **milk,** blending well after each addition.

Shape . . . . by rounded teaspoonfuls into balls. Place on ungreased baking sheets. Flatten with fork.

Bake . . . . at 400° for 8 to 10 minutes.

For use with Pillsbury's Best Self-Rising Flour, omit baking powder and salt.

Chocolate Pixies

Senior Winner by Mrs. John L. Parisot, Marseilles, Illinois

They taste like black walnut brownie bars and look like oldtime molasses cookies with "cracked" tops.

BAKE at 300° for 18 to 20 minutes   MAKES 3 dozen

Sift together . . 2 cups sifted **Pillsbury's Best All Purpose Flour***
                  2 teaspoons double-acting **baking powder** and
                  ½ teaspoon **salt**

Melt . . . . ¼ cup **butter** or margarine and
                  4 squares (4 oz.) unsweetened **chocolate** in saucepan over low heat, stirring constantly. Cool to lukewarm.

Blend in . . . . . 2 cups **sugar** and
                  4 unbeaten **eggs**, one at a time, beating well after each.

Add . . . . ½ cup **black** or **English walnuts**, chopped, and the dry ingredients; mix well. Chill at least 30 minutes.

Shape . . . . by tablespoonfuls into balls. Roll in **confectioners' sugar**. Place on greased baking sheets.

Bake . . . . at 300° for 18 to 20 minutes.

For use with Pillsbury's Best Self-Rising Flour, omit baking powder and salt.

Chocolate Almond Balls

Senior Winner by Mrs. Louis Evans, Melrose Park, Illinois

Milk chocolate balls made with chocolate syrup, coconut and almonds.

BAKE at 325° for 18 to 20 minutes   MAKES about 6 dozen

Sift together . . 3 cups sifted **Pillsbury's Best All Purpose Flour*** and
                  ¾ teaspoon **salt**

Cream . . . . . . ¾ cup **butter** or margarine and
                  ¾ cup **shortening**. Blend in

3 tablespoons (½ of 3-oz. pkg.) **cream cheese** and
                  ⅔ cup sifted **confectioners' sugar**, creaming well.

Add . . . . ½ cup **chocolate syrup****
                  1 teaspoon **vanilla** and
                  1 teaspoon **almond extract**. Beat well.

Stir in . . . . . . 1 cup **coconut**, chopped, and
                  1 cup **almonds**, chopped

Blend in . . . . . . the dry ingredients gradually. Chill.**

Shape . . . . by rounded teaspoonfuls into balls. (If desired, roll in ground almonds.) Place on ungreased baking sheets.

Bake . . . . at 325° for 18 to 20 minutes. Roll in **confectioners' sugar** while warm.

For use with Pillsbury's Best Self-Rising Flour, omit salt.
**Two squares melted unsweetened chocolate and 2 tablespoons light corn syrup may be substituted; do not chill dough.*

Chocolate Cashew Cookies

Junior Winner by Mamie Leah Young, Washington, D. C.

Melted chocolate rum wafers and cashews are at the "heart" of these oval cookies.

BAKE at 350° for 10 to 12 minutes   MAKES 5 dozen

Sift together . . 2 cups sifted **Pillsbury's Best All Purpose Flour***
                  ½ teaspoon **salt** and
                  ¼ teaspoon **soda**

Melt . . . . 1 cup (half of 8½-oz. pkg.) solid **chocolate rum candy wafers**** over hot water.

Cream . . . . . . ½ cup **butter** or margarine and
                  ¼ cup **shortening**. Add
                  ¼ cup **sugar**, creaming well.

Add . . . . 1 unbeaten **egg** or 2 egg yolks
                  1 teaspoon **rum flavoring**** and the melted chocolate wafers. Beat well.

Blend in . . . . the dry ingredients gradually. Chill.
Shape . . . . by rounded teaspoonfuls into ovals with a whole **salted cashew** inside of each (about 1 cup in all). Place on ungreased baking sheets.
Bake . . . . at 350° for 10 to 12 minutes. Cool; drizzle with Frosting in zigzag pattern.

*For use with Pillsbury's Best Self-Rising Flour, omit salt and soda.
**Mint or milk chocolate wafers and vanilla extract may be substituted for the rum wafers and flavoring.

FROSTING

Blend together 1½ cups sifted confectioners' sugar, ¼ cup cream and ½ teaspoon rum flavoring or vanilla. Thin with a few drops cream, if necessary.

Nut Cluster Cookies

Senior Winner by Mrs. Vi Poleway, Fairmont, West Virginia

Tiny cookies dipped in chocolate form candy-like clusters.

BAKE at 375° for 8 to 10 minutes   MAKES about 2 dozen

Sift together 1¼ cups sifted **Pillsbury's Best All Purpose Flour***
     ¼ teaspoon **salt**
     ¼ teaspoon **cream of tartar** and
     ¼ teaspoon **soda.** Set aside.
Add . . . . ½ cup **sugar** gradually to
     ⅓ cup **shortening,** creaming well.
Blend in . . . . . 1 unbeaten **egg**
     2 tablespoons **milk** and
     1 teaspoon **vanilla;** beat well.
Add . . . . ½ cup **salted peanuts** or toasted almonds, chopped, and the dry ingredients; mix thoroughly. Chill for easier handling.
Shape . . . . into tiny balls, ½ inch in diameter. Place on ungreased baking sheets.

Nut Cluster Cookies

Bake . . . . at 375° for 8 to 10 minutes.
Drop . . . . cookies into Chocolate Glaze, covering completely. Lift out with fork, tapping against side of double boiler to remove excess chocolate.
Place . . . . three glazed cookies, sides touching, on rack over waxed paper. Place a fourth cookie on top to form cluster. Repeat with remaining cookies. Garnish with finely chopped **nuts.**

*For use with Pillsbury's Best Self-Rising Flour, omit salt, cream of tartar, soda and milk.

CHOCOLATE GLAZE

Melt 12 squares (12 oz.) semi-sweet chocolate in top of double boiler over boiling water. Stir in 3 tablespoons sifted confectioners' sugar. Remove from heat (keep chocolate mixture over hot water).

Triple Treats

Senior Winner by Mrs. Joseph Sharps, Newbury, New Hampshire

Chocolate dough swirls through plain in a trio of tiny molded cookies. An unusual shaping method makes the chocolate pattern.

BAKE at 375° for 10 to 12 minutes   MAKES about 4 dozen

Sift together . . 2 cups sifted **Pillsbury's Best All Purpose Flour***
      ¾ teaspoon **soda** and
      ½ teaspoon **salt**
Cream . . . . . . ½ cup **butter** or margarine. Gradually add
      ¾ cup **sugar,** creaming well.
Blend in . . . . . 1 unbeaten **egg**
      1 tablespoon **milk** and
      2 teaspoons **vanilla.** Beat well.
Add . . . . the dry ingredients gradually; mix thoroughly.
Remove . . . . two-thirds of dough from bowl. Blend

            1 square (1 oz.) melted unsweetened **chocolate** into
            remaining dough. Chill 1 hour.
Roll out . . . . light dough on floured surface to a 12x6-inch rectangle. Roll out dark dough to a 12x4-inch rectangle.
Cut . . . . light and dark doughs into 12x2-inch strips. Stack the five strips, alternating light and dark.
Pinch off . . . . . marble-sized pieces of dough; shape into balls. Arrange three together, sides touching, on greased baking sheet; flatten slightly.
Bake . . . . at 375° for 10 to 12 minutes.

*For use with Pillsbury's Best Self-Rising Flour, omit soda and salt.

Texas Stars

Texas Stars

Senior Winner by Mrs. Lake Munday, Nashua, New Hampshire

This easily shaped star is made from a butter-rich coconut round, topped with a chocolate layer coated with coconut and cereal.

BAKE at 350° for 12 to 15 minutes   MAKES 4 dozen

CHOCOLATE DOUGH

Melt . . . . 2 tablespoons **butter** with
      1 cup (6-oz. pkg.) **semi-sweet chocolate pieces** over boiling water. Remove from heat.
Blend in . . . . . 1 can (15 oz.) minus 2 tablespoons **sweetened condensed milk** (reserve 2 tablespoons milk for white dough).
Add . . . . 1 cup sifted **Pillsbury's Best All Purpose Flour;*** mix thoroughly.
Stir in . . . . . . ½ cup **nuts,** chopped, and
      1 teaspoon **vanilla.** Chill at least 1 hour.

WHITE DOUGH

Cream . . . . . . ¾ cup soft **butter** or margarine. Gradually add
      ½ cup **sugar,** creaming well.
Blend in . . . . 1½ cups sifted **Pillsbury's Best All Purpose Flour*** and

reserved sweetened condensed milk. Mix thoroughly.

Stir in . . . . . . ¾ cup crisp **ready-to-eat cereal** (shredded or crumbled flakes)

Combine . . . . . 1 cup **coconut**, finely chopped, and
½ cup crushed **ready-to-eat cereal**

Roll out . . . . white dough to ⅛-inch thickness on surface sprinkled with **confectioners' sugar**. Cut into rounds with 2-inch cutter; place on ungreased baking sheets.

Drop . . . . chocolate dough by teaspoonfuls into coconut-cereal mixture; coat thoroughly. Form into balls and flatten into 2-inch circles; place on top of white circles and press down to seal.

Shape . . . . into five-pointed stars by pinching white and chocolate doughs together with thumb and index finger to form each point.

Bake . . . . at 350° for 12 to 15 minutes. *Do not overbake.*

*Pillsbury's Best Self-Rising Flour may be substituted.

Butternut Balls

Senior Winner by Mrs. Helen Van Marten, Carmel-by-the-Sea, California

There's a nut surprise in the center of each of these rich butter cookies. They stay fresh for days.

BAKE at 400° for 10 to 12 minutes   MAKES about 3½ dozen

Sift together 2½ cups sifted **Pillsbury's Best All Purpose Flour*** and
¼ teaspoon **salt**

Cream . . . . . . 1 cup **butter** or margarine. Gradually add
¾ cup sifted **confectioners' sugar,** creaming well.

Blend in . . . . . 2 teaspoons **vanilla** and the dry ingredients.

Shape . . . . by rounded teaspoonfuls into balls with a **pecan half** inside of each. Place on ungreased baking sheets.

Bake . . . . at 400° for 10 to 12 minutes. *Do not brown.* Roll in **confectioners' sugar** while warm.

*For use with Pillsbury's Best Self-Rising Flour, omit salt.

Chocolate Covered Cherry-ettes

Senior Winner by Mrs. Frank M. Caetta, Akron, Ohio

These will remind you of a popular confection—butter-rich maraschino cherry cookies covered with chocolate.

BAKE at 350° for 15 to 18 minutes   MAKES about 4½ dozen

Cream . . . . . . 1 cup **butter** or margarine. Gradually add
¾ cup sifted **confectioners' sugar,** creaming well.

Stir in . . . . 1 teaspoon **vanilla**
1 teaspoon **almond extract** and
½ teaspoon **salt**

Blend in . . . . 2¼ cups sifted **Pillsbury's Best All Purpose Flour***
½ cup well-drained **maraschino cherries,** chopped, and
¼ cup **nuts,** finely chopped

Shape . . . . by rounded teaspoonfuls into balls. Place on ungreased baking sheets.

Bake . . . . at 350° for 15 to 18 minutes.* Cool. Dip in Chocolate Dip, covering tops and sides. Top each with a piece of **maraschino cherry.** Let stand on rack until chocolate hardens, 2 to 3 hours.

*For use with Pillsbury's Best Self-Rising Flour, omit salt; decrease baking time to 13 to 16 minutes.

CHOCOLATE DIP

Melt 1 cup (6-oz. pkg.) semi-sweet chocolate pieces, 3 tablespoons butter and ½ cup milk in top of double boiler over hot water. Cool slightly. Blend in 3 cups sifted confectioners' sugar. If mixture becomes too stiff, reheat over hot water.

Butter Dream Cookies

Senior Winner by Evangline Power Diaz, San Turce, Puerto Rico

This Puerto Rican cookie recipe is particularly simple to make. The cookies are rich and colorful.

BAKE at 350° for 10 to 12 minutes   MAKES about 4 dozen

Cream.......1 cup **butter.** Add
⅓ cup **sugar,** creaming well.

Blend in.....1 teaspoon **almond extract** and
2¼ cups sifted **Pillsbury's Best All Purpose Flour;*** mix well.

Shape.......a rounded teaspoonful of dough around a **maraschino cherry,** allowing bit of cherry to show on top of each. Place on ungreased baking sheets.

Bake........at 350° for 10 to 12 minutes. *Do not brown.*

*Pillsbury's Best Self-Rising Flour may be substituted.

Split Seconds

Best of Class Winner by Mrs. Karen M. Fellows, Silver Springs, Maryland

Rich golden Swedish butter cookies with a bright red jelly filling. The dough is baked in long rolls, then sliced after baking.

BAKE at 350° for 15 to 20 minutes   MAKES about 4 dozen

Sift together..2 cups sifted **Pillsbury's Best All Purpose Flour***
⅔ cup **sugar** and
½ teaspoon double-acting **baking powder** into large mixing bowl.

Blend in.....¾ cup soft **butter** or margarine
1 unbeaten **egg** and
2 teaspoons **vanilla** to form a dough.

Place.........on lightly floured surface. Divide into four parts; shape each into a roll, 13 inches long and ¾ inch thick. Place on ungreased baking sheets, 4 inches apart and 2 inches from edge of sheet.

Make.........a depression, ¼ to ⅓ inch deep, lengthwise down center of each with knife handle. Fill depressions with **red jelly** or **jam,** about ⅓ cup in all.

Bake.........at 350° for 15 to 20 minutes. While warm, cut diagonally into bars.

*Pillsbury's Best Self-Rising Flour is not recommended for use in this recipe.

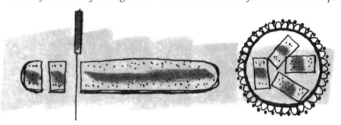

Sesame Circle Cookies

Junior Winner by Sharon Talbot, Tampa, Florida

Balls of butter-rich dough dipped into crunchy sesame seeds.

BAKE at 375° for 12 to 15 minutes   MAKES 4 dozen

Toast.......¼ cup **sesame seeds** at 375° for 5 to 8 minutes until light golden brown, stirring occasionally.

Sift together..2 cups sifted **Pillsbury's Best All Purpose Flour*** and
¼ teaspoon **salt**

Cream......½ cup **butter** or margarine and
¼ cup **shortening.** Gradually add
1 cup **sugar,** creaming well.

Blend in.....1 unbeaten **egg** and
1 teaspoon **vanilla.** Add the dry ingredients gradually; mix thoroughly.

Shape.......by rounded teaspoonfuls into balls. Dip tops in sesame seeds. Place on ungreased baking sheets.

Bake.........at 375° for 12 to 15 minutes.

*For use with Pillsbury's Best Self-Rising Flour, omit salt.

390 / MOLDED AND SHAPED COOKIES

Greek Sesame Twists

Senior Winner by Mrs. Andy Pappas, New Rochelle, New York

Rich and tender as pastry, with toasted sesame seeds on top.

BAKE at 350° for 12 to 15 minutes   MAKES 4½ dozen

Toast........3 tablespoons **sesame seeds** at 350° for 5 to 8 minutes
until light golden brown, stirring occasionally.

Sift together..3 cups sifted **Pillsbury's Best All Purpose Flour***
2 teaspoons double-acting **baking powder**
½ teaspoon **salt**
¼ teaspoon **cinnamon** and
¼ teaspoon **nutmeg**

Cream......½ cup **butter** or margarine with
¼ cup **shortening**. Add
⅔ cup **sugar**, creaming well.

Blend in.....1 unbeaten **egg** and
1 teaspoon **vanilla**; beat well.

Add........⅓ cup **cream** alternately with the dry ingredients to
creamed mixture; blend well after each addition.

Shape........dough by teaspoonfuls into strips 4 inches long.
Place ends of two strips together and twist two or
three times. Place on greased baking sheets. Brush
with beaten **egg**; sprinkle with toasted sesame seeds.

Bake.........at 350° for 12 to 15 minutes.

*For use with Pillsbury's Best Self-Rising Flour, omit baking powder and salt.

Sugar Belles

Senior Winner by Mrs. E. A. Foley, Laurel, Mississippi

*Made with confectioners' sugar, this rich and tender party cookie is
shaped to resemble a "bell;" use almond for a "clapper."*

BAKE at 350° for 12 to 15 minutes   MAKES about 4 dozen

Toast........⅓ cup **sesame seeds*** at 350° for 5 to 8 minutes until
light golden brown, stirring occasionally. Cool.

Sift together..2 cups sifted **Pillsbury's Best All Purpose Flour****
¼ teaspoon **salt**

Cream.......1 cup **butter** or margarine. Add
⅔ cup sifted **confectioners' sugar**, creaming well.

Add........1 teaspoon **vanilla**
½ teaspoon **almond extract** and the dry ingredients;
mix thoroughly. Chill for easier handling.

Mold.........dough by rounded teaspoonfuls into bells. Dip larger
end in sesame seeds; press a whole blanched **almond**
into dough for clapper. Place on ungreased baking
sheets.

Bake.........at 350° for 12 to 15 minutes.

**If desired, ⅓ cup chocolate cake decorations, colored sugars or toasted
coconut may be substituted.*

***For use with Pillsbury's Best Self-Rising Flour, omit salt; decrease butter to
⅞ cup (¾ cup plus 2 tablespoons).*

Sugar Belles

Golden Pineapples

Golden Pineapples

Junior Winner by Sally Todd, Kailua, Hawaii

Butter cookies shaped like pineapples—complete with tinted almonds for the green crowns.

BAKE at 325° for 12 to 15 minutes   MAKES about 4 dozen

Tint . . . . ½ cup slivered blanched **almonds** with
           ½ teaspoon **green food coloring.** Let dry.
Sift together . . 2 cups sifted **Pillsbury's Best All Purpose Flour*** and
           ¼ teaspoon **salt**
Cream . . . . . . .1 cup **butter** or margarine. Gradually add
           1 cup sifted **confectioners' sugar,** creaming well.
Add . . . . .1 teaspoon **vanilla** and

6 to 10 drops **yellow food coloring;** blend well.
Stir in . . . . .the dry ingredients and
           1 cup **almonds** or other nuts, finely chopped. If
           desired, chill dough for easier handling.
Shape . . . . . . .by rounded teaspoonfuls into ovals. Place 3 to 5
           tinted almonds into one end to resemble a pineapple
           crown. Place on ungreased baking sheets. Make
           crisscross design on each with fork.
Bake . . . . .at 325° for 12 to 15 minutes. *Do not brown.* Sprinkle
           with **confectioners' sugar** while warm.
**For use with Pillsbury's Best Self-Rising Flour, omit salt.*

Chinese Almond Cookies

Senior Winner by Mrs. Ray W. Crouse, Springfield, Ohio

Rich and buttery almond cookies, with an unusual texture from the corn meal in them.

BAKE at 375° for 12 to 15 minutes   MAKES about 4 dozen

Sift together . .2 cups sifted **Pillsbury's Best All Purpose Flour***
           ½ cup **white corn meal** and
           ½ teaspoon **salt**
Cream . . . . . . .1 cup **butter** or margarine. Gradually add
           1 cup sifted **confectioners' sugar,** creaming well.
Blend in . . . . .1 unbeaten **egg** and
           1 teaspoon **almond extract.** Add the dry ingredients
           gradually; mix thoroughly. Chill.
Shape . . . . .by rounded teaspoonfuls into balls.
Blend . . . . .1 unbeaten **egg yolk** with
           1 tablespoon **water.** Dip tops of balls in this mixture,
           then in
           2 tablespoons **sesame seeds.** Place on ungreased
           baking sheets. Top each with a blanched **almond.**
Bake . . . . .at 375° for 12 to 15 minutes.
**For use with Pillsbury's Best Self-Rising Flour, omit salt.*

Swedish Heirloom Cookies

Senior Winner by Mrs. Carlos Wheaton, Hopkins, Minnesota

Rich almond butter cookies, shaped into rounds, then rolled in confectioners' sugar after baking.

BAKE at 325° for 15 to 18 minutes   MAKES about 4½ dozen

Cream.......1 cup **butter** or margarine. Gradually add
1 cup sifted **confectioners' sugar** and
½ teaspoon **salt**,* creaming well.

Blend in....1¼ cups **almonds**, ground or finely chopped, and
1 tablespoon **vanilla.** Add
2 cups sifted **Pillsbury's Best All Purpose Flour***
gradually; mix thoroughly.

Shape........by rounded teaspoonfuls into balls or crescents.
Place on ungreased baking sheets.

Bake.........at 325° for 15 to 18 minutes. *Do not brown.* Roll in
confectioners' sugar while warm.

For use with Pillsbury's Best Self-Rising Flour, omit salt.

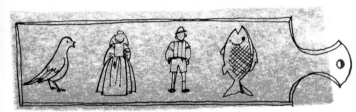

Peanut Brittle Crispies

Senior Winner by Mrs. Guy E. Eckenrode, Baltimore, Maryland

Crushed peanut brittle in a crisp, candy-like cookie.

BAKE at 375° for 9 to 12 minutes   MAKES about 2½ dozen

Sift together 1¼ cups sifted **Pillsbury's Best All Purpose Flour***
½ teaspoon **soda** and
¼ teaspoon **salt**

Cream......¼ cup soft **butter** or margarine and
¼ cup **shortening.** Add
¼ cup **sugar,** creaming well.

Blend in.....1 unbeaten **egg.** Add the dry ingredients gradually;
mix thoroughly.

Stir in.......1 cup (about ⅓ lb.) crushed **peanut brittle**

Shape........dough by rounded teaspoonfuls into balls. Place on
ungreased baking sheets.

Bake.........at 375° for 9 to 12 minutes. Cool 1 minute before
removing from sheets.

For use with Pillsbury's Best Self-Rising Flour, omit soda and salt.

Sugar Cheese Crescents

Senior Winner by Mrs. Howard L. Claypool, Danville, Illinois

"Hmmm, what's in these cookies?" Your secret will be hidden in a delicate blend of cheese and applesauce.

BAKE at 350° for 12 to 16 minutes   MAKES about 3 dozen

Sift together 2½ cups sifted **Pillsbury's Best All Purpose Flour*** and
½ teaspoon **salt**

Cream......¾ cup **butter** or margarine. Add
½ cup **sugar,** creaming well.

Blend in.....⅓ to ½ cup shredded **Cheddar cheese**
⅛ cup thick **applesauce** and
½ teaspoon **vanilla.** Add the dry ingredients; mix
thoroughly.

Shape........by rounded teaspoonfuls into balls. Roll each in
mixture of
½ cup **sugar** and
1 teaspoon **cinnamon.** Mold into crescents and place
on greased baking sheets.

Bake.........at 350° for 12 to 16 minutes.

For use with Pillsbury's Best Self-Rising Flour, omit salt.

Filled Bee Hives

Filled Bee Hives
Senior Winner by Mrs. E. Mied, Chicago, Illinois

Here are rich tender cookies that are a real conversation piece to serve. Wind pencil-slim strips of dough around filling for the bee hive effect.

BAKE at 350° for 25 to 30 minutes   MAKES 3 dozen

Sift together . . 2 cups sifted **Pillsbury's Best All Purpose Flour*** and
    ¼ teaspoon **salt** into large mixing bowl.
Cut in . . . . . . ⅔ cup **butter** or margarine until particles are fine.
Stir in . . . . . . ⅔ cup sifted **confectioners' sugar** and
    1 teaspoon grated **lemon rind**
Add . . . . .1 unbeaten **egg**
    1 tablespoon light **cream** and

1 teaspoon **vanilla**; mix well. Form into a ball.
Roll out . . . . . . .one-fourth of dough on floured surface to ⅛-inch
    thickness. Cut with 1½-inch round cutter. Place on
    greased baking sheets. Top each with a teaspoonful
    of Apple-Nut Filling.
Roll . . . . .remaining dough into pencil-like strips, 8 inches
    long and ¼-inch thick.
Wind . . . . .one strip in spiral fashion around Filling of each
    cookie, beginning at the base and gradually bringing
    to close at top.
Bake . . . . .at 350° for 25 to 30 minutes.

*For use with Pillsbury's Best Self-Rising Flour, omit salt; decrease baking time to 20 to 25 minutes.

APPLE-NUT FILLING

Combine ¾ cup applesauce, ½ cup pecans (finely chopped), 1 teaspoon grated lemon rind, ½ teaspoon vanilla, ½ teaspoon cinnamon and sugar to taste.

Peppermint Candy Cookies
Senior Winner by Mrs. Warren L. Jacques, Dayton, Ohio

There's a surprise peppermint filling inside each tender butter cookie. Crushed peppermint stick candy gives the crunchy coating.

BAKE at 350° for 12 to 15 minutes   MAKES about 3½ dozen

Cream . . . . . . .1 cup soft **butter** or margarine. Add
    ½ cup sifted **confectioners' sugar** and
    1 teaspoon **vanilla**, creaming well.
Blend in . . . .2½ cups sifted **Pillsbury's Best All Purpose Flour*** and

½ cup **walnuts** or other nuts, chopped fine. Mix thoroughly. Cover; prepare Peppermint Fudge Filling.

Shape . . . . dough by rounded teaspoonfuls into balls. Make a deep hole in center of each, and fill with about ¼ teaspoon of Filling. Reshape and seal. Place on ungreased baking sheets.

Bake . . . . at 350° for 12 to 15 minutes. *Do not brown.* While warm, roll in remainder of peppermint candy-sugar mixture. Cool; reroll in candy mixture.

Pillsbury's Best Self-Rising Flour may be substituted.

PEPPERMINT FUDGE FILLING

Combine . . . . ½ cup (¼ lb.) crushed **peppermint stick candy** and ½ cup sifted **confectioners' sugar.** Set aside.

Blend . . . . 1 ounce (2 tablespoons) **cream cheese** with 1 teaspoon **milk** until smooth and creamy.

Add . . . . ½ cup sifted **confectioners' sugar** gradually; add 3 tablespoons of the peppermint candy-sugar mixture and 1 drop **red food coloring.** Mix well.

Chewy Cranberry Gingers

Junior Winner by Carole Ballweber, Randolph, Nebraska

Cranberry sauce in a chewy ginger cookie.

BAKE at 375° for 12 to 15 minutes   MAKES 4 dozen

Sift together 2⅛ cups sifted **Pillsbury's Best All Purpose Flour***
2 teaspoons **soda**
½ teaspoon **salt**
1 teaspoon **cinnamon** and

Peppermint Candy Cookies

½ teaspoon **ginger.** Set aside.

Add . . . . 1 cup **sugar** gradually to ¾ cup **shortening,** creaming well.

Blend in . . . . . 1 unbeaten **egg** and ¼ cup **molasses;** beat well. Add the dry ingredients gradually, mixing thoroughly.

Stir in . . . . . . ½ cup **whole cranberry sauce.** Chill overnight. Dough will be soft.

Drop . . . . by rounded teaspoonfuls into **sugar;** coat thoroughly. Form into balls; place 3 inches apart on greased baking sheets.

Bake . . . . at 375° for 12 to 15 minutes.

*For use with Pillsbury's Best Self-Rising Flour, decrease soda to 1 teaspoon and omit salt.

Jamerangs

Jamerangs

Junior Winner by Mrs. Mary Rosenfeldt, Kenosha, Wisconsin

Meringue-topped butter cookies with an apricot jam filling . . . chewy and rich . . . you'll serve these with pride!

BAKE at 350° for 12 to 15 minutes   MAKES about 3 dozen

Sift together 1⅛ cups (1 cup plus 2 tablespoons) sifted **Pillsbury's Best All Purpose Flour*** and
　　　　　　 1 teaspoon double-acting **baking powder**
Cream . . . . . . ⅓ cup **butter** or margarine. Gradually add
　　　　　　 ½ cup **sugar,** creaming well.
Blend in . . . . 1 unbeaten **egg yolk** (reserving egg white)
　　　　　　 1 tablespoon **cream** and

½ teaspoon **vanilla**
Add . . . . .the dry ingredients; mix thoroughly.
Shape . . . . .by teaspoonfuls into balls. Place on greased baking
　　　　　　 sheets; flatten to ¼-inch thickness.
Combine . . . . .⅓ cup **apricot preserves** and
　　　　　　 1 teaspoon **lemon juice;** place ½ teaspoonful on each
　　　　　　 cookie. Top with a teaspoonful of Meringue, covering
　　　　　　 jam completely.
Bake . . . . .at 350° for 12 to 15 minutes.
*For use with Pillsbury's Best Self-Rising Flour, omit baking powder.

MERINGUE

Beat 1 egg white until soft mounds form. Gradually add 5 tablespoons sugar; continue beating until meringue stands in stiff, glossy peaks. Fold in ½ teaspoon cinnamon and ⅓ cup chopped walnuts.

Orange Nut Goodies

Senior Winner by Mrs. Allan Schneider, Minneapolis, Minnesota

Filled or plain . . . orange-flavored nut-topped butter cookies shaped into delectable rounds.

BAKE at 350° for 15 to 18 minutes   MAKES about 5 dozen

Sift together . .3 cups sifted **Pillsbury's Best All Purpose Flour***
　　　　　　 ½ teaspoon double-acting **baking powder** and
　　　　　　 ½ teaspoon **salt**
Cream . . . . . . .1 cup **butter** or margarine. Gradually add
　　　　　　 ¾ cup **sugar,** creaming well.
Stir in . . . . . . .1 unbeaten **egg**
　　　　　　 1 tablespoon grated **orange rind**
　　　　　　 1 teaspoon **vanilla**
　　　　　　 1 teaspoon **orange extract** and
　　　　　　 3 to 4 drops **orange food coloring;** mix well.
Add . . . . .the dry ingredients; blend thoroughly.
Shape . . . . .by rounded teaspoonfuls into balls. Press deep hole

in center; fill with ½ teaspoonful Fruit Filling. Seal, reshaping cookie into ball. If desired, dip half of each ball in

1 slightly beaten **egg white**, then into

1 cup **pecans**, finely chopped. Place nut-side up on ungreased baking sheet.

Bake . . . . at 350° for 15 to 18 minutes.

For use with Pillsbury's Best Self-Rising Flour, omit baking powder and salt.

FRUIT FILLING

Grind 1 cup raisins and ½ cup pecans. Combine with ½ cup sifted confectioners' sugar, 1½ teaspoons cinnamon, 2 teaspoons grated orange rind and 1 to 2 tablespoons orange juice.

Frosty Anise Rosettes

Senior Winner by Mrs. C. L. Comstock, Millbrae, California

Anise seed and lemon flavor these festive cookies which have a frosty glaze.

BAKE at 400° for 8 to 10 minutes   MAKES about 3½ dozen

Sift together . .3 cups sifted **Pillsbury's Best All Purpose Flour***
               2½ teaspoons double-acting **baking powder**
               ½ teaspoon **salt** and
               ¼ teaspoon **soda**

Blend . . . . ¼ cup **shortening** with
               ½ cup **sugar**, creaming well.

Stir in . . . . . . .3 unbeaten **eggs**
               2 tablespoons **anise seed**
               1 teaspoon grated **lemon rind**
               1½ tablespoons **lemon juice** and
               1 teaspoon **anise extract**, if desired. Beat well.

Add . . . . .2 cups of the dry ingredients gradually, beating at low speed of electric mixer. Stir in remaining dry .ingredients with spoon.

Knead . . . . .on floured surface for 1 minute until well blended.

Frosty Anise Rosettes

Divide . . . . .dough into eight equal parts. Roll each into a strip ½-inch thick and 20 inches long; cut into five 4-inch pieces.

Slit . . . . .each piece half way through along one side at ½-inch intervals. Seal ends together to form a circle, cut-side out. Place on greased baking sheet.

Bake . . . . .at 400° for 8 to 10 minutes. *Do not brown.* Cool. Dip tops of cookies into Sugar Glaze, allowing it to drip down sides. Decorate with **colored sugars** or **candies**.

For use with Pillsbury's Best Self-Rising Flour, omit baking powder and salt.

SUGAR GLAZE

Blend together 3 cups sifted confectioners' sugar and ⅓ cup hot milk. Thin with a few drops milk, if necessary.

Nutmeg Cookie Logs

Nutmeg Cookie Logs

Senior Winner by Mrs. Robert J. Woods, South Charleston, West Virginia

Nutmeg, vanilla and rum flavoring blend in easy cookies you'll like for holidays . . . they're shaped and frosted to resemble logs!

BAKE at 350° for 12 to 15 minutes   MAKES about 8 dozen

Sift together..3 cups sifted **Pillsbury's Best All Purpose Flour*** and
1 teaspoon **nutmeg**
Cream.......1 cup **butter** or margarine with
2 teaspoons **vanilla** and
2 teaspoons **rum flavoring**. Gradually add
¾ cup **sugar**, creaming well.
Blend in.....1 unbeaten **egg**. Add the dry ingredients gradually; mix thoroughly.

Shape........pieces of dough on lightly floured surface into long rolls, ½ inch in diameter. Cut into 3-inch lengths; place on ungreased baking sheets.
Bake.........at 350° for 12 to 15 minutes. Cool; frost. Mark Frosting with tines of fork to resemble bark. Sprinkle with **nutmeg.**

**Pillsbury's Best Self-Rising Flour may be substituted.*

FROSTING

Cream 3 tablespoons butter, ½ teaspoon vanilla and 1 teaspoon rum flavoring. Add 2½ cups sifted confectioners' sugar alternately with 2 to 3 tablespoons cream, beating until of spreading consistency.

Sugared Cashew Crisps

Senior Winner by Mrs. Gust J. Polzin, Bloomer, Wisconsin

Crisp and crunchy cookies with sugared cashews inside and a sparkling sugary topping.

BAKE at 350° for 12 to 15 minutes   MAKES about 5 dozen

Combine....½ cup firmly packed **brown sugar** and
¼ cup **water** in saucepan. Cook until a little syrup dropped in cold water forms a firm soft ball (240°). Remove from heat.
Add.........1 cup **cashews,** chopped. Stir until mixture becomes sugary and cream colored. Spread on greased baking sheet. Cool.
Sift together..3 cups sifted **Pillsbury's Best All Purpose Flour***
1 teaspoon **soda** and
½ teaspoon **salt**
Cream......½ cup **butter** or margarine and
½ cup **shortening**. Gradually add
¾ cup **sugar** and
½ cup firmly packed **brown sugar,** creaming well.
Blend in.....2 unbeaten **eggs**

2 tablespoons **water** and
1 teaspoon **vanilla;** beat well.

Stir in . . . . the dry ingredients gradually, mixing thoroughly.

Break . . . . the cashew mixture into small pieces; stir into dough. Cover and chill 2 hours.

Shape . . . . dough by rounded teaspoonfuls into balls. Dip tops in cold **water,** then into mixture of
⅓ cup **cashews,** chopped or ground, and
⅓ cup **sugar**

Place . . . . on greased baking sheets, sugar-side up. Flatten slightly.

Bake . . . . at 350° for 12 to 15 minutes. Cool 1 minute before removing from baking sheets.

For use with Pillsbury's Best Self-Rising Flour, omit soda and salt.

Coconut Sunbeams

Senior Winner by Mrs. Joe Boyden, Delta, Colorado

An apricot glaze and coconut top these golden orange-flavored butter cookies.

BAKE at 375° for 12 to 15 minutes   MAKES about 3½ dozen

Sift together . . 2 cups sifted **Pillsbury's Best All Purpose Flour***
½ cup **sugar**
½ teaspoon double-acting **baking powder** and
¼ teaspoon **salt** into large mixing bowl.

Cut in . . . . . . ¾ cup **butter** or margarine until particles are fine.

Blend . . . . 1 **egg yolk** and
1 **egg** with
2 teaspoons grated **orange rind** and
2 tablespoons **orange juice**

Sprinkle . . . . egg mixture over flour mixture, stirring with fork until mixture forms a dough. Chill for easier handling, if desired.

Shape . . . . by rounded teaspoonfuls into balls. Place on un-

greased baking sheets. Flatten to slightly less than ½-inch thickness with floured fork. Press **raisin** into center of each.

Bake . . . . at 375° for 12 to 15 minutes. Cool. Spread Apricot Glaze on tops of cookies, then dip into
2 cups finely cut **coconut**

For use with Pillsbury's Best Self-Rising Flour, omit baking powder and salt.

APRICOT GLAZE

Combine ½ cup sugar, ⅓ cup apricot preserves, 1 tablespoon orange juice and 3 tablespoons water in saucepan. Boil 3 minutes. Cool.

Coconut Honey Balls

Senior Winner by Mrs. Shirley Ravelle, Honolulu, Hawaii

Have a Hawaiian holiday; serve these rich butter cookies topped with a honey-pineapple glaze.

BAKE at 350° for 15 to 18 minutes   MAKES about 6 dozen

Cream . . . . 1 cup **butter** or margarine. Gradually add
½ cup **sugar**
1 teaspoon **vanilla** and
1 teaspoon **almond extract,** creaming well.

Add . . . . 2 cups sifted **Pillsbury's Best All Purpose Flour***
1 cup **pecans,** finely chopped, and
1 cup flaked or chopped shredded **coconut;** mix well.

Shape . . . . by teaspoonfuls into balls. Place on ungreased baking sheets.

Bake . . . . at 350° for 15 to 18 minutes. If desired, dip warm cookies into Pineapple Glaze.

Pillsbury's Best Self-Rising Flour may be substituted.

PINEAPPLE GLAZE

Combine ½ cup honey, ⅓ cup pineapple juice, 2 teaspoons vinegar and 2 tablespoons butter. Simmer 5 minutes. Cool to lukewarm.

Honey Spice Snaps

Junior Winner by Gary Woller, Hamburg, Wisconsin

Crinkle-topped and crunchy—these honey spice cookies resemble gingersnaps. Attractive and perfect for the cookie jar.

BAKE at 350° for 12 to 15 minutes   MAKES about 4 dozen

Sift together 2¼ cups sifted **Pillsbury's Best All Purpose Flour***
          1½ teaspoons **soda**
          ½ teaspoon **salt**
          1 teaspoon **ginger**
          ½ teaspoon **cinnamon** and
          ¼ teaspoon **cloves**. Set aside.
Add . . . . 1 cup firmly packed **brown sugar** gradually to
          ¾ cup **shortening**, creaming well.
Blend in . . . . . 1 unbeaten **egg** and
          ¼ cup **honey**; beat well. Add the dry ingredients

Honey Spice Snaps

gradually; mix thoroughly. Chill for easier handling.
Shape . . . . by rounded teaspoonfuls into balls. Dip half of each in water, then in **sugar**. Place sugar-side up on ungreased baking sheets.
Bake . . . . at 350° for 12 to 15 minutes.
For use with Pillsbury's Best Self-Rising Flour, omit soda and salt.

Oriental Tea Treats

Senior Winner by Mrs. John Zettel, Pacific Palisades, California

Crisp and chewy brown sugar cookies with an Oriental accent from almonds, candied ginger and tea.

BAKE at 350° for 12 to 15 minutes   MAKES about 5 dozen

Chop . . . . 1 cup blanched **almonds** and
          ¼ cup **candied ginger** very fine.
Sift together 2¾ cups sifted **Pillsbury's Best All Purpose Flour***
          ½ teaspoon **soda** and
          ¼ teaspoon **salt**
Cream . . . . . . ½ cup **shortening** with
          ½ cup **butter** or margarine. Gradually add
          1¾ cups firmly packed **brown sugar**, creaming well.
Add . . . . the dry ingredients alternately with
          ¼ cup lukewarm strong **tea**.** Blend thoroughly.
Stir in . . . . 1 teaspoon **vanilla** and the almond mixture.
Shape . . . . by rounded teaspoonfuls into balls. Place on ungreased baking sheets.
Bake . . . . at 350° for 12 to 15 minutes.

For use with Pillsbury's Best Self-Rising Flour, decrease soda to ¼ teaspoon and omit salt.

**If desired, ¼ cup water may be substituted for tea.*

Almond Crunch Cookies

Senior Winner by Mrs. S. Arthur Solga, Arlington, Virginia

Almonds flavor these crisp brown sugar cookies; an almond goes on top.

BAKE at 400° for 8 to 10 minutes   MAKES 5 dozen

Sift together . . 3 cups sifted **Pillsbury's Best All Purpose Flour***
    1 teaspoon **soda**
    1 teaspoon **salt** and
    ½ teaspoon **cream of tartar**. Set aside.

Add . . . . 1 cup **sugar** and
    1 cup firmly packed **brown sugar** gradually to
    ¾ cup **shortening** (half butter may be used) ; cream well.

Blend in . . . . . 2 unbeaten **eggs** and
    1 teaspoon **vanilla**

Add . . . . the dry ingredients gradually and
    ½ cup **almonds**, finely chopped. Mix thoroughly.

Shape . . . . by rounded teaspoonfuls into balls. Place on greased
    baking sheets; flatten to ¼ inch. Top each with an
    almond half, if desired.

Bake . . . . at 400° for 8 to 10 minutes.

For use with Pillsbury's Best Self-Rising Flour, decrease soda to ½ teaspoon and omit salt.

Praline Butter Nuggets

Senior Winner by Mrs. John Maxwell, Fort Smith, Arkansas

There are bits of pecan candy throughout these rich cookies. Delicious!

BAKE at 300° for 20 to 25 minutes   MAKES 2 dozen

Melt . . . . ¼ cup **sugar** in heavy skillet over low heat until golden
    brown.

Add . . . . ¼ cup **pecan halves**. Pour on greased waxed paper.
    Cool. Chop fine when hard.

Sift together 1½ cups sifted **Pillsbury's Best All Purpose Flour*** and

    ½ teaspoon **salt**

Cream . . . . . . ⅛ cup **butter** or margarine and
    ⅛ cup **shortening**. Add
    ¼ cup firmly packed **brown sugar**, creaming well.

Blend in . . . . . . the dry ingredients
    1 teaspoon **vanilla** and the pecan-sugar candy.

Shape . . . . by rounded teaspoonfuls into balls. Place on un-
    greased baking sheets.

Bake . . . . at 300° for 20 to 25 minutes. Roll in **confectioners'
    sugar** while warm.

For use with Pillsbury's Best Self-Rising Flour, omit salt.

Toffee Topper Cookies

Junior Winner by Ginny Ohara, Walnut Grove, California

The crunchy top on these brown sugar cookies is crushed toffee candy.

BAKE at 400° for 8 to 10 minutes   MAKES about 3½ dozen

Crush . . . . 4 ounces (¾ cup) brittle **butter toffee candy**

Sift together . . 2 cups sifted **Pillsbury's Best All Purpose Flour***
    1 teaspoon **soda** and
    ½ teaspoon **salt**

Cream . . . . . . ¾ cup **butter** or margarine. Gradually add
    1 cup firmly packed **brown sugar** and
    ¼ cup **sugar**, creaming well.

Blend in . . . . . 1 unbeaten **egg** and
    1½ teaspoons **vanilla**; beat well. Add the dry ingredients
    gradually, mixing thoroughly.

Shape . . . . by rounded teaspoonfuls into balls; place 3 inches
    apart on greased baking sheets. Flatten to about
    ½-inch thickness.

Cover . . . . each with about ½ teaspoon crushed candy.

Bake . . . . at 400° for 8 to 10 minutes. Remove from baking
    sheets immediately.

For use with Pillsbury's Best Self-Rising Flour, omit soda and salt.

Peanut Blossoms

Senior Winner by Mrs. Chester Smith, Gibsonburg, Ohio

A chocolate candy kiss on each one gives you an extra-special peanut butter cookie.

BAKE at 375° for 10 minutes, then   MAKES about 3 dozen
      for 2 to 5 minutes

Sift together 1¾ cups sifted **Pillsbury's Best All Purpose Flour***
      1 teaspoon **soda** and
      ½ teaspoon **salt**
Cream . . . . . . ½ cup **shortening** with
      ½ cup **peanut butter.** Gradually add
      ½ cup **sugar** and
      ½ cup firmly packed **brown sugar,** creaming well.
Blend in . . . . . 1 unbeaten **egg** and
      1 teaspoon **vanilla**; beat well. Add the dry ingredients;
      mix thoroughly.
Shape . . . . by rounded teaspoonfuls into balls. Roll in **sugar;**
      place on greased baking sheets.
Bake . . . . at 375° for 10 minutes. Remove from oven. Top each
      with a **solid milk chocolate candy kiss,** pressing
      down firmly so cookie cracks around edge. Return
      to oven; bake 2 to 5 minutes longer.

*For use with Pillsbury's Best Self-Rising Flour, omit soda and salt.

Brazilian Jubilee Cookies

Senior Winner by Mrs. F. H. Speers, Midland, Texas

Brazil nuts and instant coffee flavor these cookies; then frost by placing pieces of chocolate onto cookies while they are hot.

BAKE at 350° for 12 to 15 minutes   MAKES about 3 dozen

Sift together 1½ cups sifted **Pillsbury's Best All Purpose Flour***
      1 teaspoon double-acting **baking powder**

Peanut Blossoms

½ teaspoon **salt**
½ teaspoon **cinnamon** and
1 to 2 tablespoons **instant coffee.** Set aside.

Add........¾ cup **sugar** and
¼ cup firmly packed **brown sugar** gradually to
½ cup **shortening,** creaming well.

Blend in.....1 unbeaten **egg** and
2 teaspoons **vanilla;** beat well.

Chop........1 cup **Brazil nuts.** (Reserve ¼ cup to garnish cookies.)

Blend........remaining nuts and the dry ingredients into creamed mixture, mixing thoroughly.

Shape........by tablespoonfuls into balls. Place on greased baking sheets.

Bake........at 350° for 12 to 15 minutes. Remove from oven; top with a **solid milk chocolate candy kiss** or 5 semi-sweet chocolate pieces. When chocolate has softened, spread to frost. Sprinkle with reserved nuts.

For use with Pillsbury's Best Self-Rising Flour, omit baking powder and salt.

Starlight Mint Surprise Cookies

Second Prize Winner by Miss Laura Rott, Naperville, Illinois

A solid chocolate candy wafer flavored with mint is baked right in the cookie itself. What a luscious surprise when you take a bite!

BAKE at 375° for 9 to 12 minutes   MAKES 4½ dozen

Sift together..3 cups sifted **Pillsbury's Best All Purpose Flour***
1 teaspoon **soda** and
½ teaspoon **salt**

Cream........1 cup **butter** or margarine (half shortening may be used). Gradually add
1 cup **sugar** and
½ cup firmly packed **brown sugar,** creaming well.

Blend in.....2 unbeaten **eggs** and
1 teaspoon **vanilla.** Add the dry ingredients gradually;

mix well. Chill at least 2 hours.**

Open.......1 package (9 oz.) solid **chocolate mint candy wafers.** To shape cookies, enclose each wafer in a rounded teaspoonful of dough. Place on ungreased baking sheets.

Top.........each with a **walnut half.**

Bake........at 375° for 9 to 12 minutes.

For use with Pillsbury's Best Self-Rising Flour, omit soda and salt.

**Refrigerator cookies may also be made. Shape dough into rolls, 1½ inches in diameter. Wrap in waxed paper; chill 4 hours or overnight. Cut in slices ⅛ inch thick; place on ungreased baking sheets. Top with chocolate wafers. Cover with additional slices of dough; seal edges. Top with walnut halves.*

Maple Peanut Yummies

Junior Winner by Judith Korbey, Methuen, Massachusetts

Better than ever peanut butter cookies .. maple syrup is the difference.

BAKE at 350° for 12 to 15 minutes   MAKES 3½ dozen

Sift together 1¾ cups sifted **Pillsbury's Best All Purpose Flour***
½ teaspoon **soda**
½ teaspoon **salt** and
¼ teaspoon double-acting **baking powder**

Cream......½ cup **shortening** with
½ cup **peanut butter.** Add
½ cup firmly packed **brown sugar,** creaming well.

Blend in.....½ cup **maple syrup** and
1 unbeaten **egg yolk.** Add the dry ingredients gradually; mix thoroughly.

Shape........by rounded teaspoonfuls into balls. Place on ungreased baking sheets; flatten with fork.

Bake........at 350° for 12 to 15 minutes.

For use with Pillsbury's Best Self-Rising Flour, omit soda, salt, baking powder.

Peanut Butter Apple Cookies

Senior Winner by Mrs. Clara B. Walker, La Grande, Oregon

Grated fresh apple adds an interesting touch to these simply-prepared cookies.

BAKE at 375° for 12 to 15 minutes   MAKES 4 dozen

Sift together 1¾ cups sifted **Pillsbury's Best All Purpose Flour***
         ½ teaspoon **soda**
         ½ teaspoon **salt** and
         ½ teaspoon **cinnamon**
Cream......½ cup **shortening** and
         ½ cup **peanut butter.** Gradually add
         ½ cup **sugar** and
         ½ cup firmly packed **brown sugar,** creaming well.
Blend in.....1 unbeaten **egg**
         ½ teaspoon **vanilla** and
         ½ cup grated raw **apple**
Add..........the dry ingredients; mix thoroughly. Chill.
Shape........by rounded teaspoonfuls into balls. Place on greased baking sheets. Flatten with fork.
Bake.........at 375° for 12 to 15 minutes.
*For use with Pillsbury's Best Self-Rising Flour, omit soda and salt.

Cindy's Sesame Crisps

Senior Winner by Miss Hazel Norton Spence, St. Petersburg, Florida

Crisp yet tender, these cookies are rich with butter, sesame seeds and brown sugar.

BAKE at 350° for 10 to 13 minutes   MAKES about 4 dozen

Toast.......¾ cup (two 2¼-oz. pkgs.) **sesame seeds** and
         ½ cup **coconut** at 350° for 5 to 8 minutes until light golden brown, stirring occasionally.
Sift together..2 cups sifted **Pillsbury's Best All Purpose Flour***
         1 teaspoon double-acting **baking powder**
         ½ teaspoon **soda** and
         ½ teaspoon **salt**
Cream......¾ cup **butter** (half shortening may be used). Gradually add
         1 cup firmly packed **brown sugar,** creaming well.
Blend in.....1 unbeaten **egg**
         1 teaspoon **vanilla,** the sesame seeds and coconut; beat well.
Add..........the dry ingredients gradually; mix thoroughly. Chill ½ to 1 hour for easier handling.
Shape........by rounded teaspoonfuls into balls. Place 3 inches apart on ungreased baking sheets; flatten to ⅛-inch thickness.
Bake.........at 350° for 10 to 13 minutes.
*For use with Pillsbury's Best Self-Rising Flour, omit baking powder, soda, salt.

Sesame Surprise Cookies

Senior Winner by Sophia D. Eaton, Williamsburg, Massachusetts

Snappy sugar-coated cookies with sesame seed flavor and a surprise fudge filling.

BAKE at 400° for 12 to 15 minutes   MAKES about 5 dozen

Toast........2 tablespoons **sesame seeds** at 350° for 5 to 8 minutes until light golden brown, stirring occasionally.

Sift together 3½ cups sifted **Pillsbury's Best All Purpose Flour***
½ teaspoon double-acting **baking powder** and
1 teaspoon **salt.** Set aside.

Add . . . . 1 cup firmly packed **brown sugar** gradually to
1 cup **shortening,** creaming well.

Blend in . . . . . 2 unbeaten **eggs** and
1 teaspoon **vanilla**; beat well. Add the dry ingredients
gradually; mix thoroughly.

Stir in . . . . the toasted sesame seeds.

Shape . . . . by rounded teaspoonfuls into balls. Press deep hole
in center and fill with ½ teaspoonful Chocolate
Fudge Filling. Seal tops and roll cookies in **sugar.**
Place on greased baking sheets.

Bake . . . . at 400° for 12 to 15 minutes.

For use with Pillsbury's Best Self-Rising Flour, omit baking powder and salt.

CHOCOLATE FUDGE FILLING

Melt 1 cup semi-sweet chocolate pieces over boiling water. Remove
from heat. Stir in ⅓ cup sweetened condensed milk, 1½ tablespoons
water, ½ teaspoon vanilla, ¼ teaspoon salt and 1½ teaspoons grated
orange rind, if desired.

Calypso Dips

Senior Winner by Mrs. Harold Smith, Dixon, Illinois

*Perfect for any cookie tray. Coffee-flavored sticks tipped with chocolate
and nuts are fun to eat.*

BAKE at 375° for 12 to 15 minutes   MAKES about 3 dozen

Sift together . . 2 cups sifted **Pillsbury's Best All Purpose Flour***
½ teaspoon double-acting **baking powder** and
½ teaspoon **salt**

Cream . . . . . . ½ cup **butter** or margarine. Gradually add
¾ cup firmly packed **brown sugar,** creaming well.

Add . . . . ¼ cup **cream**

Calypso Dips

2 teaspoons **instant coffee** and
¼ teaspoon **black walnut flavoring,** if desired.

Blend in . . . . the dry ingredients. Chill at least 1 hour.

Shape . . . . into sticks 3 inches long and ½ inch in diameter.
Place on ungreased baking sheets.

Bake . . . . at 375° for 12 to 15 minutes. Cool. Dip one end of
each stick into Chocolate Frosting, then into
¾ cup **nuts,** finely chopped. If frosting becomes too
stiff, reheat over hot water.

Pillsbury's Best Self-Rising Flour is not recommended for use in this recipe.

CHOCOLATE FROSTING

Melt ½ cup semi-sweet chocolate pieces, 2 tablespoons sugar, 2
tablespoons water and ½ teaspoon rum flavoring in top of double
boiler over boiling water.

Butter Pecan Crunchies

Senior Winner by Mrs. James H. Hunter, Stillwater, Maine

A brown sugar-butter cookie with lots of pecans. Top these golden rounds with a simple milk chocolate frosting.

BAKE at 375° for 10 to 12 minutes   MAKES 4 dozen

Blend . . . . 2 tablespoons **butter** with
½ cup firmly packed **brown sugar.** Add
1 cup **pecans,** chopped
Sift together . . 2 cups sifted **Pillsbury's Best All Purpose Flour*** and
½ teaspoon double-acting **baking powder**
Cream . . . . . . ½ cup **butter** or margarine. Gradually add
1¼ cups firmly packed **brown sugar,** creaming well.
Blend in . . . . . 1 unbeaten **egg**
½ teaspoon **vanilla** and
½ teaspoon **rum flavoring.** Add the dry ingredients; mix well.
Stir in . . . . pecan mixture just until evenly distributed.
Shape . . . . by rounded teaspoonfuls into balls. Place on greased baking sheets; flatten slightly.
Bake . . . . at 375° for 10 to 12 minutes. Cool; frost with Milk Chocolate Frosting.

*For use with Pillsbury's Best Self-Rising Flour, omit baking powder; chill dough 1 to 2 hours before shaping.

MILK CHOCOLATE FROSTING

Melt ½ cup semi-sweet chocolate pieces over hot water. Blend in ¼ cup sweetened condensed milk. Thin with a few drops milk, if necessary.

Snappy Turtle Cookies‡

Grand Prize Winner by Mrs. Peter S. Harlib, Chicago, Illinois

Chocolate, nuts and a rich brown sugar cookie in an entertaining and unusual shape. A snap to make!

BAKE at 350° for 10 to 13 minutes   MAKES 2½ dozen

Sift together 1½ cups sifted **Pillsbury's Best All Purpose Flour***
¼ teaspoon **soda** and
¼ teaspoon **salt**
Cream . . . . . ½ cup **butter** or margarine. Gradually add
½ cup firmly packed **brown sugar,** creaming well.
Add . . . . 1 unbeaten **egg** and
1 **egg yolk** (reserve egg white); beat well.
Blend in . . . . ¼ teaspoon **vanilla** and
⅛ teaspoon **maple flavoring,** if desired.
Add . . . . the dry ingredients; mix thoroughly. Chill, if desired.
Arrange . . . . split **pecan halves** in groups of three or five on greased baking sheets to resemble head and legs of a turtle.
Shape . . . . by rounded teaspoonfuls into balls; dip bottoms into unbeaten **egg white** and press lightly onto nuts so tips of nuts show.
Bake . . . . at 350° for 10 to 13 minutes. Cool; frost tops with Chocolate Frosting.

*For use with Pillsbury's Best Self-Rising Flour, omit soda and salt.

CHOCOLATE FROSTING

Melt 2 squares (2 oz.) unsweetened chocolate or ⅓ cup semi-sweet chocolate pieces in ¼ cup milk and 1 tablespoon butter in top of double boiler over boiling water; blend until smooth. Remove from heat; add 1 cup sifted confectioners' sugar. Beat until smooth and glossy. If too thin, add additional confectioners' sugar until of desired consistency.

‡Not to be confused with "Turtles" brand candies made exclusively by DeMet's, Inc., of Chicago, Illinois.

BEST
of the
BAKE-OFF

Snappy Turtle
Cookies
Grand Prize Winner
of the Fourth
Grand National
Bake-Off®

Lemon Angel Halos

Lemon Angel Halos

Senior Winner by Mrs. James J. O'Brien, Vista, California

Crispy cookies with meringue crowns and dots of lemon filling.

BAKE at 300° for 12 to 15 minutes   MAKES about 7 dozen

Sift together . . 2 cups sifted **Pillsbury's Best All Purpose Flour***
          1 teaspoon **soda** and
          1 teaspoon **salt.** Set aside.
Add . . . . 1 cup firmly packed **brown sugar** gradually to
          ⅔ cup **shortening,** creaming well.
Blend in . . . . . 1 teaspoon **vanilla** and
          1 unbeaten **egg.** Add the dry ingredients gradually;
          mix thoroughly. Chill at least 1 hour. Meanwhile

prepare Lemon Filling, then Meringue.
Shape . . . . by level teaspoonfuls into balls. Place on ungreased
          baking sheets. Flatten to ⅛-inch thickness.
Place . . . . a rounded teaspoonful of Meringue on each cookie.
          Form a hollow in the center of each, using back of
          teaspoon dipped in cold water.
Bake . . . . at 300° for 12 to 15 minutes. Cool; fill hollow with
          ½ teaspoon Filling. (Fill cookies as needed, re-
          frigerating unused Filling.)

**For use with Pillsbury's Best Self-Rising Flour, decrease soda to ½ teaspoon
and omit salt.*

LEMON FILLING

Combine in saucepan 1 cup sugar, 1 teaspoon grated lemon rind,
¼ cup lemon juice and 3 slightly beaten egg yolks. Heat to boiling,
stirring constantly. Remove from heat. Add 3 tablespoons butter;
cover and cool.

MERINGUE

Beat 3 egg whites until slight mounds form. Gradually add ¾ cup
sugar, beating until mixture stands in stiff, glossy peaks. Blend in 2
teaspoons lemon juice; beat until mixture again forms stiff peaks.

Meringue-Topped Almondettes

Junior Winner by Kay McIntosh, St. Joseph, Louisiana

*Coconut-almond meringue atop these cookies adds a real party touch . . .
the brown sugar dough contains almonds and coconut too.*

BAKE at 375° for 12 to 15 minutes   MAKES 4½ dozen

Sift together . . 2 cups sifted **Pillsbury's Best All Purpose Flour***
          ¾ teaspoon **salt** and
          ½ teaspoon **soda**
Cream . . . . . . ¼ cup **butter** or margarine with
          ½ cup **shortening.** Gradually add

⅔ cup **sugar** and
⅓ cup firmly packed **brown sugar,** creaming well.

Add . . . . .2 **egg yolks** (reserve egg whites)
1 tablespoon light **cream** and
1 teaspoon **almond extract;** beat well.

Blend in . . . . . . .the dry ingredients gradually; mix well.

Stir in . . . . . . ½ cup blanched **almonds,** finely chopped, and
½ cup flaked or chopped shredded **coconut**

Shape . . . . .by rounded teaspoonfuls into balls; place on greased baking sheets. Flatten to ½-inch thickness with floured bottom of glass.

Top . . . . .each with a rounded teaspoonful of Almond Meringue.

Bake . . . . .at 375° for 12 to 15 minutes.

For use with Pillsbury's Best Self-Rising Flour, omit salt and soda.

ALMOND MERINGUE

Beat 2 egg whites and ¼ teaspoon salt until soft mounds form. Gradually add ⅓ cup sugar, beating well after each addition. Beat until meringue stands in stiff, glossy peaks. Fold in ½ teaspoon almond extract, 1 cup blanched almonds, finely chopped, and 1 cup chopped coconut.

Caramel-Nut Acorns

Senior Winner by Mrs. Cecil Buzek, Cincinnati, Ohio

A saucepan brown sugar-butter cookie, molded into acorn shape. The bottoms of these crisp cookies are dipped in melted caramels, then in nuts, to complete the acorn.

BAKE at 350° for 15 to 18 minutes   MAKES about 4½ dozen

Sift together 2½ cups sifted **Pillsbury's Best All Purpose Flour*** and
½ teaspoon double-acting **baking powder**

Melt . . . . .1 cup **butter** or margarine in saucepan over low heat. Remove from heat.

Stir in . . . . . . ¾ cup firmly packed **brown sugar**

Caramel-Nut Acorns

1 teaspoon **vanilla** and
⅓ cup **pecans,** finely chopped. Add the dry ingredients; blend well.

Shape . . . . .by rounded teaspoonfuls into balls. Flatten one side by pressing on ungreased baking sheet; pinch top to a point to resemble an acorn.

Bake . . . . .at 350° for 15 to 18 minutes. Cool.

Melt . . . . .½ pound (24) **candy caramels** and
¼ cup **water** in top of double boiler.

Dip . . . . .flat ends of cookies into caramel mixture, about ¼ inch deep, then into
¾ cup finely chopped **pecans**

For use with Pillsbury's Best Self-Rising Flour, omit baking powder and decrease butter 2 tablespoons.

Caramel Cream Sandwich Cookies

Junior Second Prize Winner by Helen Beckman, Mt. Vernon, Iowa

These crisp butter cookies have a delicate caramel flavor. Delicious plain, but real party fare when put together with frosting.

BAKE at 325° for 9 to 12 minutes   MAKES 4 dozen

Cream . . . . . . .1 cup **butter** or margarine. Gradually add
                ¾ cup firmly packed **brown sugar,** creaming well.
Blend in . . . . .1 unbeaten **egg yolk.** Add
                2¼ cups sifted **Pillsbury's Best All Purpose Flour.*** Stir
                until mixture forms a dough. Chill for easier handling.
Shape . . . . .into balls about the size of a marble. Place on un-
                greased baking sheets; flatten to ⅛-inch thickness.
                Mark a design with fork.
Bake . . . . .at 325° for 9 to 12 minutes. Place flat sides of two
                cookies together with Browned Butter Frosting,
                sandwich-style.

*Pillsbury's Best Self-Rising Flour is not recommended for use in this recipe.

BROWNED BUTTER FROSTING

Brown 2 tablespoons butter in saucepan. Remove from heat; blend in 1¼ cups sifted confectioners' sugar. Gradually add ½ teaspoon vanilla and 4 to 5 teaspoons cream until of spreading consistency.

Oatmeal Chip Cookies

Bride Winner by Mrs. Bettye J. Stark, Milwaukee, Wisconsin

Oatmeal cookies with crunchy almonds and chocolate pieces for the cookie snackers in your family.

BAKE at 375° for 9 to 12 minutes   MAKES about 8 dozen

Sift together . .2 cups sifted **Pillsbury's Best All Purpose Flour***
                1 teaspoon **soda** and
                1 teaspoon **salt**

Caramel Cream Sandwich Cookies

Cream . . . . . . ½ cup **butter** or margarine with
½ cup **shortening.** Gradually add
1 cup **sugar** and
1 cup firmly packed **brown sugar,** creaming well.
Blend in . . . . . 2 unbeaten **eggs;** beat well. Add the dry ingredients;
mix thoroughly.
Stir in . . . . 2 cups quick-cooking **rolled oats**
1 cup **almonds,** chopped, and
1 cup (6-oz. pkg.) **semi-sweet chocolate pieces**
Shape . . . . by rounded teaspoonfuls into balls. Place on ungreased baking sheets.
Bake . . . . at 375° for 9 to 12 minutes.

*For use with Pillsbury's Best Self-Rising Flour, increase flour to 2¼ cups;
omit soda and salt.*

Chocolate Twin Dots

Junior Third Prize Winner by Linda C. Martan, Niagara Falls, New York

*Crisp chocolate oatmeal cookies, filled with dates and currants, then
rolled in confectioners' sugar and chopped nuts before baking.*

BAKE at 375° for 10 to 12 minutes   MAKES about 5 dozen

Simmer . . . . . ½ cup **dates,** cut fine, in
¼ cup **water** until soft, 2 to 3 minutes. Cool.
Open . . . . 1 package (6 oz.) **semi-sweet chocolate pieces.** Melt
⅔ cup over hot water. (Reserve remaining ⅓ package.)
Sift together 1½ cups sifted **Pillsbury's Best All Purpose Flour***
1 teaspoon **salt** and
½ teaspoon **soda**
Add . . . . 1½ cups firmly packed **brown sugar** gradually to
¾ cup **shortening,** creaming well.

Chocolate Twin Dots

Stir in . . . . 1 unbeaten **egg**
1 teaspoon **vanilla** and the melted chocolate. Beat well.
Blend in . . . . the dry ingredients gradually.
Stir in . . . . . ½ cup quick-cooking **rolled oats**
1 cup **currants** or raisins and the date mixture. Chill,
if desired, for easier handling.
Drop . . . . by rounded teaspoonfuls into
½ cup sifted **confectioners' sugar.** Coat thoroughly
and form into balls. Dip tops into
½ cup finely chopped **nuts.** Place on greased baking
sheets. Press two chocolate pieces into each cookie.
Bake . . . . at 375° for 10 to 12 minutes. Cool 1 minute before
removing from baking sheets.

For use with Pillsbury's Best Self-Rising Flour, omit salt and soda.

Date-Orange Toppers

Date-Orange Toppers

Bride Winner by Mrs. Jerry Thomas, Kirksville, Missouri

Dates and candy orange slices make up the special topping for these brown sugar oatmeal cookies.

BAKE at 375° for 12 to 15 minutes   MAKES about 3½ dozen

Sift together 1⅔ cups sifted **Pillsbury's Best All Purpose Flour***
             2 teaspoons double-acting **baking powder**
             ½ teaspoon **salt**
             ½ teaspoon **nutmeg** and
             ½ teaspoon **cinnamon.** Set aside.
Add . . . . ⅔ cup firmly packed **brown sugar** gradually to
             ½ cup **shortening,** creaming well.
Blend in . . . . . 1 unbeaten **egg**

             1 teaspoon **vanilla** and
             2 tablespoons light **cream;** beat well. Add the dry ingredients; mix thoroughly.
Stir in . . . . 1 cup quick-cooking **rolled oats.** Chill while preparing Date-Orange Filling.
Shape . . . . by rounded teaspoonfuls into balls. Place on greased baking sheets.
Flatten . . . . to ½-inch thickness. Form a hollow in center of each. Place a rounded teaspoonful Filling in hollow. Garnish with 2 **pecan quarters.**
Bake . . . . at 375° for 12 to 15 minutes.
*For use with Pillsbury's Best Self-Rising Flour, omit baking powder and salt.

DATE-ORANGE FILLING

In saucepan combine 1 cup cut candy orange slices, ½ cup water and ⅛ teaspoon salt. Simmer 10 minutes, stirring occasionally. Add 1¼ cups (8 oz.) cut dates. Cook over low heat until dates are soft, stirring constantly. Combine 1 tablespoon cornstarch and ¼ cup cold water; add to cooked mixture. Cook and stir until thick and clear; cool.

Crunchy Lunchers

Senior Winner by Mrs. Lee Gresser, Osseo, Minnesota

Perfect for lunch boxes or for snacks with a glass of milk—whole wheat flour adds flavor.

BAKE at 350° for 12 to 16 minutes*   MAKES about 5½ dozen

Sift together . . 1 cup sifted **Pillsbury's Best All Purpose Flour***
             1 cup unsifted **Pillsbury's Whole Wheat (Graham) Flour**
             1 teaspoon double-acting **baking powder**
             1 teaspoon **soda** and
             1 teaspoon **salt.** Set aside.
Add . . . . 1½ cups firmly packed **brown sugar** and
             ½ cup **sugar** gradually to
             1 cup **shortening,** creaming well.

Blend in . . . . . 2 unbeaten **eggs** and
1 teaspoon **vanilla**; beat well. Add the dry ingredients; blend thoroughly.

Stir in . . . . . . .1 cup **coconut**
1 cup **Brazil nuts** or other nuts, chopped, and
2 cups quick-cooking **rolled oats**

Shape . . . . .by rounded teaspoonfuls into balls. Place on greased baking sheets.

Bake . . . . .at 350° for 12 to 16 minutes.*

*For use with Pillsbury's Best Self-Rising Flour, omit baking powder and salt; decrease baking time to 10 to 13 minutes.

Gingerunes

Senior Winner by Mrs. Charlotte Baird, Portland, Oregon

A lunchbox specialty . . . coconut-ginger cookies with a prune inside!

BAKE at 375° for 12 to 15 minutes   MAKES about 4 dozen

Sift together . .2 cups sifted **Pillsbury's Best All Purpose Flour***
1 teaspoon **soda**
½ teaspoon **salt**
1 teaspoon **ginger**
½ teaspoon **cinnamon** and
¼ teaspoon **cloves**. Set aside.

Add . . . . .⅔ cup firmly packed **brown sugar** gradually to
½ cup **shortening**, creaming well.

Blend in . . . . .1 unbeaten **egg** and
¼ cup light **molasses**; beat well. Add the dry ingredients; mix thoroughly.

Stir in . . . . . . .1 cup flaked or chopped shredded **coconut**. Chill.

Flatten . . . . .a rounded teaspoonful of dough for each cookie.** Place
1 uncooked, pitted tenderized **prune** in center; shape dough around prune. Dip top in **water**, then in **sugar**. Place sugar-side up on ungreased baking sheet.

Bake . . . . .at 375° for 12 to 15 minutes.
*For use with Pillsbury's Best Self-Rising Flour, omit soda and salt.
**If desired, omit prunes, and drop by rounded teaspoonfuls onto ungreased baking sheets.

Maple-Scotch Snaps

Senior Winner by Mrs. Gerald Woodside, Albert Lea, Minnesota

Crunchy candy-like cookies rolled in a crumb mixture before baking— a treat from your cookie jar.

BAKE at 375° for 12 to 14 minutes*   MAKES about 4 dozen

Combine . . . . .2 cups sifted **Pillsbury's Best All Purpose Flour*** and
2 cups firmly packed **brown sugar** in large mixing bowl.

Cut in . . . . . .½ cup soft **butter** or margarine until particles are fine. Reserve ¼ cup for topping.

Add . . . . .1 teaspoon **soda** and
½ teaspoon **salt**. Mix well.

Blend in . . . . .1 slightly beaten **egg**
2 tablespoons **milk** and
½ teaspoon **maple extract**. Mix with low speed of mixer (or with pastry blender) to form a dough.

Stir in . . . . . .½ cup **pecans**, chopped

Combine . . . . .2 tablespoons **instant chocolate mix** and the crumb mixture.

Shape . . . . .dough by rounded teaspoonfuls into balls. Roll in chocolate-crumb mixture. Place 3 inches apart on ungreased baking sheets.

Bake . . . . .at 375° for 12 to 14 minutes.* Cookies will puff and collapse during baking.

*For use with Pillsbury's Best Self-Rising Flour, decrease soda to ½ teaspoon and omit salt; decrease baking time to 10 to 13 minutes.

Currant Choosies

Currant Choosies

Senior Winner by Mrs. Lherif Loraamm, Hinsdale, Illinois

Easy to make! Easy to shape! Cookie jar cookies with "currant" appeal.

BAKE at 400° for 11 to 14 minutes*   MAKES about 4 dozen

Sift together . . 2 cups sifted **Pillsbury's Best All Purpose Flour***
        1 teaspoon **cinnamon**
        1 teaspoon **salt** and
        ½ teaspoon **soda**. Set aside.
Add . . . . 1 cup firmly packed **brown sugar** gradually to
        ⅔ cup **shortening**, creaming well.
Blend in . . . . . 1 unbeaten **egg** and
        1 **egg yolk**; beat well. Add the dry ingredients; mix
        thoroughly.

Stir in . . . . . 1½ cups **currants** and
        ½ cup **nuts**, chopped
Divide . . . . dough into four equal parts; shape each into a roll
        13 inches long. Place 4 inches apart on greased baking
        sheets. Flatten to ½-inch thickness with floured fork.
Brush . . . . with mixture of
        1 slightly beaten **egg white**
        2 tablespoons **sugar** and
        ¼ teaspoon **cinnamon**. Sprinkle with sliced **nuts**.
Bake . . . . at 400° for 11 to 14 minutes.* Cool; cut diagonally
        into 1-inch bars.

*For use with Pillsbury's Best Self-Rising Flour, omit salt and soda; decrease
baking time to 9 to 12 minutes.*

Raisin Rounds

Senior Winner by Mrs. Fern Wesemeyer, Parma Heights, Ohio

*Chewy cookies flavored with brown sugar, orange rind and sour cream.
Good for cookie-jar storage . . . if you can keep 'em that long!*

BAKE at 375° for 10 to 13 minutes   MAKES about 6 dozen

Sift together . . 4 cups sifted **Pillsbury's Best All Purpose Flour***
        1 teaspoon **soda** and
        1 teaspoon **salt**. Add
        1 tablespoon grated **orange rind** and
        3 cups (15-oz. pkg.) ground **seedless raisins**. Set aside.
Add . . . . ¾ cup **sugar** and
        ¾ cup firmly packed **brown sugar** gradually to
        1 cup **shortening**, creaming well.
Blend in . . . . . 1 unbeaten **egg**; beat well. Add half the flour mixture.

Mix thoroughly.

Add........⅔ cup **sour cream** (thick or commercial) and
1 teaspoon **vanilla.** Blend in the remaining flour mixture. Chill for easier handling.

Shape........by rounded teaspoonfuls into balls. Place on un-greased baking sheets; flatten to ⅛ to ¼-inch thick-ness with fork.

Bake.........at 375° for 10 to 13 minutes.

For use with Pillsbury's Best Self-Rising Flour, omit soda and salt.

Fig Chewies
Senior Winner by Mrs. W. H. Bergmann, Louisville, Kentucky

The combination of figs, coconut and pecans in these chewy cookies gives them an out-of-the-ordinary flavor.

BAKE at 375° for 12 to 15 minutes   MAKES about 4 dozen

Combine.....1 cup (8 oz.) dried **figs,** cut, and
½ cup **water** in saucepan. Cook until tender, about 5 minutes, stirring occasionally. Cool to lukewarm.

Sift together 1¾ cups sifted **Pillsbury's Best All Purpose Flour***
2 teaspoons double-acting **baking powder** and
½ teaspoon **salt.** Set aside.

Add........1 cup firmly packed **brown sugar** (half granulated sugar may be used) gradually to
½ cup **shortening,** creaming well.

Blend in.....1 unbeaten **egg** and
1 teaspoon **vanilla.** Add the cooked figs, then the dry ingredients. Mix thoroughly.

Drop.........by rounded teaspoonfuls into
1½ cups flaked or chopped shredded **coconut;** roll to coat. Form into balls.

Place.........on greased baking sheets. Top each with a **pecan half.**

Bake.........at 375° for 12 to 15 minutes.

For use with Pillsbury's Best Self-Rising Flour, omit baking powder and salt.

Fig Chewies

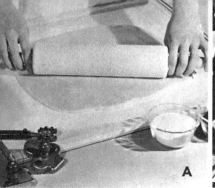

A   B

ROLLED COOKIES

—Chill dough if it is too soft to roll out easily. Roll out, a small amount at a time, to ⅛-inch thickness (or as directed in recipe). A pastry cloth and stockinet-covered rolling pin make rolling easier and help keep dough from sticking and picking up flour (photo A).

Dip cookie cutter into flour before cutting dough. Transfer cookies to baking sheet with spatula to prevent stretching and tearing dough (photo B). A metal cover from a coffee can is good for cutting giant-size cookies. Metal covers from baking-powder cans make 2 to 3-inch round cookies.

Reroll all scraps of dough at one time. Cut into diamond, square or rectangular shapes with pastry wheel or knife. (No scraps will be left.) These cookies will be slightly less tender.

Rolled cookie dough can be molded into balls and flattened to ⅛-inch thickness with bottom of glass which has been greased and dipped in sugar.

Real Good Sugar Cookies

Senior Winner by Ethel T. Reyburn, Philadelphia, Pennsylvania

Crisp sugar cookies with a delicate lemon flavor. A simple glaze decorates them.

BAKE at 400° for 6 to 9 minutes   MAKES 4 dozen

Sift together . . 2 cups sifted **Pillsbury's Best All Purpose Flour***
⅔ cup **sugar** and
1 teaspoon **salt**
Blend . . . . ½ cup **shortening** and
¼ cup **butter** or margarine with
1 tablespoon **milk** and
3 tablespoons **boiling water**
Blend in . . . . . 2 unbeaten **egg yolks**
2 teaspoons grated **lemon rind** and
1 teaspoon **vanilla**; beat well.
Stir in . . . . the dry ingredients to form dough. Chill 1 hour.
Roll out . . . . half at a time on floured surface to 1⁄16 to ⅛-inch thickness. Cut into desired shapes. Place on ungreased baking sheets.
Bake . . . . at 400° for 6 to 9 minutes. Cool; frost with **Vanilla Glaze**, page 326.

For use with Pillsbury's Best Self-Rising Flour, omit salt.

Tea Timers

Senior Winner by Mrs. Don Tierney, Fort Wayne, Indiana

Crisp cookies, flavored with orange and chopped nuts. They're rolled in graham cracker crumbs before baking for unusual texture.

BAKE at 400° for 10 to 12 minutes   MAKES about 7 dozen

Sift together . . 2 cups sifted **Pillsbury's Best All Purpose Flour***
⅔ cup **sugar**
½ teaspoon **soda** and

½ teaspoon **salt** into large mixing bowl.

Cut in . . . . . . ½ cup **butter** or margarine until particles are fine.

Combine . . . . . 1 beaten **egg**

½ cup **sour cream** (thick or commercial)

1 teaspoon **orange extract** or 1 tablespoon grated orange rind and

1 cup **pecans,** chopped. Add to the dry ingredients, stirring with fork until well combined.

Crush . . . . . . 9 double **graham crackers** (about 1½ cups)

Roll out . . . . . . dough on surface sprinkled with half the crushed graham crackers. Roll to about ½-inch thickness. Sprinkle remaining crumbs over dough; continue rolling to a 15x10-inch rectangle about ¼ inch thick. Cut into triangles about 1½ inches on each side. Place on ungreased baking sheets.

Bake . . . . at 400° for 10 to 12 minutes.

For use with Pillsbury's Best Self-Rising Flour, decrease soda to ¼ teaspoon and omit salt.

Glazed Coffee Crescents

Senior Winner by Mrs. Kurt Ruessel, Dayton, Ohio

Crisp orange-butter cookie topped with coffee-honey glaze and nuts.

BAKE at 400° for 5 to 7 minutes   MAKES 8 to 9 dozen

Sift together . . 3 cups sifted **Pillsbury's Best All Purpose Flour***

1 teaspoon double-acting **baking powder** and

½ teaspoon **soda**

Cream . . . . 1 cup **butter** or margarine. Gradually add

1 cup **sugar,** creaming well.

Blend in . . . . . 1 tablespoon grated **orange rind** and

¼ cup **orange juice.** Add the dry ingredients gradually; mix thoroughly.

Roll out . . . . . . dough, one-third at a time, on floured surface to ⅛-inch thickness. Cut with crescent or round-shaped

cutter. Place on ungreased baking sheets.

Bake . . . . at 400° for 5 to 7 minutes. Brush Coffee Glaze over warm cookies, a few at a time; sprinkle immediately with finely chopped **nuts** (about ½ cup).

For use with Pillsbury's Best Self-Rising Flour, omit baking powder and soda.

COFFEE GLAZE

Combine ½ cup sugar, ⅓ cup strong coffee and ¼ cup honey in saucepan. Bring to boil; simmer 5 minutes.

Mocha Nut Crunchies

Junior Winner by Donna Reed, Los Angeles, California

Newsworthy cookies! Crunchy chocolate cut-outs with the fragrance of coffee and a sprinkle of nuts.

BAKE at 350° for 9 to 12 minutes   MAKES about 3 dozen

Cream . . . . . . ½ cup **butter** or margarine. Gradually add

1½ to 2 teaspoons **instant coffee**

½ cup **instant chocolate mix** and

½ cup sifted **confectioners' sugar,** creaming well.

Blend in . . . . . 1 tablespoon light **cream**

Add . . . . 1¼ cups sifted **Pillsbury's Best All Purpose Flour;*** blend thoroughly.

Roll out . . . . . . on floured surface to a 14x10-inch rectangle. Cut into 2-inch squares with pastry wheel.

Press . . . . ⅓ cup **pecans,** sliced, into squares. Place squares on ungreased baking sheets.

Bake . . . . at 350° for 9 to 12 minutes.

Pillsbury's Best Self-Rising Flour may be substituted.

Grandma's Special-Tea Cookies

Junior Winner by Lois Elaine Devitt, Pleasantville, New York

These cookies are rolled very thin and baked to a delicate brown. They are tender, crisp and lightly flavored with vanilla and nuts.

BAKE at 400° for 5 to 8 minutes   MAKES about 5 dozen

Sift together 2¼ cups sifted **Pillsbury's Best All Purpose Flour***
     ½ teaspoon **salt** and
     1 cup sifted **confectioners' sugar** into large mixing bowl.
Cut in . . . . 1 cup soft **butter** until particles are fine.
Sprinkle . . . . . 2 tablespoons well-beaten **egg** and
     2 teaspoons **vanilla** over mixture; blend well and form into a ball. Chill, if desired.
Roll out . . . . . . one-third at a time on floured surface to ⅛-inch thickness.
Cut . . . . into desired shapes. Place on ungreased baking sheets. Brush lightly with beaten egg. Sprinkle with **colored sugar** or with a mixture of
     2 tablespoons **sugar** and
     ½ cup **nuts**, finely chopped
Bake . . . . at 400° for 5 to 8 minutes.
*For use with Pillsbury's Best Self-Rising Flour, omit salt.

Pineapple Sparklers

Junior Winner by Mickie Calhoun, Denton, Texas

A glistening pineapple-brown sugar glaze is spread on crisp, sugar-coated cookies after baking.

BAKE at 400° for 6 to 8 minutes   MAKES about 8 dozen

Sift together 3½ cups sifted **Pillsbury's Best All Purpose Flour***
     3 teaspoons double-acting **baking powder** and
     1 teaspoon **salt**. Set aside.

Add . . . . . . 1½ cups **sugar** gradually to
     1 cup **shortening**, creaming well.
Blend in . . . . 3 unbeaten **eggs**
     1 tablespoon grated **orange rind** and
     1 teaspoon **vanilla**. Beat well.
Add . . . . the dry ingredients gradually; mix thoroughly. Chill for easier handling.
Roll out . . . . . one-fourth at a time on floured surface to ⅛-inch thickness. Sprinkle with **sugar**; press in with rolling pin. Cut into desired shapes. Place on greased baking sheets.
Bake . . . . at 400° for 6 to 8 minutes. Cool; spread with Pineapple Glaze.
*For use with Pillsbury's Best Self-Rising Flour, omit baking powder and salt.

PINEAPPLE GLAZE

In saucepan combine 1 cup firmly packed brown sugar, ¼ cup pineapple juice and ¼ cup butter or margarine. Boil 2 minutes, stirring constantly.

Meringue Jelly Wafers

Senior Winner by Mrs. Katherine Stumpf, Enhaut, Pennsylvania

Meringue-topped wafers are sandwiched together with bright red jelly.

BAKE at 325° for 12 to 15 minutes   MAKES 5 to 6 dozen

Sift together 2½ cups sifted **Pillsbury's Best All Purpose Flour*** and
     ½ teaspoon **salt**
Cream . . . . . . ½ cup **butter** or margarine with
     ¼ cup **shortening**. Gradually add
     ½ cup sifted **confectioners' sugar**, creaming well.
Blend in . . . . . 2 unbeaten **eggs**
     1 unbeaten **egg yolk** (reserve egg white) and
     1 teaspoon **vanilla**; beat well.
Add . . . . the dry ingredients gradually; mix well.

Roll out . . . . half at a time on floured surface to ⅛-inch thickness. Cut into 2½x1-inch strips and place on ungreased baking sheets. Spread half of strips with Meringue.

Bake . . . . at 325° for 12 to 15 minutes.

Spread . . . . plain cookie strips with **jelly.** Place meringue-topped strips over jelly strips, sandwich-style, meringue-side up.

*For use with Pillsbury's Best Self-Rising Flour, omit salt.

MERINGUE

Beat 1 egg white until soft mounds form. Gradually add ¼ cup sugar, beating until meringue stands in stiff, glossy peaks.

Rainbow Cookies

Junior Winner by Audrey Sassetti, Oak Park, Illinois

Four colors of rich sugar-cookie dough, all from one mixing, are shaped into strips, then rolled to give a multicolored effect.

BAKE at 350° for 8 to 10 minutes   MAKES 2 to 4 dozen

Cream . . . . 1 cup **butter** or margarine. Gradually add
          1 teaspoon **vanilla** and
          1 cup sifted **confectioners' sugar,** creaming well.

Blend in . . . . 2½ cups sifted **Pillsbury's Best All Purpose Flour*** gradually.

Divide . . . . dough in four parts. Color one part red, one yellow and one green by adding 4 drops **food coloring** to each. Blend color into dough thoroughly. Leave fourth portion uncolored.

Shape . . . . one-fourth of each color dough into a long strip ½ inch thick. Place the four strips side by side on floured surface.

Roll out . . . . into a long strip 2½ to 3 inches wide and ⅛ inch thick. Cut into rounds with 2½-inch cutter. Place on greased baking sheets.

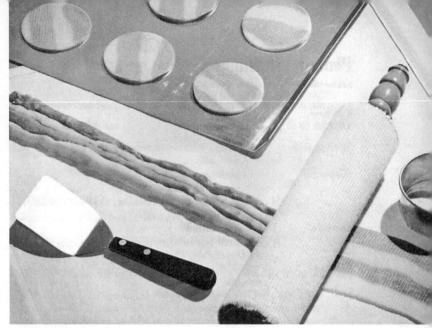

Rainbow Cookies

Repeat . . . . process with remaining dough. Reroll all extra pieces of dough together to ⅛ inch thickness and cut into rounds. Cookies made from this dough will be marbled.

Bake . . . . at 350° for 8 to 10 minutes. *Do not brown.* Cool. If desired, place cookies together sandwich-style with Peanut Butter Filling.

*Pillsbury's Best Self-Rising Flour may be substituted.

PEANUT BUTTER FILLING

Combine ⅓ cup firmly packed brown sugar and 1 tablespoon flour in saucepan. Add ½ cup water. Cook over medium heat, stirring constantly, until thick. Remove from heat; add ¼ cup creamy-style peanut butter.

Peanut Whirligigs

Senior Winner by Mrs. May Kendrick, Akron, Ohio

Peanuts, chocolate and cream cheese flavor these pinwheel cookies.

BAKE at 375° for 7 to 10 minutes   MAKES about 9 dozen

Sift together . . 2 cups sifted **Pillsbury's Best All Purpose Flour*** and
      ½ teaspoon **salt**

Cream . . . . . . ½ cup **butter** or margarine
      ½ cup **shortening** and
      ⅓ cup (3-oz. pkg.) **cream cheese.** Gradually add
      1 cup **sugar,** creaming well.

Blend in . . . . . 1 teaspoon **vanilla**
      ¾ cup **salted peanuts,** ground, and the dry ingredients;
      mix thoroughly. Chill 1 hour.

Roll out . . . . . . half of dough on floured surface to a 16x9-inch
      rectangle.

Peanut Whirligigs

Melt . . . . 3 tablespoons **butter** together with
      ¾ cup **semi-sweet chocolate pieces** over boiling water.
      Spread half of chocolate over rolled dough in thin
      layer.

Roll . . . . as for jelly roll, beginning with the 9-inch side. Wrap
      in waxed paper; chill. Repeat with remaining dough
      and melted chocolate.

Cut . . . . into slices about ⅛ inch thick. Place on greased
      baking sheets.

Bake . . . . at 375° for 7 to 10 minutes.

*For use with Pillsbury's Best Self-Rising Flour, omit salt.

French Meringue Strips

Senior Winner

*Rich cookies spread with meringue, then sprinkled with sugar, cinnamon
and almonds before baking—nice to serve for tea.*

BAKE at 350° for 10 to 15 minutes*   MAKES 8 dozen

Sift together . . 3 cups sifted **Pillsbury's Best All Purpose Flour***
      ¾ cup **sugar** and
      ½ teaspoon **salt** into large mixing bowl.

Cut in . . . . 1 cup soft **butter** or margarine until particles are fine.

Beat . . . . 2 **egg yolks** slightly. Add enough **water** to measure
      ⅓ cup. Sprinkle gradually over flour mixture,
      stirring with fork until dough is moist enough to
      hold together. Form into a ball. Chill while preparing
      Meringue.

Roll out . . . . . . dough on floured surface to 20x15-inch rectangle.
      Spread with Meringue.

Combine . . . . . 2 teaspoons **sugar**
      ½ teaspoon **cinnamon** and
      1 cup **almonds,** chopped; sprinkle over Meringue.
      Press in slightly with spatula. Cut into 3x1-inch
      bars. Place on ungreased baking sheets.

Bake . . . . .at 350° for 10 to 15 minutes.*

For use with Pillsbury's Best Self-Rising Flour, omit salt; decrease baking time to 8 to 10 minutes.

MERINGUE

Beat 2 egg whites with ⅛ teaspoon cream of tartar until soft mounds form. Gradually add 2 cups sifted confectioners' sugar, beating until thick and of spreading consistency. Fold in 1 teaspoon vanilla.

Honey Bearclaw Cookies

Senior Winner by Margery Little, Chico, California

Peanuts peek out one side of this cookie to resemble "toes." A zippy raisin-peanut mixture hides between the two cookie rounds.

BAKE at 400° for 8 to 10 minutes   MAKES about 3 dozen

Sift together 2¾ cups sifted **Pillsbury's Best All Purpose Flour***
        2 teaspoons double-acting **baking powder** and
        ¼ teaspoon **salt**
Cream . . . . . . ¾ cup **butter** or margarine. Gradually add
        1 cup **sugar,** creaming well.
Blend in . . . . . 2 unbeaten **eggs** and
        1 teaspoon **vanilla.** Add the dry ingredients gradually; mix thoroughly. Chill.
Roll out . . . . . . .one-third at a time on floured surface to ⅛-inch thickness. Cut into 2½-inch rounds. Place half of rounds on ungreased baking sheets.
Place . . . . .a teaspoonful of Raisin-Peanut Filling in the center of each round on baking sheet. Arrange 5 large **peanut halves,** flat-side down, about ¼ inch apart along edge of round to resemble bear claws. Top with another round; press edges together between peanuts to seal. Press with tip of teaspoon between peanuts, making 4 slits. Push back dough between peanuts to form "toes."

Bake . . . . .at 400° for 8 to 10 minutes.*

For use with Pillsbury's Best Self-Rising Flour, omit salt and baking powder.

RAISIN-PEANUT FILLING

Combine 1 cup finely chopped raisins, ⅓ cup finely chopped peanuts, 2 tablespoons soft butter, ⅓ cup honey and ½ teaspoon cinnamon, mixing thoroughly.

Jam Strip Cheesers

Junior Winner by Thomas E. Fogerty, Jr., St. Louis, Missouri

Only six ingredients go into these cookies. Then they are decorated with jam or jelly before baking.

BAKE at 350° for 20 to 25 minutes   MAKES 1½ dozen

Sift together . .2 cups sifted **Pillsbury's Best All Purpose Flour***
        1 tablespoon **sugar**
        ½ teaspoon **salt** and
        ¼ teaspoon double-acting **baking powder**
Cream . . . . . . ¾ cup **butter** or margarine and
        ⅓ cup (3-oz. pkg.) **cream cheese** thoroughly.
Add . . . . .the dry ingredients gradually; mix well.
Roll out . . . . . . .on floured surface to ½-inch thickness. Cut into 3x1-inch strips. Make a deep groove lengthwise down center of each with handle of knife, keeping ends closed.
Place . . . . .on ungreased baking sheets. Fill each groove with ½ teaspoon **jam** or jelly
Bake . . . . .at 350° for 20 to 25 minutes.

Pillsbury's Best Self-Rising Flour is not recommended for use in this recipe.

Lucky Stars

Best of Class Winner by Mrs. Louis Ganssle, Glen Ridge, New Jersey

A cookie with a novel shape! Delicate, buttery "stars" with a nut filling that has a hint of maple flavor.

BAKE at 400° for 7 to 10 minutes MAKES 2 to 3 dozen

Sift together 1⅓ cups sifted **Pillsbury's Best All Purpose Flour*** and
1½ teaspoons double-acting **baking powder**

Cream......¼ cup **butter** or margarine. Add
¼ cup **sugar**, creaming well.

Blend in.....1 teaspoon **vanilla**
1 teaspoon **almond extract**
⅛ teaspoon **salt*** and
1 unbeaten **egg**. Add the dry ingredients gradually;
mix thoroughly.

Roll out.......on floured surface to ⅛-inch thickness. Cut with
star-shaped cutter.

Place.........a teaspoonful of Nut Filling in center of each star.
Bring the 5 points upright; starting at the base,
pinch sides together so points stand up, allowing
filling to show. Place on ungreased baking sheet.

Bake.........at 400° for 7 to 10 minutes.

**For use with Pillsbury's Best Self-Rising Flour*, omit baking powder and salt.
Chill dough before rolling for easier handling.*

NUT FILLING

Combine 1¼ cups walnuts or pecans, ground, ⅓ cup sugar, 1⁄16 teaspoon salt, 1 tablespoon melted butter, 2 tablespoons water and 1⁄16 teaspoon maple flavoring. Mix thoroughly.

Lucky Stars

Puff-Up Tea Cookies

Senior Winner by Mrs. Joseph A. Tartre, Walnut Creek, California

You'll be amazed when you take these cream-rich flaky cookies from the oven. They puff up during baking like French puff pastry.

BAKE at 450° for 8 to 10 minutes   MAKES about 2½ dozen

Sift together . . 2 cups sifted **Pillsbury's Best All Purpose Flour*** and ⅛ teaspoon **cream of tartar** into large mixing bowl.

Cut in . . . . . . ¾ cup **butter** or margarine until particles are fine.

Sprinkle . . . . . ½ cup **cream** over mixture, stirring with fork until dough is moist enough to hold together. Form into a ball.

Roll out . . . . on floured surface to ¼-inch thickness. Cut into desired shapes. Place on ungreased baking sheets. Chill until firm, about ½ hour.**

Brush . . . . tops with **cream,** then dip in **sugar.** (A little cinnamon may be mixed with the sugar. Colored sugar may also be used.)

Bake . . . . at 450° for 8 to 10 minutes. Cookies are best eaten the day they are baked.

*Pillsbury's Best Self-Rising Flour may be substituted.

**Dough may be stored in refrigerator up to 4 days, then baked as needed; allow chilled dough to stand at room temperature 1 hour before rolling.

Date Bow Ties

Senior Winner by Mrs. Lillian Carnes, Indianapolis, Indiana

Surprisingly simple to make. Just put the date-and-nut mixture between two layers of orange pastry. Cut into strips and twist!

BAKE at 450° for 12 to 15 minutes   MAKES 2 dozen

Combine . . . . . 1 cup **dates,** cut
¼ cup **walnuts,** finely chopped
1 teaspoon grated **orange rind** and
½ cup liquid (juice of 1 **orange** plus water) in saucepan. Cook until dates are soft. Cool.

Sift together 2¼ cups sifted **Pillsbury's Best All Purpose Flour*** and 1¼ teaspoons **salt** into large mixing bowl.

Cut in . . . . . . ¾ cup **shortening** until particles are fine.

Combine . . . . ¼ cup **orange juice** and
¼ cup **water.** Sprinkle over mixture, stirring with fork until dough is moist enough to hold together. Form into a ball.

Roll out . . . . on floured surface to an 18x16-inch rectangle. Spread date mixture over half of pastry along 16-inch side. Fold over other half.

Cut . . . . into 4x1½-inch strips. Twist in center to form a "bow tie." Brush with **milk** and sprinkle with **sugar.** Place on ungreased baking sheets.

Bake . . . . at 450° for 12 to 15 minutes.

*For use with Pillsbury's Best Self-Rising Flour, omit salt.

Date Bow Ties

Steady Daters

Junior Winner by Carole Ann Hinrichsen, Dixon, Iowa

Make a hit! Serve these flaky pastry-type cookies with date-peanut filling peaking through.

BAKE at 400° for 12 to 15 minutes*   MAKES 3 dozen

Sift together 2½ cups sifted **Pillsbury's Best All Purpose Flour*** and 1 teaspoon **salt** into large mixing bowl.

Cut in . . . . 1 cup **butter** or margarine until particles are fine.

Sprinkle . . . . . 6 to 8 tablespoons cold **water** over mixture, stirring with fork until dough is moist enough to hold together.

Roll out . . . . half of dough on floured surface to ⅛-inch thickness. Cut 36 circles, using 2½-inch round cutter. Transfer to ungreased baking sheets.

Place . . . . a teaspoonful of Date-Peanut Butter Filling in center

Roll out . . . . of each circle. Moisten edges. remaining dough and cut 36 more circles. Cut 1-inch hole in center of each. Place rings on top of circles on baking sheets. Press edges together to seal.

Brush . . . . tops with **milk** and sprinkle with **sugar.**

Bake . . . . at 400° for 12 to 15 minutes.*

For use with Pillsbury's Best Self-Rising Flour, omit salt; decrease baking time to 9 to 12 minutes.

DATE-PEANUT BUTTER FILLING

In saucepan combine 1 cup cut dates, ⅔ cup water, ¼ cup sugar and 1/16 teaspoon salt. Cook over medium heat, stirring constantly, until thick. Cool. Stir in 2 tablespoons peanut butter.

Lemon Cheese Snaps

Junior Winner by Joan C. Bechert, South Miami, Florida

Swiss cheese, cream cheese and nuts combine in a crisp, delicately flavored cookie. Lemon icing fills these sandwich-style cookies.

BAKE at 375° for 6 to 8 minutes   MAKES about 2 dozen

Sift together 1¾ cups sifted **Pillsbury's Best All Purpose Flour***
½ teaspoon **salt**
⅛ teaspoon **soda** and
½ teaspoon **cinnamon**

Blend . . . . ⅓ cup **shortening** with
¼ cup shredded **Swiss cheese** and
⅓ cup (3-oz. pkg.) **cream cheese.** Gradually add
⅔ cup **sugar,** creaming well.

Blend in . . . . . 1 unbeaten **egg yolk**
1 teaspoon grated **lemon rind** and
1 tablespoon **lemon juice.** Beat well.

Add . . . . the dry ingredients and
⅓ cup **nuts,** finely chopped; mix thoroughly.

Roll out . . . . half at a time on floured surface to 1/16 to ⅛-inch

Steady Daters

thickness. Cut into rounds with 2-inch cutter. Place on greased baking sheets.

Bake . . . . at 375° for 6 to 8 minutes. Cool. Place cookies together with Lemon Icing, sandwich-style.

*For use with Pillsbury's Best Self-Rising Flour, omit salt and soda.

LEMON ICING

Blend together 1½ cups sifted confectioners' sugar, 2 tablespoons cream and 1 teaspoon lemon juice. Beat until smooth and creamy.

Date Cheese Charmers

Senior Winner by Miss Vaun E. Dole, Portland, Maine

Dates and Brazil nut filling peeks through cheese pastry layers.

BAKE at 350° for 12 to 15 minutes   MAKES 2 dozen

Shred . . . . ¼ pound (1 cup) **American cheese**; soften to room temperature. Add
½ cup soft **butter** or margarine; blend well.

Blend in . . . . 1¼ cups sifted **Pillsbury's Best All Purpose Flour.*** Chill ½ hour. Meanwhile prepare Date-Nut Filling.

Roll out . . . . dough on floured surface to ⅛-inch thickness. Cut with 2-inch cutter. Place half of rounds on ungreased baking sheets; top each with 1 teaspoon Filling.

Cut out . . . . centers of remaining rounds in diamond, square or star shapes. Place over rounds on baking sheets; seal edges with fork.

Bake . . . . at 350° for 12 to 15 minutes.

*Pillsbury's Best Self-Rising Flour may be substituted.

DATE-NUT FILLING

Combine in saucepan ½ cup cut dates, ¼ cup Brazil nuts or other nuts (finely chopped), ¼ cup firmly packed brown sugar and ¼ cup water. Cook until thick, stirring constantly. Cool.

Wheat Sweets

Junior Winner by Ellen Dougherty, Santa Ana, California

Dark, crisp, delicate . . . with a wonderfully unusual flavor from anise seed and whole wheat flour.

BAKE at 350° for 14 to 17 minutes   MAKES about 7 dozen

Sift together . . 2 cups sifted **Pillsbury's Best All Purpose Flour***
1 teaspoon double-acting **baking powder** and
1 teaspoon **salt**. Stir in
1 cup unsifted **Pillsbury's Whole Wheat (Graham) Flour** and
½ teaspoon **anise seed**. Set aside.

Add . . . . ⅔ cup **sugar** gradually to
1 cup **shortening** (half butter may be used), creaming well.

Blend in . . . . the dry ingredients with fork or pastry blender.

Sprinkle . . . . . 5 to 6 tablespoons **water** over mixture, stirring with fork until dough is moist enough to hold together. Form into a ball.

Roll out . . . . on floured surface to ⅛-inch thickness. Cut into desired shapes. Place on greased baking sheets. Sprinkle with **sugar.**

Bake . . . . at 350° for 14 to 17 minutes.

*For use with Pillsbury's Best Self-Rising Flour, omit baking powder and salt.

Poinsettias

Senior Winner by Ellen Sharbak, Hammond, Indiana

A strawberry filling peaks through the petal design that's cut in the tops of these filled cookies.

BAKE at 350° for 25 to 30 minutes*   MAKES 2 dozen

Soften . . . . . . ½ cake compressed **yeast**** in
¼ cup **milk**

Sift together . . 2 cups sifted **Pillsbury's Best All Purpose Flour*** and
¼ teaspoon **salt** into large mixing bowl.

Cut in . . . . . . ½ cup **shortening** and
¼ cup **butter** until particles are fine.

Add . . . . 1 slightly beaten **egg yolk**
⅓ cup undiluted **evaporated milk** or cream and the softened yeast. Mix well.

Sugar Silhouettes

Knead . . . . on floured surface until smooth and easy to handle, about 1 minute. Place in greased bowl and cover. Chill 4 hours or overnight.

Roll out . . . . . . half at a time on floured surface to ⅛-inch thickness.

Cut . . . . into rounds with 2½-inch cutter. Place half of rounds on ungreased baking sheet; top each with ½ teaspoon Strawberry Filling. Cut slits in remaining rounds in "petal" design. Place over rounds on baking sheets; seal edges with fork.

Bake . . . . at 350° for 25 to 30 minutes.* Cool; sprinkle with sifted **confectioners' sugar.**

For use with Pillsbury's Best Self-Rising Flour, omit salt; decrease baking time to 20 to 25 minutes.

**One-half package active dry yeast (1½ teaspoons), dissolved in ¼ cup water as directed on package, may be substituted; omit milk.

STRAWBERRY FILLING

Combine 2 tablespoons sugar, 2 teaspoons cornstarch and ⅛ teaspoon nutmeg in small saucepan. Blend in ⅓ cup drained, thawed frozen strawberries, ¼ cup strawberry juice, 1 tablespoon lemon juice and 1 tablespoon butter. Cook over medium heat, stirring constantly, until thick. Cool.

Sugar Silhouettes

Senior Winner by Mrs. H. C. Orrison, Dallas, Texas

Clever cutting idea! These crisp sugar cookies are fun to create.

BAKE at 375° for 8 to 10 minutes   MAKES about 4 dozen

Sift together . . 3 cups sifted **Pillsbury's Best All Purpose Flour***
1 teaspoon **soda** and
½ teaspoon **salt**

Cream . . . . . . ¾ cup **butter** or margarine. Gradually add
1 cup **sugar,** creaming well.

Blend in . . . . . 1 unbeaten **egg**

¼ cup thick **sour cream** or buttermilk and
1½ teaspoons **vanilla**. Beat well.

Add . . . . the dry ingredients gradually; mix thoroughly.

Remove . . . . . . half of dough from bowl; set aside. To the remaining half add

3 tablespoons **cocoa**; mix until well blended. If desired, chill doughs for easier handling.

Roll out . . . . . . light dough on floured surface to ⅛-inch thickness. Cut with 3-inch round cutter. Cut out center of cookie with smaller fancy shaped cutter. Repeat with chocolate dough.

Transfer . . . . . . light centers to chocolate rounds and chocolate centers to light rounds. If desired, sprinkle with **sugar**. Place on ungreased baking sheets.

Bake . . . . at 375° for 8 to 10 minutes.

For use with Pillsbury's Best Self-Rising Flour, omit soda and salt.

Spumoni Strips

Senior Winner by Mrs. Kathryn Chute, Pittsburgh, Pennsylvania

These three-toned cookies will remind you of that popular Italian dessert.

BAKE at 325° for 8 to 12 minutes   MAKES about 4 dozen

Sift together . . 2 cups sifted **Pillsbury's Best All Purpose Flour***
1 teaspoon double-acting **baking powder** and
½ teaspoon **salt**

Cream . . . . . . ¾ cup **butter** or margarine. Gradually add
⅔ cup **sugar** and
1 teaspoon **vanilla**, creaming well.

Blend in . . . . . . the dry ingredients gradually; mix thoroughly.

Divide . . . . dough in thirds. To one part, add
12 **maraschino cherries**, very finely chopped and thoroughly drained. To second part, add
¼ cup **nuts**, finely chopped
¼ teaspoon **peppermint flavoring** and

Spumoni Strips

4 drops **green food coloring**. Mix well. (Third part remains plain.)

Press out . . . . . . on floured surface one third of each part into a flat strip about 12 inches long and ¾ inch wide. Place 3 strips of dough side by side, plain dough in the center.

Roll out . . . . . . lengthwise into a long strip about 18 inches long and ⅛ inch thick. (Straighten outer edges if necessary.)

Cut . . . . crosswise into 1-inch strips. Place cookies on ungreased baking sheets. Repeat with remaining dough.

Bake . . . . at 325° for 8 to 12 minutes. *Do not brown.* Cool on baking sheet. Serve plain, or put together sandwich-style with **Vanilla Glaze**, page 326.

For use with Pillsbury's Best Self-Rising Flour, omit baking powder and salt.

Chocolate Cut-Ups

Chocolate Cut-Ups

Junior Winner by Sheila Stover, Moore, Oklahoma

A two-in-one cookie with a novel shaping idea! Chocolate and vanilla sugar cookie in each, both are from the same basic dough.

BAKE at 375° for 7 to 10 minutes   MAKES 3½ dozen

Sift together 1½ cups sifted **Pillsbury's Best All Purpose Flour***
     1 teaspoon double-acting **baking powder** and
     ½ teaspoon **salt**
Cream . . . . . . ½ cup **butter** or margarine. Gradually add
     ⅔ cup **sugar,** creaming well.
Blend in . . . . . 1 unbeaten **egg** and
     2 teaspoons **vanilla.** Add the dry ingredients gradually;
     mix well. Place half of dough in a second bowl.

Blend in . . . . . 2 tablespoons **cocoa** and
     ½ teaspoon **cinnamon.** Chill for easier handling.
Roll out . . . . . . .light and dark doughs separately on floured surface
     to ⅛-inch thickness. Cut with a doughnut cutter.
     Place dark "holes" in light circles and light "holes"
     in dark circles. Cut each in half.
Arrange . . . . . . .on ungreased baking sheet, forming a round cookie
     shape using opposite colored halves.
Bake . . . . .at 375° for 7 to 10 minutes.
*For use with Pillsbury's Best Self-Rising Flour, omit baking powder and salt.

Chocolate Layer Cookies

Senior Winner by Mrs. Uel C. Paul, Chilhowee, Missouri

These are double-decker cookies. Each one is two chocolate rolled cookies with fluffy peppermint filling in between.

BAKE at 400° for 6 to 8 minutes   MAKES 4 dozen

Sift together . .2 cups sifted **Pillsbury's Best All Purpose Flour***
     ½ teaspoon double-acting **baking powder** and
     ½ teaspoon **salt.** Set aside.
Add . . . . .1 cup **sugar** gradually to
     ½ cup **shortening** (part butter may be used), creaming
     well.
Blend in . . . . .1 unbeaten **egg** and
     3 squares (3 oz.) unsweetened **chocolate,** melted and
     cooled. Mix well.
Combine . . . . ¼ cup **milk** and
     1 teaspoon **vanilla.** Add alternately with the dry in-
     gredients to creamed mixture; blend well. Chill ½
     hour for easier handling.
Roll out . . . . . .half at a time on floured surface to ⅛-inch thickness.
     Cut with 2-inch round cutter; place on greased
     baking sheets.
Bake . . . . .at 400° for 6 to 8 minutes.

Spread........half of cookies with Peppermint Fluff Filling; top with remaining cookies, sandwich-style.

*For use with Pillsbury's Best Self-Rising Flour, omit baking powder and salt.

PEPPERMINT FLUFF FILLING

Combine in top of double boiler 1 egg white, ¾ cup sugar, 1 tablespoon light corn syrup and 2 tablespoons water. Cook over rapidly boiling water, beating until mixture stands in peaks. Remove from heat. Add 6 quartered marshmallows and ¼ teaspoon peppermint flavoring; continue beating until of spreading consistency.

Mad Hatter Cookies

Junior Winner by Frances Chunko, Washington, Pennsylvania

These cookies really look like hats. You can decorate them as you choose—with gumdrops, nuts and confectioners' sugar frosting.

BAKE at 350° for 11 to 14 minutes   MAKES 2 dozen

Sift together..2 cups sifted **Pillsbury's Best All Purpose Flour***
     ½ teaspoon double-acting **baking powder** and
     ¼ teaspoon **salt**
Cream......½ cup **butter** or margarine. Gradually add
     1 cup firmly packed **brown sugar,** creaming well.
Blend in.....1 unbeaten **egg** and
     1 teaspoon **vanilla.** Add the dry ingredients gradually; mix thoroughly. Chill 2 hours.
Roll out......half at a time on floured surface to a 12x9-inch rectangle; cut into twelve 3-inch squares.
Combine.....1 cup **coconut** and

⅓ cup **chocolate syrup.** Place a teaspoonful in center of each square. Top with a **pecan half.**
Fold..........corners of dough over pecan half, overlapping in center. Smooth outer edges to resemble a hat brim, and round off top of cookie with fingers. Brush cookies with melted **butter.** Sprinkle with **sugar** and place on greased baking sheets.
Bake........at 350° for 11 to 14 minutes. While hot, form a "crown" on each "hat" by pressing with fingers around each pecan half. Cool. Make a ribbon around crown of hat with **Decorator Frosting,** page 321. Decorate with **gumdrops,** cut in small pieces.

*Pillsbury's Best Self-Rising Flour is not recommended for use in this recipe.

Caramel Crisps

Senior Winner by Esther Van, La Porte, Indiana

Crunchy with nuts, these rolled brown sugar cookies are good plain or with a glaze.

BAKE at 350° for 8 to 10 minutes   MAKES 4½ dozen

Cream......½ cup **butter** or margarine and
     ⅓ cup **shortening.** Gradually add
     1 cup firmly packed **brown sugar**
     1 teaspoon **almond extract** and
     ½ teaspoon **salt,** creaming well.
Add........2 cups sifted **Pillsbury's Best All Purpose Flour***
     gradually, and
     ¾ cup **almonds,** finely chopped; mix well.
Roll out.......half at a time on floured surface to ⅛-inch thickness. Cut into desired shapes. Place on ungreased baking sheets; sprinkle with **sugar.**
Bake.........at 350° for 8 to 10 minutes. If desired, frost with **Vanilla Glaze,** page 326.

*For use with Pillsbury's Best Self-Rising Flour, omit salt.

Grandma's Caramel Cookies

Senior Winner by Mrs. Fred O. Peck, Battle Creek, Michigan

These crisp old-fashioned brown sugar cookies are cut in nice big circles.

BAKE at 400° for 8 to 10 minutes   MAKES about 6 dozen

Sift together 3½ cups sifted **Pillsbury's Best All Purpose Flour***
             1 teaspoon double-acting **baking powder**
             ½ teaspoon **salt** and
             ¼ teaspoon **soda**. Set aside.
Add . . . . 1½ cups firmly packed **brown sugar** gradually to
             1 cup **shortening**, creaming well.
Blend in . . . . . 1 unbeaten **egg**
             ¼ cup undiluted **evaporated milk** and
             1 teaspoon **vanilla** or almond extract; beat well.
Add . . . . the dry ingredients gradually; mix well. Chill.
Roll out . . . . one-third at a time on floured surface to ⅛-inch
             thickness. Sprinkle with **sugar**. Cut with 2½-inch
             round cutter. Place on ungreased baking sheets.
Bake . . . . at 400° for 8 to 10 minutes.
*For use with Pillsbury's Best Self-Rising Flour, omit baking powder, salt, soda.

Circle-O-Rangers

Senior Winner by Mrs. Murray Sutton, Talent, Oregon

Clever little "cowboys"—you cut them with a doughnut cutter! A sweet, spicy rolled molasses cookie all children will love.

BAKE at 375° for 7 to 9 minutes   MAKES about 6 dozen

Sift together . . 3 cups sifted **Pillsbury's Best All Purpose Flour***
             1 teaspoon **soda**
             1 teaspoon **salt**
             ½ teaspoon **cinnamon**
             ½ teaspoon **ginger** and
             ½ teaspoon **instant coffee**. Set aside.

Circle-O-Rangers

Add........½ cup **sugar** to
½ cup **shortening,** creaming well.
Blend in.....½ cup **molasses** and
¼ cup **boiling water.** Add the dry ingredients gradually; mix thoroughly. Chill 2 hours.
Roll out.......one-third at a time on floured surface to ⅛-inch thickness.
Cut..........with doughnut cutter. Place circle on ungreased baking sheet, with dough from hole for a head. Cut circle opposite head, and spread to make bowlegs. Make slanting cuts from sides of circle part way up, and spread for arms. Use bits of chopped raisins, currants or small candies to mark faces and buttons.
Bake.........at 375° for 7 to 9 minutes. Cool 1 minute; remove from baking sheet.

For use with Pillsbury's Best Self-Rising Flour, omit soda and salt.

Big Wheels

Senior Winner by Mrs. Alfred O. Williams, Richland, Michigan

Man-sized cookies—flavored with malted milk, brown sugar and almonds.

BAKE at 375° for 12 to 15 minutes   MAKES about 1½ dozen

Sift together..4 cups sifted **Pillsbury's Best All Purpose Flour***
¾ cup **plain malted milk powder**
2 teaspoons double-acting **baking powder**
½ teaspoon **soda** and
½ teaspoon **salt.** Set aside.
Cream.......1 cup **butter** or margarine. Gradually add
2 cups firmly packed **brown sugar,** creaming well.
Blend in.....2 unbeaten **eggs;** beat well. Add half the dry ingredients, mixing thoroughly.
Add........⅓ cup **sour cream** (thick or commercial) and
2 teaspoons **vanilla** to the creamed mixture.
Blend in.......the remaining dry ingredients and

1 cup **almonds** or other nuts, chopped; mix well. Chill at least 4 hours.
Roll out.......half at a time on well-floured surface to ¼-inch thickness. Cut into 5-inch circles with a 1-pound coffee can; place on greased baking sheets.
Bake.........at 375° for 12 to 15 minutes. Cool 2 minutes. Remove to racks; cool completely. Frost; decorate each with 5 **almonds** in "spoke" design. Press a **semi-sweet chocolate piece** into center.

For use with Pillsbury's Best Self-Rising Flour, omit baking powder, soda, salt.

FROSTING

Combine ¼ cup butter, ¼ cup undiluted evaporated milk or cream and ½ cup firmly packed brown sugar in saucepan. Cook and stir until sugar is melted; remove from heat. Add ⅓ cup malted milk powder and ½ teaspoon vanilla; blend in 2½ to 3 cups sifted confectioners' sugar until of spreading consistency.

Big Wheels

Bunny Faces

Bride Winner by Mrs. R. D. McCarthy, Buffalo, New York

Children will love to eat these easy-to-make storybook cookies!

BAKE at 375° for 7 to 10 minutes   MAKES about 5 dozen

Sift together . . 3 cups sifted **Pillsbury's Best All Purpose Flour***
      1 teaspoon **soda**
      1 teaspoon **salt**
      ½ teaspoon **ginger** and
      ½ teaspoon **cinnamon.** Set aside.
Add . . . . ½ cup **sugar** to
      ⅔ cup **shortening,** creaming well.
Stir in . . . . . . ½ cup **molasses**
      ¼ cup **boiling water** and
      ½ cup **coconut,** finely chopped
Blend in . . . . the dry ingredients gradually. Chill 2 hours.
Roll out . . . . one-third at a time on floured surface to ⅛-inch

Bunny Faces

thickness. Cut with 2½-inch round cutter. Place rounds on ungreased baking sheets. Cut off two sides of round to form a triangle shape. Place the two curved pieces on either side of the rabbit head for ears. Press to seal.
Bake . . . . at 375° for 7 to 10 minutes. Decorate rabbit faces with **Decorator Frosting,** page 321.
For use with Pillsbury's Best Self-Rising Flour, omit soda and salt.

Maple Nut Triangles

Senior Winner by Mrs. LeRoy O. Lee, Chillicothe, Ohio

Walnuts and maple flavoring go into these crisp, tender triangles.

BAKE at 350° for 10 to 12 minutes   MAKES 6 dozen

Cream . . . . 1 cup **butter** or margarine. Gradually add
      ⅔ cup firmly packed **brown sugar**
      1 teaspoon **maple flavoring** and
      ½ teaspoon **salt,** creaming well.
Add . . . . 2 cups sifted **Pillsbury's Best All Purpose Flour***
      gradually, and
      ¾ cup **walnuts,** finely chopped; mix thoroughly.
Roll out . . . . one-third at a time on floured surface to a 12x9-inch rectangle. Cut into twelve 3x3-inch squares; cut each square in half, diagonally, to make two triangles. Place on ungreased baking sheets.
Bake . . . . at 350° for 10 to 12 minutes. Cool 1 minute before removing from baking sheet. Cool; frost with Chocolate Frosting. Garnish with
      ⅓ cup **walnuts,** finely chopped
For use with Pillsbury's Best Self-Rising Flour, omit salt.

CHOCOLATE FROSTING

Melt 1 square (1 oz.) unsweetened chocolate in top of double boiler over boiling water. Add ⅔ cup sweetened condensed milk. Cook until thick, stirring constantly, about 5 minutes. Add 1 tablespoon cold water, ½ teaspoon vanilla and ½ teaspoon maple flavoring. Continue cooking, stirring until of spreading consistency.

Spiced Cherry Bells

Senior Winner by Mrs. W. J. Huggins, Columbia, South Carolina

Ring in the new! Cookie "bells" with nut filling and cherry "clappers."

BAKE at 350° for 12 to 15 minutes   MAKES about 5½ dozen

Sift together..3 cups sifted **Pillsbury's Best All Purpose Flour***
               1 teaspoon **ginger**
               ½ teaspoon **soda**
               ½ teaspoon **salt** and
               ½ teaspoon **instant coffee.** Set aside.
Add.......1¼ cups firmly packed **brown sugar** gradually to
               1 cup **shortening,** creaming well.
Blend in.....¼ cup **dark corn syrup**
               1 unbeaten **egg** and
               1 tablespoon **cream;** beat well.
Add..........the dry ingredients; mix thoroughly.
Roll out.......third at a time on floured surface to ⅛-inch thickness. Cut into 2½-inch rounds. Place on ungreased baking sheets.
Place.........a half teaspoonful of Nut Filling in center of each round. Shape into a "bell" by folding sides to meet over filling. Make top of bell narrower than "clapper" end. Place a piece of **maraschino cherry** at open end for clapper.
Bake.........at 350° for 12 to 15 minutes.
For use with Pillsbury's Best Self-Rising Flour, omit soda and salt.

NUT FILLING

Combine ⅓ cup brown sugar, 1 tablespoon butter and 3 tablespoons maraschino cherry juice; mix well. Add 1½ cups finely chopped pecans.

Spiced Cherry Bells

Ginger Pinks

Senior Winner by Mrs. Jean S. Hassler, Carnegie, Pennsylvania

Pink peppermint candy patties melt in the oven to form the attractive filling between crisp molasses cookies. Children love them!

BAKE at 350° for 6 minutes, then   MAKES 4 dozen
        for 2 to 3 minutes

Sift together 3¼ cups sifted **Pillsbury's Best All Purpose Flour***
        1½ teaspoons **soda**
        ½ teaspoon **salt**
        ½ teaspoon **cinnamon**
        ½ teaspoon **ginger** and
        ¼ teaspoon **nutmeg.** Set aside.
Add . . . . ½ cup **sugar** gradually to
        ½ cup **shortening,** creaming well.

Blend in . . . . . ½ cup **molasses.** Stir in half of dry ingredients; mix thoroughly.
Add . . . . ½ cup **buttermilk** or sour milk; mix well. Stir in the remaining dry ingredients, blending thoroughly. Chill at least 2 hours.
Roll out . . . . half at a time on floured surface to ⅛-inch thickness. Cut with 2¼-inch round cutter; place on greased baking sheets.
Bake . . . . at 350° for 6 minutes. Remove from oven. Top half of cookies with **pink peppermint candy patties** (about 1 lb.), using one patty per cookie. Bake all cookies 2 to 3 minutes longer. Top hot mint-covered cookies with plain ones. Press slightly to seal. Remove from sheets; cool.

For use with Pillsbury's Best Self-Rising Flour, decrease soda to ½ teaspoon and omit salt.

Ginger Pinks

Ginger Cookie Capers

Junior Winner by Patty Rose Welti, Plainview, Minnesota

The most delightful gingerbread cookies you ever saw. The apple butter filling makes them extra moist and delicious.

BAKE at 400° for 8 to 10 minutes   MAKES 1 dozen gingerbread men
        or 3½ dozen round cookies

Sift together . . 2 cups sifted **Pillsbury's Best All Purpose Flour***
        ⅛ cup **sugar**
        1 teaspoon double-acting **baking powder**
        ¼ teaspoon **soda**
        1 teaspoon **cinnamon** and
        ½ to 1 teaspoon **ginger**
Heat . . . . ½ cup **shortening** and
        ½ cup **molasses** in saucepan until shortening melts.
Add . . . . the dry ingredients and
        3 tablespoons hot **water;** stir until blended. Chill at

least 1 hour. Prepare Apple Butter Filling (make half of recipe for Gingerbread Men).

Roll out . . . . dough on floured surface to ⅛-inch thickness. Shape as directed below.

Bake . . . . at 400° for 8 to 10 minutes.

For use with Pillsbury's Best Self-Rising Flour, omit baking powder.

APPLE BUTTER FILLING

Cook ¾ cup apple butter, ⅓ cup cut dates and ⅛ cup sugar in small saucepan for 3 minutes, stirring constantly. Blend in 1 tablespoon butter and cool.

Gingerbread Men: Cut dough with gingerbread man cutter. Place half of the men on an ungreased baking sheet. Place about 2 teaspoons Filling in center of head and body of each. Top with remaining gingerbread men; decorate with currants or tiny slits to mark features and buttons. (No need to seal edges.) The arms and legs may be curved to make "dancing" gingerbread men.

Man-in-the-Moons or Peek-a-Boos: Cut with 2-inch round cutter. Place half of rounds on ungreased baking sheet; top each with about 1 teaspoon Filling. In remaining rounds, cut slits to resemble Man-in-the-Moon features, or cut X's for Peek-a-Boos. Place over Filling.

REFRIGERATOR COOKIES

—Chill dough if it is too soft to shape into a roll. Mold dough into rolls as big around as you want cookies to be. Wrap in foil or waxed paper. Dough may also be pressed into special molds. Chill until firm. Place rolls in freezer for an hour or two for quicker chilling. Cut straight down through dough with sharp knife to make thin slices (see photo).

Dough may be stored three weeks and baked as needed. Always cover dough.

Surprise Zookies

Junior Winner by Marlene Paulson, Fosston, Minnesota

A spicy surprise is the baked-in apple butter filling.

BAKE at 350° for 12 to 15 minutes   MAKES about 2 dozen

Sift together 1½ cups sifted **Pillsbury's Best All Purpose Flour***
     ½ cup **sugar**
     ½ teaspoon double-acting **baking powder** and
     ½ teaspoon **salt** into mixing bowl.

Cut in . . . . . . ½ cup **shortening** and
     ⅓ cup **peanut butter** until particles are fine.

Blend in . . . . . ¼ cup **light corn syrup**

Shape . . . . dough into a long roll, 2 inches in diameter. Wrap; chill at least 1 hour.

Cut . . . . into slices about ⅛ inch thick. Place half of slices on ungreased baking sheet. Place ½ teaspoon **apple butter** on each. Cover with remaining slices; seal edges with fork.

Bake . . . . at 350° for 12 to 15 minutes.

For use with Pillsbury's Best Self-Rising Flour, omit baking powder and salt.

Date-Nut Candy Toppers

Senior Winner by Mrs. Lloyd Cope, Galion, Ohio

Homemade candy baked atop a refrigerator cookie—together they make a new, interesting cookie that's chewy and date-nut rich.

BAKE at 400° for 9 to 12 minutes   MAKES about 6½ dozen

CANDY TOPPING

Combine . . . 1½ cups **sugar**
1 cup **milk** and
1 tablespoon **butter** in saucepan. Cook, stirring occasionally, to soft-ball stage (234°). Remove from heat.

Add . . . . 1 cup **dates,** cut, and
1 teaspoon **vanilla.** Beat until mixture starts to thicken.

Stir in . . . . . . 1 cup **pecans,** chopped, and
1 cup **coconut.** Beat until very thick. Chill about 15 minutes, if desired, for easier handling.

Divide . . . . into 2 parts. Shape on waxed paper into rolls 1½ inches in diameter. Wrap; chill 2 to 3 hours until firm enough to slice.

COOKIES

Sift together . . 4 cups sifted **Pillsbury's Best All Purpose Flour***
3 teaspoons double-acting **baking powder** and
1 teaspoon **salt**

Cream . . . . . . 1 cup **butter** or margarine. Gradually add
2 cups **sugar,** creaming well.

Blend in . . . . . 1 teaspoon grated **lemon rind**
2 unbeaten **eggs**
2 tablespoons **cream** and
1 teaspoon **vanilla.** Add the dry ingredients gradually; mix thoroughly.

Divide . . . . dough into thirds. Shape on waxed paper into rolls 1½ inches in diameter. Wrap; chill until Candy Topping is ready to slice.

Cut . . . . dough into slices ¼ inch thick; place on ungreased baking sheets. Top each with a slice of Topping ⅛ inch thick.**

Bake . . . . at 400° for 9 to 12 minutes.

For use with Pillsbury's Best Self-Rising Flour, omit baking powder and salt; decrease cream to 1 tablespoon.

**For variety, omit Candy Topping on part of the cookies; serve leftover Topping, sliced, as candy.*

Black Walnut Butter Wafers

Senior Winner by Mrs. Kitty Allen, Huntington, West Virginia

Tender and rich refrigerator butter cookies with lots of black walnuts. Delicious plain or iced.

BAKE at 375° for 7 to 10 minutes   MAKES about 4 dozen

Cream . . . . . . ½ cup **butter** or margarine. Gradually add
½ cup **sugar,** creaming well.

Blend in . . . . . 2 unbeaten **egg yolks;** beat well.

Add . . . . 1½ cups sifted **Pillsbury's Best All Purpose Flour*** gradually; mix to form a dough. Stir in
1 cup **black walnuts,** finely chopped

Shape . . . . on waxed paper into a roll 2½ inches in diameter. Wrap; chill 2 hours or overnight.

Cut . . . . into slices ⅛ to ¼ inch thick; place on ungreased baking sheets.

Bake . . . . at 375° for 7 to 10 minutes. Cool; frost with Black Walnut Icing.

For use with Pillsbury's Best Self-Rising Flour, add 1 tablespoon cream with the egg yolks to creamed mixture. Grease baking sheets.

BLACK WALNUT ICING

Combine 2 unbeaten egg whites, ⅛ teaspoon salt, ¼ teaspoon cinnamon and 2 cups sifted confectioners' sugar. Beat until smooth. Stir in 2 tablespoons finely chopped black walnuts.

Brazil Nut Refrigerator Slices

Senior Winner by Mrs. Leroy Wettstein, New Holstein, Wisconsin

These cookies are flavored with coconut, Brazil nuts and molasses.

BAKE at 375° for 8 to 10 minutes   MAKES about 7 dozen

Sift together . . 2 cups sifted **Pillsbury's Best All Purpose Flour***
           ½ teaspoon **soda** and
           ½ teaspoon **salt**
Cream . . . . . . ½ cup **butter** or margarine. Gradually add
           1 cup **sugar,** creaming well.
Blend in . . . . . 1 unbeaten **egg** and
           1 tablespoon **molasses**; beat well.
Stir in . . . . . . ½ cup **coconut,** finely chopped, and
           ½ cup **Brazil nuts,** slivered.
Add . . . . the dry ingredients gradually; mix thoroughly.
Divide . . . . into two parts. Shape on waxed paper into rolls
           1½ inches in diameter. Chill 3 hours or overnight.
Cut . . . . into slices about ⅛ inch thick. Place on well-greased
           baking sheets.
Bake . . . . at 375° for 8 to 10 minutes.

For use with Pillsbury's Best Self-Rising Flour, decrease flour to 1¾ cups; omit soda and salt.

Lemon Honey Slices

Senior Winner by Mrs. Kathryn H. Chesworth, Colton, California

Sweet with honey, tangy with lemon, these crisp cookies are sprinkled with sugar before they are baked to a light golden brown.

BAKE at 400° for 8 to 10 minutes   MAKES 6 dozen

Sift together 2½ cups sifted **Pillsbury's Best All Purpose Flour***
           1 teaspoon double-acting **baking powder** and
           ½ teaspoon **salt.** Set aside.
Add . . . . ½ cup **sugar** to
           ½ cup **shortening,** creaming well.
Stir in . . . . 1 unbeaten **egg**
           ¼ cup **honey**
           1 tablespoon grated **lemon rind** and
           1 tablespoon **lemon juice.** Beat well.
Blend in . . . . . . the dry ingredients gradually. Shape on waxed paper
           into roll 1½ inches in diameter. Wrap; chill over-
           night.
Cut . . . . into slices ⅛ inch thick; place on greased baking
           sheets. Sprinkle with **sugar.**
Bake . . . . at 400° for 8 to 10 minutes.

For use with Pillsbury's Best Self-Rising Flour, omit baking powder and salt.

Banana Whirls

Banana Whirls

Senior Winner by Mrs. Ardith J. Marker, Nine Mile Falls, Washington

Swirls of banana filling in refrigerator cookies—so delicious you'll want to make them often.

BAKE at 375° for 10 to 14 minutes   MAKES about 4 dozen

Sift together 3¼ cups sifted **Pillsbury's Best All Purpose Flour***
          1 teaspoon **salt**
          ½ teaspoon **soda** and
          1½ teaspoons **cinnamon**
Cream . . . . . . ½ cup **shortening** and
          ½ cup **butter** or margarine. Gradually add
          ½ cup firmly packed **brown sugar** and
          ½ cup **sugar,** creaming well.
Add . . . . 2 unbeaten **eggs;** beat well. Blend in the dry ingredients.

Stir in . . . . . . ½ cup **almonds,** finely chopped. Chill dough while preparing Caramel Banana Filling.
Divide . . . . dough into three parts. Roll out one part on floured waxed paper to a 13x8-inch rectangle. Spread with one-third of Filling. Roll as for jelly roll, starting with 13-inch side. Wrap and chill 6 hours or overnight. Repeat with remaining dough.
Cut . . . . into ¼-inch slices; place on greased baking sheets.
Bake . . . . at 375° for 10 to 14 minutes.
*For use with Pillsbury's Best Self-Rising Flour, omit salt and soda.

CARAMEL BANANA FILLING

Melt ¼ cup butter in saucepan. Remove from heat. Add ⅓ cup firmly packed brown sugar, 1 cup quick-cooking rolled oats and ¼ teaspoon salt. Stir in 1 cup (2 medium) mashed bananas; chill 15 minutes.

Candied Almond Crunchies

Senior Winner by Mrs. Gilbert L. Rathje, Davenport, Iowa

Brown sugar cookies, richly flavored and crunchy with candied almonds.

BAKE at 375° for 8 to 12 minutes   MAKES about 5 dozen

Combine . . . . ⅓ cup blanched **almonds,** finely chopped, and
          ¼ cup **sugar** in heavy skillet. Stir constantly over low heat until golden brown.
Add . . . . ¼ cup **boiling water.** Simmer, stirring constantly, until all water evaporates. Remove from skillet. Cool completely; chop fine.
Sift together . . 2 cups sifted **Pillsbury's Best All Purpose Flour***
          1 teaspoon double-acting **baking powder** and

½ teaspoon **salt**

Cream . . . . . . ¼ cup **butter** or margarine and
¼ cup **shortening.** Gradually add
¾ cup firmly packed **brown sugar,** creaming well.

Blend in . . . . . 1 unbeaten **egg** and
1 teaspoon **vanilla.** Add dry ingredients gradually;
mix well. Stir in candied nuts.

Divide . . . . dough in half; shape each half on waxed paper into
a roll 2 inches in diameter. Wrap; chill 4 hours or
overnight.

Cut . . . . into slices about ⅛ inch thick; place on greased
baking sheets.

Bake . . . . at 375° for 8 to 12 minutes.

For use with Pillsbury's Best Self-Rising Flour, omit baking powder and salt.

Pecan Paulines

Senior Winner by Mrs. Daniel H. Jones, Geneseo, Illinois

*Attractive and extra-good—brown sugar refrigerated cookies made to
resemble pralines.*

BAKE at 350° for 8 to 10 minutes   **MAKES about 3 dozen**

Sift together 1⅔ cups sifted **Pillsbury's Best All Purpose Flour***
½ teaspoon **soda** and
¼ teaspoon **salt**

Cream . . . . . . ½ cup **butter** or margarine. Gradually add
⅔ cup firmly packed **brown sugar,** creaming well.

Blend in . . . . . 1 unbeaten **egg**
½ teaspoon **vanilla** and
½ teaspoon **maple flavoring;** beat well.

Add . . . . the dry ingredients; mix thoroughly.

Pecan Paulines

Shape . . . . dough into roll 8 inches long and 2 inches in
diameter. Wrap; chill 4 hours or overnight.

Cut . . . . into slices about ⅛ inch thick; place on greased
baking sheets.

Break . . . . ¾ cup **pecan halves** into 2 to 4 pieces. Place 4 to 5
pieces on each cookie. Press down gently.

Bake . . . . at 350° for 8 to 10 minutes. Drizzle scant teaspoonful
Praline Frosting over top of each cookie.

For use with Pillsbury's Best Self-Rising Flour, omit soda and salt.

PRALINE FROSTING

Combine in small saucepan ½ cup firmly packed brown sugar, 1
tablespoon corn syrup and 1 tablespoon water. Bring to boil stirring
constantly. Remove from heat. Blend in 1 cup sifted confectioners'
sugar and 1 tablespoon water; beat until smooth, adding a few drops
of water until consistency of a glaze.

Crisp Chocolate Tweedies

Senior Winner by Mrs. Harold R. Shippey, Westport, Connecticut

The coconut and grated chocolate in these crunchy oatmeal refrigerator cookies give them a "tweedy" effect.

BAKE at 350° for 10 to 12 minutes   MAKES 7 to 8 dozen

Sift together 2¼ cups sifted **Pillsbury's Best All Purpose Flour***
          1 teaspoon **soda** and
          1 teaspoon **salt.** Set aside.
Add . . . . .1 cup **sugar** and
          1 cup firmly packed **brown sugar** gradually to
          1 cup **shortening** (half butter may be used), creaming
          well.
Blend in . . . . .2 unbeaten **eggs** and
          1 teaspoon **vanilla**
Add . . . . .the dry ingredients; mix thoroughly.

Slice o' Spice

Stir in . . . . . . .3 cups quick-cooking **rolled oats**
          ½ cup **coconut,** cut fine, and
          2 squares (2 oz.) grated **semi-sweet chocolate**
Divide . . . . .in half. Shape each into a roll 1½ inches in diameter.
          Wrap; chill at least 2 hours.
Cut . . . . .into slices about ¼ inch thick; place on greased
          baking sheets.
Bake . . . . .at 350° for 10 to 12 minutes.
For use with Pillsbury's Best Self-Rising Flour, omit soda and salt.

Slice o' Spice

Bride Third Prize Winner by Mrs. Tom McAllister, Sacramento, California

Crisp, snappy, butter cookies dipped in cinnamon-sugar before baking.

BAKE at 350° for 9 to 12 minutes   MAKES about 9 dozen

Sift together . .3 cups sifted **Pillsbury's Best All Purpose Flour***
          1 teaspoon **soda**
          1 teaspoon **cream of tartar** and
          ½ teaspoon **salt**
Cream . . . . . .½ cup **butter** or margarine and
          ½ cup **shortening** in mixing bowl. Gradually add
          2 cups firmly packed **brown sugar,** creaming well.
Blend in . . . . .2 unbeaten **eggs** and
          1 teaspoon **vanilla.** Stir in the dry ingredients.
Add . . . . .1 cup quick-cooking **rolled oats;** mix thoroughly.
Divide . . . . . . .dough in three parts; place on waxed paper and shape
          into rolls 12 inches long. Wrap; chill 6 hours or
          overnight.
Cut . . . . .into ¼-inch slices. Dip each slice into a mixture of
          ½ cup **sugar** and
          4 teaspoons **cinnamon** to coat both sides. Place on
          greased baking sheets.
Bake . . . . .at 350° for 9 to 12 minutes.
For use with Pillsbury's Best Self-Rising Flour, omit soda, cream of tartar, salt.

Hoot Owl Cookies

Second Grand Prize Winner by Natalie R. Riggin, Olympia, Washington

A novelty cookie—bake two slices of the two-tone cookie dough side by side, with chocolate chips for eyes, a cashew nut for a beak.

BAKE at 350° for 8 to 12 minutes   MAKES about 4 dozen

Sift together 2½ cups sifted **Pillsbury's Best All Purpose Flour***
           2 teaspoons double-acting **baking powder** and
           ½ teaspoon **salt**

Cream......¾ cup **butter** or margarine. Gradually add
           1 cup firmly packed **brown sugar,** creaming well.

Blend in.....1 unbeaten **egg** and
           1 teaspoon **vanilla.** Add the dry ingredients gradually;
           mix thoroughly.

Combine...1½ squares (1½ oz.) unsweetened **chocolate,** melted
           and cooled, and
           ¼ teaspoon **soda***

Remove.......two-thirds of dough to floured surface. Blend chocolate mixture into remaining dough.

Roll out.......half of light dough to a 10x4¼-inch strip. Shape half of dark dough into a roll 10 inches long; place on strip of light dough. Mold sides of light dough around dark; wrap. Chill at least 2 hours. Repeat with remaining dough.

Cut..........into slices about ⅛ inch thick and place two slices together on a greased baking sheet to resemble an owl's face. Pinch a corner of each slice to form ears. Place a **chocolate piece** in center of each slice for eyes; press a whole **cashew nut** between slices for a beak.

Bake.........at 350° for 8 to 12 minutes.

*For use with Pillsbury's Best Self-Rising Flour, omit baking powder, salt, soda.

Hoot Owl Cookies

Polka Dotties

Senior Winner by Mrs. F. Peter Ford, Orono, Maine

A new look in cookies! Brown sugar dough molded around chocolate-sprinkled dough.

BAKE at 400° for 6 to 9 minutes   MAKES about 5 dozen

Sift together..2 cups sifted **Pillsbury's Best All Purpose Flour***
2 teaspoons double-acting **baking powder** and
½ teaspoon **salt**
Cream......⅓ cup **butter** or margarine and
⅓ cup **shortening.** Gradually add
½ cup firmly packed **brown sugar** and
¼ cup **sugar,** creaming well.
Blend in.....1 unbeaten **egg** and
1 teaspoon **vanilla.** Stir in the dry ingredients; mix well.
Remove.......two-thirds of dough to surface sprinkled lightly with **sugar.**
Blend.......⅓ cup **chocolate cake decorations** into remaining one-third of dough.
Roll out.......half of plain dough to an 8x4-inch rectangle. Shape half of chocolate-speckled dough into roll 8 inches long; place on rectangle of plain dough. Mold plain dough around chocolate dough. Repeat with remaining dough.
Roll..........in mixture of
⅓ cup **pecans,** finely chopped, and
1 teaspoon **sugar,** pressing nuts firmly into dough. Wrap; chill at least 2 hours. Cut into ¼-inch slices; place on ungreased baking sheets.
Bake..........at 400° for 6 to 9 minutes.

**For use with Pillsbury's Best Self-Rising Flour, omit baking powder and salt.*

Cheese Round Abouts

Senior Winner by Mrs. Charles S. Coile, Winterville, Georgia

Rich, delectable cheese cookies with a refreshing, tangy frosting. Keep the shaped rolls of dough in refrigerator and bake as needed.

BAKE at 425° for 8 to 12 minutes   MAKES 8 to 10 dozen

Shred.......½ pound **Cheddar** or **American cheese** (2 cups); soften to room temperature. Add
1 cup soft **butter** or margarine; blend well.
Blend in....3½ cups sifted **Pillsbury's Best All Purpose Flour*** gradually to form a very stiff dough.**
Divide........dough in half; shape each into a roll 12 inches long and 2 inches in diameter. Wrap; chill at least 3 hours.
Slice..........dough ⅛ to ¼ inch thick. Place on well-greased baking sheets.
Bake..........at 425° for 8 to 12 minutes. Remove from sheets immediately. Cool; frost with Lemon Orange Frosting, if desired.

**Pillsbury's Best Self-Rising Flour may be substituted.*

***If desired, ½ cup pecans, chopped fine, may be added to half of dough. Cookies containing nuts need not be frosted.*

LEMON ORANGE FROSTING

Blend together 1 teaspoon soft butter, 1 teaspoon orange juice and ½ teaspoon lemon juice. Blend in ½ cup sifted confectioners' sugar alternately with ¾ teaspoon cream. Thin with cream, a few drops at a time, if necessary. Frosts 3 dozen cookies.

Herb Cheese Canapés

Senior Winner by Mrs. Melvin P. Spalding, Pleasantville, New York

These wafers are good with soup, delicious served with salad. Store the dough in your refrigerator and bake as needed.

BAKE at 450° for 8 to 10 minutes   MAKES about 5 dozen

Sift together..1 cup sifted **Pillsbury's Best All Purpose Flour***
           ¼ teaspoon **celery seed** and
           ⅛ teaspoon **pepper**
Cream......½ cup **butter** or margarine (half shortening may be used). Add
           1 jar (5 oz.) **pimiento cheese** spread and
           1 jar (5 oz.) **smoky cheese** spread, creaming well.
Blend in.......the dry ingredients. Chill 1 hour.
Shape........on waxed paper into a roll, 2 inches in diameter. Wrap; chill 4 hours or overnight.
Cut..........into slices about ⅛ inch thick; place on ungreased baking sheets.
Bake........at 450° for 8 to 10 minutes. Serve warm.

*Pillsbury's Best Self-Rising Flour may be substituted.

Cocoa Cheese Sandwich Cookies

Senior Winner by Mrs. Charles L. Saunders, Sunburst, Montana

Serve these tender chocolate cookies plain. Or put together in two's with a creamy-smooth cheese filling for a new flavor twist.

BAKE at 350° for 8 to 10 minutes   MAKES about 3 dozen

Sift together..2 cups sifted **Pillsbury's Best All Purpose Flour***
           ⅛ cup **cocoa** and
           ½ teaspoon **salt**
Cream......¾ cup **butter** or margarine. Gradually add
           ¾ cup **sugar,** creaming well.
Blend in.....1 unbeaten **egg** and

           1 teaspoon **vanilla.** Add the dry ingredients gradually; mix thoroughly.
Divide........in half; shape each into a roll 1½ inches in diameter. Wrap; chill at least 2 hours.
Cut..........into slices about ⅛ inch thick; place on greased baking sheets. Garnish half the slices with a **pecan half.**
Bake.........at 350° for 8 to 10 minutes. Cool. Place two cookies together with Cheese Filling, sandwich-style, using plain slices for bottoms, or serve plain.

*For use with Pillsbury's Best Self-Rising Flour, omit salt.

CHEESE FILLING

Melt 3 tablespoons butter with 1 tablespoon cream. Blend in 3 tablespoons softened cheese spread or cream cheese. Gradually add 2 cups sifted confectioners' sugar and ½ teaspoon salt. Beat until smooth, adding a few drops of cream until of spreading consistency.

Cocoa Cheese Sandwich Cookies

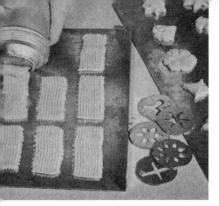

PRESS COOKIES

PRESS COOKIES—Press dough through cookie press into various shapes (see photo). Hold press upright, then force out a very small amount of dough onto baking sheet. Let go of handle and lift press. Follow directions carefully on how to assemble and use your cookie press. Use cold, ungreased baking sheets. (A warm sheet will melt the shortening in the cookies, causing them to lose shape when the press is lifted.

Swedish Gem Cookies

Senior Winner by Edward I. Kawahara, Merced, California

Rich pressed cookies—sprinkled with colored sugars, candied fruit or spiced chopped nuts before baking.

BAKE at 375° for 8 to 12 minutes   MAKES about 4 dozen

Cook........2 **egg yolks.** (Drop yolks from saucer, one at a time, into hot salted water. Simmer until hard cooked.) Press through wire sieve.

Sift together 2¼ cups sifted **Pillsbury's Best All Purpose Flour***
     1 teaspoon **salt** and
     ⅛ teaspoon **soda**

Cream......½ cup **butter** or margarine and
     ½ cup **shortening.** Gradually add
     ½ cup **sugar,** creaming well.

Add........1 unbeaten **egg**

     ½ teaspoon **vanilla** and sieved yolks; beat well.

Blend in.......the dry ingredients.

Press.........through a cookie press onto ungreased baking sheets.**

Sprinkle with...Spicy Nut Topping or colored sugar.

Bake.........at 375° for 8 to 12 minutes.

 *For use with Pillsbury's Best Self-Rising Flour, omit soda and salt.

**Or chill dough and roll out on well-floured surface to ⅛-inch thickness. Cut into desired shapes. Place on ungreased baking sheets.*

SPICY NUT TOPPING

Combine 2 tablespoons finely chopped almonds or walnuts, ¼ cup sugar and ¼ teaspoon cardamom or cinnamon.

Fruit-Filled Spritz

Senior Winner by Mrs. Donald Fish, Sr., Vancouver, Washington

Christmas cookies for holiday entertaining . . . caramel spritz with candy fruit filling.

BAKE at 375° for 12 to 15 minutes   MAKES about 6½ dozen

Sift together..4 cups sifted **Pillsbury's Best All Purpose Flour***
     ½ teaspoon **soda** and
     ½ teaspoon **salt**

Cream.......1 cup **butter** or margarine. Gradually add
     1 cup **sugar** and
     ½ cup firmly packed **brown sugar,** creaming well.

Blend in.....3 unbeaten **eggs**
     ½ teaspoon **vanilla** and
     ½ teaspoon **almond extract**; beat well.

Add..........the dry ingredients gradually; mix well. Chill dough about 2 hours. Using saw-toothed (spritz) plate, press dough through cookie press into strips across ungreased baking sheets.

Spread.......each strip with Fruitti Nut Filling. Press second strip of dough over filling to form a bar.

Bake . . . . at 375° for 12 to 15 minutes. While warm, cut into
2-inch bars.

For use with Pillsbury's Best Self-Rising Flour, omit soda and salt.

FRUITTI NUT FILLING

Combine in saucepan 1 cup water, ½ cup sugar, 1¼ cups dates, cut
into small pieces, and 2 teaspoons grated orange rind. Cook over
medium heat, stirring constantly, until thick. Cool. Stir in ½ cup
finely cut candied cherries, ½ cup flaked or chopped shredded coconut
and 1 cup chopped nuts.

Jamborees

Senior Winner by Mrs. Raymond Kilduff, Harrisburg, Pennsylvania

*Shape butter cookies with a twist of the cookie press. Rotate the press
as you force out dough—and fill hollow in center with jam.*

BAKE at 375° for 10 to 12 minutes   MAKES 7 to 8 dozen

Sift together . . 3 cups sifted **Pillsbury's Best All Purpose Flour*** and
½ teaspoon **salt**

Cream . . . . . 1¼ cups **butter** or margarine. Gradually add
1 cup **sugar**, creaming well.

Blend in . . . . . 2 unbeaten **eggs** and
2 tablespoons **vanilla**; beat well. Add the dry ingredients gradually; mix thoroughly.

Press . . . . through star plate of cookie press onto ungreased
baking sheets, forming a circle. (Do not leave open
space in center of circle.)**

Place . . . . ¼ teaspoon **apricot preserves** or marmalade into center
of each. Sprinkle with finely chopped **walnuts** (about
⅓ cup in all).

Bake . . . . at 375° for 10 to 12 minutes.

*Pillsbury's Best Self-Rising Flour is not recommended for use in this recipe.

***Dough may be dropped by rounded teaspoonfuls onto baking sheets. Dent
center of each, using back of teaspoon dipped in cold water.*

Jamborees

Chocolate Tips

Chocolate Tips

Senior Winner by Mrs. Marguerite Dugan, Washington, D.C.

The tips of jelly filled cookie strips are dipped first in melted chocolate, then in chocolate "shot" or chopped nuts.

BAKE at 400° for 6 to 8 minutes   MAKES about 4 dozen

Sift together 1½ cups sifted **Pillsbury's Best All Purpose Flour*** and
          ¼ teaspoon **salt**

Cream......½ cup **butter** or margarine. Gradually add
          ½ cup **sugar,** creaming well.

Blend in.....1 unbeaten **egg** and
          1 teaspoon **vanilla;** beat well. Stir in dry ingredients;
          mix well.

Press.........dough through cookie press, using saw-toothed (spritz)
          plate, into strips across ungreased baking sheet.

Bake.........at 400° for 6 to 8 minutes. Cut into 2-inch pieces;
          remove from sheet. Cool; spread **jelly** between two
          strips, placing bottom sides together. Dip ends in
          Melted Chocolate, then in **chocolate shot** or chopped
          nuts.

**Pillsbury's Best Self-Rising Flour may be substituted.*

MELTED CHOCOLATE

Melt ½ cup semi-sweet chocolate pieces over hot water. Add 1½ tablespoons milk, stirring until mixture is smooth.

Chocolate Press Cookies

Junior Winner by Pauline Kielb, Williamsett, Massachusetts

You can make up the dough for these rich, tender cookies so quickly. Shape them with a cookie press into any design you like—stars, posies, strips, crescents, diamonds.

BAKE at 350° for 6 to 9 minutes   MAKES about 7 dozen

Sift together..2 cups sifted **Pillsbury's Best All Purpose Flour*** and
          ½ teaspoon **salt**

Cream......½ cup **butter** or margarine. Gradually add
          1 cup **sugar,** creaming well.

Add.........1 unbeaten **egg**
          2 tablespoons **milk** and
          1 teaspoon **vanilla;** beat well.

Blend in.....2 squares (2 oz.) cooled, melted unsweetened **choco-
          late.** Mix thoroughly. Stir in dry ingredients gradu-
          ally; mix well.

Press.........through cookie press onto ungreased baking sheets
          into fancy shapes.

Bake.........at 350° for 6 to 9 minutes.

**For use with Pillsbury's Best Self-Rising Flour, omit salt.*

Almond Party Press Cookies

Senior Winner by Mrs. John H. Luihn, Portland, Oregon

Almonds and cardamom flavor these delicate cookies. Shape them into a variety of dainty forms with your cookie press.

BAKE at 350° for 10 to 12 minutes   MAKES about 7 dozen

Sift together 2¼ cups sifted **Pillsbury's Best All Purpose Flour***
             ¼ teaspoon **salt** and
             ¼ to ½ teaspoon **cardamom**
Cream......1 cup **butter** or margarine. Gradually add
             ¾ cup **sugar,** creaming well.
Blend in.....1 unbeaten **egg** and
             2 tablespoons **milk;** beat well.
Stir in.......1 cup unblanched **almonds,** finely ground, and the dry
             ingredients; mix thoroughly.
Press.........dough through cookie press, using coarse mold, onto ungreased baking sheet.
Bake.........at 350° for 10 to 12 minutes.
*For use with Pillsbury's Best Self-Rising Flour, omit salt.

Cameo Tea Cookies

Senior Winner by Esther Potenberg, Pasadena, California

Tender white cookies with a pretty cameo of chocolate on top.

BAKE at 375° for 7 to 10 minutes   MAKES about 5 dozen

Sift together 1¾ cups sifted **Pillsbury's Best All Purpose Flour***
             1 teaspoon double-acting **baking powder** and
             ½ teaspoon **salt**
Cream......¾ cup **butter** or margarine. Gradually add
             ½ cup **sugar,** creaming well.
Blend in.....1 unbeaten **egg** and
             1 teaspoon **vanilla.** Add the dry ingredients gradually; mix thoroughly.

Cameo Tea Cookies

Place.........three-fourths of dough in a second bowl. Blend into remaining dough
             1 square (1 oz.) melted, cooled unsweetened **chocolate** and
             2 tablespoons **sugar.** If necessary, add 1 to 2 tablespoons flour to give desired cookie press consistency.
Drop.........light dough by level teaspoonfuls onto ungreased baking sheets. Flatten to ¼ inch.**
Press.........a small amount of chocolate dough through a cookie press onto top of each flattened cookie.
Bake.........at 375° for 7 to 10 minutes.
  *For use with Pillsbury's Best Self-Rising Flour, omit baking powder and salt.
  **Light dough may be chilled at least 1 hour, rolled to ⅛-inch thickness and cut with small fancy cutters.

VARIETY COOKIES

Love Notes

Senior Winner by Mrs. James C. Barclay, Mason City, Iowa

Inside each of these rich, but delicate, little pastry "envelopes" is a sweet brown sugar and coconut filling.

BAKE at 375° for 13 to 16 minutes   MAKES 3 dozen

Sift together 2¼ cups sifted **Pillsbury's Best All Purpose Flour***
          2 tablespoons **sugar** and
          ¾ teaspoon **salt** into large mixing bowl.
Cut in . . . . . . ½ cup **shortening** and
          ⅓ cup **butter** or margarine until particles are fine.
Sprinkle . . . . . 5 to 6 tablespoons cold **water** over mixture, stirring with fork until dough is moist enough to hold together.
Divide . . . . into two portions; form each into a rectangle. Flatten to ½-inch thickness; smooth edges.
Roll out . . . . each on floured surface to a 15x12-inch rectangle. Cut into 3-inch squares.
Place . . . . a half teaspoon Coconut Filling in center of each. Moisten edges. Bring points to center; seal edges. Place on ungreased baking sheets.
Bake . . . . at 375° for 13 to 16 minutes.
*For use with Pillsbury's Best Self-Rising Flour, omit salt.

COCONUT FILLING

Combine 1 slightly beaten egg, ½ cup firmly packed brown sugar, 1 tablespoon flour and 1½ cups flaked or chopped shredded coconut.

Almond Tartlets

Senior Winner by Mrs. Evelyn K. Awin, Foxboro, Massachusetts

A colorful fruit-jam filling bakes between tiny tender golden tart shells and an almond topping puffs up during baking.

BAKE at 375° for 18 to 20 minutes*   MAKES 2½ dozen

Sift together . . 1 cup sifted **Pillsbury's Best All Purpose Flour***
          3 tablespoons **sugar** and
          ½ teaspoon **salt**
Combine . . . . . ⅛ cup **shortening**
          1 teaspoon **lemon juice** and
          2 tablespoons **boiling water** in mixing bowl. Whip with fork until liquid is absorbed and mixture holds a soft peak.
Blend in . . . . . 1 unbeaten **egg yolk**. Add the dry ingredients gradually; stir until mixture clings together.
Knead . . . . dough until smooth, about 1 minute. Chill. Meanwhile, prepare Almond Topping.
Roll out . . . . dough on floured surface to ⅛-inch thickness. Cut into 2¼-inch rounds and fit into small muffin cups.**
Combine . . . . . ½ cup **raspberry** or **strawberry preserves** and 1 tablespoon grated **lemon rind**. Drop by scant teaspoonfuls into each lined muffin cup. Top with a teaspoonful of Topping.
Bake . . . . at 375° for 18 to 20 minutes.*

ALMOND TOPPING

Sift together ½ cup sifted Pillsbury's Best All Purpose Flour,* ½ cup sugar, ½ teaspoon double-acting baking powder and ¼ teaspoon salt into mixing bowl. Stir in ½ cup almonds, ground. Blend in 2 tablespoons melted butter, 1 unbeaten egg and ½ teaspoon almond extract. Mix well.

*For use with Pillsbury's Best Self-Rising Flour, omit baking powder and salt in pastry and Topping; decrease baking time to 15 to 18 minutes.

**If muffin cups are 2 inches in diameter, cut dough into 2¾-inch rounds. Makes 2 dozen.

Raspberry Marble Teas

Senior Winner by Mrs. Edward F. Nash, Brockton, Massachusetts

Colorful raspberry jam, folded inside these sugar-dipped cookies, bubbles to the tops as they bake. They're best served warm.

BAKE at 375° for 15 to 18 minutes   MAKES about 2 dozen

Sift together . . 2 cups sifted **Pillsbury's Best All Purpose Flour***
            3 teaspoons double-acting **baking powder** and
            1 teaspoon **salt.** Set aside.
Add . . . . ½ cup **sugar** gradually to
            ⅓ cup **shortening,** creaming well.
Blend in . . . . the dry ingredients alternately with
            ¾ cup **milk.** Mix thoroughly after each addition. Chill
            at least 1 hour.
Pat out . . . . rounded teaspoonfuls of dough on lightly floured
            surface to 2½-inch circles.
Place . . . . a teaspoonful of **raspberry preserves** in center of
            each circle. Pull edges of dough up and over jam;
            seal. Holding sealed edges, dip under-side of each into
            1 beaten **egg,** and then into
            ⅓ cup **sugar.** Place sugared-side up on greased baking
            sheets.
Bake . . . . at 375° for 15 to 18 minutes.
For use with Pillsbury's Best Self-Rising Flour, omit baking powder and salt.

Tea Topics

Senior Winner by Mrs. John D. Sewell, Atlanta, Georgia

Dainty cookie tarts—quick and easy, with peanut butter-caramel filling . . . no special pans necessary!

BAKE at 325° for 12 to 15 minutes   MAKES 3 dozen

Sift together 1½ cups sifted **Pillsbury's Best All Purpose Flour***
            ½ cup sifted **confectioners' sugar** and
            ½ teaspoon **salt** into mixing bowl.
Cut in . . . . . . ⅔ cup **butter** or margarine until particles are fine.
Combine . . . . . 2 tablespoons **water** and
            ½ teaspoon **vanilla.** Sprinkle over flour mixture, stirring
            with fork to form a dough. Chill for easier handling.
Roll out . . . . dough, half at a time, on floured surface to ⅛-inch
            thickness. Cut into 3-inch rounds. Fit into small
            paper baking cups (tea size). Place on baking sheets.
Bake . . . . at 325° for 12 to 15 minutes. Fill each with 1 teaspoon
            Caramel Filling.
For use with Pillsbury's Best Self-Rising Flour, omit salt.

CARAMEL FILLING

In top of double boiler combine ½ pound (about 28) candy caramels and 2 tablespoons milk. Cook over boiling water until caramels melt. Stir in 2 tablespoons peanut butter. Cool.

Almond Buttercups

Junior Winner by Adele M. Ostrom, Lindstrom, Minnesota

Continental flavor . . . miniature cookie tarts with an almond filling.

BAKE at 350° for 20 to 25 minutes*   MAKES about 3½ dozen

Beat . . . . .2 **eggs** until foamy. Gradually add
½ cup **sugar** and
½ teaspoon **almond extract,** beating until thick and
ivory colored.

Fold in . . . . . .1 cup unblanched **almonds**, ground. Set aside.

Sift together . .2 cups sifted **Pillsbury's Best All Purpose Flour*** and
¼ teaspoon **salt**

Cream . . . . . . .1 cup **butter** or margarine. Add
½ cup **sugar,** creaming well.

Blend in . . . . .1 unbeaten **egg** and
1 teaspoon **vanilla.** Add the dry ingredients gradually;
mix thoroughly.

Line . . . . .bottoms and sides of tiny muffin cups or tart pans,
using rounded teaspoonful of dough in each. Spread
with back of teaspoon. Fill each with rounded teaspoonful of almond mixture.

Bake . . . . .at 350° for 20 to 25 minutes.* Cool 5 minutes before
removing from pans.

*For use with Pillsbury's Best Self-Rising Flour, omit salt; decrease baking
time to 15 to 20 minutes.*

French Tuiles

Senior Winner by Mrs. Marian Wells, Washington, D.C.

*Rich, delicate cookies from France! The word "tuiles" means "tiles."
When stacked they resemble the curved tile roofs of southern France.*

BAKE at 350° for 8 to 10 minutes   MAKES about 5 dozen

Combine . . . .¾ cup (5 to 6) unbeaten **egg whites**

1⅔ cups **sugar** and
¼ teaspoon **salt;*** stir until sugar is dissolved and
mixture is thick.

Blend in . . . . .¾ cup lukewarm melted **butter** and
¼ cup lukewarm melted **shortening.** Mix thoroughly.

Add . . . . .1 cup sifted **Pillsbury's Best All Purpose Flour*** and
¾ cup blanched **almonds,** finely chopped; beat until
smooth.

Drop . . . . .by rounded teaspoonfuls about 5 inches apart onto
lightly greased baking sheets.

Bake . . . . .at 350° for 8 to 10 minutes. Let stand ½ minute.
Remove carefully from sheet with spatula, and place
over rolling pin until firm. (If cookies harden before
they are removed from sheet, reheat in oven for a
few seconds to soften again.)

*For use with Pillsbury's Best Self-Rising Flour, omit salt and increase flour
by 2 tablespoons.*

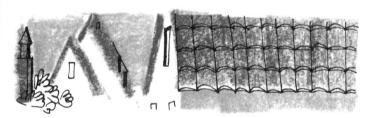

Chocolate Almond Cups

Senior Winner by Mrs. Albert Van Buren, Willmar, Minnesota

*Little butter cookie-cups with a chocolate almond meringue filling.
Rich and delicate party pastries.*

BAKE at 350° for 15 to 20 minutes*   MAKES 3 dozen

Sift together . .2 cups sifted **Pillsbury's Best All Purpose Flour*** and
¼ teaspoon **salt**

Cream......¾ cup **butter** or margarine. Add
        ½ cup **sugar,** creaming well.

Blend in.....1 teaspoon **vanilla.** Add the dry ingredients gradually;
        mix thoroughly.

Press........dough by rounded teaspoonfuls** into very small
        tart shells or small muffin cups,*** greased on the
        bottoms and sides.

Place........a rounded teaspoonful of Brownie-Nut Filling in each.

Bake........at 350° for 15 to 20 minutes.* Cool 15 minutes.
        Loosen tarts carefully; remove from pans.

*For use with Pillsbury's Best Self-Rising Flour, omit salt in pastry and
Filling; decrease baking time to 13 to 16 minutes.*

**For larger cookies, use a tablespoonful of dough in each of 2 dozen medium
muffin cups. Place about 1½ teaspoonfuls of Filling in each.*

***If less than 3 dozen tart shells are available, bake part of cookies at one
time, keeping remaining dough and Filling covered.*

BROWNIE-NUT FILLING

Grind together ¾ cup (¼ lb.) almonds and 1 cup (6-oz. pkg.) semi-sweet chocolate pieces. Beat 2 eggs in medium bowl until thick and ivory colored. Blend in ½ cup sugar, ¼ teaspoon salt and the almond-chocolate mixture.

Lacy Bonnets

Junior Winner by Joan Brueggman, Menomonee Falls, Wisconsin

*Crisp and lacy, honey flavored candy-like cookies are shaped to
resemble wide-brimmed hats with almond "bows."*

BAKE at 375° for 5 to 7 minutes   MAKES about 4 dozen

Cover........tops and necks of 6 empty soft drink bottles with
        aluminum foil. Set aside for shaping baked cookies.

Sift together..1 cup sifted **Pillsbury's Best All Purpose Flour***
        ⅔ cup **sugar**
        ⅛ teaspoon **salt**

Lacy Bonnets

Heat.......½ cup strained **honey** to boiling in small saucepan.
        Remove from heat.

Stir in......½ cup soft **butter** or margarine
        ½ teaspoon **orange extract** and
        ½ teaspoon **almond extract.** Blend in the dry ingredients.

Drop.........by teaspoonfuls about four inches apart onto well-greased baking sheets.

Place........2 slivered **almonds** near edge of each cookie.

Bake.........at 375° for 5 to 7 minutes. Cool about 1 minute;
        remove with spatula.

Shape........by placing hot cookies over tops of bottles. Form
        crown of bonnet by molding warm cookie over
        bottle top. Flare edges for brim. (If cookies harden
        before shaping, reheat in oven for a few minutes.)

For use with Pillsbury's Best Self-Rising Flour, omit salt.

Fruit Buttercups

Senior Winner by Miss Helen R. Henry, Washington, D.C.

Miniature cookie tarts with a filling of black walnuts and colorful fruits.

BAKE at 375° for 12 to 15 minutes   MAKES about 2 dozen

Sift together 2½ cups sifted **Pillsbury's Best All Purpose Flour***
         1 teaspoon **salt** and
         ¼ teaspoon **soda**

Cream . . . . . . ¼ cup **butter** or margarine and
         ½ cup **shortening.** Gradually add
         1 cup **sugar,** creaming well.

Blend in . . . . . 1 unbeaten **egg**
         1 tablespoon **cream** and
         1 teaspoon **vanilla**

Add . . . . the dry ingredients gradually; mix well. Chill while preparing Fruit Filling.

Roll out . . . . half of dough on floured surface to ⅛-inch thickness.

Cut out . . . . . . twelve 3¼-inch circles and twelve 2½-inch circles (you will need to re-roll scraps).

Fit . . . . the larger circles into bottoms of muffin cups. Fill each with 1 tablespoon Filling. Top with a smaller circle; seal edges. Cut slits in the top of each for escape of steam. Repeat with remaining dough.

Bake . . . . at 375° for 12 to 15 minutes. Cool in pans 5 minutes.

*Pillsbury's Best Self-Rising Flour is not recommended for use in this recipe.

FRUIT FILLING

Combine ½ cup sugar, ⅓ cup water, ½ cup chopped black walnuts, ½ cup mixed candied fruit, 1 cup finely cut dates, ¼ cup golden raisins, 1 teaspoon grated orange rind, ⅛ cup orange juice and 2 tablespoons lemon juice. Heat to boiling; simmer 5 minutes, stirring frequently.

Accordion Treats

Grand Prize Winner by Mrs. Gerda Roderer, Berkeley, California

Quick and easy, with novel shaping . . . crisp, wedge-shaped butter cookies baked in an accordion-pleated foil pan! Try your favorite flavor variation.

BAKE at 325° for 25 to 30 minutes   MAKES about 4 dozen

Cream . . . . . . ¾ cup **butter.** Gradually add
         ¾ cup **sugar,** creaming well.

Blend in . . . . . 2 unbeaten **eggs**
         1 teaspoon **vanilla** and
         ¼ teaspoon **salt;*** beat well.

Add . . . . 1¼ cups sifted **Pillsbury's Best All Purpose Flour*** gradually and
         ½ cup chopped **nuts,** if desired; mix thoroughly.

Fold . . . . one yard of heavy-duty aluminum foil lengthwise. Fold the double foil crosswise into 1-inch pleats to make an "accordion-pleated" pan.** Place on baking sheet.

Drop . . . . a rounded teaspoonful of dough into each fold of foil. (Dough spreads during baking.)

Bake . . . . at 325° for 25 to 30 minutes. Cool 10 minutes. Remove cookies; turn foil over for second baking. (Or clean foil with damp cloth and re-use.) Glaze or sprinkle cookies with **confectioners' sugar.**

*For use with Pillsbury's Best Self-Rising Flour, omit salt.
**Four thicknesses of regular aluminum foil may be substituted.

Variations: Substitute a teaspoon of one of the following ingredients for the vanilla and nuts: ground cardamom, caraway seed, anise seed, rum flavoring, almond extract, grated orange rind or lemon rind (or ½ teaspoon orange or lemon extract).

BEST of the BAKE-OFF

Accordian Treats
**Grand Prize Winner
of the Ninth
Grand National
Bake-Off**®

Fudge Sweetarts

Fudge Sweetarts

Junior Winner by Marcia Jensen, Milwaukee, Wisconsin

Party fare! Fudge filling is baked in a tiny pastry shell (no special pans necessary).

BAKE at 350° for 20 to 25 minutes*   MAKES about 2 dozen

Sift together . . 1 cup sifted **Pillsbury's Best All Purpose Flour***
            ¼ teaspoon double-acting **baking powder** and
            ¼ teaspoon **salt** into mixing bowl.
Cut in . . . . . . ⅓ cup **shortening** until particles are fine.
Sprinkle . . . . . 3 to 4 tablespoons beaten **egg** over flour mixture,
            stirring with fork to form a dough.
Roll out . . . . on floured surface to about 1/16-inch thickness. Cut

into 3-inch rounds. Fit into small paper baking cups (tea-size cups). Place on baking sheets.

CHOCOLATE FILLING

Melt . . . . . . 1 cup (6-oz. pkg.) **semi-sweet chocolate pieces** in
            top of double boiler over boiling water.
Stir in . . . . . . ⅓ cup **sugar**
            1 tablespoon **milk**
            1 tablespoon **butter** and
            1 teaspoon **vanilla**. Remove from heat; blend in
            1 beaten **egg**
Place . . . . a scant tablespoonful of Filling in each pastry shell.
            Top with a **pecan half.**
Bake . . . . at 350° for 20 to 25 minutes.*

*For use with Pillsbury's Best Self-Rising Flour, omit baking powder and salt; decrease baking time to 15 to 20 minutes.

Almond Strudels

Senior Winner by Mrs. H. H. Goodman, Fort Wayne, Indiana

A real gourmet cookie—butter pastry surrounds almond marzipan filling.

BAKE at 425° for 15 to 18 minutes   MAKES 4 dozen

Sift together 1¾ cups sifted **Pillsbury's Best All Purpose Flour*** and
            ½ teaspoon **salt** into large mixing bowl.
Cut in . . . . . . ¾ cup **butter** or margarine until particles are fine.
Add . . . . ¼ cup cold **water**; mix well. Divide dough into four
            parts; form each into a 5-inch roll. Wrap; chill at
            least 2 hours.** Prepare Almond Marzipan Filling.
Roll out . . . . . . each part on floured surface to a 14x8-inch rectangle.
            Brush edges with slightly beaten **egg white.**
Shape . . . . one-fourth of Filling into roll 13 inches long. Place
            roll along 14-inch edge of rectangle. Roll tightly,
            sealing ends. Place on ungreased baking sheet,
            seam-side down. Brush with slightly beaten egg white.

Repeat process with remaining dough.

Bake.........at 425° for 15 to 18 minutes. Cool; cut into 1-inch slices. Cookies are best when eaten the same day as baked.

*For use with Pillsbury's Best Self-Rising Flour, omit salt.

**Dough and Filling may be refrigerated up to four days and baked as needed.

ALMOND MARZIPAN FILLING

Combine 1 unbeaten egg, ½ cup sugar, ½ teaspoon vanilla and ¼ teaspoon salt. Gradually add 1 cup (8-oz. can) almond paste, blending thoroughly. Chill at least 2 hours.

Slice 'n' Serve Cookies

Senior Winner by Mrs. Clyde Brethorat, Lodi, Wisconsin

Date and nut batter, topped with maraschino cherries, is baked, then rolled jelly roll fashion. Slice cookies just before serving.

BAKE at 325° for 25 to 35 minutes   MAKES about 3 dozen

Coat.........1 cup **dates,** cut fine, with
            1 tablespoon **flour**
Sift together..⅔ cup sifted **Pillsbury's Best All Purpose Flour***
            ½ teaspoon double-acting **baking powder** and
            ½ teaspoon **salt**
Beat.......3 **eggs** until foamy. Gradually add
            ½ teaspoon **vanilla** and
            ¾ cup **sugar,** beating constantly until thick and ivory colored.
Fold in........the dry ingredients gently but thoroughly. Then fold in
            ½ cup **pecans,** chopped fine, and the dates.
Spread........in 15½x10½x1-inch jelly-roll pan, lined with waxed paper, then greased and floured.
Arrange....10 well-drained **maraschino cherries** across each end of batter about ½ inch from pan edge.

Slice 'n' Serve Cookies

Bake.........at 325° for 25 to 35 minutes.
Turn out......immediately onto waxed paper sprinkled with **confectioners' sugar.** Remove paper, trim edges of cake and cut crosswise into two 10x7½-inch rectangles.
Roll.........each rectangle tightly, beginning with the cherry end. Wrap in waxed paper and cool.
Spread........rolls thinly with Butter Frosting and roll in 1 cup **pecans,** chopped fine. Chill. To serve, cut in ½-inch slices.

*For use with Pillsbury's Best Self-Rising Flour, omit baking powder and salt.

BUTTER FROSTING

Cream 2 tablespoons butter. Blend in 1¼ cups sifted confectioners' sugar alternately with 3 to 4 teaspoons cream. Add ¼ teaspoon vanilla.

Tropic S'prizes

Tropic S'prizes

Junior Winner by Diane W. Hilbert, Cranford, New Jersey

An unusual way to make a filled cookie, with easy pineapple preserve filling to lend a touch of Hawaii.

BAKE at 400° for 15 to 17 minutes   MAKES 4½ dozen

Sift together..2 cups sifted **Pillsbury's Best All Purpose Flour***
    ⅓ cup **sugar**
    ½ teaspoon double-acting **baking powder**
    ¼ teaspoon **soda** and
    ¼ teaspoon **salt** into large mixing bowl.
Add........¼ cup **butter** or margarine and
    ¼ cup **shortening.** Mix with low speed of mixer or pastry blender until particles are fine.

Blend in.....1 unbeaten **egg**
    1 to 2 tablespoons **milk** and
    ½ teaspoon **vanilla.** Mix to form a dough.
Divide........dough into three parts. Roll out one part on floured surface to a 12x4-inch rectangle. Spread with
    ¼ cup **pineapple preserves.** Sprinkle with
    ¼ cup **semi-sweet chocolate pieces** and
    ¼ cup **walnuts,** chopped
Roll.........tightly as for jelly roll, starting with 12-inch side; seal edges and ends. Place seam-side down on greased baking sheet. Repeat with remaining dough.
Bake........at 400° for 15 to 17 minutes. Cool; slice ¾ inch thick. Sprinkle with **confectioners' sugar.**

*For use with Pillsbury's Best Self-Rising Flour, omit baking powder, soda, salt.

Orange Spinning Wheels

Senior Winner by Mrs. Brad R. Walker, Jonesboro, Arkansas

Candied orange peel and nuts fill these attractive butter-pastry pin-wheels. Roll the dough and filling together, slice and bake.

BAKE at 375° for 25 to 30 minutes   MAKES about 4 dozen

Sift together 1¼ cups sifted **Pillsbury's Best All Purpose Flour***
    ½ teaspoon **salt** and
    ½ teaspoon **nutmeg** into mixing bowl.
Cut in......½ cup **butter** or margarine until particles are fine.
Sprinkle.....3 to 4 tablespoons **orange juice** over mixture, stirring with fork until dough is moist enough to hold together. Chill. Prepare Orange-Nut Filling.
Roll out.......half of dough on well-floured surface to a 12x8-inch rectangle.
Spread........with half of Filling. Roll as for jelly roll, starting with 12-inch side. Cut into ½-inch slices. Place cut-side down on greased baking sheets. Repeat with remaining dough and Filling.

Bake. . . . . at 375° for 25 to 30 minutes.
*For use with Pillsbury's Best Self-Rising Flour, omit salt.

ORANGE-NUT FILLING

Combine in small saucepan 1 egg yolk, ⅓ cup sugar, 1 cup nuts, ground, 2 tablespoons orange juice, 2 tablespoons ground candied orange peel and 2 tablespoons butter. Bring just to boil. Cool.

Chocolate Peek-a-Boos

Best of Class Winner by Mrs. Frank M. Ramsey, Philadelphia, Pennsylvania

Tiny cream puff cookies with bits of semi-sweet chocolate inside. They look fancy, but you'll find them very simple to make.

BAKE at 375° for 15 to 20 minutes   MAKES about 6 dozen

Sift together . . 1 cup sifted **Pillsbury's Best All Purpose Flour***
                 ¼ cup **sugar** and
                 ¼ teaspoon **salt**
Melt . . . . ½ cup **butter** or margarine in
                 1 cup **milk** in saucepan.
Add . . . . the dry ingredients, all at once, stirring constantly. Cook until mixture leaves sides of pan in smooth compact ball. *Do not undercook.* Remove from heat.
Blend in . . . . . 4 unbeaten **eggs,** one at a time, beating well after each until mixture is smooth.
Add . . . . 1½ teaspoons **vanilla;** mix well. Cool 30 minutes.
Stir in . . . . . . ½ cup **semi-sweet chocolate pieces**
Drop . . . . by scant teaspoonfuls onto greased baking sheets.**
Bake . . . . at 375° for 15 to 20 minutes. For drier cookies turn off oven after baking; prick cookies with sharp knife, and let stand in oven for 5 minutes. Sprinkle with **confectioners' sugar.** Cool.

*Pillsbury's Best Self-Rising Flour is not recommended for use in this recipe.
**Cookies are best fresh. Dough may be refrigerated up to 3 days and baked as needed.

Swedish Toscas

Senior Winner by Mrs. E. Martinson, Detroit, Michigan

Very rich and tender pastry-shell cookies with a baked-in filling.

BAKE at 350°* for 10 minutes; then   MAKES about 1 dozen
          for 10 to 15 minutes

Cream . . . . . . 6 tablespoons **butter** or margarine; add
                 ¼ cup **sugar,** creaming well.
Blend in . . . . . 1 cup sifted **Pillsbury's Best All Purpose Flour***
Divide . . . . dough into ungreased small muffin cups or very small tart shells. Press into bottoms and half way up sides of muffin cups.
Bake . . . . at 350° for 10 minutes.
Combine . . . . ⅛ cup blanched **almonds,** slivered
                 ¼ cup **sugar**
                 2 teaspoons **flour**
                 2 tablespoons **butter** and
                 1½ tablespoons **cream** in saucepan, stirring constantly, until mixture boils.
Divide . . . . mixture into partially-baked cookie shells.
Bake . . . . at 350° for 10 to 15 minutes. Cool 3 to 5 minutes, then carefully remove from pan.

*For use with Pillsbury's Best Self-Rising Flour, decrease baking temperature to 325°.

Rise 'n' Shiners

Rise 'n' Shiners

Senior Winner by Mrs. Herb Rhodes, Anchorage, Alaska

Yeast-pastry cookies topped with a crunchy inviting mixture of nuts, crushed corn flakes and bright red cherries.

BAKE at 350° for 25 to 30 minutes*   MAKES 2½ dozen

Sift together 2¼ cups sifted **Pillsbury's Best All Purpose Flour*** and
½ teaspoon **salt** into large mixing bowl.
Cut in . . . . . ¾ cup **butter** or margarine until particles are fine.
Combine . . . . ½ cup light **cream** and
1 teaspoon **almond extract**. Blend in
1 cake compressed **yeast**, crumbled. Stir into flour
mixture to form a dough.
Roll out . . . . on floured surface to a 12x10-inch rectangle. Let
stand 20 to 25 minutes.

Brush with . . . . . slightly beaten **egg white**; spread with Cereal-Nut
Topping, pressing firmly into dough.** Cut into
2-inch squares; place on ungreased baking sheets.
Bake . . . . at 350° for 25 to 30 minutes.*

*For use with Pillsbury's Best Self-Rising Flour, omit salt; decrease baking time to 22 to 25 minutes.
**For variety, omit topping; sprinkle dough with sugar and cinnamon.

CEREAL-NUT TOPPING

Combine ½ cup firmly packed brown sugar, 1 cup chopped pecans, ⅓ cup crushed corn flakes and ½ cup maraschino cherries, cut in small pieces. Stir in ⅓ cup melted butter or margarine.

Flaky Sweetheart Crescents

Senior Winner by Mrs. Doris Komperda, Milwaukee, Wisconsin

A pecan meringue filling is rolled up inside these rich and flaky crescents. Made without kneading or rising.

BAKE at 350° for 25 to 30 minutes   MAKES 32 pastries

Sift together . . 4 cups sifted **Pillsbury's Best All Purpose Flour*** and
½ teaspoon **salt** into large mixing bowl.
Cut in . . . . 1 cup **butter** or margarine until particles are fine.
Blend . . . . 3 **egg yolks** with
½ cup **sour cream** (thick or commercial). Add
1 teaspoon **vanilla** and
1 packet active dry **yeast** (or 1 cake compressed yeast);
mix well. Add to the flour-butter mixture. Stir to
form a dough.
Divide . . . . dough into 4 parts.* Roll out each part on surface
sprinkled with **sugar**. Roll to an 11-inch circle ⅛ inch

thick; cut into 8 wedges. Spread with Pecan Filling.

Roll . . . . each wedge, starting with wide end and rolling to point. Place point-side down on greased baking sheet, curving ends to form crescents.

Bake . . . . at 350° for 25 to 30 minutes.*

*For use with Pillsbury's Best Self-Rising Flour, omit salt; decrease baking time to 20 to 25 minutes.

**Dough and filling may be stored in refrigerator up to 2 days and baked as needed. Let dough stand at room temperature for 1 hour before rolling out.

PECAN FILLING

Beat 3 egg whites until stiff, straight peaks form. Stir in 1 cup sugar, ¾ cup pecans, ground, and 1 teaspoon vanilla.

Make-a-Wish Cookies

Senior Winner by Mrs. Ethel Gates, West Warwick, Rhode Island

Everyone will wish for more and more of these yeast cookies coated with sugar and nuts—oh, so good!

BAKE at 400° for 12 to 14 minutes   MAKES 3 dozen

Soften . . . . 1 packet active dry **yeast** (or 1 cake compressed) in ¼ cup warm **water**

Sift together 2½ cups sifted **Pillsbury's Best All Purpose Flour***
¼ cup **sugar** and
1½ teaspoons **salt**

Cream . . . . . . ½ cup **butter** or margarine and
¼ cup **shortening**. Add
2 unbeaten **egg yolks**
¼ cup light **cream** and
1 teaspoon **almond extract**. Beat well.

Make-a-Wish Cookies

Blend in . . . . the softened yeast, the dry ingredients and ½ cup **pecans** or other nuts, finely chopped. Chill at least 1 hour.

Combine . . . . . ¾ cup **sugar**
¾ cup **pecans** or other nuts, finely chopped, and
2 teaspoons **instant coffee**

Roll . . . . rounded teaspoonfuls of dough into 6-inch strips, ½ inch in diameter.

Dip into . . . . a mixture of
2 slightly beaten **egg whites** and
1 tablespoon **water;** drain off excess. Coat with sugar-nut mixture.

Place . . . . on greased foil-lined baking sheets in "V" shapes. Pinch bottoms to resemble wishbones.

Bake . . . . at 400° for 12 to 14 minutes.

*For use with Pillsbury's Best Self-Rising Flour, omit salt.

PIES

Pies, pies and more pies . . . all prize-winning recipes and they're right here in this section. Favorite pies, fruit, custard, cream or chiffon have variations to suit any taste and any occasion. There are recipes for individual tarts and turnovers, too!

GENERAL HINTS

- Two important rules to remember—handle pastry as little as possible, and work quickly.
- Do not reroll pie crust trimmings as this toughens crust. Cut trimmings in strips, sprinkle with grated cheese or cinnamon and sugar, then bake. Serve with salad or tea.
- If some areas of your crust brown quicker than others (result of uneven rolling), cover those spots with small pieces of aluminum foil for remaining baking time.
- For a golden brown crust, brush cream, milk, melted butter or slightly beaten egg white over crust just before baking. If desired, sprinkle with sugar.
- A soft pastry brush is excellent for brushing liquids onto pastry.

- Use a pastry wheel to cut pastry for lattice strips, turnovers and foldovers.
- In two-crust pies, foldovers, and many tarts, slits must be cut in top pastry to allow steam that forms during baking to escape. Use your ingenuity and cut slits into different patterns to decorate pie.
- When using Pillsbury's Best Self-Rising Flour, follow directions in footnote at end of basic pastry recipe. A special footnote has been included in each individual recipe where more changes in the recipe must be made when using self-rising flour.

PASTRY—Basic recipes for one-crust, two-crust and lattice pies are included, with step-by-step photos (see page 462) to help you turn out delicate, flaky pastry that will be the envy of all your friends.

ONE-CRUST PASTRY

BAKE at 450° for 10 to 12 minutes*   MAKES 8 or 9-inch pie

Sift together . . 1 cup sifted **Pillsbury's Best All Purpose Flour*** and ½ teaspoon **salt** into mixing bowl.

Cut in . . . . . . ⅓ cup **shortening** until the size of small peas.

Sprinkle . . . . . 3 to 4 tablespoons cold **water** over mixture, while tossing and stirring lightly with fork. Add liquid to driest particles, pushing lumps to side, until dough is just moist enough to hold together.

Form . . . . into a ball. Flatten to ½-inch thickness; smooth edges.

Roll out . . . . . . on floured surface to a circle 1½ inches larger than inverted 8 or 9-inch pie pan. Fit loosely into pan; gently pat out air pockets. Fold edge to form a standing rim; flute. Prick generously with fork.

Bake . . . . at 450° for 10 to 12 minutes. Cool. Fill as desired.

For use with Pillsbury's Best Self-Rising Flour, omit salt and decrease water to 2 to 3 tablespoons; decrease baking time to 8 to 10 minutes. (Pastry made with self-rising flour is less flaky because it contains a high proportion of baking powder, an ingredient not called for in the basic recipe.)

TWO-CRUST PASTRY

BAKE according to recipe directions   MAKES 8 or 9-inch pie

Sift together . . 2 cups sifted **Pillsbury's Best All Purpose Flour*** and 1 teaspoon **salt** into mixing bowl.

Cut in . . . . . . ⅔ cup **shortening** until the size of small peas.

Sprinkle . . . . . 5 to 6 tablespoons cold **water** over mixture, while tossing and stirring lightly with fork. Add water to driest particles, pushing lumps to side, until dough is just moist enough to hold together.

Divide . . . . in half. Form into balls. Flatten to ½-inch thickness; smooth edges.

Roll out . . . . one part on floured surface to circle 1½ inches larger than inverted 8 or 9-inch pie pan. Fit loosely into pan. Fill; roll out remaining pastry as directed in recipe.

For use with Pillsbury's Best Self-Rising Flour, omit salt; decrease water to 4 to 5 tablespoons.

LATTICE PASTRY

BAKE according to recipe directions   MAKES 8 or 9-inch pie

Sift together 1½ cups sifted **Pillsbury's Best All Purpose Flour** * and ½ teaspoon **salt** into mixing bowl.

Cut in . . . . . . ½ cup **shortening** until the size of small peas.

Sprinkle . . . . . 4 to 5 tablespoons cold **water** over mixture, while tossing and stirring lightly with fork. Add water to driest particles, pushing lumps to side, until dough is just moist enough to hold together.

Form . . . . two-thirds of dough into a ball. Flatten to ½-inch thickness; smooth edges.

Roll out . . . . on floured surface to a circle 1½ inches larger than inverted 8 or 9-inch pie pan. Fit loosely into pan. Fill; roll out remaining pastry as directed in recipe.

For use with Pillsbury's Best Self-Rising Flour, omit salt; decrease water to 3 to 4 tablespoons.

MERINGUES
—Egg whites at room temperature whip up faster and give a better volume. Sprinkling sugar a tablespoonful at a time decreases the possibility of overbeating (photo A). Beat well after each addition until sugar is completely dissolved. Meringue has been beaten enough when it stands in stiff, glossy peaks that tip very slightly when beater is raised (photo B).

To prevent meringue from shrinking during baking, spread it over pie completely, sealing meringue to pie crust (photo C).

MERINGUE 🎀

BAKE at 350° for 12 to 15 minutes

Beat . . . . 3 **egg whites** with ¼ teaspoon **cream of tartar** until soft mounds form when beater is raised.

Add . . . . 6 tablespoons **sugar** gradually, beating well after each addition. Continue beating until meringue stands in stiff, glossy peaks.

Spread . . . . over filling, sealing to edge.

Bake . . . . at 350° for 12 to 15 minutes until browned.

De Luxe Meringue: Use 5 egg whites and increase the sugar to 10 tablespoons.

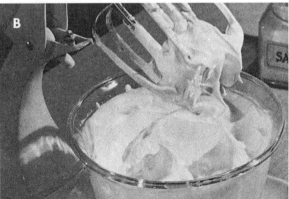

HOW TO MAKE PERFECT PASTRY

Skill in pastry making may be acquired with just a little practice. Follow these step-by-step photos and special hints.

- A 1½-quart bowl is recommended for mixing because fewer strokes are required to moisten the flour-shortening mixture.
- Too little water causes pastry to crack around edges when rolled; too much water makes dough sticky to roll and toughens pastry.
- A pastry cloth and a stockinet-covered rolling pin reduce the amount of flour and the number of strokes needed to roll dough.
- To prevent pastry from shrinking, let dough relax in pie pan about 10 minutes before fluting edge.
- Good pastry should grease the pie pan itself.
- A neat trick for lattice pie is to weave the strips of dough on a baking sheet sprinkled generously with sugar. Tilt the sheet over far edge of pie and move it toward you; lattice work will slide onto the filling.

Two-crust pie: Fill; roll out remaining dough. Cut slits; moisten rim of bottom crust. Transfer pastry to pie pan by rolling on pin; unroll onto pie (or fold in half, then in half again).

1. Sift flour with salt into mixing bowl; with pastry blender, two knives or two forks, cut in shortening until particles are size of small peas. (For richer pastry, add 1 tablespoon firm butter.)

2. Sprinkle water over flour mixture with fork. Add water to driest part, pushing lumps to side, until dough together. Form into ball (or balls). F to ½-inch thickness; smooth edges.

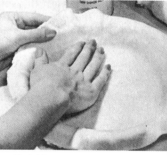

4. Roll dough 1½ inches larger than inverted pie pan; trim edges with sharp knife or scissors. Fold pastry in half; then in half again; lift carefully to pan. *Do not grease pie pans.*

5. Unfold and fit pastry *loosely* into Stretching will result in shrinkage ing baking. Gently push dough on down into bottom of pan and pat out air pockets that form.

Trim edges so pastry extends ½ inch beyond rim of pie pan. Fold edge of top pastry under lower pastry. Flute (a high flute helps prevent juicy pies from boiling over in the oven).

Lattice pie: Fill; roll out remaining do Cut into strips ½ inch wide; crissc over filling to form lattice top. Trim seal ends; fold bottom crust over to cover. Flute.

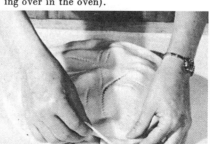

...l out pastry from center to edge in ...ctions, maintaining a circular shape ...en thickness. Use Pillsbury's Best ... Shaker to flour surface evenly to ...t sticking or tearing.

...pie shell: Fold edge of pastry under ...n standing rim. Make edging; prick ...ork. Bake; cool; fill.

...ed pie shell: Make as above; *do not* ... Fill; bake as directed in recipe.

...t pastry strips ½ inch wide and ...half of strips over filling, side by ...wisting each a few times. Place re- ...g strips crosswise over other ... twisting each.

PIE CRUST EDGINGS

Try these edgings to make your pastry attractive as well as tasty. (Coin, Scalloped and Cornucopia are for one-crust pies only.)

FLUTED—Form a high standing rim. Place right index finger inside rim; make flutes every ½ inch by pushing pastry into V with left thumb and index finger outside rim. Pinch flutes for clean edges.

SCALLOPED—Form a standing rim; place left thumb and index finger ¾ inch apart on outside of rim. With right index finger, pull pastry to center to form scallop.

CORNUCOPIA—Allow 1 inch additional overhang; do not turn under or make rim. With scissors, cut overhang into triangles at 1-inch intervals. Roll points in toward rim. Seal "cornucopias" on inner edge.

COIN—Trim pastry even with edge of pan. Cut ¾-inch circles from rolled pastry—use center of doughnut cutter or thimble. Overlap circles on slightly moistened rim; press down lightly.

POLKA DOT—Allow ½ inch overhang; fold under and form a rim. Press rounded end of bottle opener firmly into pastry rim. Repeat around outside rim.

ROPE—Form a standing rim. Place thumb on pastry rim at an angle; press pastry against thumb with knuckle of index finger.

LEAF—Form a high standing rim. With scissors, clip rim at an angle every ¼ inch. Press down clipped rim to right and left.

FORK SCALLOPED—Form standing rim. Mark edges every ¾ inch as for fluted edge. Flatten rim to pan between points with floured fork.

FRUIT PIES

—Fruit fillings may be baked with pastry in a two-crust pie, or they may be cooked and turned into baked pie shell. Recipes can be found using almost any kind of fruit.

To keep two-crust pies from leaking: Roll out bottom pastry larger so that it can be folded over the top pastry; make a high standing rim around edge, then flute.

Help keep your oven clean by making a pan (larger than pie pan) out of foil and placing it on the rack below the pie to catch any drippings.

Crispy-Top Apple Pie

Senior Winner by Mrs. Wayne R. Frazee, Markleysburg, Pennsylvania

Crisp crumb mixture tops a sour cream-apple pie.

BAKE at 450° for 10 minutes, then   MAKES 8-inch pie
     at 350° for 25 to 30 minutes

Prepare . . . . . . .recipe for **One-Crust Pastry,** page 460, using 8-inch pie pan. Do not prick crust; fill and bake as directed below.

Combine . . . .½ cup **sugar**
     1 tablespoon **flour** and
     ¼ teaspoon **salt** in mixing bowl.

Add . . . . .1 slightly beaten **egg**
     ¾ cup **sour cream** (thick or commercial)
     1 teaspoon **vanilla**

Prepare . . . . . .2 cups pared, chopped **apples** (2 medium). Add to sour cream mixture. Turn into pie shell.

Bake . . . . .at 450° for 10 minutes. Decrease temperature to 350°.

Combine . . . .¼ cup **Pillsbury's Best All Purpose Flour** and
     ¼ cup firmly packed **brown sugar.** Cut in
     2 tablespoons **butter.** Sprinkle over pie. Bake 25 to 30 minutes until custard is set.

Apple Orchard Pie

Junior First Prize Winner by Constance Thatcher, Charleston, South Carolina

Unique fresh apple flavor . . . just put shredded apples, sugar and spice into pie shell, and top it off with whipped cream.

BAKE at 450° for 10 to 12 minutes   MAKES 8-inch pie

Prepare . . . . . . .recipe for **One-Crust Pastry,** page 460, using 8-inch pie pan; bake as directed.

Prepare . . . . . .2 cups pared, shredded **apples** (4 to 6 medium)

Combine . . . . .½ cup **sugar** (use confectioners' sugar if apples are juicy) and
     ¼ teaspoon **nutmeg;** blend with apples. Turn into pie shell.

Beat . . . . .½ cup **whipping cream** until thick. Fold in
     1 tablespoon **confectioners' sugar.** Spread over pie. Sprinkle with **nutmeg.** Serve immediately.

Apple Sponge Pie

Junior Winner by Gretchen Hanlon, Quincy, Massachusetts

Butter-rich pastry is filled with apples and covered with a spongecake layer, then baked to a golden brown.

BAKE at 450° for 8 to 10 minutes, then   MAKES 9-inch pie
     at 350° for 20 to 25 minutes

Prepare . . . . . . .recipe for **One-Crust Pastry,** page 460, using 9-inch pie pan; bake at 450° for 8 to 10 minutes.

Combine . . . . .4 cups pared, sliced **apples** (4 medium)
     2 tablespoons **butter** and
     1 tablespoon **water** in saucepan.

Blend . . . . . . .½ cup **sugar** with
     1 tablespoon **flour** and
     ½ teaspoon **cinnamon.** Add to apples; cover and cook over low heat, stirring occasionally, until tender.

Turn . . . . into pie shell. Spread with Sponge Topping.
Bake . . . . at 350° for 20 to 25 minutes. Cool.

SPONGE TOPPING

Beat 2 egg yolks until light. Gradually add ¼ cup sugar, beating until thick and lemon colored. Blend in 1 tablespoon flour. Fold in 1 teaspoon grated lemon rind and 2 tablespoons cream. Beat 2 egg whites until stiff but not dry; fold into egg yolk mixture.

Red Cinnamon Apple Pie

Junior Winner by Judy Ann Fuller, Xenia, Ohio

Just one look at this pie and everyone will ask for a piece. Red cinnamon candies give the filling a bright color and true cinnamon flavor—and a lattice top lets the filling peek through.

BAKE at 425° for 10 minutes, then   MAKES 9-inch pie
    at 350° for 25 to 30 minutes

Sift together . . 2 cups sifted **Pillsbury's Best All Purpose Flour*** and
       1 teaspoon **salt** into large mixing bowl. Add
       ¼ cup blanched **almonds,** finely chopped, if desired.
Cut in . . . . . . ⅔ cup **shortening** until the size of small peas.
Blend . . . . 1 unbeaten **egg** (reserving 1 tablespoon egg white) with
       ¼ cup **water.** Sprinkle over flour mixture, stirring with fork until dough is moist enough to hold together. Divide in half. Form into balls.
Roll out . . . . . . one portion on floured surface to a circle 1½ inches larger than inverted 9-inch pie pan. Fit loosely into pan.

CINNA-APPLE FILLING

Combine . . . . ¾ cup **sugar**
       ½ cup **pineapple juice** and
       ¼ cup **red cinnamon candies.** Bring to boil, simmer 5 minutes.

Red Cinnamon Apple Pie

Prepare . . . . . . 5 cups pared, sliced **apples** (5 medium). Coat with ¼ cup **Pillsbury's Best All Purpose Flour.** Add to sugar syrup. Cook over medium heat, stirring constantly, until thickened.
Turn . . . . into pie shell.
Roll out . . . . remaining dough. Cut into strips ¾ inch wide; crisscross over filling to form lattice top. Trim and seal ends; fold bottom crust over to cover. Flute.
Brush . . . . strips with reserved egg white, slightly beaten. Sprinkle with mixture of
       1 tablespoon **sugar** and
       ¼ teaspoon **cinnamon**
Bake . . . . at 425° for 10 minutes, then at 350° for 25 to 30 minutes.
*For use with Pillsbury's Best Self-Rising Flour, omit salt.

Coconut Crunch Apple Pie

Junior Winner by Karen Getschmann, Bremerton, Washington

Old-fashioned apple pie is varied with a new coconut topping. It toasts to a crunchy, golden brown.

BAKE at 375° for 30 minutes, then   MAKES 9-inch pie
      for 25 to 30 minutes

Prepare . . . . recipe for **One-Crust Pastry**, page 460, using 9-inch
       pie pan. Do not prick; fill and bake as directed below.

Combine . . . . . ⅓ cup **sugar**
       ¼ cup firmly packed **brown sugar**
       2 tablespoons **flour**
       ½ teaspoon **cinnamon** and
       ¼ teaspoon **nutmeg**

Prepare . . . . . . 4 cups pared, sliced **apples** (4 medium). Arrange in
       layers in pie shell, sprinkling sugar mixture over
       each layer.

Sprinkle with . . 2 tablespoons **lemon juice**. Dot with
       2 tablespoons **butter**

Cut . . . . a circle to fit over filling from a double thickness of
       aluminum foil. Press firmly over filling (do not cover
       pastry).

Bake . . . . at 375° for 30 minutes. Remove from oven and
       remove foil. Flatten apple slices with spatula; cover
       with Coconut Topping. Bake 25 to 30 minutes.

COCONUT TOPPING

Beat 1 egg until light and fluffy. Stir in ⅓ cup sugar, ¼ cup milk, ⅛ teaspoon salt and 2 cups coconut, cut fine.

Rosy Apple Pie

Senior Winner by Mrs. DeLamar Turner, Savannah, Georgia

You give a healthy blush to apples in this two-crust pie by simmering the peelings and adding their juice to the filling!

BAKE at 450° for 10 minutes, then   MAKES 9-inch pie
      at 375° for 40 to 50 minutes

Prepare . . . . recipe for **Two-Crust Pastry**, page 460, using 9-inch
       pie pan.

Prepare . . . . . . 5 cups pared, sliced **apples** (5 medium). Simmer
       peelings in
       ½ cup **water** in covered saucepan 10 minutes. Add
       1 to 2 drops **red food coloring**

Combine . . . . . 1 cup **sugar** and
       2 tablespoons **flour**. Sprinkle half of mixture into pie
       shell.

Add . . . . 1 teaspoon grated **lemon rind**
       1 tablespoon **lemon juice** and

¼ teaspoon **nutmeg** to sliced apples. Arrange in layers in pie shell, sprinkling sugar mixture over each layer.

Dot with . . . . . 1 tablespoon **butter.** Pour juice from apple peelings (about 3 tablespoons) over filling.

Roll out . . . . remaining dough; cut slits. Moisten rim of bottom crust. Place top crust over filling. Fold edge under bottom crust; press to seal. Flute.

Bake . . . . at 450° for 10 minutes, then at 375° for 40 to 50 minutes.

Cross-Stitch Apple Pie

Senior Winner by Mrs. Harry F. Clarke, Evanston, Illinois

Spicy apple pie baked in a rectangular pan . . . cut X's in crust for the cross-stitch pattern.

BAKE at 450° for 10 minutes, then   MAKES 10x6 or 8x8-inch pie*
    at 375° for 40 to 50 minutes

Sift together . . 2 cups sifted **Pillsbury's Best All Purpose Flour**** and 1 teaspoon **salt** into large mixing bowl.

Cut in . . . . . . ⅔ cup **shortening** until the size of small peas.

Combine . . . . . 2 slightly beaten **egg yolks**
    3 tablespoons cold **water** and
    1 tablespoon **lemon juice.** Sprinkle over flour mixture, stirring with fork until dough is moist enough to hold together. Form two-thirds of dough into a square.

Roll out . . . . on floured surface to a 14x10-inch rectangle. Fit loosely into 10x6-inch pan.* (Or roll to 12-inch square; fit into 8x8x2-inch pan.)

If desired, pie may be baked in 9-inch pie pan.
***For use with Pillsbury's Best Self-Rising Flour, omit salt.*

APPLE FILLING

Combine . . . . . 5 cups pared, sliced **apples** (5 medium)
    ¾ cup **sugar**

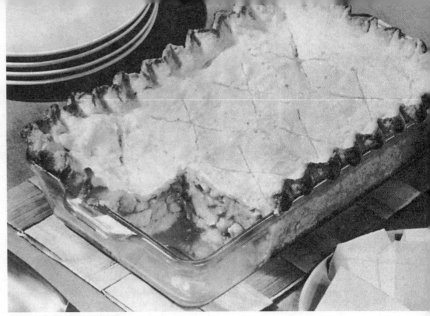

Cross-Stitch Apple Pie

    1 tablespoon **flour**
    ½ teaspoon **cinnamon**
    ½ teaspoon **nutmeg** and
    ¼ teaspoon **salt.** Turn into pastry-lined pan.

Roll out . . . . remaining dough to an 11x7-inch rectangle. (For square pan roll out dough to 9-inch square.) Cut X-shaped slits. Place top crust over filling. Fold edge under bottom crust, pressing to seal. Flute.

Bake . . . . at 450° for 10 minutes, then at 375° for 40 to 50 minutes. Cool slightly; frost with Confectioners' Sugar Icing.

CONFECTIONERS' SUGAR ICING

Measure ½ cup sifted confectioners' sugar into bowl. Blend in ¼ teaspoon vanilla and 2 to 3 teaspoons milk to form a glaze.

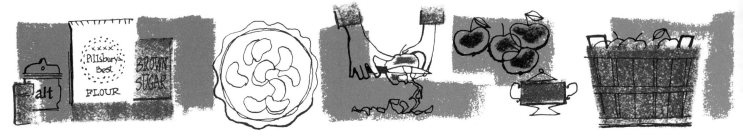

Apple Date Pie

Junior Winner by Susan Dunne, Summit, New Jersey

Dates, spices and a touch of lemon add new flavor to an apple pie.

BAKE at 425° for 15 minutes, then   MAKES 9-inch pie
    at 375° for 25 to 30 minutes

Prepare . . . . recipe for **Two-Crust Pastry,** page 460, using 9-inch
              pie pan.
Prepare . . . . . . 5 cups pared, sliced **apples** (5 medium) and
              ½ cup **dates,** cut in small pieces.
Combine . . . . ½ to ⅔ cup **sugar**
              1 tablespoon **flour**
              ½ teaspoon **cinnamon**
              ¼ teaspoon **salt**
              ¼ teaspoon ground **ginger**
              ¼ teaspoon **nutmeg** and
              1 teaspoon grated **lemon rind**
Arrange . . . . apples and dates in layers in pie shell, sprinkling each
              layer with sugar-spice mixture.
Sprinkle with . . 1 teaspoon **lemon juice.** Dot with
              1 tablespoon **butter**
Roll out . . . . remaining dough; cut slits. Moisten rim of bottom
              crust. Place top crust over filling. Fold edge under
              bottom crust; press to seal. Flute.
Bake . . . . at 425° for 15 minutes, then at 375° for 25 to 30
              minutes.

Topsy Turvy Apple Pie

Senior Winner by Mrs. Donald W. Gaard, Kensington, Minnesota

This is an upside-down pie, with apple filling between two flaky pie crusts and a rich pecan glaze on the top.

BAKE at 450° for 8 minutes, then   MAKES 9-inch pie
    at 375° for 30 to 35 minutes

Combine . . . . ¼ cup firmly packed **brown sugar**
              1 tablespoon **corn syrup** and
              1½ tablespoons **butter,** melted; spread in bottom of 9-
              inch pie pan, greased on the bottom. Arrange
              ¼ cup **pecan halves** over sugar mixture.
Prepare . . . . recipe for **Two-Crust Pastry,** page 460. Fit pastry
              loosely over sugar-pecan mixture.
Combine . . . . ⅔ cup **sugar**
              2 tablespoons **flour** and
              ½ teaspoon **cinnamon**
Arrange . . . . . 4 cups pared, sliced **apples** (4 medium) in layers in pie
              shell, sprinkling each layer with sugar mixture.
Roll out . . . . remaining dough; cut slits. Moisten rim of bottom
              crust. Place top crust over filling. Fold edge under
              bottom crust, pressing to seal. Flute.
Bake . . . . at 450° for 8 minutes, then at 375° for 30 to 35
              minutes. Loosen edges of pie; then invert on serving
              plate, bottom-side up. Serve warm with **plain** or
              whipped cream.

Orchard Mince Pie

Senior Winner by Mrs. Tamar King, Swayzee, Indiana

A full-flavored combination of apples, mincemeat and brown sugar fills this one-crust pie—chopped nuts sprinkle the top.

BAKE at 425° for 10 minutes, then at 350° for 30 to 35 minutes   MAKES 9-inch pie

Prepare . . . . . . recipe for **One-Crust Pastry,** page 460, using 9-inch pie pan. Do not prick crust; fill and bake as directed below.

Combine . . . . ¾ cup firmly packed **brown sugar**
¾ cup **sour** or **sweet cream** and
¼ teaspoon **salt**

Stir in . . . . . . 1 cup prepared **mincemeat** and
2 cups pared, chopped **apples** (2 to 3 medium)

Turn . . . . into pie shell; sprinkle with
½ cup **nuts,** chopped

Bake . . . . at 425° for 10 minutes, then at 350° for 30 to 35 minutes.

Tip-Top Applesauce Pie

Senior Winner by Mrs. Rudolph H. Nelson, Lockhart, Florida

Applesauce is combined with brown sugar in a creamy filling for a one-crust pie. Golden-brown sponge mixture tops it.

BAKE at 425° for 10 minutes, then at 350° for 25 to 30 minutes   MAKES 9-inch pie

Prepare . . . . . . recipe for **One-Crust Pastry,** page 460, using 9-inch pie pan. Do not prick crust; fill and bake as directed below.

Blend . . . . . 1¾ cups (No. 303 can) sweetened **applesauce** with
2 beaten **eggs** and
1 tablespoon **lemon juice** in large mixing bowl.

Combine . . . . ½ cup firmly packed **brown sugar**
3 tablespoons **flour**
½ teaspoon **salt** and
¼ teaspoon **nutmeg.** Add to applesauce mixture; mix thoroughly.

Pour . . . . into pie shell.

TIP-TOPPING

Beat . . . . 3 **egg whites** until soft mounds form. Gradually add
¼ cup **sugar,** beating until meringue stands in stiff, straight peaks.

Blend . . . . ⅛ cup (3-oz. pkg.) softened **cream cheese** with
3 unbeaten **egg yolks.** Add
1 teaspoon grated **lemon rind**
1 tablespoon **lemon juice** and
½ teaspoon **vanilla.** Beat well.

Add . . . . ¼ cup **sugar**
2 tablespoons **flour** and
¼ teaspoon **salt;** mix well. Fold into beaten egg white mixture.

Spread . . . . over filling; seal to edge of crust.

Bake . . . . at 425° for 10 minutes, then at 350° for 25 to 30 minutes.

Cran-Apple Pie

Junior Second Prize Winner by Barbara Campbell, Dayton, Virginia

Cranberries are cooked and sieved for special smoothness. Almonds beneath the lattice top add crunchiness.

BAKE at 400° for 25 to 30 minutes   MAKES 9-inch pie

Sift together 1½ cups sifted **Pillsbury's Best All Purpose Flour*** and
½ teaspoon **salt** into mixing bowl. Stir in
¼ cup blanched **almonds,** finely chopped

Cut in . . . . . ½ cup **shortening** until the size of small peas.

Sprinkle . . . . . 5 to 6 tablespoons cold **water** over mixture, stirring with fork until dough is moist enough to hold together.

Form . . . . two-thirds of dough into a ball.

Roll out . . . . on floured surface to a circle 1½ inches larger than inverted 9-inch pie pan. Fit loosely into pan.

*For use with Pillsbury's Best Self-Rising Flour, omit salt; decrease water to 4 to 5 tablespoons.

CRAN-APPLE FILLING

Cook . . . . 4 cups (1 lb.) **cranberries** in
⅓ cup **water** in large saucepan over low heat until berries burst, 7 to 10 minutes. Stir occasionally. Sieve; return to saucepan.

Combine . . . 2½ cups **sugar** and
⅓ cup sifted **Pillsbury's Best All Purpose Flour;** blend into cranberries.

Add . . . . 2 cups finely chopped **apples** (2 medium). Heat to boiling.

Turn . . . . hot filling into pie shell. Sprinkle
½ cup blanched **almonds,** chopped, around edge of filling.

Roll out . . . . . . remaining dough. Cut into strips ½ inch wide; criss-cross over filling to form lattice top. Trim and seal ends; fold bottom crust over to cover. Flute.

Bake . . . . at 400° for 25 to 30 minutes.

Harvest Moon Fruit Pie

Senior Winner by Mrs. Whitney S. K. Yeaple, Hillsboro, New Hampshire

Cranberries, apples and apricots make the filling for this colorful two-crust pie. A festive addition to fall and winter menus.

BAKE at 375° for 40 to 50 minutes   MAKES 9-inch pie

Prepare . . . . . . recipe for **Two-Crust Pastry,** page 460, using 9-inch pie pan.

Combine . . . . . 4 cups pared, sliced **apples** (4 medium)
1 cup fresh **cranberries,** ground, and
1 cup dried **apricots,** ground

Blend . . . . . . 1½ cups **sugar**
1 tablespoon **flour**
½ teaspoon **cinnamon**
¼ teaspoon **salt** and
¼ teaspoon **nutmeg.** Add to fruit mixture and pour into pie shell. Dot with
1 tablespoon **butter**

Roll out . . . . . . remaining dough; cut slits. Moisten rim of bottom crust. Place top crust over filling. Fold edge under bottom crust, pressing to seal. Flute.

Bake . . . . at 375° for 40 to 50 minutes.

Autumn Glory Pie

Senior Winner by Mrs. E. L. Shiddenhelm, Springfield, Ohio

Apricots and raisins make a colorful pie that tastes as good as it looks.

BAKE at 400° for 20 to 25 minutes   MAKES 8-inch pie

Sift together 1½ cups sifted **Pillsbury's Best All Purpose Flour*** and
          ¾ teaspoon **salt** into mixing bowl.

Cut in...... ½ cup **shortening** until the size of small peas.

Combine..... 1 tablespoon grated **orange rind**
          2½ tablespoons **orange juice** and
          2½ tablespoons **water**. Sprinkle over the dry ingredients, stirring with fork until dough is moist enough to hold together.

Divide........ in two parts, one twice as large as the other. Form into balls.

Roll out...... larger portion on floured surface to a circle 1½ inches larger than inverted 8-inch pie pan. Fit loosely into pan.

*For use with Pillsbury's Best Self-Rising Flour, omit salt.

APRICOT-RAISIN FILLING

Drain....... 1 No. 2½ can **apricot halves,** reserving syrup.

Combine.... ½ cup **sugar**
          2 tablespoons **cornstarch**
          ¼ teaspoon **salt** and the 1⅔ cups apricot syrup in saucepan. Cook over medium heat, stirring constantly, until thick.

Stir in....... 2 tablespoons **butter**
          2 teaspoons grated **lemon rind**
          1 cup **raisins** and the 1½ cups apricot halves, quartered. Cool.

Turn.......... into pie shell.

Roll out...... remaining dough. Cut into strips ½ inch wide; criss-cross over filling to form a lattice top. Trim and seal ends. Fold bottom crust over to cover; flute.

Bake......... at 400° for 20 to 25 minutes.

Apricot Party Surprise

Senior Winner by Mrs. Maria Kunster, Old Westbury, Long Island, New York

Canned apricot halves and a ground almond mixture fill this European pie-size "tart"—twisted strips of pastry top it.

BAKE at 375° for 40 to 45 minutes   MAKES 8-inch pie

Sift together 1½ cups sifted **Pillsbury's Best All Purpose Flour*** and
          ¼ teaspoon **salt** into mixing bowl.

Cut in..... ¾ cup **butter** or margarine until the size of small peas.

Blend .... 1 unbeaten **egg** with
          2 tablespoons **water**. Sprinkle over flour mixture while stirring with fork to form a dough. Chill 1½ hours.

*For use with Pillsbury's Best Self-Rising Flour, omit salt.

APRICOT FILLING

Drain....... 1 No. 303 can **apricot halves** (17 to 21). Set aside.

Grind....... 1 cup unblanched **almonds**

Combine..... 2 unbeaten **eggs**
          ¾ cup **sugar**
          ⅛ teaspoon **salt** and
          1 teaspoon **vanilla;** blend thoroughly with a spoon, 2 to 3 minutes. *Do not beat.* Stir in ground almonds.

Divide........ dough into two portions, one twice as large as the other. Form into balls.

Roll out...... larger portion on floured surface to a circle 1½ inches larger than 8-inch round layer pan. Fit loosely into pan.

Arrange....... apricots over pastry, reserving one for top of pie. Pour almond mixture over apricots.

Roll out..... remaining dough; cut slits. Place over filling; seal.

Reroll........ pastry trimmings; cut into ½-inch strips. Moisten 8 strips, twist and arrange like spokes of a wheel from center to edge of pie. Arrange more twisted strips around edge. Place apricot half in center; place blanched **almond halves** between "spokes."

Bake......... at 375° for 40 to 45 minutes.

Coconut Apricot Pie

Junior Winner by Miss Paula Berrey, Casper, Wyoming

A choice combination! Toasty coconut in a cookie crust with a quick apricot filling—whipped cream and coconut for garnish.

BAKE at 375° for 12 to 15 minutes   **MAKES 9-inch pie**

Toast........1 cup **coconut** at 375° for 7 to 10 minutes. Stir frequently.

Cream......½ cup **butter** or margarine. Add
3 tablespoons **sugar,** creaming well. Blend in
1 teaspoon **vanilla**

Add........1 cup sifted **Pillsbury's Best All Purpose Flour*** gradually; mix thoroughly. Stir in the coconut, reserving 2 tablespoons for topping. Chill 30 minutes.

Press.........dough firmly into bottom and sides of ungreased 9-inch pie pan.

Freshy's Blueberry Pie

Bake.........at 375° for 12 to 15 minutes. Cool.
**Pillsbury's Best Self-Rising Flour may be substituted.*

APRICOT FILLING

Drain.......1 No. 2½ can **apricot halves;** reserve 1 cup syrup.

Combine....½ cup **sugar**
2½ tablespoons **cornstarch** and
⅛ teaspoon **salt** in saucepan. Blend in syrup.

Cook.........over medium heat, stirring constantly, until very thick and clear. Stir in
2 tablespoons **butter**
1 teaspoon grated **lemon rind** and
1 tablespoon **lemon juice.** Add the apricot halves.

Turn.........into pie shell. Top with **whipped cream** and the reserved coconut.

Freshy's Blueberry Pie

Senior Winner by Mrs. R. M. Sousa, West Chicago, Illinois

Fresh or frozen—blueberries combine with whipped cream to make a "cool" dessert the year 'round.

BAKE at 450° for 10 to 12 minutes   **MAKES 9-inch pie**

Prepare.......recipe for **One-Crust Pastry,** page 460, using 9-inch pie pan; bake as directed.

Combine....¾ cup **sugar**
2½ tablespoons **cornstarch** and
¼ teaspoon **salt** in saucepan.

Blend in.....⅜ cup **water** and
1 cup frozen or fresh **blueberries.** Bring to boil; cook, stirring constantly, until very thick.

Stir in.......2 tablespoons **butter** and
1½ tablespoons **lemon juice.** Cool.

Fold in......2 cups frozen or fresh **blueberries.** Chill 1 hour.

Beat........1 cup **whipping cream** until thick; add

2 tablespoons **confectioners' sugar** and
½ teaspoon **vanilla.** Spread half of whipped cream over bottom of pie shell. Top with blueberry filling. Chill about 2 hours. Garnish with remaining whipped cream.

Banana Split Pie

Junior First Prize Winner by Janet Winquest, Holdredge, Nebraska

No cooking is needed for the butter-cream filling of this delectable pie. Just fold in fresh bananas and grated chocolate.

BAKE at 450° for 10 to 12 minutes   MAKES 8-inch pie

Prepare . . . . recipe for **One-Crust Pastry,** page 460, using 8-inch pie pan; bake as directed.
Cream . . . . . . ½ cup **butter** or margarine. Gradually add 1½ cups sifted **confectioners' sugar,** creaming well.
Add . . . . 2 unbeaten **eggs,** beating 3 minutes after each. (With mixer use a medium speed.)
Blend in . . . . . 1 teaspoon **vanilla**
Fold in . . . . . . 1 square (1 oz.) grated unsweetened **chocolate** and 2 sliced **bananas.** Turn into pie shell. Garnish with chopped **walnuts.**
Chill . . . . 2 to 3 hours. Just before serving, slice 1 **banana** over top. (Best served same day.)

Cherry-Berry Pie

Senior Winner by Mrs. Burr Carter, Elroy, Wisconsin

Cherries and strawberries in a generous two-crust pie.

BAKE at 425° for 25 to 30 minutes   MAKES 9-inch pie

Prepare . . . . recipe for **Two-Crust Pastry,** page 460, using 9-inch pie pan.

Drain . . . . 1 No. 2 can **pie cherries** and 1 package (10 oz.) thawed frozen **strawberries,** reserving juices.
Combine . . . . . 1 cup **sugar**
¼ teaspoon **salt**
2 tablespoons **quick-cooking tapioca** and
2 tablespoons **cornstarch** in saucepan; stir well.
Blend in . . . . the reserved cherry and strawberry juices; stir until sugar dissolves. Cook over medium heat, stirring constantly, until thick and clear, 5 to 8 minutes. Remove from heat.
Stir in . . . . 1 tablespoon **lemon juice** and the drained fruit.
Turn . . . . into pie shell.
Roll out . . . . . . remaining dough; cut slits. Moisten rim of bottom crust. Place top crust over filling. Fold edge under bottom crust; seal. Flute. Sprinkle with **sugar.**
Bake . . . . at 425° for 25 to 30 minutes. Cool.

Cherry-Berry Pie

Cheese Cake Cherry Pie

Cheese Cake Cherry Pie

Bride Winner by Mrs. Henri L. J. deSibour, Jr., Royal Oak, Michigan

A delightful big cherry pie! It's topped with a cream cheese "cheese-cake" mixture and baked in a cookie crust.

BAKE at 350° for 15 minutes, then for 30 minutes   MAKES 9-inch pie

Cream . . . . . . ½ cup **butter** or margarine with
         2 tablespoons **sugar** and
         ⅛ teaspoon **salt***
Add . . . . 1 cup sifted **Pillsbury's Best All Purpose Flour;*** blend well. Press crumb mixture into bottom and sides of 9-inch pie pan (do not cover rim of pan).

*For use with Pillsbury's Best Self-Rising Flour, omit salt and decrease first baking period to 12 minutes.

CHERRY FILLING

Drain . . . . 1 No. 2 can sour **pie cherries,** reserving juice.
Combine . . . . ½ cup **sugar** and
         3 tablespoons **flour** in saucepan. Add the cherry juice (about ¾ cup); mix well.
Cook . . . . over medium heat, stirring constantly, until thickened. Remove from heat; add cherries. Blend in ⅛ teaspoon **red food coloring**
Turn . . . . into pie shell.
Bake . . . . at 350° for 15 minutes. Spread Cheese Cake Topping over Filling, leaving a 3-inch circle in center of pie uncovered. Seal topping to edge of crust. Bake 30 minutes. Cool before serving.

CHEESE CAKE TOPPING

Combine ⅔ cup (two 3-oz. pkgs.) softened cream cheese, 1 unbeaten egg, ⅓ cup sugar and ½ teaspoon vanilla. Beat until thick and creamy.

Sunny Lemon Fluff Pie

Senior Winner by Mrs. E. G. Zemer, Alexandria, Virginia

This tart lemon pie, made by an unusual method, is wonderfully creamy and smooth. Coconut adds flavor and texture.

BAKE at 450° for 10 to 12 minutes, then at 350° for 12 to 15 minutes   MAKES 9-inch pie

Prepare . . . . . . recipe for **One-Crust Pastry,** page 460, using 9-inch pie pan; bake as directed.
Beat . . . . 4 **egg yolks** in top of double boiler until thick and lemon colored.
Add . . . . ⅔ cup **sugar** gradually; beat well after each addition. Cook over hot water until mixture begins to thicken around sides of pan, 5 to 7 minutes.
Blend in . . . . . 2 teaspoons grated **lemon rind**

¼ cup **lemon juice** and
¼ teaspoon **nutmeg.** Continue cooking, stirring constantly, until thick, about 10 minutes.

Beat . . . . 4 **egg whites** until foamy. Add
⅔ cup **sugar** gradually, beating until meringue stands in stiff, glossy peaks. Blend one-third of meringue into lemon mixture; cool. Turn into pie shell.

Fold . . . . ½ cup **coconut** into remaining meringue. Spread on top of filling. Sprinkle with **nutmeg.**

Bake . . . . at 350° for 12 to 15 minutes.

Two-Crust Slice o' Lemon Pie

Senior Second Prize Winner by Mrs. Charles M. Reppert, Port Washington, N.Y.

Paper-thin lemon slices go into the creamy filling of this unique pie.

BAKE at 400° for 30 to 35 minutes   MAKES 8-inch pie

Prepare . . . . recipe for **Two-Crust Pastry,** page 460, using 8-inch pie pan.

Combine . . . 1¼ cups **sugar**
2 tablespoons **flour** and
⅛ teaspoon **salt**

Blend in . . . . . ¼ cup soft **butter** or margarine; mix thoroughly.

Add . . . . 3 well-beaten **eggs,** reserving 1 teaspoon egg white for crust. Blend until smooth.

Grate . . . . . . 1 teaspoon **lemon rind** from
1 medium-sized **lemon.** Peel the lemon; cut into paper thin slices, about ⅓ cup.

Add . . . . ½ cup **water,** lemon rind and lemon slices to sugar mixture. Blend well. Turn into pie shell.

Roll out . . . . . . remaining dough; cut slits. Place over filling. Fold edge of top crust under bottom crust; seal and flute. Brush with **egg white** and sprinkle with **sugar** and **cinnamon.**

Bake . . . . at 400° for 30 to 35 minutes.

Tangy Hawaiian Pie

Senior Winner by Mrs. Herman Neitzel, Mankato, Minnesota

If you like lemon pie like Mother used to make—you're sure to like this lemony pineapple pie!

BAKE at 450° for 10 to 12 minutes   MAKES 9-inch pie

Prepare . . . . . . recipe for **One-Crust Pastry,** page 460, using 9-inch pie pan; bake as directed.

Combine . . . . . 1 cup **sugar**
½ cup sifted **Pillsbury's Best All Purpose Flour**
¼ teaspoon **salt** and
2 to 3 teaspoons grated **lemon rind** in saucepan.

Add . . . . . . 1¼ cups **water**
¼ to ⅓ cup **lemon juice** and
1 cup (9-oz. can) **crushed pineapple;** blend well. Bring to a boil, stirring constantly; cook over medium heat until thick, about 5 minutes.

Blend . . . . a little of the hot mixture into
3 slightly beaten **egg yolks.** Add to hot mixture and cook for 2 minutes, stirring constantly.

Stir in . . . . 1 tablespoon **butter.** Cover and cool to lukewarm.

Turn . . . . into pie shell. Top with **whipped cream** and garnish with chopped **nuts** or grated lemon rind. (Or top with **Meringue,** page 461, using leftover egg whites.)

Limelight Pie

Limelight Pie

Best of Class Winner by Mrs. F. A. Riecke, Pasadena, California

Here is a refreshing pie . . . the filling boasts fresh lime juice and crushed pineapple and calls for no cooking at all!

BAKE at 400° for 10 to 12 minutes   MAKES 8-inch pie

Sift together . ¾ cup sifted **Pillsbury's Best All Purpose Flour***
      2 tablespoons **sugar** and
      ¼ teaspoon **salt** into mixing bowl.

Cut in . . . . . ¼ cup **shortening** until the size of small peas.

Drip . . . . ½ square (½ oz.) melted unsweetened **chocolate** over mixture, tossing lightly with fork.

Sprinkle . . . . . 2 to 3 tablespoons cold **water** over mixture, stirring with fork until dough is moist enough to hold

together. Form into a ball.

Roll out . . . . on floured surface to a circle 1½ inches larger than inverted 8-inch pie pan. Fit loosely into pan; gently pat out air pockets. Fold edge to form a rim; flute. Prick generously.

Bake . . . . at 400° for 10 to 12 minutes.

LIME FILLING

Combine . . . . . 1 can (15 oz.) **sweetened condensed milk**
      ⅓ cup **lime juice** (about 2 limes) ** and
      ¼ teaspoon **salt**; stir until thickened.

Blend in . . . . . ⅔ cup well-drained **crushed pineapple** (9-oz. can) and 2 to 4 drops **green food coloring**; mix well.

Turn . . . . filling into pie shell. Chill 2 to 3 hours. Serve with **whipped cream.** If desired, garnish with shaved **chocolate.**

**For use with Pillsbury's Best Self-Rising Flour, omit salt in pastry; decrease baking time 8 to 10 minutes.*

***If desired, ¼ cup lemon juice may be substituted for lime juice, omitting food coloring and adding 1 tablespoon grated lemon rind.*

Mystic Chocolate Orange Pie

Senior Winner by Mrs. A. C. Biggs, Evansville, Indiana

There's a hidden layer of chocolate under the smooth orange cream filling, which needs no cooking.

BAKE at 450° for 10 to 12 minutes   MAKES 8-inch pie

Prepare . . . . recipe for **One-Crust Pastry,** page 460, using 8-inch pie pan; bake as directed. Sprinkle pie shell immediately with
      ¼ cup **semi-sweet chocolate pieces;** spread as they melt.

Grate . . . . 2 tablespoons **orange rind.** Set aside.

Prepare . . . . . . 1 cup **orange sections** (2 to 3 oranges). Reserve 6 to

8 sections for garnish. Cut remaining sections in half.

Blend . . . . 1 can (15 oz.) **sweetened condensed milk** with
⅓ cup plus 1 tablespoon **lemon juice**
1 unbeaten **egg**
⅛ teaspoon **salt** and the grated orange rind.

Fold in . . . . the pieces of orange sections.

Turn . . . . into pie shell; chill until set, 2 to 3 hours. Garnish
with **whipped cream** and reserved orange sections.

Golden Nugget Orange Pie

Senior Winner by Mrs. Beltran S. Phillips, South Charleston, West Virginia

*Pineapple and orange juice combine to give a wonderfully fresh
flavor to this pie.*

BAKE at 450° for 10 to 12 minutes, then   MAKES 9-inch pie
350° for 12 to 15 minutes

Prepare . . . . recipe for **One-Crust Pastry**, page 460, using 9-inch
pie pan; bake as directed.

Drain . . . . 1 No. 2 can **crushed pineapple** or pineapple chunks,
reserving juice.

Heat . . . . 1 cup **orange juice** (fresh, frozen or canned) and 1 cup
reserved pineapple juice in saucepan.

Combine . . . . ½ cup **sugar**
4 tablespoons **cornstarch** and
¼ cup **water**; mix until smooth. Stir slowly into hot
juices. Cook over medium heat, stirring constantly,
until thick and clear.

Blend . . . . a little of the hot mixture into
3 slightly beaten **egg yolks**; add to hot mixture. Cook
2 minutes.

Stir in . . . . the 1½ cups pineapple and
1 tablespoon **butter**. Cool. Turn into pie shell.

Prepare . . . . **Meringue,** page 461; spread over filling.

Bake . . . . at 350° for 12 to 15 minutes.

Marmalade Mince Pie

Senior Winner by Mrs. Hilaire Lacasse, Manchester, New Hampshire

An easy mincemeat pie, with the fresh tang of orange marmalade.

BAKE at 425° for 35 to 40 minutes   MAKES 8 or 9-inch pie

Prepare . . . . recipe for **Two-Crust Pastry,** page 460, using 8 or
9-inch pie pan.

Combine . . . . . 2 cups prepared **mincemeat**
½ cup **orange marmalade**
2 tablespoons **flour** and
1 tablespoon **lemon juice.** Mix well.

Turn . . . . into pie shell.

Roll out . . . . remaining dough; cut slits. Moisten rim of bottom
crust. Place top crust over filling. Fold edge under
bottom crust, pressing to seal. Flute.

Bake . . . . at 425° for 35 to 40 minutes.

Marmalade Mince Pie

Lemon-Topped Mince Pie

Senior Winner by Miss Wetona L. Crawford, Pleasant Hill, California

A tangy sponge topping is baked on this big one-crust mince pie . . . adds more flavor to an old favorite.

BAKE at 350° for 45 to 50 minutes   MAKES 9-inch pie

Prepare . . . . recipe for **One-Crust Pastry,** page 460, using 9-inch pie pan. Do not prick crust; fill and bake as directed below.

Combine . . . . . 1 package (9 oz.) dry **mincemeat,** broken in pieces
2 tablespoons **sugar** and
1 cup **water** in small saucepan. Bring to boil; boil 1 minute. Cool.

Stir in . . . . . . 2 tablespoons chopped **walnuts.** Turn into pie shell. Pour Lemon Topping over mincemeat.

Bake . . . . at 350° for 45 to 50 minutes. Cool. Serve with **whipped cream,** if desired.

LEMON TOPPING

Combine 2 tablespoons butter, ⅔ cup sugar and 2 tablespoons flour; mix well. Blend in 2 egg yolks. Stir in 1 tablespoon grated lemon rind, 2 tablespoons lemon juice and ¾ cup milk. Beat 2 egg whites until soft peaks form; gently fold into egg yolk mixture.

Deep Purple Raisin Pie

Senior Winner by Mrs. Albert Elstermeier, Rockville, Nebraska

Such simple grape juice-raisin filling . . . a pie the family will love.

BAKE at 450° for 10 minutes, then   MAKES 8 or 9-inch pie
  at 375° for 25 to 30 minutes

Prepare . . . . recipe for **Two-Crust Pastry,** page 460, using 8 or 9-inch pie pan.

Cook . . . . 1 cup seedless **raisins** in
2 cups **grape juice** in saucepan over medium heat until raisins are plump, about 10 minutes. Add
1 tablespoon **butter**

Combine . . . . . 1 cup **sugar** and
3½ tablespoons **cornstarch.** Blend in
¼ cup **grape juice** and
1 tablespoon **lemon juice.** Stir into raisin mixture.

Cook . . . . over medium heat, stirring constantly, until thick and clear. Pour into pie shell.

Roll out . . . . . . remaining dough; cut slits. Moisten rim of bottom crust. Place top crust over filling. Fold edge under bottom crust; press to seal. Flute.

Bake . . . . at 450° for 10 minutes, then at 375° for 25 to 30 minutes.

Wintertime Fruit Pie

Senior Winner by Mrs. Jack Harrington, Martinez, California

Pineapple and prunes for sweet fruity flavor, walnuts for crunchy texture make the filling of this rich two-crust pie.

BAKE at 425° for 25 to 30 minutes   MAKES 8 or 9-inch pie

Prepare . . . . recipe for **Two-Crust Pastry**, page 460, using 8 or 9-inch pie pan.

Chop . . . . 1 cup cooked dried **prunes**

Drain . . . . 1 cup (No. 1 can) **crushed pineapple**; reserve juice.

Blend . . . . ¼ cup **sugar**
2 tablespoons **cornstarch**
¼ teaspoon **salt** and
¾ cup **liquid** (pineapple juice plus water). Cook over low heat, stirring constantly, until thick and clear. Remove from heat.

Add . . . . 1 tablespoon **butter**
4 teaspoons **lemon juice** and
½ cup **walnuts**, chopped. Stir in prunes and drained pineapple. Turn into pie shell.

Roll out . . . . remaining dough; cut slits. Moisten rim of bottom crust. Place top crust over filling. Fold edge under bottom crust, pressing to seal. Flute. Brush top with **cream** and sprinkle with **sugar.**

Bake . . . . at 425° for 25 to 30 minutes.

Scandinavian "Fruit Soup" Pie

Senior Winner by Mrs. Nick Hack, St. Louis, Missouri

The traditional fruits used in Fruktsuppe—fruit soup—now in a pie!

BAKE at 400° for 25 to 30 minutes   MAKES 9-inch pie

Prepare . . . . recipe for **Lattice Pastry**, page 461, using 9-inch pie pan; fill and bake as directed below.

Combine . . . . ⅔ cup **sugar**
3 tablespoons **cornstarch** and
⅛ teaspoon **salt** in saucepan.

Stir in . . . . . . ¾ cup **orange juice**
½ cup **prune juice** and
2 tablespoons **lemon juice**. Cook, stirring constantly, until thick. Remove from heat.

Add . . . . ¾ cup sweetened **applesauce**
½ cup dried **currants**
1 cup cooked, cut **prunes** (about 30)*
1½ teaspoons grated **orange rind** and
1 tablespoon **butter**. Turn into pie shell.

Roll out . . . . . . remaining dough. Cut into strips ½ inch wide; criss-cross over filling to form lattice top. Trim and seal ends; fold bottom crust over to cover. Flute. Brush strips with **milk** and sprinkle with **sugar.**

Bake . . . . at 400° for 25 to 30 minutes.

If desired, ½ cup cooked apricots may be substituted for ½ cup of the prunes.

Scandinavian "Fruit Soup" Pie

Pearisian Pie

Pearisian Pie

Senior Winner by Mrs. Joan C. Chiakalos, Chicago, Illinois

Good winter baking apples are hard to come by . . . combine pears and applesauce for just-as-good a pie.

BAKE at 400° for 30 to 40 minutes   MAKES 9-inch pie

Prepare . . . . recipe for **Two-Crust Pastry,** page 460, using 9-inch
                 pie pan.
Combine . . . . . 1 cup sweetened **applesauce**
                 ½ cup **sugar***
                 1 tablespoon **brown sugar** and
                 1 teaspoon **cinnamon**
Add . . . . 4 cups pared, sliced fresh **pears***
Turn . . . . into pie shell. Drizzle with
                 3 tablespoons melted **butter.**

Roll out . . . . . . remaining dough; cut slits. Moisten rim of bottom
                 crust. Place top crust over filling. Fold edge under
                 bottom crust, pressing to seal. Flute. Brush with
                 1 tablespoon **butter,** melted
Bake . . . . at 400° for 30 to 40 minutes.
*Or substitute 2 No. 2 cans pears, drained and sliced. Decrease sugar to ¼ cup.

Pear Crunch Pie

Senior Winner by Mrs. Russell B. Stefanski, Long Beach, California

A spicy butter-pecan crunch is baked on top a refreshing pear filling. You'll love this new flavor in a fruit pie.

BAKE at 425° for 20 to 25 minutes   MAKES 9-inch pie

Prepare . . . . recipe for **One-Crust Pastry,** page 460, using 9-inch
                 pie pan. Do not prick crust; fill and bake as directed
                 below.
Blend . . . . 1 cup sifted **Pillsbury's Best All Purpose Flour** with
                 ½ cup firmly packed **brown sugar**
                 ½ cup **butter** or margarine
                 ¼ teaspoon **cinnamon** and
                 ¼ teaspoon **nutmeg** until mixture resembles coarse
                 crumbs. Stir in
                 ½ cup **nuts,** chopped. Reserve for topping.
Drain . . . . 1 No. 2½ can **pear halves,** reserving syrup.
Combine . . . . ¼ cup **sugar**
                 2 tablespoons **cornstarch**
                 ⅛ teaspoon **salt** and
                 ⅛ teaspoon **nutmeg** in 2-quart saucepan.
Blend in . . . . 1½ cups **liquid** (pear syrup plus water). Cook, stirring
                 constantly, until thick and clear, about 5 minutes.
                 Remove from heat.
Add . . . . 1 tablespoon **butter**
                 1 teaspoon grated **lemon rind** and
                 1 tablespoon **lemon juice**

Cut . . . . the drained pear halves in half; arrange in pie shell. Cover with the thickened pear syrup. Top with the crumb mixture.

Bake . . . . at 425° for 20 to 25 minutes. Decorate with 8 **nut halves.** Cool. Serve with **whipped cream.**

Fresh Pear Pie

Senior Winner by Mrs. Evelyn Roseboom, Grand Rapids, Michigan

You'll like this idea in fruit pies—a cinnamon and sliced fresh pear filling baked between layers of flaky pastry.

BAKE at 450° for 10 minutes, then   MAKES 9-inch pie
    at 350° for 35 to 40 minutes

Prepare . . . . . . recipe for **Two-Crust Pastry,** page 460, using 9-inch pie pan.

Combine . . . . ½ cup **sugar**
    3 tablespoons **flour**
    1 teaspoon **cinnamon** and
    ¼ teaspoon **salt**

Prepare . . . . . . 5 cups peeled, sliced fresh **pears** (6 to 7).* Arrange in layers in pie shell, sprinkling sugar mixture over each layer.

Dot with . . . . . 1 tablespoon **butter.** Sprinkle with
    1 teaspoon grated **lemon rind** and
    1 tablespoon **lemon juice**

Roll out . . . . remaining dough; cut slits. Moisten rim of bottom crust. Place top crust over filling. Fold edge under bottom crust; press to seal. Flute.

Bake . . . . at 450° for 10 minutes, then at 350° for 35 to 40 minutes. Serve plain or with whipped cream or ice cream.

If desired, substitute canned pears (2 No. 2½ cans); decrease sugar to ¼ cup and flour to 2 tablespoons. Bake at 450° for 10 minutes, then at 350° for 30 minutes.

Golden Dream Peach Pie

Senior Winner by Mrs. George B. Wesler, Milwaukee, Wisconsin

Use either fresh or canned golden peaches . . . with caramel butter syrup and a touch of whipped cream.

BAKE at 450° for 10 minutes, then   MAKES 9-inch pie
    at 375° for 25 to 35 minutes

Prepare . . . . recipe for **One-Crust Pastry,** page 460, sifting ¼ teaspoon **nutmeg** with the flour. Use 9-inch pie pan; fill and bake as directed below.

Arrange . . . . 12 fresh or canned **peach halves** (or 3 cups peach slices), well drained, in pie shell.

Melt . . . . 3 tablespoons **butter** in saucepan. Stir in
    1 cup firmly packed **brown sugar**
    ⅓ cup **Pillsbury's Best All Purpose Flour** and
    2 tablespoons **water** or peach juice; heat until sugar melts. Pour over peaches.

Bake . . . . at 450° for 10 minutes. Decrease oven temperature to 375° and bake 25 to 35 minutes. Cool thoroughly.

Beat . . . . 1 cup **whipping cream** until thick. Add
    ½ teaspoon **vanilla** and 1 tablespoon of the caramelized syrup from pie; spoon around edge of pie. Sprinkle with **nutmeg.**

Fruit in Cream Pie

Senior Winner by Mrs. Leonard Huber, Ste. Genevieve, Missouri

A fruit salad "party" pie garnished with cheese cracker crumbs.

BAKE at 450° for 10 to 12 minutes   MAKES 8 or 9-inch pie

Prepare.......recipe for **One-Crust Pastry,** page 460, using 8 or 9-inch pie pan; bake as directed.
Combine......in mixing bowl
    1 cup **sliced peaches,** well drained
    ½ cup **dates,** cut in small pieces
    ½ cup **marshmallows,** quartered
    1½ cups sliced **bananas**
    3 tablespoons **lemon juice** and
    3 tablespoons **honey.** Chill until serving time. Drain.
Beat.......½ cup **whipping cream** until thick. Fold in fruit mixture. Spoon into pie shell. Sprinkle
    2 tablespoons crushed **cheese crackers** over top.

Pineapple Crunch Pie

Pineapple Crunch Pie

Senior Winner by June L. McVey, Lincoln, Nebraska

Clear, golden pineapple filling is enclosed in this two-crust pie. It has a crunch topping made from brown sugar and pecans.

BAKE at 425° for 15 minutes, then   MAKES 8-inch pie
    for 9 to 12 minutes

Prepare.......recipe for **Lattice Pastry,** page 461, using 8-inch pie pan; shape and roll out as directed below.
Divide........in half. Form into balls.
Roll out.......one portion on floured surface to a circle 1½ inches larger than inverted 8-inch pie pan. Fit loosely into pan.

PINEAPPLE FILLING

Combine.....2 tablespoons **cornstarch**
    2 tablespoons **sugar**
    ¼ teaspoon **salt** and
    2⅓ cups (No. 2 can) **crushed pineapple** in saucepan. Cook, stirring constantly, until thick and clear. Remove from heat.
Stir in.......1 tablespoon **lemon juice** and
    1 tablespoon **butter.**
Turn..........into pie shell.
Roll out.......remaining dough; cut slits. Moisten rim of bottom crust. Place top crust over filling. Fold edge under bottom crust, pressing to seal. Flute.
Bake.........at 425° for 15 minutes. Meanwhile combine
    ¼ cup firmly packed **brown sugar**
    2 tablespoons **butter**
    1 tablespoon **corn syrup** and
    1 tablespoon **water** in saucepan. Cook over low heat, stirring constantly, until sugar is dissolved.
Add........½ cup **pecans,** chopped. Spread hot mixture over top of partially-baked pie. Bake 9 to 12 minutes until deep golden brown.

Pine-Apple Pie

Senior Winner by Mrs. Susan F. Jones, Delaware, Ohio

Apple pie with a twist . . . crushed pineapple with apples for a two-crust delight.

BAKE at 425° for 10 minutes, then   MAKES 9-inch pie
    at 350° for 25 to 30 minutes

Sift together . . 2 cups sifted **Pillsbury's Best All Purpose Flour***
          1 teaspoon **salt** into large mixing bowl.
Cut in . . . . . . ⅔ cup **shortening** until the size of small peas.
Blend . . . . 1 **egg yolk** with
          2 teaspoons **lemon juice** and
          4 tablespoons **water.** Sprinkle over flour mixture, stirring with fork until dough is moist enough to hold together. Divide in half. Form into balls.
Roll out . . . . one portion on floured surface to a circle 1½ inches larger than inverted 9-inch pie pan. Fit loosely into pan.

For use with Pillsbury's Best Self-Rising Flour, omit salt.

PINE-APPLE FILLING

Prepare . . . . . . 4 cups pared, sliced **apples** (4 medium); add
          1 cup (9-oz. can) **crushed pineapple,** undrained
Combine . . . . ⅔ cup **sugar**
          1 teaspoon **cinnamon** and
          3 tablespoons **flour.** Add to fruit mixture; place in pie shell.
Roll out . . . . remaining dough; cut slits. Moisten rim of bottom crust. Place top crust over filling. Fold edge under bottom crust, pressing to seal. Flute. Brush with
          1 tablespoon melted **butter**
Bake . . . . at 425° for 10 minutes, then at 350° for 25 to 30 minutes until apples are tender.

Pine-Apple Pie

Rhuby Fruit Pie

Senior Winner by Mrs. Elizabeth C. Bearse, Chatham, Massachusetts

A fruit-full delight! Rhubarb, peaches and pineapple in a flaky double crust.

BAKE at 350° for 1 to 1¼ hours   MAKES 9-inch pie

Prepare . . . . recipe for **Two-Crust Pastry,** page 460, using 9-inch pie pan.
Combine . . . . . 1 package (1 lb.) thawed frozen **rhubarb*** (cut, if pieces are large)
1 cup drained canned **peach slices** and
½ cup drained **pineapple tidbits**
Combine . . . . . 1 cup **sugar*** and
2 tablespoons **flour;** add to fruit mixture.
Turn . . . . into pie shell.
Roll out . . . . remaining dough; cut slits. Moisten rim of bottom crust. Place top crust over filling. Fold edge under bottom crust, pressing to seal. Flute.
Brush . . . . with **milk** and sprinkle with **sugar.**
Bake . . . . at 350° for 1 to 1¼ hours.

*If desired, use 4 cups fresh rhubarb; increase sugar to 1¼ to 1½ cups.

Rhubarb Crumble Pie

Senior Winner by Mrs. John W. Fetterman, Canton, Ohio

There is a sweet crumb topping on this refreshing rhubarb pie. Quick and simple to prepare with frozen rhubarb.

BAKE at 375° for 35 to 40 minutes   MAKES 8-inch pie

Prepare . . . . recipe for **One-Crust Pastry,** page 460, using 8-inch pie pan. Do not prick crust; fill and bake as directed below.
Drain . . . . 1 package (1 lb.) thawed frozen **rhubarb,** reserving juice.

Mix . . . . ¾ cup sifted **Pillsbury's Best All Purpose Flour**
½ cup **sugar**
¼ cup **butter** or margarine and
¼ teaspoon **salt.** Set aside for topping.
Combine . . . . . 2 tablespoons **sugar**
2 tablespoons **flour** and the rhubarb juice in saucepan. Cook over medium heat, stirring constantly, until thick. Add
2 drops **red food coloring.** Stir in rhubarb.
Turn . . . . into pie shell. Top with crumb mixture.
Bake . . . . at 375° for 35 to 40 minutes.

Cinna-Meringue Rhubarb Pie

Senior Winner by Mrs. Wendell White, Mitchell, South Dakota

The nip of cinnamon is in the meringue top of this creamy rhubarb-sauce one-crust pie.

BAKE at 450° for 10 to 12 minutes, then   MAKES 9-inch pie
    at 350° for 10 to 12 minutes

Prepare . . . . recipe for **One-Crust Pastry,** page 460, using 9-inch pie pan; bake as directed.
Combine . . . . . 2 cups sweetened **rhubarb sauce***
1 tablespoon **butter** and
1 teaspoon **vanilla** in saucepan. Cook over medium heat, stirring occasionally, until mixture comes to a boil.
Combine . . . 2½ tablespoons **cornstarch** and
¼ cup **light cream** until smooth. Blend into rhubarb

mixture; cook, stirring constantly, until thick.

Blend . . . . a little of the hot mixture into
3 slightly beaten **egg yolks.** Add to hot mixture; cook 2 minutes, stirring constantly. If desired, add 6 to 8 drops **red food coloring.** Cool to lukewarm.

Turn . . . . into pie shell; spread with Cinna-Meringue, sealing to edge.

Bake . . . . at 350° for 10 to 12 minutes.

To make sauce, cook 3 cups fresh rhubarb with ¼ cup water and 1 cup sugar over low heat, stirring occasionally, until tender. (If desired, use 1 lb. frozen rhubarb; decrease sugar to ½ cup. Or use home-canned rhubarb.)

CINNA-MERINGUE

Beat 3 egg whites with ¼ teaspoon cream of tartar and ¼ teaspoon cinnamon until soft mounds form. Gradually add 6 tablespoons sugar, beating until meringue stands in stiff, glossy peaks.

Creamy Rhubarb Pie

Senior Winner by Mrs. Raymond H. Adkins, Dover, Ohio

Creamy smooth filling, made with fresh or frozen rhubarb, is criss-crossed with strips of rich egg pastry.

BAKE at 375° for 15 minutes, then   MAKES 9-inch pie
at 325° for 30 to 35 minutes

Sift together 1½ cups sifted **Pillsbury's Best All Purpose Flour*** and ½ teaspoon **salt** into mixing bowl.

Cut in . . . . . . ½ cup **shortening** until the size of small peas.

Blend . . . . 1 **egg yolk** with
3 tablespoons **water.** Sprinkle over mixture, stirring with fork until dough is moist enough to hold together. If necessary, add more water. Form into a ball.

Roll out . . . . . . two-thirds of dough on floured surface to a circle 1½ inches larger than inverted 9-inch pie pan. Fit loosely into pan. Fold edge to form a rim; flute. Brush with part of
1 slightly beaten **egg white** (reserve remainder).

RHUBARB FILLING

Beat . . . . 2 **eggs** until light and fluffy. Stir in mixture of
¾ cup **sugar**
2 tablespoons **flour** and
½ teaspoon **salt**

Add . . . . 1 tablespoon very soft **butter** and
1 package (1 lb.) frozen **rhubarb**** (undrained), thawed just enough to cut into small pieces. Turn into pie shell.

Roll out . . . . . . remaining dough to ⅛-inch thickness. Cut into strips ½ inch wide; crisscross over filling to form lattice top. Trim and seal ends. Fold bottom crust over to cover. Flute. Brush strips with remaining beaten egg white.

Bake . . . . at 375° for 15 minutes, then at 325° for 30 to 35 minutes.

*For use with Pillsbury's Best Self-Rising Flour, omit salt in pastry; decrease water to 2 tablespoons.
**If desired, 2 cups fresh rhubarb may be used; increase sugar to 1 cup.

Strawberry Pie Delicious

Senior Third Prize Winner by Mrs. T. A. Police, New Philadelphia, Ohio

A festive combination of fresh strawberries and pineapple, pleasing to the taste and the eye.

BAKE at 425° for 10 minutes, then   MAKES 9-inch pie
     at 350° for 30 to 40 minutes

Prepare . . . . . . recipe for **Lattice Pastry,** page 461, using 9-inch pie pan; fill and bake as directed below.

Combine . . . . . 1 cup **sugar**
                 ¼ cup **cornstarch** and
                 ½ teaspoon **salt** in mixing bowl.

Stir in . . . . . . 1 quart (4 cups) fresh **strawberries,** sliced,* and
                 ½ cup drained **pineapple tidbits** or crushed pineapple

Turn . . . . into pie shell. Dot with
                 2 tablespoons **butter**

Roll out . . . . . . remaining dough. Cut into strips ½ inch wide; crisscross over filling to form lattice top. Trim and seal ends; fold bottom crust over to cover. Flute. Brush strips with **milk.**

Bake . . . . at 425° for 10 minutes, then at 350° for 30 to 40 minutes.

If desired, use 1 package (16 oz.) frozen strawberries; omit sugar and bake in an 8-inch pie pan.

Strawberry Social Pie

Senior Winner by T. O. Davis, Waynesboro, Mississippi

Flaky pie crust . . . filled with fresh strawberries, marshmallows and fluffy whipped cream. Store in refrigerator until serving time.

BAKE at 450° for 10 to 12 minutes   MAKES 9-inch pie

Prepare . . . . . . recipe for **One-Crust Pastry,** page 460, using 9-inch pie pan; bake as directed.

Strawberry Pie Delicious

Cut........10 **marshmallows** into quarters. Arrange in pie shell.
Place........1 cup sliced **strawberries** over marshmallows.
Beat........⅔ cup **whipping cream** until thick. Gradually add
          ¼ cup **light corn syrup**; beat until mixture is very thick.
Blend in.....¼ teaspoon **almond extract** and
          10 additional **marshmallows**, finely cut
Spread........over **strawberries**; seal to edge of pastry. Chill 5 to
          8 hours. Decorate with **strawberries**.

Currant Request Pie

Senior Winner by Oneita I. Zalkind, Hollydale, California

A filling of plump, juicy currants, walnuts and spices is baked in a flaky pie shell. Serve it "a la mode," if you like.

BAKE at 375° for 35 to 40 minutes   MAKES 8-inch pie

Prepare.......recipe for **One-Crust Pastry**, page 460, using 8-inch
          pie pan. Do not prick crust; fill and bake as directed
          below.
Combine.....3 well-beaten **eggs**
          1 cup firmly packed **brown sugar**
          ½ teaspoon **cinnamon**
          ¼ teaspoon **cloves** and
          1 tablespoon **butter**; mix well.
Stir in......½ cup dried **currants** or raisins
          ¾ cup **walnuts**, chopped
          1 tablespoon grated **orange rind** and
          ¼ cup **orange juice**
Pour..........into pie shell.
Bake.........at 375° for 35 to 40 minutes. If desired, serve with
          whipped cream.

CUSTARD PIES

are one-crust pies with fillings made up of sugar, milk and eggs . . . the pastry and filling are baked together.

It is difficult to know when a custard pie is baked to the correct doneness. A good test is to insert a knife halfway between center and edge of filling; when it comes out clean, custard is done. The center finishes cooking after the pie is removed from the oven. Over-baking a custard pie causes it to "weep" or become watery.

Custard Snow Pie

Senior Winner by Mrs. Lawson Odom Dailey, Dallas, Texas

A mild custard pie topped off with meringue . . . you'll like the crust with its tang of spice.

BAKE at 450° for 10 to 12 minutes, then   MAKES 8 or 9-inch pie
    at 350° for 12 to 15 minutes

Prepare.......recipe for **One-Crust Pastry**, page 460; sift
          ½ to 1 teaspoon **allspice** with the flour, if desired. Use
          8 or 9-inch pie pan. Bake as directed.
Sift together.¼ cup **Pillsbury's Best All Purpose Flour**
          ½ teaspoon **salt** and
          ¾ cup **sugar**. Set aside.
Beat........3 **egg yolks** and
          1 **egg** slightly in top of double boiler. Add
          1½ cups **milk**. Blend in the dry ingredients. Cook over
          boiling water, stirring constantly, until very thick.
Add.........1 teaspoon **vanilla**. Cool.
Sprinkle.....1 cup **coconut** in bottom of pie shell. Pour custard
          over coconut.
Prepare.......recipe for **Meringue**, page 461; spread over custard.
Bake.........at 350° for 12 to 15 minutes.

Chocolate Surprise Custard Pie

Chocolate Surprise Custard Pie

Senior Winner by Mrs. Joseph Beikirch, St. Petersburg, Florida

Grated chocolate, added to smooth, custard filling, rises to the top during baking. It's topped off with billowy meringue.

BAKE at 425° for 10 minutes, then   MAKES 8-inch pie
    at 350° for 35 to 40 minutes

Sift together . . 1 cup sifted **Pillsbury's Best All Purpose Flour***
          1 teaspoon **sugar** and
          ¼ teaspoon **salt** into mixing bowl.
Cut in . . . . . . ⅓ cup **shortening** until the size of small peas.
Combine . . . . . 3 tablespoons **water** and
          1 teaspoon **vinegar**. Sprinkle over flour mixture, stir-

ring with fork until dough is moist enough to hold together. Form into a ball.
Roll out . . . . on floured surface to a circle 1½ inches larger than inverted 8-inch pie pan. Fit loosely into pan. Fold edge to form standing rim; flute. Chill while making Chocolate Custard Filling.

*For use with Pillsbury's Best Self-Rising Flour, omit salt.

CHOCOLATE CUSTARD FILLING

Combine . . . . . 1 **egg**
          3 **egg yolks**
          ½ cup **sugar** and
          1 teaspoon **vanilla** in mixing bowl. Beat with fork to combine.
Add . . . . 1¾ cups hot scalded **milk** gradually; mix well.
Add . . . . 2 ounces grated or shaved **semi-sweet chocolate**. *Do not stir.* Carefully pour into pie shell.
Bake . . . . at 425° for 10 minutes, then at 350° for 20 to 25 minutes until slightly set.
Prepare . . . . recipe for **Meringue**, page 461; spread over filling. Bake at 350° for 12 to 15 minutes.

Coconut Crunch Pie

Senior Winner by Mrs. Miles L. Croom, Ferndale, Michigan

This pie mysteriously bakes into two layers—smooth custard on the bottom, a crunchy golden coconut layer on top.

BAKE at 350° for 35 to 40 minutes   MAKES 8 or 9-inch pie

Prepare . . . . recipe for **One-Crust Pastry**, page 460, using 8 or 9-inch pie pan. Do not prick crust; fill and bake as directed below.
Combine . . . . . 3 well-beaten **egg yolks**
          1¼ cups **sugar** and
          1 teaspoon **salt** in mixing bowl.

Add........½ cup **milk**
2 tablespoons soft **butter**
½ teaspoon **almond extract** and
¼ teaspoon **lemon extract.** Beat well.

Fold in......1 cup flaked or chopped shredded **coconut**

Beat........3 **egg whites** until stiff but not dry. Fold into egg yolk mixture. Pour into pie shell.

Bake.........at 350° for 35 to 40 minutes. Cool. Serve plain or with whipped cream.

Peaches and Cream Pie

Senior Winner by Mrs. Joseph R. Breitweiser, Milwaukee, Wisconsin

Juicy golden peaches, sour cream and brown sugar make the filling for this custard pie.

BAKE at 450° for 12 to 15 minutes, then   MAKES 9-inch pie
at 250° for 25 to 30 minutes

Prepare......recipe for **One-Crust Pastry,** page 460, using 9-inch pie pan. Do not prick crust; fill and bake as directed below.

Arrange.....8 to 10 canned **peach halves** (No. 2½ can) in pie shell, cut-side up*

Combine.....2 slightly beaten **eggs**
1 cup **sour cream** (thick or commercial) and

¼ cup **honey;** mix well. Pour over peaches.

Sprinkle.......with a mixture of
½ cup firmly packed **brown sugar** and
2 tablespoons **flour**

Bake.........at 450° for 12 to 15 minutes until crust is a golden brown, then at 250° for 25 to 30 minutes.

If desired, 4 to 5 fresh sliced peaches may be substituted.

Creamy Apri-Pear Pie

Senior Winner by Mrs. O. H. Beers, Springfield, Oregon

Apricot halves peek through a sour cream-custard filling in this colorful open-face pie—and pear halves hide below.

BAKE at 400° for 15 minutes, then   MAKES 9-inch pie
at 350° for 25 to 30 minutes

Prepare.......recipe for **One-Crust Pastry,** page 460, using 9-inch pie pan. Do not prick crust; fill and bake as directed below.

Drain........1 No. 303 can **apricot halves** and
1 No. 303 can **pear halves.** Arrange fruit alternately in bottom of unbaked pie shell, reserving 6 apricot halves for top.

Combine....¾ cup **sugar**
1 tablespoon **flour** and
2 tablespoons **butter** in small bowl.

Blend in.....3 unbeaten **eggs;** beat well.

Add.........1 cup **sour cream** (thick or commercial)
2 teaspoons grated **lemon rind** and
3 tablespoons **lemon juice.** Blend thoroughly.

Pour.........over fruit in pastry-lined pan. Arrange reserved apricot halves, cut-side down, over filling. Sprinkle with **nutmeg,** if desired.

Bake.........at 400° for 15 minutes, then at 350° for 25 to 30 minutes until filling is set.

Honey Melody Pie

Senior Winner by Mrs. Richard Gaalema, Indianapolis, Indiana

A medley of fruits and honey in a golden brown crust.

BAKE at 425° for 25 to 30 minutes   MAKES 8-inch pie

Prepare . . . . recipe for **One-Crust Pastry,** page 460, using 8-inch pie pan. Do not prick crust; fill and bake as directed below.

Cream . . . . . . 2 tablespoons **butter**
           2 tablespoons **sugar** and
           ¼ teaspoon **salt**

Add . . . . ¼ cup **honey;** beat until thoroughly combined.

Blend in . . . . . 3 unbeaten **eggs,** beating well after each.

Stir in . . . . . . ½ cup **dates,** cut in small pieces
           ½ cup drained **crushed pineapple**
           ¼ cup **pineapple juice**
           ¼ cup **pecans,** chopped, and
           2 tablespoons **lemon juice.** Mix well.

Pour . . . . into pie shell.

Bake . . . . at 425° for 25 to 30 minutes.

Tangy Lemon Pie

Senior Winner by Mrs. Ramon Nardini, Vandalia, Ohio

Tart and rich, perky lemon filling bakes to a golden brown in a single pie shell.

BAKE at 400° for 10 minutes, then   MAKES 8-inch pie
     at 350° for 25 to 30 minutes

Prepare . . . . recipe for **One-Crust Pastry*,** page 460, using 8-inch pie pan. Do not prick crust; fill and bake as directed below.

Cream . . . . . . ½ cup **butter** or margarine. Gradually add
           1¼ cups **sugar,** creaming well. Blend in

           1 tablespoon **flour**

Add . . . . 3 unbeaten **eggs,** beating well after each.

Stir in . . . . . . 1 to 2 teaspoons grated **lemon rind** and
           ⅓ cup **lemon juice.** Pour into pie shell.

Bake . . . . at 400° for 10 minutes, then at 350° for 25 to 30 minutes until deep golden brown.

*For use with Pillsbury's Best Self-Rising Flour, omit salt and decrease water to 2 to 3 tablespoons; decrease second baking time to 20 to 25 minutes.

Lemon Wow

Senior Winner by Betty Bates, San Antonio, Texas

Tart lemon filling made with buttermilk . . . as it bakes, it forms a creamy pudding on bottom and cake on top.

BAKE at 425° for 10 minutes, then   MAKES 8-inch pie
     at 350° for 20 to 25 minutes

Prepare . . . . recipe for **One-Crust Pastry,** page 460, using 8-inch pie pan. Do not prick crust; fill and bake as directed below.

Combine . . . . . 1 cup **sugar** and
           3 tablespoons **flour** in mixing bowl.

Beat . . . . 3 **egg yolks** until thick and lemon colored.

Blend in . . . . . 1 cup **buttermilk** or sour milk
           1 teaspoon grated **lemon rind** and
           ¼ cup **lemon juice.** Add to sugar-flour mixture; mix thoroughly.

Beat . . . . 3 **egg whites** until stiff but not dry. Fold into lemon mixture. Pour into pie shell.

Bake . . . . at 425° for 10 minutes, then at 350° for 20 to 25 minutes. Cool.

Danish Raisin Custard Pie

Senior Winner by Mrs. Tove Sibbern, Lackawanna, New York

Orange juice adds refreshing tang to custard filling in a butter cookie crust. Like European pies, it's baked in a layer cake pan.

BAKE at 375° for 15 to 20 minutes, then   MAKES 9-inch pie
at 400° for 20 to 25 minutes

Sift together 1¼ cups sifted **Pillsbury's Best All Purpose Flour*** and
⅛ cup sifted **confectioners' sugar** into mixing bowl. Add

1 teaspoon grated **lemon rind**

Cut in . . . . . ½ cup **butter** or margarine until the size of small peas.

Sprinkle . . . . . 2 slightly beaten **egg yolks** over mixture, stirring with fork to form a crumb mixture. Press into bottom and sides of well-greased 9-inch round layer pan.

Bake . . . . at 375° for 15 to 20 minutes until slightly browned. Remove from oven. Turn oven to 400°.

*Pillsbury's Best Self-Rising Flour may be substituted.

DANISH RAISIN FILLING

Combine . . . . . 1 cup **raisins**
2 tablespoons **sugar**
2 tablespoons **orange juice** and
¼ cup hot **water** in saucepan. Bring to boil, then simmer 5 minutes. Cool and drain.

Beat . . . . 2 **eggs** slightly. Add
2 tablespoons **sugar** and
1 teaspoon **vanilla;** beat well.

Stir in . . . . . 1½ cups hot scalded **light cream** gradually; mix well.

Turn . . . . the cooked raisin mixture into pie shell. Pour egg mixture over raisin mixture.

Bake . . . . at 400° for 20 to 25 minutes.

Date Sour Cream Special

Senior Winner by Mrs. C. W. Henriksen, Topeka, Kansas

Dates and lemon in sour cream filling with meringue topping.

BAKE at 400° for 25 to 30 minutes, then   MAKES 8 or 9-inch pie
at 350° for 12 to 15 minutes

Prepare . . . . recipe for **One-Crust Pastry,** page 460, using 8 or 9-inch pie pan. Do not prick crust; fill and bake as directed below.

Combine . . . . ½ cup **sugar**
1 tablespoon **cornstarch** and
¼ teaspoon **salt** in mixing bowl.

Blend in . . . . . 3 slightly beaten **egg yolks** and
1 tablespoon **butter,** melted

Stir in . . . . . 1½ cups **sour cream** (thick or commercial)
½ teaspoon grated **lemon rind** and
1 tablespoon **lemon juice**

Place . . . . 1 cup **dates,** finely cut, in pie shell. Pour filling mixture over dates.

Bake . . . . at 400° for 25 to 30 minutes. Decrease oven temperature to 350°. Cool pie 15 minutes.

Prepare . . . . recipe for **Meringue,** page 461; spread over filling. Bake at 350° for 12 to 15 minutes.

Raisin Cream Smoothie Pie

Junior Winner by Juanita Houch, West Plains, Missouri

This creamy pie is rich with raisins, spice and sour cream.

BAKE at 450° for 10 minutes, then   MAKES 9-inch pie
    at 325° for 20 to 25 minutes

Prepare........recipe for **One-Crust Pastry**, page 460, using 9-inch pie pan. Do not prick crust; fill and bake as directed below.

Combine.....3 slightly beaten **eggs**
        1¼ cups **sugar**
        1 teaspoon **cinnamon**
        ½ teaspoon **salt** and
        ¼ teaspoon **cloves** in mixing bowl. Mix well.

Stir in.....1½ cups **sour cream** (thick or commercial) and
        1½ cups **raisins**. Pour into pie shell.

Bake.........at 450° for 10 minutes, then at 325° for 20 to 25 minutes.

Indian Summer Pie

Senior Winner by Mrs. Sylva F. Buchanan, Cairnbrook, Pennsylvania

Apple butter, raisins and spices in a custard-like pie that's topped with a cloud of delicate meringue.

BAKE at 400° for 30 to 35 minutes, then   MAKES 9-inch pie
    at 350° for 12 to 15 minutes

Prepare........recipe for **One-Crust Pastry**, page 460, using 9-inch pie pan. Do not prick crust; fill and bake as directed below.

Combine....½ cup **sugar**
        2 tablespoons **flour**
        1 teaspoon **cinnamon** and
        ¼ teaspoon **nutmeg** in mixing bowl.

Blend in.....½ cup **apple butter**
        3 slightly beaten **egg yolks** and
        1 cup **raisins**

Combine....¾ cup undiluted **evaporated milk** and
        ½ cup **water** in saucepan. Heat just to simmering; add to raisin mixture.

Turn..........into pie shell.

Bake.........at 400° for 30 to 35 minutes.

Prepare........recipe for **Meringue**, page 461; spread over filling. Bake at 350° for 12 to 15 minutes.

Apple-Scotch Cheese Pie

Senior Winner by Miss Eunice Guill, Alexandria, Virginia

A taste surprise! Grated cheese and apple butter go into this unusual pie. It's rich—yet not too sweet.

BAKE at 400° for 10 minutes, then   MAKES 9-inch pie
    at 350° for 45 to 50 minutes

Prepare........recipe for **Lattice Pastry**, page 461. Roll out, fill and bake as directed below.

Roll out.......larger ball on floured surface to circle 1½ inches larger than inverted 9-inch pie pan. Fit loosely into pan. Fold edge to form a standing rim; flute. Prick generously.

Roll out.......remaining pastry; cut into six triangles. Place on ungreased baking sheet.

Bake . . . . pie shell and triangles at 400° for 10 minutes. Cool.

APPLE CHEESE FILLING

Cream . . . . . . ¼ cup **butter** or margarine. Gradually add
1 cup **sugar,** creaming well.
Blend in . . . . . 3 slightly beaten **eggs**
1 cup **apple butter**
¼ cup **Pillsbury's Best All Purpose Flour**
¼ teaspoon **salt** and
¾ cup shredded **American cheese**
Turn . . . . into partially-baked pie shell.
Bake . . . . at 350° for 45 to 50 minutes. Arrange baked pastry
triangles over filling.

Pum-conut Pie

Senior Winner by Mrs. H. O. Werner, Lincoln, Nebraska

Toasty coconut atop pumpkin pie in a cinnamon crust is a harvest-time special.

BAKE at 425° for 15 minutes, then   MAKES 9-inch pie
    at 350° for 20 to 25 minutes

Sift together 1¼ cups sifted **Pillsbury's Best All Purpose Flour***
1 teaspoon **cinnamon** and
¾ teaspoon **salt** into mixing bowl.
Combine . . . . ⅓ cup plus 1 tablespoon **shortening** and
¼ cup **boiling water;** beat until thick and creamy.
Add . . . . to the dry ingredients all at once. Stir quickly until
mixture holds together. Form into a ball. Flatten
to ½-inch thickness.
Roll out . . . . on floured surface to a circle 1½ inches larger than
inverted 9-inch pie pan. Fit loosely into pan. Fold
edge to form a standing rim; flute. Sprinkle with a
teaspoon of **flour.**

Pillsbury's Best Self-Rising Flour is not recommended for use in this recipe.

PUM-CONUT FILLING

Combine . . . . . 2 slightly beaten **eggs**
⅔ cup **sugar**
½ cup flaked or chopped shredded **coconut**
1 teaspoon **cinnamon**
¾ teaspoon **salt**
¼ teaspoon **mace**
1 teaspoon **vanilla** and, if desired,
1 teaspoon grated **lemon rind** in mixing bowl.
Blend in . . . . 1½ cups **pumpkin,** cooked or canned; mix well.
Combine . . . 1¼ cups hot **milk** and
2 tablespoons **butter.** Gradually add to pumpkin mixture; mix well.
Pour . . . . into pie shell.
Bake . . . . at 425° for 15 minutes, then at 350° for 10 minutes.
Sprinkle with
¼ cup **coconut.** Bake 10 to 15 minutes. Cool.

Pum-conut Pie

Apple-Butter Pumpkin Pie

Senior Winner by Mrs. Frank R. Ferren, Hobart, Indiana

Spicy apple butter gives a new tart and mellow taste to this golden-brown pumpkin pie.

BAKE at 425° for 15 minutes, then   MAKES 9-inch pie
     at 375° for 20 to 25 minutes

Prepare . . . . . . .recipe for **One-Crust Pastry,** page 460, using 9-inch pie pan. Do not prick crust; fill and bake as directed below.

Combine . . . . .1 cup **apple butter**
     1 cup **pumpkin,** cooked or canned
     ½ cup firmly packed **brown sugar**
     ½ teaspoon **salt**
     ¾ teaspoon **cinnamon**
     ¾ teaspoon **nutmeg** and
     ⅛ teaspoon **ginger**

Add . . . . .3 unbeaten **eggs.** Beat well.
Add . . . . .1 cup hot scalded light **cream** gradually; mix thoroughly. Pour into pie shell.
Bake . . . . .at 425° for 15 minutes, then at 375° for 20 to 25 minutes. Cool.

Praline Pumpkin-Custard Pie

Senior Winner by Mrs. W. W. Douglass, Searcy, Arkansas

Pecan-brown sugar crumbs form a layer beneath pumpkin-custard filling . . . an unusual pie you'll be proud to serve.

BAKE at 450° for 10 minutes, then   MAKES 9-inch pie
     at 350° for 50 to 60 minutes

Prepare . . . . . . .recipe for **One-Crust Pastry,** page 460, using 9-inch pie pan. Do not prick crust.
Combine . . . .⅓ cup **pecans,** finely chopped

⅓ cup firmly packed **brown sugar** and
     3 tablespoons soft **butter;** press gently into bottom of pie shell. Prick sides with fork.
Bake . . . . .at 450° for 10 minutes. Cool at least 2 minutes.

PUMPKIN-CUSTARD FILLING

Combine . . . . .3 slightly beaten **eggs**
     ½ cup **sugar**
     ½ cup firmly packed **brown sugar**
     2 tablespoons **flour**
     ¾ teaspoon **salt**
     ¾ teaspoon **cinnamon**
     ½ teaspoon **ginger**
     ¼ teaspoon **cloves** and
     ¼ teaspoon **mace** in mixing bowl.
Add . . . . .1½ cups **pumpkin,** cooked or canned; mix well.
Add . . . . .1½ cups hot light **cream** gradually; blend well. Pour into pie shell.
Bake . . . . .at 350° for 50 to 60 minutes. Cool.

Pumpkin Surprise Pie

Bride Winner by Mrs. Melvin Tarum, McPherson, Kansas

A pumpkin filling, rich with brown sugar and molasses, baked in a pie crust to which crushed peanut brittle is added.

BAKE at 425° for 10 minutes, then   MAKES 9-inch pie
     at 350° for 35 to 45 minutes

Prepare . . . . . . .recipe for **One-Crust Pastry,** page 460; cut in 2 tablespoons finely crushed **peanut brittle** with the shortening. Use 9-inch pie pan. Do not prick crust; fill and bake as directed below.
Combine . . . . .1 cup firmly packed **brown sugar**
     1 tablespoon **flour**
     1 teaspoon **cinnamon**

⅛ teaspoon **salt**
¼ teaspoon **nutmeg** and
¼ teaspoon **ginger** in mixing bowl.
Add . . . . 1 cup **pumpkin,** cooked or canned
1⅔ cups (13-oz. can) undiluted **evaporated milk**
2 unbeaten **eggs** and
2 tablespoons **molasses.** Beat well.
Pour . . . . into pie shell.
Bake . . . . at 425° for 10 minutes, then at 350° for 35 to 45 minutes. Cool. Serve with Peanut Crunch Whipped Cream.

PEANUT CRUNCH WHIPPED CREAM

Beat ½ cup whipping cream until thick. Blend in 1 tablespoon sugar, ½ teaspoon vanilla and ¼ cup finely crushed peanut brittle.

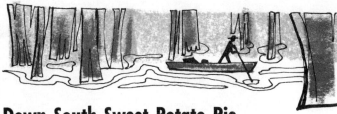

Down South Sweet Potato Pie

Senior Winner by Mrs. Leon C. Lenkoff, Louisville, Kentucky

An old Southern favorite, this smooth pie has brown sugar and spices in the filling and chopped pecans on top.

BAKE at 450° for 10 minutes, then   MAKES 9-inch pie
at 350° for 30 to 35 minutes

Prepare . . . . recipe for **One-Crust Pastry,** page 460, using 9-inch pie pan. Do not prick crust; fill and bake as directed below.
Beat . . . . 3 **eggs** slightly in a large mixing bowl.

Add . . . . 1½ cups cooked or canned **sweet potatoes,** sieved
½ cup firmly packed **brown sugar**
2 tablespoons **corn syrup**
1 teaspoon **salt**
1½ teaspoons **cinnamon**
½ teaspoon **ginger** and
½ teaspoon **nutmeg.** Beat well.
Blend in . . . . 1½ cups **milk.** Pour into pie shell.
Sprinkle . . . . . ½ cup **pecans,** chopped, over filling.
Bake . . . . at 450° for 10 minutes, then at 350° for 30 to 35 minutes.

Aunt Mary's Favorite Pie

Senior Winner by Mrs. Drue Alexander, Russells Point, Ohio

An old family favorite . . . wonderful custard pie with a hint of spice. The crust stays flaky and tender, too!

BAKE at 450° for 10 to 12 minutes, then   MAKES 9-inch pie
at 350° for 40 to 50 minutes

Prepare . . . . recipe for **One-Crust Pastry,** page 460, using 9-inch pie pan; bake as directed.
Combine . . . 1⅓ cups **sugar**
3 tablespoons **flour**
½ teaspoon **cinnamon**
¼ teaspoon **nutmeg** and
¼ teaspoon **cloves** in mixing bowl.
Blend in . . . . . 4 slightly beaten **egg yolks** and
3 tablespoons **butter,** melted. Gradually add
1¼ cups **milk,** mixing well.
Beat . . . . 4 **egg whites** with
½ teaspoon **salt** until stiff but not dry. Fold gently into egg yolk mixture.
Pour . . . . into pie shell.
Bake . . . . at 350° for 40 to 50 minutes.

Molasses Ginger Pie

Molasses Ginger Pie

Senior Winner by Mrs. Ruth Sullivan, Chicago, Illinois

If you like the smoothness of custard pie and the spiciness of pumpkin pie . . . you'll love this spicy molasses custard pie.

BAKE at 400° for 10 minutes, then   MAKES 9-inch pie
    at 325° for 40 to 45 minutes

Prepare . . . . recipe for **One-Crust Pastry,** page 460, using 9-inch pie pan. Do not prick crust; fill and bake as directed below.

Combine . . . . ⅓ cup **sugar**
    1 tablespoon **cornstarch**
    1 teaspoon **cinnamon**

¼ teaspoon **salt** and
¼ teaspoon **ginger** in mixing bowl.

Blend in . . . . . ¼ cup cold **milk** and
    3 slightly beaten **eggs**

Heat . . . . . . 1¾ cups **milk** and
    ½ cup light **molasses** in saucepan over medium heat. (Do not boil.) Blend gradually into egg mixture. Pour into pie shell.

Bake . . . . at 400° for 10 minutes, then at 325° for 40 to 45 minutes. Cool; serve with **whipped cream** or **applesauce,** or both.

New England Custard Pie

Senior Winner by Mrs. John Alton Cox, South Portland, Maine

For an added attraction try this custard pie with a maple syrup base.

BAKE at 425° for 2 minutes and 10 minutes, then   MAKES 9-inch pie
    at 350° for 10 to 15 minutes

Prepare . . . . recipe for **One-Crust Pastry,** page 460, using 9-inch pie pan. Do not prick crust. Bake at 425° for 2 minutes.

Combine . . . . . 2 tablespoons **flour**
    ½ cup **maple syrup**
    ¼ cup **water** and
    ¼ teaspoon **maple flavoring** in saucepan. Mix until smooth.

Add . . . . 1 slightly beaten **egg yolk** and
    1 tablespoon **butter.** Cook over medium heat, stirring constantly, until thickened. Pour immediately into pie shell.

Combine . . . . . 2 slightly beaten **eggs**
    ¼ cup **sugar** and
    ¼ teaspoon **salt.** Stir in
    1 cup hot scalded **milk** and

1 cup hot scalded **cream.** Pour against inside of large spoon over maple mixture.

Bake. . . . . . . .at 425° for 10 minutes, then at 350° for 10 to 15 minutes.

Custard Fluff Nut Pie

Senior Winner by Miss Rachel Brittain, Birmingham, Alabama

Pastry shell is sprinkled with pecans, then filled with fluffy custard, rich in brown sugar with a bit of rum flavoring.

BAKE at 400° for 10 to 12 minutes, then at 350° for 35 to 40 minutes   MAKES 9 or 10-inch pie

Sift together . .1 cup sifted **Pillsbury's Best All Purpose Flour*** and
½ teaspoon **salt** into mixing bowl. Add
4 teaspoons **brown sugar**

Cut in . . . . . .⅓ cup **shortening** until the size of small peas.

Sprinkle . . . . .3 to 4 tablespoons cold **water** over mixture, stirring with fork until dough is moist enough to hold together. Form into a ball.

Roll out . . . . . . .on floured surface to a circle 1½ inches larger than inverted 9 or 10-inch pie pan. Fit loosely into pan. Fold edge to form a standing rim; flute. Prick generously.

Bake. . . . . . . .at 400° for 10 to 12 minutes until golden brown.

Sprinkle . . . . .¾ cup **pecans,** chopped, over crust.

For use with Pillsbury's Best Self-Rising Flour, omit salt; decrease water to 2 to 3 tablespoons.

CUSTARD FLUFF FILLING

Combine . . . .⅓ cup **Pillsbury's Best All Purpose Flour**
¾ cup firmly packed **brown sugar**
¼ teaspoon **salt** and, if desired,
½ cup **nonfat dry milk** in saucepan.

Add . . . . . . .1½ cups **milk** gradually; blend well. Cook over medium

New England Custard Pie

heat, stirring constantly, until thick.

Blend. . . . . . . .a little of the hot mixture into
3 slightly beaten **egg yolks;** add to hot mixture. Cook 2 minutes, stirring constantly. Remove from heat; add
1 teaspoon **rum flavoring** and
1 teaspoon **vanilla**

Beat. . . . . . . .3 **egg whites** and
¼ teaspoon **cream of tartar** until soft mounds form. Gradually add
¼ cup **sugar,** beating until meringue stands in stiff peaks. Fold into cooked mixture.

Turn. . . . . .into pie shell.

Bake. . . . . . . .at 350° for 35 to 40 minutes.

CREAM PIES

are one-crust pies filled with a custard-type cooked filling thickened with flour or cornstarch. It's turned into a baked pie shell and often is topped with meringue or whipped cream.

For smooth, creamy filling, combine sugar, flour or cornstarch, then add the milk gradually to form a smooth mixture; cook over high heat until hot, then low heat until mixture boils and thickens. (Do not undercook or the filling will have an uncooked starch flavor.) To prevent scorching, use a heavy metal saucepan and stir mixture constantly during cooking.

Add a little of the hot mixture to the egg yolks, then pour the egg-yolk mixture into the remaining hot-milk mixture in saucepan. This also prevents lumping.

Fudge Sundae Pie

Senior Winner by Mrs. Frank J. Kolar, Jr., Hinsdale, Illinois

A "quickie" pie—fudge sauce and sour cream combine for filling.

BAKE at 400° for 20 to 25 minutes   MAKES 8-inch pie

Sift together . . 1 cup sifted **Pillsbury's Best All Purpose Flour***
                    1 tablespoon **sugar** and
                    ½ teaspoon **salt** in mixing bowl.
Cut in . . . . . . ⅓ cup **butter**, margarine or shortening until the size of small peas.
Combine . . . . . 2 to 3 tablespoons cold **water** and
                    ½ teaspoon **almond extract**. Sprinkle over mixture, stirring with fork until dough is moist enough to hold together. Form into a ball.
Roll out . . . . . . on floured surface to a circle 1½ inches larger than inverted 8-inch pie pan. Fit into pan. Fold edge to form a rim; flute.
*For use with Pillsbury's Best Self-Rising Flour, omit salt.

FUDGE FILLING

Combine . . . . ¾ cup **sour cream** (thick or commercial) with
                  1¼ cups (1-lb. can) **milk chocolate fudge topping** and
                  ½ teaspoon **vanilla**; mix well. Pour into pie shell.
Bake . . . . at 400° for 20 to 25 minutes. Chill until firm, about 1 hour. Serve with **whipped cream.**

Coconut-Shortbread Chocolate Pie

Senior Winner by Mrs. Robert Arnold, Green Bay, Wisconsin

Smooth chocolate filling in butter cookie pastry gets a sundae-like topping of whipped cream and coconut.

BAKE at 350° for 20 to 22 minutes   MAKES 9-inch pie

Cream . . . . . . ⅓ cup soft **butter**. Add
                    2 tablespoons **sugar**, creaming well.
Blend in . . . . . 1 unbeaten **egg yolk** and
                    1 tablespoon **cream**
Add . . . . 1 cup sifted **Pillsbury's Best All Purpose Flour*** gradually; mix well.
Blend in . . . . . 1 cup **coconut**, cut. Press evenly over bottom and sides of 9-inch pie pan.
Bake . . . . at 350° for 20 to 22 minutes. Cool.
*Pillsbury's Best Self-Rising Flour may be substituted.

CHOCOLATE FILLING

Combine . . . . ¾ cup **sugar**
                  3 tablespoons **cornstarch** and
                  ½ teaspoon **salt** in top of double boiler.
Blend in . . . . 2½ cups **milk** gradually.
Add . . . . 2 squares (2 oz.) unsweetened **chocolate**. Cook over boiling water, stirring constantly, until thick.
Blend . . . . a little of the hot mixture into
                  3 slightly beaten **egg yolks**; add to hot mixture. Cook 2 minutes, stirring constantly.

Add . . . . 1 tablespoon **butter** and
1 teaspoon **vanilla.** Cool 15 to 20 minutes. Turn into pie shell; chill. Serve topped with **whipped cream** and toasted **coconut.**

Hawaiian Chocolate Pie

Best of Class Winner by Mrs. Don W. Edwards, Lincoln, Nebraska

Crushed pineapple flavors half the filling, chocolate is added to the remainder for a really new flavor combination in a pie.

BAKE at 450° for 10 to 12 minutes   MAKES 9-inch pie

Prepare . . . . recipe for **One-Crust Pastry,** page 460, using 9-inch pie pan; bake as directed.

Drain . . . . 1 No. 1 can (1 cup) **crushed pineapple.** Set aside.

Combine . . . 1⅓ cups **sugar**
½ cup **Pillsbury's Best All Purpose Flour** and
½ teaspoon **salt** in heavy saucepan.

Add . . . . 3 cups **milk** gradually; mix well. Bring to boil, stirring constantly; cook over medium heat until thick.

Blend . . . . a little of the hot mixture into
3 slightly beaten **egg yolks**; add to hot mixture. Cook 1 minute, stirring constantly. Blend in
2 tablespoons **butter** and
2 teaspoons **vanilla**

Divide . . . . in half. Stir the drained pineapple into one portion. Cover. Cool to lukewarm.

Blend . . . . . . 1½ to 2 squares (1½ to 2 oz.) melted unsweetened **chocolate** into second portion. Cover. Cool to lukewarm.

Chop fine . . . ¾ cup **nuts**; sprinkle half of nuts over pie shell. Spoon in half of the cooled chocolate mixture. Cover with pineapple mixture and then with remaining chocolate mixture. Decorate with nuts. Cool completely. Serve with **whipped cream.**

Hawaiian Chocolate Pie

Chocolate Orange Layer Pie

Senior Winner by Mrs. Pressley Walker, Jacksonville, Florida

Smooth, extra-rich chocolate filling is topped with a fluffy orange cloud layer made with frozen orange juice.

BAKE at 450° for 10 to 12 minutes   MAKES 8 or 9-inch pie

Prepare.......recipe for **One-Crust Pastry,** page 460, using 8 or 9-inch pie pan; bake as directed.

CHOCOLATE FILLING

Heat........1 cup **milk** and
2 squares (2 oz.) unsweetened **chocolate** in top of double boiler over hot water until chocolate is melted.
Combine.....3 tablespoons **cornstarch**
½ cup **sugar**
¼ teaspoon **salt** and
2 tablespoons **milk.** Blend into milk mixture; cook over medium heat; stir constantly until thick.
Blend.........a little of the hot mixture into
2 slightly beaten **egg yolks;** add to hot mixture. Cook 3 minutes, stirring constantly.
Stir in.......2 tablespoons **butter** and
½ teaspoon **vanilla.** Cover; cool. Pour into pie shell.

ORANGE TOPPING

Soften.......1 teaspoon **gelatin** in
¼ cup undiluted **frozen orange juice** in metal cup. Place inside pan of water and heat until gelatin is dissolved. Cool slightly.
Beat........2 **egg whites** until foamy. Gradually add
¼ cup **sugar,** beating until meringue stands in stiff, glossy peaks. Fold in cooled orange mixture.
Beat........½ cup **whipping cream** until thick. Fold in egg white-orange mixture. Spread over Filling. Chill 1 hour before serving.

Fudge Pie

Bride Winner by Mrs. Carol J. Smith, Woodland Hills, California

An extra-rich chocolate refrigerator pie . . . top small servings with whipped cream for a connoisseur's delight.

BAKE at 450° for 10 to 12 minutes*   SERVES 8 to 10

Prepare.......recipe for **One-Crust Pastry,*** page 460, cutting in 2 tablespoons **butter** with the shortening; decrease water to 2 to 3 tablespoons. Use 8-inch pie pan. Bake as directed.
Heat..........in top of double boiler over boiling water
1 cup (6-oz. pkg.) **semi-sweet chocolate pieces**
⅓ cup **sugar**
⅓ cup light **cream** and
2 tablespoons **butter;** stir until mixture is smooth. Remove from heat; chill 1 hour.
Blend in.....½ teaspoon **vanilla** and
3 **egg yolks,** one at a time; beat well after each.
Beat........3 **egg whites** until stiff but not dry. Fold in chocolate mixture thoroughly.
Spoon........into pie shell. Chill 3 to 4 hours. Serve with **whipped cream.**

For use with Pillsbury's Best Self-Rising Flour, omit salt and butter; decrease baking time to 8 to 10 minutes.

Chocolate-Crusted Coffee Pie

Senior Winner by Mrs. Evan C. Lander, St. Paul, Minnesota

A smooth coffee filling in a chocolate crust. There's a second layer of tender pastry hiding in the filling.

BAKE at 375° for 12 to 15 minutes   MAKES 9-inch pie

Sift together 1¼ cups sifted **Pillsbury's Best All Purpose Flour***
¼ cup **sugar**

3 tablespoons **cocoa**

2 teaspoons **instant coffee** and

½ teaspoon **salt** into mixing bowl.

Cut in . . . . . . ½ cup **shortening** until the size of small peas. Add

¼ cup **nuts,** finely chopped, and

1 teaspoon **vanilla**

Sprinkle . . . . . 4 to 5 tablespoons cold **water** over mixture, stirring with fork until dough is moist enough to hold together.

Divide . . . . into two portions, one twice as large as the other. Form into balls.

Roll out . . . . . . larger portion on floured surface to a circle 1½ inches larger than inverted 9-inch pie pan. Fit loosely into pan. Fold edge to form a standing rim; flute. Prick generously.

Roll out . . . . . . remaining dough to an 8-inch circle. Place circle on inverted cake pan; mark 6 wedges with pastry wheel or sharp knife.

Bake . . . . both pastries at 375° for 12 to 15 minutes. *Do not brown.*

COFFEE FILLING

Scald . . . . 2 tablespoons **ground coffee** in

2 cups **milk** over boiling water. Strain.**

Combine . . . . ½ cup sifted **Pillsbury's Best All Purpose Flour***

⅔ cup **sugar** and

⅛ teaspoon **salt** in saucepan. Gradually add the milk, stirring until smooth. Cook over medium heat, stirring constantly, until thick.

Blend . . . . a little of the hot mixture into

2 slightly beaten **egg yolks;** add to hot mixture. Cook 2 minutes, stirring constantly. Cover. Cool completely.

Beat . . . . ½ cup **whipping cream** until thick; fold with

1 teaspoon **vanilla** into coffee mixture.

Turn . . . . three-fourths of Filling into pie shell. Place pastry circle on top. Top with remaining Filling in center of

circle, spreading to within 1 inch of edge. Chill until set, about 4 hours.

*For use with Pillsbury's Best Self-Rising Flour, omit salt in pastry and filling.

**If desired, substitute 5 teaspoons instant coffee for the ground coffee; add to the other dry ingredients. Milk need not be scalded.*

Jamaica Chocolate Cream Pie

Senior Winner by Mrs. James L. Atkinson, Mead, Washington

Chocolate-rum and vanilla cream fillings marbled in a flaky pie shell.

BAKE at 450° for 10 to 12 minutes   MAKES 8 or 9-inch pie

Prepare . . . . recipe for **One-Crust Pastry,** page 460, using 8 or 9-inch pie pan; bake as directed.

Blend . . . . ½ cup **sugar**

¼ cup **Pillsbury's Best All Purpose Flour** and

¼ teaspoon **salt** in saucepan.

Add . . . . 2 cups **milk** gradually. Cook over medium heat, stirring constantly, until thick.

Blend . . . . a little of the hot mixture into

2 slightly beaten **eggs;** add to hot mixture. Cook 1 to 2 minutes, stirring constantly.

Place . . . . half of mixture in a second bowl. Add

18 **solid chocolate rum candy wafers** and

½ teaspoon **rum flavoring;** stir to melt chocolate. Cover and cool, stirring occasionally.

Add . . . . ½ teaspoon **vanilla** to remaining mixture; cover and cool, stirring occasionally.

Spoon . . . . light and dark fillings alternately into pie shell for marble effect.

Beat . . . . ½ cup **whipping cream** until thick. Fold in

1 tablespoon **sugar** and

½ teaspoon **vanilla.** (Or substitute ¼ cup chocolate malted milk powder for sugar and vanilla.) Serve on pie.

Honey Chocolette Pie

Senior First Prize Winner by Mrs. William C. Oakden, Belvidere, Illinois

A tantalizing blend of flavors makes up the smooth chocolate filling for the golden almond pie crust.

BAKE at 450° for 10 to 12 minutes*   MAKES 8-inch pie

Sift together . . 1 cup sifted **Pillsbury's Best All Purpose Flour*** and
½ teaspoon **salt** into mixing bowl.
Cut in . . . . . . ¼ cup **shortening** and
3 tablespoons **butter*** until the size of small peas.
Sprinkle . . . . . 2 to 3 tablespoons cold **milk** over mixture, stirring
with fork until dough is moist enough to hold
together. Form into a ball.
Roll out . . . . on floured surface to a circle 1½ inches larger than
inverted 8-inch pie pan. Fit loosely into pan. Fold
edge to form a standing rim; flute. Prick generously.
Press gently into bottom of pie shell
¼ cup slivered blanched **almonds**
Bake . . . . at 450° for 10 to 12 minutes.* Cool.

*For use with Pillsbury's Best Self-Rising Flour, omit salt and decrease butter
to 2 tablespoons; decrease baking time to 8 to 10 minutes.*

CHOCOLATE FILLING

Melt . . . . 1 cup (6-oz. pkg.) **semi-sweet chocolate pieces** in
top of double boiler over boiling water.
Add . . . . 2 **egg yolks;** stir until mixture leaves sides of pan in
smooth compact ball. Remove from heat.
Blend in . . . . . ½ cup **sour cream** (thick or commercial); beat until
smooth.
Beat . . . . 2 **egg whites** and
¼ teaspoon **salt** until stiff but not dry. Add very slowly
⅓ cup **honey,** beating until meringue stands in stiff,
glossy peaks. Fold in chocolate mixture.
Spoon . . . . into pie shell. Chill at least 2 hours. Garnish with
whipped cream and toasted slivered **almonds,** if
desired.

Honey Chocolette Pie

Pirates' Prize Coconut Pie

Senior Winner by Mrs. George M. Hagey, Seattle, Washington

Rich coconut cream pie . . . rum flavored and topped with a high meringue.

BAKE at 450° for 10 to 12 minutes, then   MAKES 9 or 10-inch pie
     at 350° for 12 to 15 minutes

Prepare . . . . recipe for **One-Crust Pastry**, page 460, using 9 or 10-inch pie pan; bake as directed.

Scald . . . . . . 2½ cups **milk** in saucepan over low heat. Add 1 cup flaked or chopped shredded **coconut**

Combine . . . . ½ cup sifted **Pillsbury's Best All Purpose Flour** and ½ cup **milk**; stir until smooth. Add to hot coconut mixture. Cook, stirring constantly, until thick.

Beat . . . . 5 **egg yolks** 1 cup **sugar** and ¼ teaspoon **salt** together until well blended.

Blend . . . . a little of the hot mixture into egg yolk mixture; add to hot mixture. Cook 2 minutes, stirring constantly. Cover. Cool to lukewarm.

Stir in . . . . . . ½ teaspoon **rum flavoring**. Turn into pie shell.

Prepare . . . . recipe for **De Luxe Meringue**, page 461; spread over filling.

Bake . . . . at 350° for 12 to 15 minutes.

Coffee Cream Pie

Senior Winner by Mrs. R. F. Carter, Sr., Pascagoula, Mississippi

Coffee in the crust and cream filling, topped with a fluffy meringue. A perfect pie to serve the ladies.

BAKE at 425° for 8 to 10 minutes, then   MAKES 9-inch pie
     at 350° for 12 to 15 minutes

Prepare . . . . recipe for **One-Crust Pastry**, page 460, sifting 1 teaspoon **instant coffee** with the flour and salt. Use

Coffee Cream Pie

     9-inch pie pan. Bake at 425° for 8 to 10 minutes.

Combine . . . . . 1 cup **sugar** 3 tablespoons **flour** 1 tablespoon **cornstarch** 1 tablespoon **instant coffee** and ¼ teaspoon **salt** in saucepan.

Blend in . . . . 1½ cups **milk** ½ cup undiluted **evaporated milk** or light cream 3 beaten **egg yolks** and 1 teaspoon **vanilla**. Cook over medium heat, stirring constantly, until thick.

Stir in . . . . . . ½ cup **pecans,** chopped. Cover and cool. Turn into pie shell.

Prepare . . . . recipe for **Meringue**, page 461; spread over filling.

Bake . . . . at 350° for 12 to 15 minutes.

Peanut Scotch Pie

Peanut Scotch Pie

Senior Winner by Maryan Bakken, Black River Falls, Wisconsin

Peanut butter goes into the butterscotch filling. Peanuts are sprinkled over the fluffy meringue.

BAKE at 450° for 10 to 12 minutes, then   MAKES 9-inch pie
    at 350° for 12 to 15 minutes

Prepare . . . . . . .recipe for **One-Crust Pastry,** page 460, using 9-inch
         pie pan; bake as directed.
Combine . . . . ¾ cup firmly packed **brown sugar**
         ½ cup **sugar**
         ½ cup cold **milk**
         ¼ cup **Pillsbury's Best All Purpose Flour**
         3 slightly beaten **egg yolks**

         1 tablespoon soft **butter** and
         ½ teaspoon **salt** in top of double boiler; mix well.
Stir in . . . . .1½ cups hot **milk**; cook over boiling water, stirring
         occasionally, until thickened.
Add . . . . .2 to 3 tablespoons **peanut butter**; blend well.
         Cover and cool.
Turn . . . . .filling into pie shell. Prepare recipe for **Meringue,**
         page 461; spread on filling. Sprinkle with
         ¼ cup **peanuts**, finely chopped
Bake . . . . .at 350° for 12 to 15 minutes. Cool.

Banana Caramel Cream Pie

Senior Winner by Mrs. August Charles Theroff, Kansas City, Kansas

Candy caramels give rich flavor to this smooth banana cream pie. Golden meringue covers it.

BAKE at 450° for 10 to 12 minutes, then   MAKES 9-inch pie
    at 350° for 12 to 15 minutes

Prepare . . . . . . .recipe for **One-Crust Pastry,** page 460, using 9-inch
         pie pan; bake as directed.
Melt . . . . . . .10 **candy caramels** in
         2 cups **milk** in saucepan over low heat.
Combine . . . . ⅓ cup **Pillsbury's Best All Purpose Flour**
         ⅓ cup **sugar** and
         ¼ teaspoon **salt** in top of double boiler. Gradually add
         caramel mixture; blend well. Cook over boiling
         water; stir constantly until thick.
Blend . . . . .a little of the hot mixture into
         3 slightly beaten **egg yolks;** add to hot mixture. Cook
         5 minutes, stirring occasionally.
Stir in . . . . . . .1 teaspoon **vanilla.** Cover and chill.
Arrange . . . . .2 **bananas,** sliced, in pie shell. Cover with filling.
Prepare . . . . . . .recipe for **Meringue,** page 461; spread over filling.
Bake . . . . .at 350° for 12 to 15 minutes. Cool.

Grandmother's Raisin Cream Pie

Senior Winner by Mrs. Winthrop Ware, Anchorage, Alaska

Smooth sour cream filling, amply filled with raisins and nuts, goes into this meringue-topped pie.

BAKE at 450° for 10 to 12 minutes, then   MAKES 8-inch pie
    at 350° for 12 to 15 minutes

Prepare . . . . . . .recipe for **One-Crust Pastry**, page 460, using 8-inch pie pan; bake as directed.

Combine . . . . .¾ cup **sugar**
    ¼ cup **Pillsbury's Best All Purpose Flour**
    1 teaspoon **cinnamon** and
    ¼ teaspoon **cloves** in top of double boiler.

Blend . . . . . . .3 slightly beaten **egg yolks** with
    1½ cups **sour cream** (thick or commercial). Stir gradually into the dry ingredients.

Cook . . . . .over boiling water, stirring occasionally, until thick.

Stir in . . . . . . .1 cup **raisins** and
    ½ cup **walnuts**, chopped. Cover and cool. Turn into pie shell.

Prepare . . . . . . .recipe for **Meringue**, page 461; spread over filling.

Bake . . . . .at 350° for 12 to 15 minutes. Cool.

Penuche Cream Pie

Senior Winner by Mrs. Denzil Burton, Tipton, Indiana

Smooth butterscotch filling is spooned into a golden cookie crust, then topped with a toasted coconut topping.

BAKE at 375° for 12 to 15 minutes   MAKES 9-inch pie

Prepare . . . . . . .Coconut Topping

Cream . . . . . .½ cup **butter** or margarine. Add
    2 tablespoons **sugar** and
    ½ teaspoon **almond extract**, creaming well.

Blend in . . . . .1 cup sifted **Pillsbury's Best All Purpose Flour*** to make a crumb mixture.

Press . . . . .evenly over bottom and sides of 9-inch pie pan.

Bake . . . . .at 375° for 12 to 15 minutes. Cool.

PENUCHE CREAM FILLING

Blend . . . . . . .⅓ cup **Pillsbury's Best All Purpose Flour*** and
    ¾ cup firmly packed **brown sugar** in saucepan.

Add . . . . . . .1½ cups **milk** gradually. Cook over low heat, stirring constantly, until thick and smooth, 5 to 7 minutes. Cool to lukewarm.

Add . . . . .1 teaspoon **vanilla** and
    ⅓ cup soft **butter** or margarine. Beat until very smooth and creamy.

Turn . . . . .into pie shell. Sprinkle with Topping. Cool before serving.

*Pillsbury's Best Self-Rising Flour may be substituted.

COCONUT TOPPING

Combine ½ cup coconut with 3 tablespoons brown sugar in pan. Blend in 1 tablespoon butter and 1 teaspoon water. Bake at 375°, stirring occasionally, until sugar melts and caramelizes, 10 to 12 minutes. Turn out on waxed paper to cool; separate pieces with a fork to prevent lumping.

Peaches 'n Creamy Coconut Pie

Junior Winner by Naomi J. Collins, Bryan, Ohio

Start with fluffy coconut cream filling in a baked pie shell—cover with peach slices—top with a party-pink glaze. Yummy!

BAKE at 450° for 10 to 12 minutes   MAKES 9-inch pie

Prepare . . . . recipe for **One-Crust Pastry,** page 460, using 9-inch pie pan; bake as directed.

Combine . . . . ½ cup **sugar**
    4 tablespoons **cornstarch**
    2 tablespoons **flour** and
    ¼ teaspoon **salt** in saucepan.

Add . . . . 1½ cups **milk** gradually; mix until smooth. Cook over low heat, stirring constantly, until thick, 5 to 8 minutes.

Blend . . . . a little of the hot mixture into
    3 slightly beaten **egg yolks;** add to hot mixture. Cook 2 minutes, stirring constantly.

Stir in . . . . 1 teaspoon **vanilla** and
    ½ cup **coconut.** Cover. Cool ½ hour. Meanwhile, drain 1 No. 303 can sliced **peaches.** Reserve ¾ cup juice for Glaze.

Beat . . . . 3 **egg whites** until soft mounds form. Gradually add ¼ cup **sugar,** beating until mixture stands in stiff peaks. Fold in cooked mixture.

Spoon . . . . into pie shell. Arrange well-drained peach slices over filling; top with Pink Peach Glaze. Chill at least 1 hour before serving.

PINK PEACH GLAZE

In small saucepan blend 1 tablespoon cornstarch and the ¾ cup juice. Cook over low heat until thickened and clear. Add 2 drops almond extract, ½ teaspoon grated lemon rind and 2 to 3 drops red food coloring; mix well.

Choosy's Peach Cream Pie

Junior Winner by Wanda Ackerson, Joplin, Missouri

Coconut plus peaches in custard-type filling add up to a refreshingly different dessert.

BAKE at 400° for 20 to 25 minutes   MAKES 9-inch pie

Sift together . . 1 cup sifted **Pillsbury's Best All Purpose Flour*** and ½ teaspoon **salt** into mixing bowl.

Cut in . . . . ⅓ cup **shortening** until the size of small peas.

Combine . . . . . 2 tablespoons **peach juice** and
    2 tablespoons **water.** Sprinkle over mixture, stirring with fork until dough is moist enough to hold together. Form into a ball.

Roll out . . . . on floured surface to a circle 1½ inches larger than inverted 9-inch pie pan. Fit into pan. Fold edge to form a rim; flute.

*For use with Pillsbury's Best Self-Rising Flour, omit salt.

COCONUT PEACH FILLING

Combine . . . 1¼ cups **sugar**
    3 tablespoons **cornstarch**
    2 tablespoons **flour**
    1 teaspoon **salt** and
    1 teaspoon grated **lemon rind** in saucepan.

Add . . . . 3 slightly beaten **egg yolks**
    2 cups **milk** and
    ½ cup **peach juice.** Cook over medium heat, stirring constantly, until thick. Remove from heat.

Stir in . . . . 1 cup mashed **peaches,** canned, frozen or fresh
    ¾ cup flaked or chopped shredded **coconut** and
    1 teaspoon **vanilla.** Pour into pie shell.

Bake . . . . at 400° for 20 to 25 minutes. Cool. Garnish with sweetened **whipped cream** and **peach slices.**

CHIFFON PIES

CHIFFON PIES are one-crust pies with light, fluffy fillings. The filling is a gelatin-sugar mixture dissolved in liquid over heat, then chilled. Beaten egg whites and, many times, whipped cream are folded in just before filling is spooned into the baked crust. These are good pies to make ahead of time and chill until ready to serve.

The gelatin mixture should be chilled just until it mounds slightly when dropped from a spoon. After folding in egg whites and whipped cream, the mixture should still form mounds; if it doesn't, chill it awhile longer.

For a light, fluffy chiffon pie, be sure to spoon the filling into the crust carefully. Then chill pie until filling is firm.

Caramel Candy Pie

Best of Class Winner by Florence E. Ries, Sleepy Eye, Minnesota

Caramel candies are melted into the filling of this luscious pie. Scatter caramelized almond slivers on top for festive party garnish.

BAKE at 450° for 10 to 12 minutes   MAKES 8 or 9-inch pie

Prepare . . . . recipe for **One-Crust Pastry**, page 460, using 8 or 9-inch pie pan; bake as directed.

Soften . . . . 1 envelope (1 tablespoon) unflavored **gelatin** in ¼ cup cold **water**

Combine . . . . ½ pound (about 28) **candy caramels** and ¼ cup **milk** in top of double boiler. Cook over hot water until caramels melt. Stir until smooth. Remove from heat.

Add . . . . the softened gelatin; stir until dissolved.

Blend in . . . . . ½ cup cold **milk.** Chill, stirring occasionally, until thickened but not set.

Beat . . . . 1 cup **whipping cream** until thick. Add caramel mixture and beat until well blended.

Spoon . . . . into pie shell. Chill until firm. Garnish with Caramelized Almonds.

CARAMELIZED ALMONDS

In skillet combine ¼ cup blanched almonds, slivered, and 2 tablespoons sugar. Cook over low heat, stirring constantly, until golden brown. Pour immediately onto greased baking sheet. Cool; break apart.

Butterscotch Nut Chiffon Pie

Junior Winner by Dorothy J. Jones, Greer, South Carolina

Brown sugar gives this pie a real butterscotch flavor; nuts add contrasting crunchy texture.

BAKE at 450° for 10 to 12 minutes   MAKES 9-inch pie

Prepare . . . . recipe for **One-Crust Pastry**, page 460, using 9-inch pie pan; bake as directed.

Combine . . . . . 1 envelope (1 tablespoon) unflavored **gelatin** ½ cup firmly packed **brown sugar** and ½ teaspoon **salt** in saucepan.

Beat . . . . 3 **egg yolks** with 1½ cups **milk** and ¼ cup **water.** Add to gelatin mixture; cook over medium heat, stirring constantly, until gelatin dissolves, about 5 minutes. Remove from heat. Chill, stirring occasionally, until thickened but not set.

Beat . . . . ½ cup **whipping cream** until thick; fold into gelatin mixture.

Beat . . . . 3 **egg whites** until soft mounds form. Add ¼ cup firmly packed **brown sugar** gradually, beating until straight peaks form. Fold into gelatin mixture.

Stir in . . . . . . ½ cup **nuts,** chopped. Spoon into pie shell. Chill until firm, at least 1 hour. Garnish with **whipped cream** and **nuts.**

Toffee Chiffon Pie

Senior Winner by Margaret Simpson, Mountain View, California

Crunchy toffee candy in honey chiffon filling with chocolate swirled into the top—all in a tender pastry shell.

BAKE at 450° for 10 to 12 minutes   MAKES 9-inch pie

Prepare . . . . recipe for **One-Crust Pastry**, page 460, using 9-inch pie pan; bake as directed.

Soften . . . . 1 envelope (1 tablespoon) unflavored **gelatin** in ¼ cup cold **water**

Blend . . . . ¼ cup **milk**
2 tablespoons **honey** and
1 **egg yolk** in top of double boiler. Cook over hot water, stirring constantly, until mixture will coat a metal spoon.

Add . . . . the softened gelatin; stir until dissolved.

Toffee Chiffon Pie

Blend in . . . . . ¼ cup cold **milk.** Chill, stirring occasionally, until thickened but not set.

Crush . . . . 3 to 4 ounces brittle **butter toffee candy** to equal ¾ cup. Set aside.

Beat . . . . 1 cup **whipping cream** very thick. Gently fold in 2 tablespoons **honey**; fold into gelatin mixture. Then fold in ½ cup of the crushed toffee candy (reserve remainder).

Beat . . . . 1 **egg white** with ⅛ teaspoon **salt** until stiff, straight peaks form. Fold into gelatin mixture.

Spoon . . . . into pie shell, heaping into fluffy mounds.

Melt . . . . ½ cup **semi-sweet chocolate pieces** in 3 tablespoons **cream** in saucepan. Drizzle over top of pie. Sprinkle with remaining candy. Chill until firm, at least 2 hours.

Brazilian Mocha-Nut Pie

Senior Winner by Mrs. Grace Hale, Arlington, Virginia

Brazil nuts in the pie shell and folded into the coffee chiffon filling make an unusual and appealing combination.

BAKE at 425° for 12 to 15 minutes   MAKES 9 or 10-inch pie

Sift together . . 1 cup sifted **Pillsbury's Best All Purpose Flour*** and ¼ teaspoon **salt** into mixing bowl.

Cut in . . . . . . ⅓ cup **shortening** until the size of small peas.

Add . . . . ⅓ cup **Brazil nuts,** chopped

Combine . . . . . 3 tablespoons cold **water** and ¼ teaspoon **almond extract;** sprinkle over flour mixture, stirring lightly with fork until dough is moist enough to hold together. Form into a ball.

Roll out . . . . on floured surface to a circle 1½ inches larger than inverted 9 or 10-inch pie pan. Fit loosely into pan. Fold edge to form a standing rim; flute. Prick.

Bake . . . . at 425° for 12 to 15 minutes. Cool.

For use with Pillsbury's Best Self-Rising Flour, omit salt and decrease water to 2 to 3 tablespoons; decrease baking time to 8 to 10 minutes.

MOCHA CHIFFON FILLING

Combine . . . . . 1 envelope (1 tablespoon) unflavored **gelatin**
½ cup **sugar** and
¼ teaspoon **salt** in saucepan.

Beat . . . . 3 slightly beaten **egg yolks** with
1 cup **milk** and
⅓ cup cold **coffee**. Add to gelatin mixture; cook over medium heat, stirring constantly, until gelatin dissolves, about 5 minutes. Remove from heat.

Stir in . . . . . . ½ teaspoon **vanilla**. Chill, stirring occasionally, until thickened but not set.

Beat . . . . 3 **egg whites** until soft mounds form. Gradually add
¼ cup **sugar**, beating until straight peaks form.

Fold . . . . 1 cup **heavy cream**, whipped,
½ cup **Brazil nuts**, shaved, and beaten egg whites into gelatin mixture.

Spoon . . . . into pie shell. Garnish with shaved **Brazil nuts**. Chill until firm, 3 to 5 hours.

Peanut Crust Pie

Second Grand Prize Winner by Mrs. T. L. Green, Columbus, Georgia

Tasty roasted peanuts right in the crust—and it's filled with fluffy chocolate chiffon filling.

BAKE at 425° for 12 to 15 minutes   MAKES 9-inch pie

Sift together . . 1 cup sifted **Pillsbury's Best All Purpose Flour***
½ teaspoon double-acting **baking powder** and
½ teaspoon **salt** into mixing bowl.

Cut in . . . . . . ⅓ cup **shortening** until the size of small peas.

Add . . . . ¼ cup **salted peanuts**, crushed

Sprinkle . . . . . 3 to 4 tablespoons cold **water** over mixture, stirring with fork until dough is moist enough to hold together. Form into a ball.

Roll out . . . . . . on floured surface to a circle 1½ inches larger than inverted 9-inch pie pan. Fit loosely into pan. Fold edge to form a standing rim; flute. Prick generously.

Bake . . . . at 425° for 12 to 15 minues. Cool.

For use with Pillsbury's Best Self-Rising Flour, omit baking powder and salt; decrease water to 2 to 3 tablespoons.

CHOCOLATE CHIFFON FILLING

Soften . . . . . . 1 envelope (1 tablespoon) unflavored **gelatin** in
¼ cup cold **milk**

Combine . . . . . 2 squares (2 oz.) unsweetened **chocolate**
¾ cup **sugar**
¼ teaspoon **salt**
¼ teaspoon **cinnamon** and
¾ cup **milk** in saucepan. Cook over medium heat, stirring constantly, until mixture is smooth.

Blend . . . . a little of the hot mixture into
2 slightly beaten **egg yolks**; add to hot mixture. Cook 2 minutes, stirring constantly. Remove from heat.

Add . . . . ½ teaspoon **vanilla** and the softened gelatin; stir until dissolved. Chill, stirring occasionally, until thickened but not set.

Beat . . . . 2 **egg whites** until mounds form. Gradually add
2 tablespoons **sugar**, beating until straight peaks form.

Beat . . . . ¾ cup **whipping cream** until thick. Fold into beaten egg whites. Fold into gelatin mixture.

Spoon . . . . lightly into pie shell. Chill until firm, 2 to 3 hours. Before serving, top with **whipped cream** and crushed **peanuts**.

BEST of the BAKE-OFF

"Open Sesame"
Pie
**Grand Prize Winner
of the Sixth
Grand National
Bake-Off®**

"Open Sesame" Pie

Grand Prize Winner by Mrs. Bernard Alexander Koteen, Washington, D.C.

Just add sesame seeds to pastry for nut-like flavor and crunchy texture.

BAKE at 450° for 10 to 12 minutes   MAKES 9-inch pie

Toast........2 to 4 tablespoons **sesame seeds** at 450° for 2 minutes until light golden brown, watching closely. Cool.

Prepare.......recipe for **One-Crust Pastry**, page 460; add the sesame seeds before cutting in the shortening. Use 9-inch pie pan; bake as directed.

Soften.......1 envelope (1 tablespoon) unflavored **gelatin** in
¼ cup cold **water**

Beat.........1 cup **milk** with
2 **egg yolks**
¼ cup **sugar** and
¼ teaspoon **salt** in top of double boiler until well blended. Cook over hot water, stirring constantly, until mixture coats metal spoon.

Blend in.......softened gelatin. Chill, stirring occasionally, until thickened but not set.

Stir in.......1 teaspoon **vanilla** and
1 cup **dates**, cut in small pieces.

Beat.........¾ cup **whipping cream** until thick; fold into gelatin mixture.

Beat.........2 **egg whites** until soft mounds form. Add
2 tablespoons **sugar** gradually, beating until stiff. Fold into gelatin mixture.

Spoon........into pie shell. Chill until firm, at least 1 hour. Sprinkle lightly with **nutmeg**.

Orange Fluff Pie

Senior Winner by Mrs. G. W. Hyatt, Harvey, Illinois

Bake a crunchy walnut pie shell, and put a light and fluffy orange chiffon filling into it.

BAKE at 450° for 10 to 12 minutes   MAKES 9-inch pie

Prepare.......recipe for **One-Crust Pastry**, page 460; add
¼ cup **walnuts**, finely chopped, to the flour-shortening mixture. Use 9-inch pie pan. Bake as directed.

Combine.....½ cup **sugar**
1 envelope (1 tablespoon) unflavored **gelatin**
⅛ teaspoon **salt** and
1 cup cold **water** in saucepan. Cook over direct heat, stirring constantly, until gelatin is dissolved. Remove from heat.

Blend.........a little of the hot mixture into
3 slightly beaten **egg yolks**; add to hot mixture. Cook over low heat, stirring constantly, until mixture will coat a metal spoon, about 3 minutes. Remove from heat.

Add.........½ cup undiluted **frozen orange juice**, thawed. Chill until thickened but not set.

Beat.........3 **egg whites** until soft mounds form. Gradually add
¼ cup **sugar**, beating well after each addition. Beat until meringue stands in stiff, straight peaks when beater is raised. Fold into gelatin mixture. Chill until thickened but not set.

Spoon........into pie shell. Chill. Serve with **whipped cream**. Garnish with chopped **walnuts**, if desired.

Fluffy Fruit Pie

Senior Winner by Mrs. Wilmer S. Hall, Pascagoula, Mississippi

This refreshing chiffon pie features colorful fruits topped with whipped cream and pecan halves.

BAKE at 450° for 10 to 12 minutes   MAKES 9-inch pie

Prepare . . . . recipe for **One-Crust Pastry**, page 460, using 9-inch pie pan; bake as directed.

Combine . . . . . 1 envelope (1 tablespoon) unflavored **gelatin** and ½ cup **sugar** in saucepan.

Add . . . . 1¼ cups **pineapple juice**. Cook over medium heat, stirring constantly, until gelatin dissolves, about 5 minutes. Chill, stirring occasionally, until thickened but not set.

Prepare . . . . . ¼ cup unpared coarsely chopped **apple**
⅓ cup **orange sections** (1 medium)
¼ cup **maraschino cherries**, cut in eighths
¼ cup **pecans**, chopped, and
½ cup thinly-sliced **banana** (1 medium). Chill.

Beat . . . . ¾ cup **whipping cream** until thick. Whip partially set gelatin until light and frothy; fold into half of the whipped cream (reserve remaining whipped cream).

Beat . . . . 2 **egg whites** until stiff but not dry; fold into gelatin mixture with the chilled fruit. Spoon into pie shell. Top with reserved whipped cream. Decorate with **pecan halves**. Chill at least 1 hour before serving.

Happy Day Orange Pie

Senior Winner by Mrs. Charles H. Martin, Caldwell, New Jersey

There is frozen orange juice in this fresh-tasting chiffon pie—a wonderfully cool dessert.

BAKE at 450° for 10 to 12 minutes   MAKES 9-inch pie

Prepare . . . . recipe for **One-Crust Pastry**, page 460, using 9-inch pie pan; bake as directed.

Combine . . . . . 1 envelope (1 tablespoon) unflavored **gelatin**
½ cup **sugar** and
¼ teaspoon **salt** in saucepan.

Beat . . . . 3 slightly beaten **egg yolks** with
¼ cup cold **water** and
½ cup undiluted thawed **frozen orange juice**. Add to gelatin mixture; cook over medium heat, stirring constantly, until gelatin dissolves, about 5 minutes. Remove from heat. Chill, stirring occasionally, until thickened but not set.

Beat . . . . 3 **egg whites** until soft mounds form. Gradually add ¼ cup **sugar**, beating until straight peaks form. Fold into the gelatin mixture.

Beat . . . . ½ cup **whipping cream** until thick. Fold into gelatin mixture.

Sprinkle . . . . . ½ cup **coconut** over bottom of pie shell.

Spoon . . . . filling over coconut. Chill until firm. Decorate with plain or toasted **coconut**.

Gingersnap Chiffon Pie

Senior Winner by Mrs. Hilding Kilgren, South Haven, Michigan

An exotic mingling of ginger, chocolate and rum flavors! The ginger cookie "petal" crust is crisp and spicy.

BAKE at 350° for 8 to 10 minutes   MAKES 9-inch pie
                                                                                                     and 4 dozen cookies*

Sift together 2½ cups sifted **Pillsbury's Best All Purpose Flour****
            1 teaspoon **soda**
            1 teaspoon **ginger** and
            ¾ teaspoon **salt**
Melt . . . . ½ cup **shortening** in large saucepan. Blend in
            ¾ cup **sugar** and
            ½ cup **molasses**; mix well. Cool.
Add . . . . 1 unbeaten **egg**; beat well.
Blend in . . . . the dry ingredients gradually. Chill.
Roll out . . . . half of dough on floured surface to ⅛-inch thickness.
            Cut circle to fit into bottom of greased 9-inch pie pan.
            Then cut 14 to 16 circles with 2½-inch cutter;*
            place circles around inside edge of pan, slightly
            overlapping each other and bottom layer. Circles
            should cover rim of pan.
Bake . . . . at 350° for 8 to 10 minutes. Cool.

  Roll out remaining cookie dough and cut into circles or other shapes; bake on greased baking sheet at 350° for 6 to 8 minutes.
  **For use with Pillsbury's Best Self-Rising Flour, decrease soda to ¼ teaspoon and omit salt.

RUM-CHOCOLATE FILLING

Soften . . . . 1 envelope (1 tablespoon) unflavored **gelatin** in
            ¼ cup cold **water**
Combine . . . . . 1 tablespoon **cornstarch**
            ½ cup **sugar** and
            ⅛ teaspoon **salt** in saucepan.
Blend in . . . . 1¾ cups **milk**. Cook, stirring constantly, until mixture
            comes to boil. Remove from heat.

Beat . . . . 4 **egg yolks** slightly; add a little of the hot mixture.
            Return to saucepan and cook 2 minutes, stirring
            constantly. Remove from heat.
Blend in . . . . the softened gelatin; stir until dissolved. Pour half
            of mixture into a bowl; add
            1 teaspoon **rum flavoring**. Chill until it begins to
            thicken.
Stir . . . . 1 square (1 oz.) shaved unsweetened **chocolate** into
            remaining custard mixture until well blended.
Blend in . . . . . 1 tablespoon **butter** and
            1 teaspoon **vanilla**. Chill until it begins to thicken,
            then turn into pie shell. Chill until almost set.
Beat . . . . 4 **egg whites** until soft mounds form. Gradually add
            ½ cup **sugar**, beating until stiff, glossy peaks form.
Fold in . . . . the thickened custard mixture. Spoon onto choco-
            late filling. Sprinkle with shaved **semi-sweet choco-
            late**. Chill until set.

Gingersnap Chiffon Pie

Chocolate-Crusted Pie

Best of Class Winner by Mrs. Robert Monroe, Atlantic City, New Jersey

The cooky-like crust is filled with a snowy chiffon filling.

BAKE at 400° for 8 to 10 minutes   MAKES 9-inch pie

Sift together . . 1 cup sifted **Pillsbury's Best All Purpose Flour***
        ¼ cup **sugar**
        3 tablespoons **cocoa** and
        ½ teaspoon **salt** into mixing bowl.

Cut in . . . . 6 tablespoons **shortening** until the size of small peas.

Combine . . . . ½ teaspoon **vanilla** and
        3 tablespoons cold **water.** Sprinkle over mixture, stirring with fork until dough is moist enough to hold together. Form into a ball.

Roll out . . . . on floured surface to a circle 1½ inches larger than inverted 9-inch pie pan. Fit loosely into pan. Fold edge to form a standing rim; flute. Prick generously. Place "trimmings" in second pan.

Bake . . . . pie shell and trimmings at 400° for 8 to 10 minutes. Cool. Crumble trimmings for crumb topping.

For use with Pillsbury's Best Self-Rising Flour, omit salt.

VANILLA CHIFFON FILLING

Combine . . . . . 1 envelope (1 tablespoon) unflavored **gelatin**
        ⅓ cup **sugar** and
        ½ teaspoon **salt** in saucepan.

Beat . . . . 4 **egg yolks** with
        1½ cups **milk.** Add to gelatin mixture; cook over medium heat, stirring constantly, until gelatin dissolves, about 5 minutes. Remove from heat.

Stir in . . . . 1 teaspoon **vanilla.** Chill until thickened but not set.

Beat . . . . 4 **egg whites** until soft mounds form. Gradually add
        ¼ cup **sugar,** beating until stiff peaks form. Fold into gelatin mixture.

Spoon . . . . into pie shell. Chill until firm. Top with **whipped cream.** Sprinkle with crumb topping.

Chocolate-Crusted Pie

SPECIAL PIES

in this section are excellent for important occasions when you want to serve a dessert that is different.

Southern Sugar Pie

Senior Winner by Mrs. Daniel F. Moss, Jamaica, New York

This chess pie, rich with brown sugar flavor, has been a favorite in Mrs. Moss' family for nearly half a century.

BAKE at 350° for 45 to 55 minutes   MAKES 10-inch pie

Sift together 1½ cups sifted **Pillsbury's Best All Purpose Flour*** and
½ teaspoon **salt**

Combine.....3 tablespoons **water** and ¼ cup of the flour mixture to form a paste.

Cut........½ cup **shortening** into remaining flour until the size of small peas.

Add.........flour paste and mix until dough forms a ball.

Roll out.......on floured surface to a circle 1½ inches larger than inverted 10-inch pie pan. Fit loosely into pan. Fold edge to form a standing rim; flute.

For use with Pillsbury's Best Self-Rising Flour, omit salt.

SOUTHERN SUGAR FILLING

Combine.....1 cup **sugar**
1 cup firmly packed **brown sugar**

¼ cup sifted **Pillsbury's Best All Purpose Flour** and
½ teaspoon **salt**

Beat........4 **eggs** in mixing bowl until thick and ivory colored. Gradually add the dry ingredients, beating until mixture is well blended.

Add........½ cup melted **butter** or margarine
½ cup **milk** and
1 tablespoon **vanilla** gradually. Pour into pie shell.

Bake........at 350° for 45 to 55 minutes.

Walnut Chess Pie

Senior Winner by Mrs. Grant Elgin, Corvallis, Oregon

The filling forms two layers when baked . . . rich in butter and eggs, just full of walnuts . . . something like a pecan pie.

BAKE at 375° for 40 to 45 minutes   MAKES 9-inch pie

Prepare.......recipe for **One-Crust Pastry**, page 460, using 9-inch pie pan. Do not prick crust; fill and bake as directed below.

Cook......2¼ cups **sugar** and
¾ cup **water** in saucepan over high heat, stirring until sugar is dissolved. Cover for 3 minutes to dissolve sugar crystals on sides of pan. Uncover; cook until syrup spins a thread (234°). Remove from heat.

Stir in.......1 cup **butter** or margarine, cut in small pieces. When butter is melted, cool mixture quickly by placing in pan of cold water.

Beat........7 **egg yolks** thoroughly. Slowly add syrup, stirring constantly.

Stir in.......1 cup **walnuts**, chopped
1 teaspoon **vanilla** and
⅛ teaspoon **salt**. Pour into pie shell.

Bake........at 375° for 40 to 45 minutes. Cool.

Caramel Crumb Pie

Senior Prize Winner by Effie Scott, Akron, Indiana

This novel recipe will remind you of Shoo Fly Pie, so popular with the Pennsylvania Dutch.

BAKE at 375° for 40 to 45 minutes   MAKES 9-inch pie

Prepare . . . . recipe for **One-Crust Pastry,*** page 460, using 9-inch pie pan. Do not prick crust; fill and bake as directed below.

Melt . . . . ⅓ cup **sugar** in heavy skillet over low heat, stirring constantly, until sugar turns dark brown. Add slowly

5 tablespoons **boiling water,** a few drops at a time at first, stirring constantly until sugar is completely dissolved. Cool.

Dissolve . . . . . ½ teaspoon **soda*** in

⅔ cup **milk.** Blend into the syrup.

Cut . . . . ⅔ cup **butter** or margarine into

2 cups sifted **Pillsbury's Best All Purpose Flour***

1 cup firmly packed **brown sugar** and

¼ teaspoon **salt** until mixture resembles coarse crumbs.

Stir in . . . . . . ½ cup **nuts,** chopped

Pour . . . . half of the caramelized syrup into pie shell. Sprinkle evenly with crumb mixture. Drizzle remaining caramel syrup over top.

Bake . . . . at 375° for 40 to 45 minutes. Serve plain or with whipped cream.

*For use with Pillsbury's Best Self-Rising Flour, omit salt and decrease water in pastry to 2 to 3 tablespoons; decrease soda to ¼ teaspoon.

Company's-Coming Cashew Pie

Senior Winner by Mrs. Hazel Frost, Chicago, Illinois

This delectable pie is quickly and easily made—and is foolproof—so makes a wonderful "show-off" dessert.

BAKE at 350° for 50 to 55 minutes   MAKES 8 or 9-inch pie

Prepare . . . . recipe for **One-Crust Pastry,** page 460, using 8 or 9-inch pie pan. Do not prick crust; fill and bake as directed below.

Cream . . . . . . 1 cup firmly packed **brown sugar** and

3 tablespoons soft **butter**

Add . . . . ¾ cup **light corn syrup** and

1 teaspoon **vanilla;** mix well.

Blend in . . . . . 3 well-beaten **eggs**

Add . . . . 1 cup (4½ oz.) salted **cashew nuts,** finely chopped. Pour into pie shell.

Bake . . . . at 350° for 50 to 55 minutes.

Butter Pecan Orange Pie

Senior Winner by Mrs. Adolph Sanders, Austin, Texas

Tender orange butter pastry with an orange-pecan butter filling and an unusual pastry-meringue topping.

BAKE at 400° for 10 to 12 minutes, then   MAKES 8-inch pie
    at 350° for 10 to 12 minutes

Sift together . . 1 cup sifted **Pillsbury's Best All Purpose Flour***
    ¼ cup sifted **confectioners' sugar** and
    ½ teaspoon **salt** into mixing bowl. Add
    2 teaspoons grated **orange rind**

Cut in . . . . 3 tablespoons **butter** and
    3 tablespoons **shortening** until the size of small peas.

Sprinkle . . . . . 2 to 3 tablespoons cold **water** over mixture, stirring with fork until dough is moist enough to hold together. Divide into two portions, one twice as large as the other. Form into balls.

Roll out . . . . . . larger portion on floured surface to a circle 1½ inches larger than inverted 8-inch pie pan. Fit loosely into pan; pat out air pockets. Fold edge to form rim; flute. Prick generously.

Roll out . . . . . . remaining dough to an 8-inch circle. Place circle on inverted cake pan. Prick with fork.

Bake . . . . both pastries at 400° for 10 to 12 minutes. Cool. Decrease oven temperature to 350°. Prepare Baked Meringue.

*For use with Pillsbury's Best Self-Rising Flour, omit salt.

ORANGE-NUT FILLING

Cream . . . . . . ½ cup soft **butter** or margarine. Gradually add
    1½ cups sifted **confectioners' sugar,** creaming well.

Blend in . . . . . 3 **egg yolks,** one at a time, then beat until light and fluffy, 4 to 5 minutes. Add
    1 teaspoon **vanilla**
    2 teaspoons grated **orange rind**
    2 teaspoons **orange juice** and

    1 cup **pecans,** chopped; mix thoroughly.

Turn . . . . into pie shell. Chill 1 hour. Top with Meringue. Chill 1 more hour before serving.

BAKED MERINGUE

Prepare recipe for **Meringue,** page 461. Fold in 1 teaspoon grated orange rind. Spread on cooled, baked 8-inch pastry circle to the edge. Bake at 350° for 10 to 12 minutes. Cool.

Plantation Peanut Pie

Senior Winner by Mrs. Katie L. Frost, New London, Connecticut

A creamy peanut butter filling in a shell of tender pastry. Fluffy whipped cream and chopped peanuts go on top.

BAKE at 400° for 25 to 30 minutes   MAKES 8-inch pie

Prepare . . . . recipe for **One-Crust Pastry,** page 460, using 8-inch pie pan. Do not prick crust; fill and bake as directed below.

Blend together 2 unbeaten **egg yolks**
    ¾ cup **sugar** and
    ¼ cup **peanut butter**

Add . . . . ¾ cup **milk** and
    ½ teaspoon **vanilla** gradually, blending well.

Beat . . . . 2 **egg whites** and
    ⅛ teaspoon **salt** until stiff but not dry. Gently fold in egg yolk mixture.

Pour . . . . into pie shell.

Bake . . . . at 400° for 25 to 30 minutes. Cool.

Beat . . . . ½ cup **whipping cream** until thick. Blend in
    2 tablespoons **confectioners' sugar.** Spread over pie. Sprinkle with chopped **peanuts.**

Hawaiian Confection Pie

Senior Winner by H. B. Andrews, Inglewood, California

A very rich fruit pie . . . with a sweet, fluffy filling, spread with pineapple and fresh strawberries.

BAKE at 450° for 10 to 12 minutes   MAKES 9 or 10-inch pie

Prepare . . . . . . .recipe for **One-Crust Pastry,** page 460, using 9 or 10-inch pie pan; bake as directed.

Combine . . . . ½ cup **sugar**
¼ cup **light corn syrup** and
2 tablespoons **water** in saucepan. Cook over low heat until syrup forms a thread (230°).

Beat . . . . .2 **egg whites** until stiff but not dry. Pour syrup slowly over egg whites, beating until filling stands in peaks.

Add . . . . .1 teaspoon **vanilla.** Spread a thin layer of filling in pie shell.

Combine . . . . .1 cup (No. 1 can) drained **pineapple chunks** and
1 cup sliced fresh **strawberries.** Arrange in pie shell; top with remaining filling. Chill.

Lemon Mist Cheese Pie

Junior Winner by Nadine Purviance, Minburn, Iowa

This cottage cheese pie is light, fluffy and flavored with lemon.

BAKE at 425° for 10 minutes, then   MAKES 9-inch pie
at 325° for 35 to 40 minutes

Sift together . .1 cup sifted **Pillsbury's Best All Purpose Flour*** and
½ teaspoon **salt** into mixing bowl.

Cut in . . . . . . ⅓ cup **shortening** until the size of small peas.

Combine . . .2½ tablespoons **water** and
2 teaspoons **lemon juice;** sprinkle over flour mixture stirring with fork until dough is moist enough to hold together. Form into ball.

Roll out . . . . . .on floured surface to a circle 1½ inches larger than inverted 9-inch pie pan. Fit pastry loosely into pan. Fold edge to form rim; flute.

**For use with Pillsbury's Best Self-Rising Flour, omit salt.*

LEMON CHEESE FILLING

Combine . . . . .3 slightly beaten **egg yolks**
1½ cups (12 oz.) creamed **cottage cheese,** sieved
⅔ cup light **cream**
1 teaspoon grated **lemon rind** and
3 tablespoons **lemon juice.** Mix well.

Stir in . . . . . .⅔ cup **sugar**
1 tablespoon **flour** and
¼ teaspoon **salt;** mix well.

Beat . . . . .3 **egg whites** until stiff but not dry; fold into cheese mixture. Pour into pie shell.

Bake . . . . .at 425° for 10 minutes, then at 325° for 35 to 40 minutes.

Pineapple Cheese Cake Pie

Senior Winner by Mrs. Louis Dees, Fort Worth, Texas

An easy-to-make cheese cake pie with a pineapple tang and a crusty nut top.

BAKE at 425° for 10 minutes, then   MAKES 9-inch pie
at 350° for 20 to 25 minutes

Prepare . . . . . . .recipe for **One-Crust Pastry,** page 460, using 9-inch pie pan. Do not prick crust; fill and bake as directed below.

Combine . . . . .1 cup (9-oz. can) **crushed pineapple,** undrained
⅓ cup **sugar** and

1 teaspoon **cornstarch** in saucepan. Cook over medium heat, stirring constantly, until thick and clear. Cool.

Blend.......1 package (8 oz.) softened **cream cheese** with
½ cup **sugar** and
½ teaspoon **salt**; cream well.

Add.......2 unbeaten **eggs**, beating well after each.

Blend in.....½ cup **milk** and
½ teaspoon **vanilla**

Spread.......pineapple mixture in pie shell. Top with cream cheese mixture. Sprinkle with
½ cup **pecans**, finely chopped

Bake.........at 425° for 10 minutes, then at 350° for 20 to 25 minutes. Chill before serving.

Lemon Cheese Pie

Best of Class Winner by Mrs. Lyle W. Glenn, Fresno, California

Lemon juice gives refreshing flavor to velvety cream cheese mixture baked in a flaky pastry crust . . . reminds you of smooth cheese cake.

BAKE at 450° for 8 to 10 minutes, then   MAKES 8-inch pie*
at 350° for 15 to 20 minutes

Prepare.......recipe for **One-Crust Pastry**, page 460, using 8-inch pie pan;* bake at 450° for 8 to 10 minutes.

Soften.......1 package (8 oz.) **cream cheese**; beat until fluffy.

Add.......2 unbeaten **eggs**, beating well after each.

Blend in.....½ cup **sugar**
1 teaspoon **vanilla**
1 teaspoon grated **lemon rind** and
1 tablespoon **lemon juice**. Turn into pie shell.

Bake.........at 350° for 15 to 20 minutes until slightly firm. Cool. Chill at least 1 hour. If desired, serve with **whipped cream.**

Six 4-inch tarts may be made instead. Cut pastry in rounds to fit tart shells or muffin cups. Bake and fill as directed above.

Lemon Cheese Pie

Meringue-Lined Cheese Pie

Senior Winner by Mrs. John Bukovics, Toledo, Ohio

The nut meringue lining in this flaky egg pie shell adds crunchiness and keeps pastry crisp and tender.

BAKE at 375° for 20 to 25 minutes   MAKES 9-inch pie

Sift together . . 1 cup sifted **Pillsbury's Best All Purpose Flour***
                  1 tablespoon **sugar** and
                  ¼ teaspoon **salt** into mixing bowl.
Cut in . . . . . . ⅓ cup **shortening** until the size of small peas.
Combine . . . . . 1 slightly beaten **egg yolk**
                  2 tablespoons **water** and
                  1 teaspoon **vinegar.** Sprinkle over the dry ingredients, tossing with fork until dough is moist enough to hold together. Form into a ball.
Roll out . . . . . . on floured surface to a circle 1½ inches larger than inverted 9-inch pie pan. Fit loosely into pan. Fold edge to form a rim; flute. Prick generously.
Bake . . . . at 375° for 10 minutes only.

For use with Pillsbury's Best Self-Rising Flour, omit salt.

MERINGUE LINING

Beat . . . . 1 **egg white** until soft mounds form. Gradually add
                    ¼ cup **sugar,** beating until meringue stands in stiff, glossy peaks.
Fold in . . . . . . ½ cup **nuts,** chopped, and
                    ¼ teaspoon **vinegar.** Spread over partially-baked crust.
Bake . . . . at 375° for 10 to 15 minutes. Cool.

CHEESE FILLING

Combine . . . . . 1 envelope (1 tablespoon) **gelatin** with
                  ⅔ cup **sugar** in saucepan. Add
                  1 slightly beaten **egg yolk**
                  ¼ cup **water** and
                  ¼ cup **orange juice.** Cook over low heat, stirring constantly, until mixture boils. Cool to lukewarm.

Add . . . . . . 1½ cups (12 oz.) creamed **cottage cheese** and
               ½ cup **sour cream.** Beat well.
Fold in . . . . . . 1 stiffly beaten **egg white.** Turn into pie shell.
Combine . . . . ½ cup **sour cream** (thick or commercial) and
               2 tablespoons **sugar.** Spread over pie. Sprinkle with chopped **nuts** and **cinnamon.** Chill until firm, at least 2 hours.

Sour Cream Cheese Pie

Senior Winner by Mrs. Ruth Toshiko Brandt, West Los Angeles, California

A spicy butter crust with an uncooked cream cheese-sour cream filling.

BAKE at 400° for 10 to 12 minutes   MAKES 9-inch pie

Sift together . . 1 cup sifted **Pillsbury's Best All Purpose Flour***
                  2 tablespoons **sugar**
                  ½ teaspoon **cinnamon** and
                  ⅛ teaspoon **nutmeg** into mixing bowl. Add
                  1 teaspoon grated **lemon rind**
Cut in . . . . . . ⅓ cup **butter** or margarine until the size of small peas.
Blend . . . . . . 1 **egg yolk** with
                  1 tablespoon **water** and
                  ½ teaspoon **vanilla.** Sprinkle over the dry ingredients, stirring with fork, until dough is moist enough to hold together. Form into a ball.

Roll out . . . . on floured surface to a circle ¾ inch larger than inverted 9-inch pie pan. Fit loosely into pan; gently pat out air pockets. Press around rim with fork. Prick generously.

Place . . . . extra pieces of pastry on baking sheet.

Bake . . . . at 400° for 10 to 12 minutes. Cool.

*Pillsbury's Best Self-Rising Flour may be substituted.

SOUR CREAM FILLING

Combine . . . . ¾ cup **sour cream** (thick or commercial)
1 package (8 oz.) **cream cheese,** softened
¼ cup **honey**
1 teaspoon grated **lemon rind**
1 tablespoon **lemon juice** and
1 teaspoon **vanilla** in mixing bowl. Beat until thick and smooth.

Beat . . . . 1 **egg white** until soft mounds form. Gradually add
1 tablespoon **honey,** beating until stiff. Fold into the cream mixture.

Pour . . . . into pie shell. Sprinkle with crumbled pastry pieces. Chill until set, 5 to 6 hours.

Macaroon Crunch Pie

Senior Winner by Mrs. Hugh Estell, Jackson, Mississippi

Just fold crushed macaroon cookies and pecans into whipped cream, then pile into a flaky pie shell.

BAKE at 450° for 10 to 12 minutes   MAKES 8-inch pie*

Prepare . . . . recipe for **One-Crust Pastry,** page 460, using 8-inch pie pan; bake as directed.

Toast . . . . ½ cup **coconut** or chopped pecans; reserve 2 tablespoons. Sprinkle remainder into pie shell.

Beat . . . . 1½ cups **whipping cream** until thick. Add
⅓ cup sifted **confectioners' sugar;** reserve 1 cup.

Fold . . . . 1 cup crushed crisp **macaroon cookies** and
½ cup **pecans,** chopped, into remaining whipped cream. Spoon lightly into pie shell. Spread with reserved whipped cream; sprinkle with reserved coconut or nuts. Chill at least 1 hour.

Six 4-inch tarts may be made instead. Cut pastry in rounds to fit into tart shells or muffin cups. Bake at 450° for 8 to 10 minutes and fill as directed above.

Pea-Co-Nut Pie

Senior Winner by Mrs. Homer Gray, Morrilton, Arkansas

Crunchy peanuts and crisp coconut add flavor to this rich filling . . . similar to the traditional pecan pie.

BAKE at 375° for 35 to 45 minutes   MAKES 8 or 9-inch pie

Prepare . . . . recipe for **One-Crust Pastry,** page 460, using 8 or 9-inch pie pan. Do not prick crust; fill and bake as directed below.

Combine . . . . . 3 well-beaten **eggs**
1 cup **light corn syrup**
¾ cup **sugar**
2 tablespoons soft **butter**
1 teaspoon **vanilla** and
⅛ teaspoon **salt** in mixing bowl. Mix well.

Stir in . . . . 1 cup **peanuts** and
½ cup **coconut.** Pour into pie shell.

Bake . . . . at 375° for 35 to 45 minutes. Serve with **whipped cream.**

Chocolate Brownie Pie

Chocolate Brownie Pie

Senior Winner by Mrs. Verne H. Deltenre, Independence, Kansas

You'll think of your favorite brownies when you taste this chocolate and pecan filling tucked into a flaky pie shell.

BAKE at 450° for 10 to 12 minutes, then   MAKES 8 or 9-inch pie
    at 325° for 25 to 35 minutes

Prepare . . . . recipe for **One-Crust Pastry,** page 460, using 8 or 9-inch pie pan; bake as directed.

Melt . . . . 2 squares (2 oz.) unsweetened **chocolate** with
    ½ cup **butter** or margarine in top of double boiler. Blend in
    ¾ cup **sugar** and
    ¼ teaspoon **salt.** Cool 5 minutes.

Stir in . . . . 2 slightly beaten **eggs** and
    1 teaspoon **vanilla.** Blend thoroughly.

Add . . . . ½ cup sifted **Pillsbury's Best All Purpose Flour** and
    ½ cup **pecans,** chopped, mixing thoroughly.

Turn . . . . into pie shell.

Bake . . . . at 325° for 25 to 35 minutes. Chill thoroughly. Top with **whipped cream;** garnish with shaved **chocolate.**

Pecan Brownie Pie

Senior Winner by Mrs. Gerald E. Smith, Rockton, Illinois

Southern pecan pie with a chocolate flavor—top small wedges with ice cream or whipped cream.

BAKE at 375° for 25 to 30 minutes   MAKES 9-inch pie

Prepare . . . . recipe for **One-Crust Pastry,** page 460, using 9-inch pie pan. Do not prick crust; fill and bake as directed below.

Combine . . . . . 4 slightly beaten **eggs** and
    1¾ cups **sugar**

Blend in . . . . 2½ squares (2½ oz.) melted unsweetened **chocolate**
    3 tablespoons melted **butter**
    ¼ teaspoon **salt** and
    1 cup **pecans,** chopped. Pour into pie shell.

Bake . . . . at 375° for 25 to 30 minutes. Cool. (Filling will set while cooling.) Serve with **whipped cream** or ice cream.

Chocolate Creme Mint Pie

Senior Winner by Mrs. David A. Rainey, Denver, Colorado

Here's a creamy pie you'll want to serve often as company dessert.

BAKE at 450° for 10 to 12 minutes   MAKES 8 or 9-inch pie

Prepare . . . . recipe for **One-Crust Pastry,** page 460, using 8 to 9-inch pie pan; bake as directed.

Beat . . . . 3 **eggs** thoroughly. Set aside.

Cream . . . . . . ¾ cup **butter** or margarine. Gradually add 1 cup **sugar,** creaming well. Blend in beaten eggs.

Blend in . . . . . 3 squares (3 oz.) unsweetened **chocolate,** melted and cooled. Beat until smooth.

Add . . . . ½ teaspoon **peppermint extract.** Pour mixture into pie shell. Chill several hours. If desired, serve with **whipped cream.**

French Silk Chocolate Pie

Best of Class Winner by Mrs. K. E. Cooper, Silver Springs, Maryland

A magnificent chocolate pie—rich, creamy smooth and luscious, and you don't cook the filling.

BAKE at 450° for 10 to 12 minutes   MAKES 8-inch pie

Prepare . . . . recipe for **One-Crust Pastry,** page 460, using 8-inch pie pan; bake as directed.

Cream . . . . . . ½ cup **butter** or margarine. Gradually add ¾ cup **sugar,** creaming well.

Blend in . . . . . 2 squares (2 oz.) unsweetened **chocolate,** melted and thoroughly cooled, and 1 teaspoon **vanilla**

Add . . . . 2 **eggs,** one at a time; beat 5 minutes after each. (With mixer use medium speed.)

Turn . . . . into pie shell. Chill 2 hours. Top with **whipped cream** and **walnuts,** if desired.

French Silk Chocolate Pie

Calico Snow Pie

Calico Snow Pie

Senior Winner by Mrs. V. O. Pounds, Independence, Kansas

Light as a cloud! It's easily made by combining whipped cream, marshmallow creme, coconut and shaved chocolate.

BAKE at 450° for 10 to 12 minutes MAKES 9-inch pie

Prepare . . . . recipe for **One-Crust Pastry,** page 460, using 9-inch pie pan; bake as directed.
Beat . . . . 1 cup **whipping cream** until thick.
Fold in . . . . . . 1 cup (7½-oz. jar) **marshmallow creme** and
1 teaspoon **vanilla**
Add . . . . ½ cup **coconut**; fold gently.
Shave . . . . 1 square (1 oz.) **semi-sweet** or **unsweetened chocolate**
Sprinkle . . . . half the chocolate and

¼ cup **coconut** over pie shell.
Spoon . . . . cream mixture into pie shell. Top with
¼ cup **coconut** and remaining chocolate. Chill at least 2 hours before serving.

Chocolate Mallow Malt Pie

Senior Winner by Mrs. Ruth Lasky, San Bernardino, California

A light and velvety chocolate, whipped cream-marshmallow pie with a delicate malted milk flavor.

BAKE at 450° for 10 to 12 minutes MAKES 9-inch pie

Prepare . . . . recipe for **One-Crust Pastry,** page 460, using 9-inch pie pan; bake as directed.
Combine . . . . ½ pound **marshmallows**
½ cup **milk** and
¼ teaspoon **salt** in top of double boiler. Heat over hot water, stirring constantly, until marshmallows are melted. Remove from heat.
Add . . . . ½ cup **semi-sweet chocolate pieces;** stir until melted. Cool.
Beat . . . . 1 cup **whipping cream** until very thick.
Fold in . . . . . . ¼ cup **chocolate** or **vanilla malted milk powder** and 1 teaspoon **vanilla**. Fold into the marshmallow mixture.
Turn . . . . into pie shell. Arrange
¼ cup **pecans** or walnuts around edge. Chill at least 3 hours before serving.

TARTS and TURNOVERS

are small pies just right for individual servings; any type of filling may be used. They're easy to serve on any occasion and are impressive for parties! Turnovers carry well on picnics and cook-outs.

To make your own tart pans: Cut pastry into circles (size indicated in recipe) and place on circles of heavy-duty aluminum foil (cut to the same size). Prick generously; shape into tarts by bringing up sides and pinching to form flutes.

Lemon Nut Surprise Tarts

Senior Winner by Mrs. Charles Mottola, Jersey City, N.J.

These attractive little tarts have an unusually refreshing buttermilk lemon chiffon filling.

BAKE at 350° for 15 to 20 minutes   MAKES 1 dozen

Cream......⅓ cup **butter** or margarine. Gradually add
          ¼ cup **sugar,** creaming well.

Add........2 unbeaten **egg yolks;** beat well.

Sift together..1 cup sifted **Pillsbury's Best All Purpose Flour*** and
          ¼ teaspoon **salt.** Add to creamed mixture; mix well.

Add........1 to 1½ tablespoons **cream,** tossing with fork to form
          a dough.

Stir in.......1 cup **walnuts,** finely chopped

Divide........dough into twelve ungreased 3-inch tart pans or
          large muffin cups. Press into bottoms and sides of
          pans; prick generously.

Bake.........at 350° for 15 to 20 minutes. Cool 5 minutes. Remove from pans; cool.

Pillsbury's Best Self-Rising Flour is not recommended for use in this recipe.

LEMON CHIFFON FILLING

Melt.......¼ cup tart **red jelly** over hot water. Spoon into tart
        shells (about 1 teaspoonful in each). Cool.

Combine....½ package (1½ teaspoons) unflavored **gelatin**
        ¼ cup **sugar** and
        ⅛ teaspoon **salt** in top of double boiler.

Beat........2 **egg yolks** with
        ½ cup **buttermilk** or sour milk. Add to gelatin mixture;
        mix well. Cook over boiling water, stirring constantly,
        until thickened, about 8 minutes. Cool to lukewarm.

Stir in.......1 teaspoon grated **lemon rind** and
        3 tablespoons **lemon juice.** Chill until partially set.

Beat........4 **egg whites** until soft mounds form. Gradually add
        ¼ cup **sugar,** beating until straight peaks form. Fold
        into the gelatin mixture.

Spoon........into tart shells, about ¼ cup in each; decorate with
        a dot of **red jelly.** Chill 1 hour.

Lemon Nut Surprise Tarts

Grape Meringue Tarts

Senior Winner by Lilian Rogers Kuhnen, Glencoe, Illinois

Bake dainty tarts of flaky pastry, then fill them with grape filling. Top with fluffy meringue.

BAKE at 450° for 8 to 10 minutes, then   MAKES 12 to 15
    at 350° for 12 to 15 minutes

Prepare . . . . recipe for **Two-Crust Pastry**, page 460; roll out pastry
        as directed below.
Roll out . . . . . . each half on floured surface to ⅛-inch thickness.
        Cut 5-inch circles. Fit loosely into tart pans or over
        back of muffin cups. Prick generously.
Bake . . . . at 450° for 8 to 10 minutes. Cool.

GRAPE FILLING

Combine . . . . ¼ cup **cornstarch**
        ½ cup **sugar** and
        ¼ teaspoon **salt** in heavy saucepan.
Beat . . . . 4 **egg yolks** slightly. Gradually add
        3 cups **grape juice,** mixing well. Blend gradually into
        the dry ingredients, stirring until smooth. Cook over
medium heat, stirring constantly; boil for 5 minutes.
        Remove from heat.
Blend in . . . . .1 tablespoon **butter** and
        1 tablespoon **lemon juice.** Cover and cool. Divide into
        tart shells. Spread with Fluffy Meringue.
Bake . . . . at 350° for 12 to 15 minutes. Serve cold.

FLUFFY MERINGUE

Beat 4 egg whites with ¼ teaspoon salt and ½ teaspoon cream of tartar until foamy. Gradually add ½ cup sugar, beating constantly until meringue stands in stiff, glossy peaks.

Golden Lemon Tartlets

Junior Winner by Virginia Ann Lee, San Francisco, California

The recipe for lemon tarts was given to Virginia Ann by a Scottish lady friend.

BAKE at 450° for 10 to 12 minutes   MAKES 2 dozen

Prepare . . . . . . .recipe for **Lattice Pastry,** page 461; shape and roll out
        pastry as directed below.
Form . . . . .into two balls.
Roll out . . . . . . .half at a time on floured surface to ⅛-inch thickness.
        Cut each portion into twelve 3½-inch circles. Fit
        over backs of twelve small muffin cups. Prick
        generously.
Bake . . . . at 450° for 10 to 12 minutes. Cool.

LEMON FILLING

Melt . . . . ⅓ cup **butter** or margarine in top of double boiler.
Add . . . . .1 cup **sugar**
        1 teaspoon grated **lemon rind**
        ⅓ cup **lemon juice** and
        ¼ teaspoon **salt**
Blend in . . . . .4 slightly beaten **egg yolks**

Cook........over boiling water 10 minutes, stirring constantly. Cool until thickened. Spoon into tart shells. Top with **whipped cream.**

Butter Cream Orange Cups

Best of Class Winner by Mrs. J. S. Mitchell, Salt Lake City, Utah

Butter cookie tarts cradle mounds of light, fluffy whipped cream-custard filling refreshingly flavored with orange juice.

BAKE at 425° for 8 to 10 minutes　　　　　　**MAKES about 10**

Cream......½ cup **butter** or margarine. Add
　　　　　　¼ cup sifted **confectioners' sugar** and
　　　　　　½ teaspoon **salt,** creaming well.
Add......1½ cups sifted **Pillsbury's Best All Purpose Flour*** and
　　　　　　2 tablespoons **milk** gradually. Mix with fork until dough clings together. Form into a ball.
Roll out.......on floured surface to ⅛-inch thickness. Cut 4-inch circles. Fit loosely into tart pans or over backs of muffin cups. Prick generously.
Bake........at 425° for 8 to 10 minutes. Cool.
*Pillsbury's Best Self-Rising Flour is not recommended for use in this recipe.

ORANGE FILLING

Beat........3 **egg yolks** slightly in double boiler. Add gradually
　　　　　　¼ cup **orange juice,** stirring constantly, and
　　　　　　1 teaspoon **lemon juice**
Add........½ cup **sugar** and
　　　　　　⅛ teaspoon **salt.** Cook over boiling water, stirring constantly, until thickened. Cool.
Beat........1 cup **whipping cream** until very thick; fold carefully into cooled orange mixture.
Fold in......1 tablespoon grated **orange rind.** Chill. Just before serving, divide into tart shells. Garnish each with a quarter **orange slice.**

Butter Cream Orange Cups

Cinderella Tarts

Senior Winner by Mrs. Ralph M. Cook, South Charleston, West Virginia

Here's a pumpkin filling with the tang of sour cream in it.

BAKE at 450° for 10 to 12 minutes, then   **MAKES 1 dozen**
    at 350° for 10 minutes

Prepare . . . . recipe for **Two-Crust Pastry,** page 460; roll out pastry
        as directed below.

Roll out . . . . one portion on floured surface to ⅛-inch thickness.
        Cut into six 6-inch circles; fit loosely into muffin
        cups. (Or line tart pans with circles of pastry cut to
        fit.) Fold edges to form standing rims; flute. Prick
        generously. Repeat with remaining pastry.

Bake . . . . at 450° for 10 to 12 minutes.

CINDERELLA PUMPKIN FILLING

Heat . . . . 1 cup **sour cream** (thick or commercial) slowly in 2-
        quart saucepan over low heat. *Do not boil.*

Combine . . . . . 3 well-beaten **egg yolks** and
        1½ cups **pumpkin,** cooked or canned, in mixing bowl.

Blend in . . . . 1½ cups firmly packed **brown sugar**
        1 teaspoon **cinnamon**
        ½ teaspoon **ginger**
        ¼ teaspoon **salt**
        ¼ teaspoon **allspice** and
        ¼ teaspoon **nutmeg.** Pour slowly into hot sour cream,
        blending well. Cook over low heat, stirring constantly,
        until thickened. Cool.

Beat . . . . 3 **egg whites** until soft peaks form. *Do not overbeat.*
        Fold into pumpkin mixture.

Spoon . . . . immediately into tart shells, about ⅓ cup in each.

Bake . . . . at 350° for 10 minutes. Cool. Top with **whipped
        cream.**

Hidden Treasure Tarts

Senior Winner by Mrs. LaVar Bateman, Provo, Utah

*The treasure in these pecan pastry tarts is the chocolate lining. Then
each one is filled with a scoop of ice cream.*

BAKE at 375° for 15 to 18 minutes   **MAKES 1 dozen**

Sift together 1½ cups sifted **Pillsbury's Best All Purpose Flour*** and
        ½ teaspoon **salt.**

Cream . . . . . . ½ cup **butter** or margarine. Gradually add
        ⅓ cup sifted **confectioners' sugar,** creaming well.

Blend in . . . . . 2 tablespoons **water**
        1 teaspoon **vanilla**
        ⅓ cup **pecans,** finely chopped, and the dry ingredients.

Press . . . . dough into twelve 3½-inch tart pans, using about
        1 rounded tablespoonful dough in each.**

Bake . . . . at 375° for 15 to 18 minutes. Cool. Remove from pans.

Melt . . . . 1 **milk chocolate candy bar** (4 or 5 oz.) with
        2 tablespoons light **cream** over hot water. Stir until
        smooth. Cool slightly.

Spread . . . . in tart shells. Serve filled with **ice cream.**

  **For use with Pillsbury's Best Self-Rising Flour, omit salt.*
  ***If tart shells are not available, muffin cups may be used.*

Pitty-Pat Pies

Junior Winner by Becky Wade, Otterbein, Indiana

*Perfect for teen-age parties . . . heart shaped tarts (shaped in foil pans)
filled with cream filling, topped with chocolate and nuts.*

BAKE at 425° for 8 to 10 minutes   **MAKES 10**

Prepare . . . . recipe for **Two-Crust Pastry,*** page 460; cut in
        2 tablespoons **peanut butter** with the shortening.
        Shape and roll out pastry as directed below.

Form . . . . into ball.

Roll out . . . . on floured surface to ⅛-inch thickness. Cut into 5-inch circles and place on heavy-duty aluminum foil cut to the same size. Prick generously.

Shape . . . . into heart by bringing up and indenting one side; fold and crease foil along other sides to complete heart shape.

Bake . . . . at 425° for 8 to 10 minutes.

Pillsbury's Best Self-Rising Flour is not recommended for use in this recipe.

CREAM FILLING

Blend . . . . . . ⅓ cup sifted **Pillsbury's Best All Purpose Flour** with ¾ cup **sugar** and ½ teaspoon **salt** in saucepan.

Add . . . . 2 cups **milk** and 2 beaten **egg yolks**; mix well. Cook over medium heat, stirring constantly, until thick. Cool.

Beat . . . . ⅔ cup **whipping cream** and 1 teaspoon **vanilla** until thick. Fold into Filling. Spoon two-thirds of Filling into shells.

Combine . . . . . 1 square (1 oz.) melted unsweetened **chocolate** and remaining mixture. Spoon over filling. Top with **salted peanuts**.

Nut Basket Tarts

Junior Winner by Evelyn Hymers, Brighton, Massachusetts

Make up these little pies with rich, luscious filling in advance.

BAKE at 400° for 10 minutes, then   MAKES about 15
    at 325° for 20 to 25 minutes

Prepare . . . . recipe for **Two-Crust Pastry**, page 460; roll out pastry as directed below.

Roll out . . . . half at a time on floured surface to about ⅛-inch thickness. Cut into 6-inch circles; fit loosely into muffin cups. Fold edges to form standing rims; flute.

Pitty-Pat Pies

          Prick generously.
Bake . . . . at 400° for 10 minutes.

COCONUT FILLING

Combine . . . . . 3 well-beaten **eggs** 1¼ cups firmly packed **brown sugar** 1 cup **walnuts**, chopped ½ cup **coconut** 2 tablespoons **flour** 1 teaspoon **salt** and ½ teaspoon double-acting **baking powder**; mix well. Divide into tart shells.

Bake . . . . at 325° for 20 to 25 minutes. Top with **whipped cream** or hard sauce.

Old-Fashioned Apple Squares

Senior Winner by Mrs. John Schweitzer, Shelby, Ohio

An old-fashioned apple dessert gone modern! A spicy apple-nut filling is baked between layers of pastry.

BAKE at 375° for 40 to 45 minutes   MAKES 16

Sift together 1½ cups sifted **Pillsbury's Best All Purpose Flour*** and 1 teaspoon **salt** into mixing bowl.

Cut in . . . . . . ½ cup **shortening** until the size of small peas.

Combine . . . . . 1 unbeaten **egg**
¼ cup **sour cream** (or 2 tablespoons cream) and
1 tablespoon **lemon juice.** Add to flour mixture; stir with fork until dough forms a ball.

Divide . . . . in half; form into squares.

Roll out . . . . one portion on floured surface to a 12x8-inch rectangle.

Cover . . . . baking sheet with 15-inch sheet of aluminum foil. Place pastry rectangle on foil.

Combine . . . . . 2 cups pared, chopped **apples** (2 medium)
¼ cup **nuts,** chopped
⅓ cup **sugar** and
¼ teaspoon **cinnamon.** Spread over pastry.

Roll out . . . . remaining dough to a 12x8-inch rectangle. Moisten

edges of pastry on foil; top with second pastry rectangle. Pinch edges together to seal. Cut slits to indicate 16 serving pieces.

Turn up . . . . edges of foil, making a standing rim to keep juice of apples from escaping.

Bake . . . . at 375° for 40 to 45 minutes.

*For use with Pillsbury's Best Self-Rising Flour, omit salt.

Fig-Nut Foldovers

Junior Winner by Geraldine Griffin, Tucumcari, New Mexico

Combine almonds, figs and fresh apples in the tasty filling for these pastry foldovers.

BAKE at 425° for 12 to 15 minutes   MAKES 1 dozen

Prepare . . . . recipe for **Two-Crust Pastry,** page 460; roll out pastry as directed below.

Combine . . . . ½ cup **sugar**
½ cup finely chopped **figs**
1 cup finely chopped **apples**
1 cup **almonds,** chopped
1 teaspoon grated **orange rind**
1 cup **liquid** (juice of 1 orange plus water)
¼ teaspoon **cinnamon** and
¼ teaspoon **mace** in saucepan. Simmer until mixture is thick, about 5 minutes. Cool.

Roll out . . . . each half on a floured surface to a 15x10-inch rectangle. Cut into 5-inch squares.

Place . . . . 1 rounded tablespoon of cooled fig filling on each square. Fold squares in half to form rectangles. Seal edges. Prick tops. Brush with **milk** and sprinkle with mixture of
1 tablespoon **sugar** and
¼ teaspoon **cinnamon**

Bake . . . . at 425° for 12 to 15 minutes.

DESSERTS

Dessert is the sweet touch at the end of the meal that everyone looks forward to. Don't pass it off lightly ... show off your baking skills, for it's this course that gives the final impression of the meal.

In this book, cakes, pies and cookies have sections of their own. Included in this section are all the other luscious types of desserts. Follow the hints given here for baking and serving desserts.

GENERAL HINTS

- When selecting a dessert to serve, always consider the occasion! For an evening party, make it elegant; after the ladies' luncheon or for afternoon bridge, make it light and luscious; after a complete dinner, make it simple but good.
- Always dress up desserts to look their very best; it's that extra touch that will bring the "oh's" and "ah's" from your family and guests.
- Don't always feel that you have to serve your dessert in the kitchen. Be a show-off ... bake it in a colorful casserole dish or baking dish, bring it right to the table and serve it there.
- Be sure the dessert you serve balances the rest of the menu.
- Don't repeat ingredients already used elsewhere in the menu (if you're planning to serve fruit salad, then don't serve fruit dessert).
- A test for doneness of fruit desserts is to always be sure the fruit is tender before removing dessert from the oven. (Apples vary in the time they take to bake tender, depending on variety and season.)
- After paring, to keep fruits such as apples, bananas and peaches from turning brown, use a small amount of lemon juice or ascorbic acid, which can be purchased from your druggist.
- Whipping cream beats best if it is cold; it is also a good practice to chill the bowl and beater.
- To make sweetened whipped cream, beat 1 cup whipping cream until thick; fold in 2 tablespoons sugar and ½ teaspoon vanilla.

CAKE DESSERTS

CAKE DESSERTS are always well liked by all ages. There is quite a variety here; cake rolls, upside-down cakes, cake squares with fruit sauce, refrigerator cake desserts and layered cake desserts. You will want to try them all—each will bring praise from your family!

For cake-baking tips, see Cakes, page 177.

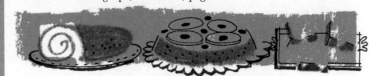

County Fair Watermelon Dessert

Junior Winner by Maurine Junker, Fairbury, Nebraska

The watermelon preserves in these cake squares make this a spicy different dessert. Serve with sweetened whipped cream.

BAKE at 350° for 25 to 30 minutes   SERVES 12 to 15

Sift together . . 2 cups sifted **Pillsbury's Best All Purpose Flour***
      1 teaspoon **soda**
      1 teaspoon **salt**
      2 teaspoons **cinnamon** and
      ½ teaspoon **nutmeg.** Set aside.

Add . . . . 1 cup firmly packed **brown sugar** gradually to
      ½ cup **shortening,** creaming well.

Blend in . . . . . 2 unbeaten **eggs,** beating well after each.

Add . . . . the dry ingredients alternately with
      1 cup **sour cream** or buttermilk. Blend well after each
      addition.

Stir in . . . . 1 cup finely chopped **watermelon pickles**

Turn . . . . into 13x9x2-inch pan, well greased and lightly
      floured on the bottom.

Bake . . . . at 350° for 25 to 30 minutes. Cut into squares. Serve
      warm with sweetened **whipped cream,** flavored
      with **nutmeg** and **vanilla.**

For use with Pillsbury's Best Self-Rising Flour, omit salt.

Penuche-Topped Cake

Junior Winner by Elaine Moehring, East Tawas, Michigan

A quick cake-like dessert with brown sugar nut topping that drips through for a marbled effect.

BAKE at 350° for 35 to 40 minutes   MAKES 12x8 or 13x9-inch cake

Sift together . . 2 cups sifted **Pillsbury's Best All Purpose Flour***
          3 teaspoons double-acting **baking powder** and
          ½ teaspoon **salt.** Set aside.
Add . . . . .1 cup **sugar** gradually to
          ½ cup **shortening,** creaming well.
Blend in . . . . .2 unbeaten **eggs,** beating well after each.
Combine . . . . .1 cup **milk** and
          1 teaspoon **vanilla.** Add alternately with the dry in-gredients to creamed mixture. Blend well after each addition.
Turn . . . . .into 12x8x2 or 13x9x2-inch pan, well greased and lightly floured on the bottom.
Combine . . . . ½ cup firmly packed **brown sugar**
          ¾ cup **nuts,** chopped, and
          ¼ cup **butter** or margarine, melted. Sprinkle over batter.
Bake . . . . .at 350° for 35 to 40 minutes. Serve warm with **whipped cream.**

For use with Pillsbury's Best Self-Rising Flour, omit baking powder and salt.

Hawaiian Holiday Dessert

Senior Winner by Teresita C. Ward, Honolulu, Hawaii

A jam crumb topping is baked on this cake-like dessert. Choose your favorite preserves.

BAKE at 350° for 25 to 30 minutes*   SERVES 8

Sift together . .1 cup sifted **Pillsbury's Best All Purpose Flour***
          1½ teaspoons double-acting **baking powder** and
          ½ teaspoon **salt.** Set aside.
Add . . . . .⅛ cup **sugar** to
          ¼ cup **shortening,** creaming well.
Blend in . . . . .1 well-beaten **egg** and
          1 teaspoon **vanilla**
Add . . . . .the dry ingredients alternately with
          ⅛ cup **milk.** Blend well after each addition.
Turn . . . . .into 8x8x2-inch pan, well greased and lightly floured on the bottom. Spread with
          ½ cup **jam**
Combine . . . . .3 tablespoons **flour**
          3 tablespoons **sugar**
          ½ teaspoon **cinnamon** and
          2 tablespoons **butter,** melted; sprinkle over cake.
Bake . . . . .at 350° for 25 to 30 minutes.* Serve warm topped with **whipped cream.**

For use with Pillsbury's Best Self-Rising Flour, omit baking powder and salt; increase baking time to 35 to 40 minutes.

Golden Cottage Cheese Squares

Senior Winner by Mrs. Mary Messersmith, Philadelphia, Pennsylvania

A light cottage cheese-raisin layer and chopped almonds are baked atop a butter loaf cake.

BAKE at 375° for 35 to 40 minutes   MAKES 12x8 or 13x9-inch cake

Grate . . . . . . .1 tablespoon **lemon rind.** Set aside.
Sift together . .2 cups sifted **Pillsbury's Best All Purpose Flour***
          2½ teaspoons double-acting **baking powder** and
          ½ teaspoon **salt**
Cream . . . . . . ½ cup **butter** or margarine. Gradually add

¾ cup **sugar,** creaming well.

Blend in . . . . . 1 unbeaten **egg**

1 unbeaten **egg yolk** and half the lemon rind. Beat well.

Add . . . . the dry ingredients alternately with

¾ cup **milk.** Blend well after each addition.

Turn . . . . into 12x8x2 or 13x9x2-inch pan, well greased and lightly floured on the bottom. Spoon Cottage Cheese Topping over batter.

Sprinkle with . ½ cup blanched **almonds,** chopped. Drizzle with

1 tablespoon **honey**

Bake . . . . at 375° for 35 to 40 minutes. Best served warm.

For use with Pillsbury's Best Self-Rising Flour, omit baking powder and salt.

COTTAGE CHEESE TOPPING

Beat 1 egg white until stiff; set aside. Beat 1 whole egg with ¼ cup sugar until thick. Gently stir in 1¾ cups dry cottage cheese, the reserved grated lemon rind and ½ cup raisins. Fold in the beaten egg white.

Layer Cream Temptation

Junior Winner by Mary Anderson, Chicago, Illinois

This spicy prune dessert is baked in layers, then piled high with brown sugar-flavored whipped cream.

BAKE at 350° for 30 to 35 minutes   MAKES two 8-inch square or 9-inch round layers

Sift together . . 2 cups sifted **Pillsbury's Best All Purpose Flour***

1 teaspoon double-acting **baking powder**

1 teaspoon **salt**

1 teaspoon **cinnamon**

½ teaspoon **soda** and

½ teaspoon **allspice.**

Cream . . . . . . ¾ cup **butter** or margarine. Gradually add

1¼ cups **sugar,** creaming well.

Golden Cottage Cheese Squares

Blend in . . . . . 3 unbeaten **eggs,** beating well after each.

Combine . . . . ½ cup **buttermilk** or sour milk

¾ cup chopped cooked **prunes** and

1 teaspoon **vanilla.** Add alternately with the dry ingredients to creamed mixture. Blend well after each addition.

Turn . . . . into two 8-inch square or 9-inch round layer pans, well greased and lightly floured on the bottoms.

Bake . . . . at 350° for 30 to 35 minutes. Cool. Fill and frost with Amber Whipped Cream.

For use with Pillsbury's Best Self-Rising Flour, omit baking powder, salt, soda.

AMBER WHIPPED CREAM

Combine 1 cup whipping cream, ½ cup firmly packed brown sugar, ½ teaspoon vanilla and ⅛ teaspoon salt. Chill 1 hour. Beat until thick.

Fruit-Filled Gingerbread

Senior Winner by Mrs. Minnie Buchanan, Long Beach, California

Orange-glazed spicy gingerbread with candied ginger and fruit inside.

BAKE at 350° for 30 to 35 minutes, then   MAKES 8x8-inch cake
for 10 minutes

Sift together 1¼ cups sifted **Pillsbury's Best All Purpose Flour***
       ¾ teaspoon **soda**
       ½ teaspoon **cinnamon**
       ¼ teaspoon **salt**
       ¼ teaspoon **cloves** and
       ¼ teaspoon **nutmeg** into mixing bowl.
Stir in . . . . . . ¼ cup mixed **candied fruit**, finely chopped, and
       2 tablespoons sliced **candied ginger**. Set aside.
Add . . . . ¼ cup **sugar** to
       ¼ cup **shortening**; cream well. Blend in
       1 unbeaten **egg**
       ⅓ cup **honey** and
       2 tablespoons **molasses**; beat well.
Add . . . . the dry ingredients gradually, mixing thoroughly.
Blend in . . . . . ½ cup hot **water**. Mix until smooth.
Pour . . . . into 8x8x2-inch pan, well greased and lightly floured
       on the bottom. Sprinkle with
       ¼ cup **nuts**, finely chopped
Bake . . . . at 350° for 30 to 35 minutes. Pour hot Orange Glaze
       over cake. Return to oven; bake 10 minutes longer.
**For use with Pillsbury's Best Self-Rising Flour, decrease soda to ¼ teaspoon
and omit salt.*

ORANGE GLAZE

Combine in saucepan ⅓ cup sugar and ¼ cup orange juice. Bring to
boil over medium heat, stirring constantly; simmer 5 minutes. Remove
from heat; stir in ½ teaspoon lemon extract.

Orange Grove Dessert

Senior Winner by Mrs. Felix Karpinski, Jr., Drexel Hill, Pennsylvania

*Orange rind, dates, walnuts go into this fragrant sour cream loaf cake.
Top with warm orange syrup and whipped cream.*

BAKE at 350° for 45 to 50 minutes   MAKES 9x9-inch cake

Prepare . . . . . . 1 cup fresh **orange juice** (2 to 3 medium oranges);
       reserve. Then put the rind of 1 orange (remove white
       membrane first) through food chopper, using
       medium blade, to obtain ¼ cup ground rind.
Grind . . . . 1 cup **dates** together with
       ½ cup **walnuts**. Add the orange rind; set aside.
Sift together . . 2 cups sifted **Pillsbury's Best All Purpose Flour***
       1½ teaspoons double-acting **baking powder**
       ½ teaspoon **soda** and
       ¼ teaspoon **salt**. Set aside.
Add . . . . 1 cup **sugar** gradually to
       ¼ cup **shortening**, creaming well.
Add . . . . 2 unbeaten **eggs**, beating well after each.
Blend in . . . . . . the dry ingredients alternately with
       1 cup **sour cream** (thick or commercial). Blend well
       after each addition.
Stir in . . . . the ground fruit-nut mixture.
Turn . . . . into 9x9x2-inch pan, well greased and lightly floured
       on the bottom.
Bake . . . . at 350° for 45 to 50 minutes. Serve warm or cold;
       cut into squares and top with warm Orange Syrup
       and **whipped cream**.
*For use with Pillsbury's Best Self-Rising Flour, omit baking powder, soda, salt.

ORANGE SYRUP

Heat together the reserved 1 cup orange juice and 1 cup sugar until
sugar melts.

Apple Skillet Cake

Junior Third Prize Winner by Dianne Illingworth, Portland, Oregon

An apple-raisin combination tops a brown sugar upside-down cake.

BAKE at 350° for 35 to 45 minutes*   **MAKES 10-inch round cake**

Melt . . . . .3 tablespoons **butter** in heavy skillet measuring
10 inches across top. Remove from heat and add
⅔ cup firmly packed **brown sugar**

Arrange . . . . .3 cups pared, thinly sliced **apples** (3 medium) in
skillet. Add
⅓ cup **raisins**

Sift together 1⅓ cups sifted **Pillsbury's Best All Purpose Flour***
2 teaspoons double-acting **baking powder** and
½ teaspoon **salt.** Set aside.

Add . . . . .¼ cup **sugar** and
⅔ cup firmly packed **brown sugar** gradually to
⅓ cup **shortening,** creaming well.

Blend in . . . . .2 unbeaten **egg yolks** and
1 teaspoon **vanilla;** beat well.

Add . . . . .⅔ cup **milk** alternately with the dry ingredients to
creamed mixture. Blend well after each addition.

Beat . . . . .2 **egg whites** until stiff but not dry. Fold into batter.

Pour . . . . .over apples.

Bake . . . . .at 350° for 35 to 45 minutes.* Turn out immediately.
Serve warm, plain or with whipped cream.

**For use with Pillsbury's Best Self-Rising Flour, omit baking powder and salt;
increase baking time to 40 to 50 minutes.*

Apple Skillet Cake

Saucy Sundae Cakes

Beat . . . . 1½ minutes. (With mixer use a low speed.)
Add . . . . 1 unbeaten **egg**
    ½ teaspoon **vanilla** and remaining cocoa mixture.
Beat . . . . 1½ minutes.
Fill . . . . muffin cups,* lined with paper baking cups, half full.
Bake . . . . at 350° for 25 to 30 minutes. Cool. Slice in half. Top
    with **ice cream** and Orange Sauce.

**If desired, batter may be baked in well-greased individual ring molds. Fill
center with ice cream and top with Orange Sauce.*
**Pillsbury's Best Self-Rising Flour is not recommended for use in this recipe.

ORANGE SAUCE

Cook 16 marshmallows (¼ lb.) and 3 tablespoons water in top of
double boiler over boiling water for 10 minutes. Remove from heat;
cool to lukewarm. Beat at high speed until fluffy. Fold in ⅓ cup
undiluted frozen orange juice, thawed, and 1/16 teaspoon salt. Sauce
should be used the same day. *Do not refrigerate.*

Saucy Sundae Cakes

Junior Winner by James Nelson Willison, Jr., Cumberland, Maryland

*Chocolate cupcakes, split and topped with ice cream and a luscious
smooth sauce of marshmallows and frozen orange juice.*

BAKE at 350° for 25 to 30 minutes   MAKES 1 dozen cupcakes*

Combine . . . . ¼ cup **cocoa** and
    ¾ cup cold **water.** Mix until smooth.
Sift together . . 1 cup sifted **Pillsbury's Best All Purpose Flour****
    ¾ cup **sugar**
    ½ teaspoon double-acting **baking powder**
    ½ teaspoon **soda** and
    ½ teaspoon **salt** into mixing bowl.
Add . . . . ¼ cup **shortening** and two-thirds of cocoa mixture.

Candy 'n' Cake

Junior Winner by Tommy L. Bever, Webster Groves, Missouri

*Marshmallows and chocolate pieces are folded into white cake. Brown
sugar and nuts are baked on top.*

BAKE at 350° for 40 to 50 minutes MAKES 12x8 or 13x9-inch cake

Sift together . . 2 cups sifted **Pillsbury's Best All Purpose Flour***
    2½ teaspoons double-acting **baking powder** and
    ½ teaspoon **salt.** Set aside.
Add . . . . 1 cup **sugar** gradually to
    ½ cup **shortening,** creaming well.
Blend in . . . . . 1 unbeaten **egg**; beat well.
Combine . . . . ¾ cup **buttermilk** or sour milk and
    1 teaspoon **vanilla.** Add alternately with dry in-
    gredients to creamed mixture. Blend well after each
    addition.

Blend in . . . . . ½ cup **semi-sweet chocolate pieces** and
12 **marshmallows**, cut in eighths (or 1 cup miniature marshmallows)

Spread . . . . in 12x8 or 13x9x2-inch pan, well greased and lightly floured on the bottom.

Combine . . . . ¼ cup firmly packed **brown sugar**
2 tablespoons **butter** or margarine and
½ cup **nuts**, chopped. Sprinkle over batter.

Bake . . . . at 350° for 40 to 50 minutes.

Pillsbury's Best Self-Rising Flour is not recommended for use in this recipe.

Western Gingerbread

Senior Winner by Mrs. Felicia M. Palmeter, Seattle, Washington

Good patio dessert! Gingerbread with crumb topping—a hit with your family every time.

BAKE at 350° for 30 to 35 minutes   MAKES 12x8 or 13x9-inch cake

Sift together . . 2 cups sifted **Pillsbury's Best All Purpose Flour***
1¼ cups **sugar**
1 tablespoon **cinnamon**
1 teaspoon double-acting **baking powder**
1½ teaspoons **ginger** and
¼ teaspoon **salt** into large mixing bowl.

Cut in . . . . . . ½ cup **shortening** until particles are fine. Reserve ½ cup of crumb mixture.

Add . . . . to remaining crumb mixture
1 unbeaten **egg**
2 tablespoons **molasses** and
1 teaspoon **soda*** dissolved in
1 cup **buttermilk** or sour milk

Beat . . . . 2 minutes. (With mixer use a low speed.)

Turn . . . . into 12x8x2 or 13x9x2-inch pan, well greased and lightly floured on the bottom.

Cut . . . . 1 tablespoon **butter** into the reserved crumb mixture.

Sprinkle over batter.

Bake . . . . at 350° for 30 to 35 minutes. Serve plain or with whipped cream.

*For use with Pillsbury's Best Self-Rising Flour, omit baking powder, salt, soda.

Ginger Cake Apple Fluff

Senior Winner by Mrs. George Alfred Keep, Oswego, Oregon

Applesauce whipped cream makes the topping for this spicy old-fashioned ginger cake.

BAKE at 350° for 35 to 45 minutes   MAKES 8x8 or 9x9-inch cake

Sift together . . 2 cups sifted **Pillsbury's Best All Purpose Flour***
1 teaspoon double-acting **baking powder**
1 teaspoon **salt**
½ teaspoon **soda**
1½ teaspoons **ginger** and
1 teaspoon **cinnamon**

Melt . . . . ½ cup **shortening** in
⅔ cup **boiling water**

Beat . . . . 1 **egg** until thick. Gradually add
½ cup **sugar**; beat until thick and ivory colored.

Add . . . . ½ cup **molasses** and the shortening-water mixture.

Blend in . . . . . . the dry ingredients; beat well.

Pour . . . . into 8x8x2 or 9x9x2-inch pan, well greased and lightly floured on the bottom.

Bake . . . . at 350° for 35 to 45 minutes. Serve warm with Apple Fluff.

*For use with Pillsbury's Best Self-Rising Flour, omit baking powder, salt, soda.

APPLE FLUFF

Beat 1 cup whipping cream until thick. Fold in ½ cup sifted confectioners' sugar, 2 tablespoons lemon juice and 1 cup sweetened thick applesauce. Chill thoroughly, or place in refrigerator tray and partially freeze.

"Town and Country" Dessert

Senior Winner by Mrs. Richard S. Wood, Tonawanda, New York

A moist cake-like graham cracker dessert. Serve it with apricot filling and whipped-cream topping.

BAKE at 350° for 45 to 50 minutes   SERVES 12 to 16

Sift together..1 cup sifted **Pillsbury's Best All Purpose Flour***
              1 cup **sugar**
              1½ teaspoons **soda** and
              1 teaspoon double-acting **baking powder** into mixing bowl.
Crush......24 single **graham crackers** very fine; add to the dry ingredients.
Beat.......2 **eggs** slightly; stir in slowly
              1¾ cups **buttermilk** or sour milk. Add gradually to the dry ingredients, mixing well.
Blend in.....¼ cup **shortening,** melted
Line.........bottoms of two 8-inch round layer pans with waxed paper. Turn batter into pans.
Bake.........at 350° for 45 to 50 minutes. Cool and spread Apricot Filling between layers. Slice and serve with **whipped cream.**

*For use with Pillsbury's Best Self-Rising Flour, decrease soda to 1 teaspoon and omit baking powder.

APRICOT FILLING

Combine 1 cup dried apricots and 1 cup water in small saucepan. Simmer until thick and jam-like, about 1 hour. Mash with fork. Add ½ cup sugar; cook a few minutes until sugar dissolves. Cool.

Blueberry Boy-Bait

Junior Second Prize Winner by Renny Powell, Chicago, Illinois

A quick coffee cake dessert filled with blueberries. Part of a rich butter crumb mixture is in the cake; the rest is sprinkled on top.

BAKE at 350° for 40 to 50 minutes   MAKES 12x8 or 13x9-inch cake

Sift together..2 cups sifted **Pillsbury's Best All Purpose Flour*** and
              1½ cups **sugar** into large mixing bowl.
Cut in......⅔ cup **butter** or margarine until the size of small peas. Reserve ¾ cup flour mixture for topping.
Add.......2 teaspoons double-acting **baking powder***
              1 teaspoon **salt**
              2 unbeaten **egg yolks** and
              1 cup **milk** to remaining crumb mixture in bowl.
Beat..........3 minutes. (With mixer use a low speed.)
Beat........2 **egg whites** until stiff but not dry. Fold into batter. Spread in 12x8x2 or 13x9x2-inch pan, well greased and lightly floured on the bottom.
Arrange.....1 cup drained **blueberries** (fresh, frozen or canned)

"Town and Country" Dessert

over batter. Sprinkle with reserved crumb mixture.

Bake . . . . at 350° for 40 to 50 minutes. Serve warm with **whipped cream.** Or serve plain as coffee cake.

*For use with Pillsbury's Best Self-Rising Flour, omit baking powder and salt.

Mount Vernon Dessert

Best of Class Winner by Mrs. Harry W. O'Donnell, Crandon, Wisconsin

A Quick-Mix upside-down cake served warm with an almond-flavored cherry sauce.

BAKE at 350° for 35 to 45 minutes   MAKES 12x8 or 13x9-inch cake

Drain . . . . 1 No. 303 can sour **pie cherries;** reserve juice.
Spread . . . . . . 2 tablespoons **butter** or margarine on bottom of 12x8x2 or 13x9x2-inch pan. Sprinkle with
½ cup firmly packed **brown sugar.** Add the cherries.
Sift together 1¾ cups sifted **Pillsbury's Best All Purpose Flour***
1 cup **sugar**
2 teaspoons double-acting **baking powder** and
½ teaspoon **salt** into large mixing bowl.
Add . . . . ⅓ cup **shortening**
¾ cup **milk** and
1 teaspoon **vanilla**
Beat . . . . 1½ minutes. (With mixer use a low speed.)
Add . . . . 1 unbeaten **egg.** Beat 1½ minutes.
Pour . . . . over cherries in pan.
Bake . . . . at 350° for 35 to 45 minutes. Serve warm with warm Cherry Sauce.

*For use with Pillsbury's Best Self-Rising Flour, omit baking powder and salt.

CHERRY SAUCE

Combine in saucepan ½ cup sugar, 2 tablespoons cornstarch and 1½ cups juice (juice from cherries plus water). Cook, stirring constantly, until thickened. Remove from heat. Add ⅛ teaspoon almond extract and ⅛ teaspoon red food coloring.

Mount Vernon Dessert

Merry Berry Dessert

Senior Winner by Mrs. Helen Bartachek, Belle Plaine, Iowa

Fold strawberries into the batter of this cake-like dessert. Serve with whipped cream and strawberry sauce.

BAKE at 350° for 35 to 45 minutes   MAKES 12x8 or 13x9-inch cake

Drain . . . . 1 package (1 lb.) thawed frozen **strawberries;*** reserve juice for topping.

Sift together . . 2 cups sifted **Pillsbury's Best All Purpose Flour****
           1¼ cups **sugar**
           1 teaspoon **soda** and
           ½ teaspoon **salt** into large mixing bowl.

Add . . . . ½ cup **shortening**
           ½ cup **sour cream** (thick or commercial)
           3 unbeaten **eggs** and

Merry Berry Dessert

           1 teaspoon **vanilla**. Beat 3 minutes.

Fold in . . . . the strawberries. Turn into 12x8x2 or 13x9x2-inch pan, well greased and lightly floured on the bottom.

Bake . . . . at 350° for 35 to 45 minutes. Serve with **whipped cream** or ice cream and Strawberry Sauce.

If desired, 1 cup fresh strawberries (sliced, sweetened and drained) may be substituted for frozen berries.

**For use with Pillsbury's Best Self-Rising Flour, omit soda and salt.

STRAWBERRY SAUCE

Combine ¾ cup of the strawberry juice, ¼ cup water and 1 tablespoon cornstarch. Cook, stirring constantly, until thick and clear.

Golden Lemon Cake Roll

Senior Winner by Anita L. Pedersen, Boelus, Nebraska

Light and tender sponge cake, golden from the egg yolks it's made with, is rolled up around creamy lemon filling.

BAKE at 375° for 15 to 18 minutes   MAKES 1 cake roll

Sift together . . 1 cup sifted **Pillsbury's Best All Purpose Flour***
           ½ cup **sugar**
           1½ teaspoons double-acting **baking powder** and
           ½ teaspoon **salt**

Beat . . . . 9 **egg yolks** until foamy. (With mixer use high speed.)

Add . . . . ½ cup **sugar** gradually, beating until thick and ivory colored.

Add . . . . ½ cup cold **water** and
           ½ teaspoon **lemon extract** gradually, beating constantly.

Fold in . . . . the dry ingredients in three portions; fold gently but thoroughly after each addition.

Spread . . . . into well-greased 15½x10½x1-inch jelly-roll pan, greased on the bottom, lined with waxed paper and greased again.

Bake . . . . at 375° for 15 to 18 minutes.

Turn out.......immediately onto towel sprinkled with **confectioners' sugar**. Remove paper.
Roll..........in towel, starting with 10-inch end. Cool. Unroll; spread with Lemon Filling. Roll again. Chill at least 1 hour.
For use with Pillsbury's Best Self-Rising Flour, omit baking powder and salt.

LEMON FILLING

Combine in top of double boiler ½ cup sugar, ⅛ teaspoon salt, 1 tablespoon grated lemon rind, 3 tablespoons lemon juice, 3 egg yolks or 1 egg and 2 tablespoons butter. Cook over boiling water, stirring constantly, until thickened. Chill thoroughly. Beat ½ cup whipping cream until thick. Fold into cooled Filling.

Strawberry Festival Dessert

Senior Winner by Mrs. Jeffrey J. Carre, Brunswick, Maine

This is a new kind of baked Alaska made with frozen strawberries.

BAKE at 325° for 40 to 45 minutes, then   SERVES 8 to 10
     at 450° for 5 minutes

Sift together . ½ cup sifted **Pillsbury's Best All Purpose Flour***
       ¼ cup **cornstarch** and
       ¼ teaspoon **salt**
Beat........2 **egg whites** with
       ¼ teaspoon **cream of tartar** until soft mounds form. Gradually add
       ¼ cup **sugar**; beat until stiff peaks form.
Beat........5 **egg yolks** with
       ½ cup **sugar**
       2 tablespoons **water**
       1 teaspoon grated **lemon rind**
       1 tablespoon **lemon juice** and
       1 teaspoon **vanilla** until thick and ivory colored.
Fold in.........the dry ingredients; blend thoroughly.

Strawberry Festival Dessert

Combine......egg yolk mixture with beaten egg whites, folding gently but thoroughly.
Turn..........into ungreased 8x8x2-inch pan.
Bake.........at 325° for 40 to 45 minutes. Invert pan for 10 minutes. Loosen edges and turn out. Cool and place on oven-proof plate or wooden plank covered with heavy paper.
Place........1 package (1 lb.) **frozen strawberries** in center of cake.
Prepare.......recipe for **Meringue**, page 461; spread over cake and berries, sealing well.
Bake.........at 450° for 5 minutes. Let stand at room temperature ½ hour before serving or store in refrigerator 1 hour. Cut into wedges to serve.
For use with Pillsbury's Best Self-Rising Flour, omit salt.

Rainbow Cream Whips

Senior Winner by Mrs. Douglas Knowles, Spokane, Washington

Tender sponge cake circles filled with tinted whipped cream.

BAKE at 350° for 10 to 15 minutes   SERVES 8

Cover.........baking sheets with brown wrapping paper. Draw sixteen 3-inch circles on paper.

Beat........4 **egg whites** until soft mounds form. Gradually add ½ cup sifted **confectioners' sugar;** beat until stiff peaks form.

Beat........4 **egg yolks**
½ teaspoon **orange extract** and
¼ teaspoon **salt** until thick and lemon colored. Fold gently but thoroughly into egg white mixture.

Fold in......⅔ cup sifted **Pillsbury's Best All Purpose Flour,*** half at a time.

Spoon.......batter onto the 16 circles; spread evenly to edges of circles.

Bake.........at 350° for 10 to 15 minutes. *Do not brown.* Remove from paper immediately and dip in **confectioners' sugar.** Cool. Arrange in two's, bottoms together, with Rainbow Whipped Cream between and on top (vary color combinations). If desired, garnish with a **maraschino cherry half.**

*Pillsbury's Best Self-Rising Flour is not recommended for use in this recipe.

RAINBOW WHIPPED CREAM

Beat 1¼ cups whipping cream until thick. Add 1 teaspoon vanilla and ¼ cup sifted confectioners' sugar. Divide into three bowls. Blend 1 drop red food coloring into first part, 3 drops green food coloring into second part and 4 drops yellow food coloring into third part.

Orange-Filled Sponge Dessert

Senior Winner by Mrs. Bruce Willingham, Hialeah, Florida

Refreshing and good . . . sponge cake layers with orange whip filling . . . ideal for leftover sponge cake.

BAKE at 375° for 15 to 20 minutes   SERVES 6 to 8

Place.........an 18x11-inch sheet of heavy-duty aluminum foil on baking sheet. Fold sides up to make a 15x8x1½-inch pan.

Sift together..1 cup sifted **Pillsbury's Best All Purpose Flour***
1 teaspoon double-acting **baking powder** and
½ cup **sugar** into small mixing bowl.

Beat........3 **egg whites** with
½ teaspoon **salt** and
½ teaspoon **cream of tartar** in large mixing bowl until soft mounds form. Gradually add
⅓ cup **sugar;** beat until stiff peaks form. *Do not underbeat.*

Combine.....3 unbeaten **egg yolks**

Rainbow Cream Whips

3 tablespoons **water**
1 teaspoon **vanilla** and
¼ teaspoon **orange extract.** Add to the dry ingredients. Beat 1 minute. (With mixer use medium speed.)

Add . . . . half at a time to egg whites; fold gently but thoroughly after each addition. Turn into foil pan.

Bake . . . . at 375° for 15 to 20 minutes. Cool.

Cut . . . . in half to make two square layers. Place one layer in 8x8-inch baking dish or 2½-quart casserole. Cover with half of Orange Filling. Top with remaining layer and Filling.

Chill . . . . at least two hours. Garnish with **whipped cream** and **orange slices.**

For use with Pillsbury's Best Self-Rising Flour, omit baking powder and salt.

ORANGE FILLING

Combine in saucepan 1 cup sugar and 3 tablespoons cornstarch. Add 1½ cups water, ½ cup orange juice, 2 tablespoons lemon juice and 1 slightly beaten egg. Cook, stirring constantly, until thick. Remove from heat; add 1 tablespoon butter, 1 tablespoon grated orange rind, 1 teaspoon grated lemon rind and ¼ teaspoon salt. Cool. Beat ½ cup whipping cream until thick. Fold the cream and 1 cup orange sections into cooled mixture.

Chocolate Fluff Roll

Senior Winner by Mrs. Carmel Fredine, Minneapolis, Minnesota

Light, delicate sponge cake, wrapped in chocolate whipped cream flavored with peppermint.

BAKE at 375° for 12 to 15 minutes   SERVES 8

Sift together . ⅔ cup sifted **Pillsbury's Best All Purpose Flour***
1 teaspoon double-acting **baking powder** and
½ teaspoon **salt**

Beat . . . . 4 **egg whites** until soft mounds form. Gradually add

½ cup **sugar**, beating until stiff peaks form.

Beat . . . . 4 **egg yolks** until thick and lemon colored.

Add . . . . ¼ cup **sugar**
2 tablespoons **water** and
1 teaspoon **vanilla** gradually; beat well.

Fold . . . . egg yolk mixture carefully into egg whites.

Sift . . . . the dry ingredients over egg mixture, folding gently but thoroughly.

Spread . . . . in 15½x10½x1-inch jelly-roll pan, greased on the bottom, lined with waxed paper, then greased again and floured.

Bake . . . . at 375° for 12 to 15 minutes.

Turn . . . . immediately onto towel sprinkled with **confectioners' sugar.** Remove paper.

Roll . . . . in towel, starting with 10-inch end. Cool. Unroll; spread with half of Chocolate Mint Cream or Chocolate Candy Stick Cream. Roll again; top with remaining Cream. Chill.

For use with Pillsbury's Best Self-Rising Flour, omit baking powder and salt.

CHOCOLATE MINT CREAM

Combine ½ cup sugar, ¼ cup cocoa, ⅛ teaspoon salt, ½ teaspoon vanilla and ¼ teaspoon peppermint extract. Blend in 1½ cups whipping cream. Beat until thick.

CHOCOLATE CANDY STICK CREAM

Follow recipe for Chocolate Mint Cream, increasing vanilla to 1 teaspoon and omitting peppermint extract. Fold ½ cup finely crushed peppermint stick candy into whipped cream.

Apricot Baba

Senior Winner by Mrs. C. L. Finch, Alliance, Nebraska

Wonderful flavor and moist texture from apricot jam and almond sauce.

BAKE at 350° for 40 to 45 minutes   MAKES 9 or 10-inch tube dessert

Soften . . . . 1 packet active dry **yeast** (or 1 cake compressed) in
⅓ cup lukewarm scalded **milk**
Add . . . . ½ cup sifted **Pillsbury's Best All Purpose Flour*** and
1 tablespoon **sugar**; beat until smooth. Cover.
Let rise . . . . in warm place (85°) until doubled, about 30 minutes.
Cream . . . . . . ½ cup **butter** or margarine. Add
3 tablespoons **sugar**, creaming well.
Add . . . . 3 well-beaten **eggs**
1 tablespoon grated **lemon rind** and
½ teaspoon **salt;*** beat well.
Blend in . . . . 1½ cups sifted **Pillsbury's Best All Purpose Flour**

Apricot Baba

Add . . . . the risen yeast mixture. Beat 6 to 8 minutes.
Turn . . . . into greased 9 or 10-inch tube pan; cover.
Let rise . . . . in warm place until doubled, about 45 minutes.
Bake . . . . at 350° for 40 to 45 minutes. Prick top with fork.
Invert into large pan. Pour Baba Sauce over top and
sides of hot cake. Spread with
½ cup **apricot preserves.** Let stand until most of the
sauce is absorbed.

**For use with Pillsbury's Best Self-Rising Flour, omit salt.*

BABA SAUCE

Combine 1 cup sugar and 1 cup strong tea in saucepan. Bring to boil;
cook 5 minutes. Remove from heat. Cool; add 2 teaspoons almond extract.

Double Quick Date Dessert

Junior Winner by John Stone, Junction City, Kansas

Just mix and bake! A delicious moist date cake.

BAKE at 350° for 35 to 40 minutes   MAKES 13x9-inch cake

Sift together 1½ cups sifted **Pillsbury's Best All Purpose Flour***
1 teaspoon **soda** and
½ teaspoon **salt**
Combine . . . . . 1 pound (2½ cups) **dates,** cut in large pieces
1¼ cups **sugar**
¼ cup soft **butter** or margarine and
1 cup **boiling water** in mixing bowl.
Add . . . . 1 teaspoon **vanilla**
½ cup **nuts,** chopped, and the dry ingredients; mix well.
Turn . . . . into 13x9x2-inch pan, well greased and lightly
floured on the bottom.
Bake . . . . at 350° for 35 to 40 minutes. Serve warm with
whipped cream or ice cream.

**For use with Pillsbury's Best Self-Rising Flour, decrease soda to ½ teaspoon;*
omit salt.

TORTES

are elegant and impressive . . . perfect for guests! They may require a little more work, but you'll not find them hard to make if you follow the recipe directions carefully.

For recipes calling for 8 or 9-inch pastry circles, you can use 8 or 9-inch round layer pans or pie pans for measuring circles.

Coconut Cream Meringue Torte

Senior Winner by Blanche E. Daggett, Joliet, Illinois

Luscious meringue tops two layers of delicate yellow cake—and in between the layers, a coconut filling. Beautiful to look at—wonderful to eat.

BAKE at 350° for 25 to 30 minutes   MAKES two 9-inch round layers

Sift together 1½ cups sifted **Pillsbury's Best All Purpose Flour***
        2 teaspoons double-acting **baking powder** and
        ½ teaspoon **salt**

Cream......⅓ cup **butter** or margarine. Gradually add
        ⅔ cup **sugar,** creaming well.

Blend in.....3 unbeaten **egg yolks** and
        1 teaspoon **vanilla**; beat well.

Add..........the dry ingredients alternately with
        ½ cup **milk.** Blend well after each addition.

Turn..........into two 9-inch round layer pans, greased and lined with 12-inch circles of waxed paper.

Beat........3 **egg whites** and
        ⅛ teaspoon **salt** until soft mounds form. Gradually add
        ¾ cup **sugar,** beating until meringue stands in stiff peaks.

Blend in.....½ teaspoon **vinegar.** Spread over batter.

Bake.........at 350° for 25 to 30 minutes. Cool. Spread Coconut-

Cream Filling between layers before serving.
*For use with Pillsbury's Best Self-Rising Flour, omit baking powder and salt.

COCONUT-CREAM FILLING

Combine in saucepan ⅛ cup Pillsbury's Best All Purpose Flour, ⅓ cup sugar and ¼ teaspoon salt. Gradually add 1½ cups milk; stir until smooth. Cook, stirring constantly, until thick. Blend a little of the hot mixture into 1 slightly beaten egg; add to hot mixture. Cook 2 minutes, stirring constantly. Blend in 2 tablespoons butter, 1 teaspoon vanilla and ½ cup plain or toasted coconut. Cover and cool.

Coconut Temptation

Junior Winner by Barbara Iglehart, Oakland, California

A torte-like dessert in a cookie crust. Rich with coconut and pineapple.

BAKE at 350° for 35 to 45 minutes   MAKES 9-inch pie

Beat........2 **eggs** with
        ⅛ teaspoon **salt** until fluffy. Add
        1 cup **sugar** gradually, beating until thick and ivory colored.

Fold in.....1½ cups flaked or chopped shredded **coconut** and
        ½ cup **nuts,** chopped

Sift together..1 cup sifted **Pillsbury's Best All Purpose Flour***
        ½ teaspoon double-acting **baking powder** and
        ¼ teaspoon **salt.** Set aside.

Add........⅓ cup firmly packed **brown sugar** to
        ⅓ cup **shortening,** creaming well.

Blend in.....1 unbeaten **egg**

Add..........the dry ingredients gradually; mix well. Spread onto bottom and sides of ungreased 9-inch pie pan.

Spoon......¾ cup drained **crushed pineapple** (9-oz. can) into shell. Top with coconut mixture.

Bake.........at 350° for 35 to 45 minutes. Cool.

*For use with Pillsbury's Best Self-Rising Flour, omit baking powder and salt.

Coconut Strata

Senior Winner by Mrs. H. Richard Chandler, Dayton, Ohio

Easy as pie . . . this extra-fancy coconut cream torte is so delicious and attractive too!

BAKE at 450° for 7 to 10 minutes, then   SERVES 8
    at 400° for 8 to 10 minutes

Prepare . . . . recipe for **Two-Crust Pastry,** page 460; shape and roll out as directed below.
Divide . . . . into four equal parts. Flatten each into a circle; smooth edges.
Roll out . . . . each on floured surface to an 8-inch circle. Transfer each circle to a baking sheet; prick generously.
Bake . . . . at 450° for 7 to 10 minutes. Cool.

COCONUT-CREAM FILLING

Scald . . . . 1 cup **milk** and
        1 cup light **cream** in saucepan.
Combine . . . . ½ cup **sugar**
        3 tablespoons **flour**
        1 tablespoon **cornstarch** and
        ¼ teaspoon **salt**; mix thoroughly. Add to milk and cream. Cook over low heat, stirring constantly, until thick.
Blend . . . . a little of the hot mixture into
        3 slightly beaten **egg yolks**; add to hot mixture. Cook 2 minutes, stirring constantly. Cool.
Add . . . . 1 teaspoon **vanilla** and
        ½ cup flaked or chopped shredded **coconut**
Place . . . . a pastry circle on a 10-inch square of aluminum foil on an ungreased baking sheet. Spoon ½ cup of the cooled Filling over circle, spreading to within ¼ inch of edge; top with another pastry circle. Continue to spread Filling and stack layers. (Spread Filling to within 1 inch of edge on top pastry circle.)
Prepare . . . . recipe for **Meringue,** page 461.

Spread . . . . around sides and over uncovered edge of top circle. Decorate center with swirl of Meringue.
Bake . . . . at 400° for 8 to 10 minutes. Cool before serving.

Empire Torte

Senior Second Prize Winner by Mrs. Louis Slavik, Bedford, Ohio

A cool rich dessert with one of the best frostings you ever tasted . . . and the cake layers are simple to make!

BAKE at 375° for 10 to 12 minutes   SERVES 10 to 12

Place . . . . an 18x12-inch sheet of heavy-duty aluminum foil on baking sheet. Fold sides up to make 15x10-inch pan; grease bottom. Make a second pan.
Sift together . . 1 cup sifted **Pillsbury's Best All Purpose Flour***
        ¾ cup **sugar** and
        1 teaspoon double-acting **baking powder** into small mixing bowl.
Beat . . . . 4 **egg whites** (½ cup) with
        ½ teaspoon **salt** and
        ½ teaspoon **cream of tartar** in large mixing bowl until soft mounds form.
Add . . . . ⅓ cup **sugar**, a tablespoon at a time; beat until stiff peaks form. *Do not underbeat.*
Combine . . . . . 4 **egg yolks** (⅓ cup)
        ¼ cup **water**
        1 teaspoon **vanilla** and
        1 teaspoon **orange extract.** Add to the dry ingredients. Beat 1 minute. (With mixer use medium speed.)
Fold . . . . into beaten egg whites gently but thoroughly.
Turn . . . . into the foil pans; spread batter evenly.
Bake . . . . at 375° for 10 to 12 minutes. (Cakes may be baked one at a time.) Cool 10 minutes. Remove foil; cut each cake into quarters to make a total of 8 thin layers. Cover tightly or frost immediately.

Stack . . . . the layers, spreading about 3 tablespoons Chocolate Surprise Frosting between each. Use remaining Frosting for sides and top. Garnish sides with chopped **nuts.** Chill at least 2 hours.

For use with Pillsbury's Best Self-Rising Flour, omit baking powder and salt.

CHOCOLATE SURPRISE FROSTING

Cream 1¼ cups butter or margarine until fluffy. Add 2½ squares (2½ oz.) cooled, melted unsweetened chocolate, 1¼ teaspoons vanilla, ¾ teaspoon maple flavoring and 2½ cups sifted confectioners' sugar; blend, then beat at high speed until of spreading consistency.

Apple ala Nut Torte

Senior Winner by Mrs. Hunter D. Young, Elyria, Ohio

A snappy dessert for the crowd . . . inexpensive, too. Serve apple cake warm with ice cream.

BAKE at 350° for 25 to 30 minutes   MAKES 13x9-inch cake

Sift together . ¾ cup sifted **Pillsbury's Best All Purpose Flour***
           1 teaspoon double-acting **baking powder** and
           ½ teaspoon **salt**
Beat . . . . 3 **eggs** with
           1 teaspoon **vanilla** until light. Gradually add
           1 cup firmly packed **brown sugar,** beating well after
           each addition.
Stir in . . . . the dry ingredients.
Fold in . . . . . . 2 cups finely chopped **apples** (2 medium) and
           1 cup **nuts,** chopped
Turn . . . . into 13x9x2-inch pan, well greased and lightly
           floured on the bottom.
Bake . . . . at 350° for 25 to 30 minutes. Serve warm with
           whipped cream or ice cream.

For use with Pillsbury's Best Self-Rising Flour, increase flour to 1 cup; omit baking powder and salt.

Empire Torte

Raspberry Ribbon Torte

Raspberry Ribbon Torte

Senior Winner by Mrs. Frances A. Nielsen, Long Beach, California

Tender, flaky circles of butter pastry baked to a crisp, delicate golden brown, then filled with simple raspberry and vanilla fillings.

BAKE at 450° for 5 to 7 minutes   SERVES 16

Sift together . . 2 cups sifted **Pillsbury's Best All Purpose Flour*** and ¼ teaspoon **salt** into large mixing bowl.

Cut in . . . . 1 cup slightly softened **butter** until the size of small peas.

Sprinkle . . . . . 4 to 6 tablespoons **ice water** over mixture, stirring with fork until dough is moist enough to hold together. Form into ball. Cover; chill 30 minutes.

Divide . . . . into six equal parts; flatten each into a circle about ½ inch thick; smooth edges.

Roll out . . . . one part on floured surface to 9-inch circle. Transfer to a cool baking sheet; prick generously. Sprinkle with 1½ teaspoons **sugar.**

Bake . . . . at 450° for 5 to 7 minutes. Repeat with remaining parts.

Spread . . . . Raspberry Filling and Vanilla Filling alternately between the cooled layers, ending with thin layer of Vanilla Filling on top. Sprinkle with ¼ cup unblanched **almonds,** ground fine

Beat . . . . 1½ cups **whipping cream** until thick. Stir in 6 tablespoons **sugar** and ¼ teaspoon **almond extract.** Spread on sides and about 1 inch around outer edge of top. Serve within 2 hours.

*For use with Pillsbury's Best Self-Rising Flour, omit salt.

VANILLA FILLING

Combine 1 package instant vanilla pudding mix and 1½ cups milk as directed on the package. Beat until thick. Chill thoroughly.

RASPBERRY FILLING

Blend together 2 tablespoons cornstarch and ¼ cup water in saucepan. Add 1 package (10 oz.) thawed frozen raspberries. Cook until thick, about 5 minutes. Chill thoroughly.

Venetian Cream-Filled Layers

Junior Winner by Mrs. Jerry McCardle, Milwaukee, Wisconsin

Two layers of delicate sponge cake are split into four, then filled and topped with chocolate and vanilla fillings.

BAKE at 350° for 25 to 30 minutes   MAKES two 8 or 9-inch layers

Sift together . ¾ cup sifted **Pillsbury's Best All Purpose Flour*** and ¼ cup **cornstarch**

Beat . . . . 5 **egg whites** until soft mounds form. Gradually add
½ cup **sugar;** beat until stiff peaks form.
Beat . . . . 5 **egg yolks** until lemon colored. Gradually add
¼ cup **sugar**
3 tablespoons **water**
1 tablespoon **lemon juice** and
1 teaspoon **vanilla.** Beat until thick, about 5 minutes.
Fold into egg white mixture.
Sift in . . . . the dry ingredients, folding gently but thoroughly.
Turn . . . . into two 8 or 9-inch round layer pans, greased on the
bottoms and lined with waxed paper.
Bake . . . . at 350° for 25 to 30 minutes. Invert to cool. Cut
layers crosswise to make four layers. Spread Choco-
late and Vanilla Filling between and on top of layers,
alternating chocolate and vanilla. Top with
¼ cup toasted **coconut.** Chill until serving time.
*For use with Pillsbury's Best Self-Rising Flour, omit lemon juice.

CHOCOLATE AND VANILLA FILLING

Combine in top of double boiler ⅓ cup sugar, ⅓ cup Pillsbury's Best
All Purpose Flour and 2 cups milk. Cook over boiling water, stirring
constantly, until thick. Cover; cook 5 minutes. Cool to lukewarm.
Cream ½ cup butter or margarine and 1 teaspoon vanilla with 1 cup
sifted confectioners' sugar. Add to milk mixture; blend well. Place
half of Filling in small bowl; blend in 1 square (1 oz.) melted unsweetened chocolate. Cool Fillings completely.

Vienna Nut Torte

Senior Winner by Mrs. Peggy Boehm, White Plains, New York

*A cooky-like dough, full of almonds or hazelnuts, is baked in two
layers, then spread with jelly and whipped cream.*

BAKE at 375° for 15 to 18 minutes   MAKES two 8-inch layers

Sift together . . 1 cup sifted **Pillsbury's Best All Purpose Flour***
1 teaspoon double-acting **baking powder** and
¼ teaspoon **salt**
Add . . . . 1½ cups **filberts** or blanched almonds, ground
Beat . . . . 2 **eggs** until thick and ivory colored. Gradually add
¼ cup **sugar,** beating well after each addition.
Cream . . . . . . ½ cup **butter** or margarine. Gradually add
½ cup **sugar,** creaming well. Blend in egg mixture.
Stir in . . . . the dry ingredients.
Spread . . . . batter in two 8-inch round layer pans, well greased
and lightly floured on the bottoms.
Bake . . . . at 375° for 15 to 18 minutes. Cool.
Spread . . . . . ¼ cup **currant jelly** over cooled layers. Fill and frost
layers with Sweetened Whipped Cream.
*For use with Pillsbury's Best Self-Rising Flour, omit baking powder and salt.

SWEETENED WHIPPED CREAM

Beat 1 cup whipping cream until thick. Blend in 1 tablespoon sugar
and ½ teaspoon vanilla.

Pineapple Meringue Torte

Pineapple Meringue Torte

Senior Winner by Mrs. Fred C. Post, Arcadia, California

No frosting to fiddle with . . . a meringue-topped butter cake with smooth pineapple filling.

BAKE at 300° for 50 to 60 minutes   MAKES 12x8 or 13x9-inch cake

Melt . . . . ⅓ cup **butter** or margarine with
　　　　　　½ cup firmly packed **brown sugar** in saucepan.
Add . . . . . . 2¼ cups (No. 2 can) **crushed pineapple.** Bring to a
　　　　　　boil, stirring occasionally.
Combine . . . . . 3 tablespoons **cornstarch** and
　　　　　　¼ cup cold **water.** Add to pineapple mixture; cook,
　　　　　　stirring constantly, until thick. Remove from heat.
Stir in . . . . . . 2 tablespoons **lemon juice.** Cool.

Sift together . . 1 cup sifted **Pillsbury's Best All Purpose Flour***
　　　　　　1½ teaspoons double-acting **baking powder** and
　　　　　　½ teaspoon **salt**
Cream . . . . . . ⅓ cup **butter** or margarine. Add
　　　　　　⅓ cup **sugar,** creaming well.
Blend in . . . . . 3 unbeaten **egg yolks** and
　　　　　　1 teaspoon **vanilla;** beat well.
Add . . . . the dry ingredients alternately with
　　　　　　⅓ cup **milk.** Blend well after each addition.
Turn . . . . into 13x9 or 12x8-inch pan, well greased and lightly
　　　　　　floured on the bottom.
Spread . . . . filling over batter. Cover with Coconut Meringue;
　　　　　　sprinkle with
　　　　　　2 tablespoons **coconut**
Bake . . . . at 300° for 50 to 60 minutes. Serve warm or cold.
For use with Pillsbury's Best Self-Rising Flour, omit baking powder and salt.

COCONUT MERINGUE

Beat 3 egg whites, ¼ teaspoon cream of tartar and ⅛ teaspoon salt until soft mounds form. Gradually add ¾ cup sugar; beat until stiff peaks form. Fold in 1 teaspoon vanilla and ¼ cup chopped coconut.

Jam Layer Dessert

Senior Winner by Mrs. Catherine A. McCabe, Akron, Ohio

A rich yeast dough baked in layers, then filled with jam and nuts. A delicate golden brown meringue frosts the top and sides.

BAKE at 375° for 8 to 10 minutes, then   SERVES 10 to 12
　　at 350° for 15 to 17 minutes

Combine . . . 1½ teaspoons active dry **yeast** (or ½ cake compressed)
　　　　　　¼ cup lukewarm **milk** and
　　　　　　2 tablespoons **sugar** in large mixing bowl.
Add . . . . ½ cup soft **butter** or margarine and
　　　　　　3 unbeaten **egg yolks;** beat well.

Blend in . . . . 1½ to 2 cups sifted **Pillsbury's Best All Purpose Flour*** gradually to form a stiff dough.

Divide . . . . dough into three parts. Roll out each part on floured surface to an 8-inch circle. Place on baking sheets or inverted cake pans. Let stand 30 to 40 minutes.

Bake . . . . at 375° for 8 to 10 minutes. Fill and frost just before serving.

Stack . . . . on baking sheet or oven-proof plate, spreading jam and nuts between layers (not on top). Use
1 cup **fruit preserves** or jam and
1 cup **nuts,** chopped, in all. (Grease baking sheet lightly around edge of bottom layer.)

Prepare . . . . recipe for **Meringue,** page 461; spread over top and sides, covering completely. Sprinkle with **nuts.**

Bake . . . . at 350° for 15 to 17 minutes.

Pillsbury's Best Self-Rising Flour may be substituted.

Rosy Dream Dessert

Senior Winner by Mrs. Garnard E. Harbeck, APO-107, New York, New York

Flaky pastry rounds—filled with berries, topped with whipped cream . . . a luscious dessert.

BAKE at 450° for 7 to 10 minutes   SERVES 8

Sift together 2½ cups sifted **Pillsbury's Best All Purpose Flour***and ½ teaspoon **salt** into large mixing bowl.

Cut in . . . . . . ½ cup **butter** or margarine and ¼ cup **shortening** until the size of small peas.

Combine . . . . . 1 unbeaten **egg**
1½ teaspoons **vanilla** and enough **sour cream** (thick or commercial)** to measure ⅔ cup; blend well. Sprinkle over flour mixture, stirring with fork until dough is moist enough to hold together.

Divide . . . . into four equal parts. Form into balls. Flatten to ½-inch thickness; smooth edges. Cover and refrigerate

three portions of dough.

Roll out . . . . remaining portion on floured surface to a 9-inch circle. Transfer to ungreased baking sheet; prick generously. Brush with melted **butter;** sprinkle with **sugar.**

Bake . . . . at 450° for 7 to 10 minutes. Repeat process with remaining dough. Cool; fill 1 hour (or less) before serving.

Spread . . . . Rosy Berry Filling between the layers. Garnish with **whipped cream.**

For use with Pillsbury's Best Self-Rising Flour, omit salt; decrease butter to ¼ cup.

**If desired, sweet cream may be substituted for sour cream. Add enough cream to egg and vanilla to measure ½ cup.*

ROSY BERRY FILLING

Drain 2 packages (16 oz. each) thawed frozen strawberries or 3 packages (10 oz. each) thawed frozen raspberries, reserving juice. In saucepan mix together ¼ cup sugar, 2 tablespoons cornstarch, 2 tablespoons quick-cooking tapioca and ¼ teaspoon salt. Add 2 cups of the reserved strawberry or raspberry juice (if necessary add water). Cook over medium heat, stirring constantly, until thick and clear. Remove from heat; add 1 tablespoon lemon juice. Cool. Fold in fruit.

Graham Cracker Nut Dessert

Senior Winner by Mrs. Pat L. Morrissey, Peoria, Illinois

Dates, pecans and graham crackers combine with rum flavoring for an exotic dessert. Easy, too—mixed in one bowl.

BAKE at 350° for 35 to 40 minutes   SERVES 8 to 10

Sift together . . 1 cup sifted **Pillsbury's Best All Purpose Flour***
  2 teaspoons double-acting **baking powder** and
  ½ teaspoon **salt** into mixing bowl. Add
  ¾ cup firmly packed **brown sugar; mix well.**
Add . . . . 1 cup **milk**
  ⅓ cup **salad oil**
  2 unbeaten **egg whites** and
  1 teaspoon **rum flavoring.** Blend, then beat at medium speed 2 minutes.
Stir in . . . . 1 cup finely crushed **graham crackers** (about 12 single)
  ½ cup **pecans,** chopped, and
  ½ cup **dates,** finely cut
Pour . . . . into 9x9x2 or 12x8x2-inch pan, well greased on the bottom.
Bake . . . . at 350° for 35 to 40 minutes. Serve warm, cut into squares and topped with Whipped Cream Sauce. Garnish each with **pecan half.**

For use with Pillsbury's Best Self-Rising Flour, decrease baking powder to ½ teaspoon and omit salt.

WHIPPED CREAM SAUCE

Cook ¾ cup sugar, 3 tablespoons water and ₁⁄₁₆ teaspoon cream of tartar in saucepan over direct heat until it spins a thread (234°). Pour slowly over 2 slightly beaten egg yolks, stirring constantly until well combined. Cool, stirring occasionally. Just before serving, beat ¾ cup whipping cream until thick. Fold in egg yolk mixture and ¼ teaspoon rum flavoring.

COBBLERS and SHORTCAKES—Plain pastry,
rich biscuit dough or muffin-like batter forms the base for the easy-to-make desserts in this section. All of the recipes are refreshing with fruit and make wonderful, quick, family desserts.

Royal Fruit Roll

Senior Winner by Mrs. Albert Hurwitz, South Miami, Florida

White seedless grapes and coconut are rolled up in a rich biscuit dough that has a hint of almond about it.

BAKE at 350° for 30 to 35 minutes   SERVES 8 to 10

Sift together 1⅔ cups sifted **Pillsbury's Best All Purpose Flour***
  ¼ cup **sugar**
  ½ teaspoon double-acting **baking powder**
  ¼ teaspoon **soda** and
  ¼ teaspoon **salt** into large mixing bowl.
Cut in . . . . . . ¼ cup **shortening** until particles are fine.
Blend in . . . . . 1 slightly beaten **egg**
  ¼ cup **sour cream** (thick or commercial) and
  ¼ teaspoon **almond extract;** stir until dough clings together. Knead on floured surface 10 strokes.
Divide . . . . dough in half; roll each to a 12x8-inch rectangle.
Spread . . . . half of Grape Filling down center of each rectangle. Fold sides to center; moisten and seal edges. Place rolls on greased baking sheet. Brush with **milk.** Cut slits.

Bake.........at 350° for 30 to 35 minutes. Remove from sheet immediately. Serve warm or cold with **cream.**

For use with Pillsbury's Best Self-Rising Flour, omit baking powder, soda, salt.

GRAPE FILLING

Combine 2 tablespoons soft butter and ½ cup sugar. Add ¼ teaspoon nutmeg, 1 teaspoon grated lemon rind, ¾ cup flaked or chopped shredded coconut and 2½ cups white seedless grapes, cut in half. (If desired, substitute 2½ cups finely chopped apples for grapes.) Mix well.

Cranberry Orange Pinwheels

Senior Winner by Mrs. Thomas G. Tyson, Greensboro, North Carolina

Orange-flavored biscuit roll-ups with cranberry and nut filling are baked in a brown sugar-orange syrup.

BAKE at 400° for 20 to 25 minutes   SERVES 10

Grate.......2 teaspoons **orange rind.** Set aside.
Combine....½ cup **water**
            ½ cup **orange juice**
            ½ cup **sugar** and
            2 tablespoons **brown sugar** in saucepan. Simmer 5 minutes. Remove from heat.
Add........¼ cup **butter** or margarine
            ¼ teaspoon **nutmeg** and half of the orange rind. Pour into 12x8x2-inch baking dish.
Sift together..2 cups sifted **Pillsbury's Best All Purpose Flour***
            4 teaspoons double-acting **baking powder** and
            1 teaspoon **salt** into large mixing bowl.
Cut in......¼ cup **shortening** until particles are fine.
Add........¾ cup **orange juice;** stir until dough clings together. Knead on floured surface about 30 strokes.
Roll out.......to a 12-inch square. Brush with orange sauce from the baking dish.

Combine.....1 cup whole **cranberry sauce,** cooked or canned
            ½ cup **walnuts,** chopped, and the remaining orange rind. Spread over dough.
Roll.........as for jelly roll. Cut into slices. Place cut-side down on sauce in baking dish.
Bake.........at 400° for 20 to 25 minutes. Serve warm with **plain** or **whipped cream.**

For use with Pillsbury's Best Self-Rising Flour, omit baking powder and salt; decrease orange juice to ⅔ cup.

Sweet Mince Roll-Up

Senior Winner by Mrs. Homer W. Beeler, Savery, Wyoming

Biscuit dough rolled up with mincemeat—basted with cinnamon sauce.

BAKE at 425° for 25 to 30 minutes   SERVES 10 to 12

Sift together..2 cups sifted **Pillsbury's Best All Purpose Flour***
            ¼ cup **sugar**
            2 teaspoons double-acting **baking powder** and
            1 teaspoon **salt** into large mixing bowl.
Add........½ cup **milk** and
            ⅓ cup **salad oil;** mix until all dry particles are moistened.
Roll out.......on floured surface to 13x9-inch rectangle. Spread with
            2 cups prepared **mincemeat** (about 1 lb.)
Roll.........as for jelly roll, starting with 13-inch side. Seal ends; place in ungreased 13x9x2-inch pan.
Bake.........at 425° for 20 to 25 minutes. Pour warm Cinnamon Sauce over roll. Bake 5 minutes, basting with sauce.

For use with Pillsbury's Best Self-Rising Flour, omit baking powder and salt.

CINNAMON SAUCE

Combine in saucepan 1 cup firmly packed brown sugar, ½ cup water, ¼ cup butter or margarine and 1 teaspoon cinnamon. Bring to boil, stirring constantly. Remove from heat.

Alaskan Cranberry Cobbler

Senior Winner by Mrs. Ethel Hansen, Anchorage, Alaska

Bright red cranberry sauce, partly covered with golden brown drop biscuits . . . there's an intriguing tartness.

BAKE at 350° for 35 to 40 minutes   SERVES 8

Sift together 2¼ cups sifted **Pillsbury's Best All Purpose Flour***
            ¼ cup **sugar**
            2 teaspoons double-acting **baking powder** and
            ½ teaspoon **salt** into large mixing bowl.
Combine . . . . . 1 cup **milk** and
            2 tablespoons **butter,** melted; add to the dry ingredients all at once, stirring until well combined.
Heat . . . . 2 cups (1-lb. can) **cranberry sauce**
Melt . . . . ¼ cup **butter** or margarine in 2-quart casserole.
Spread . . . . half of batter in casserole. Pour hot cranberry sauce over batter.
Drop . . . . remaining batter by tablespoonfuls on sauce.
Combine . . . . . 2 tablespoons **sugar** and
            ¼ teaspoon **cinnamon**; sprinkle over cobbler.
Bake . . . . at 350° for 35 to 40 minutes. Serve warm with **cream.**

For use with Pillsbury's Best Self-Rising Flour, omit baking powder and salt.

Rosy Apple Whirls

Junior First Prize Winner by Nancy Harden, Centralia, Kansas

Rich biscuit roll-ups, filled with apples, are baked over a spicy syrup made with red cinnamon candies. Best served warm with cream.

BAKE at 400° for 40 to 45 minutes   SERVES 8

Combine . . . 1½ cups **sugar**
         1½ cups **water** and
        ⅓ cup (2-oz. jar) **red cinnamon candies** in saucepan.
        Bring to boil and simmer 5 minutes. Pour into

Rosy Apple Whirls

12x8x2-inch pan, reserving ½ cup.

Prepare......3 cups pared, finely chopped **apples**; set aside.

Sift together..2 cups sifted **Pillsbury's Best All Purpose Flour***
⅓ cup **sugar**
2 teaspoons double-acting **baking powder** and
½ teaspoon **salt** into large mixing bowl.

Cut in......⅓ cup **shortening** until particles are fine.

Combine.....1 unbeaten **egg** with **milk** to measure ⅔ cup; beat with fork. Add to the dry ingredients all at once; stir until dough clings together.

Knead........on floured surface 12 to 15 strokes. Roll out to a 12-inch square. Spread with
1 tablespoon soft **butter;** cover with the apples. Roll as for jelly roll. Cut into eight 1½-inch slices and place on syrup in pan.

Bake.........at 400° for 30 minutes. Spoon 1 tablespoon of reserved syrup over each biscuit. Bake 10 to 15 minutes. Serve warm with **plain** or **whipped cream.**

For use with Pillsbury's Best Self-Rising Flour, omit baking powder and salt.

Apple-Peanut Spoon Dessert

Senior Winner by Mrs. Luther C. Pigott, West Union, West Virginia

Peanut-butter cobbler crust covers a spicy apple mixture.

BAKE at 350° for 35 to 40 minutes   SERVES 6 to 8

Combine.....4 cups pared, sliced cooking **apples** (4 medium)
½ cup **sugar**
1 tablespoon **flour**
½ teaspoon **cinnamon**
¼ teaspoon **nutmeg** and
2 tablespoons **lemon juice** in 10x6-inch pan, 1½-quart casserole or 9-inch pie pan.

Sift together.¾ cup sifted **Pillsbury's Best All Purpose Flour***
¼ teaspoon **soda** and

¼ teaspoon **salt.** Set aside.

Combine....¼ cup **shortening** and
2 tablespoons **peanut butter.** Add
⅓ cup **sugar,** creaming well.

Blend in.....1 unbeaten **egg**

Add.........the dry ingredients; blend thoroughly.

Drop........dough by tablespoonfuls to cover apples.

Bake.........at 350° for 35 to 40 minutes. Serve warm with **plain** or **whipped cream.**

For use with Pillsbury's Best Self-Rising Flour, omit soda and salt.

Old Virginia Cobbler

Best of Class Winner by Miss Lillie F. Young, Courtland, Virginia

Old-fashioned apple cobbler is always a favorite. Lemon slices added to this dessert give it refreshing tartness.

BAKE at 400° for 35 to 45 minutes   SERVES 6 to 8

Simmer.....½ **lemon** (grated rind and juice) in
½ cup **water** for 5 minutes.

Combine....¾ cup **sugar**
2 tablespoons **flour** and
¼ teaspoon **nutmeg** in saucepan; blend in the lemon-water mixture. Cook, stirring constantly, until thickened.

Add........4 cups pared, sliced **apples** (4 medium) and
2 tablespoons **butter** or margarine

Turn.........hot filling into well-greased 10x6x2-inch pan or 9-inch pie pan.

Prepare.......recipe for **One-Crust Pastry,** page 460; roll out pastry as directed below.

Roll out.......on floured surface to 10x6-inch rectangle. Cut into triangles or diamonds. Arrange over apples.

Bake.........at 400° for 35 to 45 minutes. Serve with **plain** or **whipped cream.**

Banana Split Shortcake

Senior Winner by Mrs. W. I. Dedman, Houston, Texas

Bananas and chopped nuts go into the batter of this quick shortcake topped with whipped cream and more bananas.

BAKE at 350° for 40 to 45 minutes   SERVES 9

Sift together 1¼ cups sifted **Pillsbury's Best All Purpose Flour***
           1 cup **sugar**
           1 teaspoon **soda** and
           ½ teaspoon **salt** into mixing bowl.
Cut in . . . . . . ½ cup **shortening** until particles are fine.
Add . . . . 1 cup **pecans** or walnuts, chopped
Combine . . . . . 2 well-beaten **eggs**
           ¼ cup **milk** and
           1 cup mashed ripe **bananas** (2 medium). Add all at once to flour mixture; mix until all dry particles are moistened.
Turn . . . . into 11x7x2 or 9x9x2-inch pan, well greased and lightly floured on the bottom.
Bake . . . . at 350° for 40 to 45 minutes. Serve warm or cold; cut in squares and top with **whipped cream** and **banana slices.**

*For use with Pillsbury's Best Self-Rising Flour, decrease soda to ¼ teaspoon and omit salt.

Quick Banana Buns

Junior Winner by Emma Jane Wood, St. Joseph, Louisiana

An extra-quick dessert! Sweet, muffin-like buns, flavored with bananas and spices, are baked like drop biscuits.

BAKE at 400° for 12 to 15 minutes   MAKES 15

Sift together 2¼ cups sifted **Pillsbury's Best All Purpose Flour***
           ¼ cup **sugar**

           2 teaspoons double-acting **baking powder**
           1 teaspoon **salt**
           ¾ teaspoon **soda**
           ½ teaspoon **cinnamon** and
           ¼ teaspoon **nutmeg** into large mixing bowl. Add
           ½ cup firmly packed **brown sugar**; mix well.
Cut in . . . . . . ⅔ cup **shortening** until particles are fine.
Blend . . . . 1 unbeaten **egg** with
           ⅓ cup **buttermilk** or sour milk and
           1 cup mashed ripe **bananas** (2 medium). Add all at once to flour mixture. Mix until all dry particles are moistened.
Drop . . . . by well-rounded tablespoonfuls onto greased baking sheets, about 3 inches apart.**
Bake . . . . at 400° for 12 to 15 minutes. Split and serve warm with **Cinnamon Whipped Cream,** page 329. Garnish with **banana slices.**

*For use with Pillsbury's Best Self-Rising Flour, omit baking powder, salt, soda.
**For luncheon muffins, fill well-greased muffin cups two-thirds; bake for 15 to 20 minutes.

Raisin Rolled Dessert

Senior Winner by Hazel Norton Spence, St. Petersburg, Florida

An economical dessert with flavor to remind you of old-fashioned bread pudding—may be served warm with butter as a breakfast roll.

BAKE at 425° for 20 to 25 minutes   SERVES 8

Prepare . . . . Spicy Raisin Filling; cool.
Sift together . . 2 cups sifted **Pillsbury's Best All Purpose Flour***
           ¼ cup **sugar**
           1½ teaspoons double-acting **baking powder** and

                    1 teaspoon **salt** into large mixing bowl.
Cut in . . . . . . ½ cup **shortening** until the size of small peas.
Sprinkle . . . . . ⅓ to ½ cup **milk** over mixture, stirring with fork until
                    dough is moist enough to hold together. Form into
                    square.
Roll out . . . . on floured surface to a 16x9-inch rectangle. Spread
                    with cooled Filling. Roll as for jelly roll, starting with
                    a 16-inch side. Seal edges.
Cut . . . . into sixteen 1-inch slices. Place cut-side down in
                    9x9-inch pan, greased on bottom with
                    2 tablespoons soft **butter** or margarine. Sprinkle
                    1 tablespoon **sugar** over rolls.
Bake . . . . at 425° for 20 to 25 minutes. Serve warm with **cream.**
For use with Pillsbury's Best Self-Rising Flour, omit baking powder and salt.

SPICY RAISIN FILLING

Combine in saucepan 1 cup raisins and ¾ cup water; bring to boil
and simmer 5 minutes. Add ¼ cup orange marmalade or apricot
preserves, 2 tablespoons flour, 2 tablespoons brown sugar, 1 tablespoon
butter, 2 teaspoons grated lemon rind, 2 tablespoons lemon juice, ¼
teaspoon salt, ¼ teaspoon ginger, ¼ teaspoon cinnamon and ⅛ teaspoon nutmeg. Cook over medium heat, stirring constantly, until thick.

Peach Easy Dessert

Junior Winner by Joan Lee Anderson, Erie, Pennsylvania

*A spicy peach layer is topped with rich drop biscuits, then sprinkled
with a butter crumb mixture.*

BAKE at 400° for 30 to 35 minutes   SERVES 8

Arrange . . . . . 1 No. 2½ can **peach slices,** well drained (or 3 to 4
                    peeled and sliced fresh peaches), in bottom of well-
                    greased 8x8x2-inch pan. Combine
                    ¼ cup **sugar** and
                    ½ teaspoon **cinnamon;** sprinkle over peaches.

Peach Easy Dessert

Sift together . . 1 cup sifted **Pillsbury's Best All Purpose Flour***
                    3 tablespoons **sugar**
                    2 teaspoons double-acting **baking powder** and
                    ½ teaspoon **salt** into mixing bowl.
Cut in . . . . 3 tablespoons **butter** until particles are fine.
Combine . . . . . 1 slightly beaten **egg** and
                    ¼ cup **milk.** Add to the dry ingredients; mix until all
                    dry particles are moistened. Drop by spoonfuls onto
                    peaches.
Blend . . . . 2 tablespoons **sugar** and
                    1 tablespoon **flour** together with
                    1 tablespoon soft **butter** to form crumbs; sprinkle over
                    top.
Bake . . . . at 400° for 30 to 35 minutes. Serve warm with **cream.**
For use with Pillsbury's Best Self-Rising Flour, omit baking powder and salt.

Plantation Peach Shortcake

Third Prize Winner by Mrs. B. J. O'Donell, Elkhorn, Wisconsin

This is a new kind of biscuit-shortcake with brown sugar and chopped nuts baked right inside the layers. It's really luscious!

BAKE at 450° for 10 to 13 minutes   SERVES 8

Sift together . . 2 cups sifted **Pillsbury's Best All Purpose Flour***
             3 teaspoons double-acting **baking powder** and
             ½ teaspoon **salt** into large mixing bowl.
Cut in . . . . . . ¼ cup firmly packed **brown sugar** and
             ½ cup **shortening** until particles are fine.
Add . . . . ½ cup **pecans**, chopped
Combine . . . . . 1 well-beaten **egg** and
             ⅔ cup light **cream.** Add to the dry ingredients; mix
             until all dry particles are moistened.
Spread . . . . in two well-greased 8-inch round layer pans. (For
             individual shortcakes, turn out dough on well-
             floured surface; knead a few strokes. Roll to ½-inch
             thickness. Cut with floured 3-inch round cutter.
             Place on ungreased baking sheet.)
Bake . . . . at 450° for 10 to 13 minutes.
Prepare . . . . . . 2 cups sliced **peaches** (fresh, frozen or canned). Place
             between layers or split individual shortcakes. Top
             with **whipped cream** and **peaches.**

*For use with Pillsbury's Best Self-Rising Flour, omit baking powder and salt.

Perky Pear Cobbler

Junior Winner by Meredith S. Pressey, Marblehead, Massachusetts

This winning dessert brings a new flavor idea to a fruit cobbler. Light, egg-rich biscuits cover gingery fruit sauce and pear halves.

BAKE at 400° for 25 to 30 minutes   SERVES 8

Drain . . . . 1 No. 2½ can **pear halves.** Combine pear juice and

Plantation Peach Shortcake

Combine..... water or gingerale to measure 2 cups.
¼ cup **Pillsbury's Best All Purpose Flour**
¼ cup firmly packed **brown sugar**
¼ teaspoon **salt**
1⁄16 teaspoon **ginger** and
½ teaspoon grated **lemon rind** in saucepan. Gradually blend in the liquid. Cook, stirring constantly, until thick. Add
1 tablespoon **butter** or margarine

Arrange....... pear halves, cut-side up, in 1½-quart casserole. Top with sauce.

BISCUIT TOPPING

Sift together..1 cup sifted **Pillsbury's Best All Purpose Flour***
1½ teaspoons double-acting **baking powder** and
½ teaspoon **salt** into mixing bowl.

Cut in.......2 tablespoons **butter** until particles are fine.

Combine.....1 slightly beaten **egg** and
¼ cup **milk**. Add all at once to the dry ingredients; mix until all dry particles are moistened.

Pat out........on well-floured surface to ½-inch thickness. Cut into rounds with 2-inch cutter. Arrange on top of pear mixture. If desired, place chopped **nuts** or maraschino cherries between biscuits.

Bake.........at 400° for 25 to 30 minutes. Serve warm.

For use with Pillsbury's Best Self-Rising Flour, omit baking powder and salt; decrease milk to 3 tablespoons.

Mincy Pear Cobbler

Senior Winner by Mrs. Robert E. Maurer, Pomona, California

Mincemeat and pears are topped with sugar-coated drop biscuits.

BAKE at 375° for 30 to 35 minutes   SERVES 8

Prepare......3 medium-sized **pears,** pared and sliced. Place in a

10x6-inch baking dish. Sprinkle with
¼ cup **Pillsbury's Best All Purpose Flour** and
¼ cup firmly packed **brown sugar**. (Or substitute 1 No. 2½ can pears, drained and sliced. Decrease brown sugar to 2 tablespoons.)

Combine....½ cup prepared **mincemeat** and
1 tablespoon **lemon juice**; place over pears. Top with
3 tablespoons **butter** or margarine, melted. Set aside.

Sift together..1 cup sifted **Pillsbury's Best All Purpose Flour***
1½ teaspoons double-acting **baking powder** and
1 teaspoon **salt** into mixing bowl.

Cut in.......2 tablespoons **butter** until particles are fine.

Combine.....1 unbeaten **egg** with **milk** to measure ⅓ cup. Add egg mixture and
⅓ cup prepared **mincemeat** to the dry ingredients. Stir until dough clings together.

Drop.........by level tablespoonfuls into mixture of
¼ cup **sugar**
¼ teaspoon **cinnamon** and
¼ cup **walnuts,** finely chopped. Place biscuits over pears. Sprinkle with remaining sugar-nut mixture. Drizzle with 1 tablespoon **butter,** melted.

Bake.........at 375° for 30 to 35 minutes. Serve warm with Honey Spice Whipped Cream.

For use with Pillsbury's Best Self-Rising Flour, omit baking powder and salt.

HONEY SPICE WHIPPED CREAM

Beat 1 cup whipping cream until thick. Add 2 tablespoons honey and ½ teaspoon cinnamon. Beat until thick.

Aloha Shortcakes

Senior Winner by Mrs. Ida E. Beck, Houghton, Michigan

Yummy old-fashioned shortcakes baked on top of pineapple slices, then served upside down with spoonfuls of brown-sugary juice.

BAKE at 450° for 15 to 18 minutes   SERVES 10

Melt . . . . 2 tablespoons **butter** in jelly-roll pan or other large shallow pan.

Arrange . . . . 10 **pineapple slices** (No. 2 can) in pan; reserve juice. Fill center of each slice with **maraschino cherry.**

Sift together . . 3 cups sifted **Pillsbury's Best All Purpose Flour***
⅓ cup **sugar**
4½ teaspoons double-acting **baking powder** and
1 teaspoon **salt** into large mixing bowl.

Cut in . . . . . . ½ cup **shortening** until particles are fine.

Combine . . . . . 2 beaten **eggs** and

Aloha Shortcakes

⅔ cup **milk.*** Add all at once to the dry ingredients; mix until dough clings together.

Roll out . . . . on floured surface to ⅜-inch thickness. Cut into rounds the size of pineapple slices. Place a round on each slice.

Combine . . . . . . the reserved pineapple juice with
½ cup firmly packed **brown sugar** and
1 tablespoon **lemon juice.** Pour over biscuits.

Bake . . . . at 450° for 15 to 18 minutes. Serve warm, pineapple-side up. Top with sauce from pan and **whipped cream.**

**For use with Pillsbury's Best Self-Rising Flour; omit baking powder and salt. Combine beaten eggs with enough milk to measure 1 cup.*

Pineapple Halo Dessert

Senior Winner by Mrs. Arnold Creager, Pleasantville, Indiana

Pineapple rings baked in biscuit dough. Serve warm with berries folded into sweetened whipped cream.

BAKE at 450° for 12 to 15 minutes   SERVES 6

Drain . . . . 1 No. 2 can **sliced pineapple,** reserving ⅓ cup juice.

Sift together 2¼ cups sifted **Pillsbury's Best All Purpose Flour***
⅓ cup **sugar**
3 teaspoons double-acting **baking powder** and
½ teaspoon **salt** into large mixing bowl.

Cut in . . . . . . ⅓ cup **shortening** until particles are fine.

Combine . . . . . 1 slightly beaten **egg** with the reserved juice and enough **milk** to measure ⅔ cup.

Add . . . . liquid all at once to the dry ingredients; mix well.

Roll out . . . . . . on floured surface to ⅛-inch thickness.

Cut . . . . into 12 rounds with 3½-inch cutter. Cut a small hole in center of each, doughnut-fashion.

Place . . . . a slice of well-drained pineapple on 6 rounds. Top with remaining rounds. Seal inner and outer edges. Brush with melted **butter.** Prick tops. Place on ungreased baking sheet.

Bake . . . . at 450° for 12 to 15 minutes. Serve with Strawberry-Whip Topping.

*For use with Pillsbury's Best Self-Rising Flour, omit baking powder and salt.

STRAWBERRY-WHIP TOPPING

Beat 1 cup whipping cream until thick; sweeten to taste. Fold in 2 cups sweetened, sliced strawberries.

Strawberry Sunshine Dessert

Senior Winner by Miss Elizabeth Phipps Lightcap, Washington, D.C.

Rich biscuit-like dough . . . golden crushed pineapple . . . with fluffy whipped cream and strawberries on top.

BAKE at 425° for 18 to 22 minutes   SERVES 6

Spread . . . . . 1½ cups (No. 2 can) **crushed pineapple,** drained, in well-buttered 8-inch round or 2-quart casserole.

Combine . . . . ⅓ cup **sugar** and
    1 tablespoon **flour.** Sprinkle over pineapple.

Sift together . . 1 cup sifted **Pillsbury's Best All Purpose Flour***
    2 tablespoons **sugar**
    1½ teaspoons double-acting **baking powder** and
    ½ teaspoon **salt** into mixing bowl.

Cut in . . . . . . ¼ cup **butter** or margarine until particles are fine.

Add . . . . ⅓ cup **milk;** mix to form a soft dough. Spoon over pineapple mixture.

Bake . . . . at 425° for 18 to 22 minutes. Turn upside down on serving plate. Serve warm with Strawberry Cream Topping. Decorate with whole **strawberries.**

*For use with Pillsbury's Best Self-Rising Flour, omit baking powder and salt.

STRAWBERRY CREAM TOPPING

Beat 1 cup whipping cream until thick. Fold in 1 cup sweetened, sliced strawberries.

PASTRIES and DUMPLINGS

are of many different kinds. Some are filled with fruit mixtures, while others are topped with pudding-like sauces. Some of the dumplings are steamed to doneness, while others are baked.

Steamed dumplings are much easier to shape if you dip the spoon into cold water before dropping dumplings into hot sauce (cold water keeps the dough from sticking to the spoon).

It is also very important to cover tightly and not to remove the cover of the kettle or saucepan during the simmering process; it's the steam that forms that cooks the dumplings to doneness.

Apple Orchard Snowballs

Junior Winner by Doris Ann Eberhardt, Cincinnati, Ohio

A whole sugared apple and a dab of strawberry jam are baked inside flaky pastry, then frosted. Makes a generous dessert.

BAKE at 400° for 35 to 40 minutes   SERVES 6

Prepare . . . . recipe for **Two-Crust Pastry,** page 460; shape and roll out dough as directed below.

Roll . . . . 6 cooking **apples,** pared and cored, in
    ⅔ cup sifted **confectioners' sugar**

Roll out . . . . . . pastry on floured surface to a 15x10-inch rectangle. Cut into six 5-inch squares.

Place . . . . apple in center of each square. Fill center of each apple with a teaspoon of **strawberry jam.** Moisten edges of pastry; bring edges together and seal at top. Prick with fork. Place on greased baking sheet.

Bake . . . . at 400° for 35 to 40 minutes. Cool; frost with **Vanilla Glaze,** page 326, or serve with **whipped cream.**

*For use with Pillsbury's Best Self-Rising Flour, omit salt.

Baked Apple Cuplets

Baked Apple Cuplets

Junior Winner by Linda Stopher, Cuyahoga Falls, Ohio

An interesting variation of an old favorite . . . baked apples with batter topping in individual custard cups for a quickie dessert.

BAKE at 375° for 40 to 45 minutes*   SERVES 6

Combine . . . . ¼ cup **sugar** and
          ½ teaspoon **cinnamon**
Prepare . . . . . . 6 baking **apples,** pared and cored. Roll in cinnamon sugar. Place in buttered custard cups. Spoon remaining cinnamon sugar in centers of apples. Set aside.
Sift together . ⅔ cup sifted **Pillsbury's Best All Purpose Flour***
          ⅔ cup **sugar**

¼ teaspoon double-acting **baking powder** and
          ⅛ teaspoon **salt**
Combine . . . . . 1 slightly beaten **egg**
          3 tablespoons **butter** or margarine, melted, and
          1 teaspoon **vanilla.** Add to the dry ingredients; beat well.
Place . . . . 2 tablespoonfuls of batter over each apple.
Bake . . . . at 375° for 40 to 45 minutes or until tender.
For use with Pillsbury's Best Self-Rising Flour, omit baking powder and salt; decrease baking time to 30 to 35 minutes.

Almond Delights

Senior Winner by Mrs. Opal Couch, Orchard, Nebraska

These little individual desserts have a rich cooky-like shell and delicious lemon-almond filling.

BAKE at 325° for 25 to 30 minutes   MAKES 1½ dozen cakes

Sift together 2¼ cups sifted **Pillsbury's Best All Purpose Flour*** and
          ½ teaspoon **salt**
Cream . . . . . . ½ cup **butter** or margarine and
          ¼ cup **shortening.** Gradually add
          ½ cup **sugar,** creaming well.
Blend in . . . . . 1 unbeaten **egg** and
          1 teaspoon **vanilla.** Add the dry ingredients; mix well.
Press . . . . dough into bottoms and sides of greased muffin cups (use 1½ to 2 tablespoonfuls for each).
Fill . . . . with Almond Filling.
Bake . . . . at 325° for 25 to 30 minutes.
For use with Pillsbury's Best Self-Rising Flour, omit salt.

ALMOND FILLING

Beat 2 eggs with ¼ teaspoon salt until light. Add ½ cup sugar gradually, beating constantly. Blend in 1 cup blanched almonds, ground, 1 teaspoon grated lemon rind and ½ teaspoon almond extract.

Maplenut Cornucopias

Senior Winner by Mrs. Forrest E. Thies, Oakland, California

Dainty "Horn o' Plenty" tarts with maple-marshmallow filling.

BAKE at 425° for 14 to 16 minutes   MAKES 12

Prepare . . . . recipe for **Two-Crust Pastry,** page 460; roll out as directed below.

Roll out . . . . each half on floured surface to a 12x8-inch rectangle. Cut into six 4-inch squares. Shape into cones around cornucopias made from a double layer of brown wrapping paper. Moisten overlapping edges and seal. Brush with **cream.** Place on ungreased baking sheet.

Bake . . . . at 425° for 14 to 16 minutes. Cool slightly; gently remove paper. Cool completely. Fill with Maple Marshmallow Filling. Decorate with **walnut halves** or maraschino cherries.

MAPLE MARSHMALLOW FILLING

Combine 30 marshmallows, cut in eighths, and 1½ cups whipping cream in large mixing bowl. Chill 1 hour, then beat until thick. Fold in ¾ cup walnuts, chopped, and ½ teaspoon maple flavoring.

Apple Meringue Pizza

Bride Winner by Mrs. William R. Cook, League City, Texas

Apple pie pizza topped with toasty brown sugar meringue . . . shredded cheese inside completes this always popular dessert.

BAKE at 450° for 20 minutes, then   MAKES 12-inch dessert pizza
at 350° for 18 to 20 minutes

Sprinkle . . . . . 2 tablespoons **lemon juice** over
         3½ cups pared, thinly sliced **apples** (4 medium)
Sift together 1½ cups sifted **Pillsbury's Best All Purpose Flour*** and
         ½ teaspoon **salt.** Stir in

         ¼ cup quick-cooking **rolled oats**

Cut in . . . . . . ½ cup **shortening** until the size of small peas.

Sprinkle . . . . . 4 to 5 tablespoons cold **water** over mixture, stirring with fork until moist enough to hold together.

Pat or roll out . . on floured baking sheet to a 13-inch circle.

Sprinkle . . . . . 1 cup shredded **Cheddar cheese** on crust to within 1 inch of edge. Top with sliced apples. Turn edge over filling.

Bake . . . . at 450° for 20 minutes, covering apples with a circle of foil. Remove from oven; spread Brown Sugar Meringue over apples. Bake at 350° for 18 to 20 minutes.

*For use with Pillsbury's Best Self-Rising Flour, omit salt.

BROWN SUGAR MERINGUE

Combine ¼ cup sugar, ¼ cup firmly packed brown sugar and ½ teaspoon cinnamon. Beat 2 egg whites until soft mounds form. Gradually add sugar mixture. Beat until stiff, glossy peaks form.

Apple Meringue Pizza

Spicy
Apple Twists
**Grand Prize Winner
of the Tenth
Grand National
Bake-Off**®

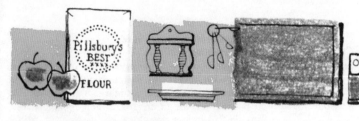

Spicy Apple Twists

Grand Prize Winner by Mrs. Don DeVault, Delaware, Ohio

Apples and spices on your list—use some pastry to form a twist around the apples with spice to flavor. Here's a dessert really to rave o'er!

BAKE at 450°* for 20 to 30 minutes   MAKES 16

Prepare...... 2 large **apples,** pared, cored and each sliced into eight wedges.

Sift together 1½ cups sifted **Pillsbury's Best All Purpose Flour*** and 1 teaspoon **salt** into mixing bowl.

Cut in...... ½ cup **shortening** until the size of small peas.

Sprinkle..... 4 to 5 tablespoons cold **water** over mixture, stirring with fork until dough is moist enough to hold together. Form into a square.

Roll out....... on floured surface to 12-inch square. Spread with 2 tablespoons soft **butter.*** Fold both sides to center.

Roll out....... to a 16x10-inch rectangle. Cut into sixteen 10x1-inch strips.

Wrap......... one strip around each apple wedge. Arrange in 13x9x2-inch pan, sides not touching. Brush with ⅓ cup **butter,** melted (using all). Sprinkle with mixture of ½ cup **sugar** and 1 to 1½ teaspoons **cinnamon**

Pour....... ¾ cup **water** into pan.

Bake......... at 450° for 20 to 30 minutes. Serve warm or cold, plain or with whipped cream.

For use with Pillsbury's Best Self-Rising Flour, omit salt; decrease baking temperature to 425°.

**Or grate or shave firm butter over center half.*

Apricot Dainties

Bride Winner by Mrs. Bernard Pollock, Mobile, Alabama

Old-time strudel dessert with apricot-nut filling served in dainty slices.

BAKE at 350° for 30 to 40 minutes   MAKES 4 dozen

Cut......... 1 cup **butter** or margarine into 2 cups sifted **Pillsbury's Best All Purpose Flour*** until particles are the size of small peas.

Add....... 1¼ cups **sour cream** (thick or commercial); stir until dough clings together. Cover; chill 5 to 6 hours.**

Combine..... 1 cup **apricot preserves** and 1 tablespoon **lemon juice;** mix to break up any large pieces of apricots.

Divide........ dough into four parts. Roll out one part on pastry cloth to a 14x12-inch rectangle. Spread with ¼ cup of the apricot mixture. Sprinkle with one-fourth of the Nut Filling.

Roll......... as for jelly roll, starting with 14-inch side; seal edges. Place on ungreased baking sheet. Repeat process with remaining dough.

Bake......... at 350° for 30 to 40 minutes. Cut in 1-inch slices. Serve warm or cold, sprinkled with **confectioners' sugar.**

Pillsbury's Best Self-Rising Flour may be substituted.

**Dough may be stored in refrigerator up to 4 days and baked as needed.*

NUT FILLING

Mix together 1½ cups nuts, chopped, 1 cup chopped coconut, ½ cup chopped raisins and ¼ cup chopped maraschino cherries.

Blushing Beauty Dumplings

Blushing Beauty Dumplings

Senior Winner by Mrs. Will Lutzenberger, St. Louis, Missouri

Tart pie apples are peeled, wrapped in jackets of orange pastry, then basted with bright red apple syrup as they bake.

BAKE at 350° for 50 to 60 minutes   MAKES 6 dumplings

Peel and core.6 medium baking **apples**; reserve peelings.
Combine . . . 1½ cups **water** and peelings in saucepan. Cover; cook until tender, 5 to 10 minutes. Drain juice; to it add
 ½ cup **sugar**. Cover and cook 10 minutes. Remove from heat; add
 ⅛ teaspoon **red food coloring**. Set aside.
Sift together . . 2 cups sifted **Pillsbury's Best All Purpose Flour*** and
 1 teaspoon **salt** into large mixing bowl. Add

 2 teaspoons grated **orange rind**
Cut in . . . . . . ⅔ cup **shortening** until the size of small peas.
Sprinkle . . . . . 6 to 7 tablespoons cold **orange juice** over mixture, stirring with fork until dough is moist enough to hold together. Form into a square.
Roll out . . . . on floured surface to an 18x12-inch rectangle. Cut into six 9x4-inch strips.
Wrap . . . . a pastry strip around each apple, sealing bottom and side.
Combine . . . . . 2 tablespoons **sugar** and
 1 teaspoon **nutmeg**. Place 1 teaspoonful in center of each apple. Top each with
 1 teaspoon **butter**
Place . . . . in 12x8-inch baking pan, sides not touching. Pour reserved syrup around dumplings.
Bake . . . . at 350° for 50 to 60 minutes. Baste with syrup after baking 40 minutes. Serve warm, plain or with cream.
*For use with Pillsbury's Best Self-Rising Flour, omit salt.

Glazed Apple Dumplings

Senior Winner by Miss Blanche Joyner, Franklin, Virginia

These extra-good apple dumplings have a touch of cheese in them . . . and marshmallow brown-sugar sauce on top.

BAKE at 375° for 40 to 45 minutes   SERVES 10

Sift together 2½ cups sifted **Pillsbury's Best All Purpose Flour***
 2 teaspoons double-acting **baking powder** and
 1 teaspoon **salt** into large mixing bowl.
Add . . . . ¼ cup shredded **American cheese**
Cut in . . . . . . ⅓ cup **shortening** until particles are fine.
Add . . . . 1 cup light **cream** gradually, mixing lightly with fork. Form into ball.
Roll out . . . . on floured surface to ⅛-inch thickness. Cut into ten 6-inch circles.

Prepare......3 cups pared, cubed **apples** (3 medium). Place about ⅓ cup of apple cubes on each circle. Sprinkle each with
1 tablespoon **sugar** and **nutmeg**

Moisten.......edges of dough; bring edges together at top and seal. Place in jelly-roll pan.

Pour.......½ cup **milk** and
¼ cup **water** over dumplings.

Bake.........at 375° for 40 to 45 minutes. Serve warm with Brown Sugar Sauce.

For use with Pillsbury's Best Self-Rising Flour, omit baking powder and salt.

BROWN SUGAR SAUCE

Combine in saucepan 1 cup sugar, 1 cup firmly packed brown sugar and 1 tablespoon cornstarch. Blend in 1 cup water. Cook over low heat, stirring constantly, until smooth and slightly thickened. Add 6 marshmallows and 3 tablespoons butter; cook slowly, stirring constantly, until melted. Blend in 2 teaspoons vanilla.

Applecots

Senior Winner by Mrs. Henry L. Kibler, Paoli, Indiana

Dressed up dumplings . . . fresh apple slices and canned apricots in each.

BAKE at 375° for 15 minutes, then
      for 20 to 25 minutes   MAKES 6 dumplings

Drain.......1 No. 2½ can **apricot halves.** Reserve syrup.

Prepare......2 medium **apples;** pare and cut each into nine pieces.

Sift together..2 cups sifted **Pillsbury's Best All Purpose Flour***
2 teaspoons double-acting **baking powder** and
1 teaspoon **salt** into large mixing bowl.

Cut in......⅔ cup **shortening** until the size of small peas.

Add.........½ cup **milk;** stir until dough clings together.

Roll out.......on floured surface to a 12x18-inch rectangle. Cut into six 6-inch squares.

Place.........3 apple pieces, 2 or 3 apricot halves and
1 teaspoon **butter** in the center of each square. Fold corners to center and pinch together.

Arrange.......dumplings in a 9x9x2 or 11x7x2-inch pan.

Bake.........at 375° for 15 minutes. Pour hot Apri-Cinnamon Syrup over dumplings. Bake for 20 to 25 minutes. Serve warm with Apricot Topping or cream.

For use with Pillsbury's Best Self-Rising Flour, omit baking powder and salt.

APRI-CINNAMON SYRUP

Combine in saucepan 1¼ cups apricot syrup, ½ cup sugar and ¼ teaspoon cinnamon. Bring to boil. Remove from heat; stir in 2 tablespoons butter or margarine.

APRICOT TOPPING

Beat ½ cup whipping cream until thick. Fold in 1 tablespoon sugar and 4 to 6 mashed apricot halves.

Applecots

Apple Dimplings

Senior Third Prize Winner by Mrs. Mary Suciu, Otter Lake, Michigan

Flaky butter-egg pastry with an apple slice hidden inside . . . a party version of an old-fashioned apple dumpling!

BAKE at 450° for 10 to 15 minutes   MAKES 14 to 16 tarts

Sift together . . 3 cups sifted **Pillsbury's Best All Purpose Flour***
⠀⠀⠀⠀⠀⠀⠀⠀⠀½ teaspoon **salt** and
⠀⠀⠀⠀⠀⠀⠀⠀⠀¼ teaspoon **nutmeg** into large mixing bowl.
Cut in . . . . 1 cup **butter** (half shortening may be used) until the size of small peas.
Blend . . . . 2 unbeaten **eggs** with
⠀⠀⠀⠀⠀⠀⠀⠀⠀⅓ cup **milk** and
⠀⠀⠀⠀⠀⠀⠀⠀⠀¼ teaspoon **almond extract.** Sprinkle over the flour mixture, stirring with fork until dough is moist enough to hold together. Reserve leftover egg mixture. Chill about 1 hour; prepare Apple Slices.
Roll out . . . . . . half of dough on floured surface to ¹⁄₁₆-inch thickness.
Cut . . . . 14 to 16 circles, ¼ inch larger than apple slices. Place on ungreased baking sheets. Top each circle with a cooled apple slice.
Combine . . . . ⅓ cup **sugar** and
⠀⠀⠀⠀⠀⠀⠀⠀⠀1 teaspoon **cinnamon.** Sprinkle a half teaspoon over each apple slice.
Roll out . . . . . . remaining dough and cut additional circles, ¾ inch larger than apples. Cut a ''hole'' from center of each. Place over apple slices. Seal edges.
Place . . . . 1 teaspoon **red jam** or jelly in center of each.
Brush . . . . pastry with reserved egg mixture or milk; sprinkle with remaining cinnamon and sugar.
Bake . . . . at 450° for 10 to 15 minutes.

**For use with Pillsbury's Best Self-Rising Flour, omit salt.*

APPLE SLICES

Peel and core 8 cooking apples. Cut into 1-inch slices to resemble pineapple slices. Heat ¼ cup dark corn syrup in a skillet. Place half

Apple Dimplings

of apple slices in syrup and sprinkle with 2 tablespoons brown sugar. Cook over low heat until tender, turning to cook both sides. Do not cover. Remove from syrup; cool. Repeat with the remaining apple slices, using an additional ¼ cup dark corn syrup and 2 tablespoons brown sugar.

Cinnamon Apple Dumpling Dessert

Senior Winner by Mrs. Edward D. Gallager, San Francisco, California

These dessert dumplings are spiced with red cinnamon candies and steamed in a skillet like regular dinner dumplings.

SIMMER 20 minutes   SERVES 8

Combine . . . . ½ cup **sugar**
            ¼ cup **Pillsbury's Best All Purpose Flour** in 10-inch skillet or shallow pan that has a tight cover.

Add . . . . 2 cups **apple juice** gradually; blend well. Cook, stirring constantly, until thick.

Add . . . . 2 tablespoons **butter**
            1 tablespoon **red cinnamon candies** and
            4 cups sliced, unpeeled **apples** (4 medium); heat to boiling point.

Sift together . . 1 cup sifted **Pillsbury's Best All Purpose Flour***
            3 tablespoons **sugar**
            1½ teaspoons double-acting **baking powder**
            ¼ teaspoon **salt** and
            ¼ teaspoon **nutmeg** into mixing bowl.

Cut in . . . . 2 tablespoons **shortening** until mixture resembles coarse crumbs.

Add . . . . ½ cup **milk**; mix only until all dry particles are moistened.

Drop . . . . dough by tablespoonfuls onto hot apples.

Simmer . . . . uncovered for 10 minutes. Cover tightly; simmer 10 minutes. Serve warm with **cream.**

**For use with Pillsbury's Best Self-Rising Flour, omit baking powder and salt.*

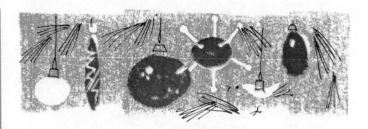

Cranberry Coconut Holidainty

Senior Winner by Mrs. Willard Aiken, Des Moines, Iowa

Festive, colorful cranberries and orange juice make the sauce, then sweet coconut dumplings are spooned on top.

SIMMER for 20 minutes   SERVES 8

Combine . . . . . 3 cups fresh **cranberries**
            1¼ cups **water** and
            2 cups **sugar** in large wide saucepan or skillet. Bring to boil; cook 5 minutes. Remove from heat; add
            ½ cup **orange juice**

Sift together . . 1 cup sifted **Pillsbury's Best All Purpose Flour***
            ¼ cup **sugar**
            1¼ teaspoons double-acting **baking powder** and
            ¼ teaspoon **salt** into mixing bowl. Add
            ½ cup **coconut**

Beat . . . . 1 **egg** until light and fluffy. Add
            ¼ cup **butter** or margarine, melted and cooled, and
            2 tablespoons **orange juice** or water. Add to the dry ingredients; mix until all dry particles are moistened.

Heat . . . . cranberry mixture again to boiling point.

Drop . . . . dough by tablespoonfuls into simmering cranberry mixture. Cover tightly; simmer 20 minutes. Serve warm; spoon cranberry sauce over dumplings. Top with **whipped cream,** if desired.

**For use with Pillsbury's Best Self-Rising Flour, omit baking powder and salt.*

Dandy Caramel Dumplings

Junior Winner by Nancy Kennedy, Oconomowoc, Wisconsin

Smooth rich sauce over light tender dumplings is downright good eating.

SIMMER for 20 minutes   MAKES 9

Combine.....2 tablespoons **butter** or margarine
            1½ cups firmly packed **brown sugar**
            1½ cups **water** and
            ⅛ teaspoon **salt** in 10-inch skillet or large, wide saucepan. Bring to boil, stirring constantly. Turn off heat.
Sift together 1¼ cups sifted **Pillsbury's Best All Purpose Flour***
            ⅛ cup **sugar**
            2 teaspoons double-acting **baking powder** and
            ½ teaspoon **salt** into mixing bowl.
Cut in.......2 tablespoons **butter** until particles are fine.
Combine....⅓ cup plus 1 tablespoon **milk** and

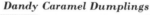

Dandy Caramel Dumplings

1 teaspoon **vanilla**. Add to the dry ingredients all at once; stir until dough clings together.
Heat..........caramel mixture again to boiling point.
Drop..........dough by tablespoonfuls into simmering sauce. Cover tightly; simmer 20 minutes. Serve warm with **plain** or **whipped cream**.

For use with Pillsbury's Best Self-Rising Flour, omit baking powder and salt.

Delicate Meringue Tarts

Junior Winner by Sylvia Boone Ross, Calhoun, Kentucky

Snowy-white, tender meringue is baked in individual flaky tart shells and topped with colorful fruit or jam.

BAKE at 450° for 10 to 12 minutes, then   MAKES 1 dozen
    at 350° for 12 to 15 minutes

Prepare.......recipe for **Two-Crust Pastry**, page 460; roll out and cut as directed below.
Roll out.......half at a time on floured surface to ⅛-inch thickness. Cut into six 5-inch circles; fit into 3½-inch tart shells.* Prick generously. Repeat with remaining pastry.
Bake.........at 450° for 10 to 12 minutes.

MERINGUE FILLING

Beat........4 **egg whites** with
          ¼ teaspoon **cream of tartar**
          1 teaspoon **vanilla** and
          ¼ teaspoon **almond extract** until soft mounds form. Add
          ½ cup **sugar** gradually, beating until meringue stands in stiff peaks.
Divide........meringue into tart shells.
Bake.........at 350° for 12 to 15 minutes. Cool. Top with fresh or frozen **fruit** or jam.

If tart shells are not available, muffin cups may be used.

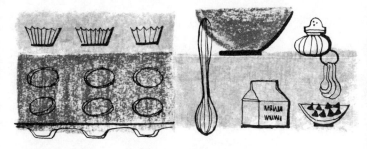

Double Chocolate Crinkle Tarts

Senior Winner by Rosa Tusa, Milwaukee, Wisconsin

Delicate little chocolate tarts with a crinkle effect give a party air. Take your choice of two whipped cream fillings.

BAKE at 375° for 12 to 15 minutes　　　　　　MAKES 1 dozen

Melt . . . . 1 cup (6-oz. pkg.) **semi-sweet chocolate pieces.** Cool.

Sift together 1¼ cups sifted **Pillsbury's Best All Purpose Flour*** and
　　　　　　⅛ teaspoon **salt**

Cream . . . . . . ⅓ cup **shortening** and
　　　　　　2 tablespoons **butter** or margarine. Add ¼ cup of melted chocolate. Blend in the dry ingredients.

Divide . . . . into twelve 3-inch muffin cups, lined with paper baking cups. Press dough evenly into bottoms and sides.

Bake . . . . at 375° for 12 to 15 minutes. Cool. Remove from paper baking cups and fill with Chocolate Chip Cream or Chocolate Mocha Cream. Chill.

*Pillsbury's Best Self-Rising Flour is not recommended for use in this recipe.

CHOCOLATE CHIP CREAM

Combine 1 cup whipping cream, ¼ cup sifted confectioners' sugar and 1 teaspoon vanilla. Chill. Beat until thick. Fold in slowly the remaining chocolate. Use fewest strokes possible to allow chocolate to solidify into small flecks.

CHOCOLATE MOCHA CREAM

Combine ¼ cup whipping cream and the remaining chocolate in top of double boiler. Heat over hot water, stirring occasionally, until thin and smooth. Cool to room temperature. Combine ¾ cup whipping cream, ¼ cup sifted confectioners' sugar, 1 teaspoon vanilla and ½ teaspoon instant coffee. Beat until thick. Fold in chocolate-cream mixture.

Golden Pear Tartlets

Senior Winner by Mrs. Sigmund Broda, Bronx, New York

There's a pear and a dab of jelly inside these tarts . . . and on the outside is crispy pastry.

BAKE at 450° for 18 to 20 minutes　　　　　　SERVES 6

Drain . . . . 1 No. 303 can **pear halves;** cut into slices.

Sift together 1½ cups sifted **Pillsbury's Best All Purpose Flour***
　　　　　　1 tablespoon **sugar**
　　　　　　1 teaspoon **salt** and
　　　　　　½ teaspoon double-acting **baking powder** into large mixing bowl.

Cut in . . . . . . ½ cup **shortening** until the size of small peas.

Sprinkle . . . . . 4 to 5 tablespoons **water** over mixture, stirring with fork until dough is moist enough to hold together. Form into ball.

Roll out . . . . on floured surface to ⅛-inch thickness. Cut into six 5-inch circles.

Place . . . . about 5 pear slices on each. Place a teaspoon of tart **jelly** on slices. Sprinkle with
　　　　　　½ teaspoon **sugar**

Moisten . . . . edges of dough; bring edges together at top and seal. Place on ungreased baking sheet.

Bake . . . . at 450° for 18 to 20 minutes. Serve warm with **whipped cream.**

*For use with Pillsbury's Best Self-Rising Flour, omit baking powder and salt.

Tasty Berry Gems

Senior Winner by Mrs. Elsie Fraher, Wareham, Massachusetts

Sparkle the menu with cranberry-pineapple lattice pastry squares.

BAKE at 425°* for 25 to 30 minutes   SERVES 10 to 12

Cook . . . . 1 cup **cranberries** and
1 cup (9-oz. can) **crushed pineapple**, undrained, in 2-quart saucepan until berries burst. Stir occasionally.

Combine . . . . ½ cup **sugar** and
1 tablespoon **cornstarch.** Add
1 package (10 oz.) thawed, frozen **strawberries**; mix well.

Add . . . . to cranberry mixture. Cook over medium heat, stirring constantly, until thick and clear. Stir in 1 teaspoon **vanilla.** Cool.

Prepare . . . . recipe for **Two-Crust Pastry,** page 460;* shape and roll out dough as directed below.

Divide . . . . dough into two parts, one twice as large as the other.

Place . . . . larger portion on ungreased baking sheet. Roll out

Tasty Berry Gems

to a 14x11-inch rectangle. Spread cooled filling to within ½ inch of edges. Brush edges with **cream.**

Roll out . . . . remaining dough. Cut into strips ½ inch wide; crisscross over filling to form lattice top. Trim and fold up bottom crust to cover ends; flute. Brush lattice top with cream.

Bake . . . . at 425° for 25 to 30 minutes.

*For use with Pillsbury's Best Self-Rising Flour, omit salt and baking powder; decrease baking temperature to 400°.

Berrytime Dessert

Senior Winner by Mrs. V. B. Fetterman, Silver City, New Mexico

If you like berry pies, you'll like this dessert. It's made of rounds of flaky pastry, covered with boysenberry sauce.

BAKE at 450° for 8 to 10 minutes   SERVES 8

Prepare . . . . recipe for **Lattice Pastry,** page 461; roll out and cut as directed below.

Roll out . . . . on floured surface to ⅛-inch thickness. Cut into rounds with 3-inch cutter. Place on ungreased baking sheets. Prick rounds with fork.

Bake . . . . at 450° for 8 to 10 minutes. Cool.

Drain . . . . 1 No. 2 can **boysenberries**; reserve juice.

Combine . . . . ¼ cup **sugar**
2 tablespoons **cornstarch**
¼ teaspoon **salt** and
¼ teaspoon **cinnamon** in saucepan.

Blend in . . . . . 1 cup of the reserved juice. Cook over medium heat, stirring constantly, until thick. Remove from heat.

Stir in . . . . 1 tablespoon **butter**
1 tablespoon **lemon juice** and the boysenberries.

Serve . . . . boysenberry sauce between and on top of cooled pastry rounds, allowing three rounds per serving. Top with **whipped cream.**

PUDDING DESSERTS

PUDDING DESSERTS includes recipes for puddings, cake-like puddings and steamed puddings.

If you do not have a large steamer or kettle, puddings may be steamed in the deep well cooker in your range or in a double boiler (check to see that double boiler does not boil dry). Or use the quick method and make your steamed puddings in a pressure saucepan; just follow pressure saucepan directions.

You may cover steamed puddings tightly with aluminum foil if you don't have a ready-made cover for the mold.

To test for doneness remove foil or cover after minimum steaming time. If pudding does not spring back when touched lightly, re-cover and continue to steam.

Steamed puddings are good keepers; just store them in a cool, dry place. To reheat in mold, cover and steam 30 minutes; or remove from mold, wrap tightly in aluminum foil, and heat in 350° oven about 30 minutes.

Indian Halvah

Senior Winner by Mrs. Rukmini Krishnaswamy, Columbus, Ohio

Salted nuts, coconut, cardamom and almond give this dessert a taste and texture all its own.

COOK—see below   SERVES 8

Melt . . . . ½ cup **butter** or margarine in heavy deep skillet.
Add . . . . ¾ cup sifted **Pillsbury's Best All Purpose Flour***
    ¾ cup (4 oz.) mixed **salted nuts**
    ½ cup **coconut**
    ¼ teaspoon **salt** and
    ½ teaspoon ground **cardamom**. Cook over low heat,

stirring constantly, until mixture is well browned. Remove from heat.

Blend in . . . . . ½ cup **sugar**; mix well. Cool slightly.
Combine . . . . . 2 cups **milk** and
    ½ teaspoon **almond extract**. Add gradually to flour mixture; mix well. Cook over medium heat, stirring constantly, until mixture is thick and glossy, about 10 minutes.
Serve . . . . hot or cold with **whipped cream**. To serve cold, mold in 8x8x2-inch pan; chill and cut into squares.

*For use with Pillsbury's Best Self-Rising Flour, omit salt.

Caramel Apple Pudding

Senior Winner by Mrs. Clifton G. Mandrell, Russell, Kentucky

Tasty and quick . . . this pudding-type dessert is good with ice cream.

BAKE at 375° for 40 to 50 minutes   SERVES 6

Sift together . ¾ cup sifted **Pillsbury's Best All Purpose Flour***
    ½ cup **sugar**
    1 teaspoon double-acting **baking powder**
    1 teaspoon **cinnamon** and
    ¼ teaspoon **salt** into mixing bowl.
Add . . . . 1½ cups coarsely chopped **apples**
    ½ cup **almonds**, chopped, and
    ½ cup **milk**; blend thoroughly.
Spread . . . . into greased 1½-quart casserole or 10x6x2-inch baking dish.
Combine . . . . ¾ cup firmly packed **brown sugar**
    ¼ cup **butter** or margarine and
    ¾ cup **boiling water**; stir until butter is melted. Pour over batter.
Bake . . . . at 375° for 40 to 50 minutes. Serve warm with **ice cream** or whipped cream.

*For use with Pillsbury's Best Self-Rising Flour, omit baking powder and salt.

Cinnamon Pudding Cake

Cinnamon Pudding Cake

Bride Winner by Mrs. Shirley Blount, St. Charles, Missouri

Butterscotch flavor and nut crunch top make this spicy dessert unique.

BAKE at 350° for 35 to 40 minutes   SERVES 8 to 10

Combine . . . 1¾ cups firmly packed **brown sugar**
          1½ cups **water** and
          2 tablespoons **butter** in saucepan. Bring to boil. Cool.
Sift together . . 2 cups sifted **Pillsbury's Best All Purpose-Flour***
          2 teaspoons double-acting **baking powder**
          ½ teaspoon **salt** and
          2½ teaspoons **cinnamon**
Cream . . . . . . 2 tablespoons **butter** or margarine with

1 cup **sugar**
Add . . . . the dry ingredients alternately with
          1 cup **milk.** Blend well after each addition.
Spread . . . . into a greased 9x9x2-inch pan. Pour brown sugar
          mixture over batter. Sprinkle with
          ½ cup **nuts,** chopped
Bake . . . . at 350° for 35 to 40 minutes. Serve warm with
          whipped cream.

For use with Pillsbury's Best Self-Rising Flour, omit baking powder and salt.

Family Caramel Pudding

Junior Winner by Nancy E. Markel, Arvada, Colorado

Make this tender pudding-cake in a jiffy by pouring caramel sauce over a raisin-date batter before baking. Serve with cream, if you like.

BAKE at 350° for 40 to 45 minutes   SERVES 6 to 8

Combine . . . 1¼ cups **water**
          ⅔ cup firmly packed **brown sugar** and
          2 tablespoons **butter** in saucepan. Bring to boil; simmer
          5 minutes. Add
          1 teaspoon grated **lemon rind**
Sift together . . 1 cup sifted **Pillsbury's Best All Purpose Flour***
          ½ cup **sugar**
          1½ teaspoons double-acting **baking powder** and
          ½ teaspoon **salt** into mixing bowl.
Add . . . . ½ cup **milk** and
          2 tablespoons **butter,** melted. Beat 1 minute.
Fold in . . . . . . ¼ cup **raisins** and
          ¼ cup **dates,** cut fine
Spread . . . . in well-greased 8x8x2-inch pan. Pour brown sugar
          syrup over batter.
Bake . . . . at 350° for 40 to 45 minutes. Serve warm with **plain**
          or **whipped cream.**

For use with Pillsbury's Best Self-Rising Flour, omit baking powder and salt.

Spun Gold Apricot Dessert

Senior Winner by Mrs. Groff S. Brown, Monrovia, California

This refreshing dessert has an inviting apricot flavor. A delicate pudding forms at the bottom with a cake layer on top.

BAKE at 325° for 45 to 55 minutes   SERVES 8

Combine . . . . ½ cup sifted **Pillsbury's Best All Purpose Flour***
               ¾ cup **sugar** and
               2 tablespoons **butter**, melted, in mixing bowl.

Blend . . . . 3 well-beaten **egg yolks** with
               ¼ cup **milk.** Add to flour mixture; mix until smooth.

Stir in . . . . . 1½ cups (12-oz. can) **apricot nectar** and
               1 tablespoon **lemon juice**

Beat . . . . 3 **egg whites** with
               ½ teaspoon **salt** until soft mounds form. Add
               ¼ cup **sugar** gradually, beating until stiff peaks form.

Fold in . . . . apricot mixture.

Fill . . . . well-greased custard cups three-fourths full. (If desired, 1 teaspoon **apricot jam** may be placed in bottom of each cup before filling.) Place cups in pan of hot water.

Bake . . . . at 325° for 45 to 55 minutes. Cool. Invert on plates; serve with **whipped cream,** if desired.

*Pillsbury's Best Self-Rising Flour is not recommended for use in this recipe.

Marsh-Mocha Puddin' Cake

Bride Winner by Mrs. Robert P. Monfore, Dante, South Dakota

Something different in chocolate pudding cakes! Sour cream and brewed coffee give additional flavor . . . marshmallows marble the top.

BAKE at 325° for 45 to 50 minutes   SERVES 8

Sift together . . 1 cup sifted **Pillsbury's Best All Purpose Flour***
               ½ cup **sugar**
               2 tablespoons **cocoa**
               ½ teaspoon **soda** and
               ½ teaspoon **salt** into mixing bowl.

Blend in . . . . . ¾ cup **sour cream** (thick or commercial) and
               1 teaspoon **vanilla**

Stir in . . . . 1 cup **nuts,** chopped

Combine . . . . ½ cup firmly packed **brown sugar** and
               2 tablespoons **cocoa** in an 8x8x2-inch pan. Add
               1½ cups hot **coffee.** Stir to dissolve.

Sprinkle . . . . . 2 cups **miniature marshmallows** or cut marshmallows over mixture in pan.

Spoon . . . . batter over marshmallows, leaving some uncovered to form a marbled top.

Bake . . . . at 325° for 45 to 50 minutes. Serve warm or cold with **cream** or ice cream.

*For use with Pillsbury's Best Self-Rising Flour, omit soda and salt.

Marsh-Mocha Puddin' Cake

Apple Dapple Pudding

Best of Class Winner by Mrs. Norman Prince, Milwaukee, Wisconsin

A pudding full of plump, spicy apple slices, raisins and slivered almonds, and there's a rich crumb mixture on top. Best served warm.

BAKE at 375° for 20 minutes, then   SERVES 8 to 10
for 30 to 40 minutes

Sift together . ¼ cup **Pillsbury's Best All Purpose Flour***
    ½ cup **sugar**
    1 teaspoon double-acting **baking powder** and
    1 teaspoon **cinnamon** or apple pie spice
Combine . . . . ⅓ cup **water**
    1 slightly beaten **egg**
    1 tablespoon **lemon juice** (reserve grated rind) and
    1 teaspoon **almond extract,** if desired.

New England Fruit Pudding

Add . . . . 4 cups pared, sliced **apples** (4 medium)
    ½ cup **almonds,** chopped, and
    ½ cup **raisins** or currants. Add the dry ingredients; mix well.
Turn . . . . into well-greased 10x6x2-inch baking dish or a 2-quart casserole; cover tightly with aluminum foil.
Bake . . . . at 375° for 20 minutes. Remove foil. Sprinkle Dapple Topping over apples. Bake 30 to 40 minutes until apples are tender. Serve warm with **whipped cream.**

DAPPLE TOPPING

Combine . . . . ¾ cup sifted **Pillsbury's Best All Purpose Flour***
    ¼ cup **sugar**
    ¼ cup firmly packed **brown sugar**
    1 teaspoon **cinnamon**
    1 teaspoon grated **lemon rind** and
    ¼ teaspoon **salt*** in mixing bowl.
Cut in . . . . . . ½ cup **butter** or margarine until particles are fine.
**For use with Pillsbury's Best Self-Rising Flour, omit baking powder and salt.*

New England Fruit Pudding

Bride Winner by Mrs. Helen Ann Foley, Meridan, Connecticut

Grated apple, raisins and dates in a spicy light pudding . . . with your choice of toppings.

BAKE at 350° for 40 to 45 minutes   SERVES 8 to 10

Sift together . . 1 cup sifted **Pillsbury's Best All Purpose Flour***
    ¾ teaspoon **soda**
    ½ teaspoon **salt**
    ½ teaspoon **cinnamon** and
    ¼ teaspoon **nutmeg.** Set aside.
Add . . . . ⅔ cup **sugar** gradually to
    ½ cup **shortening,** creaming well.

Blend in . . . . . 1 unbeaten **egg** and
1 tablespoon **milk;** beat well. Add the dry ingredients gradually; mix thoroughly.
Stir in . . . . . 1½ cups pared, coarsely shredded **apples**
½ cup **dates,** cut, and
½ cup **raisins**
Turn . . . . into 8x8x2-inch pan, greased on the bottom.
Bake . . . . at 350° for 40 to 45 minutes. Serve warm with **ice cream** or whipped cream and Butterscotch Sauce.

For use with Pillsbury's Best Self-Rising Flour, decrease soda to ½ teaspoon and omit salt.

BUTTERSCOTCH SAUCE

Combine in saucepan ½ cup sugar, ½ cup firmly packed brown sugar, ¼ cup light cream and 2 tablespoons light corn syrup. Cook over medium heat to soft-ball stage (234°). Cool slightly; stir in ¼ cup light cream and ½ teaspoon vanilla.

Saucy Cherry Squares

Senior Winner by Mrs. Robert O. Boyd, St. Paul, Minnesota

A chewy cake-dessert—with pie cherries baked in and more cherries and their juice in a sauce for the top. Quick and easy.

BAKE at 350° for 35 to 40 minutes   SERVES 8 to 10

Drain . . . . 1 No. 303 can sour **pie cherries;** reserve juice.
Sift together . . 1 cup sifted **Pillsbury's Best All Purpose Flour***
1 teaspoon double-acting **baking powder** and
½ teaspoon **salt**
Combine . . . . . 1 tablespoon **butter** or margarine with
1 cup **sugar.** Mix well.
Add . . . . 2 unbeaten **eggs;** beat well.
Blend in . . . . . . the dry ingredients; mix thoroughly.
Stir in . . . . 1 cup of the drained cherries and
½ cup **nuts,** chopped

Turn . . . . into well-greased 9x9x2-inch pan.
Bake . . . . at 350° for 35 to 40 minutes. Serve warm or cold with **whipped cream** or ice cream and warm Cherry Sauce.

For use with Pillsbury's Best Self-Rising Flour, omit baking powder and salt.

CHERRY SAUCE

Combine in saucepan ⅓ cup sugar, 1 tablespoon cornstarch, the reserved juice and remaining cherries. Cook, stirring constantly, until thick and clear. Blend in 2 to 4 drops red food coloring.

Tuti Fruti Pudding

Senior Winner by Mrs. W. R. Fridley, Brentwood, Missouri

Fruit cocktail is baked right into this very simple delicious one-egg cake-dessert. The easiest yet . . . and the family will love it.

BAKE at 350° for 30 to 40 minutes   SERVES 12 to 15

Drain . . . . 1 No. 303 can **fruit cocktail;** reserve juice.
Sift together . . 1 cup sifted **Pillsbury's Best All Purpose Flour***
1 cup **sugar**
1 teaspoon **soda** and
½ teaspoon **salt**
Beat . . . . 1 **egg** until thick and ivory colored.
Add . . . . the fruit cocktail (about 1¼ cups) and ½ cup of the reserved juice.
Blend in . . . . . . the dry ingredients.
Turn . . . . into 12x8x2 or 13x9x2-inch pan, well greased and lightly floured on the bottom.
Combine . . . . ½ cup firmly packed **brown sugar** and
¾ cup **pecans,** chopped; sprinkle over batter.
Bake . . . . at 350° for 30 to 40 minutes. Serve warm or cold with **whipped cream** or ice cream.

For use with Pillsbury's Best Self-Rising Flour, increase flour to 1¼ cups; decrease soda to ¼ teaspoon and omit salt.

Pine-Scotch Pudding

Senior Winner by Mrs. James T. Gresham, Menasha, Wisconsin

Heap whipped cream and pineapple-butterscotch sauce on squares made with pineapple and nuts.

BAKE at 325° for 30 to 35 minutes   SERVES 12

Sift together . ¾ cup sifted **Pillsbury's Best All Purpose Flour***
              1 teaspoon double-acting **baking powder** and
              ¼ teaspoon **salt**
Beat . . . . 2 **eggs** with
              1 teaspoon **vanilla** until fluffy. Gradually add
              1 cup **sugar**, beating until thick and ivory colored.
Fold in . . . . . . 1 cup drained **crushed pineapple** and
              1 cup **nuts**, chopped. Fold in the dry ingredients.
Turn . . . . into well-greased 12x8x2 or 13x9x2-inch pan.
Bake . . . . at 325° for 30 to 35 minutes. Cool; cut into squares.

Cheery Pineapple Dessert

Serve topped with **whipped cream** and Pineapple-Butterscotch Sauce.

For use with Pillsbury's Best Self-Rising Flour, omit baking powder and salt.

PINEAPPLE-BUTTERSCOTCH SAUCE

Melt ¼ cup butter or margarine in saucepan. Blend in 1 tablespoon flour. Add 1 cup firmly packed brown sugar, ¼ cup pineapple juice and ¼ cup water; mix well. Boil 3 minutes, stirring constantly. Blend a little of the hot mixture into 1 beaten egg; add to hot mixture. Cook 1 minute. Cool; add ½ teaspoon vanilla.

Cheery Pineapple Dessert

Junior Winner by Sandy Smith, Port Huron, Michigan

All ages will go for this tasty pineapple pudding cake, colorful with bits of cherries.

BAKE at 350° for 35 to 40 minutes   SERVES 8 to 10

Drain . . . . 1 No. 1 can (1 cup) **crushed pineapple**; reserve juice.
Sift together 1¼ cups sifted **Pillsbury's Best All Purpose Flour***
              1 teaspoon double-acting **baking powder** and
              ¼ teaspoon **salt**
Cream . . . . . . ¼ cup **butter** or margarine. Gradually add
              ½ cup **sugar**, creaming well.
Add . . . . the dry ingredients alternately with
              ½ cup **milk**. Blend well after each addition.
Spread . . . . in 9x9x2-inch pan, well greased on the bottom.
Top with . . . . ¼ cup chopped **maraschino cherries**, the drained
              pineapple and
              ¾ cup firmly packed **brown sugar**
Combine . . . . . . in saucepan the pineapple juice and **water** to
              measure ¾ cup. Bring to boil; pour over batter.
Bake . . . . at 350° for 35 to 40 minutes. Serve warm with
              whipped cream.

For use with Pillsbury's Best Self-Rising Flour, omit baking powder and salt.

Saucy Perk-Up Pudding

Junior Winner by Peggy Olmsted, Topsham, Maine

This dessert combines the intriguing tartness of rhubarb with a trace of mint. A crunchy butter-crumb mixture goes on top.

BAKE at 375° for 35 to 45 minutes   SERVES 8

Drain . . . . 1 package (16 oz.) thawed, frozen **rhubarb,** * reserving ¼ cup of juice.

Combine . . . . . 1 cup drained **crushed pineapple**
1 teaspoon dried **mint leaves** (or ½ teaspoon mint flavoring) and drained rhubarb. Turn into 8x8 or 10x6-inch baking dish.

Beat . . . . .1 **egg** until light and fluffy. Gradually add
⅓ cup **sugar*** and
2 tablespoons **flour.** Beat until smooth.

Blend in . . . . . . .the reserved rhubarb juice*
1 tablespoon **lemon juice** and a few drops **red food coloring.** Pour over fruit.

Sift together . . 1 cup sifted **Pillsbury's Best All Purpose Flour****
½ cup **sugar** and
¼ teaspoon **salt** into mixing bowl.

Cut in . . . . . . ½ cup **butter** or margarine until the size of small peas. Sprinkle over mixture in pan.

Bake . . . . .at 375° for 35 to 45 minutes. Cut into squares; serve plain or with whipped cream.

*If desired, 2 cups fresh rhubarb may be substituted for frozen. Increase first measurement of sugar to ¾ cup and omit rhubarb juice.

**For use with Pillsbury's Best Self-Rising Flour, omit salt.

Steamed Brownie Roll

Senior Winner by Mrs. H. A. Wilson, Houston, Texas

Serve this as a steamed dessert—or a chocolate-date quick bread. Make ahead of time and store in your refrigerator or freezer.

STEAM 1½ to 2 hours   SERVES 8

Melt . . . . .2 squares (2 oz.) unsweetened **chocolate** in
1 cup **water** in saucepan over medium heat. Remove from heat.

Stir in . . . . . . .1 cup **dates,** cut into pieces
½ cup **nuts,** chopped
1 teaspoon **soda*** and
½ teaspoon **salt.** Cool to lukewarm.

Add . . . . .1 cup **sugar** gradually to
¼ cup **shortening,** creaming well.

Blend in . . . . .1 unbeaten **egg** and
1 teaspoon **vanilla;** beat well.

Add . . . . .2 cups sifted **Pillsbury's Best All Purpose Flour***
alternately with chocolate mixture. Beat until smooth.

Divide . . . . . . .batter into 3 well-greased No. 2 cans, or a 1-pound coffee can and 1 No. 2 can. (Or use a well-greased 1½-quart mold.) Cover tightly with aluminum foil. Place on rack in large steamer or kettle; add boiling water to one-third height of cans. Cover tightly.

Steam . . . . .for 1½ to 2 hours. Unmold while hot. Serve hot with your favorite **hard sauce** or ice cream. (Or serve cold as a bread, sliced thin.)

*For use with Pillsbury's Best Self-Rising Flour, omit soda and salt.

My Mother's Pudding

My Mother's Pudding

Junior Third Prize Winner by Martha Parkison, Encampment, Wyoming

A spicy molasses, raisin and nut steamed pudding served with nutmeg sauce or hard sauce.

STEAM for 2 to 2½ hours   SERVES 10

Sift together 1½ cups sifted **Pillsbury's Best All Purpose Flour***
       1½ teaspoons double-acting **baking powder**
       1 teaspoon **salt**
       1 teaspoon **cinnamon**
       ¾ teaspoon **soda**
       ½ teaspoon ground **cloves** and
       ½ teaspoon **nutmeg** into mixing bowl.

Add . . . . ¾ cup grated or ground **suet**
       ½ cup **nuts,** chopped, and
       1 cup **raisins.** (Mixed candied fruit, chopped, may be substituted for part of raisins.)
Combine . . . . . 1 slightly beaten **egg**
       ¾ cup **milk** and
       ¾ cup light **molasses.** Add to the flour mixture all at once; stir until dry particles are moistened.
Turn . . . . into well-greased 2-quart mold or casserole.** Cover tightly. Place on rack in large steamer or kettle; add boiling water to one-third height of mold. Cover tightly.
Steam . . . . for 2 to 2½ hours.
Serve . . . . hot with Nutmeg Sauce or hard sauce. Cool and store in mold.

**For use with Pillsbury's Best Self-Rising Flour, omit baking powder and salt; decrease soda to ¼ teaspoon.*

***Or use two well-greased 1-pound coffee cans; steam each in a separate kettle.*

NUTMEG SAUCE

Cream ¼ cup butter or margarine. Gradually add ½ cup sugar, creaming well. Blend in 1 egg yolk, 1½ tablespoons flour and 1 teaspoon vanilla. Gradually add 1¼ cups boiling water. Pour into top of double boiler; cook over boiling water, stirring constantly, until thickened. Stir in ¼ teaspoon nutmeg.

CRISPS and COOKIE DESSERTS

have a cookie or crumb base with a filling, most often a fruit filling, on top. Many recipes call for a layer of crumbs to be sprinkled over the top.

A garnish of whipped cream adds a festive party touch. Many of these recipes are also good served simply as bar cookies.

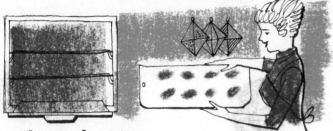

Apple Candy Crisp

Senior Winner by Mrs. Casimir T. Subbie, Fort Worth, Texas

There's a delicious difference to this apple crisp—it's the flavor of crushed peanut brittle.

BAKE at 400° for 30 to 40 minutes   SERVES 4 to 6

Prepare . . . . . . 6 cups pared, sliced **apples** (5 to 6 medium). Arrange in well-buttered 8x8x2 or 10x6x2-inch pan.

Sprinkle . . . . . ¼ cup **sugar**
½ teaspoon **salt** and
1 tablespoon **lemon juice** over apples.

Sift together . ¾ cup sifted **Pillsbury's Best All Purpose Flour***
½ cup **sugar** and
1 teaspoon **cinnamon** into mixing bowl.

Stir in . . . . . . ¼ cup **butter** or margarine, melted, to form crumbs.

Add . . . . ¼ pound (¾ cup) finely crushed **peanut brittle**

Press . . . . crumb mixture over apples. Sprinkle with
¼ cup **water**

Bake . . . . at 400° for 30 to 40 minutes. Serve warm with **cream**.

*For use with Pillsbury's Best Self-Rising Flour, omit salt.

Brazil Nut Fluff

Junior Winner by Carolyn Monroe, Jerome, Idaho

To make this luscious dessert, sandwich nuts between a buttery cooky-like layer; top with cherry chiffon and whipped cream.

BAKE at 400° for 12 to 15 minutes   SERVES 8

Sift together . . 1 cup sifted **Pillsbury's Best All Purpose Flour***
⅓ cup **sugar**
½ teaspoon double-acting **baking powder** and
½ teaspoon **salt** into mixing bowl.

Cut in . . . . . . ⅓ cup **butter** or margarine until particles are fine.

Sprinkle . . . . . 3 tablespoons **milk** over mixture, stirring with fork until dough is moist enough to hold together.

Press . . . . into ungreased 9x9x2-inch pan. Sprinkle with
½ cup **Brazil nuts** or almonds, chopped, and press down gently.

Bake . . . . at 400° for 12 to 15 minutes. Cool.

*For use with Pillsbury's Best Self-Rising Flour, omit baking powder and salt.

FLUFF TOPPING

Soften . . . . 1 envelope (1 tablespoon) unflavored **gelatin** in
¼ cup cold **water**

Combine . . . . . 3 slightly beaten **egg yolks**
¼ cup **sugar** and
⅛ teaspoon **salt** in top of double boiler.

Add . . . . 1½ cups scalded **milk** gradually. Cook over hot water, stirring constantly, until mixture will coat a metal spoon. Remove from heat. Add softened gelatin; stir until dissolved. Chill, stirring occasionally, until thickened but not set.

Fold in . . . . . . ½ cup sliced **maraschino cherries,** well drained

Beat . . . . 3 **egg whites** until stiff but not dry. Gradually add
¼ cup **sugar,** beating well. Fold gently but thoroughly into gelatin mixture.

Spoon . . . . over cooky layer; decorate with toasted **nuts**. Chill until firm about 2 hours. Serve with **whipped cream**.

Black-Bottom Refrigerator Dessert

Black-Bottom Refrigerator Dessert

Senior Winner by Mrs. Jack Jalving, Kalamazoo, Michigan

A luscious, rich brownie layer topped with a whipped cream chiffon cloud. Prepare this dessert early, then chill until serving time.

BAKE at 350° for 25 to 30 minutes   SERVES 6 to 8

Sift together . ¾ cup sifted **Pillsbury's Best All Purpose Flour***
       ½ teaspoon double-acting **baking powder** and
       ½ teaspoon **salt**
Melt . . . . ½ cup **shortening** with
       2 squares (2 oz.) unsweetened **chocolate** in saucepan
       over low heat. Remove from heat; cool.
Blend in . . . . .1 cup **sugar** and

      1 teaspoon **vanilla.** Mix until smooth.
Add . . . . .2 unbeaten **eggs,** beating well after each.
Blend in . . . . . . .the dry ingredients gradually; mix thoroughly.
Turn . . . . .into well-greased 9x9x2-inch pan.
Bake . . . . .at 350° for 25 to 30 minutes. Cool in pan; spread
      with Cream Chiffon. Chill at least 2 hours.
*For use with Pillsbury's Best Self-Rising Flour, omit baking powder and salt.

CREAM CHIFFON

Soften 2 teaspoons (⅔ envelope) gelatin in ¼ cup cold water in cup. Place cup in pan of hot water to dissolve gelatin; cool to lukewarm. Beat 2 egg whites with ¼ teaspoon salt until soft mounds form. Add ¼ cup sugar gradually; beat until mixture stands in stiff peaks. Fold in lukewarm gelatin mixture. Beat ¾ cup whipping cream until thick; blend in 1 teaspoon vanilla. Fold into gelatin mixture.

Blueberry Belle Crunch

Senior Winner by Mrs. George C. Young, Morristown, Minnesota

The crunch topping of this blueberry dessert is crisp and golden. Good any time of the year!

BAKE at 375° for 25 to 35 minutes   SERVES 8

Combine . . . . .1 package (12 oz.) frozen, or fresh **blueberries***
       ¾ cup **sugar**
       2 tablespoons **flour**
       ¼ teaspoon **salt** and
       2 tablespoons **lemon juice**
Spread . . . . .in greased 9-inch pie pan.
Combine . . . .¾ cup sifted **Pillsbury's Best All Purpose Flour****
       ½ cup quick-cooking **rolled oats**
       ½ cup firmly packed **brown sugar**
       ½ teaspoon **salt** and
       ½ teaspoon **vanilla** in mixing bowl.
Cut in . . . . . . ½ cup **butter** or margarine until mixture resembles

coarse crumbs. Sprinkle over blueberry mixture.

Bake........at 375° for 25 to 35 minutes. Serve hot.

If desired, 1½ cups (15-oz. can) drained blueberries may be used. Combine 2 tablespoons cornstarch, ½ cup sugar, ¼ teaspoon salt and ¾ cup blueberry juice. Cook, stirring constantly, until thickened. Add blueberries and 2 tablespoons lemon juice.

**For use with Pillsbury's Best Self-Rising Flour, omit salt in crumb topping.*

Cherry Meringue Dessert

Senior Winner by Mrs. A. F. Smith, El Paso, Texas

A cookie crust, sprinkled with pecans, has a border of meringue and a colorful cherry pie filling in the center.

BAKE at 375° for 12 to 15 minutes, then   SERVES 8 to 10
    at 350° for 12 to 15 minutes

Sift together 1¼ cups sifted **Pillsbury's Best All Purpose Flour***
        ½ teaspoon double-acting **baking powder** and
        ¼ teaspoon **salt**

Blend......⅓ cup **shortening** with
        ⅓ cup **sugar**, creaming well.

Blend in.....2 unbeaten **egg yolks** and
        1 tablespoon **milk**; beat well. Add the dry ingredients all at once; stir until mixture forms a dough.

Press.........into bottom of well-greased 9-inch round layer pan.**

Chop.......½ cup **pecans**; reserve 2 tablespoons for Meringue. Sprinkle remainder over dough.

Bake.........at 375° for 12 to 15 minutes. Cool.

CHERRY FILLING

Drain.......1 No. 303 can sour **pie cherries**, reserving ¾ cup juice.

Blend.....2 tablespoons **cornstarch** with
        ½ cup **sugar** in saucepan.

Blend in.......the reserved cherry juice, stir until sugar dissolves. Cook, stirring constantly, until thick and clear.

Cherry Meringue Dessert

Remove from heat.

Add.........¼ teaspoon **almond extract** and the cherries. Cool.

Transfer.......the cookie circle to baking sheet. Drop Meringue by tablespoonfuls around edge on top of circle. Sprinkle with reserved pecans.

Bake.........at 350° for 12 to 15 minutes. Fill center with Cherry Filling.

Pillsbury's Best Self-Rising Flour is not recommended for use in this recipe.

**Dough may be rolled out to a 9-inch circle on greased baking sheet and baked.*

MERINGUE

Beat 2 egg whites until soft mounds form. Add ¼ cup sugar gradually, beating well after each addition. Beat until meringue stands in stiff, straight peaks.

Cherry Blossom Dessert

Junior Winner by Betty Blore, Minot, North Dakota

This is a quick and easy dessert that combines the color and flavor of plump red cherries with the crunchiness of oatmeal and brown sugar.

BAKE at 350° for 25 to 30 minutes　　　　　SERVES 9 to 12

Drain . . . . 1 No. 303 can sour **pie cherries,** reserving juice.
Combine . . . . ¼ cup **Pillsbury's Best All Purpose Flour** and
　　　　　　　1 cup **sugar** in saucepan. Add the cherry juice (about
　　　　　　　¾ cup) and, if desired,
　　　　　　　¼ teaspoon **red food coloring**
Cook . . . . over medium heat, stirring constantly, until thick.
　　　　　　　Remove from heat; stir in cherries. Cool.
Sift together 1½ cups sifted **Pillsbury's Best All Purpose Flour***
　　　　　　　1 teaspoon **salt** and
　　　　　　　½ teaspoon **soda** into mixing bowl.
Blend in . . . . . 1 cup firmly packed **brown sugar** and
　　　　　　　¾ cup quick-cooking **rolled oats**
Cut in . . . . . . ½ cup **shortening** until particles are fine.
Press . . . . half of crumb mixture into bottom of ungreased
　　　　　　　12x8x2 or 13x9x2-inch pan. Spread with cherry
　　　　　　　filling. Cover with remaining crumb mixture. Press
　　　　　　　down gently.
Bake . . . . at 350° for 25 to 30 minutes. Cut into squares; serve
　　　　　　　warm or cold with **whipped cream.**

*For use with Pillsbury's Best Self-Rising Flour, omit salt and soda.

Almond Treasures

Senior Winner by Mrs. Donald Pence, Socorro, New Mexico

A rich almond filling is nestled under latticework of tender cookie dough.

BAKE at 350° for 45 to 50 minutes　　　　　MAKES 1½ to 2 dozen

Sift together . . 3 cups sifted **Pillsbury's Best All Purpose Flour***
　　　　　　　⅔ cup **sugar**
　　　　　　　1 teaspoon double-acting **baking powder** and
　　　　　　　1 teaspoon **salt** into large mixing bowl.
Cut in . . . . 1 cup **butter** or margarine until particles are fine.
Blend . . . . 2 slightly beaten **egg yolks** with
　　　　　　　⅓ cup **milk.** Add to flour mixture; stir to form dough.
Roll out . . . . . . half of dough on floured surface to fit into well-
　　　　　　　greased bottom of 9-inch round layer pan.
Beat . . . . 3 **egg whites** until stiff peaks form. Sift in
　　　　　　　1½ cups sifted **confectioners' sugar** gradually, folding
　　　　　　　just enough to blend.
Fold in . . . . . . 1 cup unblanched **almonds,** ground, and
　　　　　　　1 teaspoon **almond extract.** Spread over dough in pan.
Roll out . . . . . . remaining dough to 9x6-inch rectangle. Cut into
　　　　　　　9x½-inch strips. Place half of strips across filling;
　　　　　　　cross diagonally with remaining strips. Brush strips
　　　　　　　with beaten **egg white.**
Bake . . . . at 350° for 45 to 50 minutes. Cool; cut into wedges or
　　　　　　　bars.

*For use with Pillsbury's Best Self-Rising Flour, omit baking powder and salt.

Apricot Dessert Bars

Junior Second Prize Winner by Gregory Patent, San Francisco, California

Plenty o' apricots between crumb base and topping. Yummy with whipped cream.

BAKE at 400° for 10 minutes, then   MAKES about 1 dozen
for 20 to 25 minutes

Combine . . . 2½ cups drained cooked **apricots**
         ¾ cup **sugar** and
         ¼ cup **apricot juice** or water. Cook over medium heat
         about 5 minutes, stirring occasionally, until slightly
         thickened. Cool.

Sift together . . 2 cups sifted **Pillsbury's Best All Purpose Flour***
         1 teaspoon **salt** and
         ½ teaspoon **soda**

Cream . . . . . . ¾ cup **butter** or margarine. Gradually add
         1 cup **sugar,** creaming well.

Blend in . . . . the dry ingredients to form a crumb mixture.

Stir in . . . . . 1½ cups flaked or chopped shredded **coconut** and
         ½ cup **walnuts,** chopped

Press . . . . 3 cups of crumb mixture in bottom and half way up
         sides of greased 13x9x2-inch pan.

Bake . . . . at 400° for 10 minutes.

Spread . . . . apricot mixture over partially baked crust. Sprinkle
         with remaining crumb mixture. Return to oven; bake
         20 to 25 minutes. Cool; cut into bars. Serve with
         whipped cream.

*For use with Pillsbury's Best Self-Rising Flour, omit salt and soda.

Apricot Dessert Bars

Peach Elizabeth

Senior Winner by Mrs. Rosemary H. Sport, Roxbury, Massachusetts

A sunny peach filling nestled between two butter-crunch-spice layers— a dress-up version of a fruit crisp.

BAKE at 350° for 45 to 50 minutes   SERVES 9

Sift together . . 1 cup sifted **Pillsbury's Best All Purpose Flour***
                  ½ teaspoon **soda**
                  ½ teaspoon **salt**
                  ½ teaspoon **cinnamon** and
                  ¼ teaspoon **nutmeg**
Cream . . . . . . ½ cup **butter** or margarine in mixing bowl.
Blend in . . . . . 1 teaspoon grated **lemon rind**
                  1 teaspoon **lemon juice***
                  ½ cup firmly packed **brown sugar**
                  ½ cup crushed **cornflakes** and the dry ingredients until mixture resembles coarse crumbs.
Press . . . . half of mixture into bottom of well-greased 8x8x2-inch pan. Arrange
                  9 **peach halves** (fresh or No. 2½ can, well drained), cut-side down, over mixture in pan. Sprinkle with remaining crumb mixture.
Bake . . . . at 350° for 45 to 50 minutes. Serve warm or cold with **plain** or **whipped cream.**
For use with Pillsbury's Best Self-Rising Flour, omit soda, salt, lemon juice.

Pear-adise Chocolate Dessert

Senior Winner by Mrs. James L. Schoenholz, Los Angeles, California

Chocolate-filled pear halves are sprinkled with orange juice and a butter-crumb topping for surprising flavor and texture.

BAKE at 375° for 35 to 45 minutes   SERVES 8

Combine . . . 1½ cups sifted **Pillsbury's Best All Purpose Flour***
              1 cup **sugar**
              1 tablespoon grated **orange rind** and
              ¼ teaspoon **salt** in mixing bowl.
Cut in . . . . 1 cup **butter** or margarine until particles are fine.
Drain . . . . 16 small canned **pear halves** (or use 8 fresh pears: peel, core and halve). Place 1 pear half, cut-side up, in each of 8 well-greased individual baking dishes placed on a baking sheet.**
Place . . . . 2 **solid chocolate mint candy wafers** in hollow of each pear. (Or use milk chocolate or rum wafers.) Top with remaining pear halves, cut-side down.
Pour . . . . 1½ tablespoons **orange juice** over each (¾ cup in all). Sprinkle with crumb mixture.
Bake . . . . at 375° for 35 to 45 minutes. Serve warm with **whipped cream.**
For use with Pillsbury's Best Self-Rising Flour, omit salt.
**If desired, dessert may be baked in a 9x9-inch baking dish.*

Plum Perfection

Senior Winner by Mrs. Franz Guhl, Dassel, Minnesota

A royal dessert in flavor and appearance . . . purple plums in a crumb crust.

BAKE at 350° for 20 to 25 minutes   SERVES 8 to 10

Sift together 1¼ cups sifted **Pillsbury's Best All Purpose Flour***
              ¼ cup **sugar** and

¼ teaspoon **salt** into mixing bowl.

Cut in . . . . . . ½ cup **butter** or margarine until particles are fine.

Stir in . . . . . . ½ cup blanched **almonds,** finely chopped

Press . . . . crumb mixture into bottom and halfway up sides of ungreased 8x8x2 or 10x6x2-inch pan.

Bake . . . . at 350° for 20 to 25 minutes.

PLUM FILLING

Drain . . . . . . 1 No. 2½ can **purple plums,** pitted; reserve juice. Arrange plums in rows on crust.

Combine . . . . . 3 tablespoons **sugar** and
2 tablespoons **cornstarch.** Gradually add reserved juice (1⅔ cups). Bring to boil, stirring constantly. Cook until thick and clear.

Stir in . . . . 1 tablespoon **lemon juice** and
½ teaspoon **almond extract**

Pour . . . . over plums. Chill until firm. Serve with **whipped cream.**

*For use with Pillsbury's Best Self-Rising Flour, omit salt.

Sugar-Nut Berry Dessert

Senior Winner by Mrs. Sam Long, Galion, Ohio

Fresh raspberry flavor fills a cookie crust . . . meringue sprinkled with sugar and nuts tops this wonderful dessert.

BAKE at 350° for 25 to 30 minutes   SERVES 8 to 10

Sift together 1¼ cups sifted **Pillsbury's Best All Purpose Flour***
¼ teaspoon **soda** and
¼ teaspoon **salt**

Cream . . . . . . ½ cup **butter** or margarine. Add
⅓ cup **sugar;** blend thoroughly.

Blend in . . . . . 2 unbeaten **egg yolks** and
1 teaspoon **vanilla;** beat well. Add the dry ingredients; mix well.

Press . . . . into bottom and sides of ungreased 9-inch pie pan or 8x8x2-inch pan.

RASPBERRY-MERINGUE FILLING

Combine . . . . . 1 package (10 oz.) thawed frozen **red raspberries****
¼ cup **sugar** and
2 tablespoons **cornstarch.** Cook over low heat, stirring constantly, until thick.

Turn into . . . . . prepared shell. Sprinkle with
½ cup **walnuts,** chopped

Beat . . . . 2 **egg whites** until stiff. Spread over nuts.

Sprinkle . . . . . ¼ cup **walnuts,** chopped, and
1 tablespoon **sugar** over egg whites.

Bake . . . . at 350° for 25 to 30 minutes.

*For use with Pillsbury's Best Self-Rising Flour, omit soda and salt.

**One cup red raspberry jam may be substituted for the raspberry-sugar-cornstarch mixture.

Sugar-Nut Berry Dessert

Ruby Razz Crunch

Senior Second Prize Winner by Mrs. C. W. Myers, Fort Collins, Colorado

Frozen rhubarb and raspberries baked in a delectable bar-type dessert—with a frozen pink whipped cream topping!

BAKE at 325° for 55 to 65 minutes   SERVES 8 to 10

Drain . . . . 1 package (1 lb.) thawed frozen **rhubarb** (cut, if pieces are large) and

1 package (10 oz.) thawed frozen **red raspberries** (reserve ¼ cup berries). Combine fruits; set aside.

Mix . . . . the fruit juices and measure 1 cup, adding **water** if necessary.

Combine . . . . ½ cup **sugar** and

3 tablespoons **cornstarch** in saucepan. Blend in fruit juices. Cook over medium heat, stirring constantly, until thick and clear. Remove from heat; cover.

Blend . . . . . 1½ cups sifted **Pillsbury's Best All Purpose Flour***

1 cup firmly packed **brown sugar**

1 cup quick-cooking **rolled oats**

1 teaspoon **cinnamon** and

½ cup **butter** or margarine, melted, together until mixture resembles coarse crumbs.

Press . . . . two-thirds of crumb mixture into ungreased 9x9x2-inch pan. Cover with combined fruit and thickened fruit juice.

Sprinkle . . . . . . with remaining crumb mixture.

Bake . . . . at 325° for 55 to 65 minutes. Cool slightly; cut into squares. Serve warm or cold with mounds of Pink Frozen Cream Topping.

Pillsbury's Best Self-Rising Flour may be substituted.

PINK FROZEN CREAM TOPPING

Beat 1 cup whipping cream until thick; add ¼ cup sugar, the reserved raspberries and 1 to 3 drops red food coloring. Beat until thick. Drop in mounds on waxed paper; freeze until firm. (If desired, serve unfrozen.)

Ruby Razz Crunch

VARIETY DESSERTS
—Here you'll find a group of miscellaneous recipes ... from cheese cakes to dessert pancakes.

A good test for doneness of cheese cakes is to insert a knife halfway between the center and edge of the filling when minimum baking time has been reached. If the knife comes out clean, the cheese-cake is done. You'll notice that the center still seems runny and underbaked; actually, with this type of mixture, baking continues after cheese cake has been removed from oven. Cheese cakes should be thoroughly chilled before serving; they set up while chilling.

Preheat skillet you are going to use for baking dessert pancakes until a few drops of water "dance" on skillet's surface; it is then at the correct temperature.

When making cream puffs, stir the flour, shortening and water vigorously over medium heat until mixture leaves sides of pan and is smooth and compact. *Do not undercook.* It is important to beat well after the addition of each egg until batter is smooth and glossy. Use medium-sized eggs; too large eggs give a thin batter that will not hold shape on the baking sheet.

Bake cream puffs until firm to the touch; turn off oven, prick puffs and allow them to dry in oven 10 minutes.

Magnolia Manor Dessert

Senior Winner by Mrs. Carmion Gareis, New Ulm, Minnesota

A fragrant and spicy dessert, made with pecans and molasses and served with sweetened whipped cream cheese and a tangy orange sauce.

BAKE at 350° for 30 to 35 minutes   SERVES 6 to 8

Sift together . . 1 cup sifted **Pillsbury's Best All Purpose Flour***
      ⅔ cup **sugar**
      ¼ teaspoon **cinnamon**
      ⅛ teaspoon **ginger** and
      1/16 teaspoon **cloves**
Cut in . . . . 3 tablespoons **butter** or margarine until the size of small peas.
Add . . . . ⅓ cup **pecans,** chopped
Press . . . . two-thirds of crumb mixture in well-greased 8x8x2-inch pan.
Combine . . . . ½ cup **boiling water** and
      1 teaspoon **soda.*** Add
      ¼ cup **molasses**; mix well. Pour over crumb mixture in pan. Sprinkle with remaining one-third crumb mixture.
Bake . . . . at 350° for 30 to 35 minutes. Serve warm with Whipped Cheese Topping and warm Orange Sauee.
**For use with Pillsbury's Best Self-Rising Flour, decrease soda to ½ teaspoon.*

WHIPPED CHEESE TOPPING

Soften ⅓ cup (3-oz. pkg.) cream cheese with 1 tablespoon cream and ½ teaspoon vanilla. Blend in 3 tablespoons confectioners' sugar; cream well.

ORANGE SAUCE

Combine in saucepan ½ cup sugar, 1 tablespoon flour, 1 tablespoon cornstarch and ⅛ teaspoon salt. Add ¾ cup boiling water and 2 tablespoons butter or margarine. Cook over medium heat, stirring constantly, until thick and clear. Remove from heat; add grated rind and juice of 1 orange and juice of 1 lemon.

Apple Impromptu

½ cup **sugar**, creaming well.

Blend in . . . . . 1 slightly beaten **egg** and
1 teaspoon **vanilla**

Sift together . ½ cup sifted **Pillsbury's Best All Purpose Flour*** and
½ teaspoon double-acting **baking powder**. Blend into the creamed mixture. Spread over apples. Bake 20 to 25 minutes. Serve warm or cold, topped with **plain** or **whipped cream,** or ice cream.

**For use with Pillsbury's Best Self-Rising Flour, omit baking powder.*

Cheese Cake Supreme

Senior Winner by Mrs. Dorothy Miller, Philadelphia, Pennsylvania

Top quality cheese cake is baked in a candy-like malted milk flavored crust.

BAKE at 350° for 20 minutes, then   SERVES 9 to 12
for 35 to 40 minutes

Sift together 1¼ cups sifted **Pillsbury's Best All Purpose Flour***
½ cup **chocolate malted milk powder**
½ teaspoon double-acting **baking powder** and
¼ teaspoon **salt**

Cream . . . . . . ½ cup **butter** or margarine and
2 tablespoons **sugar**. Blend in the dry ingredients.

Press . . . . into greased bottom of 9x9x2-inch pan.

Bake . . . . at 350° for 20 minutes.

CHEESE CAKE FILLING

Cream . . . . 1 package (8 oz.) **cream cheese** and
1 cup creamed small curd **cottage cheese**. Gradually add
¾ cup **sugar**, creaming well.

Add . . . . 2 unbeaten **eggs**
1 teaspoon grated **lemon rind**
2½ tablespoons **lemon juice** and

Apple Impromptu

Senior Winner by Mrs. Russell Mallquist, Worcester, Massachusetts

A crispy cake-like topping baked on a layer of apples. Has the wonderful flavor of apple pie, but so easy and quick to make.

BAKE at 400° for 20 minutes, then   SERVES 6
for 20 to 25 minutes

Prepare . . . . . . 4 cups pared, sliced **apples** (4 medium). Place in well-greased 8 or 9-inch pie pan.

Combine . . . . ¼ cup **sugar** and
¼ teaspoon **cinnamon;** sprinkle over apples. Cover with aluminum foil.

Bake . . . . at 400° for 20 minutes.

Cream . . . . 1 tablespoon **butter**. Add

1 teaspoon **vanilla.** Blend well.

Stir in . . . . . . ¼ cup **Pillsbury's Best All Purpose Flour.** Add
2 cups **milk,** mixing until smooth.

Pour . . . . over partially baked crust. Sprinkle with a teaspoon
chocolate malted milk powder.

Bake . . . . at 350° for 35 to 40 minutes. Chill thoroughly at
least 4 hours.

For use with Pillsbury's Best Self-Rising Flour, omit baking powder and salt.

Cookie-Crust Cheese Cake

Senior Winner by Mrs. Henry Donkers, Portland, Oregon

*A rich, velvety cream cheese dessert with true cheese cake flavor . . .
patterned after a Bavarian master baker's "cheese soufflé."*

BAKE at 325° for 1 hour   SERVES 8

Sift together . . 1 cup sifted **Pillsbury's Best All Purpose Flour***
2 tablespoons **sugar**
½ teaspoon double-acting **baking powder** and
¼ teaspoon **salt** into mixing bowl.

Cut in . . . . . . ⅓ cup **butter** or margarine until size of small peas.

Beat . . . . 1 **egg** slightly; combine 2 tablespoons (save remainder)
with
2 tablespoons **milk.** Sprinkle over flour mixture, stirring
with fork until dough is moist enough to hold
together. Form into ball. Chill 1 hour.

Roll out . . . . . . half of dough on floured surface to a 9-inch circle;
fit into bottom of 9-inch spring-form pan at least
2¾ inches deep.

Roll out . . . . . . remaining dough to a 14x6-inch strip. Cut into two
14x3-inch strips; press against inner side of pan.
Seal to bottom dough.

CREAM CHEESE FILLING

Beat . . . . 4 **egg whites** in large bowl until soft mounds form.

Cheese Cake Supreme

Gradually add
½ cup **sugar,** beating until stiff peaks form.

Blend . . . . ½ cup **sugar**
2 tablespoons **flour** and
¼ teaspoon **salt** with
1½ cups **cream cheese** (one and one-half 8-oz. pkgs.)

Add . . . . 1 tablespoon grated **lemon rind**
1 tablespoon **lemon juice**
4 unbeaten **egg yolks,** remaining egg from crust and
1 cup **sour cream** (thick or commercial). Beat until
creamy. Gently fold into egg whites.

Turn . . . . filling into pastry-lined pan.

Bake . . . . at 325° for 1 hour. Turn off heat; cool in oven ½
hour. Chill completely.

For use with Pillsbury's Best Self-Rising Flour, omit baking powder and salt.

Swiss Chocolate Cheese Cake

Senior Winner by Mrs. Orval Emerson, Coshocton, Ohio

Something wonderfully different in the cheese cake field . . . a rich chocolate filling with coconut is delectable in a crunchy cookie crust.

BAKE at 350° for 40 to 45 minutes　　　　　SERVES 12 to 15

Sift together . . 1 cup sifted **Pillsbury's Best All Purpose Flour***
　　　　　　　¼ cup **sugar** and
　　　　　　　¼ teaspoon **salt** into mixing bowl.
Cut in . . . . . . ⅓ cup **butter** or margarine until particles are fine.
Press . . . . crumb mixture into bottom of greased 8x8x2-inch pan. Set aside.
Cream . . . . . . 1 package (8 oz.) **cream cheese** and
　　　　　　　2 squares (2 oz.) melted unsweetened **chocolate**
Add . . . . 2 unbeaten **eggs,** beating well after each.
Blend in . . . . . ⅔ cup **sugar**
　　　　　　　2 tablespoons **flour** and
　　　　　　　¼ teaspoon **salt**; beat well.
Stir in . . . . . . ⅔ cup **light cream**
　　　　　　　½ cup flaked or chopped shredded **coconut** and
　　　　　　　1 teaspoon **vanilla.** Pour into prepared pan.
Bake . . . . at 350° for 40 to 45 minutes. Chill until set, at least 2 hours.

*For use with Pillsbury's Best Self-Rising Flour, omit salt in crust.

Lucy's Caramel Custard Ice Cream

Senior Winner by Mrs. Carl Witt, Atchison, Kansas

Here's homemade ice cream like grandmother made. There's brown sugar for caramel flavor and nuts for added goodness.

FREEZE—see below　　　　　　　　MAKES 1 gallon*

Caramelize . . . 2 cups firmly packed **brown sugar** in heavy skillet over low heat; stir constantly. *Do not scorch.*
Scald . . . . 4 cups (1 quart) **milk** in large saucepan. Remove from heat.
Combine . . . . . 1 cup sifted **Pillsbury's Best All Purpose Flour****
　　　　　　　2 cups **sugar** and
　　　　　　　3 well-beaten **eggs.** Mix thoroughly.
Add . . . . flour mixture to milk, blending thoroughly. Return to heat and cook, stirring constantly, until thick.
Combine . . . . . . caramelized sugar and custard; cool thoroughly.
Add . . . . 4 cups (1 quart) **milk**
　　　　　　　4 cups (1 quart) **whipping cream** and
　　　　　　　1 teaspoon **vanilla** to caramel mixture; blend well.
Pour . . . . into ice cream freezer, 1-gallon size.* Freeze to "mush" consistency.
Add . . . . 1 cup **pecans** or walnuts, chopped. Repack freezer; continue to freeze well.
Remove . . . . dasher from freezer; pack well with ice and salt.

Allow ice cream to stand in freezer about 3 hours before serving.

Or prepare half of recipe above. Freeze mixture in 3 refrigerator trays until there are no soft spots (about 3 hours). Cut frozen mixture from tray; place in chilled bowl. Beat until mixture is free from lumps (not soft and mushy). Spoon into 2 trays and freeze again. Stir in the chopped nuts.

**Pillsbury's Best Self-Rising Flour is not recommended for use in this recipe.

Peppermint Cream-Topped Puffs

Senior Winner by Mrs. Richard Milton Dietz, Lancaster, Pennsylvania

Delicate sponge puffs . . . topped with whipped cream and crushed peppermint candy. A different kind of cooky dessert.

BAKE at 350° for 10 to 12 minutes   SERVES 12

Beat . . . . 4 **egg whites** in large bowl until soft mounds form. Gradually add
½ cup sifted **confectioners' sugar,** beating until stiff peaks form.

Beat . . . . 4 **egg yolks**
¼ teaspoon **salt** and
½ teaspoon **vanilla** until thick and lemon colored. Fold gently but thoroughly into egg whites.

Add . . . . ⅔ cup sifted **Pillsbury's Best All Purpose Flour,*** half at a time; fold gently after each addition.

Drop . . . . by tablespoonfuls about 2 inches apart onto baking sheets covered with brown paper. Flatten slightly.

Bake . . . . at 350° for 10 to 12 minutes. Remove from paper immediately. To serve, arrange puffs in clusters of three. Top with Peppermint Whipped Cream.

*For use with Pillsbury's Best Self-Rising Flour, omit salt.

PEPPERMINT WHIPPED CREAM

Beat 1 cup whipping cream until thick. Fold in ½ cup crushed peppermint stick candy.

Grandma's Dessert Pancakes

Senior Winner by Miss Ida E. Koncz, Coraopolis, Pennsylvania

These pancakes are thin and rich. Make the raisin-cream filling and custard sauce in advance—fill and stack just before serving.

BAKE at medium heat   SERVES 8

Sift together . . 1 cup sifted **Pillsbury's Best All Purpose Flour***
2 tablespoons **sugar**
1 teaspoon double-acting **baking powder** and
½ teaspoon **salt.** Set aside.

Combine . . . . . 2 well-beaten **eggs**
1½ cups **milk**
2 tablespoons **shortening,** melted; add to the dry ingredients all at once. Stir until well blended.

Heat . . . . skillet over medium heat. Brush with **shortening.**

Pour . . . . batter, scant ¼ cup at a time, into skillet. Tilt pan to make a 6-inch round pancake. Brown about 1 minute, turn and brown on other side.

Stack . . . . pancakes, spreading about ¼ cup Raisin Cream Filling between each layer (make two stacks). Cut in wedges. Serve immediately, topped with warm Custard Sauce.

*For use with Pillsbury's Best Self-Rising Flour, omit baking powder and salt.

RAISIN CREAM FILLING

Combine in saucepan 2 beaten egg yolks, ¼ cup raisins, 3 tablespoons sugar, 2 teaspoons cornstarch, ⅛ teaspoon salt, ⅛ teaspoon nutmeg, ½ cup milk, 2 tablespoons honey, 1 teaspoon grated lemon rind and 1 teaspoon vanilla. Cook until thickened. Remove from heat. Add 2 cups (1 pound) creamed small curd cottage cheese.

CUSTARD SAUCE

Beat 2 eggs slightly in top of double boiler. Add 1 cup milk, 2 tablespoons sugar and ⅛ teaspoon salt. Cook over boiling water, stirring constantly, until mixture will coat a spoon. Remove from heat; add 1 teaspoon vanilla.

Window Waffle Wedges

Senior Winner by Mrs. Roy H. Reeve, Mattituck, Long Island, New York

Sweet, crisp, golden waffles served with ice cream and pineapple sauce.

BAKE at medium low heat   MAKES 7 waffles

Sift together . . 1 cup sifted **Pillsbury's Best All Purpose Flour***
       1 teaspoon double-acting **baking powder** and
       ½ teaspoon **salt**

Cream . . . . . . ½ cup **butter** or margarine. Gradually add
       1 cup **sugar,** creaming well.

Add . . . . 4 unbeaten **egg yolks** and
       1 teaspoon **vanilla.** Beat well.

Blend in . . . . the dry ingredients.

Beat . . . . 4 **egg whites** until stiff but not dry. Fold gently but thoroughly into batter.

Bake . . . . in preheated waffle iron at medium low heat until steaming stops and waffle is golden brown, 3 to 5 minutes. Serve warm with **ice cream** and Pineapple Mint Sauce, or fresh fruit and whipped cream.

**For use with Pillsbury's Best Self-Rising Flour, omit baking powder and salt.*

PINEAPPLE MINT SAUCE

Combine ¼ cup sugar and 1 tablespoon cornstarch in saucepan. Add 1 cup pineapple juice, 1 cup crushed pineapple and a few mint leaves, if desired. Cook, stirring constantly, until clear.

Delicate Orange Crepes

Junior Winner by Charmaine LeBaron, Glendale, California

Wonderfully light dessert pancakes with an orange-honey sauce.

BAKE at medium high heat   SERVES 5 to 6

Beat . . . . 1 cup creamed **cottage cheese** with mixer (or press through a sieve) until very fine.

Add . . . . 1 cup **sour cream** (thick or commercial)
       1 tablespoon **sugar**
       ¾ teaspoon **salt**
       1 tablespoon grated **orange rind** and
       3 tablespoons **orange juice;** mix well.

Blend in . . . . . 4 well-beaten **eggs** and
       1 cup sifted **Pillsbury's Best All Purpose Flour;*** beat until smooth.

Heat . . . . lightly-greased skillet over medium high heat.

Pour . . . . batter, ¼ cup at a time, into skillet. Tilt to make a 6-inch round pancake. Brown 1 to 2 minutes on each side.

Roll . . . . warm pancakes. Arrange on oblong serving dish or on individual dessert plates, three or four on each. Serve with hot Orange Honey Sauce. (Pancakes may be made ahead of time, then rolled and reheated at 350° for 5 to 8 minutes before serving.)

**Pillsbury's Best Self-Rising Flour is not recommended for use in this recipe.*

ORANGE HONEY SAUCE

Blend in saucepan ½ cup honey, ⅓ cup butter or margarine, ¼ teaspoon cinnamon, 2 teaspoons grated orange rind and 2 tablespoons orange juice. Cook over medium heat, stirring until butter is melted.

Lemon Dream Dessert

Senior Winner by Mrs. Margaret Belitz, Chicago, Illinois

These unusual, tart, lemony bars were inspired by dream bars.

BAKE at 350° for 15 minutes, then   MAKES 1½ dozen bars
    for 25 to 30 minutes

Cut . . . . ⅓ cup **butter** or margarine into
       1 cup sifted **Pillsbury's Best All Purpose Flour*** and
       2 tablespoons **sugar** until mixture resembles coarse crumbs.

Press.........mixture firmly into ungreased 8x8x2, 9x9x2 or
11x7x2-inch pan.

Bake.........at 350° for 15 minutes.

Combine.....2 beaten **eggs**
½ cup firmly packed **brown sugar**
¾ cup **coconut**, chopped
½ cup **nuts**, chopped
¼ teaspoon **salt**
⅛ teaspoon double-acting **baking powder** and
½ teaspoon **vanilla**; mix well. Spread over crust.

Bake.........at 350° for 25 to 30 minutes. Frost immediately with
Lemon Frosting. Cool 15 minutes; cut into bars.

*For use with Pillsbury's Best Self-Rising Flour, omit baking powder and salt.

LEMON FROSTING

Combine 2 teaspoons grated lemon rind, 2 tablespoons lemon juice
and 1 cup sifted confectioners' sugar. Mix until smooth.

Strawberry Puff Ring

Senior Winner by Mrs. M. B. Hirschberg, Cincinnati, Ohio

*A novel, cream puff dessert. Confectioners' sugar glaze on top, a luscious
cream filling and fresh strawberries inside.*

BAKE at 400° for 30 to 35 minutes   SERVES 8 to 10

Sift together. ¾ cup sifted **Pillsbury's Best All Purpose Flour***
½ teaspoon **salt**

Heat........6 tablespoons **butter** or margarine and
¾ cup **boiling water** in saucepan just to boiling.

Add..........the dry ingredients all at once; cook, stirring constantly, until mixture leaves sides of pan in smooth
compact ball. Remove from heat; cool 1 minute.

Blend in.....3 unbeaten **eggs**, beating until smooth after each.

Spoon........dough in ring shape about 8 inches in diameter on
greased baking sheet.

Bake.........at 400° for 30 to 35 minutes. Turn off oven. Prick
puff with sharp knife. Leave puff in oven 10 minutes
to dry out center. Cool; slice off top of ring. Fill
with Cream Filling and
2 cups fresh **berries** or fruit. Replace top; frost with
Vanilla Glaze, page 326. Decorate with additional
berries. (One package frozen berries may be used.
Drain and thicken juice to use instead of Glaze.)
Chill until serving time.

*For use with Pillsbury's Best Self-Rising Flour, omit salt.

CREAM FILLING

Combine in saucepan ½ cup sugar, ⅛ cup Pillsbury's Best All Purpose
Flour and ½ teaspoon salt. Blend in 2 cups milk. Cook over low heat,
stirring constantly, until thick. Remove from heat. Blend a little hot
mixture into 2 slightly beaten eggs (or 4 egg yolks); add to hot mixture.
Cook, stirring, 1 minute. Cover; cool. Blend in 2 teaspoons vanilla.

Strawberry Puff Ring

INDEX

The figure following each entry (0) indicates the number of the BAKE-OFF in which it was a prize winner. Entries in italics are special hints or variations of base recipes.